Joseph B. Killebrew

Report on the Culture and Curing of Tobacco in the United States

Joseph B. Killebrew

Report on the Culture and Curing of Tobacco in the United States

ISBN/EAN: 9783337187217

Printed in Europe, USA, Canada, Australia, Japan

Cover: Foto ©Andreas Hilbeck / pixelio.de

More available books at **www.hansebooks.com**

DEPARTMENT OF THE INTERIOR,
CENSUS OFFICE.

FRANCIS A. WALKER, Superintendent,
Appointed April 1, 1879; resigned November 3, 1881.

CHAS. W. SEATON, Superintendent,
Appointed November 4, 1881.

REPORT

ON THE

CULTURE AND CURING OF TOBACCO

IN THE

UNITED STATES.

BY

J. B. KILLEBREW,
SPECIAL AGENT.

WASHINGTON.
GOVERNMENT PRINTING OFFICE.
1884.

TABLE OF CONTENTS.

CHAPTER I.—STATISTICAL REVIEW OF THE TOBACCO CROP OF 1879.

CHAPTER II.—CLASSIFICATION—TYPE MAPS—VARIETIES OF THE TOBACCO PLANT.

CHAPTER VIII.—CULTURE AND CURING OF TOBACCO IN LOUISIANA.

CHAPTER IX.—CULTURE AND CURING OF TOBACCO IN MARYLAND.

CHAPTER X.—CULTURE AND CURING OF TOBACCO IN MISSOURI.

CHAPTER XI.—CULTURE AND CURING OF TOBACCO IN NEW YORK.

CHAPTER XII.—CULTURE AND CURING OF TOBACCO IN NORTH CAROLINA.

CHAPTER XIII.—CULTURE AND CURING OF TOBACCO IN OHIO.

CHAPTER XIV.—CULTURE AND CURING OF TOBACCO IN PENNSYLVANIA.

CHAPTER XV.—CULTURE AND CURING OF TOBACCO IN TENNESSEE.

CHAPTER XVI.—CULTURE AND CURING OF TOBACCO IN VIRGINIA.

CHAPTER XVII.—CULTURE AND CURING OF TOBACCO IN WEST VIRGINIA.

CHAPTER XVIII.—CULTURE AND CURING OF TOBACCO IN WISCONSIN.

LETTER OF TRANSMITTAL.

DEPARTMENT OF THE INTERIOR,
CENSUS OFFICE,
Washington, D. C., October 15, 1881.

Hon. FRANCIS A. WALKER,
Superintendent of Census.

SIR: I have the honor to submit my report on the culture and curing of tobacco in the United States, together with special reports upon this industry in Arkansas, Florida, Illinois, Indiana, Kentucky, Louisiana, Maryland, Missouri, the New England states, New York, North Carolina, Ohio, Pennsylvania, Tennessee, Virginia, West Virginia, and Wisconsin.

The product of Florida and Louisiana, taken together, amounts to only 77,136 pounds, a very insignificant fraction of the total crop of the Union for 1879.

It is believed that the soil and the climate of Florida are more especially adapted to the growing of tobacco, with the fragrance and texture of Cuba tobacco, than those of any other part of the United States. Enough has been done in this state to show that with proper selection of varieties and intelligent culture and management a product of most excellent quality, closely approximating that of Cuba, can be grown upon a large extent of its territory.

The Perique of Louisiana is unlike any other tobacco in the world, in the peculiar manner of curing and handling and in flavor, but the product is small, and cannot probably be much increased in quantity.

These considerations have made it advisable to include the two states above named in the list of those upon which special reports are made.

To obtain the information necessary, a schedule, prepared in this office, embracing fifty-two distinct questions, was sent to growers of tobacco, and to such other persons as were presumed to possess knowledge on the subject, in every county of the tobacco-growing sections. Subsequently, a second and more elaborate series of questions was incorporated in a supplemental schedule, and distributed with especial care to persons who had positive knowledge of the subject-matter. This supplemental schedule embraced one hundred and seven distinct questions, the object of which was to elicit accurate and trustworthy information about all the details of the industry, from the sowing of the seed until the product passes into the hands of the merchant or manufacturer. It was found necessary to prepare a third series of questions, ten in number, which were submitted to correspondents who had already exhibited a desire to aid in the labor of investigation.

An extended correspondence was required to clear up obscurities and to compare and verify facts. Your special agent made personal examination of numerous districts of territory in which the plant is grown, obtaining in this way a more accurate knowledge of many important details than could possibly be derived from mere correspondence.

The investigation in its scope and character was unprecedented. Tobacco planters, of life-long experience, when asked to make answer as to certain details of the industry, required conference with others to reply intelligently. The examination of farm records, and not unfrequently laborious journeys of many miles, were necessary to obtain the facts desired. The schedules as returned, almost without an exception, evidence a pains-taking care to give full, clear, and accurate information. Special thanks are due to those whose prompt and carefully prepared replies form the basis of these reports.

Acknowledgments are due to Wallace Tappan for valuable data as to the management of tobacco in New York; to Frank R. Diffenderffer for special information as to the industry in Pennsylvania; to R. L. Ragland for an excellent account of tobacco culture in Virginia, Maryland, and West Virginia; to Thomas E. Browder, of Kentucky, for assistance in unraveling the intricacies of the various types grown in that state and in other states; to Professor G. C. Swallow for a description of the soils of Missouri, with their geological derivation; to Professor Goessmann, of Massachusetts Agricultural College, for an interesting account of the soils of the Connecticut valley; to Professor W. C. Kerr, of North Carolina, for a very suggestive report on the tobacco soils of that state; and to H. M. Doak, of Tennessee, for valuable assistance in the preparation of this report. Nor must I omit to mention the services of C. F. Vanderford, of Tennessee, in revising and condensing this report and comparing its statements with the original sources of information.

To Dr. S. S. Rathvon, of Pennsylvania; to M. H. Clark & Bro., of Clarksville, Tennessee; to Sawyer, Wallace & Co., and J. S. Gans & Co., of New York; to Gierke & Niemann, of Baltimore; to John Ott, of Richmond; to F. W. Ferrel, of Danville, Virginia; to Jacob Zimmer, of Miamisburg, Ohio; to C. & R. Dormitzer & Co., of Saint Louis, Mo.; to W. G. Mier, of Louisville, Ky.; and to E. H. Griest, of Cincinnati, Ohio, I am indebted for valuable suggestions.

Very respectfully, your obedient servant,

J. B. KILLEBREW.

CULTURE AND CURING OF TOBACCO IN THE UNITED STATES.

CHAPTER I.

STATISTICAL REVIEW OF THE TOBACCO CROP OF 1879.

Tobacco is grown to some extent in every state and territory of the Union, except possibly Utah, Montana, and Wyoming. As a staple crop it is produced in only sixteen states, in one of which (Arkansas) the industry is of recent origin. Of the total crop of the United States in 1879 (472,661,158 pounds) these sixteen states produced 469,816,203 pounds. The remainder (2,844,955 pounds) was grown upon small patches in all parts of the country, embracing a range of 22 degrees of latitude and 52 degrees of longitude, and exhibiting the remarkable facility with which the tobacco plant accommodates itself to varying conditions of climate and of soil.

A considerable quantity of tobacco is grown in Alabama, Georgia, Mississippi, South Carolina, and Texas. This product rarely finds its way even to primary markets. It is raised for home use, mostly cured by sun and air, and is consumed almost entirely for pipe-smoking. A very small part of it is stripped and made into twist for chewing, the manipulation being of the rudest character.

In Alabama the plant is grown in all but three counties. The average yield in 1879 was only 206 pounds per acre, an evidence of careless culture and wretched management. More than one-third of all the tobacco produced in the state was grown in the eight counties lying along the Tennessee river—163,264 pounds on 757 acres. In Madison county, upon 224 acres, was produced 36,356 pounds—162 pounds per acre. The very small yield can only be explained by stating the fact that the plant is raised only in patches, simply for a cheap article.

In Georgia three-fourths of the product was made in that part of the state north of Atlanta, though grown to a small extent in ninety-six of the one hundred and thirty-seven counties. The average yield for the state was only 235 pounds, that of Cherokee county (17,900 pounds on 35 acres, an average of 511 pounds) alone showing an approach to profitable production.

In Mississippi the average yield was 282 pounds. Of the total product more than nine-tenths was grown north of the latitude of Jackson, and of this not more than 5,000 pounds were produced along the Yazoo and in the country between that river and the Mississippi. The only county producing a yield indicating even moderately careful culture was De Soto, making 12,026 pounds on 27 acres—445 pounds per acre. The soils of De Soto, Marshall, Tippah, Tishomingo, and of all the northern and eastern counties, except the bottom lands, are well adapted to the production of a fair grade of tobacco, only needing manurial applications and good cultivation to produce remunerative crops.

In South Carolina three-fourths of the total product was grown in nine counties in the northwestern corner of the state. The average yield per acre in this section was 262 pounds, Oconee county making 4,775 pounds on 13 acres—367 pounds per acre. The plant is grown to a limited extent in 23 of the 33 counties of the state.

In Texas the average yield was 323 pounds. The plant was grown in 91 counties; but more than three-fourths of the total product was raised in 35 counties in the eastern part of the state, from Fannin county, on Red river, to Newton county, on the Sabine. Lamar county, in northeastern Texas, adjoining the Indian territory, made the largest yield: 15,003 pounds on 29 acres—an average of 517 pounds. Attempts made by German colonists to produce a marketable tobacco met with little success, the product being coarse and of inferior quality. This may have resulted from an improper selection of varieties, or possibly from unfavorable seasons. Extensive bodies of land well adapted to certain types of tobacco are found in the northern and eastern sections of Texas.

In New Jersey, upon soils and under conditions very much like those of southeastern Pennsylvania, tobacco is grown to some extent, Mercer county producing 69,810 pounds upon 60 acres in 1879, an average of 1,163 pounds, and Burlington county 94,487 pounds upon 76 acres, an average of 1,243 pounds per acre. Only 8,018 pounds were grown in other counties.

Michigan and Minnesota have succeeded well in growing a fair quality of tobacco for home consumption. In Michigan tobacco was planted to a limited extent in forty-seven counties, with an average yield of 404 pounds per acre. Lenawee county, on the Ohio border, reported a yield of 6,863 pounds on 10 acres; Monroe county, on lake Erie, in the southeast corner of the state, 5,757 pounds on 11 acres; and Van Buren county, in the southwest, 4,586 pounds on 9 acres. In Minnesota the average yield was 429 pounds, and the plant is grown in fifty counties. A yield of 613 pounds per acre was reported in Saint Louis county, in latitude 46° 30′—an evidence of the peculiar climatic conditions of this region, and of the wonderful capacity of the plant to adapt itself to a new habitation. In Houston county, in the southeastern corner of the state, on the Mississippi river, a yield of 6,253 pounds on 12 acres was reported; in Meeker county, a degree and a half farther north, 6,403 pounds were grown upon 12 acres.

In Iowa tobacco was grown in eighty-seven of ninety-nine counties. Seven counties—Marshall and Grundy, in the central portion of the state; Decatur, Wayne, and Davis, on the Missouri border; Jones, in the central eastern part; and Madison, in the central southern part—together produced 160,391 pounds, 38 per cent. of the total product of the state. The yield per acre (in Marshall 953 pounds, and in Grundy 1,478 pounds) indicates a favorable soil and evidences good culture. The average yield of the state is 608 pounds, exceeding that of Virginia 40 pounds per acre. Experiments made with the White Burley tobacco have given satisfactory results.

In Kansas tobacco was planted in sixty-two counties. Two counties, Franklin and Chautauqua, produced more than 10,000 pounds each, the former averaging 778 and the latter 567 pounds per acre. The product is red, coarse, and of inferior quality, and is used only for home consumption.

In Otoe county, Nebraska, there were grown 10,065 pounds of tobacco on 11 acres, an average of 915 pounds, but nothing is known of the character of the product.

California produced some bright yellow tobacco of good quality in 1874; but the industry has not grown in importance: an indication that the culture has not been profitable. San Benito county reported 59,100 pounds grown in 1879 on 64 acres, an average of 923 pounds per acre; Los Angeles 8,200 pounds, grown on 10 acres. So far as can be ascertained only a few small crops were grown in 1880. Replies received to inquiries as to tobacco-growers in San Benito state that no tobacco was planted in that county, and that only two persons were known to be engaged in its production in Santa Clara.

Tobacco is grown to a small extent in Arizona, New Mexico, Nevada, Colorado, Idaho, Dakota, Oregon, and Washington territory, but the characteristics and capabilities of the soils of this vast region are comparatively unknown.

The following tabular statement shows the acreage, production, yield per acre, value of crop in farmers' hands or in primary markets, value per hundred pounds, value per acre, cost per hundred pounds and per acre, and profit per hundred pounds and per acre of the tobacco crop of 1879 in the states producing it as a staple, with the rank of each state in acreage, production, etc. Kentucky, Ohio, Missouri, and Illinois produce, in separate districts of their respective territory, two or more distinct classes of tobacco, differing widely in the character and in the value of the cured product. The figures are given in the table for these districts separately:

RANK OF EACH STATE.							STATES.	Acreage.	Production (pounds).	Value of crop in farmers' hands.	Value per 100 pounds.	Value per acre.	Cost of production per 100 pounds.	Difference between cost and value per 100 pounds.
Production.	Acreage.	Total value.	Value per acre.	Value per 100 pounds.	Cost per 100 pounds.	Difference of cost and value.								
1	1	1	9	13	13	12	Kentucky	226, 120	171, 120, 784	$11, 080, 782	$6 48	$49 04	$4 90	$1 58
							White Burley district	53, 474	46, 863, 687	4, 920, 813	10 50	92 02	6 60	3 90
							Shipping districts	170, 421	123, 428, 119	6, 169, 169	5 00	30 20	4 25	0 76
							Remainder (a)	2, 225	829, 978	...	...	...	...	...
2	2	2	14	12	10	13	Virginia	140, 791	79, 988, 868	5, 399, 249	6 75	38 35	5 33	1 42
3	7	3	4	5	5	3	Pennsylvania	27, 560	36, 943, 272	4, 630, 360	12 55	168 19	8 42	4 13
4	8	5	7	9	9	10	Ohio	34, 676	34, 735, 235	2, 670, 434	7 69	77 01	5 91	1 78
							White Burley district	11, 255	10, 826, 083	1, 299, 202	12 00	115 43	7 70	4 30
							Spangled district	7, 551	6, 326, 040	316, 403	5 00	41 90	4 69	0 31
							Seed-leaf district	15, 460	17, 302, 783	1, 054, 830	6 10	68 23	5 27	0 83
							Remainder (a)	410	277, 729	...	...	...	...	...
5	4	8	16	14	14	18	Tennessee	41, 532	29, 365, 052	1, 536, 287	5 24	37 04	4 50	0 74
6	3	4	8	2	4	2	North Carolina	57, 208	26, 986, 213	3, 805, 056	14 10	66 51	9 33	4 77
7	5	7	10	11	11	9	Maryland (b)	38, 174	26, 082, 147	1, 825, 750	7 00	47 83	5 01	1 99
8	11	6	2	3	2	4	Connecticut	8, 666	14, 044, 652	1, 929, 982	13 74	222 71	9 85	3 89
9	6	12	13	17	17	16	Missouri	15, 621	12, 015, 657	600, 256	5 00	38 67	3 58	1 42
							Manufacturing district	2, 977	1, 701, 391	136, 114	8 00	45 72	5 25	2 75
							Shipping district	12, 644	10, 314, 266	464, 142	4 50	37 00	3 41	1 09
10	10	9	6	8	12	6	Wisconsin	8, 810	10, 608, 423	899, 118	8 48	102 06	4 95	3 53
11	9	13	15	16	16	16	Indiana	11, 955	8, 872, 842	443, 642	5 00	37 11	3 60	1 40
12	13	10	5	7	6	6	New York	4, 937	6, 481, 431	721, 059	11 12	146 05	8 00	3 12
13	15	11	3	4	3	7	Massachusetts	3, 358	5, 369, 436	683, 575	12 73	203 57	9 72	3 01
14	12	14	17	15	15	17	Illinois	5, 612	3, 935, 625	202, 661	5 15	36 11	4 17	0 98
							Seed-leaf district	752	1, 043, 975	87, 036	8 34	115 74	4 61	3 73
							Shipping district	4, 860	2, 891, 650	115, 625	4 00	23 70	4 00	...
15	14	15	12	10	6	14	West Virginia	4, 071	2, 296, 146	170, 374	7 42	41 85	6 00	1 42
16	17	16	19	18	18	11	Arkansas (c)	2, 064	970, 220	41, 547	4 28	20 13	2 70	1 58
24	30	0	1	6	1	8	New Hampshire (d)	88	170, 843	20, 501	12 00	232 97	10 00	2 00
32	29	0	11	1	7	1	Florida (d)	90	21, 182	3, 995	18 86	44 39	7 50	11 36

a Not included in the districts as defined in this report. Very little of this tobacco is marketed, being retained by the growers for home consumption.
b A small amount of seed-leaf is grown.
c Not more than one-half the product of Arkansas is marketed.
d New Hampshire and Florida are introduced into this table as indicating extremes of price for the one and of yield per acre for the other. The results of tobacco culture in these two states afford a curious study.

The tables on the following pages show the acreage and tobacco crop of the year 1879.

TOBACCO CROP OF THE UNITED STATES, BY COUNTIES (CENSUS OF 1880).

ALABAMA.

County.	Acres.	Pounds.	County.	Acres.	Pounds.	County.	Acres.	Pounds.
Total	2,197	452,426	Crenshaw	83	6,256	Macon	6	680
			Cullman	41	8,888	Madison	224	36,350
Autauga	6	1,844	Dale	2	250	Marengo	43	7,479
Baldwin	1	350	Dallas	13	1,078	Marion	44	8,285
Barbour	22	3,512	De Kalb	19	4,322	Marshall	48	9,710
Bibb	36	5,248	Elmore	12	2,586	Monroe	11	2,496
Blount	48	9,012	Etowah	47	11,333	Montgomery	2	318
Bullock	3	833	Fayette	37	7,184	Morgan	62	17,795
Butler	7	2,550	Franklin	17	3,087	Perry	24	4,623
Calhoun	29	6,592	Geneva	4	948	Pickens	51	8,637
Chambers	39	8,055	Greene	41	6,820	Pike	5	764
Cherokee	62	14,318	Hale	16	5,540	Randolph	44	11,521
Chilton	4	537	Henry	24	4,490	Russell	2	303
Choctaw	23	4,322	Jackson	90	17,127	Saint Clair	53	11,208
Clarke	10	2,340	Jefferson	55	17,640	Shelby	10	2,298
Clay	85	13,408	Lamar	46	10,420	Sumter	13	2,627
Cleburne	85	15,113	Lauderdale	106	19,870	Talladega	30	5,520
Coffee	5	1,403	Lawrence	105	27,276	Tallapoosa	21	5,350
Colbert	84	8,820	Lee	11	1,700	Tuscaloosa	20	5,568
Conecuh	7	1,210	Limestone	107	32,034	Walker	69	10,900
Coosa	28	5,258				Wilcox	15	2,695
Covington	8	1,764				Winston	3	571

ARIZONA.

County.	Acres.	Pounds.	County.	Acres.	Pounds.	County.	Acres.	Pounds.
Pima	1	600						

ARKANSAS.

County.	Acres.	Pounds.	County.	Acres.	Pounds.	County.	Acres.	Pounds.
Total	2,064	970,220	Greene	8	5,735	Perry	14	5,918
			Hempstead	12	3,000	Phillips	12	11,172
Arkansas	15	5,952	Hot Spring	23	5,823	Pike	16	4,809
Ashley	15	4,194	Howard	23	7,749	Poinsett	4	2,470
Baxter	13	6,470	Independence	44	21,726	Polk	10	2,040
Benton	547	395,982	Izard	81	13,212	Pope	33	12,570
Boone	81	34,089	Jackson	11	4,700	Prairie	9	4,860
Bradley	23	1,433	Jefferson	2	250	Pulaski	13	4,965
Calhoun	6	1,470	Johnson	27	7,041	Randolph	27	13,848
Carroll	28	16,540	La Fayette	10	3,217	Saint Francis	21	9,276
Clark	18	3,732	Lawrence	8	4,600	Saline	24	9,418
Clay	21	11,390	Lee	12	2,962	Scott	13	5,896
Columbia	40	13,333	Lincoln	9	3,276	Searcy	16	8,984
Conway	24	8,501	Little River	10	2,747	Sebastian	27	8,570
Craighead	44	24,942	Logan	98	18,977	Sevier	23	6,284
Crawford	13	1,912	Lonoke	17	6,107	Sharp	33	10,0[illegible]
Crittenden	13	6,105	Madison	45	25,150	Stone	11	5,4[illegible]0
Cross	19	4,406	Marion	11	3,321	Union	49	10,[illegible]15
Dallas	19	8,410	Miller	4	1,335	Van Buren	27	10,469
Desha	9	3,057	Mississippi	4	1,387	Washington	51	23,357
Dorsey	16	4,421	Monroe	5	2,590	White	48	28,1[illegible]4
Drew	12	5,608	Montgomery	13	2,085	Woodruff	5	2,435
Faulkner	44	11,974	Nevada	6	1,907	Yell	16	4,070
Franklin	9	2,404	Newton	84	12,406			
Fulton	4	3,400	Ouachita	13	3,588			
Garland	21	4,751						
Grant	22	9,310						

CALIFORNIA.

County.	Acres.	Pounds.	County.	Acres.	Pounds.	County.	Acres.	Pounds.
Total	84	73,317	Humboldt	1	850	Nevada	1	1,000
			Los Angeles	10	8,200	San Benito	64	59,100
Butte	1	200	Mendocino	1	360	San Joaquin	2	900
Calaveras	1	500	Merced	1	500	Sonoma	1	667
Del Norte	1	1,040						

CONNECTICUT.

County.	Acres.	Pounds.	County.	Acres.	Pounds.	County.	Acres.	Pounds.
Total	8,666	14,044,652	Litchfield	1,556	2,211,161	New London	10	29,622
			Middlesex	573	806,753	Tolland	405	658,634
Fairfield	602	973,933	New Haven	167	215,105	Windham	2	1,850
Hartford	5,112	9,039,514						

DAKOTA.

County.	Acres.	Pounds.	County.	Acres.	Pounds.	County.	Acres.	Pounds.
Total	5	1,897	Bonhomme	3	1,057	Clay	2	840

DELAWARE.

County.	Acres.	Pounds.	County.	Acres.	Pounds.	County.	Acres.	Pounds.
Total	4	1,278	Kent	3	740	New Castle	1	538

DISTRICT OF COLUMBIA.

County.	Acres.	Pounds.	County.	Acres.	Pounds.	County.	Acres.	Pounds.
Washington	2	1,400						

FLORIDA.

County.	Acres.	Pounds.	County.	Acres.	Pounds.	County.	Acres.	Pounds.
Total	90	21,182	Jackson	4	834	Orange	1	500
			Jefferson	5	507	Santa Rosa	7	919
Alachua	11	980	Lafayette	4	1,180	Sumter	1	200
Calhoun	3	615	Leon	10	3,006	Suwannee	2	715
Clay	1	300	Madison	5	1,045	Walton	3	467
Columbia	8	785	Marion	13	1,258	Washington	2	415
Gadsden	14	6,677	Monroe	1	300			

GEORGIA.

County.	Acres.	Pounds.	County.	Acres.	Pounds.	County.	Acres.	Pounds.
Total	971	228,500	Floyd	20	5,069	Murray	18	2,375
			Forsyth	26	7,570	Newton	1	235
Appling	7	1,080	Franklin	22	4,288	Oconee	3	995
Baldwin	1	420	Fulton	5	1,590	Paulding	34	7,288
Bartow	30	9,744	Gilmer	7	2,302	Pickens	22	6,640
Bulloch	6	380	Gordon	14	4,053			
Calhoun	2	311	Greene	7	1,949	Pike	6	1,330
			Gwinnett	40	11,588	Polk	22	8,130
Carroll	15	2,792	Habersham	19	2,063	Rabun	18	3,643
Catoosa	7	2,337	Hall	46	8,201	Spalding	3	580
Chattahoochee	3	510	Hancock	7	1,920	Stewart	1	300
Chattooga	4	980	Haralson	35	10,138			
Cherokee	35	17,900	Harris	5	1,108	Sumter	1	470
			Hart	20	5,204	Talbot	4	719
Clarke	1	445	Heard	11	1,630	Taliaferro	1	205
Clinch	1	275	Henry	2	420	Taylor	3	1,000
Cobb	4	740	Houston	3	374	Telfair	1	215
Coffee	5	1,003	Jackson	14	4,083			
Colquitt	5	1,168	Jasper	1	277	Thomas	2	656
			Jones	5	1,923	Towns	48	3,127
Coweta	18	2,454				Troup	5	2,133
Crawford	8	706	Lincoln	10	4,080	Union	43	7,707
Dade	8	435	Lumpkin	46	10,021	Upson	3	311
Dawson	19	3,902	McDuffie	2	355			
Decatur	2	803	Macon	1	355	Walker	7	2,377
			Madison	1	480	Walton	5	1,957
De Kalb	6	1,676	Marion	3	645	Ware	1	235
Dooly	2	387	Meriwether	23	5,972	White	24	4,738
Elbert	5	1,020	Milton	8	975	Whitfield	20	5,207
Fannin	53	9,807	Monroe	4	1,009			
Fayette	11	2,537	Montgomery	5	560	Worth	9	1,780

IDAHO.

ILLINOIS.

County.	Acres.	Pounds.	County.	Acres	Pounds.	County.	Acres.	Pounds.
Total	5,612	3,985,825	Hancock	6	1,655	Moultrie	11	4,430
			Hardin	4	2,810	Ogle	3	1,335
Adams	17	8,320	Henry	3	793	Peoria	8	1,219
Alexander	13	2,150	Iroquois	30	9,825	Perry	18	6,705
Bond	14	4,660	Jackson	19	8,770	Piatt	3	1,580
Boone	1.	1,050	Jasper	77	37,817	Pike	19	12,053
Brown	6	3,137	Jefferson	43	22,101	Pope	102	63,013
Bureau	1	400	Jersey	16	5,649	Pulaski	76	46,800
Calhoun	5	3,150	Jo Daviess	462	630,530	Randolph	8	3,001
Carroll	24	33,505	Johnson	366	188,204	Richland	16	8,114
Cass	9	4,460	Kankakee	3	1,650	Rock Island	1	510
Champaign	10	4,070	Knox	8	1,778	Saint Clair	1	485
Christian	11	5,060	La Salle	3	855	Saline	1,070	785,897
Clark	44	10,321	Lawrence	15	10,985	Sangamon	4	2,652
Clay	42	21,085	Lee	7	2,414	Schuyler	4	1,665
Clinton	12	4,857	Livingston	2	685	Scott	6	3,043
Coles	36	13,850	Logan	2	710	Shelby	56	25,022
Cook	21	20,100	McDonough	17	9,491	Stephenson	286	373,031
Crawford	83	65,213	McHenry	4	3,160	Tazewell	5	2,575
Cumberland	30	15,464	McLean	2	845	Union	6	2,155
De Witt	6	3,409	Macon	6	2,140	Vermilion	18	8,405
Douglas	7	3,840	Macoupin	22	9,742	Wabash	15	6,040
Edgar	35	15,326	Madison	11	6,825	Warren	1	450
Edwards	1	425	Marion	38	20,117	Washington	9	4,920
Effingham	31	14,078	Marshall	3	1,075	Wayne	42	28,665
Fayette	29	14,150	Massac	120	89,280	White	47	37,780
Franklin	184	98,672	Menard	2	620	Williamson	1,363	752,904
Fulton	25	18,259	Mercer	1	345	Woodford	2	1,080
Gallatin	35	19,820	Montgomery	21	8,825			
Greene	14	6,338	Morgan	6	2,214			
Grundy	3	880						
Hamilton	382	244,600						

INDIANA.

County.	Acres.	Pounds.	County.	Acres.	Pounds.	County.	Acres.	Pounds.
Total	11,955	8,672,642	Hendricks	12	5,820	Pike	974	687,674
			Henry	13	11,225	Porter	3	1,417
Adams	7	2,635	Howard	11	6,670	Posey	43	25,935
Allen	19	17,003	Huntington	6	3,035	Pulaski	11	6,060
Bartholomew	40	37,364	Jackson	19	10,602	Putnam	29	11,624
Blackford	3	1,100	Jasper	7	4,627	Randolph	21	8,601
Boone	25	16,912	Jay	4	2,110	Ripley	20	11,840
Brown	251	190,285	Jefferson	33	23,821	Rush	2	1,110
Carroll	10	5,159	Jennings	21	10,535	Saint Joseph	2	925
Cass	3	483	Johnson	5	3,965	Scott	14	4,780
Clark	37	24,165	Knox	7	4,945	Shelby	47	40,791
Clay	13	5,800	Kosciusko	6	3,302	Spencer	3,355	2,593,559
Clinton	15	7,978	Lagrange	1	610	Starke	2	1,357
Crawford	20	10,920	La Porte	2	735	Steuben	1	380
Daviess	85	20,280	Lawrence	20	11,542	Sullivan	48	22,125
Dearborn	1	200	Madison	9	4,745	Switzerland	79	79,298
Decatur	7	2,847	Marion	5	2,256	Tippecanoe	7	3,045
De Kalb	1	387	Marshall	8	2,624	Tipton	21	9,631
Delaware	5	2,231	Martin	20	10,671	Union	4	2,325
Dubois	1,144	778,024	Miami	4	1,630	Vanderburgh	9	4,355
Elkhart	3	1,075	Monroe	28	16,237	Vermillion	10	5,563
Fayette	9	6,450	Montgomery	13	6,249	Vigo	8	4,245
Floyd	1	295	Morgan	14	6,490	Wabash	29	20,280
Fountain	25	8,404	Newton	2	850	Warren	18	5,650
Franklin	5	1,097	Noble	2	863	Warrick	4,273	3,253,323
Fulton	5	1,814	Ohio	1	1,000	Washington	78	50,606
Gibson	123	91,015	Orange	67	41,830	Wayne	248	268,024
Grant	4	1,775	Owen	43	21,090	Wells	9	6,402
Greene	125	92,350	Parke	26	11,582	White	8	4,215
Hamilton	9	4,579	Perry	282	164,480	Whitley	1	800
Hancock	6	3,110						
Harrison	10	6,536						

IOWA.

County.	Acres.	Pounds.	County.	Acres.	Pounds.	County.	Acres.	Pounds.
Total	892	420,477	Delaware	7	3,954	Marion	9	7,250
Adair	2	1,126	Des Moines	3	1,427	Marshall	24	22,875
Adams	4	2,486	Dubuque	10	7,030	Mills	3	1,315
Allamakee	8	4,531	Fayette	7	3,404	Mitchell	8	1,534
Appanoose	12	6,841	Floyd	4	1,920	Monona	4	1,030
Audubon	8	1,542	Franklin	4	2,630	Monroe	4	1,855
Benton	8	1,590	Fremont	11	6,699	Montgomery	3	1,265
Black Hawk	3	1,280	Greene	1	681	Muscatine	2	890
Boone	6	4,107	Grundy	23	32,525	O'Brien	1	704
Bremer	2	571	Guthrie	6	3,210	Page	6	3,685
Buchanan	8	1,952	Hamilton	8	1,584	Palo Alto	1	425
Buena Vista	1	550	Hancock	1	268	Polk	8	1,725
Butler	10	7,375	Hardin	2	555	Pottawattamie	4	2,485
Calhoun	1	700	Harrison	6	2,805	Poweshiek	7	3,430
Cass	1	370	Henry	12	7,306	Ringgold	11	6,028
Cedar	4	3,468	Howard	4	1,709	Sac	1	650
Cerro Gordo	8	5,320	Iowa	8	4,746	Shelby	8	3,171
Cherokee	3	5,000	Jackson	8	3,222	Story	13	4,599
Chickasaw	12	7,060	Jasper	12	6,228	Tama	18	3,854
Clarke	14	8,655	Jefferson	17	3,155	Taylor	4	1,765
Clayton	10	4,135	Johnson	5	3,470	Union	6	1,699
Clinton	1	250	Jones	31	31,507	Van Buren	22	9,173
Crawford	1	982	Keokuk	18	8,230	Wapello	8	5,175
Dallas	6	4,556	Kossuth	2	1,237	Warren	7	3,402
Davis	19	12,186	Lee	15	4,256	Washington	5	3,640
Decatur	47	27,288	Linn	8	4,277	Wayne	31	18,835
			Louisa	8	1,070	Webster	7	1,402
			Lucas	11	7,000	Winnebago	7	0,602
			Madison	87	14,175	Winneshiek	3	1,513
			Mahaska	11	5,795	Worth	6	2,810

KANSAS.

County.	Acres.	Pounds.	County.	Acres.	Pounds.	County.	Acres.	Pounds.
Total	333	191,869	Ellis	6	4,565	Montgomery	4	2,910
Allen	5	1,886	Franklin	16	11,670	Morris	1	770
Anderson	3	1,425	Greenwood	4	3,050	Nemaha	4	1,992
Atchison	10	6,088	Harper	1	300	Neosho	12	7,259
Barton	1	610	Harvey	3	1,025	Osage	6	2,651
Bourbon	8	2,655	Jackson	5	2,890	Osborne	1	585
Brown	2	830	Jefferson	8	5,145	Ottawa	1	805
Butler	7	4,785	Jewell	6	3,120	Phillips	2	1,458
Chase	1	360	Johnson	5	2,460	Pottawatomie	9	5,040
Chautauqua	20	11,845	Kingman	4	5,000	Republic	13	7,066
Cherokee	7	2,285	Labette	8	4,697	Riley	2	235
Clay	4	1,700	Leavenworth	6	3,785	Rush	9	5,575
Cloud	7	4,415	Lincoln	1	266	Sedgwick	1	820
Coffey	4	2,565	Linn	6	6,660	Shawnee	2	886
Cowley	3	960	Lyon	6	2,025	Smith	3	2,412
Crawford	7	4,580	McPherson	1	600	Sumner	1	540
Davis	1	705	Marion	2	800	Wabaunsee	6	1,407
Dickinson	1	500	Marshall	6	2,070	Washington	11	5,660
Doniphan	9	8,335	Miami	14	6,000	Wilson	7	4,005
Douglas	11	2,718	Mitchell	3	675	Woodson	5	3,045
Elk	9	5,216				Wyandotte	8	5,150

KENTUCKY.

County.	Acres.	Pounds.	County.	Acres.	Pounds.	County.	Acres.	Pounds.
Total	226,120	171,120,784	Bath	112	70,819	Boyle	13	6,262
Adair	1,142	696,746	Bell	24	4,567	Bracken	7,159	6,120,635
Allen	283	100,355	Boone	1,706	1,770,958	Breathitt	54	8,169
Anderson	43	22,480	Bourbon	19	17,001	Breckinridge	5,444	3,932,565
Ballard	5,195	3,760,743	Boyd	42	19,711	Bullitt	28	8,502
Barren	3,120	2,805,586						

KENTUCKY—Continued.

County.	Acres.	Pounds.	County.	Acres.	Pounds.	County.	Acres.	Pounds.
Butler	1,652	1,030,029	Henry	4,371	4,015,708	Muhlenburgh	3,856	2,731,716
Caldwell	4,272	3,215,602	Hickman	658	461,048	Nelson	14	4,722
Calloway	5,035	3,477,520	Hopkins	6,744	5,028,435	Nicholas	938	759,118
Campbell	891	704,527	Jackson	41	9,268	Ohio	4,767	3,167,989
Carroll	2,780	2,584,116	Jefferson	26	11,632	Oldham	365	296,860
Carter	50	22,403	Jessamine	6	1,355			
Casey	125	67,449	Johnson	50	12,566	Owen	7,007	5,785,351
Christian	18,475	12,577,574	Kenton	2,358	3,322,771	Owsley	20	9,065
Clark	38	17,187	Knox	37	18,008	Pendleton	5,302	4,072,291
Clay	51	12,274	La Rue	563	350,360	Pike	100	18,643
Clinton	143	77,408	Laurel	68	23,202	Powell	38	8,543
Crittenden	2,368	1,647,036	Lawrence	101	23,392	Pulaski	106	30,516
Cumberland	655	671,970	Lee	29	10,670	Robertson	2,365	1,722,398
Daviess	13,280	9,823,461	Leslie	11	2,050	Rockcastle	52	17,181
Edmonson	727	456,670	Letcher	23	2,907	Rowan	41	24,430
Elliott	112	35,683	Lewis	1,516	1,036,900	Russell	110	75,469
Estill	58	18,380	Lincoln	97	35,214			
Fayette	2	702	Livingston	1,127	709,578	Scott	210	160,535
Fleming	1,548	1,866,855	Logan	8,104	6,032,083	Shelby	661	520,262
Floyd	73	12,845	Lyon	1,355	980,403	Simpson	2,240	1,668,055
Franklin	1,208	890,361	McCracken	3,377	2,419,825	Spencer	41	28,185
Fulton	537	410,337	McLean	4,934	3,729,616	Taylor	1,526	932,026
Gallatin	1,249	1,265,367	Madison	82	30,173			
Garrard	89	45,612	Magoffin	73	11,464	Todd	8,456	6,808,425
Grant	2,438	2,130,215	Marion	171	101,980	Trigg	8,481	5,607,143
Graves	11,318	8,901,434	Marshall	2,085	1,411,692	Trimble	2,070	1,658,307
Grayson	1,770	1,065,244	Martin	30	9,484	Union	3,634	2,006,298
Green	2,845	1,417,070	Mason	5,485	6,261,365	Warren	3,565	2,605,368
Greenup	43	21,698	Meade	694	483,250	Washington	87	43,860
Hancock	3,037	2,155,180	Menifee	30	18,368	Wayne	50	20,264
Hardin	540	374,302	Mercer	20	14,300	Webster	6,447	4,740,682
Harlan	2	790	Metcalfe	942	614,577	Whitley	19	3,498
Harrison	1,657	1,201,972	Monroe	222	187,141	Wolfe	50	29,520
Hart	3,027	2,239,626	Montgomery	123	128,472			
Henderson	12,468	10,312,031	Morgan	60	9,931	Woodford	1	530

LOUISIANA.

Total	283	55,054	Iberia	2	516	Sabine	12	2,833
PARISH.			Jackson	9	2,480	Saint Helena	1	225
Avoyelles	30	5,262	La Fayette	24	2,334	Saint James	64	14,680
Bossier	4	1,005	Lincoln	6	2,060	Saint Landry	7	1,262
Caddo	3	1,268	Livingston	3	885	Saint Martin	7	775
Calcasieu	9	2,910						
Caldwell	8	1,780				Tangipahoa	2	275
Catahoula	1	370	Morehouse	1	380	Union	2	665
De Soto	14	4,286	Natchitoches	1	405	Vermillion	5	1,112
East Baton Rouge	1	400	Ouachita	1	445	Vernon	1	210
Franklin	2	585	Point Coupée	1	500	Webster	8	1,155
Grant	1	220	Red River	1	375	Winn	22	4,846

MAINE.

Sagadahoc	1	250						

MARYLAND.

Total	86,174	26,082,147	Carroll	162	137,171	Montgomery	1,053	806,026
COUNTY.			Cecil	43	59,030	Prince George's	9,637	8,575,246
Allegany	2	1,115	Charles	7,913	5,145,509	Saint Mary's	5,528	4,429,310
Anne Arundel	6,271	4,441,010	Frederick	429	370,840	Somerset	2	1,355
Baltimore	12	9,601	Garrett	4	1,027	Washington	5	7,050
Calvert	6,848	3,880,845	Harford	52	68,085	Wicomico	3	1,388
Caroline	1	1,422	Howard	208	138,030	Worcester	1	205

MASSACHUSETTS.

County.	Acres.	Pounds.	County.	Acres.	Pounds.	County.	Acres.	Pounds.
Total	3,353	5,369,436	Franklin	1,211	1,926,238	Hampshire	1,448	2,305,442
Berkshire	60	85,747	Hampden	633	1,051,474	Norfolk	1	540

MICHIGAN.

County.	Acres.	Pounds.	County.	Acres.	Pounds.	County.	Acres.	Pounds.
Total	170	83,969	Ingham	2	768	Muskegon	1	240
Allegan	4	1,963	Ionia	2	1,185	Newaygo	2	1,354
Antrim	3	1,925	Isabella	1	425	Oakland	2	345
Barry	3	2,160	Jackson	5	3,171	Oceana	3	1,735
Bay	1	280	Kalamazoo	1	485	Ottawa	8	1,378
Benzie	1	965	Kent	4	3,147	Saginaw	4	1,873
Berrien	6	2,126	Lapeer	6	2,008	Saint Clair	7	2,908
Branch	4	2,213	Leelanaw	5	1,987	Saint Joseph	2	1,376
Calhoun	3	730	Lenawee	10	6,863	Sanilac	4	2,257
Cass	8	3,460	Macomb	8	1,365	Shiawassee	3	2,225
Eaton	5	2,850	Manistee	1	287	Tuscola	8	5,365
Emmet	9	2,080	Manitou	2	322	Van Buren	9	4,386
Genesee	2	540	Midland	1	230	Washtenaw	2	968
Gratiot	4	1,337	Monroe	11	5,737	Wayne	3	1,756
Hillsdale	9	2,180	Montcalm	1	650			
Huron	4	1,554						

MINNESOTA.

County.	Acres.	Pounds.	County.	Acres.	Pounds.	County.	Acres.	Pounds.
Total	163	69,922	Goodhue	2	405	Ramsey	2	1,320
Anoka	3	1,025	Hennepin	8	966	Redwood	1	810
Becker	1	333	Houston	12	6,253	Renville	2	377
Benton	3	630	Isanti	3	2,096	Rice	7	2,400
Blue Earth	2	690	Kandiyohi	4	2,010	Saint Louis	3	1,930
Brown	3	936	Le Sueur	6	3,401	Scott	4	2,480
Carver	8	2,661	Lincoln	1	212	Sherburne	5	2,817
Chippewa	2	1,276	McLeod	4	1,573	Sibley	3	536
Chisago	1	442	Meeker	12	6,403	Stearns	6	3,265
Cottonwood	2	610	Morrison	4	1,071	Steele	3	1,050
Dakota	1	300	Mower	4	1,075	Swift	2	1,025
Dodge	2	1,070	Nicollet	4	545	Todd	1	706
Douglas	6	2,305	Olmsted	1	353	Waseca	3	1,512
Faribault	1	300	Otter Tail	4	1,965	Washington	1	930
Fillmore	7	2,525	Polk	1	210	Watonwan	1	430
Freeborn	2	575				Winona	2	600
						Wright	8	2,237

MISSISSIPPI.

County.	Acres.	Pounds.	County.	Acres.	Pounds.	County.	Acres.	Pounds.
Total	1,471	414,068	Itawamba	32	7,520	Noxubee	38	8,219
Adams	5	1,264	Jasper	17	3,649	Oktibbeha	15	2,790
Alcorn	40	14,852	Jefferson	9	2,027	Panola	10	3,347
Amite	16	3,230	Jones	17	4,088	Pike	1	400
Attala	32	10,711	Kemper	16	6,716	Pontotoc	41	15,207
Benton	33	10,634	La Fayette	21	5,803	Prentiss	38	13,406
Bolivar	1	600	Lauderdale	27	7,686	Rankin	26	5,798
Calhoun	27	7,926	Lawrence	35	5,288	Scott	34	11,044
Carroll	7	2,460	Leake	56	18,080	Simpson	4	1,329
Chickasaw	33	10,926	Lee	45	11,100	Smith	28	10,402
Choctaw	39	12,300	Le Flore	3	907	Sumner	27	5,732
Claiborne	3	1,010	Lincoln	32	8,442	Tallahatchie	9	1,924
Clarke	28	8,870	Lowndes	6	1,734	Tate	6	1,030
Clay	29	11,750	Madison	28	10,968	Tippah	71	25,127
Copiah	22	5,440	Marion	2	437	Tishomingo	44	18,526
Covington	13	4,743	Marshall	33	9,738	Union	25	7,578
De Soto	27	12,026	Monroe	90	16,864	Warren	1	207
Franklin	13	3,082	Montgomery	26	6,853	Wayne	12	3,294
Grenada	7	2,118	Neshoba	27	6,091	Wilkinson	3	628
Hinds	17	3,368	Newton	20	8,525	Winston	27	9,480
Holmes	11	4,321				Yalobusha	14	5,323
						Yazoo	8	1,300

MISSOURI.

County.	Acres.	Pounds.
Total	15,621	12,616,657
Adair	27	28,838
Andrew	16	12,257
Atchison	18	12,008
Audrain	34	20,477
Barry	48	42,500
Barton	16	10,135
Bates	28	15,640
Benton	19	10,300
Bollinger	20	8,189
Boone	66	40,958
Buchanan	23	12,035
Butler	28	12,530
Caldwell	4	1,930
Callaway	1,175	870,231
Camden	11	4,838
Cape Girardeau	33	17,222
Carroll	670	639,325
Carter	5	3,503
Cass	7	2,310
Cedar	53	30,683
Chariton	4,674	4,384,924
Christian	11	7,001
Clark	13	6,278
Clay	3	1,243
Clinton	26	13,972
Cole	11	5,430
Cooper	29	21,252
Crawford	18	7,400
Dade	10	5,422
Dallas	18	11,210
Daviess	25	13,330
De Kalb	10	6,550
Dent	14	9,075
Douglas	28	13,130
Dunklin	26	14,051
Franklin	147	94,154
Gasconade	16	8,624
Gentry	23	10,890
Greene	40	16,528
Grundy	24	11,756
Harrison	74	42,052
Henry	20	9,543
Hickory	13	4,502
Holt	22	18,337
Howard	795	604,704
Howell	18	9,004
Iron	7	2,021
Jackson	56	41,986
Jasper	4	2,420
Jefferson	9	5,801
Johnson	25	13,025
Knox	42	28,983
Laclede	17	8,583
La Fayette	22	16,060
Lawrence	19	10,305
Lewis	8	4,330
Lincoln	408	308,090
Linn	429	362,133
Livingston	322	305,073
McDonald	23	11,645
Macon	865	728,584
Madison	27	10,040
Maries	7	4,135
Marion	51	40,060
Mercer	57	29,779
Miller	27	13,543
Mississippi	23	21,616
Moniteau	17	7,310
Monroe	327	421,232
Montgomery	208	181,701
Morgan	32	8,600
New Madrid	29	14,243
Newton	29	13,404
Nodaway	45	23,674
Oregon	51	10,530
Osage	66	52,910
Ozark	39	19,577
Pemiscot	3	2,190
Perry	16	6,694
Pettis	26	13,719
Phelps	40	18,706
Pike	653	408,473
Platte	11	6,200
Polk	44	24,576
Pulaski	23	10,910
Putnam	57	34,143
Ralls	12	6,683
Randolph	889	701,052
Ray	41	22,844
Reynolds	14	6,867
Ripley	20	8,657
Saint Charles	90	52,452
Saint Clair	22	12,101
Saint François	36	15,688
Sainte Genevieve	18	7,320
Saint Louis	4	1,368
Saline	638	540,175
Schuyler	43	32,252
Scotland	28	15,284
Scott	80	16,846
Shannon	9	3,370
Shelby	148	126,567
Stoddard	79	54,183
Stone	25	5,620
Sullivan	59	30,200
Taney	8	3,685
Texas	20	10,745
Vernon	20	12,122
Warren	155	86,672
Washington	34	8,995
Wayne	33	14,005
Webster	49	38,885
Worth	7	3,900
Wright	57	40,588

NEBRASKA.

County.	Acres.	Pounds.
Total	101	57,978
Antelope	1	340
Boone	2	1,380
Burt	4	1,835
Cass	9	3,925
Cedar	1	360
Clay	2	690
Cuming	2	600
Custer	1	425
Dawson	6	2,600
Dixon	1	300
Douglas	2	1,700
Fillmore	1	248
Franklin	1	750
Furnas	1	445
Gage	4	2,740
Hamilton	2	1,475
Harlan	1	670
Holt	5	2,540
Jefferson	2	1,145
Johnson	1	510
Kearney	1	446
Lancaster	3	1,287
Merrick	1	675
Nemaha	4	2,100
Nuckolls	1	480
Otoe	11	10,065
Pawnee	3	1,455
Platte	1	270
Red Willow	1	225
Richardson	9	4,881
Saline	4	2,467
Saunders	3	1,110
Sherman	1	620
Thayer	1	400
Washington	1	944
Webster	5	3,880
York	2	1,890

NEVADA.

NEW JERSEY.

County.	Acres.	Pounds.	County.	Acres.	Pounds.	County.	Acres.	Pounds.
Total	152	172,315	Gloucester	2	570	Passaic	1	318
			Hunterdon	2	890	Salem	1	560
Bergen	1	250	Mercer	60	69,810	Sussex	1	400
Burlington	76	94,487	Morris	2	1,700	Warren	1	330
Essex	5	3,300						

NEW MEXICO.

County.	Acres.	Pounds.	County.	Acres.	Pounds.	County.	Acres.	Pounds.
Taos	7	890						

NEW YORK.

County.	Acres.	Pounds.	County.	Acres.	Pounds.	County.	Acres.	Pounds.
Total	4,837	6,481,431	Greene	1	355	Otsego	3	2,183
			Hamilton	2	710	Putnam	42	55,309
Allegany	2	609	Herkimer	1	340	Saint Lawrence	4	1,049
Broome	53	67,518	Jefferson	5	1,850	Saratoga	2	840
Cattaraugus	2	823	Lewis	3	1,072	Schenectady	6	6,850
Cayuga	299	407,769				Schoharie	2	1,014
Chautauqua	4	1,763	Livingston	1	457	Schuyler	7	8,250
Chemung	1,102	1,571,685	Madison	53	50,064	Steuben	698	904,125
Chenango	16	12,049	Monroe	12	20,250	Suffolk	2	405
Clinton	20	7,430	Niagara	5	2,795	Sullivan	3	1,099
Columbia	4	5,670	Oneida	8	1,692	Tioga	25	20,433
Cortland	1	263				Tompkins	102	115,771
Delaware	3	1,012	Onondaga	1,769	2,346,257	Ulster	1	500
Duchess	279	407,156	Ontario	1	567	Warren	1	615
Erie	2	1,212	Orange	6	5,350	Wayne	13	14,710
Essex	1	684	Orleans	98	110,365	Westchester	8	1,825
Franklin	10	4,084	Oswego	256	312,341	Yates	1	418

NORTH CAROLINA.

County.	Acres.	Pounds.	County.	Acres.	Pounds.	County.	Acres.	Pounds.
Total	57,298	26,986,213	Gates	3	620	Pender	8	690
			Graham	4	1,095	Perquimans	1	400
Alamance	1,688	695,013	Granville	8,941	4,606,358	Person	5,968	3,012,387
Alexander	28	11,799	Greene	8	1,055	Pitt	.8	568
Alleghany	8	2,049	Guilford	910	422,716	Polk	4	931
Anson	11	4,880						
Ashe	60	11,064	Halifax	21	8,487			
Beaufort	17	5,263	Harnett	32	9,510	Randolph	45	11,101
Bertie	2	554	Haywood	100	39,518	Richmond	6	1,305
Bladen	6	1,040	Henderson	29	4,087	Robeson	2	577
Brunswick	7	2,502	Hertford	7	2,160	Rockingham	9,332	4,341,259
Buncombe	947	475,428				Rowan	216	115,251
			Hyde	4	517			
Burke	58	20,079	Iredell	465	242,714	Rutherford	36	12,908
Cabarrus	12	3,239	Jackson	21	4,601	Sampson	26	14,352
Caldwell	75	25,384	Johnston	36	12,861	Stanley	8	1,735
Carteret	1	303	Jones	1	250	Stokes	4,890	2,131,181
Caswell	10,174	4,336,664				Surry	2,136	905,250
			Lenoir	45	13,500			
Catawba	49	20,380	Lincoln	15	6,085			
Chatham	141	49,837	McDowell	100	30,541	Swain	11	1,166
Cherokee	42	8,411	Macon	46	9,154	Transylvania	10	3,853
Chowan	1	398	Madison	1,620	607,011	Union	9	3,407
Clay	25	5,771				Wake	238	94,354
Cleaveland	28	5,122	Martin	1	211	Warren	1,756	992,254
Columbus	15	3,860	Mecklenburg	10	2,291			
Craven	6	2,732	Mitchell	77	29,047	Washington	4	685
Davidson	464	260,538	Montgomery	54	14,370	Watauga	23	7,210
Davie	1,265	633,330	Moore	70	15,724	Wayne	196	102,979
Duplin	16	4,655	Nash	27	7,502	Wilkes	110	88,211
Edgecombe	3	550	Northampton	86	20,484	Wilson	17	8,745
Forsyth	1,668	822,768	Onslow	2	730			
Franklin	118	56,032	Orange	2,323	1,178,732	Yadkin	425	177,595
Gaston	7	2,180	Pamlico	12	1,520	Yancey	84	33,698

OHIO.

County.	Acres.	Pounds.	County.	Acres.	Pounds.	County.	Acres.	Pounds.
Total	34,676	34,735,285	Gallia	163	99,176	Morgan	872	746,872
Adams	1,179	1,654,070	Geauga	4	2,405	Morrow	6	2,347
Allen	4	5,125	Greene	538	591,746	Muskingum	3	1,067
Ashland	5	6,450	Guernsey	435	372,369	Noble	1,857	1,634,156
Ashtabula	11	12,325	Hamilton	21	15,200	Paulding	15	7,611
Athens	167	140,812	Hancock	2	1,255	Perry	23	12,971
Auglaize	13	8,751	Hardin	7	2,302	Pickaway	9	5,180
Belmont	1,206	1,847,926	Harrison	11	14,180	Pike	14	8,588
Brown	6,181	6,244,856	Henry	12	16,625	Preble	1,893	2,225,861
Butler	800	554,275	Highland	119	95,899	Putnam	4	1,677
Carroll	1	535	Hocking	10	4,125	Richland	1	750
Champaign	11	2,847	Holmes	3	1,103	Ross	18	8,670
Clarke	45	64,642	Jackson	6	2,425	Scioto	20	16,633
Clermont	3,898	3,524,151	Jefferson	1	650	Seneca	1	1,283
Clinton	86	33,098	Knox	2	2,601	Shelby	116	83,130
Columbiana	21	1,850	Lake	15	21,500	Stark	6	6,200
Coshocton	6	2,374	Lawrence	36	23,906	Summit	1	2,472
Crawford	6	1,965	Licking	7	3,675	Trumbull	1	778
Cuyahoga	1	254	Logan	4	2,835	Tuscarawas	1	448
Darke	1,778	2,244,576	Lorain	1	510	Union	5	4,111
Defiance	145	151,279	Lucas	1	551	Van Wert	9	6,776
Delaware	4	2,464	Madison	4	849	Vinton	77	62,627
Fairfield	4	1,295	Mahoning	3	1,386	Warren	1,001	1,125,254
Fayette	6	3,631	Marion	1	580	Washington	733	751,744
Franklin	4	640	Medina	44	65,502	Wayne	52	65,344
Fulton	6	2,121	Meigs	6	8,729	Williams	2	832
			Mercer	13	7,900	Wood	1	450
			Miami	499	646,223	Wyandot	4	3,165
			Monroe	2,037	1,571,008			
			Montgomery	8,604	9,314,372			

OREGON.

County.	Acres.	Pounds.	County.	Acres.	Pounds.	County.	Acres.	Pounds.
Total	43	17,825	Coos	1	671	Lane	17	5,149
Benton	1	379	Douglas	2	785	Linn	8	1,889
Clackamas	8	2,640	Jackson	6	3,625	Tillamook	2	895
Clatsop	1	275	Josephine	1	1,075	Yam Hill	1	842

PENNSYLVANIA.

County.	Acres.	Pounds.	County.	Acres.	Pounds.	County.	Acres.	Pounds.
Total	27,586	36,943,272	Delaware	11	12,347	Northampton	8	4,073
Adams	58	56,107	Elk	2	1,347	Northumberland	488	589,541
Allegheny	6	2,360	Erie	4	2,736	Perry	52	49,120
Armstrong	5	2,730	Fayette	8	5,575	Philadelphia	52	49,600
Beaver	5	2,627	Forest	1	283	Pike	2	518
Bedford	4	2,798	Franklin	77	68,065	Potter	4	2,872
Berks	220	240,027	Fulton	4	3,172	Schuylkill	9	6,764
Bradford	132	173,142	Greene	12	7,383	Snyder	98	115,960
Bucks	934	1,160,970	Huntingdon	12	14,045	Somerset	2	906
Butler	5	4,224	Indiana	15	10,181	Sullivan	1	476
Cambria	5	2,454	Jefferson	2	1,376	Susquehanna	2	1,530
Cameron	7	6,550	Juniata	78	80,609	Tioga	284	292,198
Centre	22	27,733	Lackawanna	2	503	Union	99	109,414
Chester	487	633,632	Lancaster	16,092	28,946,326	Venango	1	421
Clarion	1	454	Lawrence	3	1,080	Warren	1	720
Clearfield	1	490	Lebanon	624	709,488	Washington	3	2,665
Clinton	680	993,401	Lehigh	31	35,620	Wayne	2	783
Columbia	21	8,190	Luzerne	29	35,786	Westmoreland	54	62,096
Crawford	6	3,207	Lycoming	319	463,686	Wyoming	85	39,875
Cumberland	346	448,118	McKean	1	335	York	4,567	6,753,766
Dauphin	544	614,362	Mercer	9	4,116			
			Mifflin	49	55,025			
			Monroe	1	425			
			Montgomery	16	20,980			
			Montour	61	58,179			

RHODE ISLAND.

County.	Acres.	Pounds.	County.	Acres.	Pounds.	County.	Acres.	Pounds.
Providence	2	785						

SOUTH CAROLINA.

County.	Acres.	Pounds.	County.	Acres.	Pounds.	County.	Acres.	Pounds.
Total	169	45,679	Edgefield	9	1,706	Oconee	13	4,775
			Greenville	83	9,838	Orangeburgh	2	310
Abbeville	16	3,280	Horry	19	7,251	Pickens	10	2,400
Aiken	3	800	Lancaster	2	298	Spartanburgh	12	2,153
Anderson	14	8,539	Laurens	8	2,709	Sumter	1	352
Charleston	1	250	Marion	7	1,085	Union	9	1,949
Darlington	2	929	Newberry	2	845	York	7	1,530

TENNESSEE.

County.	Acres.	Pounds.	County.	Acres.	Pounds.	County.	Acres.	Pounds.
Total	41,632	29,305,052	Hamblen	81	34,030	Meigs	13	4,150
			Hamilton	12	4,045	Monroe	86	11,810
			Hancock	51	7,541	Montgomery	11,581	8,208,461
Anderson	26	7,878	Hardeman	84	23,102	Moore	17	7,425
Bedford	51	21,849	Hardin	88	28,300	Morgan	20	8,537
Benton	389	278,721						
Bledsoe	16	6,373				Obion	1,432	1,133,472
Blount	21	4,362	Hawkins	100	42,781	Overton	64	42,947
			Haywood	62	32,991	Perry	29	8,881
Bradley	23	6,110	Henderson	123	43,440	Polk	26	5,295
Campbell	23	6,077	Henry	2,726	1,002,079	Putnam	94	75,384
Cannon	43	19,908	Hickman	51	21,858	Rhea	17	6,347
Carroll	109	80,167				Roane	22	6,165
Carter	87	12,932	Houston	306	206,028	Robertson	6,016	4,342,588
Cheatham	1,343	950,352	Humphreys	33	21,320	Rutherford	47	24,199
Claiborne	43	12,730	Jackson	291	233,072	Scott	35	5,935
Clay	108	67,776	James	0	2,190	Sequatchie	8	2,140
Cocke	45	13,101	Jefferson	10	6,045	Sevier	39	9,810
Coffee	48	21,100				Shelby	41	15,178
			Johnson	26	9,335	Smith	1,819	1,798,081
Crockett	35	10,090	Knox	45	10,306	Stewart	2,848	1,676,773
Cumberland	15	2,835	Lake	5	1,750	Sullivan	207	70,009
Davidson	41	19,690	Lauderdale	68	83,052	Sumner	495	280,326
Decatur	60	31,750	Lawrence	81	16,109	Tipton	46	16,139
De Kalb	65	26,514				Trousdale	1,041	882,805
Dickson	775	494,428	Lewis	7	3,870	Unicoi	65	23,022
Dyer	364	813,365	Lincoln	39	17,948	Union	15	4,026
Fayette	68	20,901	Loudon	24	6,517	Van Buren	14	6,470
Fentress	23	7,807	McMinn	2	615	Warren	77	28,455
Franklin	61	25,061	McNairy	95	34,803	Washington	40	27,312
						Wayne	63	16,844
Gibson	56	92,036	Macon	1,212	898,592	Weakley	4,770	3,506,707
Giles	66	26,814	Madison	67	32,419	White	72	31,084
Grainger	48	13,121	Marion	22	8,344	Williamson	107	134,196
Greene	77	26,102	Marshall	47	24,583	Wilson	361	300,470
Grundy	2	430	Maury	72	90,384			

TEXAS.

County.	Acres.	Pounds.	County.	Acres.	Pounds.	County.	Acres.	Pounds.
Total	685	221,283	Camp	3	635	Freestone	16	5,943
			Cass	9	2,210	Gillespie	1	217
			Cherokee	13	4,715	Gonzales	1	280
Anderson	13	5,140	Collin	1	270	Grayson	29	7,655
Angelina	23	8,495	Colorado	4	631	Gregg	5	905
Austin	8	2,049	Comal	2	595	Grimes	7	2,297
Bastrop	5	1,287	Cooke	8	3,500	Guadalupe	1	350
Bowie	12	3,798	Delta	8	4,685	Hardin	9	795
			Denton	1	255	Harris	5	1,584
			De Witt	3	700	Harrison	9	3,601
Brazoria	2	610	El Paso	1	225	Hayes	1	200
Brazos	4	1,965	Falls	4	1,142	Henderson	14	3,800
Burleson	4	1,510	Fannin	23	9,406	Hopkins	25	9,057
Burnet	1	299	Fayette	4	1,720	Houston	14	4,806
Calhoun	9	450	Franklin	2	1,165	Hunt	11	4,044

TEXAS—Continued.

County.	Acres.	Pounds.	County.	Acres.	Pounds.	County.	Acres.	Pounds.
Jasper	80	2,800	Nacogdoches	24	8,124	Smith	12	5,059
Kaufman	2	790	Newton	9	2,622	Tarrant	1	480
Kendall	2	755	Panola	9	3,000	Titus	6	2,410
Lamar	28	15,003	Polk	1	707	Trinity	18	5,273
Lavaca	8	3,632	Rains	11	4,645	Tyler	10	1,590
Leon	2	932	Red River	7	1,045	Upshur	23	5,822
Liberty	2	600	Robertson	4	1,502	Van Zandt	14	3,217
Limestone	12	6,800	Rusk	7	1,635	Victoria	8	350
Madison	6	900	Sabine	4	1,105	Walker	8	2,756
Marion	8	520	San Augustine	21	4,231	Waller	1	600
Matagorda	2	1,162	San Jacinto	5	1,406	Washington	7	4,134
Montgomery	13	2,635	Shelby	33	9,313	Wharton	2	650
Morris	7	2,712				Wood	24	9,025

VERMONT.

County.	Acres.	Pounds.	County.	Acres.	Pounds.	County.	Acres.	Pounds.
Total	84	131,432	Chittenden	2	886	Washington	1	206
			Franklin	1	893	Windham	74	127,219
Addison	1	440	Lamoille	1	1,025	Windsor	1	260
Bennington	1	303	Rutland	2	760			

VIRGINIA.

County.	Acres.	Pounds.	County.	Acres.	Pounds.	County.	Acres.	Pounds.
Total	140,791	79,988,868	Giles	199	122,056	Page	8	5,237
			Gloucester	25	18,829	Patrick	1,645	714,073
Albemarle	3,216	2,460,972	Goochland	1,052	656,024	Pittsylvania	22,680	12,271,583
Alleghany	11	6,662	Grayson	82	10,485	Powhatan	1,479	914,182
Amelia	3,524	1,726,317	Greene	529	382,492	Prince Edward	4,357	2,482,326
Amherst	4,010	3,111,801	Greensville	11	5,075	Prince George	27	20,500
Appomattox	3,198	1,965,637	Halifax	15,042	7,653,842	Prince William	5	1,292
Augusta	4	1,827	Hanover	1,489	1,064,735	Pulaski	211	122,776
Bath	6	5,615	Henrico	106	101,155	Rappahannock	12	3,830
Bedford	9,174	5,315,560	Henry	6,830	2,955,080	Richmond	14	7,322
Bland	10	4,164	Highland	1	567	Roanoke	1,022	686,410
Botetourt	1,187	742,953	Isle of Wight	5	420	Rockbridge	517	380,065
Brunswick	2,734	1,538,161	King and Queen	80	14,711	Rockingham	14	9,564
Buchanan	10	2,186	King George	20	6,775	Russell	34	11,405
Buckingham	3,978	2,130,529	King William	97	63,066	Scott	135	49,659
Campbell	6,446	3,927,333	Lee	54	15,286	Shenandoah	5	8,106
Caroline	1,204	901,437	Loudoun	6	2,454	Smyth	40	17,859
Carroll	83	29,375	Louisa	2,978	1,921,488	Southampton	5	775
Charlotte	5,922	3,220,446	Lunenburg	3,409	1,976,205	Spotsylvania	554	396,668
Chesterfield	804	523,096	Madison	132	101,697	Stafford	7	4,280
Clarke	10	9,555	Mecklenburg	6,439	3,430,408	Sussex	5	4,715
Craig	56	38,540	Middlesex	4	1,512	Tazewell	48	18,357
Culpeper	6	2,470	Montgomery	1,833	854,496	Warren	2	2,303
Cumberland	2,979	1,814,074	Nansemond	1	215	Washington	679	353,457
Dinwiddie	2,752	1,540,395	Nelson	3,497	2,600,295	Westmoreland	14	18,450
Essex	13	5,015	New Kent	14	11,860	Wise	6	3,308
Fairfax	4	5,370	Northampton	12	1,740	Wythe	16	7,383
Fauquier	17	6,077	Northumberland	11	6,745	York	5	1,061
Floyd	627	342,250	Nottaway	2,911	1,562,670			
Fluvanna	1,391	917,561	Orange	372	260,715			
Franklin	6,862	3,520,833						
Frederick	1	705						

WASHINGTON TERRITORY.

County.	Acres.	Pounds.	County.	Acres.	Pounds.	County.	Acres.	Pounds.
Total	8	6,930	Pierce	6	6,165	Whatcom	1	355
King	1	410						

WEST VIRGINIA.

County.	Acres.	Pounds.	County.	Acres.	Pounds.	County.	Acres.	Pounds.
Total	4,671	2,296,146	Harrison	18	10,131	Preston	10	6,255
			Jackson	250	193,146	Putnam	322	190,864
			Jefferson	2	510	Raleigh	82	10,705
Barbour	25	10,737	Kanawha	820	186,713	Randolph	22	5,738
Berkeley	2	1,471	Lewis	26	8,445	Ritchie	185	138,461
Boone	38	8,057	Lincoln	231	128,417			
Braxton	13	5,020	Logan	78	7,813	Roane	80	11,967
Brooke	1	709	McDowell	21	5,342	Summers	230	120,015
			Marion	35	5,250	Taylor	4	1,608
Cabell	140	89,757	Marshall	12	4,713	Tyler	207	147,606
Calhoun	23	9,222	Mason	54	25,685	Tucker	7	2,061
Clay	20	6,640	Mercer	356	150,813			
Doddridge	30	18,608	Mineral	3	1,826	Upshur	22	7,500
Fayette	397	253,400	Monongalia	22	11,330	Wayne	185	70,530
			Monroe	154	78,580	Webster	9	2,751
Gilmer	43	23,139	Morgan	1	515	Wetzel	197	136,781
Grant	4	1,723	Nicholas	46	15,610	Wirt	108	74,078
Greenbrier	12	5,936	Pendleton	5	1,741			
Hampshire	11	6,787	Pleasants	18	14,562	Wood	103	72,062
Hardy	8	1,855	Pocahontas	8	4,693	Wyoming	81	7,502

WISCONSIN.

County.	Acres.	Pounds.	County.	Acres.	Pounds.	County.	Acres.	Pounds.
Total	8,810	10,008,423	Grant	87	34,850	Polk	12	3,694
			Green	122	117,571	Portage	2	692
			Green Lake	6	2,249	Richland	19	11,814
Adams	13	9,685	Iowa	6	3,127	Rock	8,608	4,643,870
Barron	7	8,565	Jackson	4	1,904	Saint Croix	4	742
Brown	5	1,728	Jefferson	209	292,501			
Buffalo	5	1,908	Juneau	9	4,784	Sauk	5	2,916
Burnett	2	389	Kewaunee	4	2,096	Shawano	3	819
			La Crosse	1	800	Sheboygan	2	456
Calumet	1	225	La Fayette	10	13,800	Taylor	2	875
Chippewa	7	4,002	Langlade	1	480	Trempealeau	9	4,847
Clark	5	2,575	Lincoln	1	344			
Columbia	5	2,680	Marathon	7	2,984	Vernon	59	35,170
Crawford	22	14,645	Marinette	3	836	Walworth	13	9,360
			Marquette	6	2,612	Washington	8	447
						Waukesha	2	2,000
Dane	4,931	5,371,242	Monroe	4	1,872	Waupaca	8	5,290
Dodge	19	8,440	Oconto	8	1,524			
Dunn	5	3,183	Outagamie	2	868	Waushara	8	1,098
Eau Claire	3	1,135	Pepin	9	2,878	Winnebago	3	2,271
Fond du Lac	1	441	Pierce	3	752	Wood	2	1,135

RECAPITULATION BY STATES.

State.	Acres.	Pounds.	State.	Acres.	Pounds.	State.	Acres.	Pounds.
The United States	638,841	472,661,158	Kentucky	226,120	171,120,784	North Carolina	57,208	26,986,213
			Louisiana	258	55,954	Ohio	34,676	34,735,235
Alabama	2,197	452,426	Maine	1	250	Oregon	43	17,825
Arizona	1	600	Maryland	38,174	26,082,147	Pennsylvania	27,560	36,943,272
Arkansas	2,064	970,220	Massachusetts	8,358	5,369,436	Rhode Island	3	765
California	84	73,317						
Connecticut	8,666	14,044,652	Michigan	170	83,969			
Dakota	5	1,807	Minnesota	163	69,922	South Carolina	169	45,679
Delaware	4	1,278	Mississippi	1,471	414,663	Tennessee	41,532	29,365,052
District of Columbia	2	1,400	Missouri	15,621	12,015,657	Texas	685	221,283
Florida	90	21,182	Nebraska	101	57,970	Vermont	84	131,432
Georgia	971	228,590				Virginia	140,701	70,988,858
Idaho	2	400	Nevada	2	1,500			
Illinois	5,613	8,965,825	New Hampshire	88	170,843			
Indiana	11,955	8,872,842	New Jersey	152	172,315	Washington	6	6,900
Iowa	692	420,477	New Mexico	7	600	West Virginia	4,671	2,296,146
Kansas	333	191,669	New York	4,937	6,481,431	Wisconsin	8,810	10,008,423

CHAPTER II.

CLASSIFICATION—TYPE MAPS—VARIETIES OF THE TOBACCO PLANT.

CLASSIFICATION.

The various types of tobacco produced in different sections are treated locally in the districts in which they are severally grown. They are here grouped into a distinct classification, according to differences in character and use, the modes and forms of manufacture, and of consumption. While each distinct soil formation gives peculiar qualities to the plant as to texture, color, flavor, and general structure, these may be modified by culture and curing into still greater variations of character. A knowledge of what quality or property is wanting may enable the grower so to apply his fertilizers, or to manage the curing process, as greatly to enhance the value of the product; and a want of this knowledge may also cause the grower to destroy, by imperfect cultivation or curing, the very quality which gives the product its highest value.

Commercial circles recognize classes, types, and grades. The basis of a class is its adaptation to a certain purpose; the basis of a type is the combination of certain qualities or properties in the leaf, as color, strength, elasticity, body, flavor, etc., or in the methods of curing, as sun-cured, air-cured, flue-cured, etc. Grades represent the different degrees of excellence in a type, as low, medium, good, or fillers, binders, and wrappers. In the yellow fancy type there may be ten or twelve of these grades, while in some heavy, coarse shipping tobacco only two are made, leaf and lugs. A district may produce only one type, which may be referred to several classes. The yellow tobacco, for instance, is one type, yet it is used both for smoking and for chewing, and is therefore put into two classes; if exported, it would be put into three classes. A district may also produce many types of the same class, as in New England, where several types of seed-leaf and Havana seed are produced, yet they all belong to cigar tobacco, and are used solely for that purpose. Again, a locality may produce one type of one class.

In the following schedule of classification no attempt is made to divide into separate classes that portion of the crop taken for exportation. All this is thrown together into one class, called export tobacco, though the types suited for the different countries are given.

CLASSES, TYPES, AND SUB-TYPES.

CLASS I.—DOMESTIC CIGAR TOBACCO AND SMOKERS.

Seed-leaf and Havana seed.

Connecticut Seed-Leaf.
"New England" Seed-Leaf.
Pennsylvania Seed-Leaf.
New York Seed-Leaf.
Ohio Seed-Leaf.
Wisconsin and Illinois Seed-Leaf.
Florida Seed-Leaf.

Other cigar and smoking tobacco.

White Burley lugs.
American-grown Havana.
Perique.
Common Virginia, North Carolina, Missouri, Eastern Ohio, Maryland, Tennessee, Kentucky, Indiana, and Illinois lugs.
Kentucky and Indiana cheroot and stogie wrappers and fillers.
Fine-fibered Clarksville wrappers.
Indiana Kite-Foot.

CLASS II.—CHEWING TOBACCO.

Fine-cut and plug fillers.

Fine-cut Burley.
Fine-cut Mason county.
White Burley fillers.
Red Burley fillers.
Virginia sun- and air-cured fillers.
Virginia flue-cured fillers.
Missouri air-cured fillers.
Kentucky, Indiana, Tennessee, Virginia, Maryland, and West Virginia fire-cured fillers.
Tennessee and Kentucky air-cured fillers.

Plug wrappers.

Virginia yellow and mahogany.
North Carolina yellow and mahogany.
Western Kentucky yellow.
Hart county (Kentucky) bright and yellow.
Henry county (Tennessee) yellow.
Missouri and Arkansas yellow.
West Virginia yellow.
Clarksville and Missouri dark and red.
Mason county (Kentucky) Burley.

CLASS III.—EXPORT TOBACCO.

English shippers.

Bird's-eye cutting leaf.	Navy leaf.
Brown roll wrapper.	Irish filler.
Spinning leaf.	Scotch Elder.
Shag—a heavy cutter.	Scotch and Irish spinners.
Plug wrapper.	Strips—used for same purposes as above.
Plug fillers.	

Continental shippers.

French Regie—A, B, and C.	Switzerland:
Italian Regie—A, B, and C.	Swiss wrappers.
Austrian Regie.	Swiss fillers.
Spanish Regie.	Holland:
Snuff-leaf and lugs.	Dutch saucer.
Germany:	Belgium:
German saucer.	Belgian cutter.
German spinner.	Denmark, Norway, and Sweden:
Ohio, Maryland, and West Virginia spangled.	Heavy Kentucky and Tennessee types
Smokers—fat lugs.	

African shippers.

Liverpool African.	Gibraltar African.
Boston African.	

Mexico, South America, and West Indies.

Baling wrapper.	Baling filler.

CLASS I.—CIGAR AND SMOKING TOBACCO.

SEED-LEAF AND HAVANA SEED.

CONNECTICUT SEED-LEAF.—This includes both the seed-leaf and the Havana seed. The seed-leaf of Connecticut valley is a very large, fine-fibered, light-colored leaf, sweetish to the taste, soft, and silky, and when light tobacco was fashionable it outstripped all rivals. It burns with a solid, yellowish ash, a little reduced from the original size, the ash having a beautifully granulated or oölitic surface. Havana seed, grown from seed acclimated for four years, has a thin leaf, fine in texture and delicate in flavor, and very glossy and silky. The seed-leaf in Housatonic valley grows darker in color and has more body than that grown in Connecticut valley. It burns well, and is stronger than the Connecticut-valley tobacco, having a larger content of nicotine. Altogether, this is probably the most valuable seed-leaf grown. The whole product of Connecticut sweats well, that in Housatonic valley coming out of that process greatly improved in color, having a very dark chestnut-brown hue. This tobacco burns probably better than any other seed-leaf, but not with so white an ash as many other kinds. The soils are abundantly supplied with salts whose base is potash, which renders the carbon in burning porous, and causes it to burn well. Connecticut seed-leaf will make five thousand cigar wrappers to the one hundred pounds.

NEW ENGLAND SEED-LEAF is the name given to the product of Massachusetts, New Hampshire, and Vermont. It differs from the growth of Connecticut in being coarser in texture and heavier in body, and therefore is not so well suited for wrappers as the Connecticut Seed-Leaf. It is deficient in oily substance, and does not sweat to a good rich color; nor are the burning qualities so good. The ash is not so firm or light, but appears to be more humid. A large proportion of the crop grown in the last-named states is of the variety known as Havana seed, which, though not so large, makes far better fillers for cigars than the seed-leaf varieties.

PENNSYLVANIA SEED-LEAF is of a dark-brown color, has a rich leaf, and gives from six to eight thousand wrappers to the hundred pounds. The flavor is not so good as that of Connecticut Seed-Leaf, and it has an acrid taste, leaving a disagreeable bitter in the mouth after smoking. It sweats to a beautiful brown color, and burns with a white ash, which, however, splits and falls like snowflakes; is very oily and elastic, strong and smooth, and is in great demand by cigar-makers. It rarely suffers injury from sweating, and its strength of tissue enables it to bear the strain required in wrapping cigars.

NEW YORK SEED-LEAF.—This type does not rank as high as those of Pennsylvania and Connecticut. The flavor is excellent, and some of the very best wrappers are made from Wilson's hybrid and one or two other varieties. It burns compactly, with a white ash, except when raised on swamp muck or heavy clay soils, when it is liable to burn black and to curl and roll in burning. This defect in a portion of the crop has kept the standard low. Considerable quantities are exported to Bremen, and some to other foreign markets. The product shrinks about 10 per cent. in sweating. Two types are recognized in New York: Big Flats and Onondaga. The first is of a large growth, is at times very popular, and stands sweating well. Onondaga is short, very substantial, and makes excellent fillers.

OHIO SEED-LEAF is noted for its exceeding dryness. It is a leafy product, and is in more demand for exportation than any other seed-leaf. It burns well, with a white chalky ash, which is sometimes a little flaky; has usually a good dark-brown color, and the type is more uniform in character than that of Pennsylvania. The handsomest seed-leaf produced in Ohio is grown in Medina and Wayne counties. It is large, fine, and very much resembles that grown in Connecticut, but is rather light in color. Generally, the Ohio seed-leaf ranks third as to quality among the seed-leaf products of the United States. While its color is not equal to that of Pennsylvania, nor its texture so fine as that of Connecticut, in burning qualities that from the Miami valley is superior to both, burning with an ash as white as that of Pennsylvania and with a solidity equal to that of Connecticut.

LITTLE DUTCH, a very sweet variety, is grown to some extent in Miami valley. It has a sleek, glossy surface, silky fiber, dark-brown in color, is very highly prized by cigar manufacturers on account of its delicate flavor, and burns well; but having a very thin, fine leaf, it is very sensitive to fermentation, and is easily injured during that process. If put in boxes before the stems are thoroughly cured it "butt-rots" and injures very rapidly. It has a decided tendency to produce white veins, but, being mainly used for fillers and binders, these veins are not so objectionable as in the ordinary seed-leaf. In the market this variety ordinarily brings double the price of the same grades of seed-leaf. Indiana grows some seed-leaf around Richmond, which is classed with the Ohio product.

WISCONSIN AND ILLINOIS SEED-LEAF is noted for its capacity for absorbing and retaining water, being always limp, even in the dry, cold weather of winter. It has a thin leaf, is the most tender of all the seed-leaf products, and requires to be handled with great care. In consequence of its tenderness and the careless manner in which it is generally handled it does not stand high in the estimation of manufacturers. Much of this type is injured on passing through the sweat, by which process it loses about 20 per cent. in weight, while other types of seed-leaf lose from 9 to 12 per cent. The product of Wisconsin and Illinois has great uniformity of color, and in this respect is a superior type. It resembles the Connecticut seed-leaf, and when resweated has a fine finish; burns with a solid ash, especially after it has been resweated, and contains very little nicotine.

FLORIDA SEED-LEAF.—This type is distinguished by the large number of white specks which cover the leaf. These specks, though the result of disease and blemish, are a sure indication of fineness of texture. The color is rather light for the present requirements of the manufacturer. At one time it was exceedingly popular, and commanded very high prices, both in this country and in Germany. When thoroughly sweated it burns well. The Havana sorts have a great delicacy of flavor and fineness of leaf, much like the tobacco grown in Cuba.

Havana seed is a type intermediate between the seed-leaf and that grown from imported Havana seed. It is smaller in size, richer in glossiness, finer in texture, and sweeter in flavor than the seed-leaf proper, and though yielding a third less per acre, the higher prices paid for it seem to make it equally as profitable to cultivate as the seed-leaf. In the West it is called Spanish or Sweet-scented, and in Connecticut, New York, and Pennsylvania it is called Havana seed. It is very valuable, because it furnishes a large percentage of wrappers, while the lower grades make very sweet cigar fillers, second in quality only to the Little Dutch and Havana tobacco. This type may be grown on thin, poor soil, and made profitable when the larger varieties of seed-leaf grown upon such soils would entail loss to the producer.

OTHER CIGAR AND SMOKING TOBACCO.

WHITE BURLEY LUGS.—This sub-type is fine, bright, of good flavor, thin in leaf, light or yellowish brown in color, inclined to be trashy and chaffy, and makes, with the North Carolina and Virginia bright lugs, the finest grades of smoking-tobacco for pipes. It is very popular on account of its mildness, and is composed of the lower leaves of the plant and those badly mutilated by worm-cuts. Some of this sub-type, of a bright, thin character, is granulated for making cigarettes.

AMERICAN-GROWN HAVANA.—Experiments have been made in almost every part of the country with tobacco grown from seed imported from Cuba. The first year the product is small, and emits, even while growing, a strong, sweet flavor, and the leaves rarely attain a length of over ten or twelve inches. It cures up a dark-brown color when grown upon heavy clay soils; but, grown upon sandy soils, the color is a lighter hue, and the flavor is thought to be superior in not having so much rankness. Florida produces a small quantity for market, and little patches are common in every part of the country for domestic use. It deteriorates rapidly in flavor when grown successively from seed matured in this country, but increases in size and usefulness as a wrapper. Its deterioration in aroma is not so rapid in the extreme southern states as in the more northerly ones. Some experiments in cultivating and curing this type are given at the close of the chapter on Tennessee.

PERIQUE.—This type is grown in Louisiana, and is cured in its juices under heavy pressure. It is very black and glossy in appearance, emits a strong spirituous flavor, makes a very strong smoking-tobacco, and is not popular except with those habituated to its use. Some of the product of Louisiana is air-cured, and is used in making very strong cigars, as further detailed in the chapter on Louisiana.

COMMON LUGS FROM THE HEAVY TOBACCO DISTRICTS.—This sub-class is made up from the lower grades of many types. It is trashy, earth-burned, of every conceivable color, deficient in body and weight of leaf, and milder than the better grades of the types from which it comes. By a due admixture of colors and strength of leaf many brands of smoking-tobacco are made, as bright and dark, brown and red, spangled and yellow, mild and strong. Some air-cured lugs of this sub-class are granulated for cigarettes, the stock being furnished from light, thin products from Kentucky, Tennessee, Indiana, Illinois, Missouri, Eastern Ohio, and Maryland. The lugs selected for this purpose are as light in color as possible.

STOGIE WRAPPERS AND FILLERS.—For stogie wrappers a short western leaf of full breadth and light body, fine fiber, and uniformly dark color is selected. To a very small extent a red or cinnamon color is required. It must be air-cured or entirely free from any flavor imparted by fire, and it is necessary that it shall have passed through the sweat and become somewhat soured in flavor. This particular style of leaf is used at Pittsburgh and at Wheeling—very largely at the latter point—for wrappers in the manufacture of a specific class of common cigars, technically called stogie cigars. A stogie filler consists of a leaf of the same quality as the wrapper, but is of lower grade, too narrow or otherwise unfitted for wrappers. What are technically called "self-workers" are largely used in this trade. They consist of packages or casks with a proper proportion of wrappers and fillers packed in them, each for working the other.

FINE-FIBERED CLARKSVILLE WRAPPER.—This type has great smoothness and delicacy of general structure, great elasticity and strength, with a moderate supply of oily substances, good breadth of leaf, and is of a port-wine color. It is used largely in the United States and in Canada, in connection with the red wrapper, in the manufacture of plug tobacco for smoking as well as for chewing. A large proportion of these wrappers is exported. They are not popular for making cigars in the United States, because they impart a rank flavor to the cigar. Wrappers of the same character are produced in Virginia and are used for like purposes. A few are taken for the manufacture of stogie cigars.

INDIANA KITE-FOOT.—This is a broad, short leaf, grown in Owen and Clark counties, Indiana. It is cured with fire, and the color is generally brown, sprinkled with yellow spots. The fibers are small, and the leaves are very elastic. It is employed for making common cigars.

CLASS II.—CHEWING-TOBACCO.

FINE-CUT AND PLUG FILLERS.

WHITE BURLEY.—This is the product of a new variety which within the past decade has come into profitable and extensive cultivation. It is bright brown or golden in color, of thin tissue, good breadth and length of leaf, comparatively free from gums and oils, possessed of great absorptive capacity, and is of a mild and pleasant flavor. It is exceedingly popular with the manufacturers of plug and cutting tobacco. There are two sub-types of the White Burley, known as cutters and fillers. Cutters are almost entirely destitute of gums and oils, and therefore are stiff and harsh. Fillers have more body and more gum than the cutters, and are, consequently, softer and more elastic. Their popularity with manufacturers arises from their capacity to absorb a very large percentage of the sauces with which they are treated. Dr. Moore reports that the Owen county (Kentucky) plug fillers will absorb over two and a half times their weight of water without dripping when done up in a roll. The product is popular with consumers when manufactured into plug or fine-cut, because it is very mild, and can be used without producing the nervous irritation consequent on the use of stronger tobacco. It is not so sweet naturally as the flue- and sun-cured tobacco of Virginia, or of the air-cured product of Missouri. The chapters on Ohio and Kentucky give further details.

FINE-CUT MASON COUNTY.—This type only differs from the White Burley grown in other districts in having very little gum, less body and elasticity, and is used for a cutting leaf mainly.

RED BURLEY FILLERS.—These differ from the White Burley fillers only in not having such bright colors, the color being rather a dark cinnamon. The product of the Red Burley is also of a somewhat lighter and more flimsy character when grown upon similar soils.

VIRGINIA SUN- AND AIR-CURED FILLERS.—These are made chiefly in Caroline, Hanover, Louisa, and Spotsylvania counties, Virginia. The product is of medium size as to leaf, light-brown as to color, very sweet and fragrant, with a fair proportion of gums and oils, and popular as a chewing-tobacco. The air-cured fillers of Missouri approximate those of Virginia in the qualities of sweetness and fragrance.

VIRGINIA FLUE-CURED FILLERS.—These are of medium size, brown or mahogany in color, oily and elastic, fine in texture, delicate in fiber, and have a liveliness of appearance not observable in the White Burley product. They are made principally in Henry county, Virginia, and command very high prices on account of their exceeding natural sweetness.

MISSOURI AIR-CURED FILLERS.—These are distinguished chiefly on account of their sweetness, and are frequently mixed with the product of other states to give a pleasant taste to the manufactured article. They also make a very tough "chew".

FIRE-CURED FILLERS OF THE HEAVY TOBACCO DISTRICTS.—These are employed in making a coarse, strong chewing-tobacco for the consumption of miners, sailors, and lumbermen, who prefer an article with a rank tobacco taste, strong in nicotine, and of great toughness of leaf.

TENNESSEE AND KENTUCKY AIR-CURED FILLERS.—This type is of light to medium weight, free of coarseness in texture and fiber, not gummy or waxy, of sweet and mild natural flavor, clear of any bitterness, generally porous in structure, and of bright or pale-red color. It is entirely air-cured. Its natural absorbing capacity is fully preserved by air-curing. Curing by artificial heat would not only impair its flavor, but impart a highly injurious odor of smoke. Length or breadth of leaf is not an essential. This product is generally grown upon the sandstone lands or siliceous soils, and is distinguished from the White Burley fillers by having heavier body, less delicacy of structure, and by being less colored.

PLUG WRAPPERS.

NORTH CAROLINA AND VIRGINIA YELLOW AND MAHOGANY.—The yellow and mahogany wrappers may be considered grades of the yellow type. The highest grade is small in size, with a lemon-yellow color, soft and silky, and has a surface which sparkles in the sunlight, the minute golden grains scattered over the upper portions of the leaf adding to the brilliancy of its appearance. Other grades follow this, such as orange, dull yellow, and on by imperceptible gradations to the mahogany. The lemon-yellow leaf stands at the head as a wrapper for plug. The chief distinguishing characteristic of the yellow leaf of North Carolina and Virginia is that it will not blacken under pressure when subjected to the processes of manufacturing, but retains its golden luster. The mahogany wrapper is larger than the yellow leaf, displaying a ground of yellow, spotted with red or brown. It usually has more oily substances in its composition, and therefore blackens more under pressure. Western Kentucky, Hart county, Kentucky, and Henry county, Tennessee, produce a leaf unexcelled in the beauty of its yellow color. It is generally larger than the North Carolina and Virginia yellow tobacco, but will not maintain its color in the manufacturing process. The yellow tobacco of Ohio and West Virginia is intermediate in character between that of North Carolina and the West, the former having more oil in its composition than the latter. The yellow tobacco of Missouri and Arkansas very much resembles that grown in Kentucky. It has a brilliant hue, but is open to the objection of blackening under pressure. The yellow wrappers stand very high in absorptive capacity.

CLARKSVILLE AND MISSOURI DARK AND RED.—This type is found in leaf of full weight of body, strong and elastic texture, with good supply of oils and "fat", soft, smooth, and flexible in structure, of fine stem and fiber, and the dark wrapper has a port-wine color. The leaf must be of good width, of well-rounded proportions, and free of all blemish, such as spot and worm-cut. Length of leaf has no specific standard, for some forms of manufacturing full length being required, and for others short length being preferred. The highest value of the type is found in the leaf of full length. Red wrapper has the same essential qualities as those described for dark wrappers, except that of color, which must be a full, deep, and solid red. These wrappers are used largely in Canada.

MASON COUNTY (KENTUCKY) BURLEY WRAPPERS.—For many years the wrappers grown in this county have been noted for their great fineness, softness, silkiness, and elasticity. They are of medium size, running from a reddish yellow in color to a dark brown. The substitution of the White Burley variety for those previously grown has improved rather than impaired the character of the wrappers. They are used both for plug and for cigars.

CLASS III.—EXPORT TOBACCO.

ENGLISH SHIPPERS.

ENGLISH SHIPPERS consist of leaf and strips, which are used, with a single exception, for identical purposes. Until within a short period the larger consumption was of strips or stemmed tobacco, the stem being removed as a special preparation to avoid the payment of duty on it. Recently, however, the consumption of leaf has increased in the United Kingdom, under an arrangement by which the manufacturer is allowed to return the stem into the hands of the proper officers for destruction or for export. In some forms of manufacture, however, the stem is pressed in the leaf into a thin plate and then split, so as to divide the leaf into two parts, as in making strips. For these reasons the consumption of leaf in the different forms of manufacturing in England is increasing.

BIRD'S-EYE CUTTING LEAF.—This is the only type used exclusively in the leaf in English consumption, and consists of a very bright, smooth, thin, and clean leaf, with as little gum and oil as possible. The essential peculiarities of quality are that the color of both the inside and the outside surfaces of the leaf shall be of uniform and similar shades of bright color, and that the stem shall be of a brightish brown color on the outside and white on the inside. Each section into which the stem is cut presents in appearance on its cut surface the eye of a bird. This type was formerly scarce, and was furnished chiefly by the Lower Green River district, in Kentucky; but since the production of light and colored types it has largely increased in the Burley district, and especially in Virginia and North Carolina.

BROWN-ROLL WRAPPER.—This is a bright red or full bright leaf, thin and smooth in texture, of good breadth, resembling in general structure the leaf used for cutting into fine-cut by our domestic manufacturers. It is used in England as a wrapper for spinning brown roll. By filling the wrapper properly with suitable fillers a continuous strand is made and spun of about one inch in diameter, which is packed into a coil, similar to a coil of rope, from which sections are cut for retail. For this purpose it is always stemmed. The brown-roll filler is the material with which the wrapper is filled, and consists of stock of the same type as the wrapper, except that it is of lower grade.

SPINNING-LEAF OR STRIPS.—This type consists of a long, rich, and oily leaf, of full brown color, good weight of body, strong and elastic texture, and of general smoothness in structure. Recently brighter colors have been more in demand for this purpose than formerly. The types used in England for this purpose were of the heavy, oily, and "fatty" descriptions grown in the Clarksville district, until recently these became so much appreciated in value on account of the German demand for them that the heavy but less oily types of the Lower Green River district were substituted. The recent improvements in machinery used in spinning enable manufacturers to use material of a lower grade. The purpose for which this type is used is similar to that for which the brown-roll wrapper is used, except that the strand into which it is spun is of smaller size. This is put up and cut for retail in the same manner as the brown roll. A still smaller strand is spun, called lady's twist, but to much less extent now than formerly. The strand of this twist was not larger than the point of the little finger, and was consumed principally in Scotland, Ireland, and the north of England. The wrapper for this consisted of a smaller and shorter leaf of the same general qualities as those used for the larger strand.

SHAG.—This is a coarsely-cut English manufactured product. The supply is drawn chiefly from Indiana and the Green River district in Kentucky. It has but little gum, yet more than the cutting leaf used in the United States. Shag tobacco is really a heavy cutting leaf, and it finds substitutes from Japan, Java, Paraguay, and the Dutch possessions. The principal requisite is that it shall be low in price, so that manufacturers may sell it for the same price as that obtained before the increase of duty.

PLUG WRAPPERS.—This type consists of a rich, dark-brown leaf, smooth in structure, medium in size, and strong and elastic in texture. Its consumption is very small, as plug tobacco is used to a very limited extent in the United Kingdom.

PLUG FILLERS.—These consist of a short, common, and imperfect leaf of the same type as the wrapper.

NAVY LEAF.—The "navy plug", in quarters, half pounds, and pounds, is a style of tobacco which gained its reputation during and after the war. The best of Green river redried fillers were the material used for its manufacture, but during the past few years the fashion has turned toward White Burley fillers, and they now compose the largest portion of leaf tobacco used for manufacturing "navy plug" in its various sizes.

IRISH FILLER.—To a very limited extent a short, well-ripened, clean, and oily leaf is used in Ireland for fillers. The Bird's-eye and Irish filler are sold in English markets in the leaf for the special consumption to which they are adapted, and all other types either in strips or leaf. If in the latter, the stem is removed from the leaf by the manufacturer in preparation for manufacturing, or so prepared as to be used with the rest of the leaf. The consumption of strips is much larger than that of leaf.

SCOTCH ELDER.—Scotch Elder is a type of great absorptive or drinking qualities, having a leaf of good size, very porous, with but little gum, reddish in color, and with medium texture. Mr. Todd is authority for saying that, since the tax in the United Kingdom has been increased, 100 pounds of tobacco will be so heavily watered as to make 155 pounds when sold to consumers.

SCOTCH AND IRISH SPINNERS.—These are almost or quite identical in type with English spinners, and the description made of the latter may be applied to the former.

CONTINENTAL SHIPPERS.

FRENCH TYPES may be reduced to two distinct lines of classification, as heavy and light, with considerable irregularity as to grade and deficiency in distinctness as to type.

TYPE A.—This consists of a leaf 23 to 25 inches in length, of moderately smooth appearance, dark-brown color, and not of so much weight of body and substance as the Italian Regie.

TYPE B.—Of the same qualities for both light and heavy as type A, except that the length is 22 to 23 inches.

TYPE C.—This consists of good, sound, clear lugs or common leaf, of moderately heavy body, or running from the Clarksville and western Kentucky type of medium weight of body to lower Green river product of medium weight of substance. These types are used for cigar wrappers, fillers, and binders, for the manufacture of snuff, and for cutting into smoking-tobacco. The heavy types are generally taken from the nondescript part of the Clarksville and western Kentucky districts, and the lighter types from nondescript of the Lower Green River district, of Illinois, and of Indiana. The types vary so much in the French orders that in some years the whole of it may be supplied by the product of the latter-named districts. Those made in the orders of 1880 and 1881 do not class, on an average, much, if at all, above the grade and quality required in former years in the lowest type, C. France is taking from good lugs up to medium leaf, but no very fine tobacco, from the United States.

ITALIAN REGIE TYPES.

TYPE A.—This is a large, showy, smooth, and silky leaf, 25 to 26 inches long, of fine fiber and texture, and of solid dark-brown color. Moderate weight only is required in this type, and just enough oil and fat to create elasticity and strength of texture. It is used by the Italian Monopoly Company as wrappers in the manufacture of cigars.

TYPE B.—This type varies between heavy and light tobacco, sometimes the former and sometimes the latter being required by the annual orders of the Monopoly Company. When the former is required, the type consists of leaf of heavy body, dark-brown color, and of more general richness and weight of substance than type A, and 22 to 25 inches in length. This type is used largely in the manufacture of snuff. Type B, light, consists of leaf of second and third grades, of the same length and showy appearance, of light-brown or red color, and of moderate weight of body and substance. This type is used in the manufacture of cigars of milder flavor than those made of the heavier types, and also largely for cutting into smoking-tobacco.

TYPE C.—This consists of choice lugs or short common leaf, 18 to 20 inches in length, and of moderate weight of body, and is used as fillers and binders in the manufacture of cigars. Of these several types, A is chiefly selected from the lighter-bodied and smooth product of the Clarksville district and the western Kentucky district; B heavy, from the heavier-bodied products of these districts; B light, chiefly from the product of moderate weight of substance of the Lower Green River district and Indiana and Illinois; and C from the lighter-bodied lugs and common leaf of the heavy-producing districts and the heavier bodied of the light producing districts.

AUSTRIAN REGIE.

The Austrian Regie takes only one type or grade from the United States. This is a wrapping leaf, very smooth and fine in fiber, of very solid, firm, and glossy texture, above medium heavy body, but not of the heaviest and most fleshy type, and of a perfectly uniform brown color. A very essential quality is toughness and "stretchiness" of texture, and it must be well cured by fire, but not injured in curing. The length of the leaf is not an essential part of the fitness, but good length is much preferred. This type is used in Austria as wrappers in the manufacture of cigars, and is supplied chiefly from Virginia, and in smaller part from the Clarksville district. Large crops of tobacco are raised in Hungary, more than enough to supply Austria with the lower grades.

SPANISH REGIE.

No classification of the tobacco bought by the Spanish Regie is made. It consists of sound and common lugs of all types and districts, except the Burley and bright-producing districts of Kentucky and North Carolina, and of the low and nondescript leaf of light type. The order is generally made for one-third of leaf of low grade and two-thirds of lugs. It is all used for smoking; the better grades for wrappers, binders, and fillers in the manufacture of cigars, and the lower for granulation for the manufacture of cigarettes.

SNUFF LEAF AND LUGS.

Snuff leaf is heavy, very rich and fat, of fine fiber and dark color, and is used for making the finer grades of snuff. The leaf described as German spinner is used partly in Germany for making the best grades of snuff. Snuff lugs are of the same qualities as the leaf, heavy, fat, and dark in color, considerably fermented, and are used for making the common grades of snuff.

GERMAN TYPES.

GERMAN SAUCER.—This is a sweet, fair-bodied leaf, of fine fiber and stem, gummy without fatness, and either clear, cherry-red in color, or mottled with yellow, or what is technically called piebald. It is generally a leaf of good length and weight of body, with gummy surface. It is prepared for consumption in Germany by the application of sauce of a peculiar description. The fiber must be yellow after saucing, and the leaf black. The largest proportion of this type is taken from Virginia.

GERMAN SPINNER.—This consists of leaf of the heaviest body, 24 to 26 inches in length, full in width, of fine fiber and stem, very oily and fat, so that it will sweat supple and strong, tough and elastic in texture, and of a very deep or dark-brown color. This type is used in Germany and the north of Europe for spinning into strand. It is supplied chiefly from the Clarksville district, but in part also from the Upper Green River district, and to a very small extent from the Lower Green River district. German spinning fillers are of the same type as the wrappers used in spinning, but consist of very fat, clean, and heavy-bodied lugs, which are supplied from the Clarksville and Upper Green River districts.

OHIO, MARYLAND, AND WEST VIRGINIA SPANGLED.—This is a leaf of moderate length, full breadth, and small stem. It has a medium strength in texture, is rather deficient in oil, and is in color yellow, yellow spangled with red, red spangled with yellow, and fine red. It is cured with fire, but has a mild, sweet flavor. The fine yellow and yellow spangled goes to Bremen, where it is rehandled, put in lighter casks, and sent to Russia for consumption, a portion, however, being taken to Austria and England, the latter countries taking also the red spangled. England takes, besides, the fine red. Germany takes all grades for consumption except fine yellow and dark brown, which latter are taken by France and Italy, and Spain takes the unsound and nondescript qualities. Scraps of this type are used in this country for smoking-tobacco.

SMOKERS—FAT LUGS.—The very fat, heavy, and oily lugs of the Clarksville and other heavy tobacco-producing districts, beside being used in the manufacture of common snuff in the United States and Germany, for baling fillers, and for spinning fillers, as noted elsewhere, are also taken on the continent for making common cigars.

SWITZERLAND.

SWISS WRAPPER.—This is a long and broad leaf, 26 to 30 inches in length, silky, of fine fiber and stem, and of a dark-brown or chestnut color. It is desirable that the spaces between the small or lateral stems should be broad, and the combination of thin with strong and elastic texture is desired, that a maximum supply of wrapper may be obtained from a given weight of product. It is used in Switzerland as a wrapper in the manufacture of cigars, and is supplied chiefly from the Clarksville district, but to a small extent from other heavy-producing districts.

HOLLAND.

DUTCH SAUCER.—This is similar in all respects to the German saucer, except that it is thinner and more silky in texture. It is exported exclusively to Rotterdam.

BELGIUM.

BELGIAN CUTTER.—This is a short leaf of a mottled or piebald color, and of fair body, without fat or oil. The general quality and structure are such as have been described for German and Dutch saucers, except that the grade is lower than is used for those purposes. It is used in Belgium for cutting.

DENMARK, NORWAY, AND SWEDEN.

A bright, mottled or red, fleshy, sweet leaf, not fat, prepared in Germany from the product usually of Virginia and the Kentucky and Tennessee districts, is a great favorite in Denmark, Norway, and Sweden. In addition to this the heavy Clarksville types, cured with fire, are largely consumed in these countries.

AFRICAN SHIPPERS.

African shippers may be divided into three classes, as follows:

1. Suitable for southern Africa, should be of long, dark leaf, strong body, small tie, put in hogsheads of small size, and prized to weigh about 1,550 pounds gross; neatly handled.

2. Sutable for the intermediate portion of the country, should be of long leaf, medium to light color, fine fibers, handled as class one, and weigh about 1,450 pounds gross.

3. Suitable for the more northern part of Africa, should be of light leaf, not so long as classes one and two, and handled in medium-sized hogsheads, weighing not more than 1,450 pounds gross. It is better that this class should not be overhandled.

During the past few years tobacco has also been packed in boxes for shipment to the coast of Africa. The quality is the same as described above, about 400 pounds going into a box by hard prizing, and the tobacco is more subject to atmospheric influences than when prized in hogsheads.

While most of the tobacco shipped to Africa is first rehandled in this country, still there is a fair proportion of leaf of suitable quality and handling sent to market direct by farmers. This is mainly taken for account of merchants in Boston, Massachusetts, who send cargoes of various articles to the African coast.

MEXICO, SOUTH AMERICA, AND THE WEST INDIES.

BALING WRAPPERS.—This is a heavy leaf, 28 to 30 inches in length, of fair width, very fat and oily, of heavy texture, and of very dark color. A necessary condition of this class is that it should be neatly tied in small bands, neatly and strongly packed in casks, and moderately pressed. It is used as wrappers in preparing stock for the trade of the several markets named, and is packed in bales weighing from 100 to 200 pounds, and covered with cloth, so that two bales may be balanced across the back of a pack mule for transportation across the mountainous regions of the districts in which it is consumed.

BALING FILLERS.—Common rich and heavy leaf and fine lugs of heavy body and full supply of oils and fatness are used for this purpose. Some of the exports to the West Indies are called "black fats", and are made dark by very heavy pressure and by the application of water, clear or tobacco-stained.

Nondescript leaf is incapable of classification. It has the merit of cheapness, and is usually bought and held by speculators, who take advantage of the scarcity of some well-defined type to put a nondescript variety on the market approaching in general qualities the type in demand.

The lowest and commonest grades of lugs are often used in the United States, especially if air-cured, in the manufacture of the cheapest grade of pipe-smoking tobacco. With this product a large proportion of stems is frequently mixed to increase the bulk and to reduce the cost. Some of this low grade is also used in making sheep-wash.

23

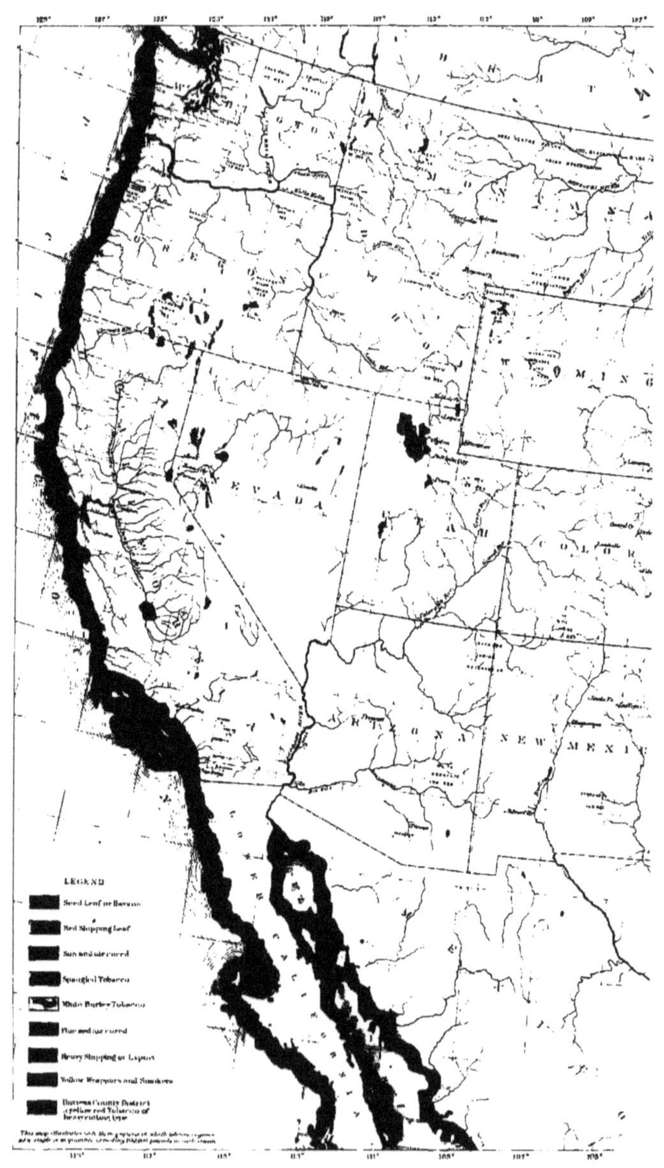
LEGEND
Seed Leaf or Havana
Red Shipping Leaf
Sun and air cured
Spangled Tobacco
White Burley Tobacco
Heavy Shipping or Export
Yellow Wrappers and Smokers

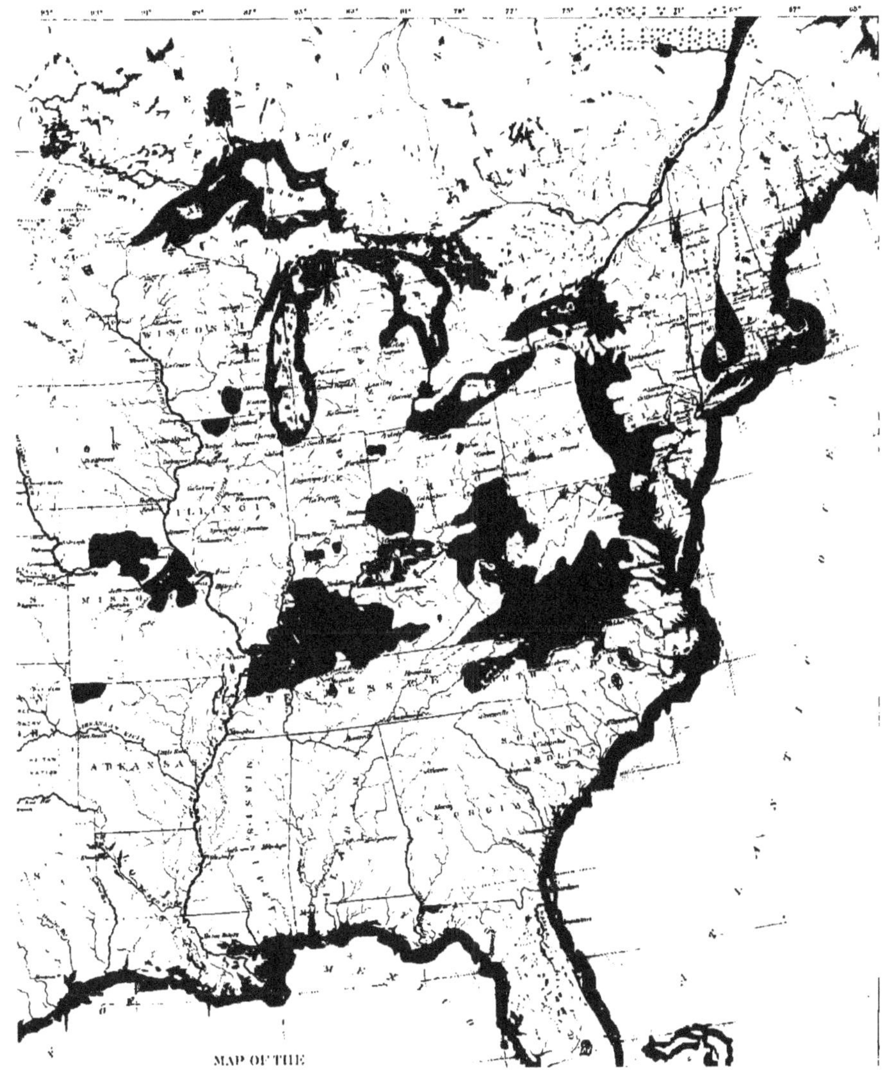

MAP OF THE

Stems or midribs used to be exported in large quantities to Germany for the manufacture of cheap grades of snuff and smoking tobacco, and were also employed as manure or for the protection of fruit trees from the borer and other insect enemies. Since the tax was raised in Germany on tobacco and stems the consumption of the latter, except the finest bright from Virginia leaf, has fallen off considerably, and for a year or two past the article has become almost valueless, stemmers and manufacturers being unable to obtain the cost of prizing and casks. Large quantities of stems, with the trash and sweepings of stemmeries, are now used for manurial purposes.

TYPE MAPS.

In the map which accompanies this chapter the localities in which the leading types are produced are designated by colors. It must not be inferred, however, that no other types than those indicated are made in the districts to which particular types are referred, but only that those types predominate or give character to the district. The types run into each other by such imperceptible gradations that it is often difficult to define with precision the line of separation.

The portions of the maps colored blue indicate that a heavy shipping leaf, either air-cured or fire-cured, is produced. Red indicates a lighter shipping leaf, red and colored, also cured by fire; dark yellow the regions in which the yellow tobacco is grown in greater or smaller quantities. Light yellow shows the main White Burley district, though this variety is grown in many other localities, as in West Virginia, eastern Ohio, Missouri, and Indiana, but was not the prevailing type in 1879. A yellow ground, spangled with red, shows where the spangled tobacco, taken in Germany, Russia, England, and France, is grown—a fine, showy article, with but little gum and body. A neutral tint, or drab color, as is shown in the center of the yellow-tobacco growing region of North Carolina and Virginia, shows where flue- and air-cured fillers are made, probably the most highly prized fillers, on account of sweetness and flavor, produced in the United States. The same kind of fillers, though not so decided in character, is produced in Missouri, as indicated by the color. Green shows the locality of sun- and air-cured sweet fillers. Some of these are also produced in Missouri, along with the flue-cured. Seed-leaf and Havana districts are represented on the maps by a chestnut-brown color. In many places within the limits of the blue air-cured fillers are produced suitable for use in domestic plug, but they do not constitute the predominating type.

It would be impossible to represent by colors the almost infinite varieties of types and sub-types produced in the shipping district, for these types frequently differ in the same township or civil district.

A county is seldom colored unless it produces as much as 100,000 pounds, though there are a few exceptions, as in the case of West Virginia, where a peculiar type is grown over a widely extended district. Strips of other counties that lie contiguous to a well-known tobacco district, as in Wisconsin and in the Miami valley, are frequently colored when the limits of culture are well known.

VARIETIES OF TOBACCO.

More than a hundred varieties of the tobacco plant are named in the schedules returned to this office. Of these more than half are either synonyms or designations descriptive of different peculiarities of the same variety. For instance, the Little Orinoco of Virginia is called Brittle Stem in West Virginia and Missouri and Narrow Leaf in Maryland.

Below are given the names of fifty of the best known varieties, with description of certain marked peculiarities of style, growth, character of leaf, etc., the uses for which they are best adapted, and the states in which they are mainly grown:

Varieties.	Description.	Uses.	Where grown.
Adcock	Wide space between leaves; ripens uniformly from top to bottom.	Wrappers and fillers for plug; excellent fine smokers.	North Carolina.
Baden	Short leaves, light; inclined to be chaffy; cures a fine yellow, but liable to green spots.	Plug wrappers and fillers; smokers	Maryland.
Baltimore Cuba	Long leaf; good body; fine, silky texture; tough; yields well; sweats a uniform color; disseminated by the U. S. Agricultural Department.		Ohio (Miami valley).
Bay	Large, heavy leaf; red spangled and yellow when cured.	Manufacturing and shipping	Maryland.
Beat-all (same as Williams)	Large, spreading leaf; fine fiber; dark, rich, and gummy.	Export to Great Britain and Germany; well cured; makes fine wrappers.	Tennessee, Virginia.
Belknap	Sub-variety of Connecticut Seed-Leaf	Same as Connecticut Seed-Leaf	Connecticut, Massachusetts, New York.
Bull-face	Sub-variety of the Pryor; large, heavy leaf, oval shaped; tough; small stems and fibers; a luxuriant grower.	Heavy shipping; makes good wrappers for plug.	Virginia, North Carolina, Tennessee.
Burley—Red	Thin leaf, narrowing toward the tip from center	Cutting tobacco	Kentucky, Virginia, Ohio.
Burley—White	Long, narrow leaf; white in appearance while growing; grows flat, with points of leaves hanging down.	Fancy wrappers, and for cutting purposes	Ohio, Kentucky, Virginia, Maryland, Missouri, Indiana.
Clardy	Large, smooth, heavy leaf, extremely broad; stalks long; a hybrid.	Common plug; exported for Swiss wrappers.	Kentucky, Tennessee.
Connecticut Seed-Leaf	Broad leaf; strong, thin, elastic, silky; small fibers.	Cigar wrappers; lower grades for binders and fillers.	Connecticut, New Hampshire, New York, Pennsylvania, Ohio, Wisconsin, Minnesota; also in Indiana, Illinois, and Florida.

Varieties.	Description.	Uses.	Where grown.
Connecticut Broad Leaf	Modification of above; leaves broader in proportion to length; fibers more at right angles to midrib.	Same as above	Connecticut, New York, Wisconsin.
Cuba	Small leaf, grown from imported seed; retains much of the aroma of Cuba-grown tobacco.	Cigar wrappers, fillers, and binders	Pennsylvania, New York, Wisconsin, Florida, Louisiana.
Cunningham	Short, broad leaf; thick and stalky growth	Fillers and smokers	North Carolina.
Duck Island	Broad leaf; fine appearance; full grower; originated from Havana seed.	Cigar work	New York, Pennsylvania.
Flannagan	Similar to Little Orinoco, but broader leaf, finer fiber; silky and tough.	Fancy wrappers; plug fillers	Virginia.
Florida Leaf	Fine texture, silky and elastic; becomes spotted with white when ripening.	Cigar wrappers, binders, and fillers	Florida.
Frederick	Akin to White Stem; rough leaf; heavy and rich; stands up well.	Mainly for export to Europe	Virginia, Tennessee.
Glessner	Large handsome leaf; fine texture; soft and elastic	Cigar wrappers and fillers; smokers	Pennsylvania, New York, Wisconsin.
Gooch	Broad, round leaf; leaves thick on stalk; yellow on hill when ripe; cures easily.	Fancy wrappers and smokers	Virginia, North Carolina.
Gourd Leaf	Broad, short, fine, and silky leaf; yellows on the hill	Plug wrappers and fillers; smokers	Virginia.
Governor Jones	Long, narrow leaf, of good body	Plug wrappers and fillers, and for common smoking.	Kentucky.
Havana Seed	Very thin, fine leaf; fine texture; delicate flavor	Cigar wrappers	Connecticut, Massachusetts, Pennsylvania, Wisconsin.
Hickory Leaf	Fine fiber and texture; cures up very bright	Plug work, smokers, and shipping	West Virginia.
Johnson Green	Said to be a cross of Orinoco and White Stem; large, heavy leaf; strong flavor.	Strips and shipping leaf	Virginia.
Kite-Foot	Rather short, wide leaf; thin; apt to cure a greenish color unless fully ripe.	For very common cigars; culture decreasing.	Indiana.
Little Dutch	Narrow leaf, small and short; in flavor resembling Yara tobacco.	For binders and fillers for cigars; very popular.	Ohio (Miami valley).
Long Green	Coarse and heavy; vigorous grower	Heavy shipping leaf	Virginia.
Lancaster Broad Leaf	Upright grower; delicate silky fiber	Cigar wrappers, binders, and fillers; smokers.	Pennsylvania, Wisconsin.
Lovelady	Long, dark, narrow leaf; very heavy	Export; grown for African shippers	Virginia, Tennessee, Indiana.
Mann	Leaf of good body; heavy and gummy	Plug wrappers and fillers; export	North Carolina.
Orinoco	Short, broad leaf; upright growth and open habit; light colored; much ruffled.	Plug wrappers and fillers; for strips and for export leaf.	Virginia, Missouri.
Orinoco—Big	Short, broad leaf; doubtless same as last named	Sweet plug wrappers and fillers; export	Virginia, Missouri, North Carolina, Tennessee, West Virginia.
Orinoco—Little	Long, narrow, tapering leaf; fine texture; stands up well.	Principally for plug work and smokers; sweetest variety grown.	Virginia, North Carolina, Tennessee, West Virginia, Missouri.
Pennsylvania Seed-Leaf	Same as Connecticut Seed-Leaf	Same as Connecticut Seed-Leaf	Same as Connecticut Seed-Leaf.
Perique	Medium-sized leaf; fine fiber; small stem; tough, gummy, and glossy.	Smoking; cigars and cigarettes; for mixing with other kinds.	Louisiana.
Pittsylvania Yellow	Medium-size; leaves elongated, good distance apart; fine texture; small tough stems.	Fine wrappers and fillers; good export variety.	West Virginia.
Pryor—Blue	Large, fine leaf, long, and well proportioned; good color; slightly ruffled.	Cigar and plug fillers; stemmers for export.	Virginia, North Carolina, Kentucky, Tennessee, Missouri, Indiana.
Pryor—Yellow	Heavy, wide leaf; fine texture; fine bright color; tough; weighs well.	Cigar and plug wrappers and fillers; stemmers for export.	Same as last.
Pryor—White (or Medley Pryor).	Very broad leaf; soft and silky texture, and tough fiber; a beautiful grower.	Plug wrappers and fillers	Virginia.
Shoestring	Heavy leaf; rather narrow; long and large stem	Dark navy plug; good stripping leaf	Tennessee, Kentucky, Missouri, Virginia.
Sleek-stem	Large, long leaf; heavy weigher; no ruffles	Heavy dark fillers; shipping leaf	Tennessee.
Spanish Seed	Uniform dark color; medium size leaf; ripens ten days earlier than other varieties.	Highly prized for dark cigar wrappers	New York, Illinois, Wisconsin.
Thickset	Leaf long, pointed, narrow; coarse fiber; very short stalk; coarse and heavy.	Common plug work and shipping	Kentucky, Missouri, Maryland, West Virginia, Tennessee, eastern Ohio.
Twist-bud	Heavy, large leaf; screw-shaped terminal stem	Export mainly; also for plug fillers	Kentucky, Missouri, Maryland.
Vallandigham	Large, pointed, smooth leaf	Cigar wrappers and fillers; smokers	Wisconsin.
White Stem	Leaf long, slender, drooping; tough and fibrous; largest leaf grown.	Plug wrappers, strips, and shipping leaf	Virginia.
Wilson's Hybrid	Said to be an improved Havana; erect habit; easy of cultivation.	Cigar wrappers, binders, and fillers	New York.
Yellow Mammoth	Very large leaf; rapid grower; yields largely	Stemmed for export, for Swiss wrappers	Tennessee.
Williams	Same as Beat-all, grown in Tennessee for twenty-five years as Williams.	British and German export	Tennessee.

Chapter III.

CULTURE AND CURING OF TOBACCO IN ARKANSAS.

The production of tobacco in Arkansas is comparatively a new industry, and is confined to a few counties, chiefly in the northwestern corner of the state. The quality of the tobacco grown is very similar in every respect to that produced in Virginia. The tobacco-growing portion of this state is in the same latitude as that portion of North Carolina which produces the finest yellow leaf in the United States, and the heavy, dark types are taking a high rank for the Regie trade.

While the chief agricultural products of the state are cotton and corn, there are large areas which, in soil and climate, are well adapted to the growth of small grain and of tobacco. This is especially true of the elevated plateaus in the northern part of the state west of Black river, comprising the counties of Randolph, Izard, Newton, Boone, Madison, Carroll, Benton, and Washington. These counties in 1870 produced two-thirds of the tobacco grown in the state. The soil on which the great bulk of the crop was grown is chiefly derived from the disintegration of the magnesian and subcarboniferous limestones. The weathering of these limestones does not at any place give a heavy or impervious soil, as the siliceous constituents in both formations give porosity and furnish sand enough to make the soil loose and of easy cultivation. With a subsoil of red clay they retain manures for a long time, and no soils in the United States respond more readily in all seasons to manurial applications.

The census of 1840 returned for the state of Arkansas 148,439 pounds; of 1850, 218,936 pounds; 1860, 989,980 pounds; 1870, 594,886 pounds; and by the returns of the enumerators in 1880 the state, in 1879, produced 970,220 pounds, showing a small decrease as compared with that produced in 1859, but an increase of 63 per cent. as compared with the crop of 1869. Of the product of 1879 the counties of White, Independence, Madison, Boone, Washington, and Benton produced 531,494 pounds, the last-named county alone producing 395,982 pounds, being more than three-fifths of the amount reported for the whole state by the census of 1870.

BENTON COUNTY DISTRICT.

The surface of Benton county, the only one in the state that produced over 100,000 pounds of tobacco, is rolling, with numerous tracts of elevated table or prairie land. Alike in surface features are Boone, Madison, and Washington. The town of Fayetteville, in the latter county, has an elevation of 1,350 feet above the sea, and a prairie in Madison county has an elevation of over 1,000 feet. The streams run in deep valleys, cut down through these plateau lands, from which they are fed by never-failing springs.

No extensive series of observations have ever been made in the tobacco-growing region of Arkansas. The elevation of Benton county is between 800 and 900 feet greater than that of Fort Smith, the latter being 460 feet above the sea. The center of Benton county is about one degree farther north. At Fort Smith a period of observation covering nineteen years and three months shows the temperature of spring to be 60.79 degrees; of summer, 78.48; of autumn, 60.65; and of winter, 40.55; mean for the year, 60.12. The difference in elevation and in latitude would probably make a difference in the annual temperature of between two and three degrees. The rain-chart constructed under the direction of Professor Joseph Henry shows that the annual precipitation in Benton county varies from 32 to 44 inches.

VARIETIES OF TOBACCO GROWN.

The White Burley, which grows in the tobacco districts of Arkansas, is very large, giving it a rough appearance, and, in consequence of its size, many of the leaves, in growing, touch the ground. The Virginia Golden Leaf is also grown to a considerable extent, and is very rich, oily, and smooth, with stem and fiber small. It also matures early and cures easily, and is the favorite for fillers. The Yellow Pryor and the Orinoco are nearly equal in good qualities, but do not produce as fine a leaf. The two latter varieties are richer in oily substances than the White Burley, and are not so fragrant or heavy in body as the Virginia Golden Leaf, but are very useful for plug work.

The relative proportion of types has varied greatly within the last decade, as illustrated by the following:

Type.	1879.	1869.
	Per cent.	*Per cent.*
Dark shipping	15	42
Fillers	30	10
Bright wrappers	5	8
Cutting	20	....
Nondescript	30	40

It will be seen that the nondescript and shipping leaf have been largely reduced, while the higher grades have all increased, except bright wrappers.

In northern Arkansas this improvement has been very marked since 1877, especially in grades suited for domestic consumption. The production of the heavy shipping qualities is avoided as much as possible. The comparatively poor, dry, silicious soils, producing from 500 to 600 pounds per acre of half bright or good bright wrapping leaf, which sells from 10 to 30 cents per pound, yield a far better return to the planter than the rich red-clay soils or manured lots, which produce larger crops of ordinary shipping leaf, bringing only 3 or 4 cents per pound. The thin soils are easily cultivated, as no rank weeds shoot up to interfere with the growth of the crop.

The beds of limestone are approximately horizontal, and the clayey beds which overlie them absorb water slowly, especially upon the level prairie lands. In their wild state a rank vegetation springs up upon these level, almost treeless plains, and in time forms a thick mat of humus, which, commingled by cultivation, makes a very rich soil. When cherty beds occur along with the clay, the land is much better drained. Where there is a predominance of clay the soils are cold, but the gravel of the chert, when present, warms up such soils, and gives a quick growth to the crops planted upon them. Usually the cherty soils have in their original condition a scanty growth of hickory and black-jack, with an undergrowth of hazel. These loose, dry, silicco-calcareous and argillaceous soils are seldom affected injuriously by either wet or dry seasons unless the maximum is extreme. When freshly cleared the tobacco grown on them has an exceedingly fine, silky texture, a golden color when cured, and a rich aroma. In the language of one of the schedules, "The soil preferred is a gravelly loam, rich, red, deep, and light, with a subsoil of reddish clay"—freshly cleared land, on which the original growth was as indicated above. Another describes the best soil for heavy tobacco as the black loam of bottom lands, and for fine tobacco flat hickory land, the latter gray in color, with a reddish-yellow subsoil, warm and dry. The land is carried in tobacco two years, the quality of the second year's growth being much heavier and better suited for shipping leaf than for wrappers. It is observed that the color of the under-clay has much to do with the quality of the tobacco. Very red under-clays, free from gravel, will not make a type so fine as lighter clays, but the product is heavier. No difference, however, is seen in the product of level or rolling lands, provided they be equally well drained and of similar soils.

It is estimated that 40 per cent. of the soils preferred for the growth of the better types of tobacco is occupied in the county of Benton, and that 70 per cent. of the wooded lands is adapted to its growth.

The usual practice to prevent a rapid deterioration of soil is to sow wheat at the end of the second year, and upon this crop of wheat, in the following spring, clover. Two crops of clover are allowed to mature, which are sometimes depastured with stock, but often suffered to fall down and decay upon the land for its enrichment.

While the finest tobacco is grown upon lands which had an original tree covering of hickory and black-jack, it is noted that a soil with a tree growth of walnut and wild cherry—always indicative of fertility—will make a broad shipping leaf, color dark brown, fiber large, but leaf pliant and full of oil.

In relation to these two classes of soil, namely, the black-jack and hickory soil, with light reddish clay, and the walnut and cherry soil, with a deep red under-clay, some curious facts were brought to light by Dr. Peter, the chemist of the geological survey. Taking two samples of the first class, one virgin and the other having been under cultivation for twenty years, it was found that by cultivation the soil had lost in organic matter, oxide of iron, carbonate of lime, and magnesia, but the silica, potash, soda, and phosphoric acid were increased, the first by 3 per cent., the second by 20 per cent., soda by 38 per cent., and phosphoric acid by 81 per cent. The loss, however, in all these elements was very large in a comparison of two analyses of virgin soil and of soil long under tillage taken from Washington county, where the timber growth was walnut and cherry and the subsoil a deep red clay.

Very little fertilizing is done for the tobacco crop, mainly because fresh lands are largely employed in its growth. In making the heavier grades of shipping leaf sometimes from two to four tons of manure are applied broadcast upon an acre, but the effect is to increase the yield at the expense of quality. A few farmers apply the manure in the hill.

PLANTING AND CULTIVATION OF TOBACCO.

Seed-beds are burned and prepared in all respects as in Tennessee and Kentucky. These beds are sown at any time from December 20 to March 15, and the plants are large enough for transplanting from May 10 to June 25. For fancy or fine crops the earlier the plants are set the better, as bright colors are more easily made when the tobacco is cured before the advent of cool weather. Old lands require larger plants than new.

The preparation of the soil for receiving the plants depends upon the quality of the tobacco to be produced and whether the land be old or new. For the finer kinds a light plowing, only 3 to 4 inches deep, is given. For heavy shipping leaf deep and thorough breaking is done, 7 or 8 inches in depth for old land, first during the winter, if possible, and again in April or May. New lands are well grubbed, broken with coulter once or twice, then with turning plow twice; followed with a heavy harrow after each breaking. Subsoiling is not practiced in preparing the land for growing a crop of tobacco, but is found to be very beneficial for other crops. Harrowing the land several times is regarded as indispensable to putting the soil in good condition. Old land is laid off with long, narrow plows (bull-tongues), and two furrows are thrown on this with a turning plow, making a straight ridge, elevated 3 or 4 inches above the general level. The tops of these ridges are slightly flattened with a common hoe and the plants are set on the ridges from 20 to 24 inches apart for fine tobacco. In growing heavier tobacco, or tobacco of any kind on new land, the land is laid off 3 feet each way, or 3½ by 3 feet, or on very rich soils 3½ by 3½ feet, and small hills are made at the points of intersection. This is always done when it is desired to apply manure to the hill, it being placed in the depressions made at the intersectional points and the hills made above them. If showers should happily come after the hills or ridges are prepared the plants are set out rapidly, but in seasons of drought a gill of water is applied to each hill in new land before planting. On old lands a pint of water is required for each hill to insure the life of the plant. As soon as the plants are firmly established, a common hoe is used to loosen the soil around them, which gives them an early start. The field is then plowed as often as may be necessary to keep down the weeds and to keep the land in good tilth.

From ten to sixteen leaves are left to each plant in topping, and the suckers are removed as fast as they attain a length of 2 or 3 inches. From four to seven weeks intervene between topping and harvesting, the period for the latter being the last of August, and continuing until the last of September, and even into October, when the transplanting has been delayed, or when unfavorable weather has checked the growth of the plants. In cutting a common knife is used. The stalk is sometimes split, but oftener speared on a smooth stick 4 feet long, from six to twelve plants to the stick. The time preferred for cutting is late in the afternoon, when the tobacco will not "sunburn". It is hung and hauled in in the morning while cool, in which condition it does not bruise so easily by handling. If possible, tobacco is never harvested immediately after a rain. When rains are continued, it is difficult to cure the crop to bright colors, nor does it ever recover its oily smoothness of leaf, but becomes harsh and impaired in quality.

CURING OF TOBACCO.

Two-thirds of the whole product of Burley tobacco is air-cured in open barns, one-sixth by charcoal, and one-sixth by flues and open wood fires, and it is usually allowed to remain on scaffolds, constructed in the fields, for three or four days before being put into these barns. Flue and charcoal curing are elaborated in the chapter on North Carolina, and are the modes used for making yellow wrapper.

After being well cured, the tobacco is carefully assorted as to length, color, richness, and defective leaves, tied mostly in hands of eight leaves, hung up on sticks for "ordering", or temporarily bulked.

There are three or four grades made in every crop, consisting of wrappers, bright and half bright fillers, and lugs or smokers, for bright tobacco; leaf, lugs, and trash, for the Burley sorts; and good leaf, low leaf, and lugs, for the heavy shipping tobacco. Unusual pains are taken, especially in Benton county, in properly assorting the crop. A really excellent article of tobacco, slovenly or unskillfully handled, will bring a very small price.

The insects and the diseases which attack the plant are the same as in other tobacco-growing sections. The bud-worm or wire-worm is probably more troublesome than any other insect.

TOBACCO-HOUSES.

These houses are constructed of logs, and are from 16 to 20 feet square, and from four to six tiers in height. Many of these log barns are furnished with flues, at a cost of from $5 to $30. Larger frame barns, 50 feet or more in length and 40 feet in breadth, are also built for air-curing, but these large structures are not deemed so efficient in the curing of yellow tobacco, it being much more difficult to secure a uniformity of temperature in them. The smaller barns will hold about 400 sticks of tobacco, equivalent, on an average, to the product of one acre; the larger barns, for air-curing, have often a capacity for housing 6,000 sticks, the product of from 14 to 16 acres. For flue or charcoal curing the barns are made very tight, but are open for air-curing. The cost of these structures ranges from $50 to $400. About 1 in 800 is annually destroyed by fire.

MARKETING OF TOBACCO.

By far the largest proportion of the crop is sold loose to local dealers, agents, or manufacturers, and is delivered to them in good prizing or bulking order; that is to say, when the tobacco is soft enough to handle without breaking the leaf but with the stem dry enough to crack two-thirds of its length when bent. Dealers pack in hogsheads 44 inches in the head and 58 inches in height, which cost $2 each. The number of pounds of each type or grade of tobacco packed in a hogshead of this size is: of fine wrappers, 900 pounds; of manufacturing leaf, fine, 1,000 pounds; common manufacturing leaf, 1,200 to 1,500 pounds; lugs, from 1,500 to 2,000 pounds.

The time for delivering to dealers is during the fall and winter months, and even up to April, when the weather has been unsuitable for handling tobacco previously. When kept late, it is frequently injured in the open barns by mold, which is always present to some extent in warm, wet weather. Dealers prefer to prize in March, April, and May, before the period arrives for the tobacco to go into the sweating process. It generally reaches the market in Saint Louis in May, June, and July.

PRICES OF TOBACCO.

The average price received by the farmers for tobacco tied in bundles and not prized is $4\frac{1}{4}$ cents per pound. Bright and half-bright wrappers bring an average of $12\frac{1}{2}$ cents, ranging from 8 to 40 cents, a very small proportion bringing the higher figures. For White Burley the average price is 6 to 8 cents; manufacturing, 5 cents; common, $3\frac{1}{2}$ cents; lugs averaging $1\frac{1}{4}$ cent. The general average is reached by calculating the proportion of the crop of the district as one-twentieth bright wrappers, one-tenth White Burley, one-fourth manufacturing, two-fifths common, and one-fifth lugs. It costs 2 cents per pound to handle and pay all expenses on the tobacco after it leaves the planter's hands until it is sold in Saint Louis. There are no stemmeries in the district, but there are a few establishments where plug is made.

COST OF RAISING THE TOBACCO CROP.

Good tobacco lands are worth from $10 to $25 per acre; inferior from $1 to $5. When money rent is paid, $5 per acre is the customary price. This probably includes the use of barns for housing the crop. Labor is cheap, and good men, well skilled in the growing and handling of the crop, can be hired the year round at $150, inferior hands at $100, and by the day, in summer, 75 cents is paid for the best hands. Wages, however, are not advanced in proportion to skill in the laborer. The following detailed estimate of cost on best soils was made for Benton county by Mr. William Smith:

DR.	
To cost of making seed-bed	$1 50
Rent of land (interest on price)	2 50
Cost of preparing one acre for plants	3 50
Drawing and setting plants	1 50
Cultivating, harvesting, and preparing for market	33 00
Delivering crop to market	1 50
Total cost	43 50
CR.	
By 1,600 pounds tobacco, at 4⅓ cents (best lands)	69 33

Profit per acre, $25 83; cost of production per pound, 2.7 cents.

Good crops of White Burley averaged at the same time 8 cents per pound, making a profit per acre of $84 50. A yield of 500 or 600 pounds per acre is often more profitable than a yield of 1,600 pounds; for 600 pounds at 12 cents, or 500 pounds at 15 cents, the average price of the fine yellow wrappers grown on thin soil, will aggregate a larger amount than 1,600 pounds at 4⅓ cents. The tendency among all planters of the district is to abandon the growth of the heavy, low-priced styles of tobacco and to substitute the finer and more salable types.

Tobacco is also raised by "croppers", the landlord furnishing only land, barns, and sticks, receiving therefor one-third of the crop, divided while green on the sticks at the time of cutting. One hand is allowed from two to three acres.

Charcoal, for curing, is worth 5 cents per bushel, delivered at the barn. One hundred bushels are required to cure 450 to 500 sticks of fine tobacco, an average of ten plants to the stick, or the product of one acre. Fewer plants are put to the acre and fewer on a stick for heavy, coarse tobacco, which is for the most part air-cured or cured by open wood fires. White Burley is also air-cured.

Wooden prizes cost from $5 to $12; screw and lever, $11; screw and ratchet, $14.

There are no warehouses for the inspection and sale of tobacco in the district.

OTHER DISTRICTS.

Some experiments have been made in central Arkansas, near Little Rock, within the past year, with Havana tobacco, which were very satisfactory, the product having the rich, mellow, aromatic flavor of the Cuba-grown leaf, and the cigars made from it being highly esteemed.

Every county in the state raises more or less tobacco, but principally in small patches for domestic consumption. A section of country embraced in Clay, Greene, Crawford, and Poinsett counties is occupied by Crowley's ridge, a considerable elevation, distinguished for its remarkable fertility. The subsoil of this ridge is a clayey bed, which underlies the quaternary marls and sands of the Saint Francis bottoms. Analyses develop the fact that the subsoil of this ridge contains more phosphoric acid, potash, soda, oxide of iron, and magnesia than the top virgin soil, and that fields long cultivated, though containing less potash, phosphoric acid, and soda than the subsoil, have a larger proportion than the virgin soils of other districts. The timber growth is black oak, hickory, black and white walnut, and tulip tree. Tobacco is planted on the slopes of this ridge, and the quality has been highly commended for domestic fillers and wrappers. From this point the product goes to Paducah or to Louisville, Kentucky.

Another region is beginning to produce tobacco in a small way for market, principally on the southwestern side of White river, and embracing a part of Van Buren, Stone, Searcy, and Newton counties. It may be considered an extension of the Benton County district.

The following statement shows the production, acreage, yield per acre, and value of the tobacco crops of Arkansas for 1876, 1877, 1878, and 1879. Only the figures for 1879 are from census returns:

Year.	Production.	Acreage.	Yield per acre.	Value in primary markets.	Average value per pound.
	Pounds.		*Pounds.*		*Cents.*
1876...	956,800	2,080	460.00	$62,192	6.50
1877...	1,045,950	2,202	475.00	49,683	4.75
1878...	916,320	1,992	460.00	36,653	4.00
1879...	970,220	2,064	470.07	41,547	4.28

The crop of 1877 was the largest that has been produced for years, but it was of inferior quality, being coarse and bony. The crop of 1879 was not so good, however, as that of 1878, being affected by dry weather; but in 1876 it was about of the same character as the crop of 1879, with a fair proportion of yellow wrappers and smokers.

Nothing can be more deceptive, without proper explanation, than the table given above. The amount of tobacco grown in the state for market is very small, and the comparatively large amount produced for home consumption reduces the average very low. Benton, which sends more tobacco to market than all the other counties together, reports an average yield per acre of 724 pounds—a third greater yield than is reported for the whole state, and equal to that reported in some of the best tobacco districts in the South. Bradley county reports a yield of less than 100 pounds to the acre, and many others report between 300 and 400 pounds per acre.

CHAPTER IV.

CULTURE AND CURING OF TOBACCO IN FLORIDA.

The quantity of tobacco grown in Florida would not of itself justify an extended notice of the state as a tobacco-growing region. The article produced, however, more nearly than any other grown in the United States, resembles that produced in Cuba. No other portion of the United States so nearly resembles Cuba in the character of its flora, the equableness of its temperature, or the variety of its marketable productions.

CLIMATE.

In the latitude of Jacksonville, 30° 15′ north, recent observations by the signal officer of the United States give a yearly mean average of 69.6 degrees, and the yearly range of the thermometer, as made up from the daily mean, to be 30.7 degrees. The rainfall for ten years averages 48 inches.

PROGRESS OF TOBACCO CULTURE.

Tobacco was first cultivated for market in Florida in 1829, in Gadsden county. A Virginia gentleman made it profitable on account of the silky texture of the leaf and the large amount that could be produced to the acre. The census of 1840 showed a total production for the state of 75,274 pounds, of which Gadsden county produced 66,324 pounds. In the census of 1850 the state reported 998,614 pounds, and of this Gadsden county was credited with 776,170 pounds and Marion county with 109,000. During the decade between 1840 and 1850 its culture extended into Calhoun, Leon, and Jefferson counties, adjoining Gadsden, and into Marion, near the center of the peninsula.

Between 1850 and 1860 the highest point of production was reached, and for several years the annual sales varied from 3,000 to 4,000 boxes of 400 pounds each. In 1860, owing to the increasing efforts made to raise sugar, and to the high price of sea-island cotton (to the production of which the earnest attention of the planters had been directed), the reported production of tobacco declined to 828,815 pounds for the state, of which Gadsden county raised 553,701 pounds; Washington, 36,680; Calhoun, 119,800; and Liberty, 34,900. Jefferson and Marion had abandoned its culture. The total production reported in 1870 was 157,405 pounds, and nearly every county, except Gadsden, ceased to raise tobacco for market. In that year Gadsden county produced 118,799 pounds; Calhoun, 13,822 pounds; and Washington, 7,590 pounds. A few other counties reported a small quantity, the largest being Jackson, producing 4,202 pounds—scarcely enough for home consumption. The product in 1870 was only 19 per cent. of the amount produced in 1860. The enumerators' returns for 1880 show the production to have fallen to 21,182 pounds, grown on 90 acres, with an average yield per acre of 235 pounds, the lowest yield reported for any state or territory, except Maine and New Mexico. The crop of 1879 amounts to but 14 per cent. of that of 1869.

This decrease in production has been attributed to a multiplicity of causes, among them the want of confidence in the constancy of the labor in the state, tobacco requiring the most assiduous attention from the time it is planted until it is harvested. The petty thieving which prevails among certain classes in the tobacco-growing region had a depressing effect also. Hundreds of pounds were often carried off from the open sheds in a single night. Moreover, the hammock lands in the center of the tobacco-growing area have been very generally opened, and experience has demonstrated that in Florida the soils which produce the highest-priced seed-leaf tobacco must be fresh. When grown upon soils long opened it is thick and leathery.

The gray and mulatto hammock lands, slightly rolling and freshly cleared, are preferred for tobacco. If planted upon lands having a putty-like subsoil, the plants will grow well until the tap-roots come in contact with the impervious clay beneath, when they wither and scald if the sun should be hot. This is especially the case during a rainy season. This bluish clay is highly retentive of moisture, and an excess of water in either the soil or the subsoil is fatal to the tobacco plant. This subsoil has precisely the same effect upon the orange trees, the foliage of which becomes yellow when an orchard is established on such soils.

The red subsoil is very arenaceous, and is inclined to be porous, sufficiently, at least, to allow the superfluous water to percolate through it. A few hummocks have a sandy subsoil. These are very warm, and when planted in tobacco produce a quick growth. The leaves of the plants upon such soils become covered with white specks, locally called "turkey-egged". At one time tobacco so specked was very much in demand, 1.12 rix dollars per pound having been paid for it by the Germans. The fashion having changed for this peculiar style of tobacco, such soils are no longer desired for its culture.

About two-fifths of Gadsden county are pine lands, almost perfectly level. These lands have a grayish soil, with a salmon-red clay foundation. At the depth of 20 feet a bed of yellow sand occurs, and still lower a white sand, with a soft, whitish limestone rock, which hardens by exposure to the air. The soil of the pine lands is thin, varying from three to five inches in thickness, but will grow a good quality of tobacco when fertilized with cotton-seed, the quantity applied being about a pint to each hill of tobacco. The tobacco is equal in quality to any grown on the hummock lands, and many farmers prefer the pine lands for its growth. The droppings of cattle on the sandy pine lands enrich the land, while their tramping gives a degree of compactness to the soil which is highly beneficial. While some of these lands are very sandy, the soil of others is argillaceous, cold, and compact. Tramping the latter is attended with bad results. The chief difference between the pine and the hummock lands in the raising of tobacco is that the latter will grow it without fertilization and the former will not.

While the quantity of tobacco grown in Florida has been gradually decreasing for several years, the increasing demand for cigar leaf at Jacksonville and at Key West induced, as is reported, a larger planting for 1880 than for many years past.

VARIETIES OF TOBACCO GROWN.

Several varieties of tobacco are cultivated in Florida: the Florida Leaf, the Connecticut Seed-Leaf, the Havana, and the Virginia. The seed of the Florida Leaf was originally introduced from Virginia, and, while it has retained the size of the Virginia tobacco, it has, through a succession of years, acquired a silkiness and elasticity from the soil and climate which make it very valuable for wrapping purposes.

The Connecticut Seed-Leaf was introduced a few years since. It has a much broader leaf than the Florida variety, will grow a larger number of pounds per acre, and is more easily cured a chestnut color, the color most sought after at the present time by the manufacturer. Nor is it liable in as great degree as the Florida Leaf to the white speck, which is now considered a defect in the Florida variety.

The Havana is small, but commands a higher price. More plants may be grown to the acre, and two or even three crops may be grown in a single year upon the same land by leaving a sucker on the stalk near the ground in succession as the various crops mature. Another reason for its popularity is that it can be grown on old manured lands, while the other varieties are confined almost exclusively to the freshly-cleared areas.

The Florida Leaf and the Connecticut Seed-Leaf are grown for wrappers mainly, though the worst leaves are taken for fillers for common cigars. The Florida Leaf, though not so large as the Connecticut Seed-Leaf, has a better body and more gum. The Cuba tobacco is grown for both fillers and wrappers, and is said to preserve to a considerable extent the aroma of the Cuba-grown tobacco, becoming, however, larger and longer, until it assimilates the Florida Leaf. It is thought, however, that the deterioration, if it may be called such, will not occur in regions further south.

Many years ago a variety called the Spanish was extensively grown. It is reported to have had great silkiness and elasticity as a wrapper.

The Virginia is only grown for home consumption.

Tobacco planted upon sandy soils or gray hummock has less weight and a lighter color than when planted upon rich, loamy soil or manured lots, where it will grow heavier, coarser, and darker. A great deal depends upon the time at which it is planted.

The cultivation and curing of the crop is done very much as in eastern Ohio, from eighteen to twenty-four leaves being left on each plant when topped, the latter number for the Cuban varieties. In three or four weeks the lower leaves begin to turn from a dark to a light yellowish green. When in this condition three or four of the under leaves are plucked from the stalk and carried to the curing-house. The gatherings from this time on until all the leaves are stripped from the stalk occur at intervals of three or four days. Men, women, and children all find active employment during the harvesting season. A wagon is taken to the field, and those who are to pluck the leaves from the stalk wait until the dew is off, and then with both hands strip off the ripe leaves, laying them straight, a dozen or more in a pile. Others follow and take up the piles, either in their arms or in large square baskets, and carry them to the wagon, placing them regularly in the wagon bed. The leaves are then immediately conveyed to the barn or drying shed. Here they are taken out and placed on a platform elevated 2 or 3 feet above the ground. They are then taken one by one and an incision is made near the butt of the midrib long enough for a stick three-fourths of an inch square to pass through readily. The instrument used for making the incision is a hawk-bill knife, or a piece of tin made in the same form, attached to a handle. The sticks are made 4 feet 2 inches long, and thirty leaves are put upon each stick, care being taken in stringing the leaves to put them "back to back and face to face". In other words, the leaves must not be put upon the sticks so that they will conform one to another, for if so placed when the desiccating process begins they will enfold each other, exclude the air, and become damaged or ruined by pole-sweat or "house-burn". The sticks are next elevated upon the tiers or racks in the barn and placed 6 inches apart. Tobacco is sometimes hung on a scaffold in the open field until it wilts, and is then taken into the barns, which are sometimes made dark, under the impression that too much light in curing is injurious, though it is always necessary that the tobacco have plenty of air in such cases during the night. In very damp weather, in the warm climate of Florida, tobacco will mold very quickly, and sometimes it is necessary to build small fires on the dirt floors of the barns to prevent this. For these fires charcoal is preferred. Any considerable amount of smoke, however, will greatly injure the flavor. A large stove, with a flue discharging the smoke outside, will dry the tobacco and prevent injury by mold or by smoke. There should be more or less moisture in the barn until the main stem of the leaf is of a nut-brown color.

The barns in Florida are built usually of round, rough pine poles. A house 30 feet square and 15 feet high is deemed sufficient to house two acres, there being seven rows of stalls, made of poles, elevated one above the other, to the roof of the building. The total cost of a barn of this size will not exceed $30. In about five days the leaves from two or more sticks are put upon one, and room is made in this way for another gathering.

The tobacco is first assorted when the green leaves are split, all the perfect long leaves being put in one class, the worm-eaten and ragged into another, and the short leaves into a third. The tobacco is again assorted after curing, the same classification being made, with a due regard to color and texture of the leaves. From eighteen to twenty-five leaves are put in a bundle, each bundle being wrapped near the head with an inferior leaf, which is tucked between the others. Should the tobacco be in a state of proper humidity to keep well, it is immediately bulked down; but if the condition is too high, it is again put on sticks in bundles, the bundles being straddled over the sticks, ten or fifteen to the stick, and again elevated on the tiers, until favorable weather shall bring it to proper condition. If after tying up the leaves in bundles the planter has his boxes prepared, the tobacco is often packed directly in them, the heads being placed against the inside ends of the box, with the tails lapping in the center. Loosely packed in the boxes, the tobacco is pressed down with a lever, and an additional quantity is packed in, until the amount in each box is 400 pounds. These boxes are 32 inches deep, 2½ feet wide, and 3½ feet long. The packing usually takes place between the first of October and the last of December. Careful handling and curing makes a difference of from 10 to 20 per cent. in the selling price. Cuba tobacco ranges in price from 20 to 50 cents per pound, depending upon the care and skill exercised in curing and sweating.

The diseases of the tobacco plant in Florida are rare when planted on soils well drained. Hostile insects and worms multiply with amazing fecundity in that warm climate. They resemble those found in other localities.

COST OF RAISING TOBACCO.

The estimated cost and profit of raising tobacco in Florida on best soils are as follows:

Dr.	
Rent of 2 acres of land	$10
One hand for five months	40
Board of same, at $10 per month	50
Use of horse and utensils	18
Use of barn and sticks	3
Boxes for packing	6
Marketing	3
	130
Cr.	
By 1,000 pounds of tobacco, at 15 cents	240
Profit on 2 acres	110

Cost of production, $8 12½ per hundred pounds.

This is a full estimate of the cost of production, some farmers making it as low as $7 50 per hundred pounds. The same laborer can make by moderate work three bales of cotton, 500 pounds each (1,500 pounds), 75 bushels of corn, and 50 bushels of sweet potatoes, which, at the prevailing prices, would bring in the market $250; but as it will require to produce these commodities the work of the laborer for twelve months the growing of tobacco would seem to be much more remunerative. On the best tobacco soils the same quantity of Cuba tobacco may be grown with the same expenditure of labor that will sell in the market for 25 cents a pound, making the profit $270. This increased profit on the growing of the Cuban variety has caused planters to abandon the seed-leaf to a great extent. The Cuba tobacco does not go through "the sweat" so well as the seed-leaf varieties. The burning qualities, too, in the Cuba, which is used more largely for fillers than for wrappers, is quite important. This quality is said to be more largely developed by the application of cotton-seed to the soil.

Mr. G. W. Floyd states that he has raised at the rate of 1,200 pounds of Florida Leaf to the acre on pine land tramped by cattle. He sold it for 12½ cents per pound.

Angus Nicholson raised in 1866 three crops of Cuba tobacco by turning out suckers, and made 400 pounds on a quarter of an acre. This was grown on a sandy ridge, fertilized with cotton-seed, and he was offered 75 cents a pound for it. On hummock lands the same gentleman grew 1,800 pounds of Florida Leaf to the acre. The tobacco attained a height of 8 feet, and had from sixty to seventy leaves to the plant. The land was heavily manured with cotton-seed, deep furrows having been run and filled with the seed, and then covered with two more furrows. This crop brought in the market 18¾ cents per pound.

Thomas M. Smith, of Decatur county, Georgia, raised a crop of 10 acres of Florida Leaf, which made an average yield of 1,500 pounds to the acre, and was sold for 15 cents per pound. This crop was grown on red, stiff, hummock land, without the application of any fertilizer.

The prices paid for the crops grown have also greatly animated the tobacco-growers. They have ranged about as follows: Florida and Connecticut fillers, 5 cents; binders, 8 cents; wrappers, 16 cents; price around, 14 cents; Cuba tobacco fillers and binders, 15 cents; wrappers, 25 to 30 cents; average for wrappers, 20 to 25 cents. A few cases of extra fine tobacco brought prices far in excess of any mentioned here.

The relative proportion of fillers, binders, and wrappers is variable, and depends upon the degree of skill and care exercised in growing, curing, and sweating. In the best crops of seed-leaf there are about two-thirds wrappers and one-third binders and fillers.

The crop in Florida is very irregular in quantity. In 1873 it was 80,000 pounds; in 1874, 160,000 pounds; in 1875, 320,000 pounds. Since that time it has been constantly decreasing, the small amount produced being taken by cigar manufacturers in Jacksonville. The average crop since 1876 has not exceeded 30,000 pounds, so small a quantity as to be lost sight of in the volume of trade.

Chapter V.

CULTURE AND CURING OF TOBACCO IN ILLINOIS.

The state of Illinois has less variety in topography than almost any other state of the Union. The surface features are generally gently-rolling prairies, whose greatest elevations rarely exceed 700 feet above the sea-level. This is increased in the northern part of the state and decreased in the southern portion. The feature of the central region is that of a great level, the slopes being of very slight grade. In the southern and western portions of the state the surface is rugged over small areas, and there are some bluff-like peaks.

Tobacco has been cultivated to some extent in Illinois since its first settlement, though up to 1864 its culture was confined, for the most part, to the more southerly counties. The census of 1840 reports the whole number of pounds produced at 564,326, the following counties only reporting a production in excess of 50,000 pounds, viz: Gallatin, 63,190; Wayne, 60,110; White, 68,061; Williamson, 115,419. The succeeding census shows that the production of this staple did not keep pace with the increase of population, for while the latter increased during the decade between 1840 and 1850 nearly 80 per cent., the tobacco product increased only 48 per cent. The number of pounds reported in 1850 was 841,394, only two counties reporting over 50,000 pounds, Saline and Williamson, the latter producing over five-eighths of the whole. The census of 1860 returned 6,885,262 pounds; an increase, as compared with 1850, of 718 per cent. The counties at that period producing over 50,000 pounds were Crawford, Franklin, Gallatin, Hamilton, Jasper, Jefferson, Johnson, Pope, Saline, Wayne, White, and Williamson, the last-named county still taking the lead, producing over 1,700,000 pounds, Johnson and Saline coming next, each producing over 1,000,000 pounds.

Previous to 1860 no tobacco as a staple crop had been cultivated in the northern tier of counties. The high prices, however, which prevailed in 1863 induced Mr. A. Simmons, a resident of Stephenson county, to make an experimental planting of the seed-leaf variety. It grew large and cured up an excellent color. He had the whole crop manufactured into cigars, and found a remunerative and ready market for them at home. His complete success stimulated his neighbors the succeeding year to plant a crop, and the cultivation gradually extended so as to embrace the larger portion of Stephenson and Jo Daviess counties.

In 1870 the total production of Illinois was 5,249,274 pounds, a falling off, as compared with the census of 1860, of over 20 per cent. This was probably due to the occurrence of unfavorable season, and not to a reduced acreage. The following counties reported a production of over 50,000 pounds, viz: Edwards, Franklin, Gallatin, Hamilton, Jackson, Johnson, Jefferson, Massac, Pope, Pulaski, Saline, Stephenson, Wayne, White, and Williamson; Saline and Williamson being still in the lead, each producing a little over 1,150,000 pounds. Crawford and Jasper during this decade abandoned to a large extent the culture of the crop, while Edwards, Massac, Pulaski, and Stephenson were added to the list of tobacco-growing counties. The returns of the enumerators of the census of 1880 show a total production for the state of 3,935,825 pounds, the counties having under cultivation over 100 acres being Franklin, Hamilton, Johnson, Massac, Pope, Saline, Williamson, Jo Daviess, and Stephenson. Of the counties named Jo Daviess and Stephenson are in the extreme northwestern part of the state, the others in the southern part.

The rocky strata underlying the surface of all these southern counties belongs to the carboniferous formation, and consists of shales, sandstones, slates, and limestones; but the soil of this whole area is almost entirely composed of drift, some of which is derived from the same rocks as those underlying, brought from their location in more northern sections of the state. The topographical features of this region are varied, some sections having level and others rolling prairies. In the former the soil is very rich and of black color, while on the rolling and ridgy prairies the soil is usually a chocolate brown, but of equal fertility with the black soils. The timbered ridges have almost invariably a light chocolate-brown colored soil. The tree growth of the ridges is chiefly black and white oak and the various kinds of hickory. Where the tops of the ridges become plateaus, or coves are formed on their sides, the elm, black walnut, sugar maple, and wild cherry grow to great size. Johnson and Pope counties are broken with frequent ridges and bluffs, while to the south the country becomes gently rolling, and then so level that the streams drain off slowly, frequently overflowing large areas. The ridge land is fertile, especially on the plateau tops, and the tree growth is white and black oak and hickory. The soil is sandy and warm, and is easily cultivated. The soil in the southern part, though somewhat wet, is warmed up and the clays made loamy from the mixture of sands from the highlands of the north, and is of great fertility. The timber growth is white oak, sugar maple, walnut, hickory, elm, etc. Pulaski and Massac counties are almost identical in their geological formation and in the character of their soils. The northern townships have a surface covered by gently sloping hills, with an arenaceous, loamy soil that is very fertile. These hills are heavily timbered with white and black oak, hickory, poplar, black gum, walnut, and dogwood. In the southern part of these counties the soil is the rich alluvial river bottoms, with a growth of pecan, willow, sycamore, maple, cottonwood, ash, and elder. The central area is largely occupied by a section called the "oak barrens", the soil of which is a fine arenaceous loam of a yellow color and of great depth. The term "oak barrens" is derived from a peculiar variety of Spanish oak, of small size and rough and bushy appearance. It is the prevailing undergrowth, the larger trees being scattered, and consisting of post, white, and black oaks, hickories, and a few yellow poplars and elms. In the western portion of this area the large growth is more abundant, with frequent black and white walnut and sugar maple. The soil of these "oak barrens" is claimed to have great capabilities for production. The best soils of Saline county are those derived from drift. This drift is a yellowish, gravelly clay, and Saline county has a much larger proportion of it than the adjoining county of Gallatin. The poorest soil is that derived from the shales of the coal formation. The timber growth on the river bottoms is black walnut, white, red, and black oak, hickory, and poplar; that on the highlands chiefly hickory and the oaks. The soils of the county of Williamson resemble those of Saline, especially the western part of that county, though they are more varied. The prairies are small and scattered over all parts of the county. The post-oak flats are considered the poorest land, and the chocolate-colored clay loam, on which the prevalent tree growth is oak and hickory, with occasional walnut, linden, and wild cherry, is considered the best.

The characteristics of the soils, topography, and timber growth of all the counties in the southern division of the state are a parallel of those described. They may be thus summed up: Wherever a prairie has dark, chocolate-colored soil, it is fertile, and where there is a similar soil, with a timber growth of the heavy oaks, pignut or scaly-bark hickory, with more or less black walnut, large crops of corn or tobacco may be expected from it when cleared.

In the counties of Jo Daviess, Stephenson, and in part of Carroll the underlying rocks are the limestones of the Trenton group, with occasional hills of the Niagara. There are large areas entirely free from drift, and the quaternary sands and pebbles which do exist are derived from sources other than those of the more southern parts of the state. It has also been assumed that the rolling prairies of these counties have been made by a different cause from that producing those of the central part of the state. Unlike the latter, the surface of these northwestern prairies sometimes rises into high ridges, and then again they become low swamps. The soil is a loam, with a predominance of sand, and these prairies are noted for their excellence as grazing lands. The general slope of Jo Daviess county is to the southwest, and is excellently watered by numerous streams. The eastern part of the county is generally level prairie, with a rich, warm, deep soil; the central part uneven, and the timber scrubby. The western sections are well timbered, but hilly, and in many places there are prominent bluffs. The southern surface is varied, frequently rising into gravelly hills. The general color of the soil is reddish, and it is seldom considered fertile by those accustomed only to the rich, black prairie soils of the central region. Stephenson has the reputation of being one of the best agricultural counties in the state. The soil is very rich, and it has a darker chocolate color than that found in the southern counties. The oak openings are very rich, and produce large crops of wheat, and are the lands specially adapted to tobacco. The land of this county is almost all prairie, with occasional patches of timber, and it is well watered, but not so abundantly as Jo Daviess. The timber growth consists of the oaks, walnuts, and maples, and the prairies have a gently undulating surface.

CLIMATE.

The records of temperature and aqueous precipitation are very meager in the tobacco districts of this state. Observations made at Winnebago, in the county next east of Stephenson, from 1856 to 1867, showed the following average temperature for the different seasons of the year: Spring, 48 degrees; summer, 69.22; autumn, 47.48; winter, 20.67; average for the years included, 46.34. The rainfall for nine years, from January, 1857, to December, 1866, at the same point, for the seasons, was as follows: Spring, 9.72 inches; summer, 12.31; autumn, 9.66; winter, 6.14; average for years named, 37.83.

TOBACCO DISTRICTS.

Since the cultivation of the seed-leaf varieties has become general in some of the northern counties the trade has recognized two distinct tobacco districts in the state:

1. The seed-leaf district, comprising Stephenson, Jo Daviess, and a very small portion of Carroll county. The tobacco raised in these counties is packed in boxes, and is consumed, for the most part, in the United States.

2. The shipping district, embracing all those counties that lie in the southern part of the state in which tobacco, whether of the seed-leaf or of heavier varieties, is packed in casks instead of boxes.

THE SEED-LEAF DISTRICT.

This district is composed of high, rolling prairies, interspersed with "oak openings", with a soil derived for the most part from the drift formation. Local accumulations of a yellow clay are found, which generally form the more elevated portions of the district, and upon which a timber growth of elm, burr oak, basswood, maple, birch, pin oak, black-jack oak, shell-bark hickory, and wild cherry is found.

The increase in acreage was about 15 per cent. greater in 1879 than in 1878. The yield, though the same in Stephenson county, was somewhat increased in Jo Daviess in 1879, the crop being of a very superior quality.

The Connecticut and the Pennsylvania Seed-Leaf, and a variety known as Sweet-Scented, or Spanish, are planted throughout the district. The latter variety is doubtless the same as that known as Havana Seed, which is so extensively grown in New England. This seed was introduced into Illinois by the Agricultural Department, and it is becoming the most popular variety grown. It is only about two-thirds as large as the seed-leaf varieties, has a pea-green color, grows with upright leaves, and is preferred by farmers, because it has a better flavor, a finer texture, is more elastic, and brings a better price in market. The flavor resembles that of the Havana, but is not so decided. It occupies a position intermediate between the seed-leaf varieties and the Havana, both in size and in aroma, and is said to make a cigar mild and pleasant to the taste, neither so strong as the genuine Havana nor so insipid as the seed-leaf. The same variety of tobacco grown on the dark prairie soils is thought to have a better flavor and to cure up to a deeper color than if grown upon the clayey soils of the timbered lands. Upon the latter soils it is lighter in color, heavier in body, and approximates the heavier sorts used in the manufacture of plug chewing-tobacco. Successively grown on well fertilized prairie lands, tobacco improves in flavor, in elasticity, in texture, and in burning qualities. Land from which the water will gradually drain off, not level, but nearly so, is preferred, whether originally prairie or timbered land, but the soil must be dark in color, loose from an accumulation of humus or of arenaceous material, or, better, from a combination of the two. The timber growth which characterizes good soils for tobacco is pin oak, black-jack, hickory, and burr oak. Prairie land is, by a majority of planters, preferred to timbered lands. The gentle slopes bordering the streams, with a southern exposure, are generally selected, and are highly fertilized with stable manure—better a year old than fresh—forty or more loads per acre being applied for the first crop of tobacco; but afterward half that quantity will suffice to keep the land in good tilth and to increase its fertility. A load of manure is about half a cord. Tobacco succeeds tobacco year after year without any rotation, as the product so grown shows a constant improvement. Should there be an undue proportion of argillaceous matter in the soil, a crop of rye is found to be beneficial if turned under in the spring, but even the crop of rye does not break the continuity of the tobacco crop.

No attempt is now made to grow tobacco without fertilizing, for experience has demonstrated that when tobacco is grown, even upon virgin soils, without manure, the texture is coarse and the flavor poor. The yield per acre has been increased during the past ten years; the average now is 1,392 pounds per acre. The seed-leaf varieties run from 1,500 to 2,000 pounds, and the sweet-scented from 800 to 1,400 pounds per acre. The quality of the tobacco has greatly improved within the same period, due to increased care and skill in manuring. There is also a better knowledge of the soil, and there are better houses for curing the crop.

SEED-BEDS.

A deep, dark soil, having a southern exposure, is selected for a seed-bed, and the same place is used for a number of years. It is not burned, but spaded up, and a liberal quantity of fresh stable manure is worked into the soil. The sowing is done as early after the 1st of April as possible, and may be extended even into May; the transplanting is done from the 1st to the 25th of June.

In the preparation of the soil for the crop manure is applied in the spring, though the land always receives one plowing in the previous fall. A second plowing to the depth of 5 inches is given after the application of the manure, and afterward a third, with frequent harrowings, to keep the land well worked until the plants are ready to set, at which time rows are made 3½ feet apart, and the plants are set in the rows—seed-leaf 24 inches, and sweet-scented, or Spanish, 20 inches apart. A few growers make hills in the rows for receiving the plants; others set out on the sides of the furrows. The first method is the neatest and the best should unfavorable weather set in after transplanting. In the cultivation of the crop a fine-toothed cultivator is first run between the rows; afterward a two-horse cultivator, provided with shields, which run under the leaves of the tobacco plant, is employed, the shovels to which throw a small quantity of dirt to the plant. The latter implement is employed as often as the land may need stirring. In thirty or forty days the plants are topped to fourteen, eighteen, or twenty leaves, according to the vigor of each. No pruning is done. The crop is suckered twice, and cut immediately after the last suckering. It is then air-cured, and its management in all its details is almost identical with that given in the description of the adjacent Wisconsin district.

One method of killing the tobacco fly is practiced which is not mentioned in the schedules from any other district. A bed of petunias, a genus related to the tobacco plant, is sown near the tobacco-field, the sowing being so timed that the flowers, of which the moth is very fond, may be in bloom about the time the fly makes its appearance. At twilight these beds are visited, and as the moths hover over the flowers they are knocked down and killed with paddles. This is said to be the most effective method of destroying them.

The acreage and the amount produced in the district, yield and value, for four years are as follows, only the figures for 1879 being from census returns:

Year.	Production.	Acreage.	Yield per acre.	Value in primary markets.	Value per pound.	Value per acre.
	Pounds.		*Pounds.*		*Cents.*	
1876	810,000	570	1,473	$67,200	8.00	$117 89
1877	841,000	590	1,425	73,587	8.75	124 72
1878	822,000	651	1,258	79,461	9.66	121 50
1879	1,043,975	752	1,388	87,030	8.34	115 74

Farmers for the most part sell to local dealers, who reassort and pack in boxes 3½ feet long and 2½ feet deep and wide, containing 400 pounds to the box. These boxes are made of white pine, and cost $1 each. The following table gives the range of prices received by farmers for different varieties, crop through, for four years to 1879:

Year.	Seed-leaf.	Sweet-scented.
	Cents.	*Cents.*
1879	6 to 8	11
1878	7½	12½
1877	6¾	20
1876	8	None raised.

The farmer does not sell by grades, but in stripping three grades are made, viz, wrappers, binders, and fillers. Wrappers are worth about twice as much as binders, and the latter twice as much as fillers. The proportion of grades varies in different crops, according to soil and management. The best crops in a good season will run as high as 66 per cent. wrappers, the remainder being equally divided between fillers and binders. The average, however, is: wrappers, 50 per cent.; binders and fillers, each 25 per cent. The tobacco of this district is mainly consumed in the United States, though a small proportion of the lower grades is taken for export. It is understood that about one-third of the tobacco of the district is Sweet-Scented Spanish or Cuba Seed, as it is variously called, and the remainder seed-leaf. A part of the product is taken in the district by manufacturers, but by far the larger proportion is sent to New York, Chicago, Saint Louis, Cincinnati, and Baltimore.

TOBACCO-HOUSES.

Up to within a recent period the houses for curing the crop were very inferior. Rude structures, made oftentimes of rails, and covered with straw, were thought to be good enough, and even now there are many sheds with good frames having only a roofing of straw. The great losses suffered in consequence of this inadequate provision have induced the better class of farmers to erect good houses, in which the tobacco is not only protected from bad weather, but the farmer is enabled to have the tobacco under control during the curing process. A cut illustrating one of the best of these barns, belonging to A. Simmons, is here given.

End view—Entrance.

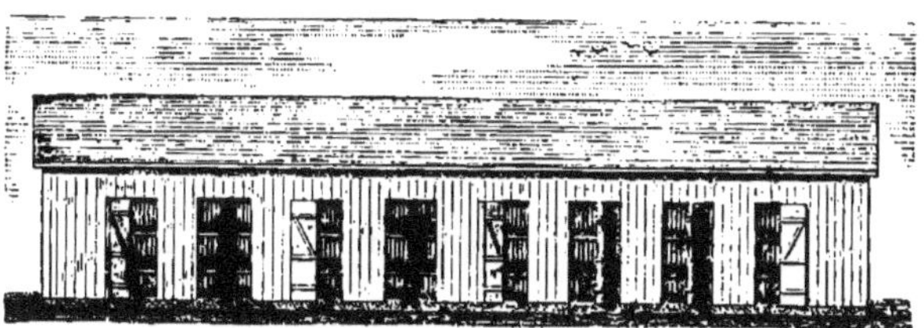

Side view.

A house of this kind, 28 feet wide and 108 feet long, having 18-feet posts, with four tiers beside the peak or roof tier, is considered ample for harvesting 6 acres of tobacco. In the "shed" represented there are ten bents, 12 feet apart. Each one of these bents has three posts. The upper three tiers are framed into these posts, but the ground tiers are let in by slots, so that they may be lifted out. This permits a wagon to be driven in, which is a great convenience in filling up the higher tiers. Such a shed as the one represented, with good shingle roof and side doors, may be built at a cost of about $700.

A shed for 3 acres is constructed of posts 18 feet high, but its width is reduced to 24 feet, and its length to 60 feet. Many growers prefer small sheds, as it is thought the tobacco is less liable to pole-sweat.

White veins are of very common occurrence in the crop, and are due, it is thought, to the prevalence of drought while curing tobacco cut full ripe; at least it has been observed that they appear in greatest quantity under these conditions. White veins sometimes occur without any known cause, injuring the crop very much, but not so much as pole-sweat.

COST OF RAISING TOBACCO.

Lands capable of producing the best tobacco and yielding the largest number of pounds per acre readily sell at $50 per acre. Such lands will yield 1,800 pounds of seed-leaf and 1,300 pounds of the sweet-scented varieties per acre. The wages of a good man are $1 per day and board. Mr. A. Simmons, the oldest grower in the district, furnishes the subjoined estimate, applicable for the best lands. He estimates that a good man can cultivate and take care of 4 acres of tobacco by working five months in the year:

Dr.	
One man five months, at $1 per day	$130
Board of hand	40
Manure, 20 loads, at $1 per load	20
Use of horse and plows	10
Feed of horse, two and one-half months	10
Rent of land, $4 per acre	16
Use of sheds, lathes, wagon, etc	25
Hauling to market	5
	256

Cr.	
By 7,200 pounds tobacco, at 8 cents	576
Profit on each hand on best soils	320
Profit on each acre	80
Cost per pound to grow, 3⅝ cents.	

Taking the average yield of the district, the cost will be $4 61 per 100 pounds.

Assuming the yield of the Spanish varieties to be 1,300 pounds per acre on best soils, 4 acres would produce 5,200 pounds, which, at 11 cents, would bring $572, which is nearly the same amount as is realized from an equal acreage of seed-leaf. To the inquiry made as to the relative proportions of the two varieties planted, no definite answer was returned, but about one-third of the acreage is of the Spanish varieties. The difference between cultivating the two may be expressed by saying that the Spanish varieties are of readier sale, require less shed room, but are more likely to be injured in the sweating process. The seed-leaf varieties fluctuate in price less than the Spanish, can be grown with more certainty, yield more uniformly, and are preferred by farmers who have no speculative turn. It may be mentioned in this connection, however, that the Spanish varieties are growing every year in favor, and to this tendency is to be ascribed the change which is taking place among farmers in the selection of soils for the growth of tobacco. Twelve or fifteen years ago the best tobacco was grown upon the black, timbered lands, and the prairie soils were thought to grow inferior tobacco. It is now found that tobacco grown upon the black soils of southern slopes, on gently rolling prairie, has not only a larger leaf, but has also a better flavor.

SHIPPING-LEAF DISTRICT.

The counties belonging to this district are Franklin, Hamilton, Johnson, Massac, Pope, Saline, and Williamson, with smaller areas in Clay, Gallatin, Hardin, Jackson, Marion, Jefferson, Pulaski, Wayne, and White.

Much of the crop of 1879 in this district was injured by mold and by the disease known as "leprosy". The exceedingly low prices which have prevailed for several years for the tobacco grown in southern Illinois have had a very depressing effect upon the industry, and the crop has been greatly reduced.

The varieties planted consist of the Blue and Yellow Pryors, Tully, One-sucker, White Stem, and generally such as are grown in the heavy tobacco districts of Kentucky and Tennessee. Descriptions of these varieties may be found in the chapters on these two states.

The tobacco of southern Illinois is used for making strips for the English markets, for export to the continent and to Africa, for manufacturing into heavy plug for Mexican balers, for stogie fillers, and for manufacturing a rough smoking-tobacco; but for all these purposes it is considered inferior to the tobacco grown in Kentucky, and even in Indiana, Williamson county being an exception, in which the product is of considerable value. The tobacco is generally of good size, red or brownish in color, showy, porous, with a large stem and fiber. In Johnson, Massac, and Pope counties some rich, fat tobacco is produced on the limestone soils, and on the oak and hickory ridges a style of tobacco much resembling the light-colored leaf of the Owensboro' (Kentucky) district is made. It is estimated that 65 per cent., though classed as shipping leaf, may with more propriety be referred to the nondescript. It occupies a very low place in the market, due probably more to bad handling than to the want of adaptation in the soils for the production of a high grade. A large part of the product is grown on freshly-cleared lands, on which the original timber growth was hickory, oak, walnut, and poplar, but the soils preferred are light-colored rolling uplands, with a clayey, mulatto subsoil. On such lands the tobacco grows with a finer texture, and has a better color, though light, having but little body. On bottom lands, and on old lands well manured, a dark-red, spongy leaf is produced, heavy, but not fatty, which, though well adapted to the manufacture of strips, is unsuited for domestic manufacture. Old lands, when planted in tobacco, are generally treated with stable manure, at a cost varying from \$1 50 to \$5 per acre.

The preparation of seed-beds and the cultivation of the crop are copied after the methods pursued in the heavy tobacco districts of Kentucky, but much less care is taken with the crop. About two-thirds of the tobacco, after it is cut, is simply hung up in open barns, after being previously exposed to the sun on scaffolds, and no further attention is given to curing it. It is afterward taken down, assorted, stripped, and packed in a rough way in hogsheads, which are made to weigh from 1,400 to 1,800 pounds for leaf and lugs. Some fire the tobacco with logs, and here and there a few farmers have constructed barns with flues for curing. Such farmers make a moderate profit on the crop, but it is a question of great doubt whether one farmer in ten growing tobacco in southern Illinois makes it profitable. The average price received by the farmer is: for leaf, \$3 75 to \$5; lugs, \$1 50 to \$2.

As estimated, the cost of production varies from \$2 50 to \$4 per hundred pounds, and the yield per acre for the different counties growing over 100 acres averages 619 pounds. Saline county shows the largest production, and also the largest average yield per acre in 1879, and Williamson stands next. The quality of tobacco grown in this latter county is much better than that raised in any other county in southern Illinois, and is better than the best raised in Indiana; but all other southern Illinois tobacco is considered inferior.

Hogsheads cost from \$1 75 to \$2. A large portion of the crop, probably three-fourths, is sold to local dealers, who pay so much per pound through, receive it in redrying houses, and pack it for market.

Strips are put up at Galatia and Raleigh, in Saline county, and also at Equality, in Gallatin county. At these points 75,000 pounds of strips were put up in 1879.

TOBACCO PRODUCTION.

The following statement shows the amount of production, acreage, yield per acre, and value of the product in the primary markets of all the tobacco areas in the state of Illinois not embraced in the seed-leaf district for the years indicated. The figures for all the years are estimated except those for 1879, which are made up from the census returns:

Year.	Production.	Acreage.	Yield per acre.	Value in primary markets.	Value per pound.	Value per acre.
	Pounds.		*Pounds.*		*Cents.*	
1876...........	10,734,800	17,743	605	\$420,392	4	\$24 20
1877...........	7,032,400	11,435	615	210,972	3	18 45
1878...........	3,447,470	5,651	610	103,424	3	18 30
1879...........	2,891,850	4,860	595	115,625	4	23 79

The following statement shows the total amount of production for the state of Illinois, yield, value of product in primary markets, value per pound, and value per acre for the years indicated. The yield of each year, except the last, which is from census returns, is estimated:

Year.	Production.	Acreage.	Yield per acre.	Value in primary markets.	Value per pound.	Value per acre.
	Pounds.		*Pounds.*		*Cents.*	
1876...........	11,574,800	16,313	682	\$496,302	4.29	\$27 11
1877...........	7,873,400	12,025	655	284,539	3.61	23 66
1878...........	4,270,370	6,305	677	182,885	4.28	29 00
1879...........	3,935,823	5,612	701	202,661	5.15	36 11

All reports agree that, while the tobacco area is very rapidly diminishing in southern Illinois, it is gradually increasing in the northern part of the state, where the seed-leaf and Spanish varieties are cultivated.

CHAPTER VI.

CULTURE AND CURING OF TOBACCO IN INDIANA.

The counties in Indiana growing the largest quantities of tobacco for market are Brown, Dubois, Gibson, Greene, Perry, Pike, Spencer, Warrick, and Wayne. Of the total product of the state in 1879, over 85 per cent. was grown in the counties of Dubois, Gibson, Perry, Pike, Spencer, and Warrick. This block of counties lies in the southwestern part of the state, between the Ohio river on the south and White river on the north, being adjacent to the Lower Green River district of Kentucky.

GEOLOGICAL AND PHYSICAL FEATURES.

Excluding the ash-colored alluvial bottoms, which are formed of the fine silty deposits gathered by the streams from the highly-comminuted material of the drift and clay, this block of counties belongs to the carboniferous formation. Along the Ohio river the lands in the eastern part of the district are broken into hills more or less abrupt, which rise to an equal height with the great interior plateau which forms by far the largest part of the surface of the state. These elevations sometimes form long, winding ridges, which constitute the watersheds of the numerous tributaries of the Ohio river. The lowlands on the streams sometimes spread out to a great width, rising gradually for the most part by easy slopes to the summits of the ridges, and these ridges are frequently almost severed by the beds of smaller streams, making a succession of knobby hills. At other places the crests of the ridges are broad enough to give a wide expanse of gently-rolling land, and these continue to widen as the distance from the larger streams is increased, forming large plateaus by uniting one with another as the heads of the smaller streams are passed. In the western part of the district the surface is more level, there being but few high hills.

In Dubois county one-tenth is estimated to be creek and river bottoms, one-half modified drift and alluvium of ancient lakes and rivers, and the remainder bold hills and ridges and elevated plateaus, made up of the conglomerate sandstones and slates of the coal measures. The eastern part of the county is very rugged, but in the southern and western parts plateau lands are of frequent occurrence, sometimes level, but generally rolling. Some of the best soils in the county are derived from the loess, which generally forms a sandy loam of brown color. Many of the highest plateaus and hills are capped by this soil, which supplies a tree growth of walnut, sugar maple, wild cherry, and papaw. These plateaus are usually called "walnut levels", which are noted for the excellence of the crops grown upon them. The soil of many of the creek and river bottoms is very wet in winter, and bakes to great dryness in summer. It has an ashen color, is very fine-grained or powdery, though pebbles and broken shaly material often occur, imbedded in the finer silty deposits. The usual timber growth is elm, red maple, and gum, and where there is a considerable proportion of sand and gravel beech, sugar maple, overcup oak, and the tulip tree are found.

The surface in the western part of Gibson county is generally level or gracefully undulating. About one-half of this portion of the county is bottom land, lying on the Wabash and the White rivers. Some sandy barrens also occur. Elevated plateaus are characteristic of the eastern and northeastern boundaries. These are often pierced by deep valleys. The soils of this county are fairly typical of the soils of the principal tobacco-growing area of the state, and may be divided into four groups:

1. River bottoms, made up of sands and clays spread out by overflows, generally fine silt or impalpable sands, but often gravelly or slaty. This soil is formed by a commingling of materials derived from the various beds through which the streams pass with a large amount of vegetable matter. Where there is not an excess of argillaceous matter the soil is warm and rich, but local beds of "crawfishy" soil occur, as well as beds of sand.

2. Second bottoms. This soil generally rests against the terrace beds or ancient alluviums, which may be recognized by the beds of sand and gravel, reaching to a considerable height. The texture of this soil is much coarser than that of the river bottoms.

3. Coming next is the loess, consisting of ashy-gray siliceous clays, often containing minute shells. When undisturbed it has a buff color, but under culture it rapidly assumes the gray ashen color mentioned, and becomes compact in structure.

4. The bowlder drift next succeeds. This is a heavy bed of blue and gray clays, very tenacious, and containing a large amount of pebbles and bowlders foreign to the region.

The yellowish loam which rests upon the ridge coming in from Pike county constitutes a broad belt of very fertile lands about Princeton and Owensville, and its characteristic timber is oak and poplar (tulip tree), maple, beech, hickory, ash, gum, etc.; in the river bottoms, walnut, sycamore, cottonwood, papaw, elm, and honey-locust.

Perry and Spencer have many more rugged hills than the counties described, and Perry, Spencer, and Warrick have the largest areas of good alluvial soils, the two latter counties producing five-eighths of all the tobacco grown in the state. Spencer grows the best tobacco, but Warrick makes the largest quantity.

In Pike county the bottom lands on Pataka river are of a great width, but the soil is whitish in color and cold, being completely saturated with water during the spring and winter months and parched by drought in summer. South of the Pataka the soils are reddish in color, and upon these tobacco is grown of a character resembling the heavy product of Kentucky.

Perry county, though very broken and uninviting for agricultural industry, has soils well adapted to the culture of tobacco, which is grown on the sandy loams of the river bottoms and upon the gentle slopes of the hills, where the reddish siliceous soils occur. The Saint Louis limestones crop out along the banks of the Ohio and in the valley over the greater part of the county east of Deer creek, and the coal-bearing strata mount up oftentimes in rugged hills to the height of from 200 to 400 feet. The soils derived from the weathering of the Saint Louis limestone and those from the weathered drift, or the limestones intercullated with the coal measures, are found to be best adapted to the growth of fine tobacco.

Brown and Greene counties lie farther north, and differ from those described in having more extensive drift and lacustrine deposits, which give character to the soil. The coal measures are wanting in Brown county, the underlying rocks belonging to the subcarboniferous, and the soils have a varied character. The drift appears in the northern part of the county, and gives rise to soils of much strength and durability. The alluvial soil, mainly derived from the aluminous shales and sandstones, is often sticky and cold, unless ameliorated or enriched by sands and calcareous clays from the glacial drift or limestone. On the bluffs flanking the streams are benches of ancient alluvium, containing pebbles of quartz. Lacustrine loess and silts are found in various parts of the county, making soils of fair fertility, and here and there are rich valleys, often partly surrounded by knobs from 200 to 300 feet high. Weed Patch knob rises to the height of 1,147 feet above the sea, and nearly 500 feet above Nashville, the county-seat. Tobacco is grown principally in the southeastern part of the county, though it is also grown to some extent in the central and northwestern portions.

Wayne county, in the eastern part of the state, has soils derived from the disintegration of the drift deposits. The kinds of tobacco grown are the seed-leaf varieties, including Havana seed.

METEOROLOGY.

The reports of the United States signal office cover only one point in the state—Indianapolis; yet, while its elevation above the sea is only 698 feet, the records at that point may be taken as a basis of calculation for the tobacco-growing regions of the southern and eastern portions of the state. The observations at Indianapolis were commenced February 10, 1871, and are given to October 31, 1880. Mean temperature: Spring, 52.2 degrees; summer, 75.1; autumn, 53.7; winter, 32.8; extreme range, 118; average range, 49.9; highest temperature, 97; lowest, 20 below zero; mean annual rainfall and melted snow, 45.22; prevailing winds, south. The following is condensed from observations extending from 1864 to 1873, at Vevay, 525 feet above the sea, 72 miles south of Indianapolis: The average mean of spring for the period included in the observations was 54.46 degrees; summer, 76.41; autumn, 55.38; winter, 32.48. The mean of the nine years' observations at Indianapolis was 53.4; that at Vevay, though not for the same years, was 54.68. The annual rainfall, including melted snow, for the period reported was: At Vevay, 52.77 inches, being for spring, 15.63; summer, 11.40; autumn, 15.12; winter, 10.62.

VARIETIES OF TOBACCO GROWN.

Numerous varieties of tobacco are produced in the state, chief among them being the Yellow and Blue Pryor, Orinoco, One-sucker, Lovelady, Connecticut Seed-Leaf, Kite-Foot, and White Burley. The first named are grown almost exclusively in Warrick, Spencer, Perry, Pike, Dubois, Gibson, and Orange counties; the White Burley to some extent in the counties first named, and largely in Switzerland county; and the seed-leaf varieties in Wayne, Randolph, and Shelby counties, and a portion in Greene. In the first named group of counties smokers and Regie styles of tobacco are mostly grown, though about 40 per cent. was formerly taken for fillers in the manufacture of domestic plug. A considerable quantity is bought up by local dealers and made into strips. A large part of the growth, on account of its comparative freedom from gum, partakes of the nature of cutting leaf, and when cutters are scarce and high some of it is taken in this country for cutting purposes. It is better suited, however, for cutting in England, where a heavier type is used than in America. Of the whole amount produced in the southwestern part of the state 45 per cent. is classed as nondescript, 20 per cent. as heavy cutters, and 35 per cent. as fillers. Ten years ago 60 per cent. of the crop was fillers and 40 per cent. nondescript. A very small amount, made from the Lovelady and One-sucker varieties, is used for the African trade. The White Burley makes bright smokers or cutters, and is coming into favor, because it brings a higher price than the varieties heretofore grown. It is coarser in structure and duller in color than the same variety grown in Ohio and Kentucky, and only makes a substitute for the fine domestic cutting-leaf. In Switzerland county this variety is grown almost exclusively. About 3 per cent. of bright wrappers are made.

There is also a small quantity of a smooth, dark leaf grown in Spencer county suitable for the Italian market, and also a smaller amount of lighter color, taken by the French Regie, classed French B. The commoner sorts, classed as nondescript, find the readiest market in Spain. The amount of heavy German tobacco grown is unappreciable. The product is generally poor, and it will absorb a great deal of water, which it parts with readily, for which reason a large part is converted into strips for cutting purposes in England.

A light-bodied tobacco, suitable for manufacturing plug in the United States, is grown to some extent on the elevated lands in Dubois, Spencer, Warrick, and Pike counties. A light-brown color is generally secured, but all colors are made.

To characterize properly the tobacco of this district is difficult; but it may be said generally that the great bulk of it is very porous and spongy, lean and bony, with little or no gum; colors not decided, but rather light, mottled, and dingy; generally, but not always, badly handled and badly assorted. It is usually grown by renters and tenant farmers in small patches, the average crop for each farmer being about 2,500 pounds. There is therefore a lack of uniformity, as also a lack of conveniences for handling, and a want of skill among the cultivators. It stands low in the markets of the world, and as an export tobacco only ranks next above that grown in Illinois. The tobacco is sold loose to local dealers.

The Indiana Seed-Leaf is grown in Wayne and portions of contiguous counties, in Shelby, and a little in Orange and other counties. The quantity produced in 1879 was 746,298 pounds. It is produced upon soils derived mainly from the drift. The production some years runs up as high as 1,600,000 pounds, but this is unusual, and only occurs when seed-leaf tobacco commands a high price. The crop is exceedingly irregular as to quantity.

The Kite-Foot tobacco, grown in small quantities by Germans in Clarke and Owen counties, deserves mention on account of the peculiar method of handling. It has a broad, short leaf, cures up a brownish color, with yellowish spots, and resembles the spangled tobacco of the eastern Ohio district. It has small fiber and stretchy leaves, and is cured with fire. In harvesting, the leaves are gathered from the stalks, as is done in eastern Ohio and in Florida. It is used in this country for making very common cigars.

SOIL AND CULTIVATION.

The manner of cultivating and curing tobacco in southwestern Indiana is identical with that practiced in the Lower Green River district of Kentucky, except that in Indiana the culture is not so uniformly well done, nor are the houses for curing it so well built. The stalks are also speared to a larger extent. All is air-cured except about 10 per cent., and, as a result, a large amount is very often injured by pole-sweat or mold. The crop of 1879 was very greatly damaged, and the average price was largely reduced in consequence of this injury.

The methods of planting, cultivating, curing, and managing the seed-leaf varieties may be seen by reference to the article on the Miami seed-leaf district of Ohio, with which the seed-leaf district of Indiana properly belongs.

The soil greatly influences the quality. Tobacco grown on the hills is brighter colored than that raised on clay bottom lands, and a good sandy loam is the best for its production, especially if lately cleared. Land that has been heavily manured, or an old barn lot, produces a dark, heavy leaf, fit only for shipping. In some sections the proportion of dark shipping tobacco has fallen off one-third, in others one-half, while bright wrapping and smoking have doubled in quantity. Cutting-leaf has increased one-sixth, and seed-leaf, not heretofore grown in some counties in the southwestern part of the state, comprises 5 per cent. of the crop. In the selection of soil for tobacco greater care is taken than formerly, and more attention is paid to its cultivation and handling; it is also better assorted, sized, and graded.

Throughout the tobacco-growing region of the state the soil preferred is a sandy loam on rolling lands and on plateaus where the drainage is good. On lands so situated, and where there is a considerable accumulation of vegetable mold, the yield is best. Full 60 per cent. of the land now occupied in tobacco is of this character. On newly-cleared land the custom is to plant tobacco the first and second years, and to follow the third year with wheat and grass. Full three-fourths of the wooded land is suited to the growth of tobacco, and soils which have a primitive growth of white oak, dogwood, sugar maple, and hickory are preferred. Tobacco grown on such lands freshly cleared is of finer quality, but is lighter than that grown on lands which have been cultivated for a time. The freshly-cleared lands are greatly preferred for White Burley. The rolling lands produce a better quality, but a leaf of less weight than the level and more moist lands.

Very small quantities of fertilizers have as yet been used, probably on not more than 10 per cent. of the area cultivated in tobacco. Barn-yard manure is the chief one used, though some few growers have tried superphosphates. The custom is to use from five to six cords of stable manure to the acre, at a cost of from $5 to $6. When superphosphates are used, the quantity applied is from 200 to 300 pounds per acre. Many farmers use less of both kinds. The effect of these fertilizers is a greater yield, especially on the clay soils; but where manures are used the cured leaf is darker and seldom of market value, except for shipping.

By continual cropping in tobacco the soil deteriorates very rapidly unless manured; but the custom being to follow it with wheat and grass, there has been little, if any, average deterioration, and the annual yield per acre has in some instances increased. The rotation generally adopted is to follow tobacco with rye or clover, clover being considered the best, the system practiced being to cut off the first growth of clover of the second year, turn under the second growth, and seed the land to grass.

Farmers deliver their crops to dealers at any time after it is stripped, the season beginning generally in January and ending in May. Two classes are made in the regie or southwestern counties, trash or lugs and leaf; the prices in 1879, when sold by grades, being: for lugs, 2½ to 3 cents; leaf, 4 to 6 cents; bright wrappers and fillers, 9 to 9½ cents, and some seed-leaf as high as 15 cents.

In this district lands suitable for growing tobacco are worth in the market from $10 to $25 per acre. Very little land is rented for money. The share system of renting prevails here, and generally throughout the South, under which one-third of the crop produced is given for the use of the land, the landlord furnishing barns in which to house the crop. When the landlord furnishes teams and everything except labor the tenant gets only half the crop. The tenant provides his own food, but is furnished with house and fuel. Labor ranges in price from $10 to $18 per month, with board, the average being about $15; day laborers get $1 per day.

The following estimate of the cost of production per acre has been furnished by a gentleman at Booneville:

Cost of seed-bed	$0 50
Weeding, and attention to same	30
Rent of land (interest on price)	1 50
Stable manure	1 50
Cost of breaking land	2 00
Harrowing, lining out, and hilling	1 50
Drawing and setting out plants	1 25
Cultivating	5 00
Topping, worming, and suckering	2 50
Harvesting	5 00
Assorting and stripping	3 00
Bulking	20
Use of barn, laths, wagons, etc	1 50
Delivering crop to market	2 00
	27 75

Average yield per acre, 742 pounds.
Cost to produce, $3 74 per hundred pounds.

In the southwestern counties barns are generally constructed of logs, at a cost of about $50. They are open, and give little protection to tobacco in bad, damp weather. In the seed-leaf district framed sheds are usually employed for curing the crop, but they are generally of poor character.

STRIPS.

Strips are made at the following points in the state: Evansville, Booneville, Rockport, Grandview, Richland, Dale, and Huntingburgh. During the year 1879 the amount of strips put up in the state, as nearly as can be ascertained, was 1,710,000 pounds. For this work children from nine to twelve years of age are largely employed, being paid 40 cents for every hundred pounds of strips made. It is usual to pay less than this for stemming tobacco of broad leaf, and more for stemming lugs and tobacco having a narrow leaf. The amount of strips made by children will range from 50 to 100 pounds per day, while full-grown experts can make from 150 to 200 pounds, the quantity largely depending upon the quality of the tobacco stemmed.

Narrow tobacco loses from 40 to 50 per cent., wide tobacco about 33⅓ per cent., 10 per cent. of this being chargeable to the moisture in the leaf at the time of purchase. One large firm states that in a business which has covered thirteen years the largest average yield of strips for any one year was 62 per cent. of the tobacco bought. The absorptive capacity is variable, ranging from 33 per cent. for lean tobacco down to 15 per cent. for fatty sorts. There are four classes of strips made in the district: Long bright, long dark, short bright, and short dark. Lug strips are classified in the same way. These classes are again subdivided as to texture, fineness of fiber, width of leaf, and absorptive capacity, the lean strips being separated from those of more body. When in proper condition of dryness they are packed in hogsheads 58 inches high by 43 inches in the head. About 1,250 pounds net of strips are packed in each hogshead. Casks cost about $2 each. Dealers pay for oak staves $20 per thousand, and $1 is required to pay the cost on each hogshead for setting up, including cost of hoops and headings. The lumber for headings costs from $10 to $12 50 per thousand feet.

It may be added that the best farmers pay but little attention to tobacco culture, nor are the best lands employed for its production. It appears to be a favorite crop only with a class of roaming farmers, who can always find a ready market for it, though at prices which ordinarily will barely pay for the cost of production.

CROPS OF INDIANA.

The figures in the following table for the years 1876, 1877, and 1878 are based on information derived mainly from the state bureau of statistics, and may be relied on as very nearly correct. The production, acreage, and yield per acre for 1879 are from the returns of the census of 1880. The value in primary markets, value per pound, and value per acre are ascertained from schedules returned to this office and other data:

Year.	Production.	Acreage.	Yield per acre.	Value in primary markets.	Value per pound.	Value per acre.
	Pounds.		*Pounds.*		*Cents.*	
1876	15,015,370	16,769	800	$750,779	5.00	$40 00
1877	9,401,368	12,704	740	305,544	3.25	24 05
1878	8,100,000	11,008	740	280,632	3.50	25 90
1879	8,872,842	11,955	742	443,642	5.00	37 11

Of the tobacco produced in Indiana in 1879, 746,298 pounds are estimated to be of the seed-leaf variety, 23,860 of the White Burley type, and the remainder of the Régie sorts, including heavy cutters, air-cured for manufacturing, and stogie fillers, classed as heavy tobacco.

CHAPTER VII.

CULTURE AND CURING OF TOBACCO IN KENTUCKY.

Kentucky takes the first rank as a tobacco-growing state, producing more than double the quantity of any other state, and more than one-third of the entire amount produced in the Union. The crops for the census years from 1840 were as follows:

	Pounds.
1840	53,436,909
1850	55,501,196
1860	108,126,840
1870	105,305,869
1880	171,120,784

Virginia took the first rank up to 1870, when Kentucky took the lead. Probably the largest and the best crop ever produced in the state was that of 1877. The production then reached 181,484,630 pounds, while for 1876 and 1875 the production was, respectively, 120,967,449 and 148,319,429 pounds. The entire area covered by the crop for 1879 (226,120 acres) shows an average yield per acre of 756.77 pounds. The area of its cultivation is widening every year, extending into the mountainous districts on the east and contracting the limits of the blue-grass region in the central portion of the state.

HISTORY.

In 1785 General Wilkinson, of Lexington, Kentucky, entered into a contract with the Spanish government in Louisiana to deliver several boat-loads of tobacco in New Orleans. Whether the tobacco he delivered was grown on the Ohio river or in the Spanish settlements on the Mississippi river is uncertain. Probably some of it was produced in Kentucky, for Mr. Wailes, former state geologist of Mississippi, after speaking of the production of the crop in that state, even as early as 1783, says:

> It is certain, from some cause, either from fraud in packing, the falling off in quality, or from the competition of Kentucky tobacco, introduced into New Orleans under General Wilkinson's contracts with the Spanish authorities, or by their connivance, the price was so reduced that the further cultivation of it in Mississippi for exportation was, in a few years, wholly abandoned.

The early cultivation of tobacco in the West, and its progressive development, have never been made subjects of record. Being a commodity of small local consumption, and dependent chiefly for its value upon foreign demand, the early growers were without adequate markets at home, and were forced to rely upon a rude navigation to reach the seaboard. It was by far the most profitable crop which could be grown, and almost the only one which would command ready money at all times when placed in market.

The culture of tobacco in Kentucky was begun as a business by the early settlers from the old tobacco states, and notably by those from Virginia. It is well known that about the year 1810 it was grown in marketable quantity at several points in the southern and central portions of the state. During that year John Small and Edmond Curd, from Virginia, and in 1812 Martin Hogan, from the same state, and Thomas Morrow, from North Carolina, settled in Logan county, and commenced the cultivation of tobacco. The crops grown by these persons were generally prized in hogsheads, hauled to the Cumberland river, and shipped by flatboat or keelboat to New Orleans, sold at low prices, and the proceeds of sale were brought back in coin, there not being sufficient commerce then to afford means of exchange. Some of these persons, however, found markets for their crops by hauling them loose in wagons a distance of twenty or thirty miles to local buyers, who were engaged to a small extent in manufacturing tobacco for supplying the home demand. From 1810 to 1820 other immigrants from the older states, among whom were Richard and William C. Browder and John P. Moore, from Virginia, engaged in the culture of tobacco as a permanent business. They were soon followed by others, and, being located at some distance from any shipping point on the Cumberland river, these persons manufactured their own crops, with the smaller crops of their neighbors, which they purchased. The manufactured product was then sent to Russellville and Nashville, Tennessee, and other neighboring points, where it was sold to supply the local consumption. The increase in production was small for the first decade, but from 1820 to 1830 there was a marked increase. By 1830 the culture had become established as a leading and permanent industry in Logan county, where it is still the most important staple.

Simultaneously with the beginning of the growth of tobacco in Logan county it was also commenced in Green, Barren, Hardin, and Warren counties under similar circumstances. Barren county, being convenient to shipping points on Barren river, and having advantages which attracted settlers in large numbers, soon became prominent as a tobacco-producing district. In Hardin county Peter McDaniel was one of the first growers. His first crop was grown in 1811, and during that year the entire crop of the county did not exceed ten hogsheads. This crop was sold to Allen & Beardsley, in the hand, at $2 per hundred pounds. Hardin county, being remote from shipping points, made slow progress in the increase of production, and it was not until 1827 that such facilities were available to induce much interest in the business. In that year V. McDaniel became a local dealer in tobacco and bought a few small crops at 75 cents, $2, and $2 50 per hundred pounds for the different grades, prized and delivered at Stephensport, on the Ohio river. From this date the culture of tobacco gradually grew to be an important business. In Adair and Cumberland counties the business seems to have had a somewhat later beginning, and to have commenced in the former county about the year 1817, when two gentlemen from Virginia settled there and engaged in its culture. Their first crops were hauled to the Cumberland river and shipped to New Orleans, where good prices were realized (about $8 per hundred pounds), the close of the war of 1812 having caused a large advance in prices, which was maintained up to the time when these crops were sold. These prices caused a large and rapid increase in the production, and the succeeding crop was a large increase on former ones. It was shipped to New Orleans, and sold for $6 and $7 per hundred. In Cumberland county the culture, as a fixed employment, is traced back to 1820, when the crop was shipped to New Orleans by flatboat out of the Cumberland river and sold for $3 to $5 per hundred. A succeeding season of better prices induced a large increase in the production, which, aided by better and cheaper facilities for shipping, caused by the advent of steam navigation, established tobacco culture as the leading industry of the county. The crops of this county at one time furnished the types most suitable for supplying the orders made by the French government. The date of the first crops of Breckinridge county is uncertain, but it was probably between the years 1810 and 1815, and were sold generally to local dealers. The nearness of the Ohio river, and the shipping facilities afforded by it, caused the establishment at an early day of home markets, which secured for the first crops raised an average of about $3 per hundred pounds. Some planters shipped their crops to New Orleans by flatboat on their own account, but this method involved so much delay in realizing proceeds of sales that most planters preferred to sell in home markets at current prices, although very low. About 1840 better home markets were established by dealers, who stemmed tobacco and put it up for the English markets, and from this time the culture largely and rapidly increased. In Christian county the growing of tobacco was commenced about the year 1815, when one hogshead was shipped by flatboat to New Orleans, supposed to have been the first ever shipped from the county. About 1820 small crops, not exceeding one hogshead in any individual crop, were raised and shipped. Previous to this a few small patches were grown in the county, and the product was sold to a small manufacturing establishment, which was started at Hopkinsville in 1818, for the purpose of supplying the local demand. From this time the production gradually increased, owing to the advent of new settlers, principally from Virginia, and to the increased area of open lands. Between the years 1825 and 1830 the culture became an important branch of industry, and in the latter year it became general, stimulated by the success of previous growers and by better facilities of transportation. The first attempts to grow the crop were so unprofitable that many who engaged in it abandoned it for the culture of cotton and hemp, which, in turn proving unprofitable, was abandoned, and the growing of tobacco was resumed.

The district bordered by the lower part of the Ohio river was not settled so early as other tobacco-producing sections of the state, and it has not been possible to obtain fully the historical facts in regard to the culture in this section. In Union county the culture was commenced in 183 , from which time to 1850 the tobacco grown in the county was nearly all hauled to Henderson, on the Ohio river, and sold to stemmers at $1 to $4 per hundred on credit, one-half payable in March, and the other half on the 1st of June following.

These districts were the field of the earliest establishment of this important industry west of the Alleghany mountains

Very little is known as to the early methods of culture and curing or the varieties most generally grown. The methods were for a long time primitive and unskillful. The culture was with indifferent implements, used without dexterity or skill, and the curing was generally done by hand-firing, or with no firing, as the producer might fancy. The rude and imperfect methods of culture, however, found a compensation in the freshness and strength of the virgin soils, and the yield of product under these conditions was as favorable in weight as it has been since under more skillful and perfect modes, but was inferior in quality.

CLIMATE.

The climate of Kentucky is remarkably pleasant, though variable. The mean annual temperature is about 55° The thermometer often falls to 20° in winter, and sometimes, though rarely, goes below zero; in summer it rises to 90°, and very rarely to 100°. Winter sometimes continues from late in November until the last of March, but is often so mild that good grazing for cattle and sheep may be had throughout that period. The prevailing winds in spring and summer are from the southwest; in winter, during the coldest periods, from the northwest. Rain is very frequent in winter, but the summers are sometimes characterized by protracted droughts. Observations by the signal service at Louisville from September 11, 1871, to October 31, 1880, show a mean average temperature for the seasons as follows: Spring, 56.1 degrees; summer, 77.4; autumn, 56.9; winter, 37.3; average range, 56.9; highest temperature recorded, 102; lowest, 10 below zero; mean of prevailing winds, south; mean annual precipitation, 48.36 inches. Observations at Springdale, in Mason county, the center of the White Burley tobacco district, for a period of nearly 28 years, extending from July, 1841, to December, 1870, show: Mean average temperature—spring, 53.26 degrees; summer, 72.42; autumn, 54.64; winter, 34.50; for the year, 53.71. Mean amount of precipitation for 24 years and 3 months of this period: Spring, 12.90 inches; summer, 13.46; autumn, 10.07; winter, 12.15; for the year, 48.58. At Danville, observations for 12 years, to December, 1870, show an average temperature for the different seasons as follows: Spring, 56.28 degrees; summer, 75.58; autumn, 58.56; winter, 37.84; average for the year, 57.07. The average rainfall for 8 years, to December, 1866, for the seasons, was: Spring, 12.87 inches; summer, 12.76; autumn, 8.08; winter, 11.92; average for the year, 45.63.

TOBACCO DISTRICTS.

There are eight tobacco-growing districts in Kentucky recognized by the trade, each having some peculiarities of soil producing types more or less distinct. These districts are:

I. Paducah, or western district, embracing the counties of Fulton, Hickman, Graves, Ballard, McCracken, Marshall, and Calloway.

II. Ohio River district, embracing the counties of Livingston, Crittenden, Caldwell, Lyon, Hancock, Breckinridge, and Meade, in two separate bodies, the Lower Green River district lying between them with its coal measures.

III. Lower Green River district, embracing the counties of Henderson, Union, Daviess, Webster, Hopkins, McLean, and Muhlenburgh; resembling adjacent districts of Indiana and Illinois.

IV. Green River district, embracing the counties of Butler and Ohio.

V. Upper Green River district, embracing the counties of Barren, Warren, Hardin, Grayson, Edmonson, Hart, Green, La Rue, Marion, Taylor, and Allen.

VI. Clarksville district, embracing the counties of Trigg, Christian, Todd, Logan, and Simpson, and seven counties in Tennessee.

VII. Cumberland River district, embracing the counties of Metcalfe, Russell, Adair, Clinton, Cumberland, Monroe, Casey, Wayne, and Pulaski.

VIII. White Burley district, embracing what was formerly known as the Boone County district, the Mason County district, the Pendleton County district, and the Kentucky River district. The following counties are now included in the White Burley district, though it is rapidly widening, and may soon embrace several other districts: Boone, Kenton, Campbell, Gallatin, Grant, Pendleton, Bracken, Carroll, Owen, Harrison, Robertson, Mason, Lewis, Fleming, Montgomery, Nicholas, Bourbon, Scott, Franklin, Henry, Trimble, Oldham, Shelby, and Woodford. The cultivation of the White Burley is even invading the blue-grass region of Fayette and the surrounding counties.

PADUCAH, OR WESTERN DISTRICT.

GEOLOGICAL FEATURES, SOILS, AND TYPES OF TOBACCO.

This whole district has been referred to the Tertiary formation, though there are strips lying on the Mississippi and Ohio rivers which properly belong to the Quaternary, and a belt on the Tennessee river belonging to the sub-Carboniferous. The soil, where sufficiently elevated to be well drained, is highly productive. Its physical condition, in the main, is excellent, being very fine-grained, and much of it resembling in color and pulverulence a bed of ashes.

Ballard county, which occupies the northwestern corner of the district, has a deep vegetable loam, which rests, at variable depths, upon clay and sand. Parallel with the Ohio and the Mississippi rivers is a belt of timbered land 5 or 6 miles in width, the timber growth of which is black oak, white oak, tulip tree, hickory, maple, hackberry, elm, cypress, and beech. In the alluvial bottoms cottonwood and sweet gum abound, and the soil is black and sandy. The soil of the timbered belt is a dark gray, and contains nearly 50 per cent. of siliceous matter in its composition. The alluvial soils grow a big, coarse, leafy tobacco, which cures up a uniform red color, and is chiefly used for making strips. On the timbered uplands a richer and finer leaf is grown that commands a better price, but it is principally suited to the Regie trade. Between this belt of timbered land and Mayfield creek, going south, is a broad stretch of barren land. These "barrens" in Ballard county form an elevated plateau, which as an open pasture is unexcelled. The timber growth is very inferior, and consists of a few harsh black-jack oaks, hickory, post oak, and red oak, with an undergrowth of sumac, dogwood, and hazel. The soil of the "barrens" is very free and generous, and is well adapted to the growth of fine tobacco. The "yellow leaf" of Ballard county is second in reputation only to the "gold leaf" of North Carolina, and it differs from the latter only in being of larger size and richer in the essential oils of tobacco. The existence of so much oily substance in its composition is a disadvantage, inasmuch as it causes the leaf to blacken under pressure, becoming a mottled yellow-brown and black. South of Mayfield creek the land is more undulating, the soil deeper, and the timber is large and abundant. In color, the soil, with the exception of that in the southeasterly portion of the county, is dark gray and black, with a dirty buff-colored subsoil, and will grow a good heavy shipping leaf. Around Milburn the soil is of a light gray, and is not so productive, and the tobacco grown on this land is of a more flimsy character. Underneath all the soils of the county, excepting only the alluviums on the larger streams, there is a bed of drifted material, composed of rounded pebbles of quartz, gneiss, and sandstone, which are sometimes cemented together by the oxide of iron, but are more generally lying loose, as though left by a receding stream. These beds of gravel are from ten to fifteen feet in thickness, and lie at variable depths beneath the surface. Sometimes the pebble beds give place to local accumulations of fine sand, and where this is the case, and the beds come near the surface of the ground, the land becomes exhausted very rapidly under cultivation. Should the surface be rolling, deep gullies form with surprising rapidity, and the most careful attention is demanded to preserve the soil from becoming utterly worthless. The census returns of 1880 show the average yield in the county to be 723.92 pounds per acre, which is a little less than the average for the western district, which is placed at 739 pounds.

Hickman county is generally level, though sometimes rolling. The soils and the timber growth are much like those in the southern part of Ballard county, on the north. With the exception of the alluvial bottoms, the soil is dark gray or ash colored, and sometimes whitish, very light, and generous. It has a large proportion of silica and insoluble silicates in its composition, with a variable quantity of lime, phosphoric acid, potash, and oxide of iron. Where there is a considerable amount of alumina in its composition the soil has greatly increased power to catch and hold organic matter, thus forming a loam of great fertility. The quality of tobacco produced is coarse, and is only suitable for stemming purposes and for the Regie trade. Only 658 acres are reported, which is the smallest quantity grown in any county in the district, except Fulton, which is heavily timbered, and has a soil similar to that of Hickman. Cotton and the grasses have taken the place of tobacco to a large extent. The tobacco grown is very inferior in quality, being coarse, with large stems and fibers, though the yield per acre is satisfactory, being a fraction over 702 pounds.

McCracken county has soils of very unequal fertility. In the eastern part of the county the surface is undulating and the soil is light-brown in color, with a mulatto subsoil, and of medium fertility. The timber growth is black oak, hickory, and black-jack oak. By far the largest amount of tobacco is grown in this part of the county, and when the lands are first opened the quality is very fine, the color bright, and suitable for making fine wrappers for plug. On old manured lots a rich and heavy German type is produced. In the eastern portion of the county the surface is flat, and post oak forms the predominating tree growth, intermixed with occasional white oak. Flat post-oak lands are not at all suitable for the growth of tobacco, and indeed are scarcely suitable for any other crop. These flat lands are confined to the region drained by the Clark river. In the middle part of the county the surface is broken, the soil is thin, and tobacco is not grown to any considerable extent. The chief difference between the soils of this county and those of Ballard is that they are more gravelly and sandy, lighter in color, have less clay in their composition, and are not so fertile. The flat lands are often "water-logged", and will scarcely produce anything. The average yield of tobacco per acre for the county is about 717 pounds.

Graves county, lying south of McCracken, raises more than twice the amount of tobacco grown by any other county in the district. Thirty years ago there was no timber in the county, except along the margins of streams or on wet lands, but since the annual fires have been interdicted a scrubby growth of hickory, red oak, and post oak has sprung up, and has covered all the uncultivated portions, and on the wet lands or low swales water oak, cypress, gum, walnut, cherry, maple, tulip tree, ash, beech, cucumber tree, and many other varieties are found. The best tobacco soils are indicated by the growth of red oak and mocker-nut hickory (*Carya tomentosa*). The soil of at least two-thirds of the county is a grayish-yellow, underlaid with pebbles and sand. On the streams a whitish soil predominates. On the ridges, mainly in the eastern part, where the prevailing timber growth is hickory, a fine yellow tobacco is grown, which commands a very high price. The product of this county is taken for the French, German, and Italian markets. The black German type is produced on rich soils, where the original timber growth was the tulip tree, hickory, oak, gum, walnut, with an undergrowth of hazel and sumac. If well cultivated, the soils of this county will resist successfully the effects of drought and of wet weather. A hard clay lies beneath the surface, which, unless well broken, compacts closely, and the water is held by the hard pan beneath. Deep plowing and a thorough pulverization of the surface soil have been found of greatest benefit in enabling the tobacco plant to resist the blighting effects of drought or of exceeding wet weather.

Marshall and Calloway counties, which occupy the eastern side of this district, may be considered together. On the eastern edge of these counties is a fragmentary belt of the sub-Carboniferous rocks, and beds of marl are frequent, interstratified with sands and clays of varying colors. In some portions there are areas of flat, wet lands, corresponding with some portions of West Tennessee. Generally the soil is rich and loamy, with a considerable admixture of siliceous matter, which makes it very loose and light. Accumulations of whitish clay occur, and the soil is then cold and unproductive. The belt lying along the Tennessee river is hilly, and in places rugged, with the outcropping of the sub-Carboniferous limestones, and beds of chert, liberated by the dissolving of these limestones, are common. Generally the soils in this belt are thin and unproductive, except where basins occur, or where the alluvium of the river prevails. A very fine type of yellow tobacco, suitable for wrapping purposes, is grown upon the sandy loams and gravelly ridges of these two counties, and shipping leaf, much resembling that grown in Graves county, is produced on the richer soils. Of the two counties, Calloway produces more than twice as much tobacco as Marshall, and has a larger area of fertile soils. The quantity of yellow tobacco made in Calloway is also far in excess of that produced in Marshall, the latter county having a very limited area among the ridges adapted to its growth. Marshall county, however, produces a long, red, light-bodied tobacco, suited for the French market. On the generally level surface west of the broken area occupied by the Carboniferous rocks the timber is small and of the same character as that which prevails in Graves county, but is much larger in the rugged region bordering the Tennessee river, consisting of the varieties common to the river basins.

A limited area in Graves, Ballard, McCracken, and Calloway counties produces about 33 per cent. of rich, heavy, gummy tobacco, suited for the German market, and approximating closely the Clarksville type, but inclined to higher colors.

CLASSIFICATION OF TYPES.

Probably no part of the United States grows a greater variety of types of tobacco than the district under consideration, almost every sort demanded by foreign and domestic markets being produced, as classified in chapter II. These classes are as follows:

German Shipper, to which only about 5 per cent. of the product belongs.

Swiss Wrapper, grown on fertile uplands well manured.

African, which may be grown on rich bottom soils, and includes about 20 per cent. of the product.

German Saucer, which grows in greatest perfection on good rich second-year uplands without manures.

Regie tobacco, which includes: I. French A, B, C, chiefly grown in Marshall and Calloway counties; II. Italian; III. Spanish; IV. Austrian, German Spinner, and manufacturing leaf, both fillers and wrappers, the latter varying from lemon-yellow to very dark.

There has been very little change in the types of product during the past ten years, but probably the nondescript has been reduced to some extent, and the yellow or bright wrapper increased. The following will approximate the proportions of each grade for the district:

	Per cent.
Dark and red shipping	35
Fillers, sun- and air-cured	20
Bright wrappers	5
Cutting	15
Nondescript	25

The constancy of the proportion of types is due mainly to the large quantity of new land cultivated in tobacco, fully one-third of the crop being planted upon virgin soil, a third on land which has grown only one crop, and the remainder upon manured lots.

VALUE OF THE CROP.

The prices received by planters have a very wide range, from $2 per hundred for inferior lugs to $40 per hundred for fine bright wrapper. The average price received by the farmers is placed by a good authority at $5 per hundred. Mr. T. H. Puryear, of Paducah, who has kept a record of the receipts and prices at that point since 1875, furnishes the following statement, which will fairly represent the prices received by a large majority of the planters:

Year.	Lugs.	Leaf or good.
1875	$9 00	$18 00
1876	6 00	11 00
1877	4 00	8 00
1878	3 00	5 50
1879	3 50	9 00
1880	4 00	6 00

The cost to the planter of inspecting and selling on the Paducah market is $1 50 per hogshead. Out of the tobacco now raised in the district domestic manufacturers take only a part of the sun- and air-cured fillers and some of the bright wrappers.

STRIPS.

It is estimated by a large dealer that 5 per cent. of the total product grown in the Paducah district is made into strips for the European market. The great development of leaf attained by the tobacco plant on the rich lowlands and the deep brown colors produced on the upland bottoms, and, above all, the spongy nature of the leaf when grown in such situations, admirably fit it for making strips.

Two establishments for making strips are in operation in this district: one at Paducah, which made about 380 hogsheads in 1879, and one at Hazlewood, which made 75 hogsheads, making the total product 455 hogsheads, requiring about 825,000 pounds of tobacco in the stem to produce 500,000 pounds of strips, there being an estimated loss from taking out the midrib of 33 per cent., and the loss from weight between the condition in which it is received from the planter and the condition in which it is prized as strips is placed at from 5 to 10 per cent. The loss from taking out the stem, however, is variable. If the tobacco is long and broad, with small stems, the loss does not exceed 25 per cent., but should the leaves of the tobacco be narrow and of light texture, with large stems, the loss may even exceed 40 per cent.

The price paid for stemming varies from 40 to 50 cents per hundred pounds of strips made. An active man or woman may make from 250 to 300 pounds of strips a day in large leafy stock; the average, probably, is under 200 pounds.

COST OF PRODUCTION.

Nothing can be more unsatisfactory than the conflicting and often irreconcilable differences in the estimates made of the cost of production. Differences in the soil, in the labor employed, and in the distance from market, complicate the question. Comparing estimates, it appears that the average cost of growing the crop for this district is not far from $4 per hundred pounds on the best lands, and from $5 to $6 on inferior tobacco soils. Three acres are usually allotted to each hand, and the average yield per acre for the district is 739 pounds, or 2,217 pounds to the hand. The price of labor is $12 per month the year round, and by the day 75 cents. The following will give an idea of the profits of farming in this district, though it is difficult to estimate the actual cost of producing the tobacco crop:

Dr.	
Wages of one man and board for year	$200 00
Rent of ten acres of land for wheat, at $3	30 00
Rent of fifteen acres of land for corn, at $3	45 00
Rent of three acres for tobacco, at $4	12 00
Use of team and feed for same	50 00
Use of barns and tools	15 00
Total	352 00
Cr.	
By 2,217 pounds of tobacco, at $5	110 85
By 120 bushels of wheat, at $1	120 00
By 600 bushels of corn, at 30 cents	180 00
Total	410 85
Profit on one hand	58 85

In this statement the expense account is charged with the actual rent of the land, and not merely with the interest on value. The best tobacco lands in the district may be bought at a price not exceeding $25 to $30 per acre, and for such as will give the average yield the prices range at from $18 to $20 per acre.

Planters frequently have tobacco and other crops raised on "shares", receiving one-third for the use of the land alone, or one-half when they furnish all except the labor. If the landlord furnishes rations to the cropper and his family, they become a charge against the tenant's share of the crop.

The varieties of tobacco cultivated, and the methods of curing and handling adopted, have not been such as to give the product a high character, either at home or abroad. Old habits of raising a shipping leaf cured with smoke and fire are difficult to surmount, and, as a consequence, the cultivation of tobacco cannot be said to be remunerative. One danger demands notice. The looseness of the soil, while making it easy of tillage, makes it also easy to wash. Fields are cultivated for a few years and often abandoned, to be furrowed with gullies, down which the soil is carried with every rain. Many of these scarified old fields, growing up in persimmon and sassafras sprouts, may be seen in passing through the country. When these gullies have once cut through the thin loamy bed of the surface and reached the stratum of sand or gravel beneath their destructive power is almost unlimited. A little attention at first checks them.

The following statement exhibits the total product of the Paducah, or western district, for the years 1876, 1877, and 1878; also the total product and acreage for 1879. The table is mainly from returns to the state auditor, and only the figures for 1879 are from census returns:

	Pounds.
Product in 1876	11,538,036
Product in 1877	21,395,381
Product in 1878	9,664,497
Product in 1879	20,843,497
Acreage in 1879	28,205
Average yield per acre in 1879	739

THE OHIO RIVER DISTRICT.

TOPOGRAPHY.

Most of this district is very broken in surface, has but a small extent of level area, and the two sections are very much alike in topography. The northern border of the eastern group of counties and the northern and part of the western line of the western group are skirted by the Ohio river. The Cumberland river runs through Lyon and Livingston counties of the latter group, and the Elizabethtown and Paducah railway passes through its southern end. These natural and artificial highways afford convenient facilities for transportation.

TYPES OF TOBACCO PRODUCED.

In the eastern group the most decided types are of light body; in the western counties the larger part of the product is heavy-bodied tobacco. In Breckinridge county especially, and to a smaller extent in Hancock and Meade counties, the light leaf has been highly valued as fillers for chewing plug, but has recently lost value on account of changes in the tastes and requirements of manufacturers and consumers. This type is of moderately light body, of delicate fiber and texture, of sweet flavor, and of clear bright or red colors, and a very small proportion is suitable for bright wrappers, or for fine-cut chewing or the higher grades of smoking-tobacco.

The heavy types of tobacco grown in this section of the Ohio River district are the product of alluvial lands, or of strong uplands heavily manured. They want smoothness of texture, but are more oily and waxy and less spongy than the same types produced in the Lower Green River district, and have about the same general adaptation, being largely used for making strips, and, to some extent, are available for supplying the demands of the French and the Italian governments.

In Breckinridge county 10 per cent. of the product is classed as dark shipping, 30 per cent. fillers, 5 per cent. bright wrappers, 5 per cent. cutting, and 50 per cent. nondescript, with but little variation in these proportions during the last ten years.

Of the product of Hancock county for 1879, 33 per cent. is dark shipping, 20 per cent. fillers, 20 per cent. cutting, and 27 per cent. nondescript; and of the crop of 1869 there was 20 per cent. dark shipping, 10 per cent. fillers, 10 per cent. cutting, and 60 per cent. nondescript.

In Meade county the crop of 1879 contained a larger proportion of nondescript than either of the two counties above named.

In the western group both light and heavy tobaccos are grown, the latter predominating. The heavy tobacco of this section is coarse and rough in texture and fiber, with only a moderate supply of oils, and furnishes a very small proportion of stock for manufacturing or for the better export types. A small part of the product is available to supply the demands of the French and Italian governments, but the bulk of this heavy tobacco is of low grade, and finds its way to inferior markets. This group of counties produces a tobacco of lighter body, a small proportion of which is suitable for plug fillers, for bright wrappers, and fine smokers, but of quality somewhat inferior to that of the similar types grown in the eastern counties of the district.

Of the crop grown in Crittenden county in 1879 the proportion of dark shipping is estimated at 25 per cent.; of fillers, 10 per cent.; and of nondescript, 65 per cent. Of the crop of 1869 40 per cent. was dark shipping, 12 per cent. fillers, and 48 per cent. nondescript.

Of the crop in Lyon county in 1879 there was 40 per cent. dark shipping, 20 per cent. fillers, 10 per cent. bright wrappers, 5 per cent. cutting, and 25 per cent. nondescript. In 1869 the proportions were: Dark shipping, 30 per cent.; fillers, 30 per cent.; bright wrappers, 15 per cent.; cutting, none; and nondescript, 25 per cent.

So far as can be ascertained, the average of the classification given for Crittenden and Lyon counties will very nearly describe the product of the other two counties of this section.

VARIETIES OF TOBACCO PRODUCED.

Most of the varieties grown in this district are common to the state. There are some local varieties, among which are the Lacks, of heavy weight, well colored, broad leaf, of fine fiber, and a strong grower; Greenwood, long and narrow leaf, difficult to cure, of uniform color, and adapted for export purposes; Big Whig, leaf of light body, cures a bright color, and is very showy in general appearance.

Of the varieties Yellow Pryor is preferred, because its product is suitable for fillers for plug manufacturing and for redrying in the leaf for shipment to England for cutting, and it is said to have more "chew" in it and a better flavor than most other varieties. Blue and Henderson Pryor, Big Whig, and Lacks are used for strips, for which purpose they are well suited, and also for supplying various export demands. Greenwood, One-sucker, Twist-bud, and Long Green have no special adaptation, and pass into export stocks in the leaf. When handled and cured with especial care a small proportion of the yield of these varieties finds a sale as fillers for manufacturing. There is complaint, probably well founded, that no care is taken to preserve the purity of varieties; that mixed sorts have resulted, and that the difficulty of growing and curing any desired type or grade has been much increased by this too common neglect.

A growing disposition is manifested by planters, especially those of the eastern group of counties, to engage in the cultivation of the White Burley, and the light types produced in this district are no longer sought for by manufacturers.

GEOLOGY AND SOILS.

The soils of the whole of this district, with small exception, are derived from the Chester group of rocks, which consist of alternate beds of impure or earthy limestones, shales, and sandstones. In the eastern group the sandstones and shales are predominant as surface formations, imparting to the soils a siliceous character. In this group is also found a part of the Carboniferous formation, extending over a considerable area of Hancock county. In Breckinridge county there is a separate and distinct bed of coal, of a highly resinous character, and resembling cannel coal, and also a large exposure of the Tar-spring sandstone, which forms the base of the Chester group, and is the source of several noted "tar" springs. There are also beds of green and red marly shales, very rich in potash and soda, the soils upon which are esteemed, as being finely adapted to the production of tobacco.

The geology of the western group of counties is somewhat similar to that of the eastern, but more calcareons and less siliceous. The soils of this block of counties may be divided into calcareous and siliceous, the former occupying the lowlands and a small portion of uplands, while the latter is found exclusively on the higher lands. The calcareous soils vary in character as they are derived from the limestones of the Saint Louis or the Chester group, and the sandy soils differ as they are derived from the sandstones and shales of the Chester or the Carboniferous group. The limestone lands consist of black loam, rich in vegetable mold, overlying a red-clay subsoil. The freestone soils are of a yellowish or grayish color, upon a subsoil of yellow or blue clay; and when resting upon a blue clay these sandy soils are of the poorest grade.

The limestone soils may be divided into two classes: lowlands, consisting of Quaternary beds; and uplands, consisting principally of outcroppings. The lowlands produce a type of heavy, coarse, large-leaved tobacco; the uplands yield a product of finer fiber and texture, more compact in structure, but with smaller leaf. Where the limestone uplands are derived from the Saint Louis group the soil is generally fertile and strong, producing a smooth and oily type; but the tobacco grown upon limestone soils derived from the Chester group has well-developed stem and fiber, but is deficient in width of leaf, in weight, and in supply of oils. The siliceous uplands produce the light types.

In Breckinridge and the other counties of the eastern group old lands of calcareous character, well manured, are preferred for rich and heavy types, and new or freshly-cleared lands for the finer types of light and colored tobacco. The timber growth upon preferred lands consists of hickory, sugar-tree, dogwood, beech, black-jack, hazel, white oak, and walnut.

In Breckinridge county three-fourths of the tobacco crop is grown upon old lands and one-fourth on freshly-cleared soils, and in Hancock county one-third upon old and two-thirds upon new lands. In the first-named county all the wooded lands are reported to be adapted to the growth of tobacco; in the latter the proportion is estimated at 90 per cent.

In the western section of this district the soils preferred for tobacco are limestone, with a timber growth of black oak, hickory, dogwood, post oak, walnut, and gum. Two-thirds of the crop in Caldwell county is produced upon limestone soils; in Crittenden, one-half; in Livingston, three-fifths. The proportion of freshly-cleared lands occupied by tobacco is estimated at from 30 to 50 per cent.

The rate of soil deterioration is variously estimated in different localities. One planter reports that "after three years of continuous culture in tobacco the soil is considered useless for that or any other crop"; while another insists that "tobacco does not impoverish land, and when followed by wheat the yield of the latter is much better". Others place the rate of deterioration at from 5 to 33 per cent. The weight of evidence indicates that there is throughout this section a tendency of the soils to deteriorate rapidly, except under careful management. A large part of the general surface is abruptly broken. Lands upon the Quaternary formation are acknowledged as of very durable fertility. From 50 to 85 per cent. of the wooded lands of this section are considered adapted to the growth of tobacco.

Planters usually plan to follow tobacco with wheat seeded to clover. Sometimes rye is sown in the fall and turned under in May following, or allowed to ripen and fall on the land, and this is said to reinstate the soil after one crop of tobacco. The available supply of farm manures is too small to afford extensive help in the work of soil recuperation; small grains, clover, the grasses, and sometimes "rest", by suffering a growth of weeds, bushes, and briers, are the methods in general use.

INSECT ENEMIES AND DISEASES.

The flea-beetle is probably not so troublesome as in other sections of the country less broken in surface and not so heavily wooded. The cut-worm, horn-worm, and some species of grasshoppers are common. "Frenching" is reported to prevail under conditions which favor it. "Fire" is not complained of to serious extent, the surface configuration of the district being such as to afford ready means of drainage.

COST OF PRODUCTION.

No reports were made from either section of this district as to the value of tobacco lands, cost of labor, etc. It may be assumed, however, that the estimates already made for the Paducah district will apply very nearly to that of the Ohio river.

VALUE OF THE CROP OF 1879.

In Hancock county the average value is stated as $4 50 per hundred pounds, with dark shipping at $3 50 and the light types at $5. In Breckinridge county the average value is estimated at $6, with trash at $2; lugs, $2 50 to $4; dark leaf, $4 25 to $5; good leaf, $5 50 to $8; and colored leaf, $9 to $12. In Lyon county the average value is estimated at $4. In Crittenden, lugs, nondescript, $1 50 to $2; good lugs, $3 to $4 50; common leaf, $3 50 to $4 50; good leaf, $5 to $7; and what is known as cutting leaf, $5 to $12. In Caldwell county, the average is estimated at $4 75, and in Livingston county at $4 50.

GENERAL FACTS AND STATISTICS.

The manures used in this district are always applied upon old lands, and are almost entirely the product of the stable and the barn-yard, used both in the hill and broadcast. Commercial fertilizers are used to some extent, almost exclusively in the hill, about an ounce to each plant; from three to four hundred pounds per acre in the few instances where employed broadcast. Of domestic manures, that from the stable is usually applied in the hill, and the coarser material from the barn-yard is spread broadcast. In Breckinridge county about 1 per cent. of the tobacco land is fertilized with commercial manures, the results being of uncertain character. In Hancock county about 20 per cent. of the area cultivated in tobacco is manured from the stable and the farm-yard, at an average cost of $6 per acre, producing an increase of 60 per cent. in yield, with a large improvement in quality where heavy body is desired. In Lyon county about one-third of the tobacco acreage is fertilized with domestic manures, increasing the yield about 50 per cent., but making a coarser product. In Crittenden county manures are used on one-fifth of the tobacco land; these consist of stable manure, bone dust, and "Homestead Tobacco Grower", and are estimated to increase the yield one-third, with 50 per cent. improvement in quality. In Caldwell county about one-fourth of the tobacco is manured with domestic and commercial fertilizers, at a cost of from $3 to $5 per acre, resulting in an increase of one-fourth in yield, with improvement in weight and supply of oils in the cured product. In Livingston county two-thirds of the surface is manured with stable and lot manure, a shovelful being applied to each hill, at a nominal cost, producing one-third increase in yield, with larger size and weight of plant.

The average yield per acre of the crop of 1879 in this district was estimated at 720 pounds, and the damage to the quality of the crop from different causes was estimated as follows: Green cutting, 10 per cent.; house-burn, 14 per cent.; stem-rot, 10 per cent.; worm-eaten, 2 per cent. These estimates were made before the crop was marketed, and may admit of material modification since its full delivery. Mold forming on the cured leaf produced greater loss than any other form of injury.

The following statement shows the production, acreage, yield per acre, value of crop in farmers' hands or in primary markets, value per pound, and value per acre of the tobacco crops in the Ohio River district. The production for the years 1876, 1877, 1878 is obtained from official returns made to the auditor of Kentucky, and that for 1879 is from returns made to the Census Bureau:

Year.	Production.	Acreage.	Yield per acre.	Value of crop in farmers' hands.	Value per pound.	Value per acre.
	Pounds.		*Pounds.*			
1876	11,465,224	17,630	650	$745,230 08	6.50	$42 25
1877	18,967,015	21,779	871	1,043,235 33	5.50	47 00
1878	8,214,747	13,691	600	451,811 08	5.50	33 00
1879	13,184,520	18,297	721	650,226 00	5.00	36 03

THE LOWER GREEN RIVER DISTRICT.

TOPOGRAPHY

The Ohio river separates this district from those of a similar character in Illinois and Indiana. Much of the surface is more or less broken, though not rugged, and there are large areas very slightly rolling or almost level. An irregular range of hills extends along the western and southern border, forming a dividing line between the waters of the Cumberland and those of the Green river. This range forms the only abruptly broken surface of any extent in the district. Green river, which is navigable at all seasons, passes through the northeastern part; the Ohio river skirts its northern border; the Saint Louis and Southeastern railway traverses its center from north to south, and the Elizabethtown and Paducah railway crosses it a short distance south of a central line east and west. All parts of the district are within a few miles of railroad or river, and are well provided with facilities for transportation.

The soils of this district are peculiarly adapted to the growth of tobacco, and have less general adaptation to other crops than those of most other sections of the state. From the early settlement of this territory tobacco has been the staple crop, furnishing employment for a large amount of capital and labor, and several towns owe their prosperity and commercial importance almost entirely to their positions as tobacco markets.

TYPES OF TOBACCO PRODUCED.

The types of this district may be divided into the two leading lines of heavy and light tobacco, and subdivided into several sub-types.

On the Ohio river bottoms the tobacco grown is large, coarse, and heavy, of strong texture, thick and leathery, with little oil, easily dried, and of great capacity for absorption. This product is used almost entirely for making English strips, some portions of the longer leaf being suitable for shipment to Africa. On creek bottoms and the alluvials of Green river, and on flat lands of good soil overlying a red-clay subsoil, a richer and smoother heavy tobacco, of less absorptive capacity and more oily, is produced, and consequently it is not so generally used for strips as the former. When of sufficient strength and delicacy it is used for dark wrappers, and if free of gum, smooth and of fine texture, it is used for cigar wrappers. The lower grades are sometimes sold for fillers in making common dark plug for smoking in Canada. The lowest grades of both these sub-types are used for cutting into cheap smoking tobacco and for export. A small proportion of the higher grades of the Green river heavy tobacco is suitable for filling orders for the French and Italian governments.

The light type of tobacco is grown upon the more siliceous soils of the rolling or broken lands. When of good length and breadth and sufficiently tough it is suitable for strips; if of light and thin body and light color it is used for brown roll wrappers. Bright lugs and the lower grades of bright and light leaf are made into strips for brown roll, but the more fancy kinds of bright yellow leaf, with stems of the same color as the leaf, are used for cutting into "bird's-eye" smoking-tobacco. The coarser and rougher grades of all the light types are used for cutting into smoking-tobacco, and the darker and tougher grades for spinning. This type, until within a few years, entered largely into domestic consumption. Its mildness of natural flavor and great capacity for receiving artificial flavors made it especially fit for the use of manufacturers until the demand for an article of lighter texture, more decided color, and finer fiber established a standard not reached by any but the very best and most carefully handled product of this district.

It is not possible, with the information at hand, to determine the average proportion of each type in the cured product. The current opinion is that the general product is increasing in heaviness of body.

Opinions differ as to whether the quality of the product has improved or deteriorated since 1870. Dealers assert that the average quality is not so good as it was ten years ago, and account for the deterioration by the decrease in the proportion of the crop grown on fresh lands. Many planters admit the falling off in quality, and attribute it to various causes, as a series of unfavorable seasons, the too frequent use of mixed seed, or an impoverished soil. On the other hand, equally well-informed planters claim that there has been no deterioration, except perhaps a relative one, in so far as the requirements of consumers have raised the general standard of quality. In some localities it is maintained that the quality of the product has improved, because of better arrangements for handling and curing; that planters are beginning to understand that the higher grades alone pay a profit over the cost of production, and are planting less and making a better quality; and there is little doubt that the seasons are less favorable than when larger forest areas protected the fields and modified the effects of excessive rains or cold winds, or the sweep of storms.

VARIETIES AND THEIR PECULIARITIES.

Blue, Yellow, and Henderson Pryors are most generally cultivated. Tennessee Red, Orinoco, Little Hill, Twist-bud, and Long Green are also planted. The low prices realized for export types have brought into favor varieties the product of which is more suitable for domestic manufacturing. The Pryors make a leaf of good length and breadth, of delicate fiber and texture, and are well adapted for making wrappers and fillers. They are easily cultivated, healthy in constitution, and cure readily. The Yellow Pryor is especially popular on account of its habits of growth, the plant being of medium size and good height, with leaves set well apart on the stalk, and maturing well early in the season. All the Pryors are useful for stemming into strips, having a small and light stem and smooth leaf. The Little Hill has a rounded leaf, not very wide, of fine fiber, and ranks among the best varieties for stemming and for general purposes. The Orinoco is hardy in constitution and not liable to diseases of growth; is most valuable when grown on soils which develop oily consistency and heaviness of texture, making a grade suitable for the better German consumption. The Twist-bud makes a heavy yield, cures easily into bright or red colors, makes excellent plug-fillers, but is not fit for wrappers nor for making strips on account of its narrow leaf and heavy stem. Tennessee Red is coarse, and derives its value from its heavy weight. Long Green is largely grown by some on account of its weight. The leaf is coarse, of good length, but rather narrow, and when of sufficient length it is valuable for shipment to Africa.

Even in the same neighborhood, and upon similar soils, there is no attempt at the production of any uniform type. The multiplicity of varieties grown in a single neighborhood, and often upon one farm, has resulted in cross-fertilization, and a consequent production of variations. No valuable varieties can be expected from this miscellaneous inter-fertilization, and even the most careful attempts to that end would be difficult and uncertain amid such surroundings.

The best planters use much care in propagating the seed and preserving the purity of desirable kinds. Some frequently procure seed from other sections of the country, hoping in this way to produce a plant true to name.

GEOLOGY AND SOIL FORMATIONS.

The whole of this district lies within the western coal-basin. All the members of this formation are exposed upon the surface at one point or another of the district. In some places the sandstones appear; in others the shales, conglomerates, or carboniferous limestones are found near the surface in some localities; in others, some one of the coal measures is exposed, exhibiting within a narrow territory frequent and abrupt changes of surface configuration, and equally abrupt changes in the composition and character of the soils.

A feature of some uniformity in the geology of this district is the prevalence of salt-bearing sandstones, underlying almost its whole surface. All the soils are more or less saline, and in parts of Henderson and Hopkins counties this peculiarity is very marked.

There are also considerable deposits of iron ore, principally in Daviess, Muhlenburgh, and Hopkins counties. These ore deposits, when in any considerable body, lie at some depth below the surface, but throughout the section of country where iron ores exist the upper soil is more or less ferruginous.

The largest body of soil of uniform character is the alluvium of the streams, and is found chiefly in Daviess, Henderson, and Union counties, along the Ohio river. In the two latter counties this formation is large, and in Henderson county it is estimated to cover an area of 60,000 acres. McLean and Muhlenburgh counties have considerable tracts of alluvial soils along the line of Green river. These alluvials are very productive, the soil consisting of a very deep loam, overlying a solid red-clay subsoil. The growth of the forests is poplar, elm, sugar-tree, gum, etc., with an occasional undergrowth of cane.

A small area in Muhlenburgh county deserves special notice, because of the peculiar capacity of its soil. It consists of a narrow strip of land, extending outward from Green river, in some places so swampy as to be impenetrable, and supposed to have been at one time a part of the channel of the river. The prevailing growth is cypress, of which there are large and heavy forests still remaining. Such portions of this territory as could be made available were originally settled by a colony of Pennsylvania Germans, whose descendants still occupy the lands and continue the cultivation of tobacco. The soil is a dark loam on a subsoil of pale red clay. The tobacco produced here is of a thin, light texture, of a very delicate fiber, with a natural tendency to cure into bright colors. It is free from oil and gum, and the lighter part of the product has been much used for fine-cut chewing, and is radically different from types made upon similar soil formations elsewhere.

The better upland soils are mainly of sandstone derivation, modified by various outcroppings of the strata of the coal group, and consist of a dark mold, mixed with sand, on a subsoil of yellow clay. The growth consists of hickory, black oak, white oak, walnut, and a few poplars, with an undergrowth of dogwood, sassafras, and occasionally sumac. Upon rolling or broken lands this class of soils is liable to serious damage by washing, requiring constant watchfulness and good management to preserve them.

The soils derived from the outcroppings of shales and conglomerates are not very productive. They are usually gray in color, upon a subsoil of light yellow or blue clay. The conglomerate soils make a poor and starchy quality of tobacco, thin and harsh. The growth upon these lands consists of oaks and hickories, very few of which are large trees. Considerable areas of this class of lands are found in Muhlenburgh, Webster, and Hopkins counties. In Daviess county the ridge lands have a soil of sandy loam, upon a subsoil of rich yellow clay, with a forest growth of poplar, sweet gum, ash, white oak, and dogwood. These lands produce a tobacco of light body, delicate texture and fiber, which cures easily into bright colors, and on that account has been highly valued of late years.

Of the lands planted in tobacco in 1879 from one-third to one-half was such as is known as fresh land—land either cleared for the crop of that year, or not more than three years previously. In different localities the estimated proportion of forest land suitable for tobacco growing varies from 33 to 100 per cent. On the Quaternary formations almost the entire body of forest lands is adapted to the culture of tobacco, but upon the uplands the proportion is less than one-half.

Upon the whole, it is admitted that there has been a marked depreciation of fertility of the upland soils throughout the district. This is attributed to a very great extent to the surface washing to which most of the ridge and hill lands are liable. The river and creek bottoms, naturally very fertile, are generally so nearly level as not to wash easily, and do not show any falling off in productive capacity.

When the uplands are so far worn as to cease to produce crops which will pay for cultivation they are either abandoned and turned out or inclosed, so as to prevent cattle ranging upon them, and suffered to grow up in persimmons, sassafras, briers, and broom grass; in the latter case, they may be again brought under cultivation after the expiration of ten or fifteen years. If such lands are put down in clover before the exhaustion has gone so far as to make it impossible to get a fair catch restoration may be accomplished much more quickly. It is a common practice to follow tobacco with wheat seeded to clover. Sometimes rye follows tobacco, to be turned down early in the spring for either tobacco or corn, and sometimes the grasses are made to occupy two or more years in the rotation. A large number of farmers, however, do not make timely use of the necessary agencies for maintaining the fertility of their farms. The low market value of lands, and the large areas of forest soils adapted to tobacco culture, almost valueless until opened for cultivation, have been inducements to neglect the necessary care of the older fields and to rely upon the "new grounds" as the best to maintain the annual product.

While the planters of this district generally concur in the opinion that continuous culture of any given soil in tobacco will produce exhaustion, they do not admit that the crop is more exhaustive than many others. Good lands will make three profitable crops of tobacco, and it is doubted whether three successive crops of corn or wheat could be taken from the same class of lands without even greater exhaustion of fertility.

The yield per acre, so far as can be ascertained, has not materially decreased since 1870. Collating the returns made to the auditor of Kentucky for several years and the official returns of the recent census, it would appear that there has been no deterioration of soils if the "yield per acre" is conclusive evidence; but if it be kept in mind that the tobacco crop not only occupies the best of the old lands, but very nearly monopolizes those newly cleared, it may be concluded that much of the soil exhaustion everywhere evident in this district is chargeable to the culture of tobacco.

LABOR, WAGES, AND COST OF PRODUCTION.

A very considerable portion of the tobacco crop of this district is made by the labor of the proprietors themselves, with such assistance as can be rendered by members of their families and occasional help hired by the day or month.

Farm laborers, when hired by the year, are paid from $100 to $150, with board; employed by the month, from $10 to $15, with board; by the day, from 50 to 75 cents.

Tobacco lands in this district differ greatly in value—from $5 to $50 per acre—according to the productiveness of the soils, the character and quality of the average product, distance from market, etc. The average value of the better class of lands may be estimated at $25, and of inferior lands at $8 per acre. Lands capable of producing 1,000 pounds rent at from $6 to $8 per acre; but it is rarely the case that such lands are rented for money, the share system being more common. Lands producing with good culture an average of 500 pounds per acre rent at $4 or $5.

The following is an estimate of cost of tobacco grown upon the best lands:

Wages one man, six months	$75
Board one man, at $2 per week	52
Rent of 3 acres of land, at $6	18
Feed of horse for two months	8
Use of wagon, implements, barn, etc	15
	168

One hand cultivates 3 acres, making 3,000 pounds, worth 6 cents, $180.

This shows a profit of only $18 on the product made by one hand on 3 acres of first-class land, after estimating a full yield, and the crop, as sold, at a price somewhat above the average.

It is very difficult to estimate correctly the cost of raising tobacco in this district. If an account be kept of the actual cost of labor performed by man and team, the interest upon value of land, the depreciation in value of team, implements, etc., and a fair estimate of the cost of necessary repairs to barn, fixtures, etc., it will be found that the cost per pound of the cured product is not much less than 5 cents. At the average prices realized there is little profit in the business, and its economic value to the people of the district consists in the fact that it furnishes employment at fair wages for a very large proportion of the working population.

The estimated values of the several grades of the product of 1879 are: For trash 50 cents to $1 per hundred; for lugs, $2 to $4; for leaf, $4 to $8. That portion of the crop sold to stemmers at Henderson realized an average price around of about $4 35 per hundred pounds. This was mainly heavy shipping tobacco. The better and lighter product was sold at higher prices, making the average value of the crop of the district about $5 per hundred.

Commercial fertilizers are used to a very limited extent, with favorable results generally reported. Farm-yard and stable manures are carefully saved, and are used by the better farmers almost exclusively upon the lands planted in tobacco.

The damage to the quality of the crop of 1879, attributable to various causes, was: From green cutting, 20 per cent.; house-burn, 20 per cent.; stem-rot, 12 per cent.; worm-eaten, 10 per cent. By house-burn and stem-rot the damage to this crop was exceptionally large.

In the following statement material for the first three years is obtained from official returns made to the auditor of Kentucky. The production and yield per acre for 1879 are derived from official returns made to the United States Census Bureau:

Years.	Production.	Acreage.	Yield per acre.	Value of crops in farmers' hands.	Value per pound.	Value per acre.
	Pounds.		*Pounds.*			
1876	33,887,528	46,741	725	$2,202,689 32	6 50	$47 12
1877	43,034,008	51,688	850	2,526,257 21	5 75	48 87
1878	26,439,603	40,670	650	1,454,178 10	5 50	35 75
1879	39,062,224	50,343	776	1,909,372 95	4 89	37 93

THE GREEN RIVER DISTRICT.

This district occupies a small area between the Upper and the Lower Green River districts. The surface of the country is much broken, a very small proportion of the lands being level or moderately rolling. The slackwater navigation of Green river and the Elizabethtown and Paducah railway furnish transportation at all seasons of the year.

The types grown, both of heavy and of light tobacco, are closely related to those of the Upper and the Lower Green River districts. The heavy tobaccos are coarser and less oily than those of the upper district, and less flexible, not so smooth, and of less absorptive capacity than those of the lower district. They are of coarse fiber and stem, stiff and starchy, and usually of narrow leaf. This is especially true of the product grown upon the Chester group of rocks. That grown upon the Quaternary soils has a larger and wider leaf, but is otherwise equally coarse and harsh. These heavy tobaccos, especially those grown in Butler county, are of lower quality than the related grades of the same type grown in adjoining districts, and the larger part of the product falls into the nondescript class. The light types are approximations to similar types of the two adjacent districts, having less delicacy of structure than those of the Upper, and less absorptive capacity than those of the Lower Green River country. These lighter types furnish a very small proportion of bright wrappers of common grade, a few packages of bright smokers, and a moderate amount of fillers for plug chewing.

Little attention has been paid to the selection of varieties. The characteristics of the crops of this territory are narrowness, coarseness, and roughness of leaf.

Green River district is occupied by two distinct geological formations: the Carboniferous and the Chester groups and the limestones of the Saint Louis group. Butler county is about equally divided between these two formations, while Ohio county lies more largely upon the Carboniferous, having a narrow belt of the Chester group upon its eastern border. In both of these counties there is a general thinning out and termination of the coal measures, while the Chester group appears with its alternating beds of sandstone, shale, and limestone.

Upon the Saint Louis limestones the soils consist of loose, light loam upon a subsoil of red clay; upon the Carboniferous formation are light-colored loams, resting upon a compact and tenacious yellow clay; and upon the Chester group are thin, grayish loams, upon a subsoil of blue clay. There are considerable areas of alluvial soils along the water-courses, consisting of deep, dark loams upon a foundation of red clay. The growth upon the alluvials is made up of heavy oaks, poplars, walnut, and elm; upon the Chester, white and red oaks; and upon the Carboniferous, mostly scrubby oak and hickory. The types grown upon the Carboniferous soils are of a light, delicate, and porous structure, of mild and sweet flavor, with very little gum and oils; upon the Chester they are stiff, harsh, and coarse, with somewhat more of gum and oils; and upon the Quaternary they are large and coarse, with a long and broad leaf of porous texture, heavy fiber and stem, and of strong and pungent flavor.

The surface overlying the Carboniferous system is much the largest in extent; that occupied by the Chester is the next in extent; the Quaternary is of limited area; and the Saint Louis so small as not to be worth estimating. Much of the soil of the district is very tender under cultivation, and is liable to severe damage by surface washing.

The proportion of lands abandoned as exhausted is small. Rotation of crops is not much practiced. The Carboniferous soils are easily tilled and produce freely, and on that account are more heavily taxed by continuous cultivation than the limestone soils. It is the received opinion that both the quality and the quantity of the yearly product of tobacco have decreased during the past ten years to a material extent.

The values of lands in this district vary between wide limits. Low-grade lands, producing from 150 to 500 pounds of tobacco per acre, are worth from $1 to $5 an acre; lands of the best grade, capable of making 1,000 pounds, are worth from $20 to $25 per acre. The rental value of the best lands is $5, and of the poorer lands from $1 to $2 per acre. Men employed by the year are paid from $100 to $120, with board, and day laborers get from 50 to 60 cents per day, with board, and 75 to 80 cents without board. The cost of barns, fixtures, implements, etc., does not vary from that of other districts in the state.

The following estimate is made of the cost of production on the best lands:

Rent of 2½ acres, at $5	$12 50
Wages and board, one man, three months	50 00
Cost of 10,000 plants, at 10 cents per hundred	10 00
Stripping, packing, and prizing	7 50
	80 00

Product, 2,500 pounds, worth $5 per 100 pounds, $125.

From this estimate are omitted interest upon cost of barns and fixtures, the use of team and feed for same, and cost of repairs to implements. Upon the low-grade lands it is said that "the tobacco crop would always bring the producer in debt if it were not made by the women and children, who would be otherwise unemployed".

The value of the crop of 1879 is estimated at $4 50 for dark shipping; fillers, $2 to $4; bright wrappers and smokers, $5 to $8; cutting, $5 to $8; nondescript, $2 to $4. No prices are given for trash, lugs, and low leaf. The value of the crop round is estimated at 5 cents per pound.

In the following statement the production of the Green River district for the first three years is obtained from official reports to the auditor of Kentucky. For 1879 the weight of product, acreage, and yield per acre are derived from official returns to the United States Census Bureau, and the rest of the statement is estimated:

Year.	Production.	Acreage.	Yield per acre.	Value of crop.	Value per pound	Value per acre.
	Pounds.		Pounds.		Cents.	
1876	4,988,414	7,675	650	$311,775 87	6.25	$40 62
1877	7,555,465	9,444	800	415,550 57	5.50	44 00
1878	3,697,682	6,723	550	104,128 30	5.05	28 87
1879	4,218,028	6,419	657	210,901 40	5.00	32 86

THE UPPER GREEN RIVER DISTRICT.

This district occupies a central position between the eastern and western boundaries of the state, and extends from the Tennessee line to within 25 or 30 miles of the Ohio river. Its surface is greatly diversified. Some portions of the district are covered with a growth of heavy timber; in other parts the forest is thin, and the trees are dwarfed and scrubby. It is well watered by Green and Barren rivers, both of which are navigable, and by numerous small streams. The Louisville and Nashville railway passes nearly through its center north and south, with branches from several points on the main line, affording, with the river navigation, abundant facilities for the shipment of its products. Tobacco employs a larger amount of capital and labor than any other farming industry.

TYPES OF TOBACCO PRODUCED.

In Green, Barren, Warren, Taylor, and to some extent in the other counties, is produced a type of heavy tobacco, rich, and oily, strong, elastic, and of fairly smooth structure, solid and firm. Being very flexible, it is desirable both for dark wrappers and for spinners. Some portions of this type possess the oils and weight of body necessary for the manufacture of snuff. It furnishes a portion of the export to Germany, the north of Europe, to Switzerland, and a limited amount goes to Canada. Some part of it is taken for the French and Italian Regie. The lowest grades are adapted for the Spanish Regie, and are also used for cutting into the cheaper smoking-tobaccos for domestic consumption.

In a small district of Hart and Barren counties are produced some excellent bright wrappers, of small and rather short leaf, very fine, and rather oily, and of a mild and delicate flavor. This type is thin and light in body and colored, but is of sufficient strength to be used as wrappers for plug chewing. The amount is very limited, and is estimated to be not more than one-twentieth of the general product of Hart county, where nearly all of it is grown. The lower grades and lugs of this type are used as plug fillers, and the better flavored of these grades for cutting into pipe-smoking tobacco. This line of types requires soils of peculiar character, with high culture and careful management in curing, and is made by a small class of planters, whose large experience in its production, aided by the employment of fixtures of the most approved construction, has brought them much personal reputation as well as profit.

A third type made in this district consists of a light and thin leaf of bright or red colors, formerly used to a large extent by manufacturers as fillers for plug tobacco. Deficient in gum and oils, it is of medium weight of body, and has neither the strength of texture nor high coloring to fit it for use as wrappers. It is not so firm in texture as the heavy types of this district, and has but moderate absorptive capacity. The special uses of this type are for fillers for plug chewing, and a very small proportion is fitted for bright wrappers when of sufficient smoothness, desired color, and strength. As now grown and cured this type supplies some of the brighter qualities required for German export, and a part of the heavier grades are adapted for the French Regie. Its absorptive capacity is too low for export to England. Recent changes in the tastes of consumers are bringing into use material of still lighter texture and body, and efforts are being made by planters to modify this type to suit the new demand. The lower grades are still largely used for common plug fillers, for cutting into a low grade of smoking-tobacco for home consumption, and for export to Germany, Belgium, Spain, and the Mediterranean ports. In Green county this type is estimated at 30 per cent. of the total product of tobacco, in Grayson at 25 per cent., and in Hart at 50 per cent. In Barren and Warren counties it is probably less than 30 per cent., and in Taylor, Allen, and Marion about 35 per cent.

In this district there is also produced a large bulk of nondescript. The lugs and trash of this class hold a much more definite position than the leaf of higher grades, are largely used for cutting into common smoking-tobacco for domestic consumption, and are exported to supply a foreign demand for the cheapest material. In Grayson county the proportion of nondescript is estimated at 40 per cent., in Hart county at 30 per cent., and the proportion is large in all parts of the district.

There has been some improvement in the quality of the general product within the past ten years. This is probably the result of better cultivation and more skillful curing and the adoption of better varieties, with a consequent diminution of nondescript grades, in which there has been a recognized deterioration of quality.

VARIETIES OF TOBACCO PRODUCED.

The principal varieties grown are the Blue and Yellow Pryor and Orinoco. Until recently a variety known as One-sucker was extensively planted, and Big Burley and Apron Leaf were at one time popular in certain sections. The first three above named have been found best adapted for the production of salable types.

The Yellow and Blue Pryor have nearly the same habits of growth, and make a product of very similar characteristics; but the leaf of the Yellow Pryor is somewhat more tapering at the point than that of the Blue Pryor. Both have a smooth and silky texture and good body, and a length and width of leaf suitable for all manufacturing purposes. With appropriate handling and curing these varieties, grown upon soils of diverse character, produce different kinds and qualities of leaf, adapted to various uses. When of sufficient weight and strength of texture, they make both dark and bright wrappers; when very oily and heavy, they are suitable for spinning and for grinding into fine grades of snuff; when of light body and bright color, they make fillers for plug chewing; and when of thin texture, with a good breadth of leaf, delicate fiber, elastic, and of a deep brown color, they are very useful for cigar wrappers. No other varieties have shown so wide a range of adaptation. The Yellow Pryor is preferred for making bright wrappers, because it is easily cured into a bright golden color.

The Orinoco is well adapted for spinning, and, when not too heavy, makes good wrappers. The close set of the leaves upon the stalk, and the heavy ruffling at the bases of the stems, are objectionable characteristics.

The Big Burley, Apron Leaf, and One-sucker are all coarse varieties. The One-sucker has a long, narrow leaf, erect instead of drooping, and is said to produce but one crop of suckers, for which reason it was at one time popular with those who desired quantity of product rather than quality. When of sufficient length of leaf, it is useful for packing into stock for the African trade, which is about its only adaptation. The same may be said of the other two varieties, which make a product of low grade.

GEOLOGY AND SOIL FORMATIONS.

This district lies almost entirely upon the sub-Carboniferous formation, and its soils differ as one or the other member of this system approaches the surface. The southeastern portion is based upon the lower member of the sub-Carboniferous limestone, which is composed of dark, earthy shales, with thin strata of limestone rocks. The central and most of the northwestern part lies upon the middle member of this system, technically called the barren limestone, much purer and more massive in its beddings than the rock of the lower stratum. On the western border of this district is a skirting of the Chester group of rocks, lying at the base of the Carboniferous and overlapping with a narrow margin the sub-Carboniferous limestone. In the northeastern portion the prevailing formations are limestones, with an exposure of sub-Carboniferous sandstone and shales. In Hart county the Carboniferous system approaches the surface, manifested by its strata of coal and the characteristic rocks of that formation.

The area occupied by the barren limestone forms much the larger part of the territory of this district. The soil is very nearly of a uniform character, consisting mainly of a light loam upon a deep red-clay foundation. On the broken surfaces it is much mixed with gravel, and is especially adapted to the production of rich and oily types of tobacco of heavy body and smooth texture. It is easily cultivated, naturally well drained, but rather tender, and upon the slopes is subject to injury by rapid washing. Its red-clay subsoil gives to these lands great durability, makes them easily restored to fertility by manure or by proper rotations, and enables them to resist the effects of drought. The limestone upon which this body of soil is based contains many nodules of flint, and is very cherty in some localities, is of close texture, and disintegrates slowly. The soil is therefore slowly supplied with mineral fertilizers from this source, and must have periods of rest from tillage by well-considered rotations, in which clover and the grasses hold prominence, in order to maintain a given standard of productiveness.

The characteristic timber growth consists of red, black, and post oaks, and hickory of rather small size, with a prevailing undergrowth of hazel and dogwood. Where the growth of hickory is largest the soil is generally quick and productive, and makes a leaf of smooth and fine texture, fine fibered, and with a good supply of oils. The soils preferred are level or slightly-rolling surfaces of vegetable mold, or gravelly slopes of rather stiff consistency, with good depth. Under average conditions the yield varies from 600 to 1,000 pounds per acre, but the chief value of these soils consists more in the peculiar qualities of the tobacco produced upon them than in the weight per acre. By some it is believed that their capacity is declining. The deterioration of quality may be attributed, in some measure, to a succession of unfavorable seasons. For several years past there has been a general deficiency of strength and elasticity of texture and a smaller supply of oils. Most of the tobacco now produced is grown upon old lands, and these, when manured well, produce the heavier and more oily types. No large area of new lands suitable for tobacco culture is now available, and the proportion of the product derived from newly-cleared lands is annually decreasing. The constantly lessening proportion of such types accounts for the presumed deterioration in the quality of the general product.

In Green and Taylor counties there are considerable bodies of soil, known as "beech lands", which produce oily and heavy types of tobacco. These soils consist of a dark loam or vegetable mold, overlying a red-clay foundation of good depth. The prevailing tree growth is of red beech, mixed with walnut, sugar-tree, and hickory. Uplands, slightly rolling, are preferred, but the lowlands along the water-courses do well for tobacco, except in wet seasons, when the product is likely to be coarse and of inferior quality. These lands contain a larger proportion of chert in the limestone base and intermixed with the clay of the subsoil than those of the central area of the district already described, but their general productiveness, ease of tillage, liability to damage by surface washing, etc., are very nearly the same. The same methods for the maintenance or restoration of fertility are in common use, and are found effective. About one-half of the wooded lands of Green and Taylor counties is adapted to the production of tobacco; but, as elsewhere in the district, the proportion of the annual planting upon newly-cleared lands is decreasing.

In Hart county, and in a limited portion of the northwestern corner of Barren, is a distinct body of lands noted for the production of tobacco specially suited for bright wrappers. The soil is calcareo-siliceous, overlying the measures of the adjacent coal-fields, which here extend eastward in thin and irregular strata. The surface is ridgy; the soil thin, and of a mulatto color; the subsoil, compact yellow clay. The timber growth is scrubby hickory, white oak, post oak, black oak, chestnut, and chestnut oak. The soil contains much gravel and sand, and the subsoil is calcareous. The tobacco grown upon this soil is of light body, very fine and silky in texture and fiber, but so firm and compact as to possess especial value for wrappers. The soils preferred for making "Hart county bright wrappers" are freshly-cleared sandy uplands, with a timber growth of hickory, black-jack, and post oak and a sparse undergrowth of hazel. The yield, especially of the finer types, does not exceed 500 or 600 pounds per acre; but this moderate yield is more than compensated by the increased value per pound.

Outside of these three distinct soil formations the lands of this district are of uncertain adaptation for tobacco of well-defined character in market. The lighter types are sometimes available as plug fillers, and in rare instances for a low grade of wrappers; the heavier types have little usefulness for any purpose. The soils are of low value, not durable, and can be reclaimed only at a cost greater than their value.

VALUE OF THE CROP OF 1879.

The great variety of types of tobacco produced in this district, and the large proportion of nondescript, make it difficult to state accurately the average values of the crop. As nearly as can be ascertained, the average values may be estimated as follows: For nondescript, $3; for lugs, $4 25; light-body fillers, $5; bright wrappers, $15 per hundred pounds.

LABOR AND THE LABOR SYSTEM.

Laborers employed in tobacco culture are mostly colored, and are generally hired for the year at a stated rate of wages per annum, ranging from $100 to $150, with board or rations, to men of the best class. Some crops are grown on shares. Day laborers, men, are paid 50 cents per day, with board; without board, 75 cents. By the month men are paid from $8 to $11, with board. A large part of the crop of this district is made by the proprietors themselves, with the help of such members of their families as are able to work.

COST OF PRODUCTION.

Upon good soils, of fair productive capacity, the following result may be obtained under skillful management:

Cost of labor, one man, one year, with board	$200 00
Wear and tear of implements and fixtures	20 00
Use of team, and feed for same	65 00
Rent of 15 acres wheat land, at $2 50	37 50
Rent of 15 acres corn land, at $3	45 00
Rent of 3 acres tobacco land, at $6	18 00
	385 50
Average product of tobacco by one laborer, 2,000 pounds, at 5 cents	100 00
Average product of wheat, 200 bushels, at 75 cents	150 00
Average product of corn, 450 bushels, at 30 cents	135 00
	385 00

Results as favorable as those here estimated have been frequently obtained upon good lands with average seasons, but in far the greater number of instances the cost of producing tobacco must exceed 5 cents per pound. A large part of the lands of this district do not admit of raising a variety of crops in such amounts as to be profitable. On such lands the production of tobacco is maintained because the labor employed is that of the farmer and his family.

In the following statement the weight of product in the Upper Green River district for the first three years is obtained from official returns to the auditor of Kentucky. For 1879 the production, acreage, and yield per acre are obtained from the returns made to the United States Census Bureau. The rest of the statement is estimated:

Year.	Production.	Acreage.	Yield per acre.	Value of crop.	Value per pound.	Value per acre.
	Pounds.		*Pounds.*		*Cents.*	
1876	12,618,191	21,027	600.00	$820,182 41	6.50	$39 00
1877	21,311,137	33,448	727.00	1,438,068 22	6.00	43 61
1878	10,313,750	20,627	500.00	511,472 10	5.23	20 25
1879	11,602,507	17,076	678.40	590,029 85	5.00	33 92

THE CLARKSVILLE DISTRICT.

Tobacco culture in that part of the Clarksville tobacco district lying south of the Kentucky line is described in the chapter on Tennessee.

In Kentucky the territory is a wide and continuous water-shed, from which the drainage is carried into the Cumberland river by a number of small streams, with narrow channels and high, rocky banks. Its general surface is level, or rolling in long, low curves, with some small and narrow belts of broken country. The Cumberland river cuts through the western part of Trigg county, the Louisville and Memphis railway passes through Logan and Todd counties, the Saint Louis and Southeastern railway through Christian and Todd, and the Louisville and Nashville railway through Simpson county, affording good facilities for transportation.

There is much uniformity in type, and almost the entire product is characterized by heaviness and firmness of texture, strength and elasticity, oily consistency, and general smoothness of structure, with moderate delicacy of fiber and stem, and may be considered as one leading line of types.

By its peculiar permanent qualities the Clarksville product meets a very wide range of demands. Some of these are so established in character that in chapter II they have been described under the following types: Fine-fibered Clarksville Wrapper, Clarksville and Missouri dark and red, Italian Regie A and B, French types A and B, Austrian Regie, German Saucer, Snuff Leaf and Lugs, German Spinner, Swiss Wrapper, Dutch Saucer, Belgian Cutter, African Shippers, and Mexican Wrappers.

In the northern part of the district, on the line of juncture between the Saint Louis and the Carboniferous formations, is produced a type of light body, somewhat resembling the lighter types of the Lower Green River district. This to some extent is used for domestic manufacturing purposes, as fillers, but it is of low grade.

The richest and most oily lugs are used in the United States for grinding into common snuff; the leafy lugs, of less weight of body, are used for cutting into common smoking-tobacco. In Germany the former grade is used for fillers in spinning, and in both Germany and Spain for the manufacture of common snuff; the latter grade is used in France, Spain, and Italy for binders and fillers for common cigars, and those of least substance and of fair quality for granulation for fillers for cigarettes. Decayed or damaged lugs are used for sheep-wash.

The tobacco product of this district has a wider range of adaptation to purposes of a high grade than that of any other section of the state, as it is susceptible of being cured into such diversity of color.

During the past ten years marked changes in the quality of the general product have taken place. In Todd county the proportion of dark shipping in 1879 is reported to have decreased considerably. In Christian county the following estimate is made: Dark shipping, 40 per cent. in 1879, 25 per cent in 1869; fillers, 25 per cent. in 1879, 25 per cent. in 1869; cigar leaf, 5 per cent. in 1879, 10 per cent. in 1869; bright wrappers and smokers, none in 1879, 25 per cent. in 1869; nondescript, 30 per cent. in 1879, 15 per cent. in 1869. It is claimed, however, that this estimate is for a given locality, and does not fairly represent the product of the whole county.

The only improvement is reported from Trigg county, where the product is said to be heavier and cleaner and the general quality somewhat better than ten years ago. Dealers who have handled the crops of this district for the past ten years agree in opinion that there has been a marked decline in the general standard of quality, and it is a recognized fact that the average deterioration of quality has been more marked than in most of the other districts of the state, amounting in Logan and Christian counties to from 10 to 25 per cent.

GEOLOGY AND SOIL FORMATIONS.

The whole surface of this district is situated upon the Saint Louis group of rocks belonging to the sub-Carboniferous formation (and mostly upon the cavernous member of this group), with the exception of a narrow belt of the Keokuk group on its southern and western border and of coal-bearing strata upon its northern line. The western half of Trigg and the southeastern part of Simpson lie upon the Keokuk group, which also underlies a narrow strip on the southern lines of Logan, Todd, and Christian counties. The northern parts of Todd and Christian counties are situated upon the Carboniferous, and the hills in the northern part of Logan are capped with members of the Chester group.

The soils of this district, having these diverse sources of formation, vary in character and capacity. Wherever situated upon the Saint Louis group, a deep bed of clay rests upon the underlying rock, overlaid by a surface soil, in some places of a very deep-red color, and in others a light or pale red. The darker soils are lighter and of looser texture than the light-colored soils, and are of superior fertility. The lands on this formation are covered with a timber growth of black-jack, red oak, post oak, hickory, and gums of small size, with an undergrowth of hazel and dogwood. Originally very fertile, these soils have maintained the production of tobacco of superior excellence until recently.

The soils lying upon the Keokuk group are rather stiff and compact upon a foundation of pale-red clay. They cover a surface of gravelly and cherty ridges, and the prevailing tree growth is of large size, consisting mostly of red oak, with a few poplars (*Liriodendron tulipifera*), white oaks, elms, and gums, with an undergrowth of dogwood. Tobacco grown upon these soils has less breadth of leaf, less fatness and oils, not so much strength and elasticity, is not so heavy, and has less tendency to cure into full dark and brown colors than that grown upon the Saint Louis group. The frame (stem and fibers) of the leaf is coarser in proportion to the weight and body of web with which it is filled.

There are in Christian county three distinct bodies of land upon the Saint Louis group, producing three distinct qualities of tobacco. One of these is a rich and strong barren soil, with a scrubby growth of black, red, and post oak and hickory, upon which is made an oily and fat tobacco of very heavy texture, well suited to the higher grades of German demand. Another consists of a small area of level land, somewhat lower than the general surface, inclined to be marshy and wet, with a soil of dark color upon a foundation of stiff and tenacious yellow clay, producing a leaf of rather light weight, very silky, of delicate fiber, and specially fitted for use as Swiss wrappers. The third consists of an area of ridgy surface, with a soil of a grayish-brown color upon a subsoil of red clay, and with a timber growth of black and red oaks and scattering poplars, walnut, and hickory. This soil is sandy, and lies upon a margin adjacent to the coal-bearing strata. Its product is specially adapted for dark wrappers.

The type of tobacco for which this district is particularly noted is grown in highest perfection upon the soils of the eastern part of Trigg and the southern part of Christian, Todd, and Logan counties, where the original growth seems to have been a dense covering of barren grass (*Andropogon scoparius and A. furcatus*), succeeded by hazel.

In the eastern part of Logan and in Simpson county the peculiar characteristics of the type are lost to a large extent in a product of coarser quality, with less supply of oils and fatness. Here the soils are more compact, of a pale brown or darker color, upon a subsoil of no great depth above the bed-rock. These soils are more siliceous than those with which they are compared, nor have they the full red color which distinguishes the best tobacco soils of Christian and other counties.

There are some areas of Quaternary along the water-lines of this district very little used for the culture of tobacco. When grown upon such soils the product is very coarse.

The marginal areas in this district lying upon the Chester and Carboniferous groups are small and unimportant, and the types of tobacco produced upon them are scarcely recognized as a part of the crop of the Clarksville district.

The best lands are always selected for the growth of tobacco, the older lands being kept in permanent lots for this purpose and maintained in fertility by manuring and a system of rotation. Where available, small additions of freshly-cleared land are added to the tobacco-fields every year. The proportion of new lands is, however, steadily decreasing. In Christian county one acre of fresh land to fifty of old land is cultivated each year. In Logan county one-fifth of the land devoted to tobacco culture is estimated as fresh land; that is, such land as has been cleared but a few years, and is capable of producing a fair yield without manures.

Of the wooded lands of Trigg county 60 per cent. are adapted to the growth of tobacco; of Todd county, 90 per cent.; of Christian county, 80 per cent.; and of Logan county, 60 per cent. The forest area of the best tobacco lands of this district is already so much reduced that no considerable acreage of "new ground" is now available without such destruction of timber as could be justified only by absolute necessity. It is estimated that the average production per acre is 10 per cent. less than for the decade ending with 1869. This holds good for all the other cultivated crops, as well as for tobacco.

In only two counties, Christian and Logan, is any estimate made of the proportion of tobacco lands exhausted and turned out as old fields; in these counties it is stated as not exceeding 1 per cent. Land so turned out grows up quickly in briers, broom grass, sassafras, and persimmon, and is within a very few years restored to fair productiveness.

The methods adopted for maintaining fertility are much the same as those in use throughout the state. On level lands tobacco occupies a given field one year, followed by wheat, seeded to clover, the clover turned down in the fall of the third year, and the land manured for tobacco, to be planted in the fourth year. This plan, with the liberal use of manure, has proved quite successful. Some farmers have recently attempted to grow two crops of wheat, alternating with tobacco every third year, but the result was not satisfactory. Careful observers, especially those who have long occupied the better lands overlying the Saint Louis group, are of opinion that tobacco should not be grown upon the same soils at shorter intervals than four years, and that the best rotation is as follows: First year, tobacco, manured, the field sown in wheat in the fall of the same year; second year, clover, seeded upon the young wheat, lightly pastured in the fall; third year, clover for mowing, and to be pastured off only in dry weather; fourth year, clover, turned down in the fall, to be prepared in the spring for tobacco. Upon good soils some planters have succeeded in growing fair crops of tobacco year after year upon the same fields by seeding to rye in the fall, to be plowed under about the first of May. Stock pease are much used for green manuring, and are especially valuable upon the lighter uplands. Bone-dust, land plaster, and some of the more prominent commercial fertilizers, are used, but to a very limited extent.

VARIETIES OF TOBACCO PRODUCED.

Beside the varieties already described in the reports upon adjoining districts there are some of much local reputation. The Burt makes a very large plant, coarse in stem, fiber, and web of leaf, ripens imperfectly, and when of sufficient length is suitable for African shippers. The Clardy and the Thickset are described among the Varieties, chapter II, pages 23, 24. The Morrow, which is a very old variety, makes a plant of full size. The leaf is of good length and width, terminating very abruptly at the lower end, heavy, but rather coarse in stem and fiber, and makes good German shippers when not too coarse. It is difficult to cure, and is consequently liable to house-burn; ripens slowly, and is not easily "wormed", because of the heavy ruffling upon the stalks and leaf stems. The Vick makes a large plant, and has a narrow, bony, but heavy and thick leaf. The cured leat is deficient in flexibility, is of no decided character or quality, having no ruffling upon the stalk or stem, and is preferred for that reason, and because it makes good yield of weight. The Tally is a local variety very similar to the Vick. The Little Yellow makes a large plant, and has leaves of full length, but somewhat narrow, set well apart on the stalk, with very little ruffle. The texture is heavy, with a moderately delicate stem and fiber, and makes good yield of weight. The plant is not hardy, and is liable to field-fire and "speck". When not too heavy bodied or too narrow in leaf the Little Yellow makes good Swiss wrappers; when sufficiently heavy and well cured it fills a portion of the Austrian demand. It is thought to be produced by cross-fertilization, as are also the Clardy and Burt varieties.

The Orinoco, Blue and Yellow Pryors, and Beat-all, or Williams, are also grown in this district, and are generally preferred. The high prices prevailing during the period of general inflation induced many planters to seek the largest yield without reference to quality, resulting in diverse cross-fertilizations, and the consequent loss of distinctive and characteristic varieties. Efforts are now made to reduce the number of varieties. Limited experiments have been made in growing the White Burley, but with indifferent success. The two types made by the White Burley and the heavy product of this district differ so widely that they cannot probably be profitably grown in the same territory.

COST OF LABOR AND PRODUCTION.

The labor system is very similar to that of other tobacco-growing districts of the state, except that a larger proportion of the crop is made by hired labor. When tobacco is grown on the share system the employer furnishes land, team, implements, barn, and fixtures, with house and fuel for the laborer and his family, and gives the laborer one-half of the product. Wage hands are paid an average of $125 per annum, with board.

Barns cost from $50 to $300, with capacity for curing and storing from 2,000 to 15,000 pounds; annual cost for repairs, about 5 per cent. Tobacco-sticks cost from $3 to $4 per 1,000; one-horse plows, cost $5; breaking plows, $12; harrows, from $5 to $15; hoes, from 75 cents to $1, with an average annual depreciation of value on all implements of 10 per cent.

The best lands in farms are worth $50 per acre, with a rental value of $6 per acre for tobacco lands producing an average of 900 pounds, and the lowest grades of lands are valued at $10 per acre, with a rental value of $2 for such as are capable of producing 400 pounds per acre.

The following is an estimate of the cost of production, under average conditions, with good management:

Wages of one man and board	$200 00
Use of team and feed	65 00
Rent of 3 acres of tobacco land, at $6	18 00
Rent of 15 acres of wheat land, at $2 50	37 50
Rent of 15 acres of corn land, at $3	45 00
Wear of implements and fixtures	10 00
Total cost	375 50
2,000 pounds of tobacco, at 5½ cents	$110 00
180 bushels of wheat, at 75 cents	135 00
450 bushels of corn, at 30 cents	135 50
Total value of product	380 50

VALUE OF THE CROP OF 1879.

The average value of this crop in farmers' hands did not exceed 5½ cents per pound, and it is probable that a close estimate of net proceeds, clear of cost for casks and conveyance to market, would not show a value much, if any, over 5 cents. The following is given as the estimate of an experienced dealer, made after the crop had been almost entirely sold, the prices being based upon sales made in the Hopkinsville market: Best grades for baling and Swiss wrappers, 10 to 13 cents; good German types of leaf, 6½ to 10 cents; Regie leaf, 4½ to 6½ cents; good lugs, 3¾ to 4¾ cents; common lugs, 3 to 3½ cents per pound.

The weight of product in the Clarksville district for the first three years is obtained for the statement below from official returns made to the auditor of Kentucky. For 1879 the weight of product, acreage, and yield per acre are derived from returns made to the United States Census Bureau:

Year.	Production.	Acreage.	Yield per acre.	Value of crop.	Value per pound.	Value per acre.
	Pounds.		*Pounds.*		*Cents.*	
1876	10,000,747	16,667	600.00	$750,030	7.50	$45 00
1877	33,888,803	39,869	850.00	2,202,772	6.50	55 25
1878	18,111,010	27,832	650.72	996,106	5.50	35 79
1879	31,761,180	45,756	694.14	1,746,865	5.50	38 18

THE CUMBERLAND RIVER DISTRICT.

This district is situated in the southeastern part of the state, and is bounded on the south by the Tennessee line, west and north by the Upper Green River district, and east by the eastern coal-fields.

Most of the surface is very broken, with an occasional small body of level or rolling lands. Its eastern half, lying near the base of the Cumberland mountains, is penetrated by spurs of this range, and is very rugged, while the remainder is cut into sections of hilly and rolling lands. The Cumberland river passes through it from northeast to southwest, and on either side tributary streams have cut the face of the country into deep and narrow valleys, separated from each other by a very broken and elevated country.

TYPES OF TOBACCO PRODUCED.

The heavy types of tobacco are produced mostly upon low or bottom lands, and are rather coarse in fiber and stem, rough, wanting in flexibility, deficient in oils, but of good weight. In parts of Adair and Metcalfe counties a type of heavy tobacco is grown possessing smoothness, delicacy of fiber and texture, with a good supply of oils. This is grown upon fertile uplands, and is very similar to the better styles of heavy tobacco grown in the Upper Green River district. The light types are of fine fiber, light texture, and bright and red colors, and approximate similar types grown in adjoining districts. Some portion of this product has found use as bright wrappers and fillers for domestic manufacturing, for cutting into fine-cut chewing, and for the better grades of smoking tobacco. The more progressive farmers have been successfully endeavoring within four or five years to improve the quality of the product, especially of the lighter types, by a careful selection of appropriate varieties and the adoption of improved methods of curing.

Only three counties of this district furnish estimates of the proportion of different types produced. These estimates are as follows for the crop of 1879:

County.	Dark shipping.	Fillers.	Bright wrappers and smokers.	Cutting.	Nondescript.
	Per cent.	*Per cent.*	*Per cent.*	*Per cent.*	*Per cent.*
Cumberland	50	10	10	....	30
Metcalfe	25	25	10	5	35
Monroe	75	20	....	5	....

These estimates being for but a small portion of the district cannot be taken as a reliable basis upon which to estimate the character of the entire product.

VARIETIES OF TOBACCO GROWN.

These are Blue and Yellow Pryor, Orinoco, Twist-bud, One-sucker, Shoestring, Poor Man's Friend, Long Green, Morrow, Silk Leaf, and White Burley. The Pryors and Orinoco are preferred. The Shoestring makes a very long, narrow leaf, with heavy stem and fiber, and is of very full but coarse texture, but is of no special value except for making African shippers. The One-sucker, Poor Man's Friend, and Long Green are very similar in habits of growth and in quality of cured product, and are valuable only because of the ease with which they are cultivated and prepared for market. The crop of White Burley for 1879 was so small as not to attract attention.

GEOLOGY AND SOIL FORMATIONS.

The whole of this district, except a small belt along its eastern margin, is situated upon the sub-Carboniferous formation. On its eastern border the coal-measure shale and sandstone of the eastern coal-field crop out and form a small body of characteristic soils, covering about half the area of Wayne county and a small section in Clinton. The remainder of the territory of these two counties lies upon the Saint Louis limestone, and has the surface features usually marking the presence of this group—rolling surface lines, numerous broad basins, sink-holes, and a scrubby growth of oak and hickory. As is the case with similar geological levels in the Clarksville and Upper Green River districts, it is supposed to have been at no very remote period a continuous prairie, covered with a rank growth of barren grass.

Throughout the remainder of this district various strata appear in the surface formations, exposing in one place or another almost every member of the sub-Carboniferous groups. In Casey county the Upper Silurian exposes formations of magnesian limestone, the Devonian, with its black shales, and the Lower Silurian in small belts of blue limestone. In Adair county the lower members of the Saint Louis group predominate, exhibiting earthy and shaly limestones and frequent outcroppings of red or gray shales, with occasional exposures of sub-Carboniferous sandstone. The rugged surface of Cumberland county exposes a succession of cherty limestones of the Saint Louis group and of black, gray, and green shales, as members of separate sub-Carboniferous strata.

The lithological features of Monroe and Metcalfe counties consist mainly of heavy masses of red and green shales, lying upon a thin bedding of black shale, and covered by formations of impure and shaly limestones, underlying beds of chert, mixed with red clay. Upon the slopes of a high ridge passing through these counties these heavy beddings of shale are exposed, capped with the limestones and overlying chert above noted. The geological features of Metcalfe, Monroe, and Cumberland counties have this characteristic in common: the deepest cuts of the streams expose the upper members of the Lower Silurian, while upon the hills are found the shales and limestones of the sub-Carboniferous formation.

With such diversity of origin the soils of this district differ very much in character and productive capacity. In Monroe, Metcalfe, Wayne, Clinton, and Adair counties are found bodies of land upon which the forest growth is mainly of poplar, beech, and buckeye, producing a heavy type of tobacco of delicate stem and fiber, of smooth texture, good weight, and a fair supply of oils and gum. These lands lie upon a red-clay foundation of from 6 to 10 feet in depth.

Beds of Quaternary along the water-lines, composed of a very deep loam, mixed with vegetable mold, upon a subsoil of red clay, are covered with a tree growth of beech, sugar-tree, walnut, and elm. These soils produce a heavy, coarse tobacco, rather porous in texture, and generally rough.

Upon the sub-Carboniferous sandstones the soils are stiff, clayey loams of a mulatto color, upon a subsoil of yellow clay 3 to 6 feet in depth, with a timber growth of white oak, hickory, and chestnut. Upon these lands the product of tobacco is light, of fine fiber, of delicate and silky texture, mild and sweet in flavor, and with a tendency to cure into bright and yellow colors.

Lying upon and derived from the shales are soils consisting of dark, coarse, and loose loam, upon a subsoil of dark or bluish material 1 to 4 feet in depth, and covered with a forest growth of post oak, hickory, and elm. These soils produce a plant of full size, with long and broad leaves, of medium weight, almost destitute of oils or gum, rather porous in structure, and having a tendency to cure into red colors.

The proportion of new lands occupied in tobacco culture varies in different localities from 10 to 75 per cent., the term "new" lands being taken to represent such as are not yet so much exhausted as not to produce successively fair crops of tobacco.

Of the wooded lands, from 75 to 100 per cent. are adapted to the production of tobacco. This estimate does not include such areas as cannot be made available for tillage of any kind, such as very steep or rocky hillsides.

All reports from this district agree that under tobacco culture the lands are declining in productiveness. This is a result not attributable to exhaustion of plant food by the growth of crops, but to surface washing. The broken and uneven surfaces of most fields are rapidly scoured away by heavy rainfalls, and large areas are consequently regarded as "worn out". To maintain the production of tobacco fresh lands have been cleared, and the process has been repeated until not much more timber land remains than is required for economic purposes. Most of the forest lands are so broken and thin in soil that, although they might produce several crops of tobacco while fresh, they would soon become exhausted and comparatively worthless. It is probable, therefore, that the highest limit of production has been reached, and that tobacco culture in this district will scarcely retain its present importance.

The decrease of yield per acre is variously reported. In some localities it is stated as high as 25 per cent., as compared with the yield of the decade ending with 1869; in others, from 10 to 20 per cent. A corresponding deterioration of quality is reported, especially in the heavier types, which have lost largely in weight and firmness of texture.

COST OF LABOR AND PRODUCTION.

The labor system is much the same as in other parts of the state. Men receive from $75 to $120 per annum when employed by the year, with board; by the day, 40 to 75 cents, with board. When crops are grown on the share system, the laborer gets one-half, the employer furnishing necessary team, implements, etc. Barns and fixtures for storing and curing cost from $75 to $400.

The best lands in farms are worth from $15 to $30 per acre, producing 800 to 1,200 pounds of tobacco per acre, with a rental value of $4 to $6. Inferior lands are valued at $5 to $10 per acre, producing 400 to 800 pounds, and are rented at $2 per acre.

The cost of production varies between 4½ and 8 cents per pound, the latter being the cost upon inferior lands. There is general complaint that the culture of tobacco brings little or no profit. It would probably be abandoned in a great measure but for the fact that it furnishes employment for many workers, who cannot undertake the heavier labors of the farm.

VALUE OF THE CROP OF 1879.

Bright wrappers were sold at 10 to 25 cents, the smaller quantity bringing the larger price; good shipping leaf, 6 to 8 cents; common leaf, 5 cents; and lugs, 2½ to 3 cents. The value of the crop round in primary markets may be fairly estimated at 5 cents per pound.

In the following table the weight of product in the Cumberland River district for the first three years is obtained from official returns to the auditor of Kentucky. For 1879 the weight of product, acreage, and yield per acre are derived from the official returns made to the United States Census Bureau. The remainder of the statement is estimated:

Years.	Production.	Acreage.	Yield per acre.	Value of crop.	Value per pound.	Value per acre.
	Pounds.		*Pounds.*		*Cents.*	
1876	4,399,737	7,333	600.00	$263,984	6.00	$36 00
1877	7,472,310	10,307	725.00	410,977	5.50	39 87
1878	3,204,084	6,408	500.00	160,204	5.00	25 00
1879	2,441,542	3,844	635.16	118,304	4.85	31 76

CULTURE AND CURING OF TOBACCO IN THE SHIPPING DISTRICTS OF KENTUCKY.

The methods of culture and the processes of curing tobacco in the seven districts of Kentucky already described have no peculiarities not common to them all. This part of the report is therefore made applicable to the whole tobacco region of the state, except the district in which the White Burley is the principal variety grown. The character of the product of this new variety differs materially from that of any other, and the manner of cultivation, handling and curing of the crop, varies in many particulars from the methods practiced in producing the types grown in the other districts of the state. For these reasons it is thought best to conclude the account of what may be properly called the shipping districts of Kentucky, treating separately the White Burley district.

PREPARATION OF THE SOIL FOR PLANTING.

It is the practice of good planters to break the land intended for tobacco as deeply as possible and as early in the fall as practicable. It is regarded as of prime importance to complete the breaking of deep and stiff clay soils before the colder period of winter. Soils of shale and sandstone derivation do not so imperatively require fall or winter plowing, nor is it necessary that they must be worked to such depth as is essential for those based upon the limestone formations; but even with the deepest and most friable of the silicious soils there are advantages to be gained by early breaking.

Whatever the character of the surface or subsoil, it is important that all vegetable matter shall be turned under in time to become thoroughly rotted before the final preparation for planting is begun, not only to secure the utmost value of such material, both as a fertilizer and as a mechanical amendment to the soil, but that it shall be so entirely decomposed as to offer no impediment to subsequent processes of culture. In many instances, where stubble, weeds, or grass cover the intended tobacco-field, if the breaking is deferred until February, or later, it is necessary to burn over the land, so that clean and satisfactory work may be done with the plow. Although it may be claimed that the ashes of the burned weeds or stubble return to the soil all the fertilizing constituents of real value, experience has demonstrated that the mechanical effects of slow fermentation and decomposition in the soil make the fibrous material of straw, dry grass, and weeds of much greater manurial value than that of several times the equivalent in ashes.

Upon the heavier lands, and especially upon those having a stiff clay subsoil, plows of steel or of chilled cast iron, drawn by two or three and sometimes by four horses, are used in breaking. The deeper the plowing the more satisfactory is this first preparation for tobacco, the depth being limited only by the capacity of the implement and the strength of the team. Good farmers are careful that not too much of the clay subsoil shall be turned uppermost, and that the deepening of the tillable surface shall be accomplished by gradually increasing the depth of culture year after year.

Upon the lighter lands, such as are found in the Lower Green River district, and upon the sandy soils and light alluvials throughout the state, the ground is not broken so deeply, usually from 3 to 4 inches only, and the work is rarely done until spring.

After the soil has been broken, it remains untouched until the season for planting approaches. The preparation for planting is so timed that the plants, as soon as ready, may be set in freshly-worked soil.

If manures are to be applied broadcast, as is usually the case with the coarse and imperfectly decomposed accumulations of the stable and farm-yard, they are hauled upon the land in February, or later, when the soil is dry enough to permit such work, and scattered as evenly as possible. The plow usually follows closely, turning under the manure with as little delay as practicable.

One rebreaking is generally thought sufficient, and if further preliminary work is necessary it is done with the harrow. If still cloddy and not properly fined, the field is rolled and again harrowed, or the surface is dragged with a heavy log, sometimes with two or more logs in a gang, and finally harrowed.

The preparation of newly-cleared land differs only in the manner of breaking. After the timber has been removed, brush, trash, and leaves are piled or raked into heaps and burned, clearing the surface as nicely as possible of all obstructions. The plow used for breaking is known as a "jumping coulter". This implement consists of a heavy iron or steel shovel, firmly bolted to a very strong frame or "stock". In front of the shovel, and in line with its center, is fixed into the beam a strong blade of steel, or iron laid with steel, sharp upon the front edge and rounding backward at the lower end. The blade extends downward, so that the point stands just in front of the shovel, and at an equal depth. The implement is built strongly throughout, so that it may be used with a stout team of mules or horses. Roots of considerable size are easily cut by the blade, and are torn up and thrown to the surface by the shovel. If large roots are encountered, the backward curve of the blade allows it to slide over the obstruction, and the plow is not impeded in its work. After the ground is plowed and cross-plowed in this manner it is repeatedly harrowed, and the roots are gathered up and removed; it is then plowed with the jumping coulter, harrowed, and the remaining roots picked off. The land is then ready for final preparation.

Both the row and the check system of cultivation are practiced, but the latter plan is the one adopted in all cases where the shape of the field or the lay of the land does not make it impracticable or unadvisable. The width between the rows and the distances between the plants are varied to suit the character of the soil, the variety of tobacco to be planted, and the type to be produced. Upon lands in fair condition 3½ feet each way is the ordinary distance. If it is intended to make a type of heavy weight, strong texture, and fat body, the distance between the hills must be great enough to admit of long-continued tillage. Recently a standard of 4 feet each way has been adopted by some good farmers with excellent results. A larger amount of food available for each plant, the free access of sunlight and air, and greater ease and thoroughness in the later cultivations, with less bruising and breaking of the leaves in the operations of topping, suckering, and worming, are all secured by the wider setting. It has been found that the total yield per acre is quite as large as when the plants are more crowded, and that the product is of better grade, because of better development in size, strength, and quality of leaf.

The field is marked each way, usually with a shovel or bull-tongue plow. An expert plowman can work from six to eight acres one way in ten hours, setting his stakes as he goes. When but one man is marking off, the stake rows are run at double width, and he "splits the middle" at each back furrow; when two men are at work, the most expert runs the stake rows at four widths, and "splits the big middle" by the return furrow, the helper splitting the "little middles", after a little practice, very accurately. The field is then marked in the same way at right angles, and is ready for hilling.

Manure is applied in the hill to some extent, but this is tedious and expensive. A given quantity of manure will go over a much larger area, and, if thoroughly decomposed and fine, will increase the yield in favorable seasons two or three times as much as the same quantity applied broadcast. Evil results are apt to follow the use of coarse and badly-rotted manure in the hill, especially if dry weather should occur before the plants are well rooted. A pint of leached ashes or a moderate shovelful of rich and well-rotted stable manure dropped in the check is applied with good effect. The hill is made with the hand-hoe, covering the manure to a depth of 6 or 8 inches.

It is essential that manures used in the hill shall be buried deep enough not to be dried by an ordinary season of drought, lest the plant be too much stimulated at first and thereafter almost entirely deprived of nourishment.

Spot and field-fire are almost certain to show themselves in fields where unfit material has been used for manuring in the hill, or where the best material has been injudiciously applied.

Commercial fertilizers are used to a very limited extent, and almost always in the hills, the quantity varying from a heaping teaspoonful to a tablespoonful for each plant. Opinions differ as to the effect of these fertilizers. In some instances more weight and a better quality of product have been obtained by their use, but in the large majority of cases no apparent benefit has been derived, either because used in too small quantities, or because they were adapted neither to the deficiencies of the soil nor to the demands of the tobacco plant.

Upon new lands manures are seldom applied, but their use is as decidedly favorable as upon old lands, and always proves a profitable expenditure.

In the heavy tobacco districts about one-half of the land planted in tobacco is manured in one way or another. Ordinarily the final preparation of the soil to receive the plants is made with the plow. A "list" is made upon the marking furrows by running a one-horse turn-plow on each side, throwing the earth together into a narrow bed. Furrows are then turned at right angles to the ridges. The tops of the latter are then cut off with the hoe, and the exact position for the plant is marked by clapping the earth, thus firming the surface and fitting it for the operation of planting. When the soil has been thoroughly pulverized this method is rapid, economical, and as perfect as can be desired.

If the land is cloddy and not well fined, it is necessary to make the hills with the hoe, breaking the clods and chopping the earth closely and drawing up the soil upon one end of the cut ridge, the hill being raised a little above the general surface.

Not unfrequently the tobacco plants are set in the loose earth at the crossings of the marking furrows without other preparation. It is claimed that by this method the plants are more likely to survive, because better protected from the drying winds and the heat of the sun, and because the roots are less likely to suffer for want of needed moisture. The early cultivation of plants set in this way is not so conveniently done, however, and the method is of questionable economy, except when circumstances require a resort to it to save a "season", (*a*) or for want of time to make more thorough preparation.

The land being made ready, and the plants of proper size, the first sufficient rainfall puts the ground in condition for planting. The most careful hands are set to work to draw the plants from the bed, only such as are strong and well developed being taken, and these are bruised as little as possible. The drawing is so managed as not unnecessarily to disturb the surface of the bed, so as to leave the remaining plants in the best condition for thrifty growth. The plants are carried to the field in baskets. A man or boy, with a basket, goes in advance, dropping a plant upon each hill of two rows. Two planters follow, each upon his own row. A smooth, round stick, 12 inches long, $1\frac{1}{2}$ or 2 inches in diameter, and pointed, is carried in the right hand, with which the planter makes a hole of proper depth; the plant is then placed in position with the left hand, and the soil pressed closely about the roots by a thrust of the stick on one side of the hole. The farmer frequently tests the thoroughness of the work by catching the tip of a leaf of the newly-set plant between the forefinger and the thumb, and if the soil has been sufficiently compacted about the roots the tip of the leaf will break off, leaving the plant in place, but if it is pulled up in this way it is evidence of imperfect work. Good planting is very essential to insure a quick start and a perfect and uniform stand. The earlier cultivation can only be successfully managed when the plants are as nearly as possible of uniform size and every hill is occupied.

If replanting is necessary, it is done at the first opportunity, always using large and vigorous plants. If the cut-worm kills a plant, the destroyer must be found before setting another plant, or the work may have to be repeated more than once. Grasshoppers sometimes attack newly-set plants, feeding upon the partially wilted leaves, and frequently eat out the bud. The field is inspected daily, so that the presence of insect enemies may be known and proper precautions taken to protect the plants. Vacancies are supplied as quickly as possible, and every effort is made to get an even start over the whole field. The early plantings make the better yield and quality of product.

CULTIVATION OF TOBACCO.

As soon as the plants are established in their new position cultivation is commenced. Usually a one-horse turn-plow is run close to the plant row on each side, throwing the soil from the plants. This is called "barring off", a term in common use in tobacco and cotton culture to describe the operation of turning the soil away from the plant row. When nicely done, this leaves the plants standing upon a narrow strip of undisturbed soil, easily and rapidly cleaned of grass or weeds by the hoe hands, who follow the plow. The soil displaced by the turn-plow covers up and destroys the grass and weeds which have started in the "balks" or middles of the rows. If the middles are free of grass, a single or double shovel is sometimes preferred for the first cultivation, and the work is certainly of superior efficacy when this implement can be used.

The first cultivation completed, a second is immediately begun, barring off the rows at right angles to the first plowing with the turn-plow or with the double shovel. No hoe work is necessary, unless the plowing has been so long delayed as to permit the weeds to get a start.

a A "season", in the vocabulary of the tobacco planter, means such a degree of moisture in the soil that the plants may be removed from the seed-beds to the field without endangering their vitality in transplanting. The word is also used when there is humidity enough in the atmosphere to bring the cured product in a condition or order that it may be handled without damage.

A third cultivation follows. The turn-plow is again used in the same direction as at first, but the soil is now thrown toward the plant row. Three or more furrows are run in each row, so as to break up the entire middle and leave it loose and fine, easily penetrated by the extending roots of the plants. This plowing is sometimes followed by the hand hoes, which bring up a small quantity of fine soil around the plant; but this work is rarely done unless the hills become foul with weeds or grass. Long-continued cultivation, especially in the production of heavy types of tobacco, gives profitable results, both in quantity and in quality. The hoe is used at intervals, as needed, to secure perfectly clean culture of the entire surface, and plowing is continued until the attention of the whole force of laborers is required in other pressing demands of the crop, even to seven plowings, if size of plants and the season permit. Priming and topping must be promptly done as soon as the plants are large enough. If this is neglected beyond the proper time, narrowness and shortness of leaf and thinness of texture are the consequences. As soon as any number of the plants have become large enough the laborers go over the field and top them. The first part of this work is the priming—breaking off the lower leaves so as to leave the stalk bare for 6 or 8 inches above the surface of the hill.

Practices and opinions vary as to priming. Those who favor high priming claim that the lower leaves, being farther removed from the ground, do not become so much injured, and there is therefore a smaller proportion of low grade in the product. On the other hand, it is urged that the removal of several lower leaves delays maturity, and that the upper leaves, which are always the best, are lighter and less oily, without compensation in the quality of the lower leaves.

Much the larger number of tobacco-growers maintain that low or moderate priming gives best results in the quality of the middle and upper leaves; that the loss, because of damage to the under leaves, is more than offset by the greater weight and fatness of leaves grown as closely as may be to the sources of nourishment.

A third class of farmers do not prime at all, and give as reasons for their practice that the loss of vitality occasioned by "bleeding" is avoided; that the ground leaves protect those above, so that a larger number of sound, clean leaves are grown upon each plant; that a greater weight of product is obtained; and that the close shading of the soil keeps it moist and in better condition to sustain growth. The objections urged to this method are that the lower leaves afford concealment to the worms; that these leaves are most likely to be neglected in worming; that the close covering and shading of the soil prevents access of sun and air; that in wet seasons evaporation is checked; and that there is frequent loss by field-fire and kindred diseases.

The plant is topped by breaking out the terminal bud. An experienced man performs this operation very rapidly, leaving the desired number of leaves without counting. If eight or twelve are to be left, the top leaves are found at right angles to the lower pair; if ten are to remain, the top pair is in line directly over the bottom ones. The quality of the product as to weight and oiliness depends in a great measure upon the number of leaves left upon the plant. The general practice in the heavy tobacco districts is to top low, and the larger number of planters adopt a standard of ten leaves in the first toppings. A few farmers claim that more weight of higher quality is made by topping at eight leaves; but if the soil is rich and strong ten leaves will develop well and mature into good quality, and this has been deemed the most economic standard for topping.

The maturity of the plant is hastened or retarded as one or another standard of priming and topping is adopted. On strong, rich lands the first plants which "come into tops", especially if they should be few in number, are primed rather high and topped at twelve leaves, thus delaying maturity, so that they may ripen at the same time with the second topping, which is done as soon as a sufficient number of plants are large enough, at ten leaves, with somewhat lower priming, to hasten maturity. The toppings are continued at ten leaves, with lower priming, at successive periods, until late in July or early in August, when only eight are left, the object being to hasten maturity, so that the plant may ripen before the date of probable frost. The standard for both priming and topping is gradually reduced as the season advances, until the latest plants may be topped at four or five leaves without priming at all, each plant being treated according to its individual development and promise.

Upon the removal of the terminal bud, or "button", the top leaves, which were very diminutive, are forced into very rapid growth. The plant makes vigorous efforts to reproduce itself, throwing out branches from the axils of the upper leaves. These branches, or suckers, are pinched out before making a growth of more than 2 or 3 inches, and are never suffered to remain longer than absolute necessity compels. Usually suckers appear in succession, first at the top of the plant, and then leaf by leaf at the axil of each, until the final effort of the plant is made by throwing up one or more branches from the base of the stalk. If "suckering" is promptly attended to, much of the tedious and often unsuccessful searching for worms is avoided, these branches being an excellent hiding-place for the horn-worm, as well as for other insect enemies. The utmost vigilance is necessary to prevent the dwarfing of the crop leaves by the growth of neglected suckers and to save them from mutilation by the worms, and great care is enjoined upon the laborers not to break the stems or tear the leaves. Careless topping frequently injures the tender top leaves, a very slight damage to which manifests itself later in a torn, jagged, or misshapen appearance. Rough handling of the growing plant does not always betray itself until the expanded leaves magnify trifling injuries into serious blemishes. The keenest and closest supervision is therefore necessary, especially when, as is often the case, transient labor, inexperienced and careless, must be employed.

CUTTING OF TOBACCO.

The work of cutting and housing tobacco is commenced as soon as there is a sufficient number of ripe plants. A proper condition of maturity is indicated by the general appearance of the plants: the leaves thick and heavy, of grainy surface, and cracking easily when folded between thumb and forefinger, the points of the leaves curling downward. The afternoon is preferred for cutting, because the plants may be allowed to wilt fully without danger of sunburn.

The cutting tool is usually an ordinary butcher-knife. Two rows are cut by each man, who selects the ripe plants, splits the stalks half way down, cuts them off just below the bottom leaves, and places them upon the ground to the right or left of the double row he is traversing. As two cutters are generally employed, four rows of cut plants are thus brought together into a "heap row". As soon as wilted enough to allow handling, the plants are piled into heaps of eight, ten, or twelve, according to size, each pile having just the number intended to be hung on one stick. The hangers follow, a tobacco-stick having been dropped at each pile by a helper. A stick is thrust into the ground, so as to stand firmly at an angle of about forty-five degrees, and the plants are hung upon it by opening the split in the stalk and straddling them across the stick.

As much is cut during the afternoon as can be handled and removed from the field before the heat of the next day. The scaffolds are generally made in the corners of the fences inclosing the field. These are made by laying three rails or poles on top of the fence, supported at the outer end by forks or other convenient means, so as to permit two tiers of tobacco upon sticks to be hung on each scaffold. As the tobacco is hung the sticks are crowded together as closely as possible. If the field is small, and the distance from the scaffold permits, the tobacco upon the sticks is carried by hand and hung, but if it is necessary to employ a wagon for the purpose these sticks are placed upon the wagon in "coops" or piles, outward and alternately at one or the other side of the pile, care being observed to keep the plants straight and smoothly laid, to prevent bruising. The tobacco is allowed to remain on the scaffold from three to five days, as the weather permits, when it is removed to the barn and placed upon the tiers, ready for the final processes of curing. Some years ago the practice of scaffolding before housing was almost abandoned. Recently this method of preparatory curing is adopted by the majority of planters, because the plant is completely wilted and the texture softened, the leaf yellowing into a clear, golden color, and easily curing into clear colors, with the required toughness and elasticity.

When the crop is to be sun-cured alone, it is placed upon scaffolds in the open field, and it is there exposed until cured or until threatening weather compels its removal to the barns or sheds. To obviate the necessity for removal some planters construct a rough frame over the scaffold, which may be quickly covered with planks or boards. If properly cared for when not in use, tarpaulins are quite as cheap as boards, and, as a protection against showers, are brought into service in much less time.

When tobacco is hung on the tier poles in the barn care is observed to open the plants upon the sticks and to place the sticks apart upon the tiers, so as to admit of free ventilation. From seven to eight large plants or eight to twelve smaller ones are hung upon each stick. The sticks being 4½ feet long, and the tier poles placed 4 feet apart, when the plants are evenly distributed upon the sticks, and the latter separated from 6 to 8 inches apart upon the tiers, there is little danger of house-burn.

If possible, the plants are allowed to come to perfect maturity before cutting them; but in wet seasons, upon the appearance of what is known as "field-fire", they must be cut prematurely, to prevent further serious loss in both quality and weight.

CURING OF TOBACCO.

The object of curing, by whatever process, is to fix the qualities of the plant as to strength and elasticity of texture, flavor, and color. Excellent quality may be lost by unskillful or improper curing, especially when done by artificial heat, and the curing processes must be so managed as to dry out the water without other material alteration of the constituent properties of fiber and tissue.

Several years ago a product of dark colors was so much in demand that the practice became generally prevalent of curing tobacco, as soon as it could be put into the barns, by hard-firing; but it was found that this method resulted in starchiness and stiffness of texture, destroying the pliancy and elasticity of the leaf, and in the loss of oils by too rapid drying. This experiment proved conclusively that artificial heat should be used in curing to assist the natural process, rather than to force it violently.

A necessary preparation for curing by artificial heat is a thorough wilting of the plant, with perfect softness and flexibility of the stem, fiber, and tissue of the leaf. In coming into this condition the color of the leaf is changed from a green into a bright shading of yellow, and it is customary to delay the application of the heat until this change of color has taken place.

Open wood fires are in common use for curing the heavy-bodied types. Two large logs of partially seasoned wood are laid side by side and in contact upon the earthen floor of the barn, and the fires are kindled with a few chips and twigs of small brush between the logs, so that they may become well ignited. The fire is then so managed as to burn continuously without blazing, which is to be avoided, because of the risk of setting fire to the dried tobacco or of injury by forcing the curing too rapidly. A moderate heat at first, gradually increased to such temperature as has been found by experience best suited to complete the process of curing the desired type, is kept under control by constant watchfulness. The purpose is to carry the curing to such a state of completion that it may be safely left to atmospheric influences, and this is reached when the tissue or body of the leaf is thoroughly dried, the stem being still in a green state. After this no firing is done, except as needed to ward off the danger of house-burn or to prevent mold or mildew, which is sometimes threatened during long-continued damp weather. Under favorable circumstances the leaf will become humid and limp at night, partly by absorption from the atmosphere and partly by diffusion of the juices remaining in the green stems, and dry out during the day. This is deemed highly favorable for completing the curing by natural means.

In a few instances the firing is continued for the purpose of fixing specific colors in the leaf, but this is done at some loss, probably, of general qualities. When the stem is left to cure by gradual drying, the colors produced by artificial heat are always, during the remainder of the process of curing, changed into much darker shades unless the atmosphere should be in a continuously drying condition, for which reason, when it is desired to retain a certain color, the fires are kept up until the stem is also cured.

For convenience in handling and to make the curing in larger bodies, and in order to obtain uniformity of color, larger and closer barns are used in curing with open wood fires than are found best in other methods. The lower parts of these barns are rather close, to prevent winds or currents of air from interfering with the ascent of the heat through the body of tobacco hanging above. In barns too closely built, and not provided with ample ventilation, the elasticity and the strength of the leaf are often much impaired, especially with a large bulk of heavy-bodied plants.

Charcoal as fuel is not much used, and only for the purpose of curing bright wrappers for domestic manufacture. In the Upper Green River district 75 per cent. of the product is air-cured; of the remainder, one-half is cured with charcoal and one-half with wood. When charcoal is used, small piles, of such size and so arranged as to produce the desired volume of heat, are distributed over the floor of the barn, kindled carefully, and thereafter managed so that the temperature shall not be increased too rapidly nor allowed to become too high. Unless the purpose is to obtain fixed colors, the firing is not continued after the curing is sufficiently advanced to admit of safely leaving the remainder of the process to natural means. The advantages of charcoal are the better preservation of the natural flavors of the plant, which are always impaired by the volatile matters emitted from wood in combustion, entire freedom from blaze, with greater safety, and the economy in fuel and labor. The different characteristics of the plants, and the peculiar structure of the houses in which they are cured, make great variation in the fuel required. A large, heavy, fully-developed leaf requires a much larger amount of fuel to bring about thorough desiccation than a small, light-bodied leaf, and a much less amount of fuel is necessary to cure tobacco in a tight, close barn, built of logs, than in a frame house boarded up with thin planks. One authority estimates one hundred and fifty bushels of charcoal for curing one thousand pounds of tobacco.

Flues are also used by some planters for curing bright wrappers. The barns are usually small and closely built, and the flues are of brick or stone, capped with sheet-iron, constructed and operated in the same manner as in the flue-curing districts of Virginia and North Carolina. Peculiarities of soil in which the plant is grown, and, even in a greater degree, the character of the season during cultivation, affect in a very marked manner the results of this method of curing. If the plant, when cut, is full of sap, it is much more difficult to cure into bright colors than when this primary condition is more favorable, and the product of rich soils, of heavy body and strong growth, whatever the variety, has a strong tendency to cure into dark colors.

A barn of ordinary size can be fitted with brick-walled and iron-capped flues, including cost of arches for the furnaces and chimneys for carrying off the smoke, at a cost of from $40 to $75, varying with cost of materials and of labor. The investment, once made, is thereafter chargeable with a very moderate tax for repairs.

Throughout the state, except in the Clarksville district, the method most generally practiced is that of air-curing. The proportion of air-cured tobacco is estimated in different localities at from 50 to 90 per cent., and in response to the demand of domestic manufacturers there has been a very large increase in the proportion of the crop cured in this way. The natural flavors so much valued by consumers can only be preserved in purity by what are called the "natural methods" of curing: by sun and air.

Scaffolding the plants for some days before they are put into the barn greatly assists this method, and is an excellent preparation for the work to be done in the house. Crowding the barns cannot be permitted, and abundance of open space is necessary to give free access to currents of air among the hanging plants. The sticks are placed well apart upon the tiers, and the plants separated upon the sticks. Doors and windows are thrown open, except when driving rains make it necessary to close them temporarily. Open sheds are very commonly used in air-curing, and are by many farmers considered best. If the weather is dry and cool, the curing can be done in close-built barns; but if it be damp and sultry, damage by house-burn is almost certain, unless prevented by artificial heat. The heat, whether of open wood fires, charcoal, or flues, injures the product to a greater or less extent; but house-burn is far worse, and must be prevented by judicious and timely firing.

The effects of these different methods, as exhibited in the cured product, are very marked and of widely varying character. By artificial heat firmness and solidity of structure are increased, the strength of texture is preserved, if the curing is properly done, and the porous system of the leaf is fixed in a permanent state of contraction, which reduces its capacity for too ready absorption and increases its ability to pass uninjured through a high degree of fermentation. It is therefore safer in long transportation by sea, or in exposure, where strong fermentation is to be apprehended. By the method of air-curing the natural flavors of the leaf are preserved, uncontaminated with the acid vapors of burning wood, and its porous system is so developed as to possess large absorptive capacity for moisture and for artificial flavorings. It is much more liable to injury by fermentation than fire-cured tobacco, and is therefore not so well suited to purposes requiring textural strain nor to withstand exposure. It is especially adapted to uses demanding natural and sweet flavors, with a high absorbing capacity. The difference in commercial value of the product cured by the two methods is estimated as follows: Fine grades of air-cured leaf, \$2 per hundred pounds higher than leaf of the same variety cured by fire; medium grades, \$1 per hundred pounds higher. In the lower grades the difference is not marked. This is for products suited to domestic manufacture, and does not apply to coarse and heavy types, in which the methods of curing make little or no difference in the average commercial value. In many heavy types curing by artificial heat, properly applied, makes a tobacco of stronger texture and better keeping qualities, and therefore more valuable.

In the Paducah district a large proportion of the crop is cured by log fires or in open barns by air. In Ballard county one-half of the crop is cured with open wood fires, one-tenth with charcoal or with flues, and the remainder is air-cured. In Graves county three-fourths of the crop is air-cured, and the balance by various applications of artificial heat. In Calloway county one-fourth is air-cured, one-fourth is cured with charcoal, and one-half with wood fires. In the remaining counties of this district neither charcoal fires nor flues are used, the product being partly air-cured and partly cured by open wood fires. A small proportion of the crops of Ballard and McCracken counties is sun-cured, a method which is said to impart peculiar sweetness to the leaf and to make it especially desirable for manufacture into chewing-tobacco.

In the Ohio River district both methods are employed. The product of Hancock county is mostly air-cured. In Caldwell and Crittenden counties the two methods are about equally followed. In Lyon county about 40 per cent. of the crop is air-cured; in Livingston county one-third; and in Breckinridge county from one-third to one-half. Charcoal fires and flue-curing are used to a limited extent in the last two counties. The air-curing in this district is mostly confined to the product of siliceous soils, which, by reason of more porous structure, is much more easily cured in this way than the oily and heavy tobacco grown on calcareous lands.

In the Green River district air-curing is generally adopted, the character of the product being especially suited to this method of treatment.

In the Upper Green River district air-curing is the method adopted for the lighter product; the heavy types are fired. The proportion of air-cured tobacco varies in different localities from one-fourth to nine-tenths.

In the Clarksville district the product is cured almost entirely by artificial heat. It has so much weight and thickness of texture that it cannot be well cured otherwise. It enters very largely into the export trade, and must be cured in such a manner as will preserve it from injury by fermentation, through which it passes in ocean transportation.

In the Cumberland River district both methods are followed. In some parts of the district charcoal is extensively used, and there has been great improvement in handling and curing tobacco. Some excellent bright wrappers have been produced, and there is promise of an increased amount of this type.

TOBACCO-BARNS.

Tobacco-houses vary in character to suit the needs of the farmer, and rail pens, roughly covered, are frequently used for curing and storing the smaller crops of air-cured tobacco. A great many tobacco-houses are constructed of logs, covered with clapboards. The larger planters, especially those who grow the heavier types, have one or more tobacco-barns of large capacity, strongly framed, and weatherboarded or planked upright, with proper arrangements for ventilation. The cost of either class of houses or sheds depends upon the value of the material and the kind of labor employed in their construction. The cheaper sheds are provided by an outlay of \$5 or \$10, while the best barns may cost from \$300 to \$800. For air-curing the houses are purposely built smaller and of more open structure than for curing by artificial heat.

Want of sufficient house-room necessitates the crowding together of the first curing of the season to make room for the later cutting. This necessity involves much risk, and the greatest vigilance is demanded to guard against injury by over-hasty curing in the first instance, followed by serious damage by house-burn, as a result of prematurely crowding imperfectly-cured tobacco. To escape these dangers farmers frequently make temporary use of other farm buildings.

Barns in which flues are placed are built very tight and of small size, and are either framed, closely boarded, and battened, or are made of logs, nicely fitted, and well chinked and daubed. Means of ventilation must be provided for these closely-built houses, so that control may be had as completely as possible of the temperature and of the volume of fresh air to be admitted during the several stages of the curing process.

PREPARATION OF TOBACCO FOR MARKET—WHERE AND HOW SOLD.

At proper and convenient seasons the cured tobacco is stripped and prepared for market.

A moist atmosphere is necessary to produce and maintain proper "order" in the leaf, which cannot be handled without great injury in a dry condition. Cured tobacco is liable to loss of quality and weight while hanging in the barn, and it is an object with good planters to withdraw it from such risk as soon as possible. A favorable season is utilized to take down so much as can be stripped and bulked in proper condition. Bulking is done as soon after stripping as possible, or as soon as the proper "order" is obtained. In some cases the tobacco, when found in proper order, is taken down and put into temporary bulks upon the sticks, so as to preserve and continue this condition until it can be stripped, tied, and packed into bulk for prizing. This is objectionable, because when bulked in the stalk the tobacco lies so loosely as to be easily dried by harsh winds, and stripping is often made impossible without reordering. This can be done successfully by careful management in close houses, or by covering the bulk with carpets, blankets, or otherwise; but generally the method is uncertain, and in most cases the tobacco is left hanging in the barn and stripped by installments, as opportunity permits.

In stripping heavy types the best planters assort into two, three, or even four classes of leaf, putting into each class leaves of similar length, color, and weight, and making two other classes or grades of the inferior lower leaves, the better of the two called "lugs", and the damaged and dirty leaves called "trash". After being thus assorted, the leaves are tied into bundles or "hands" of five to six leaves each, the stems even, and the head of the bundle closely and neatly wrapped with a leaf folded for the purpose, making a tie 1½ or 2 inches broad, and fastened by tucking the stem end of the tie-leaf through the center of the bundle.

If the tobacco is sufficiently cured and in proper order, each day's stripping is bulked at the close of the day; if not in proper condition, the bundles are usually hung on sticks and replaced upon the tiers in the barn, to be brought into bulking order. Sometimes, instead of rehanging, the bundles are piled in ranks, called "windrows", to remain until the excess of moisture is evaporated and the tobacco can be safely bulked. This method is preferred, unless the stripped tobacco is so damp as to endanger its quality by piling in this way, because when well managed it brings the stock into good condition for packing smoothly and closely into bulk. When hung on sticks the bundles, because of not being properly balanced, frequently become crooked, and the leaves are blown open by the winds, so that it is difficult to put them down into a smooth and compact bulk. Nevertheless, rehanging is the only safe way to treat stripped tobacco too soft to be put down in bulk.

For bulking heavy tobacco the desired condition is evidenced by softness and pliability of leaf, the stem only moderately flexible. The texture and fiber should be supple, without excess of moisture, while the stem for one-third or one-half its length should crack slightly in bending. Much care is necessary to secure the right condition for bulking to prevent sweating into a harsh and dry state, which greatly injures the tobacco, and, on the other hand, to avoid mold or "funking", liable to occur when the bundles are packed down too damp.

With light types of tobacco, especially such as are intended for manufacturing fillers, it is requisite that the order should be such as to secure perfect immunity from injury in sweating. Such tobacco is not suitable for use until fermentation has taken place, and is unfit for use if soured or funked in passing through that process. Very few planters attempt the process of sweating in bulk, but prefer to sell the loose tobacco or to prize lightly in casks for delivery to local dealers, who redry it during the spring and summer, putting it in such condition and form as to pass through the necessary fermentation without loss.

The lighter types, because of the necessity for rehandling, are not, as a general thing, so carefully ordered as the heavy tobaccos, and are not usually so neatly handled in tying into bundles or in packing into casks or cases For the most part, this class of tobacco is sold to dealers who make a business of reassorting and repacking for home manufacturers. In the production of bright wrappers, however, the handling is very careful, the work of assorting very thorough, and the tying and packing is neatly done.

In the assorting of yellow tobacco in the Paducah district about five grades are usually made: First, a uniform bright yellow, leaves perfect and elastic; second, color not so uniform, and leaves not so perfect and elastic; third, mahogany color, yellow and brown spots, making a dappled surface; fourth, imperfect leaves of various colors, from bright yellow to mahogany, called good lugs; fifth, trashy and dirty lugs, composed of sun-parched, soiled ground leaves.

It is the custom of a large class of planters in all districts of the state to hasten the preparation of their crops for market. These crops are sold in bulk to local dealers, or are packed and shipped to the nearer markets, frequently in poor condition, without having passed through the necessary process of bulking to produce the smoothness and compactness essential for neat packing into casks for prizing. This stock is bought to a large extent by rehandlers. The proportion of the annual product disposed of in this way probably exceeds one-half, and much the larger part of this is sold and delivered from the 1st of December to the 1st of April. Of the remainder of the product, which is prized by the planters themselves, fully one-half is sold by the 1st of May, commencing as early as the 1st of January.

A few planters take pride in skillful handling. They assort closely and carefully, and give special attention to stripping, bulking, and prizing. Prizing is generally postponed until spring, to secure proper atmospheric humidity, with mild temperature.

The casks used are from 56 to 60 inches in length by 40 to 42 inches across the head, and cost, including the lumber for heads and nails for fastening, $2 50 to $2 75 each. Of heavy tobacco, 1,400 to 1,650 pounds of leaf and 1,600 to 2,000 pounds of inferior grades are packed in each cask. The prizing is so managed that the bundles of tobacco will open loosely and freely when taken out of the package. Different grades are, as far as possible, put into separate casks.

Lighter types, suitable for manufacturing fillers, are prized in the same way as the heavy tobacco, but are not so heavily pressed, from 1,000 to 1,400 pounds being put into a cask of the dimensions above given. Bright wrappers are packed in smaller casks and pressed lightly, the net weight varying from 500 to 700 pounds.

The presses used in prizing are mostly such as are known as "beam prizes", consisting of a single stout wooden lever or a combination of two or more levers, somewhat clumsy and slow of operation, but very effective, and of moderate cost. These presses are usually built upon the farm, and of home material, and may be estimated to cost from $25 to $40 each. Local dealers in tobacco use screw-presses mostly, because of the economy of space and convenience and rapidity of operation. These presses cost from $50 to $75 each.

In the Paducah district fully three-fourths of the crop prized by the planters is marketed from the middle of April to the middle of June. That sold loose from wagons to dealers is delivered during the winter months, when it is often in unfit condition to be put into hogsheads, and, as estimated, forms about one-third of the whole product of the district. Paducah and Mayfield are the principal markets. The former city, beside the Kentucky product, receives a considerable amount of tobacco from western Tennessee, Arkansas, and the lower counties of southeastern Missouri. From Missouri and Arkansas the receipts are about 100 hogsheads annually. When placed upon the market, a sample, consisting of several bundles, is drawn from the cask, in accordance with legal requirements, and this sample is properly labeled, so as to identify it with the package from which it is taken, and the contents of which it must fairly represent. The package of tobacco is sold by sample to the highest bidder, the planter reserving the right to accept or reject the price thus offered.

The larger part of the product of the Ohio River district is sold to local dealers. The loose leaf, which goes into the hands of local dealers and prizers, is sold by them in the Hopkinsville, Clarksville, Paducah, and Louisville markets, and a small portion is shipped direct to New York. That portion of the product stemmed into strips is always shipped direct to England, and the redried leaf is sold mostly in American markets, a small part going to England. The crop is thus distributed according to its adaptation to various uses, foreign or domestic.

In the Lower Green River district much the larger part of the crop is sold in bulk to stemmers and redriers at Owensboro', Henderson, and other places of minor importance. These two towns are the largest markets in the West for the sale of tobacco in bulk. Tobacco is usually carried to these towns on wagons. Samples are drawn by dealers from each load, so as to represent the grades of which the load is made up, and the price is fixed according to the quality of the sample, the highest offer, of course, determining the sale. In some cases crops are sold to the agents of factories, who are sent out into the country to buy the product of the more important plantations.

At Henderson there are 17 factories, most of them of large capacity, employing a total of 700 laborers, and making an aggregate of 6,000 hogsheads of strips annually. These factories require from 10,000,000 to 11,000,000 pounds of tobacco every year to employ them to their full capacity. At Owensboro' there are about 20 factories, using about 10,000,000 pounds of tobacco annually; and at several other points in this district are factories regularly engaged in buying tobacco in bulk from the producers, making it into strips or redrying the leaf for the English markets.

Strips, as removed from the stem, are tied together in large bunches and hung on sticks about 4 feet in length, which are placed in tiers in drying-rooms for drying out and reordering. They are rarely taken down and put in bulk before the 1st of June, when no mistake can be made as to their exact degree of humidity. From and after this date they are taken down in a very dry condition, barely moist or pliable enough to prevent injury in handling and prizing, and put into bulks, from which they are packed and prized in casks, 1,200 to 1,300 pounds in each. Strips are always packed into casks, with the leaves loose from each other, the ties on the bundles being first removed. From November until June the employés are busy in stemming and ordering the stock, and during the remainder of the season they are employed in getting the tobacco into bulk and prizing into casks.

At Henderson the average yield of strips from 100 pounds of leaf is 68 pounds; at Owensboro' it is estimated at 66 pounds. The difference is because of the heavier class of tobacco stemmed at the former place. The loss in weight includes the weight of the stems removed, in addition to an average loss of 10 per cent. by difference of order when received from the planter and when in proper condition for prizing for export.

Redrying leaf is done in the same manner as with strips. Almost always the bundles as tied by the planters are ordered, redried, and packed without other rehandling. Some large factories are exclusively employed in redrying leaf for use in domestic manufacture.

Strips are annually shipped direct to English markets, being very rarely offered for sale in America. The strips of this district will absorb 15 to 33 per cent. of moisture and flavoring matters in process of manufacture. Redried leaf is shipped to some extent direct to England; but a large part of it is taken in American markets for domestic manufacture, for which purpose it may be prized to weigh 1,400 to 1,600 pounds net.

A large number of local dealers throughout the Lower Green River district make a business of purchasing tobacco from the planters, prizing it into casks or otherwise packing it in the same condition as received from the planter, and shipping or hauling it to interior distributing markets, either to Hopkinsville, Clarksville, or the Ohio River towns.

Probably 75 per cent. of the crop of this district is sold in bulk, and is marketed and delivered from November to May, the time for marketing the entire crop extending from November until the 1st of October following.

Of the product of the Green River district fully three-fourths is sold to local dealers, who receive it in bulk, and most of it is delivered between the 1st of December and the 1st of April. The dealer buys the tobacco under contract for delivery in a specified state of preparation and order. Much of the crop being delivered in such poor condition as greatly to reduce its value, many of the local tobacco-buyers have houses constructed for the purpose of rehandling it, and some of them attempt to utilize ordinary barns, constructed for curing, but not suited for rehandling the stock. Some of these local dealers make a business of purchasing and redrying such kinds of tobacco as are required for certain classes of domestic manufacture, in which enterprise they have been quite successful. The crop of this district goes mostly to the Louisville market, a small part of it direct to New York, and a few shipments for sale are made at Evansville, Indiana.

The crop of the Upper Green River district is marketed almost entirely at Louisville, occasional shipments being made direct to New York. The system of railway transportation, which reaches nearly every portion of this district, having Louisville as a common terminus, gives that city permanent advantages in the control of the product of this territory. Freight charges are moderate, shipments can be made at any time, and tobacco delivered at Louisville can be sampled and sold during any business day of the year. The charges at Louisville are 50 cents drayage on each cask from the railway depots to the warehouse; $2 per cask and 1 per cent. on its gross proceeds for receiving, inspecting, and selling, with a privilege of four months' storage free of charge to the shipper.

In the Clarksville district the crop is marketed from December to September following, the larger part being delivered and sold from April to July. From the middle of April to the middle of July is the period of fermentation, during which time tobacco handles and shows to the very best advantage if in proper condition. A small part of the crop is sold to stemmers in bulk, and is made into strips for the English markets, and a considerable quantity is sold to local dealers, who reassort the leaf and prize it for sale in some of the interior markets, as Clarksville, Hopkinsville, or Louisville. The larger part of the crop is prized by the planters themselves, and is shipped and sold for their own account. Casks 58 by 40 or 60 by 42 inches cost about $2 50 each, and are prized to contain 1,500 to 1,700 pounds of the better, and 1,600 to 2,000 pounds of the inferior, grades of tobacco. The product of this district is sold mostly at Clarksville and Hopkinsville under similar regulations to those prevailing elsewhere in the state. At Clarksville the charges to the shipper for selling are $2 10 on each cask and 1 per cent. commission on gross proceeds; in Hopkinsville, $2 50 on each cask and 1 per cent. commission. A small part of the crop is shipped to Louisville for sale, and a few shipments are made to New York direct.

As the product of this district is mostly taken for export, and is sold in foreign markets in the original packages, the handling and ordering are much more careful and thorough than with the product of lighter body in other districts, much of which is, of necessity, rehandled to put it in marketable condition. The leaves are carefully assorted into two, three, or four uniform grades, tied into small and neat hands, properly conditioned by hanging up in tiers or by placing in windrows, where it is allowed to remain until brought into the desired order, and then packed smooth and straight into close bulks, from which, at the proper time, it is packed into casks and prized. The right condition for bulking or packing is obtained when the body of the leaf is soft and pliable and the stem supple, but solid and firm for one-half of its length. If the stem be soft from moisture contained in it, the soundness of the tobacco, either in bulk or in the cask, is much endangered by excessive fermentation.

In cold, wet seasons the order or condition is very uncertain, and cannot be relied on, as the leaf does not show the full amount of contained moisture, and if packed at such time will become soft and overdamp when the temperature becomes warmer. It is almost equally objectionable to have the leaf too dry, as this prevents smooth and neat handling and close packing, and it is apt to become harsh, stiff, and rough after fermentation. Bulking and packing can be safely done only when the atmosphere is warm and soft enough to produce pliancy of leaf without excess of humidity. It is desirable that the tobacco shall not contain moisture enough to affect its keeping qualities, and shall yet retain enough to sweat it into a soft and supple condition. The work of assorting and stripping is done in winter; that of ordering and bulking during the winter, but mostly in spring; and that of packing and prizing into casks during spring and early summer.

The Cumberland River district lies chiefly on either side of the river from which it takes its name. This river is the principal means of transportation, and is navigable only for short seasons during the year. It is an object, therefore, with producers to hasten the preparation of their crops for market, in order to avail themselves of the earliest opportunities for shipment. The produce of the western portion of this district is hauled in wagons to a branch of the Louisville and Nashville railway which terminates at Glasgow, and a small amount is delivered at one or more points on the main line of the railway. The lack of reliable and cheap transportation imposes a heavy tax upon the producer in getting his tobacco to market. A large part of the crop of the district is sold to local dealers, the amount thus disposed of being estimated at from one-half to two-thirds of the whole. No stemming is done, and the entire product is marketed at Louisville and Nashville

THE WHITE BURLEY DISTRICT.

This district occupies a territory embracing, in whole or in part, twenty-four counties in the northern part of the state. If a straight line should be drawn from Louisville to Paris, in Bourbon county, and thence to Portsmouth, on the Ohio, it would form nearly the southern boundary of the White Burley district of Kentucky, while the other boundaries would be limited by the Ohio river. It embraces about 3,000 square miles, and is traversed by the Kentucky and the Licking rivers, both of which are navigable for small steamboats for some months every year. The tributaries of these rivers ramify into almost every square mile of the district.

PHYSICAL FEATURES.

No part of Kentucky has a more diversified surface than that embraced within the district under consideration. Probably it would be within limits to say that in the White Burley district one-third of the territory is level or slightly undulating, one-third broken, and the remainder knobby and often very rough. Passing through the center from north to south is a lofty elevation, known as Dry ridge, along whose crest for many miles the Cincinnati Southern railroad passes. From this backbone, easterly and westerly, numerous spurs shoot out. Between Dry ridge and the southeastern limits of the district one deep, bifurcated trough occurs, forming the water-sheds of the south fork and the main stream of the Licking river. East of that river the surface becomes more elevated, until it culminates in the rugged heights of the eastern coal-field of Kentucky. West of Dry ridge the basin of the Kentucky river occurs, about midway between the ridge and the western limits of the district on the Ohio river. From Dry ridge to the Kentucky river the general slope of the surface is toward the northwest, but west of that river the slope is more decidedly north, though in Oldham and Trimble counties the longest slope is toward the west. The whole White Burley district may be described as a table-land, gashed by numerous streams. The ease with which the rocks are crumbled by natural forces, though giving an uneven surface to the country, assures a high degree of productiveness wherever the constituent elements of the rocks possess the basis of fertility.

GEOLOGICAL FORMATIONS AND SOILS.

With few exceptions, all of the rocky formations of this district belong to the Lower Silurian age, and, for the most part, the rocky beds lie in a position so nearly horizontal that over broad districts no dip is perceptible. The soils vary greatly in fertility, those derived from the marly calcareous limestones, characterized by the presence of fossil shells and of arenaceous material, being generally the most fertile and friable. When the limestones contain a large proportion of magnesia, the soils are arid; when of argillaceous matter, wet and cold. Owing to the unevenness of the surface of the country and the generally horizontal position of the strata every bed in a vertical range of probably 800 feet is brought to the surface. In the eastern portions of Lewis and Fleming counties the stiff soils of the Devonian shales appear; below them the brownish-red soils, derived from the magnesian limestones of the Upper Silurian, which in turn are succeeded, in going west, by the rich, black, fertile loams that rest upon the marly limestones of the Lower Silurian. In many counties of the district, notably in Scott, Owen, Gallatin, Carroll, Grant, and Boone, the rocks that give character to a considerable area are different varieties of a peculiar earthy siliceous "mudstone", interstratified in the blue limestone formations. The aggregate of these varieties of "mudstone" or "rotten sandstone" are said to have a thickness of 100 feet. The elevation of this bed above the Ohio river is from 200 to 300 feet, and the color of the layers is buff or a dirty yellow. They contain a small percentage of lime and a large percentage of sulphuric acid and silica. From some of the members of this bed a cold, wet beech land is derived. On well-drained slopes the soil from this "mudstone" is much better, and supports a growth of hickory, oak, tulip-tree, sugar-tree, and some walnut and hackberry. Above and below the "mudstone" the soils are more productive, being derived from the blue limestones, which are rich in mineral fertilizers.

The following analysis of the best soil in the blue-grass region was made for the geological survey of Kentucky by Dr. Robert Peter:

Organic and volatile matters	7.771
Alumina and oxides of iron and manganese	12.961
Carbonate of lime	2.464
Magnesia	0.173
Phosphoric acid	0.319
Sulphuric acid	0.170
Potash	0.393
Soda	0.130
Sand and insoluble silicates	75.266
	99.647
Moisture driven off at 300°	4.700

ANALYSIS OF A SUBSOIL.

Organic and volatile matter	6.450
Alumina and oxides of iron and manganese	13.773
Carbonate of lime	3.476
Magnesia	0.354
Phosphoric acid	0.447
Sulphuric acid	0.032
Potash	0.498
Soda	0.095
Sand and insoluble silicates	75.434

It is the universal belief among the farmers of this region that when a field fails to produce a good crop of corn or tobacco it is only necessary to seed it in blue grass and let it remain for four or five years, that all its pristine fertility may be restored. Only one or two of the schedules received from this region mention the practice of manuring. The very great fertility of these limestone soils is attributed by Dr. Peter, of the geological survey:

1. To its state of extreme division. The very fine sand will pass through the finest bolting cloth of 5,000 apertures to the square inch, leaving 0.04 of 1 per cent. of quartzy grains not as large as a mustard-seed.

2. Its large proportion of phosphates and the alkalies.

3. The great amount of organic matter which it contains. This gives a dark color to the surface soil, which increases its power to absorb and retain heat, and also gives it such porosity that it will retain a large amount of moisture. Heat and moisture, combined with the large proportion of the most essential elements of plant food and the excellent mechanical condition of the soil, make it among the most productive and desirable soils in the United States.

WHITE BURLEY TOBACCO.

Mention is made in the chapter on Ohio of the origin of the variety of the tobacco plant known as the White Burley. It is believed that fully four-fifths of the plug tobacco used in the east, north, and west is made from this variety, and its introduction and culture has worked one of the most remarkable revolutions known to the agriculture of this country.

Within the last ten years the whole of what is now called the White Burley district has abandoned every other variety. This tobacco is porous, but of fine texture, is almost destitute of gum, and cures up a remarkably uniform bright or yellowish-red color, varying from bright yellow to bright red and cinnamon.

At first the White Burley was planted closely, the rows being 3 feet apart, and the plants set in the rows from 1½ to 2 feet apart, and it was topped from eighteen to twenty leaves. This was done to give thinness to the leaf and to adapt it more fully to making cutting tobacco. In 1868 the manufacturers of cutting tobacco rejected the White Burley on account of its bright color, and in 1871 and 1872 the production was very limited. Toward the close of the latter year Spaulding & Merrick, of Chicago, determined to establish a brand of cutting tobacco made from this peculiar type. This they did, and successfully competed with all other brands on the market, and there sprang up at once an active demand for the White Burley from all the cutting trade.

Cutters now prefer about one-third of the heavier sorts and two-thirds of the lighter kinds. The heavier sorts are used in manufacturing plug and navy, and to some extent for bright smokers, and the lower and medium grades, when prices will justify, are taken in small quantity for export to Germany. The medium grades are also in demand for making brown roll in England and for making bright-cutting strips, but nine-tenths of the whole product is consumed in the United States.

The crop of 1875 was noted for its excellent cutting qualities, and was larger by 25 per cent. than that of the preceding year, which latter crop was readily taken at good prices. The crop of 1876 was about 12 per cent. greater than that of 1875. The high prices stimulated the planters to a more careful culture and a more extended planting, and the crop of 1876, in consequence of this unusual culture, had a heavier leaf and larger absorbing qualities. This especially fitted it for the plug manufacturer, and experiments which had been made showed it to be suitable for making very popular brands of chewing-tobacco. Orders came in from New York, Richmond, Petersburg, Lynchburg, Chicago, and other points so rapidly that the prices of the heavier grades were relatively advanced, and the attention of growers of the White Burley was, after this period, directed to the production of a heavier type than the cutting leaf, to meet the constantly-growing demand of the plug manufacturers. Since 1877 what was believed to be exceptional in 1876 has become the standard type. The consequence is that, while all shipping styles of tobacco have been dull or depressed, the leaf tobacco of the White Burley district has commanded prices double, and sometimes quadruple, those paid for the best shipping leaf produced in other regions of the state. Nor is the profit confined to the increased prices received for the White Burley tobacco. The labor necessary for making this variety is much less than that demanded for the export tobacco, and the risk of curing, by not using fire, is reduced to the minimum. The farmers living in the northern part of the state raise the same product as those in the southern and western parts, and receive from two to three times the remuneration for labor expended; yet all these cultivate soils that do not differ materially in fertility and capacity of production, nor in accessibility to good markets.

COMPARISON OF TOBACCO CROPS.

The crop of 1877 was 21 per cent. less than that of 1876, but showed a marked improvement in quality; and the product of 1878 was nearly equal in amount to that of 1877, with still further improvement. The crops of these two years were the best that were ever raised in the district, that of the latter year ranking highest. Both crops were well ripened, free from the effects of disease, and commanded very high prices. Stimulated by these high prices, the product of 1879 was the largest in acreage and in yield of any crop ever grown in the district; the boundaries were extended, unusual attention was given to preparations for the crop, and the quality of the product, up to the time of housing, was equal to that of any previous year. Unfortunately, however, the crowded condition of the barns, consequent upon the large crop and the very warm weather which set in about the 1st of October, caused at least 10 per cent. to be greatly damaged by house-burn. Superadded to this calamity, the supervening mild weather, with much rain, produced a barn-mold, which in its effects was almost as damaging as house burn. With good, close barns much of this damage could have been avoided; but the hurry and rush of many farmers to plant out a crop, taking the risk of curing it in temporary structures, resulted in very serious injury to the tobacco. A great deal of it was cured in rail pens and open barns, with no means of protection against the fogs and beating rains, and the result was that, notwithstanding the large crop planted and well harvested, there was less good, sound tobacco on the market than in the previous year. Prices ruled very high for the first half of the year, and only showed a decline when the fact was well established by the middle of June, 1880, that another very large crop was planted. Bright lugs advanced during the commercial year in Cincinnati from 5 to 7½ cents, at the commencement of the season, to 6 to 10 cents, and bright fillers from 11 to 15 cents to 14 to 20 cents.

The White Burley, while growing, has a pale-green or greenish-white color, and the leaves grow closely on the stalk; consequently a plant having the same number of leaves is not so tall as those of many other varieties. It is very delicate when young, is more sensitive to the heat of the sun or continued wet than any other kind, and is not a favorite variety with the less careful cultivators because of this tenderness of constitution, which causes it to perish easily when transplanted. A stand is therefore difficult to obtain. Two weeks are generally required for it to become established after transplanting, but when it begins to grow it outstrips the other varieties, and is ready for harvesting two weeks earlier than any other variety planted at the same time. Originating from the Red Burley by cross-fertilization, there is a very decided tendency to revert to the original type. The first years after it originated the White Burley, after curing, was silky, fine, and light-bodied, with a yellow color on the upper surface and white beneath. It grows thicker and less delicate every year, and it is believed that the retroversion to its original type will in a few more years be complete.

In the White Burley district there are two distinct classes of tobacco grown. In the counties of Owen, Franklin, Henry, Oldham, Scott, and Trimble cutting tobacco, or what may be used for cutting purposes, is grown almost exclusively. The counties of Boone, Kenton, Gallatin, Grant, Campbell, Pendleton, Harrison, Bracken, Robertson, Nicholas, Mason, Lewis, and parts of others make a heavier article, used for fillers mainly, but some cutting leaf. The tobacco grown in the last-named counties has more gum than that grown in Owen and the surrounding counties, which is light, thin, and chaffy. Unquestionably the soil has a powerful influence upon the quality. All the returns concur in this. One from Owen county says:

> An open soil will produce a quick growth, which is essential in making a porous product. Slow growth insures a hard, compact quality, of dark color. Eastern or southeastern slopes produce the best quality of tobacco. Ridge lands and lands sloping to the west induce a slow growth, and are therefore not so desirable.

Another schedule, which applies to the whole district, says:

> On newly-cleared lands a lighter-colored tobacco is grown, which makes a fine cutting leaf. Old lands make fillers, sometimes wrappers, mahogany in color, rich, and oily. Second year's land (that is, land which has only been cultivated one year) makes a cherry-red tobacco, suitable for fillers.

A correspondent from Robertson county says:

> Strong, loamy soils do not produce so fine a quality of tobacco as white-oak and sugar-tree clay.

One from Carroll county says:

> On freshly-cleared lands the tobacco will cure a better color, but light in body and better adapted for cutting purposes, making, however, few pounds per acre. Old lands grow tobacco of better body, less color, more useful for plug fillers, and with more pounds per acre.

Another schedule from Owen county says:

> On new lands tobacco grows very thin, light, and bright; on second year's land it is heavier, with more body, and the quality more useful. On old sod land the tobacco is still heavier, is red in color, and is better adapted to the use of the manufacturer of plug and for export.

Precisely the same statement comes from Kenton county. Fleming county, which probably has a greater variety of soils than any other county in the district, reports:

> Rich, sandy soils produce the finest quality of tobacco; black loam grows the heaviest and darkest in color; white-oak lands the lightest and highest-priced qualities, used both for wrappers and for making fine-cut.

Mason county, which has been celebrated for fifty years for the delicacy and fineness of its tobacco, reports:

Oak lands produce the finest quality, commanding the highest prices, especially that raised on fresh or newly-cleared lands. By "finest quality" is meant a product showing great silkiness of leaf, brightness of color, exceedingly soft to the feel, smooth, lustrous, and elastic, fine in grain and texture. This style of tobacco will bring $5 per hundred more than that grown on beech lands.

One schedule from Bracken county says:

On new or fresh lands the color is brighter, but the product is not so heavy as on old, strong lands. It cures up a rich, golden color, while that grown on old land is red in color, but with better body. The soil being the same, that grown on southern hillsides is finer and cures up brighter in color.

All the other counties in the district report substantially the same in relation to influences of soil upon quality.

GRADES OF PRODUCT.

These vary greatly in the different counties of the district. The following table will show the proportion of different grades as reported from the typical counties:

Counties.	Dark Shipping.	Fillers.	Bright smokers and wrappers.	Cutting.	Nondescript.
	Per cent.	*Per cent.*	*Per cent.*	*Per cent.*	*Per cent.*
Boone	10.00	20.00	30.00	40.00	....
Bracken	12.50	25.00	25.00	25.00	12.50
Carroll	....	33.00	17.00	50.00	....
Fleming	30.00	30.00	15.00	15.00	10.00
Henry	....	20.00	30.00	40.00	10.00
Mason	....	33.33	33.33	33.33	....
Owen	....	20.00	10.00	60.00	10.00
Pendleton	....	20.00	5.00	60.00	15.00
Robertson	25.00	33.33	16.66	20.00	5.00

Taking the average of the whole district, and the proportion would be about as follows: Dark shipping, 10 per cent.; fillers, 30 per cent.; bright smokers and wrappers, 20 per cent.; cutting, 35 per cent.; nondescript, 5 per cent. The scarcity of the latter grade is due to the fact that the colors of the White Burley are exceedingly uniform, and the inferior grades are put in the smoking grade. The only nondescript in the district comes from the attempt to grow White Burley upon soils unsuited for it, and the product from such soils is known in the market as Bastard Burley, and is deficient in color and other desirable qualities. Much of this, however, is used for plug fillers.

SOILS BEST SUITED FOR WHITE BURLEY TOBACCO.

It is considered by all correspondents that the finest tobacco is grown upon rolling lands, with a good clay subsoil and a timber growth of hickory, white oak, tulip-tree, beech, walnut, hackberry, black locust, and ash. Wherever the white-oak tree grows in any quantity the soil is called oak soil. While a few planters prefer old land, because the yield is much larger, a large majority prefer freshly-cleared oak lands upon the southern and eastern sides of hills. On the undulating lands, where the soil is derived from the crumbling of the highly calcareous, sandy, blue limestones, and where blue grass has formed a sod for many years, a very useful quality of tobacco is produced for manufacturing purposes, and these are preferred next to the freshly-cleared oak lands. All the soils of the district have more or less imbedded gravel. One correspondent says: "For quality, oak lands; for quantity, fat, rich, calcareous soils, with a mixture of walnut and burr oak." The soils preferred vary somewhat in different counties. In Owen county, for example, the soils are classified in the order of preference as Nos. 1, 2, and 3. No. 1 supports a growth of sugar-tree, beech, tulip-tree, hackberry, and white walnut. This approximates the typical blue-grass soil. No. 2 has a growth of white oak and other associate trees, and has more clay in its composition, is not so fertile, does not yield so many pounds per acre as No. 1, but makes a good, rich-colored tobacco. No. 3 has a tree-covering of ash, locust, tulip-tree, and some others. The soil resembles river and creek bottoms, and, like the latter, grows a coarse, rough, bony tobacco, used more for plug than for cutting. The eastern exposure in newly-cleared lands always makes the most salable tobacco. Level lands grow tobacco much like that grown on river bottoms, coarse and harsh, but leafy.

The soils in nearly every part of the district are very durable. When apparently worn out and exhausted, if turned out, and a sufficient time is allowed to permit fresh assimilable elements to be unlocked by disintegration from the underlying shales and limestones, they become as fertile as ever.

It is thought that in quality tobacco has improved fully 25 per cent. within the past decade. Even the tendency of the White Burley to revert to the characteristics of its parentage, of which mention has been made, and which by some is called a deterioration, has been to the advantage of the planters, and a most extraordinary demand has been created for the product of the reverting variety. It approaches the true ideal of a filler. The color is good; it has large drinking capacity; is mild in its effects; has a delicate flavor and good body, and is popular with consumers. Ten years ago a very inconsiderable portion of the tobacco of this district went into plug; now fully one-half of it is worked into plug and smokers for domestic use.

FERTILIZATION OF TOBACCO.

In no other district in the United States, not even in the rich tobacco districts of Missouri, is manuring neglected so much. This is accounted for in part by one correspondent, who says that tobacco is either planted upon freshly-cleared lands, where no manure is thought to be necessary, or upon old sod land, which is found to produce excellent tobacco without any fertilization. In Bracken county a very small amount of land plaster is sometimes put in the hill. In Kenton county one-tenth of the tobacco area is estimated to be fertilized. Bone dust is used sparingly by a few farmers, and stable manure at a cost of from $5 to $10 per acre. Lewis county reports that about 33 per cent. of the tobacco land has an application of stable manure. A small number of farmers in Owen county apply a special fertilizer, known as "tobacco-plant food", to the hill after planting, and about 150 pounds to the acre are used, at a cost of $3. Barn-yard manure is now used in Robertson county to a very limited extent. The remaining counties report no fertilizers used, though all admit that well-manured soils will increase the yield from 33 to 50 per cent., beside greatly improving the quality of tobacco produced.

PREPARATION OF THE SOIL FOR TOBACCO.

Old sod land is usually broken in the fall or early spring to the depth of about 6 inches and allowed to remain until about the 1st of May, by which time the sod will be thoroughly rotted. It is afterward well harrowed and pulverized and laid off for planting. The most approved plan now is to lay off the rows 3½ feet apart and make small hills in the row from 2 to 3 feet apart. Some prefer a shorter distance for the hills in the rows, under the impression that the shorter the distance to within a foot and a half the smaller will be the stems and fibers. Others aim to produce tobacco of a little heavier body, that may be used either as a heavy cutter or as a bright filler, or even as a heavy filler. To do this the distance is increased between plants. Some few, on old manured lands, go as far as 4 feet for the distance of the rows apart, with hills 3 feet apart in the rows. The distance apart of the plants is probably a less important factor than high or low topping in the determination of special types, and much less than the character of the soil upon which the plant grows.

It is claimed by some good planters that a silkier article of tobacco may be made by cultivating the sod land the first year in corn, following the corn with tobacco. The usual rotation is tobacco, wheat or corn, clover or blue grass, and then tobacco again after two years of clover and several years of blue grass.

The cultivation of the crop is the same as in other districts, and is much better now than before the introduction of the White Burley, for it was a general belief that working the soil well made the Red Burley coarse and rendered it unfit for cutting purposes. The result of better working has been largely to increase the yield of the crop. This is usually plowed three times and hoed once.

Planted usually between the 15th of May and the 1st of July, the topping is done between the 10th of July and the middle of August, and the harvesting from the 20th of August to the 10th of October. The plant is not pruned, and in this the practice is different from that of any other district in the state. From twelve to sixteen leaves are left to the plant. Some farmers top as high as twenty leaves, but it is found that the leaves are not so large nor so uniform in size and color, nor is the cured product of such desirable quality. It is thought also that a larger number of pounds can be made by topping to twelve leaves than by topping to twenty.

Tobacco in this district is usually suckered two or more times before it ripens. The period between topping and harvesting varies upon different soils, and by reason of high and low topping, and the prevalence of wet or dry weather for from four to seven weeks, the earliest maturity takes place on warm southern exposures, upon a quick black or brown limestone soil. Northern exposures, clayey soils, wet weather, as well as high topping, all delay the period of ripening, but the average length of time between topping and cutting may generally be put at four weeks.

HARVESTING OF TOBACCO.

When fully ripe, the plants are cut with a knife by splitting the stalk, as in the other districts of the state, the time preferred for this operation being the afternoon. A method of cutting and hanging prevails to some extent in Bracken county which is unusual. Each cutter takes three rows, and as each plant is severed it is straddled over a stick set up in the ground in the center of the space occupied by six plants, this number being allotted to each stick. In this way the plants are cut and hung without being laid upon the ground. This saves time, and secures neatness in handling. These sticks, 4½ feet long, with their loads of tobacco, are either taken directly to the barns and hung 12 inches apart on the tier poles, or are placed upon scaffolds erected with poles in the open fields or in the angles of a worm fence. About two-thirds of the farmers scaffold their tobacco. The sticks are allowed to remain from five to eight days on the scaffolds, and are then taken to the barns and arranged on tier poles 8 inches apart. It will be observed that one-third of the space in the barns is saved by scaffolding, and, beside, it is thought that tobacco is not only sweeter by taking the sun for a few days, but that the danger from house-burn is much decreased. But tobacco should never be scaffolded in rainy weather. If freshly cut, the leaves get in a condition known as a "strut", and are easily injured in that condition in consequence of their exceeding tenderness. Scaffolds are also liable to give way in wet weather and precipitate the tobacco in a compact mass to the ground, by which it is bruised and broken, and if it is not taken up at once it is liable to heat and coddle in the mass, which is as destructive as the action of frost. When well wilted, and before the leaves begin to turn brown, rain will do no injury.

CURING OF TOBACCO.

No fire is used in curing White Burley tobacco. About eight weeks are required to cure it well by the ordinary process of air-curing when put into the barns, which are provided with ample facilities for ventilation. The openings are not closed day or night, unless there is an excess of wet weather, when the doors are closed. Too much dry weather during the process of curing injures the tobacco by decreasing the elasticity and the toughness of the leaf and destroying the uniformity in color, making the leaves mottled. An old grower says:

> If the weather is very dry, it will be changeable in color; if too wet, the color will be too dark; but after cutting, if the weather is fine, with occasional showers, the tobacco will cure a beautiful bright color.

ASSORTING AND STRIPPING OF TOBACCO.

The tobacco being fully cured, it is taken down when in proper condition and assorted into four or five grades, as follows, beginning at the bottom of the stalk and going upward to the top:

1. The sand leaves, trash, or flyings. This grade is made up of the soiled and parched leaves, varying in number from one to three.
2. Good trash or lugs, taken next above the ground leaves, varying in number from two to three leaves.
3. Bright and prime leaves, taken from the central part of the stalk, in number from four to six.
4. Tips, or top leaves, red, in number from one to three.

Two classes of "reds" are sometimes made, known as first and second reds.

Some planters only make three classes, trash, lugs, and good; the first being the ground leaves, the second the imperfect leaves, and the third the bright middle and top leaves. If the tobacco is topped low, there is great uniformity in color and length of all the leaves near the top; but if topped high, the upper leaves are small and imperfectly developed.

These several grades are tied into bundles of ten to twelve leaves each, rehung upon sticks, and crowded upon the tier poles until damp, warm weather supervenes, which is most favorable for ordering. The sticks are then given greater distance, and when the leaves become sufficiently pliant to handle without breaking the tobacco is taken down, bulked, and weighed, each grade being kept separate. In this condition probably nine-tenths of all the tobacco grown in the district is sold to local dealers, who receive it in houses prepared for prizing, and pack from 700 to 1,100 pounds for fine grades, and from 1,200 to 1,800 pounds for trash and lugs, in each cask. These casks are by no means uniform in size. Some of them are 5 feet high and 48 inches in diameter; others 5 feet high and 42 inches in diameter; and again others are 56 inches high and 48 inches in diameter. Local dealers buy at all times, from the period when the crop can first be examined after curing until the following May or June. It is estimated that the cost of prizing, shipping, and selling the crop, including the cost of hogsheads, will amount to $2 per hundred pounds. This also includes shrinkage in the weight of the tobacco from the time it goes out of the planter's hands until it reaches the market where it is inspected and sold. This shrinkage is estimated to vary from 3 to 8 per cent., and if permitted to go through the sweat before being sold 5 per cent. more must be added.

A crop that has been properly cultivated, kept free from worms, neatly and carefully handled, well assorted into grades, tied into neat hands, artistically packed and prized into hogsheads of the weight required for each grade, will bring in the market from 33 to 50 per cent. more than one that has been grown upon similar soil and handled in a slovenly manner. There is a wide range in prices. For instance, when the crop is assorted into two grades, only 8 cents and 4 cents for the two grades may be considered a fair average price, while the same crop, if assorted into four grades, would bring 15, 12, 10, and 4 cents for each grade, respectively, of bright, red, lugs, and trash.

VALUE OF THE TOBACCO CROP OF 1879.

The following statement will show the prices received by planters in the counties named for the crop of 1879:

Counties.	Trash.	Lugs.	Red.	Bright.	Average.
Boone	$4 00	$7 00	$10 00	$12 00	$10 00
Bracken	5 00	9 00	15 00	19 00	12 00
Carroll	3 00 to 4 50	5 00 to 7 50	12 00	10 00	10 00
Fleming	5 00	7 00	9 00	14 00	10 50
Henry	5 00	6 50	8 00	12 00	10 00
Kenton	3 50 to 5 00	6 00 to 8 00	16 00	18 00	11 00
Lewis	....	....	....	....	7 00
Mason	3 00	8 00	12 00	18 00	12 00
Owen	3 00	7 00	12 00	20 00	12 00
Pendleton	....	....	....	....	10 00
Robertson	3 00 to 4 00	6 50	10 00	12 00	9 00

Sometimes tobacco is graded into smokers, cutters, fillers, and nondescript, each of these having sub-grades. The prices for such grades are: Smokers, 5 to 12 cents; cutters, 10 to 30 cents; fillers, 8 to 20 cents; nondescript, 3 to 8 cents.

The average price given in the last column of the table is the price usually paid through for the crop when bought by local dealers, and is a much fairer index of its value than the prices affixed to grades, because the quantity in each grade is exceedingly variable in the different crops. Many of the schedules give no price for grades at all. Taking the whole district through, the average price received for the crop of 1879, loose, by farmers, is not far from 10 cents per pound.

The only county in the district which makes an average yield of 1,100 pounds to the acre is Mason. The following counties make a yield averaging between 1,000 and 1,100, viz: Boone, Gallatin, and Montgomery. The counties whose average yield is between 900 and 1,000 pounds per acre are Bourbon, Carroll, Henry, Kenton, and Shelby; those making an average yield of between 800 and 900 pounds are Bracken, Fleming, Grant, Nicholas, Oldham, Owen, and Trimble; between 700 and 800 pounds, Campbell, Franklin, Harrison, Pendleton, Robertson, and Scott. Those making a yield below 700 pounds are Lewis and Woodford. Woodford county, at the time the census was taken, could not with any propriety be considered as a tobacco-growing county of the White Burley district. It really entered upon the culture of the crop in 1880.

COST OF TOBACCO PRODUCTION.

Three different detailed reports make the cost of growing the crop on best soils, respectively, $3, $3 52, and $3 60 per hundred pounds, and upon such inferior soils as are planted in tobacco $6 to $8 per hundred. One of these statements, from Owen county, is appended. One man can successfully cultivate and house, by exchanging labor, 5 acres of tobacco, which, on best soils, will yield 1,000 pounds per acre. So we have:

CR.		
By 5,000 pounds of tobacco, at 10 cents		$500 00
DR.		
To hire of hand, six months	$90 00	
To board of hand, six months, at $10	60 00	
To use of horse, plows, barns, etc	20 00	
To rent of land (interest on price)	6 00	
		176 00
Profit on each hand employed		324 00
Cost of production per pound, 3.52 cents.		

This represents the profits under the most favorable circumstances. Taking the average of the district, 876.32 pounds per acre, and assuming the expense to be the same, the profit on each hand will amount to $262 16. But this is probably not a fair estimate, as the number of acres allotted to each hand will not exceed three. One schedule from Robertson county says 4 acres to each hand is the maximum. Owen county reports the number of acres for each hand at 5, and sometimes 6, while schedules from other counties give from 2½ to 3. Assuming, then, 3 acres as the average amount of land allotted to each hand, and that the yield per acre is the average of the district, or 876.36 pounds, we shall have:

CR.		
By 2,628.96 pounds, at 10 cents		$262 91
DR.		
To hire of hand, six months	$90 00	
To board of hand, at $10 per month	60 00	
To use of horse, plows, barns, etc	20 00	
To rent of land (interest on price)	3 60	
		173 60
Profit on each hand		89 31
Cost of production, 6.6 cents.		

This is probably more nearly correct for the whole district than either of the other estimates; but there is no doubt that the profits on individual crops are often very great. Mr. J. M. Chambers reports a crop grown in Mason county, without manure, on land which has been cleared for ninety years, but upon which blue grass had grown and been depastured for many years. Upon 7 acres of this land a crop of 14,000 pounds was raised, which brought in the market an average of 12 cents per pound, or $1,680, being an average of $240 per acre. Taking the usual acreage allotted to each hand, and putting the cost of cultivation the same as in other estimates, the profit on each person employed in making this crop was $544.

The price of the best blue-grass lands ranges from $100 to $150 per acre. The very best soils, however, for tobacco in Owen, Pendleton, and other contiguous counties, may be bought at prices ranging from $20 to $50 per acre, and inferior lands at about one-half those figures, the higher prices being for lands well improved and favorably situated. Rents are very much higher in proportion than lands. An acre of good tobacco land, capable of producing 800 pounds to the acre, will readily rent for $12, while land producing 1,000 to 1,500 pounds will bring from $18 to $20 per acre.

Wages throughout the most populous portion of the district for farm hands by the year range from $10 to $15 per month and board, the former price being paid for boys from fifteen to eighteen years of age, and the latter price for well-trained men. By the day, in summer, the price paid for the same character of labor is 75 cents and $1. On the outskirts of the tobacco-growing district the price for grown men by the year is $140 and board; by the day, 75 cents. Those working "on shares" receive the same proportion of the crop as elsewhere in the southern states.

Strippers receive 75 cents per day, and packers and prizers $1. Hogsheads are worth from $1 75 to $2 25, varying according to the convenience of timber and the kind employed.

Every important county has from three to eight redrying houses, in which local dealers receive the tobacco from the planters in wagons and prize it for market. Louisville and Cincinnati are the chief markets.

The only strips made in the district are put up at Carrollton, at the mouth of the Kentucky river. Two hundred and sixty thousand pounds of White Burley were made into strips at this point, which netted 75 per cent. of strips, a much larger percentage than is made from the heavier leaf at Henderson and at Owensboro', in the Lower Green River district. A few strips from White Burley are also made at Louisville for the English trade, the quantity, however, being inconsiderable, on account of the high prices of the leaf.

The light green of the White Burley leaf, approximating the color of the horn-worm, makes the task of worming somewhat more difficult than in other portions of the state. The greatest damage sustained by the tobacco of this district, however, is from house-burn, and from the imperfect protection afforded by open barns against harsh winds and drifting rains, inducing a very injurious mold.

The extraordinary increase in the production of this type of tobacco has outstripped the means provided for its proper protection while it is curing.

Screw prizes are used by local dealers, costing generally from $50 to $100, and beam prizes, such as are described in the chapter on Tennessee, are of frequent use among planters.

Few farming districts in the United States show a more general thrift than the region under consideration. There are but few private debts, and a manifest desire has been awakened among farmers to improve their estates by the erection of better houses and barns, and to preserve the fertility of the soil by a proper rotation of crops and by more judicious cultivation.

The following statement exhibits the total product and acreage of tobacco in the White Burley district for the years 1876 to 1879, and the average yield per acre for the latter year, only those for 1879 being from census returns:

	Pounds.
Product in 1876	30,909,433
1877	24,356,870
1878	23,906,253
1879	46,862,687
Acreage, 1879	53,474
Average yield per acre, 1879	876.36

CHAPTER VIII.

CULTURE AND CURING OF TOBACCO IN LOUISIANA.

HISTORICAL NOTES.

Tobacco, rice, and indigo were the principal staple productions of Louisiana a hundred and sixty years ago. About the time of the settlement of New Orleans the "Western Company" introduced the cultivation of the plant, and some quantity was grown as early as 1718. In 1752 its culture was encouraged by the offer of the royal government of France to receive into the king's warehouse all the tobacco raised in the province at the rate of 30 livres—equal to $7—per hundred weight. The same encouragement was extended by the Spanish authorities in 1776. A greater impetus was given to its production in 1793 and 1794 in consequence of the ravages of insects upon the indigo plant, which was now abandoned for the more certain crops of sugar, rice, and tobacco. Only a limited area, however, was at that period planted in sugar-cane, and, as large capital was necessary for its production, many years passed before sugar became the distinguishing staple of the state. In the mean time the production of rice and of tobacco continued to increase. In 1802, 2,000 hogsheads of tobacco were exported from New Orleans, and its culture had become general all along the river as far up as Natchez, at least for domestic consumption.

At that early date the tobacco grown was not noted for any peculiar excellence. Cultivated upon alluvial soils, badly harvested, and cured in poorly-appointed houses, it presented a rough, bony appearance, though full of gum and highly charged with nicotine. Coming in competition, as it did from 1785, with the far better quality raised on the Ohio river, it gradually lost favor, and its production sensibly declined up to 1824.

THE FRENCH ACADIANS AND PERIQUE TOBACCO.

About this period a new process of curing was introduced by Pierre Chenet, a descendant of the Acadian French. These people, expelled in 1755 from Acadia, now Nova Scotia, adhering to their ancient customs, associating only with one another, have but few industries, and they live contented on the simplest food and with the plainest dress. They learned to cure tobacco in its own juices, as taught by Pierre Chenet, and in his honor have named the tobacco so cured *Perique*, though some claim the word to be a corruption of *peruke*, and that the peculiar method of curing was known much earlier.

WHERE THIS PECULIAR TOBACCO IS GROWN.

The cultivation of this tobacco is confined almost exclusively to the parish of Saint James, which lies about 50 miles above New Orleans, and is intersected by the Mississippi river, two-thirds of the parish being on the north and northeastern side of the river and the remainder on the south and southwestern side, the river here having a course southeast and east, and continuing in this direction several miles below New Orleans. The portion of the parish which lies east and northeast of the river is triangular in shape, with its northeastern apex resting on lake Maurepas, between which and lake Pontchartrain Pass Manchac forms a connecting link. The whole parish covers an area of about 330 square miles, and is nearly evenly divided between improved, unimproved, and swamp lands. The face of the country is level, interrupted occasionally by sloughs, bayous, and swampy lakes. Near the Mississippi river the land is more elevated, and slopes back gently for 2 or 3 miles to cypress swamps, which extend almost continuously in a line more or less parallel with the river. In the very midst of these swamps there are elevated spots, rising 4 or 5 feet above the general level. In consequence of this elevation they are well drained, and the soil is exceedingly fertile, being both calcareous and siliceous, and in its primitive state it is covered with dense canebrakes, above which tower the oak, the magnolia, the gum, and the hickory. The French and the Spanish pioneers of Louisiana were in the habit of driving their cattle to these places, during the season when other forage was scarce, to feed upon the canes, and from this circumstance they came to be known as *vacheries*, or "cattle lands". These spots are of frequent occurrence, and many of them have been cleared up and put into cultivation, one of the most noted of which is Grande Pointe. They are highly prized for their agricultural capabilities, and on them the best sugar-cane and the best tobacco are grown, their comparative freedom from the pestiferous and ineradicable coco-grass making them exceedingly valuable.

CLIMATE.

The climate of Louisiana is very mild and agreeable during the winter months, but rather oppressive in the hot months of July and August. The hot days are always relieved by heavy dews at night, thus securing vegetation, in part at least, against the parching effects of extreme dryness. The mean average temperature at Baton Rouge for twenty-eight years, from January, 1832, to December, 1860, was as follows: Spring, 68.90 degrees; summer, 81.26; autumn, 68.13; winter, 54.20; average, 68.12. According to the United States signal service the mean temperature at New Orleans from November 1, 1870, to October 31, 1880, was as follows: Spring, 69 degrees; summer, 81.8; autumn, 69.6; winter, 55.8. During this period the extreme range of the thermometer was 71 degrees, and the average range 32.

RAINFALL.

The reports of the signal service give the mean annual precipitation at New Orleans from November 1, 1870, to October 31, 1880, at 65.44 inches, and at Shreveport for the period extending from September 1, 1871, to October 31, 1880, at 49.97 inches. The mean of the prevailing winds at New Orleans for the period embraced by the observations of the signal service was southeast, and at Shreveport south.

SOILS NOW CULTIVATED IN TOBACCO.

For growing tobacco two varieties of alluvium are employed: the gray soils, which lie immediately on the eastern or northeastern bank of the Mississippi, and the magnolia soils, which occupy the gentle eminences amid the swamps, known as *vacheries*. The soil preferred for tobacco is the last, which is a dark, sandy loam, highly calcareous, easily worked, and producing a style of tobacco silky in texture, medium in size, and of a flavor superior to that grown on other soils. Black lands, mixed with yellow sand, are next in point of superiority for producing tobacco. The clayey lands, however, are said to make tobacco of greater strength, but lack the silky texture and delicate fiber. The black lands, if well drained, are excellent for tobacco, provided they have sand enough in their composition to make them friable. When there is a lack of sand, these lands compact so closely that they are difficult of tillage, and the plant does not grow with the most healthful vigor.

THE PERIQUE TOBACCO DISTRICT.

There are two principal centers in Saint James parish around which the Perique tobacco is grown and prepared for market. One of these lies immediately upon the Mississippi river, the post-village, Convent, being about the middle of the belt. On each side of this place the land is divided into small farms, each with a frontage of a few hundred feet on the river, and running back so as to embrace 10 or 12 acres. Only about 12 arpents were cultivated near Convent and 65 at Grande Pointe in 1879. A considerable quantity of the tobacco grown around Convent is used in the manufacture of cigars, but its texture and flavor are not equal to that grown on the elevated lands beyond the swamps. This is owing, no doubt, to the stiffer nature of the soil and to the hurtful influence of the coco-grass or nut-grass (*Cyperus rotundus*, var. *hydra*), which no amount of labor can destroy.

Grande Pointe, already mentioned, is famous for the excellence of its Perique tobacco. It occupies an insular position beyond the swamps, and is about 3 miles from the Mississippi river. The river in its course, after leaving Convent, runs east, which makes Grande Pointe lie to the north. The land of this *cacherie* is owned by fifteen proprietors, fourteen of whom own 12 acres each, and the remaining one about 50 acres, making in all 218 acres. A dense growth of cane and lofty trees, hanging with tufted mosses, surrounds the settlements. Red oak, cottonwood, ash, black gum, persimmon, live oak, sassafras (which is here a tree in size), and magnolia are found growing on elevations of from 3 to 5 feet above the swamps which surround the place. Cypress trees abound in the swamps and on the oozy lands which girdle the swamps.

The first settlement made at this point was in 1824. The land was divided into small holdings, and has been cultivated every year since. The amount cultivated in tobacco at present is 64 acres, or about 77 arpents—an arpent being 4,088 square yards, or nearly five-sixths of an English acre. The amount raised in this locality does not exceed 20,000 pounds in any one year; for the year 1879 it was 14,680 pounds. The whole crop of Perique tobacco grown in Louisiana is not over 48,000 pounds, that grown at Grande Pointe making usually five-twelfths of the whole; and yet the Perique tobacco is known throughout the markets of America and of Europe. About three-fourths of the product of the state is made into Perique rolls; the remainder is used in the leaf.

PECULIARITIES OF THE PERIQUE TOBACCO.

Seed from Kentucky or from Tennessee makes a tobacco too rich and too large to cure well, but if sown for several years in succession it gradually assumes the type of that grown from the native seed. The old Perique has a fine fiber, medium leaf, and small stems. It is strong, rich, gummy, tough, and dark, with a shining luster, and when taken from the presses its glossy appearance is strikingly beautiful. Because of its strength, it is largely intermixed with milder kinds and made into smoking-tobacco and cigarettes, and by those accustomed to it it is sought for chewing purposes.

GRADES OF PRODUCT.

There is a material variation in the quality of this variety of tobacco grown on different soils. When grown on a sandy loam, it has the delightful aroma so much prized, and this aroma decreases in strength as the amount of clay in the soil is increased. There are three grades into which it is made:

1. Robe, or the most perfect leaves, which are used for wrappers, constitutes 10 per cent. of the crop.
2. Good leaf, which forms the fillers for chewing-tobacco. The proportion of this grade is about 50 per cent.
3. Smokers, which amount to 40 per cent. of the crop, and are made out of the lower leaves, which are usually bespattered with dirt.

The proportion of good tobacco has decreased during the past decade, owing to the great reduction in the price of the Perique. Ten years ago a *carotte* of 4 pounds brought in the market from $5 to $10, according to the grade; but the same can now be bought for less than $2, with 64 cents deducted for tax, to which Perique tobacco, by the decision of the commissioner of internal revenue, is subject. This has had such a depressing effect that the tobacco area in the Perique region is constantly diminishing. (*a*)

DECREASE OF TOBACCO PRODUCT AND CAUSES.

The acreage of the tobacco crop of 1879, as compared with that of 1876, shows a decrease of 40 per cent.; with 1877, of 50 per cent.; with 1878, of 33 per cent. The yield per acre, however, in 1879 was greater than in 1878, but 10 per cent. less than in 1876 and 1877. The crop of 1879 had twice as much good tobacco as that of 1878, but of much the same quality as the crops of 1876–'77. While the amount produced per acre has probably been increased during the past decade, in comparison with the decade preceding, it is not managed so nicely as it was when prices were higher. At one time every leaf was brushed and cleaned, so great was the ambition of the farmers to excel; now no such pains are taken, and, as the disposition to abandon its cultivation grows stronger every year, less and less pride is taken in its manipulation.

---

a A bill (Senate 390) provided that "Perique tobacco may be sold by the manufacturer or producer thereof, in the form of *carottes*, directly to a legally qualified manufacturer, to be cut or granulated and used as material in the manufacture of cigarettes or smoking-tobacco, without the payment of tax". This passed the Senate April 6, 1882, but failed to become a law during the session.

SOILS AND MODES OF CULTIVATION.

A very small quantity of freshly-cleared land is put in tobacco, the old lands being preferred, because the soil is more easily prepared. On new lands the tobacco has larger stems and fibers; the texture is coarser, and it has a strong acrid taste. For making sweet tobacco old lands are best; for quantity, new lands. Some blood fertilizers and cotton-seed meal have been tried, but they tended to make the tobacco coarser, while the flavor was impaired. Lime, spread broadcast upon a pea fallow, increases the yield about one-fourth, but impairs the quality. If the soil is put in tobacco for several years in succession, without fertilizing with pease, no difference is perceptible in the yield for the first two years, but there is a very perceptible diminution in the quantity the third and succeeding years. The quality, however, improves in both sweetness and texture. After the third year the superior quality scarcely compensates for the loss in quantity. The yield was 25 per cent. greater per acre in 1879 than it was in 1869. It is only within the present decade that pease have been introduced and used to increase the fertility of the soil. On old land, ten years ago, sixty *carottes* of 4 pounds each was about the average yield per arpent, but with the constant use of the pea crop as a fertilizer a product of 75 *carottes* per arpent is now common. When the tobacco is taken off, in June or July, one bushel of pease is sown to the arpent, and the vines are not turned under as a green crop, but are cut and taken off for hay when the small pods begin to form. It is claimed that the pea vines shade the land during the heated term, and this improves it, leaving it mellow and loose for the succeeding crop of tobacco.

SEED-BEDS.

The soil is not burned, but is highly manured with cow-dung, which is put on 6 inches thick and turned under with a spade or a plow; after this the bed is well worked with a hoe and a rake until the soil is thoroughly pulverized. The manure is applied to this bed in October and turned under; and during the latter part of December the bed is again worked, and channels are cut through it every 3 feet, so as to secure drainage. The seed, after being mixed with ashes, is sown about the 1st of January or the last days in December, and the bed is beaten with the back of a spade or pressed by a roller. When the plants begin to appear the beds are covered with palmetto leaves, so as to protect them against the frosts of February, and when the leaves are about 2 inches in length they are drawn and transplanted in the fields, and the seed-bed is plowed and sown with pease, which remain on it until October, when preparation begins for another year. The same spot is used for five or six years in succession, and is only abandoned when the coco-grass or Bermuda grass takes complete possession of it. When the land intended for seed-beds is burned it becomes too light and porous, and the plants die out under the scorching rays of the sun.

PREPARATION OF THE SOIL AND CULTIVATION.

The tobacco soils in Louisiana are very deep, and, though somewhat compact on the river lands, are very friable on the elevated uplands, among the swamps. In the month of January the land for tobacco is plowed to the depth of 6 or 8 inches, care being taken that it is sufficiently dry to work. If plowed too wet, and a hot sun supervenes, the river land, and especially the black, sticky soil, will bake as hard as a sun-burned brick, and no amount of labor will render it pulverulent until the ameliorating influences of the frosts have decomposed the hard lumps. The soil is usually reversed with a turning-plow, and the subsoil-plow is only used after the tobacco has been planted to break out the middles at the last plowing, and thus to secure good drainage. No cultivated plant is more susceptible to the injurious effects of an excess of water in the soil than tobacco. When overflowed, though the water may retire within a few hours, the plant immediately wilts and gradually dies. Another plowing is given the soil about the middle of February by running furrows from 4 to 5 feet apart, and two more furrows with a turning-plow, thrown on each side of the initial furrows, thus forming a series of beds. Toward the end of February, when the soil is in good condition, a horse-rake is run along the tops of the ridges, giving each a wide, level top. After this beds are thrown up on the tops of the original ridges with a one-horse plow, four furrows together. With a hand-rake the tops of these are raked off, and the land is ready for planting. The plants are then set out 3 feet apart on the beds after a rain, but in seasons of drought it is often necessary to water each plant a day or two after it is transplanted. The planting usually takes place about the last week in February and the first week in March, though the time may be extended to April, or even to May. The usual distance between plants is 3 by 4 feet, making 12 square feet to each plant, thus giving 3,630 plants to the acre, or a little over 3,000 to the arpent. The distance between the rows, however, varies from 4 to 4½ and 5 feet, according to the character of the soil, the wider distance being used on very fertile soils. No effort is made to make the plants align across the beds, as the cultivation is all done one way, and the water furrows are carefully protected, so as to take away any excess of moisture from the immediate vicinity of the plant. The cultivation of the crop is very simple, but frequent, as in the semi-tropical climate of Louisiana grass grows with remarkable rapidity. A subsoil-plow, after the plant is well rooted, is run on each side of the row to the depth of 8 or 10 inches. A *piochon*—a combination of the harrow and the cultivator—is then used to pulverize the soil between the rows, after which hoes are employed to scrape out any grass that may remain in the narrow belt which is left untouched between the plants. As often as it rains this triplex process of cultivation is pursued until the tobacco is nearly large enough to top. At that time the dirt is thrown to the plant with a one-horse turning-plow, followed with the hoe, by which the dirt is more carefully disposed about the stalks. The middles are then opened with a subsoiler, and the cultivation is finished. Should grass shoot up after this, it will rather be an advantage than a disadvantage, as without it the lower tobacco leaves are liable to be spattered with dirt during heavy showers.

PRIMING AND TOPPING OF TOBACCO.

The tobacco plant is not "primed". In the Perique region about the 15th of May the seed-bud is pinched out, leaving from twelve to eighteen leaves on each plant. The time, however, for "topping" varies with the soil, and on sandy lands is from one to two weeks earlier than upon stiff, cold, argillaceous soils.

SUCKERING OF TOBACCO.

One week after topping the suckers are pulled off and diligent search is made for the green worm. This process must be repeated every week until the tobacco ripens, which is usually from four to five weeks after it is topped. It is said that in the climate of Louisiana three suckers will come out in succession to every leaf, which is not the case in the colder climates of the middle and Atlantic states, where two suckers to the leaf is the maximum.

RIPENING TOBACCO.

In the latter part of June or early in July the tobacco plants, if well cultivated, will show a yellowish, mottled appearance, the leaves being very crisp and easily broken. After it is ripe, heavy rains, followed by hot suns often injure the crop by scalding. Heavy dews are beneficial, as the secretory organs of the plant are rendered more active in storing up in the vesicular structure the rich juices and gum that give flavor and strength to the cured product.

CUTTING AND CURING OF TOBACCO.

Contrary to the practice in other tobacco-growing regions, the plants are cut during the hottest part of the day and taken immediately to sheds. The stalk is not split in cutting, but is severed with a hatchet about 3 inches above the ground, leaving from two to three of the lower leaves on the stump, which are thought to be worthless on account of the large amount of dirt adhering to them, they having served their purpose in keeping the other leaves free from sand and dirt. After the tobacco has been taken to the sheds a number of boys and girls are kept busily employed in sharpening pieces of cane from 3 to 4 inches long. These are driven one into each stalk near the lower end, at such an angle as to form a hook. By these hooks the plants are suspended upon a series of ropes stretched lengthwise in the shed, these ropes being a foot apart, and the plants on the ropes 6 inches from each other. As the plants wilt the distance between them is lessened. Now begins the peculiar manipulation of the Perique tobacco. As soon as the leaves become embrowned, and while the stem or midrib is yet green, each one is carefully picked from the stalk and the green stem is pulled out. The first leaves are pulled off in about ten days from the time the tobacco is put in the shed, and from one to three leaves at intervals of a few days, until the whole stalk is stripped. As fast as the green stem is pulled out the leafy parts are made into loose twists, each twist containing from twenty to thirty half leaves. These twists are packed in boxes 11 inches square, capable of holding 50 pounds, which, when nearly full, are put under a simple lever press, the lever being 12 feet long, to which weights are attached, so as to secure a pressure on the tobacco of 7,000 pounds to the square foot. Screw-presses are never used, for the reason that a continuous pressure is required in curing this tobacco. After remaining in press for twenty-four hours it is taken out, opened, and thoroughly aired for a few minutes, until the exuded juices, black, tarry, and thick, can be reabsorbed, when it is again placed under pressure. This treatment is continued with each box for ten days in succession, every twist being opened, aired, and turned, so that the juices will saturate the whole mass. From a light brown the tobacco grows darker each day, until it shines in oily blackness. After ten days the manipulation becomes less frequent, once in three or four days being sufficient. At the expiration of three months the tobacco is cured and emits a rich, spirituous flavor, which has been imparted to it by the reabsorption of the aerated juices. Perique tobacco is cured and preserved by the resinous gums contained in the natural leaf. The robe or wrapper leaves are handled with great care, and are kept in twists by themselves while being cured under pressure.

The next step is to put the tobacco into cylindrical rolls, or *carottes*, containing usually 4 pounds, though two, and even one pound *carottes* are made for home consumption. To do this the tobacco is taken from pressure, and each leaf is opened, straightened, and aired. Then a cloth, 24 inches long and about 15 inches wide, is laid upon a table and covered with robe leaves, the bottom side of the leaf being turned uppermost, and the fibers so disposed as to run to a point in a longitudinal median line of the cloth. A mat of leaves is then placed on the layer of robe, a half inch or more in thickness, and extending nearly to the edges of the underlying cloth. A second cloth is laid over this mat, and the tobacco is compacted by tramping, after which the ends of the mat are doubled over about three inches at each end and tramped again. The whole mass—cloth, robes, and fillers—is then rolled into a cylinder 15 inches long and about 3 inches in diameter, a hole being kept through the center, into which the ends of the robe leaves are tucked. The ends of the cloth are now tied and a rope wound in a coil about the *carotte* from end to end with a windlass made for the purpose. This rope is taken off at the expiration of twenty-four hours and again wound more tightly around the *carotte*, when it is ready for market. A man of ordinary skill can put up ten *carottes* a day with a boy to assist at the windlass. The making of *carottes* is generally the work of winter and leisure days, and employs every member of the household in taking the tobacco from the presses, opening, straightening, and weighing it, preparatory to the rolling, which requires considerable tact and skill in the operative. The tobacco often remains in the boxes under pressure for twelve months or more, growing sweeter with time, and is only put into *carottes* when there is a demand for it, or when the planter desires to sell.

COST OF PRODUCING AND MARKETING TOBACCO.

The cost of raising and marketing Perique tobacco probably exceeds that of any other tobacco grown. The value of the land on which it is cultivated is estimated at from $30 to $50 per arpent, the rental value of which is $5 a year. Wages for workers in tobacco amount to 75 cents and $1 a day and board, the latter reckoned at 75 cents a day. The following estimate for a crop on 4 arpents of land was made at Grande Pointe:

Dr.	
Rent of 4 arpents of land, at $5	$20 00
One man five months, at $20 per month	100 00
Two men one month, at $25 per month	50 00
Three men one month, curing, etc.	75 00
Rent of shed, 10 per cent. on $200	20 00
Boxing	4 50
Putting up 300 *carottes*, at 10 cents	30 00
Rope for wrapping, 10 cents per *carotte*	30 00
Internal-revenue tax-stamps	192 00
	521 50
Cr.	
By 300 *carottes*, 4 pounds each, at 41 cents per pound	492 00
Loss for each four arpents cultivated	29 50

Actual cost of production, exclusive of tax, 27½ cents per pound.

The growing of Perique tobacco would cease entirely but for the fact that women and children do a large part of the work when they could not be profitably employed at any other industry. The growers of Perique have very small farms, and can produce no other crop on the same amount of land that will give them regular employment. While there is no profit in making tobacco, by its culture they are able to get a fair average compensation for the time employed.

It will be observed that the yield per arpent at Grande Pointe is 75 *carottes*, or 300 pounds, equivalent to 360 pounds per acre; but the stem, which makes 25 per cent. of the weight of the leaf, must be added, which will give 480 pounds per acre. There is also a shrinkage of 20 per cent. in the process of curing, which will make the actual yield per acre 600 pounds as the product is usually estimated. The maximum production is 30 *carottes* to the 1,000 plants, about 92 to the arpent, or 109 to the acre. Compared with the yield of a ton or more per acre in Pennsylvania and the Connecticut valley, this appears exceedingly small. The production per acre can easily be increased to 1,000 or even 1,500 pounds by the application of strong fertilizers in sufficient quantity, but the increase in yield will be at the expense of quality. The peculiar sweetness and flavor of the Perique would be destroyed, and with the destruction of these qualities it would take rank among the lowest grades of American tobacco.

DISEASES OF TOBACCO.

FIRING, OR BROWN RUST, is one of the few diseases to which tobacco in Louisiana is subject, and occurs occasionally, but not to such an extent as to work serious injury to the crop. During excessively hot, wet weather in June or July the disease manifests itself. The leaves nearest the ground will sometimes dry up and others become spotted, and occasionally, during the prevalence of heavy rains, accompanied by strong winds, they are turned over, and the drops of rain will bruise the under surface. These bruised spots become "rusted" in a few days, and if the plant is not cut the whole leaf will become involved.

SUNSTROKE.—When the soil upon which tobacco is grown is not well drained the presence of water in excessive quantity, accompanied by a hot sun, will produce "sunstroke", the effect of which is first to wilt the leaf, which afterward blackens and dries up in the field if not cut.

BIZONE.—The disease known in North Carolina as "waterloon", and in Kentucky and Tennessee as "walloon", and "frenching", akin to the last, occur on close, compact, wet soils.

Draining the land thoroughly is the best remedy for the prevention of all these diseases.

INSECTS.

Insects have rarely been troublesome to the tobacco plant in Louisiana. In the spring of 1880 the flea-beetle was very destructive to young plants, but never before within the memory of the tobacco-growers. In a climate so mild, and where vegetable life is so profuse, it might be expected that cut-worms would be very destructive, but such is not the fact, the very abundance of vegetation acting as a protection to the tobacco plant. Nor are horn-worms troublesome upon the varieties of tobacco grown for Perique. It is an easy task for one man to keep ten thousand plants clear of these pests. Bud-worms, which are small, greenish, and white striped, and when grown are less than an inch in length, are much more troublesome, and require constant and unremitting search until the tobacco is topped. When they attack the bud of the plant they pierce the embryotic leaves through and through and completely check their development. But while the green-worm (*Sphinx carolina*) does not attack with vigor the tobacco grown for working up into Perique, it is very destructive to the sweet-scented varieties, such as Havana, Brazil, and Yara, and if either of them is planted in a row beside the Perique the worm will devour the first and scarcely touch the second.

INJURY FROM STORMS.

About once in six years the tobacco in the field is injured by hailstorms. In this latitude, however, hailstorms occur about the time of the vernal equinox, and the tobacco plant has abundant time to mature after the period for storms has passed.

VALUE OF TOBACCO PRODUCT.

The average value per pound in Saint James parish for Perique is about 41 cents, including a duty of 16 cents per pound. The value per pound of the different grades is, including duty: Chewing, 46 cents; smoking, 36 cents; robe, 56 cents. The latter tobacco sometimes brings a fancy price, but is rarely ever sold alone, and is generally consumed in wrappers for the other two grades.

PECULIARITIES AND SPECIAL USES OF THIS VARIETY.

Nearly the entire product of the Perique region is taken by manufacturers, and is by them treated as raw material. They make it into fine-cut, in which form it has a glossy appearance, totally different from any other fine-cut tobacco. This gloss or varnish is due to the superabundance of juices, which steep and saturate the *carotte*, and so securely are they sealed up that no vicissitudes of climate or season are able to diminish them. The fine-cut, in its turn, is manufactured into cigarettes, and the tobacco to a very limited extent into cigars. It is also packed in paper packages, tin cans, and glass jars for use in the pipe, and is also used to mix with weaker kinds of tobacco, by which the flavor, but not the strength, of the Perique is preserved. A very small quantity is made into snuff, which by a French gentleman of the old régime is preferred to any other kind.

POINTS OF EXCELLENCE.

The great points of excellence claimed for Perique tobacco are—

1. Its great strength. It has a large content of nicotine, amounting to 4.32 per cent., and more sweet juices than any other kind. It is therefore valuable for mixing with lighter and weaker types.

2. It is free from the acrid, biting, creosotic taste so common in other kinds of southern-grown tobacco, and has a rich, fragrant odor, combined with a smooth, delicate taste.

3. By men of literary habits it is said that Perique tobacco stimulates the action of the brain, and that its narcotic effects are less than those of any other sort of tobacco. Men of vigorous constitution affirm that it produces an exhilaration of spirits akin to that which comes from drinking good old wine, without the disagreeable results too apt to follow the use of the latter stimulant.

In this report upon the tobacco of Louisiana attention has been directed mainly to the product of Saint James parish, for the reason that this parish puts up the best Perique made in the state. A small quantity is made in Winn, Avoyelles, and De Soto parishes, and it was formerly grown to a limited extent in Lafourche, Terrebonne, and Natchitoches, but in quality is said to be far inferior to the Perique of Saint James.

By far the larger portion of Perique tobacco finds a market at the various little stores that line the banks of the Mississippi in the region known as "the coast". The people who raise and cure it use it as a species of currency, the country merchants accepting the *carotte* as so much money, agreeing to stamp each one before it is delivered, deducting the value of the stamp from the actual selling price. When a considerable number of *carottes* has accumulated at the storehouses they are shipped to New Orleans and sold to some wholesale dealer, who in turn supplies the demand from New York and other points. The compact bundles into which the tobacco is put make it very convenient for handling.

OTHER TOBACCO.

The growing of Cuba tobacco has been frequently tried on the gray soil along the river banks, but with indifferent success. Grown from seed imported from Havana or Vuelta de Abajo, it emits a pleasant odor while growing, and when properly cured the first year from the seed is no mean substitute for the Cuba-grown tobacco; but each succeeding year it shows a gradual decline in fineness of texture and sweetness of flavor, until it approximates in size and general appearance the Perique tobacco, but never attains the peculiar spirituous flavor of that variety. The difficulty of procuring fresh seed from Cuba every year, and the inexperience of the planters in handling and curing the Cuba tobacco, together with the want of an established market for home-grown Cuba, have repressed its cultivation.

PRODUCTION OF TOBACCO.

Assuming that three-fourths of the product of the state is raised for sale and the remainder for the individual consumption of the producers, the latter being generally a fixed quantity, the following statement will give, approximately, the production, acreage, and yield for the several crops grown from 1876 to 1879, inclusive, the figures for 1879 being taken from the census returns:

Year.	Production.	Acreage.	Yield per acre.
	Pounds.		*Pounds.*
1876	94,248	396	238
1877	109,956	462	238
1878	74,210	362	205
1879	55,954	253	221

The price of tobacco grown in Louisiana is so irregular that it is impossible to arrive at anything like a satisfactory result as to values. When put up in *carottes*, the price ranges, without the tax, from 20 to 60 cents per pound; in the leaf it sells from 5 to 20 cents per pound. A considerable part of the product is consumed by the producer, so that any attempt to fix the value would be deceptive, although some dealers estimate that 18 cents per pound would probably approximate the average value for all grades.

CHAPTER IX.

CULTURE AND CURING OF TOBACCO IN MARYLAND.

We have no historical account of the precise date of the introduction of tobacco into Maryland, nor of its first culture by that colony. It is probable that the first planters were William Claiborne and his associates, who emigrated from Virginia and made the first settlement in the state on Kent island (now a portion of Queen Anne county) in 1631, just one year before the charter under which Maryland was permanently established was granted by James I to Cecilius Calvert, second Lord Baltimore.

For a long time in Maryland, as in Virginia, excessive efforts to produce large crops of tobacco and the neglect of home supplies brought scarcity, and consequent distress.

The culture of tobacco at an early period extended over eastern and southern Maryland, and for a long series of years the counties on the eastern shore of the Chesapeake bay were large producers. As late as 1849 Queen Anne county raised 8,380,851 pounds, and Somerset county 1,763,822 pounds. In 1869 Queen Anne raised none, and Somerset 14 pounds. No other county on the eastern shore raised any tobacco in 1869, except Wicomico, 370 pounds, making the product of this district of the state 384 pounds, where more than 10,000,000 pounds had formerly been raised. Other crops, giving quicker and better returns, have completely ousted tobacco from this portion of the state, which is so admirably adapted to truck farming that it will probably not produce tobacco again as a staple crop.

The amount produced in Maryland has fluctuated widely. Before the Revolutionary War it rose to 20,000 hogsheads; at the end of that war it did not exceed 10,000 hogsheads, since which time it reached 51,000 hogsheads in 1860, descended to 27,064 in 1868, and rose to 27,782 in 1869.

The peculiar characteristics of nearly all Maryland tobacco afford it only a limited field of consumption. It is used only by smokers of the pipe, who are contented with a cheap article, and is consumed chiefly by the peasantry of Germany and Holland, who cannot afford to pay for a richer tobacco, and who would smoke their home-grown weed were not the Maryland leaf the cheaper of the two. A marked characteristic of Maryland tobacco is its mildness.

There are some fine Bay, Burley, and cigar-leaf tobaccos raised in Maryland. The soils are capable of producing a much larger proportion of the finer types than has generally been grown, requiring, of course, a change of varieties and appropriate management.

Nearly all the tobacco grown in Maryland is produced in the counties of Anne Arundel, Calvert, Carroll, Charles, Frederick, Howard, Montgomery, Prince George's, and Saint Mary's.

There are three distinct types grown: Air-cured, Red and Yellow Bay, and Spangled Bay.

Air-cured tobacco constitutes fully four-fifths of the total product, and is grown in the district composed of Saint Mary's, Charles, Calvert, Prince George's, Anne Arundel, and Howard counties.

The Red and Yellow Bay and Spangled Bay are produced in Montgomery, Frederick, and Carroll.

In portions of Carroll, Cecil, and Harford small patches of cigar tobacco are cultivated, the product finding a market in Pennsylvania.

Hailstorms in summer are not of frequent occurrence, and when they appear it is usually in narrow belts, causing but partial damage in contracted areas. Wind storms, occurring about the autumnal equinox, sometimes cause considerable damage, particularly when they are violent and occur before the 22d of September. Heavy rains occasionally inflict great injury, drowning some and washing away other portions of the crop, and bespattering all with mud and sand.

GEOLOGY.

Saint Mary's, Charles, Calvert, and portions of Prince George's and Anne Arundel are of Tertiary formation, the northern portions of Prince George's and Anne Arundel are Cretaceous, and the other tobacco-producing counties are primary. The soils of the three states of Virginia, Maryland, and New Jersey are strikingly similar in many respects, and this is especially true of the light gray, micaceous, and feldspathic soils. For the cereals and many other crops they are considered poor, but good for certain types of tobacco. This class of lands is attracting more attention as their capabilities for improvement are becoming better known. Of these soils a recently published *Geology of New Jersey* says: "It is observed that the rocks are in many places subject to decay, and that in such localities the soil is susceptible of high cultivation." The following are given as analyses of specimens of such soils, the same mentioned above as being common to Maryland and Virginia:

	Soda feldspar.	Potash feldspar.	Soda and lime feldspar.
	Per cent.	*Per cent.*	*Per cent.*
Silica	68.6	64.6	62.1
Alumina	19.6	18.5	23.7
Soda	11.8	....	....
Potash	....	16.9	....
Lime	....	....	14.2
	100.0	100.0	100.0

TOPOGRAPHY AND SOILS OF THE SEVERAL COUNTIES.

SAINT MARY'S.—The southeastern portion is low and level; the northwestern undulating. The soil, originally a rich, black mold, has been impoverished by continued cultivation, without rest or manuring; but it is gradually improving under the free use of lime, with better management.

CHARLES.—Like Saint Mary's, generally low and sandy, but rolling enough to drain well. Soils once rich, but now greatly worn by excessive cropping without manure.

CALVERT.—Level or gently rolling. Soils, sand and clay loam; quick and productive where not too much exhausted.

PRINCE GEORGE'S.—Lands generally lie well, and were once very rich. Though worn, they produce well with a little help. The best soils are a clay and sand loam.

ANNE ARUNDEL.—Southern part level; northern rolling. Above Annapolis the soil is light gray and not considered productive; below that city the lands are richer, darker in color, stiffer, and more clayey.

Nearly all the soils of the five counties above named are alluvials, and were originally very productive.

HOWARD.—General surface undulating, and the soils of the southern part are very much like those above described. In the west and northwest of the county the formation is primary, and the soils are more like those of western Maryland and middle Virginia. There are narrow belts of limestone running through the county, upon which the soil is productive and susceptible of high improvement.

MONTGOMERY.—Rolling and hilly, and the soils vary as greatly as the geological formations upon which they rest. The eastern part of this county is primary, the rocks mostly gneiss, mica, and hornblendic slates, and the soils are mostly light and sandy, with clay subsoil. Though not rich, they can be made to grow paying crops of tobacco by the aid of manures. The western portion is talcose slate, with areas well adapted to tobacco, the poorest soils producing the finest grades.

FREDERICK.—Rolling, almost mountainous; well drained. Has a variety of soils—limestone, granitic, gneissoid, and slaty. The sandy and slaty soils are the best for tobacco. Here, as in Montgomery, the poorer soils produce the finest tobacco.

CARROLL.—Undulating and hilly; geology primary; soils variable. Those on the slopes and foothills of Parr's ridge are best suited for tobacco.

Although western Maryland produces a type that sells higher than that grown in the southern and eastern portions of the state, very little tobacco is raised there, farmers preferring other crops.

The soil varies in depth from 3 to 8 inches on the rolling lands in the upper or "bay" district, and from 6 to 12 inches or more in the southern alluvial district. The lands of the rolling or hilly sections are generally of easy tillage, and are more or less liable to wash. In southern Maryland the land lies well, except immediately on the creeks and rivers, where it is swampy.

In Prince George's, Anne Arundel, and generally in the counties of the air-curing district, tobacco is planted upon almost all classes of soils, farmers usually selecting the most fertile lands. In Prince George's county light clay hillsides, made rich with manure after clover fallow, are preferred when new lands are not to be had. The product is much better upon new lands, but such soils are now exceedingly scarce. In Anne Arundel county a clay loam, or a dark loam with clay subsoil, is preferred; in Montgomery a light-red soil is usually chosen. In Howard a rich, dark, sandy, or clay loam is preferred where quantity is the object; but if quality is sought the preference is given to gray, rolling lands, fertilized. Throughout the tobacco section all classes of arable lands are planted.

The original forest growth of the best tobacco soils is now very scant, most of it having long since disappeared to make room for crops, or for fuel, rails, lumber, etc. What remains is composed of oak, chestnut, locust, pine, etc.

VARIETIES OF TOBACCO CULTIVATED.

Varieties are often named from some peculiarity of growth, habit, or appearance of the plant, as Broad Leaf, Narrow Leaf, Twist Bud, etc., or take their names from individuals who have made some marked success in producing them, as Wilson, Turner, etc.

Broad Leaf, grown in Prince George's, and perhaps in other counties, is tall, with the leaves broad, and not very many on the stalk; is chaffy and rather light in weight; cures a pretty color, burns easily, and is liked by many planters.

Narrow Leaf, grown in Prince George's, Anne Arundel, and Montgomery counties, is not very tall; has many leaves, thickly set on the stalk. The leaves are narrow, but heavy, cure a pretty red, are thick and fine, and grow larger upon rich land. Some planters in Montgomery claim that a better article can be grown of this variety than of any other; but it does not, however, bring as good a price as the lighter sorts.

Baden, grown in Prince George's county, sometimes called "poor-land tobacco", cures a beautiful whitish-yellow, but is liable to greenish spots or stripes on the leaves, which lessen its value. The leaves are short, light, and chaffy. If the weather is favorable when it is first cut and put into the barn, it cures a fine yellow and outsells other sorts.

White Burley, grown to some extent in several counties, is much liked by those who have tried it. It requires strong land, cures better than most other varieties, can be cut before maturity, and yet retain its color.

Pear Tree, more generally known as Boyer, grown in Montgomery county, where it is the principal variety cultivated; Wilson and Five-Sucker, grown in Anne Arundel; Thickset, grown in Calvert, are varieties locally popular. A new variety, called White Kentucky, was introduced into Calvert county in 1869. This variety cures well and is popular, the only objection to it being that it requires a very rich and highly-manured land to grow it to proper size. In Howard county the Burley, the Connecticut Seed-Leaf, and the Maryland, the seeds of which varieties were sent to that county by the United States Agricultural Department, have been grown to considerable extent. The Maryland is thrifty, of quick growth, sometimes reaching a height of six feet; is not as fine and as good as the Burley, but is more prolific. Connecticut Seed-Leaf is successfully grown in Howard for pipe-smoking and cigars.

Tobaccos grown upon lands rich in vegetable matter are generally of a poor quality, large, coarse, dark in color, and light and trashy. When grown upon thin lands, dressed with stable manure broadcast and fertilized in the drills with a proper quantity of good superphosphate, they are of a better and more salable quality, and when raised upon new lands they are of the first quality. On the sandy bottoms of the lower country—Prince George's, Saint Mary's, Charles, and Calvert counties—the tobacco is duller in color and heavier than that produced upon the micaceous soils of Howard. Light dry soils and sandy loams produce light-red and yellow tobaccos of the finest quality and highest price, and heavy, dark loams yield darker grades and more weight, but of inferior quality and of small value.

TOBACCO FERTILIZERS.

In southern Maryland commercial fertilizers are used on about one-fifth of the area cultivated in tobacco. These are kainit, phosphates, and various special manures, manufactured in Baltimore or sold there. Fertilizers are applied in quantities varying from 100 to 400 pounds per acre, either broadcast or in the drill, at a cost of from $3 to $12 per acre.

In the Bay district nearly all the tobacco lands are manured with domestic or commercial fertilizers, or both. From 250 to 400 pounds of commercial manures are applied, usually in the drill, at a cost of from $6 50 to $10 per acre.

The use of fertilizers, generally ammoniated superphosphates, or special compounds manufactured and sold as tobacco manures, increases the yield very materially, especially in favorable seasons; but this increase of weight is almost always attended by a depreciation of quality. Tobacco grown without the help of these fertilizers does not mature quite so early, but is more pliable, keeps in order better, and has more body. Upon the dark loams of Charles county commercial fertilizers have produced little or no effect; but plaster, lime, and ashes have given favorable results, increasing the yield, but without any appreciable improvement of quality.

In the Bay district fertilizers are considered indispensable, and are generally used only in connection with farm-yard and stable manures. In Howard county good farmers do not attempt to raise any crop without manuring and the use of fertilizers. In Prince George's, and in some portions of other counties of southern Maryland, the effects of fertilizers are rarely seen after the first crop to which they are applied. If none are used upon succeeding crops, there is an immediate falling off in the yield, which will continue unless the soil is manured or improved by judicious rotation. In Calvert county an experiment was made upon a certain field by planting it for six years successively in tobacco, and the yield for the sixth year was as good as that for the first, but there was a marked depreciation in the quality. In southern Maryland are large areas of land, which have been planted in tobacco at recurring intervals for more than a hundred and fifty years, still capable of producing a fair crop without fertilizers, and this upon soils upon which manures have never been used—an evidence of the remarkable natural fertility of these particular soils.

The yield of tobacco has decreased from 10 to 25 per cent. during the last ten years in Prince George's, Calvert, and Charles counties. In Anne Arundel county some planters have succeeded in producing larger crops than formerly, while the majority confess to a gradual lessening of yield. The general decrease in the counties above named is attributed to the failure of clover for several years during the decade, and the rather stinted use of home-made manures as one of the consequences of that failure. In Montgomery county the yield has increased from 10 to 12 per cent.

In Prince George's, Calvert, Anne Arundel, Montgomery, and Howard counties wheat usually follows tobacco. Clover alone, or clover and grass seeds, are sown upon the wheat lands, to remain two or more years, when the land is again put in tobacco. In Charles county a favorite method is to sow rye after tobacco; then pease or buckwheat, to be limed and turned down for wheat; then clover, to stand two years; then tobacco again. The best farmers use plaster upon clover, and bone dust and kainit upon wheat in the rotation. Some sow cow pease, a bushel and a half per acre, at the last plowing of the tobacco crop, the vines plowed under for wheat, 200 to 400 pounds of bone dust or kainit, or a mixture of the two, turned under with the pea-vines, and the wheat top-dressed in February with salt and plaster. Some lime heavily, using 100 bushels or more per acre, but this makes a coarse and rather low-priced tobacco. In Howard county, where practicable, tobacco is grown two years on clearings; then wheat, followed by clover or grass.

Tobacco-growers, in all parts of the state in which that crop is produced, agree in the opinion that with proper rotation tobacco is not more exhaustive than corn or other crops usually grown upon their lands. In southern Maryland tobacco has been grown continuously as long as on any other area of territory in the United States, and fair crops are still grown upon these lands without fertilizers.

The soils of southern Maryland abound in lime and magnesia, and the remaining elements are generally found in requisite quantity in almost all soils. The subsoil contains much potash, and the soil, derived from a conglomerate, was once rich in the acids. Another reason why these lands have maintained their fertility for so long a period is that the soil has not been washed away by heavy rains, as is the case on rolling lands.

PLANT-BEDS, ETC.

Nine-tenths of the plant-beds in Maryland are prepared without burning. Fuel is scarce and costly, and a good situation, thorough preparation, and heavy manuring are relied upon. Very few of the beds are covered. The beds, both raw and burned, are generally sown as soon as prepared. In Prince George's county seed is sown from January 1 to April 1, and in Howard county from February 15 to April 15. Hot-beds are used to a limited extent, and are commended as a surer protection against the flea-beetle.

In Prince George's transplanting begins about the 10th of May, and is continued till July 4; in Howard the work begins about the 20th of May, and is usually completed by the 1st of July.

PREPARATION OF THE SOIL FOR TOBACCO CULTIVATION.

Land intended for tobacco is plowed deeply and as thoroughly as possible during the winter or in February, cross-plowed in April and home manures applied, and again cross-plowed, usually with shovels, dragged, rolled, or harrowed until fine tilth is secured. If fertilizers are used broadcast, they are generally applied at the last harrowing.

In Howard county the usual practice is to lay off the rows three feet apart, fertilize in the drill, cover the manure with a corn-coverer or with two furrows of a light turn-plow, and lay off in checks 2 feet 8 inches or 3 feet. Hills are made in the checks, chopped fine, and leveled with the hand hoe. The practice in other counties is not materially different.

Some planters first weed with the hand hoe, then plow both ways, two furrows each time, or once through each way with the double shovel, cultivate again both ways, and finish up with the hand hoe, dressing the hills. This generally suffices upon clean land, well prepared; but, if necessary, cultivation is repeated every ten days until the plants are so large as to prevent further working. Upon most of the soils of this tobacco region it has been found that frequent shallow plowings after the plant has started into rapid growth are best, and that, in average seasons, deep plowing after the first cultivation is not advisable.

PRIMING, TOPPING, AND SUCKERING TOBACCO.

In Prince George's county priming is not done until the bottom leaves are large enough to be pulled off and saved as "ground leaves". These are gathered when the tobacco is matured and ready to be cut. The ground leaves are saved easily, and are quickly put into market. The plants are topped low, and the suckers are pinched out as fast as they appear. Cutting begins about the time the first suckers are large enough to pull off. The whole field is topped at once.

The same methods prevail throughout most of the tobacco region of Maryland. Priming is rarely done. The tops are pinched out as soon as the seed-bud appears, and cutting follows within from ten days to three weeks after topping.

In hot, damp weather the plants ripen more slowly than when warm and dry. They mature faster in dry weather, unless very cool, and "ground leaves" will accumulate.

In Prince George's county cutting begins about the first of August and continues till the last of September. In Howard the work of harvesting begins during the latter part of August, and is usually finished by the middle of September. Only five to thirty days intervene between topping and cutting.

HARVESTING AND HOUSING OF TOBACCO.

In harvesting and housing tobacco the plants are cut two rows at a time and laid on the ground, the butts a little to the right of the operator. The next two rows are then cut and laid in like manner, the butts of the last in close proximity to the first, and a boy follows, depositing tobacco-sticks at proper intervals for use in spearing. The implement used for this purpose is a spear-shaped piece of iron, with a socket, into which the tobacco lath fits. Sometimes a small trestle is used as a support for the spear, but experts do not require it. Experts place the end of a lath in the socket of the spear, resting the other end on the ground; hold the spear end with the left hand, grasp a stalk with the right at the butt end, and place it on the top of the spear, about 4 inches from the end. As soon as the spear has penetrated the stalk, release the hold of the lath with the left hand and place it on the stalk to the left of the spear point, and then press down with both hands until the spear head has passed through the stalk and the latter is fairly strung on the lath, as indicated in the illustration.

Six or eight plants are speared upon each stick. These sticks, filled with tobacco, are set up in the field, in rows, in shooks of eight or ten sticks each. A cart or wagon is driven between the rows and is loaded from either side, great care being taken not to bruise the plants in handling. The tobacco is carted to the barn and the sticks are placed on the tiers, or it is hung out of doors on scaffolds. Cutting is done in the morning, as soon as the dew is off, or after four o'clock in the afternoon on bright, hot days, so that the plants may not be sunburned.

In southern Maryland the tobacco-houses are generally large frame structures, from 15 to 20 feet high, 20 to 30 feet wide, and 30 to 60 feet long. A barn of medium size, 24 by 40 feet and 16 feet high, is capable of curing 3,000 to 3,500 pounds of tobacco, and if built of good material, underpinned with stone or brick, such a house will cost about $400. Tobacco-houses are usually constructed somewhat open, to permit the free circulation of air, and some are so built as to admit or shut out the air at pleasure. Tobacco-sticks cost about $1 per thousand.

Insurance may be effected upon tobacco-houses, but at high rates, and, therefore, comparatively few farmers insure their barns.

CURING OF TOBACCO.

In Prince George's county the product is all air-cured. If a damp spell occurs after the barn is filled with tobacco it is sometimes fired with wood to save it; but this is rarely done, as the product then sells only at very reduced prices. Furnaces have been tried to some extent in Anne Arundel and Montgomery counties, and in most cases the results were not satisfactory. In Montgomery about one-twentieth of the product is air-cured, the rest being cured with open wood fires; in Howard four-fifths of the crop is air-dried and one-fifth is cured with wood fires; and in Calvert, Charles, and Saint Mary's counties the tobacco is all air-cured. Lower Maryland tobacco, cured by open wood fires, is unsalable; but the highest price paid in Baltimore for tobacco grown in Maryland is for the bright "Spangled", raised in the Bay district, and cured with open wood fires.

Pole-sweat or house-burn does more or less damage every year, and is caused by hanging too close, by crowding on the sticks, or by rehanging too soon while the tobacco is in a sweat. House-burn can be prevented by having plenty of room and by proper attention to ventilation, and can be arrested by judiciously managed artificial heat. Tobacco is often much damaged by continued wet and foggy weather in barns not made tight, and especially is this the case when the tobacco, after being cured, is not run close together, so as to exclude the damp air as much as possible. The best plan to avoid injury, and that adopted by careful managers in the lower Maryland section, is to run the tobacco up in the roof-space of the barn and press the sticks close together as tight as possible, cover the floor with dry straw or hay, and make the barn as close as can be.

STRIPPING, ASSORTING, AND BULKING OF TOBACCO.

Maryland planters seldom bulk the tobacco before it is stripped. If bulked at all, it is only as a temporary expedient to keep the leaves in pliable order to be properly sorted and tied up into bundles or "hands". These "hands" contain eight to ten of leaf, ten to twelve of ground leaves, and twelve to fourteen of "tips"—the small, inferior top leaves. The air-cured tobacco of southern Maryland is usually sorted into four grades: Brights, seconds, dulls, and tips. In the Bay district more grades are made: Yellow-spangled, crop, seconds, dulls, and tips.

After the tobacco is stripped and tied it is usually put down in bulk. Bulks are constructed as follows: Logs, poles, or skids, as long as needed, are placed 2 feet above the floor of the barn, resting on blocks or other supports, and the poles, 3½ feet apart, are covered with tobacco-sticks, laid across closely, making a platform. Two or three bundles at a time are passed to the bulker, who smoothes out the leaves and lays them on the platform, with the heads even and pointing outward, making a course all around the platform outside. Another bulker follows, laying the heads about midway of the first course, and completes a round in the same manner as the first. The heads of the inner course point outward, tails inward and lapping; making, in all, four courses of bundles in the width of the platform. A narrow bulk is made by packing on these two courses with the heads outward and a middle course. A still narrower one, made with only two courses, is the "tailing-down" mode, called by some "windrows". The narrower the bulk the less liable is the tobacco to heat; but it is more liable to dry out and get out of order for prizing.

Tobacco stripped late in the season and in good order is rarely hung up again, but is bulked as stripped or packed for sale.

The length of time tobacco is permitted to remain in bulk depends upon its condition when thus packed down and the option of the planter. If bulked in soft condition, it will not keep sound after the weather becomes warm, but will ferment and spoil. Thoroughly dried out, and then caught in proper condition—leaves supple and stems dry—and bulked or packed, it will keep safely. A great deal of tobacco is damaged every year in bulk and hogshead by neglecting to bulk or pack in proper condition.

Bulking gives a fan-like shape to the bundles, prevents injury from atmospheric influences, and is regarded as an essential part of the "conditioning" process necessary to make it ready for prizing into hogsheads. If bulked in proper condition, the "sweat", through which tobacco always passes when closely packed, is only moderate, the leaf is improved, and the sweet flavor of a really good tobacco is manifest. If the sweating, either from being bulked or packed in bad condition, is immoderate, or allowed to go on till great heat is attained, the leaf and stem become moldy or "funked", and the quality is seriously damaged or the tobacco utterly ruined.

The proportion of "funked" tobaccos, or such as are damaged by excessive fermentation, is greater in air-cured than in fire-cured tobacco, the leaf being more thoroughly dried by artificial heat. The proportion of damaged tobacco varies with the seasons, it being in some years less than 5 per cent., and in others more than 10 per cent. of the crop.

For prizing tobacco the old lever beam is most in use. This is usually made on the farm, is easily constructed, and at small cost, varying from $5 to $10, according to material and workmanship. Screws of wrought or of cast iron are also used by some planters, and cost from $25 to $50 each. The screw is far more convenient than the lever, and is gradually coming more into use.

SELLING OF TOBACCO.

Maryland tobacco is nearly all prized and sent to Baltimore, where it is stripped of the hogshead or tierce, broken in several places, and samples drawn therefrom, which are intended to represent fairly the contents of the package. These samples are drawn by inspectors, and are taken by the commission merchants to whom the tobacco is consigned. The tobacco is sold by sample. The cost of selling is $1 50 per hogshead, charged by the commission merchant and paid by the planter or owner. There is also a charge of $2 per hogshead for inspection, storage, etc., called outage, which is paid by the purchaser; but the whole cost of $3 50 per hogshead comes at last out of the tobacco. The usual cost of hogsheads is $1 50 each.

Tobacco inspection in Maryland is under state control. The board of trade of Baltimore has recently petitioned the governor and members of the legislature to repeal the present tobacco-inspection laws of the state.

The best qualities of yellow tobacco, grown in Montgomery county, sell from $18 to $20 per hundred, and inferior sells down to $3; a difference owing not to soil and cultivation only, but to the condition of the tobacco when cut and to the varying skill in curing, handling, and packing.

DISEASES OF TOBACCO.

"Red-fire", "black-fire," and "white-speck" prevail more or less every year, and "frenching" and "walloon" trouble tobacco-planters in all parts of the state where tobacco is grown. "Hollow-stalk" is found occasionally in fields of healthy tobacco. Fortunately, the loss from diseases is comparatively small, except "fire", which does more damage, one year with another, than all the others combined.

ENEMIES OF TOBACCO.

The Maryland planter has no peculiar experience with insects not indicated in Chapter XX.

CIGAR TOBACCO.

The small product of cigar tobacco raised along the border in northeastern Maryland finds its way into Pennsylvania, and is absorbed with the product of that state. A few samples of this type are sent to Baltimore.

COST OF RAISING TOBACCO.

The rate of wages paid for field hands averages about $8 per month for good men; by the day, for men, 50 cents, and for women, 25 cents, with board. Most of the farm labor is hired by the month and by the day; but occasionally a man is hired by the year at from $80 to $110, with board.

Lands capable of producing, without manure, 1,000 pounds or more of tobacco sell at from $30 to $50 per acre; and inferior lands, capable of producing, without fertilizers, 450 to 500 pounds per acre, are valued at from $8 to $10 per acre. Location and improvements are factors influencing the prices of farming lands.

Tobacco hands command no higher wages than other field laborers, but experienced sorters and packers are paid higher prices.

Lands are rarely rented at a fixed price per acre. The usual custom is for the cropper to pay rent in kind: from one-half to one-fourth of the crop, according to the fertility of the soil and other contingencies.

Estimates of the cost of raising tobacco vary widely. In southern Maryland the average cost of production is placed at $4 80 per hundred pounds; in western Maryland the average is estimated at $6 08 per hundred pounds. The average number of acres planted to the hand in southern Maryland is 4 acres; in western Maryland, 3 acres. Planters are of the opinion that, under adequate supervision, the cost of production is somewhat decreased in a large crop.

The following statement shows the total yield of tobacco in pounds, the acreage, yield per acre, value in farmers' hands, value per pound, and value per acre in the state of Maryland, for the years 1876, 1877, 1878, and 1879:

Year.	Amount produced.	Acreage.	Yield per acre.	Value of crop in farmers' hands.	Value per pound in farmers' hands.	Value per acre.
	Pounds.		*Pounds.*		*Cents.*	
1876	33,153,379	37,349	888	$1,610,600	4.87	$43 12
1877	30,123,210	43,500	690	1,674,750	4.25	38 04
1878	30,420,171	34,307	867	1,444,680	4.75	42 00
1879	26,082,147	38,174	653	1,825,750	7.00	47 83

In this table the figures given for the first three years are estimates from the most reliable data attainable, and only those for 1879 are from the census of 1880.

Chapter X.

CULTURE AND CURING OF TOBACCO IN MISSOURI.

The French and Spanish settlers of Missouri raised tobacco for their own consumption, but it was not until about the year 1822 or 1823 that it began to be grown as a staple crop. This cultivation was begun in Pike and the adjoining counties by emigrants from Virginia. It became a staple crop in Chariton county about the year 1834, and continued to increase in quantity until that county produced fully one-third of all that was grown in the state. No other state in the Union, however, has shown such rapid fluctuations in the amount of tobacco produced as Missouri, and this makes it rather difficult to point out with any degree of precision the tobacco-growing districts. When tobacco commands a good price, two-thirds of the counties of the state produce it as a staple crop, but with the fall of prices stock-raising and grain-growing are substituted in its place. In 1850 Missouri ranked as fifth among the states in the production of this staple, raising 17,113,784 pounds; in 1860 it fell to seventh, though producing 25,086,196 pounds; and in 1870 it took the sixth place, though falling off in production more than one-half, reporting for that year 12,320,483 pounds. The following table will show the production for the past four years:

	Pounds.
1876	43,245,000
1877	33,978,000
1878	22,560,000
1879	12,015,657

Only the figures for 1879 are from census returns.

In 1876 Missouri ranked third in production, Kentucky and Virginia only excelling it, but it fell to the ninth place in 1879. The very rapid decline for the few years past is due to the overproduction in the country at large of the types which are specially grown in Missouri and to the heavy decline in prices; also in part to the revolution which has taken place among the plug manufacturers of the United States in the substitution of White Burley for fillers. The seed of the White Burley was introduced into the state from Mason county, Kentucky, in 1878 and 1879, but from some unknown cause it failed to germinate well, and, as a consequence, the acreage in tobacco was very largely decreased in every portion of the state. At least one-half the crop of 1880 is estimated to be of the White Burley.

CHARACTER OF MISSOURI TOBACCO.

As a tobacco state, Missouri, previous to the change alluded to, presented some original characteristics, to some extent still prevailing. All types, except those used in the manufacture of domestic cigars, are grown, from the heaviest, darkest shipping leaf to the light, bright wrapper, so much sought by domestic manufacturers. The heavy tobacco of Missouri has also great absorbent or "drinking" qualities.

Missouri lugs make the best ordinary smoking-tobacco, this grade from the districts producing manufacturing tobacco being lighter than the lugs grown in the shipping districts. The shipping tobacco of Missouri is rather coarse, with large stems and fiber, being grown generally on the rich bottom lands. It contains less gum than that produced elsewhere, and is put up as dry as is possible without breaking. It resembles the Henderson (Kentucky) tobacco, but is not so uniform in color, varying all the way from a bright yellow to a dark red or brown. The color is naturally from a rich dark brown to a high-colored red leaf. When cut green and cured up it is generally very dark, while that which is allowed to ripen fully cures up a more desirable color. Grown on lowlands or prairies, it produces a rich brown and large leaf, which is much sought for export. The manufacturing leaf is grown on the hill lands, particularly on the white-oak soils. The chief difference between the manufacturing and the export tobacco is that the former is of fine fiber and texture, brighter in color, and is not so heavy as the latter.

PHYSICAL FEATURES AND SOILS.

The heavy tobacco district occupied by the counties of Carroll, Livingston, Saline, Howard, Chariton, Linn, Macon, Randolph, Shelby, Monroe, and Boone is one extended plain, with a rolling surface and a gentle declination toward the southeast. Through this plain the Missouri, Grand, Chariton, Lamine, and Salt rivers have cut their valleys to the depth of 200 feet, while numerous smaller streams intersect all parts of the district, with channels deep and wide in proportion to the water discharged. The undulating character of the surface and the channels of the streams furnish a complete drainage. For the most part the coal measures underlie the whole district, save in portions of Saline, Howard, and Boone, where the Subcarboniferous, Devonian, and Silurian rocks successively appear, and also in the largest parts of Shelby and Monroe, which are underlaid chiefly by the Subcarboniferous rocks. All of these consolidated strata are so deeply covered by the Quaternary deposits that they have exerted little or no influence in the formation of the soil. Resting on the consolidated strata are thick beds of glacial, lacustrine, terrace, and alluvial formations. The glacial strata of bowlders, sands, and clays are sparingly developed, and rest upon the coal measures and older rocks where they come to the surface. The lacustrine strata, known as bluff, bury the glacial drift deeply. The surface deposit is the bluff loam, varying in thickness from a few feet to 200 feet. This deposit is rich in lime, magnesia, potassa, soda, phosphoric acid, silica, and alumina. The bottom prairie, or lower terrace, and the alluvial formations are similar in composition to the bluff, save that the material is coarser and more porous. This district is about equally divided between timber and prairie, the timber occupying the larger area in the river bottoms, and the prairie in the highlands.

The upland soils were formed of the bluff marls, and the bottom soils of the bottom prairie and alluvial formations of the river valleys. There are several distinct varieties of soil, distinguished by the grasses and weeds in the prairies and by the trees in the forests.

In the manufacturing district, composed of the counties of Callaway, Pike, Montgomery, Lincoln, and Warren, on the north side of the Missouri river, and Osage and Franklin, on the south side of that stream, the geological and topographical features are greatly varied, but the soils north of the Missouri river resemble those already described. In those counties lying north of the Missouri river the country gradually rises from the mouth of that river along the dividing ridge toward the northwest. From the water-shed between the two streams the slope is very gentle toward the Mississippi on the east and the Missouri on the south. Numerous tributaries to these streams drain the entire area. The general surface is undulating, with abrupt declivities to the larger streams, and the geological features are much more varied than in the heavy tobacco area. The strata below the surface deposits are composed of the rocks of the coal measures, Subcarboniferous, Devonian, and Upper and Lower Silurian.

The Quaternary deposits so completely cover these rocks that they have very little influence on the soil save along the bluffs of the streams and the more broken portions of the district. The calcareo-magnesian, along the bluffs of the Missouri, are the most extensive. These warm, rich soils produce a superior article of tobacco. The bluff loam covers all the uplands of this district (save the few areas mentioned above) to depths varying from 5 to 100 feet; consequently the upland soils derive their mineral characteristics from it. The alluvium and bottom prairie formations underlie all the bottom lands and form the bases of their soils, and these formations are nearly alike. The district is about equally divided between prairie and timber lands, and a considerable portion lies in the river bottoms. Elm lands occupy considerable areas in Pike and Callaway counties and smaller areas in all the other counties. Resin-weed lands also occupy considerable areas in the prairie region adjacent to the elm lands in the timber. Clearing up and cultivating these lands has removed the natural growth of trees, weeds, and grasses, which indicate the quality of the soils; but the crops produced on them fully sustain their early reputation for fertility. Hickory and prairie land of the same quality are found in all the counties of the district, and occupy fully one-third of the upland. These hickory lands are interspersed with and adjacent to the elm lands, and pass by imperceptible gradations from the one to the other, both soils producing large crops of good tobacco. White-oak lands occupy ridges where the lighter materials of the soil have been washed away. They sustain a growth of white and black oak, shell-bark and black hickory, dogwood, sassafras, red-bud, and fragrant sumac. The surface soil of these white-oak lands is not so rich as the last-named variety, but the subsoil is better, as has been shown by analyses at various depths. This soil occupies considerable areas in this district, and a large part of the tobacco is raised on white-oak lands. The yield ranges from 500 to 1,000 pounds per acre, and the quality of the staple is better, as a rule, than that produced on richer lands. Bottom timber lands cover large areas of the river counties, and yield the largest crops of tobacco produced in the district. Many of these counties formerly produced large quantities of tobacco, but in late years the farmers have found other crops more profitable, and their tobacco-barns, in many cases, have been left to decay.

Franklin and Osage counties have a good diversity of surface configuration. The surface was originally an undulating plain, but the Missouri, Osage, Gasconade, Meramec, and other streams have cut through its deep, broad valleys, usually bounded by abrupt and mural bluffs. In places the ascent to the plain above is by gentle acclivities. The geological features are very different from those of other districts described. The consolidated strata are the magnesian limestone series of the Lower Silurian system, consisting of sandstones and magnesian limestones, containing many beds and nodules of flint. The bluff loam is well developed on the bluffs of the streams, and is spread more sparingly over the interior upland portions of the district. The alluvium is spread over the valleys of all the large streams. The soils of these two counties are somewhat different from those already described. There is very little hackberry, crow-foot, elm, or resin-weed land in the district; but hickory lands prevail to a limited extent, more or less modified, and pass into one or the other of the following varieties: White-oak lands prevail on the ridges leading to the Missouri bluffs, and in some of the interior parts of the counties; and post-oak lands occupy the broad, flat ridges away from the river bluffs, where the bluff formation is so changed as to be much more compact and argillaceous and less calcareous and sandy. The growth is post oak, with very few black and Spanish oaks, hickory, red-bud, and dogwood. These lands cover large areas, and are highly esteemed for tobacco. They will not prove so durable as the soils already described. Magnesian limestone soils are based upon the magnesian limestone series or the mineral-bearing rocks of southern Missouri. They produce a great variety of trees and shrubs, among which are black and white walnut, black gum, elms, sugar maple, honey locust, rock chestnut, scarlet, laurel and white oaks, ash, hickory, buckeye, hazel, dogwood, and haws, and grapes are often conspicuous.

CLIMATE.

Missouri is subject to all the advantages and disadvantages of an inland or continental climate. The influences of its two great rivers—the Mississippi, on its eastern border, and the Missouri, running through the center of the state, and their various tributaries—favorably modify its climatic condition. The elevation above the sea varies from 300 to 400 feet in the southeastern portion of the state, and from 1,200 to 1,600 in the southwestern portion. Accurate meteorological observations for any extended period have been only made at Saint Louis. According to the report of the signal officer at that point the mean temperature at Saint Louis from November 1, 1870 (the time at which the observations commenced), to October 31, 1880, has been as follows for the several seasons: Spring, 55 degrees; summer, 77.1; autumn, 55.9; winter, 34.5. The highest temperature recorded during the ten years in which observations have been made was 101 degrees, and the lowest 16, the average yearly fluctuations being 50.7, and the average mean temperature 55.6. The mean annual rainfall for the same period was 39.67 inches, and the mean of the prevailing winds has been south. The daily changes of temperature are ordinarily not more than 20 degrees, but occasionally reach 30, and even 40 degrees. The winters are variable, alternating between cold spells and mild and open weather. Notwithstanding the large rainfall, the climate may be classed as a dry one, as the most abundant rains fall in a very short space of time, and clear skies are the rule and cloudy and overcast ones the exception. Evaporation is rapid, and the dew point is consequently a high one. The prevailing winds are south and southeast in the warmer seasons and west and northwest in the colder ones.

CHARACTER OF PRODUCT AND PROPORTION OF GRADES.

HEAVY TOBACCO DISTRICT.[a]

By far the largest proportion of tobacco raised in Missouri heretofore consisted of a heavy, substantial leaf, grown principally in the following counties, viz: Chariton, with a crop ranging in quantity from 4,500,000 to 14,000,000 pounds, as in 1876, the average annual production of the county for ten years being about 9,000,000 pounds; Randolph, Howard, and Boone, with an average annual production of 6,000,000 pounds; Saline, with an average crop of 2,000,000 pounds; Carroll, Livingston, and Linn, with an average production of 2,500,000 pounds; and Macon, Shelby, and Monroe, with an average crop of 2,000,000 pounds.

This group of counties may, for convenience of description, be called the heavy tobacco district. All the product of this district is bought up by rehandlers in the principal towns.

Though the largest proportion of the tobacco of this district has been prepared for the British market, yet a small part of it has been taken by the trade in the United States on account of its sweetness and toughness—the lugs and common dark leaf by the manufacturers of lower grades of smoking-tobacco and plug tobaccos, and the finer parts of the crop for the better grades of chewing-tobacco.

It is estimated that of the crop grown in this district in 1879 the percentages of grades were as follows: Dark shipping, 33 per cent.; fillers (one-half White Burley), 30 per cent.; smokers, 8 per cent.; wrappers, 2 per cent.; cutting, 10 per cent.; nondescript, 17 per cent. Ten years previously the proportions of grades were as follows: Dark shipping, 50 per cent.; sweet fillers, 10 per cent.; cuttings, 10 per cent.; wrappers and smokers, 10 per cent.; nondescript, 20 per cent.

The requirements of the home manufacturers and the dullness of the markets abroad have produced the changes indicated, and the shipping and stemming types, suitable for home consumption, have greatly improved.

MANUFACTURING DISTRICT.

The annual average production of this district is about 3,850,000 pounds. It produces a very fine grade of manufacturing tobacco, having a fine fiber, and the crop contains a fair proportion of colored and yellow leaf, which approximates in character the finer styles of Virginia leaf.

Callaway, Osage, and Franklin counties raise a fair proportion of bright wrappers, which have been valued highly by manufacturers in former years, but are rather too small for western manufacturers. Small crops of a mixed character are raised in Saint Charles, Laclede, Dallas, Webster, Greene, and other counties of Missouri. Jackson county, in the western part of the state, raises a small quantity of very fine tobacco, resembling that grown in Callaway county. It is generally conceded, however, that the latter county raises the finest tobacco grown in the state, rivaling in the brilliancy of its yellow color the hickory leaf of autumn. The light wrappers, fillers, and smokers grown in this county command very high prices, some of the wrappers selling in the Saint Louis market for 50 cents per pound.

The product of Montgomery, Lincoln, Warren, and Pike is used for plug fillers almost exclusively, but the crop has been gradually decreasing in quantity for several years. All the tobacco grown in Pike county is consumed at the manufacturing establishments situated in the county.

The following will show the production of the several counties in the manufacturing district during the past four years, only the figures for 1879 being from census returns:

Counties.	1876.	1877.	1878.	1879.
	Pounds.	*Pounds.*	*Pounds.*	*Pounds.*
Callaway	1,922,865	1,450,385	853,340	570,231
Franklin	108,792	106,587	104,610	94,134
Lincoln	916,420	924,270	606,280	808,000
Montgomery	428,061	475,421	213,022	181,761
Osage	118,876	120,476	96,572	52,010
Pike	880,788	916,996	583,390	408,473
Warren	174,821	184,362	140,321	86,072
Total	4,551,523	4,184,497	2,600,141	1,701,391

All tobacco raised in the state outside of the manufacturing district may be referred to the heavy shipping grades, except about 15 per cent. of White Burley.

KINDS OF SOILS PREFERRED FOR TOBACCO IN DIFFERENT COUNTIES.

Referring to the schedules returned from Missouri, we find the following descriptions of soils preferred for tobacco:

CALLAWAY.—For growing manufacturing tobacco, white-oak ridge land, with scattering hickory along the water-courses, freshly cleared; for shipping tobacco, river and creek bottoms and black-hickory lands, with a few black oaks.

CHARITON.—For fine tobacco, a grayish soil, clayey and sandy loam on uplands, the original growth of which is white oak, linden, hackberry, with papaw undergrowth. Alluvial soils are cultivated to some extent. Rich, hilly lands are best adapted to the growth of White Burley. It will "scab" on bottom lands.

CARROLL.—Clay loam, freshly cleared, preferred; original growth, hickory and white oak.

FRANKLIN.—Upland clayey soils, having a rolling surface, known as oak and hickory lands, make the finest tobacco.

HOWARD.—White-oak lands, freshly cleared. A large proportion of the crop is planted on old lands, which produce the heaviest tobacco.

LINCOLN.—Freshly-cleared white-oak soils, fine, sandy, and clayey on uplands; white oak, ash, and walnut growth.

LINN.—Hickory and pin-oak soil on uplands, gray in color, with a pale yellowish subsoil.

MACON.—Light, sandy loam, on rolling lands, with a timber growth of hickory and white oak. Clayey soils produce heavy tobacco; sandy loams a bright fancy type, in demand by home manufacturers.

OSAGE.—Both river bottoms and uplands are planted in tobacco, the former making the heaviest article, and the latter the finest and best for the manufacturer. White oak is the characteristic growth on the best upland soils.

RANDOLPH.—Good sandy soil or limestone land. The best and finest tobacco is grown on new lands, which for two successive years produce the high-priced fancy grades, and sometimes, but rarely, a good-colored leaf is grown on old lands. The soil preferred has a strong white-oak growth, and is underlaid with limestone. Other characteristic trees on best tobacco soils are hickory, linn, hackberry, pin oak, and post oak.

SALINE.—All kinds of soil are cultivated in tobacco, viz, prairie, bluff loam, timbered, and bottom lands. The timbered bluff-loam land is preferred, which has a tree-covering of white oak, sassafras, and hickory. Soils upon which black oak and wild cherry grow are also admirably adapted to the growth of tobacco.

Tobacco grown upon prairie soil is the least desirable of any grown in the state, being coarse, deficient in gum, with a leaf too thick and too lifeless for the requirements of the domestic manufacturer, yet too deficient in fatty qualities to make a good shipping leaf.

A growth of white oak and linden, with papaw undergrowth, indicates the best soil for the finest grades of manufacturing leaf. The heaviest shipping leaf is grown upon soils the original timber of which was burr oak, red elm, and walnut. The sandy soils do not grow as heavy a leaf as the more silty, argillaceous soils.

It may be said generally for all the counties of Missouri that the heavy types are grown upon rich, clayey soils, and the finer types upon the thin ridges. For growing cutting tobacco new ground is preferred; for fillers, new ground and clover fallow; for shipping leaf, bottom lands, manured lots, and very fertile uplands; and for the production of fine yellow wrappers and smokers thin uplands, freshly cleared, with a characteristic growth of hickory and white or post oak.

All soils for tobacco must be well drained. It is estimated that the tobacco grown upon lands freshly cleared is worth in the market about 50 per cent. more per pound, on an average, than that grown on old lands. The condition of the soils is generally very good, being loose and porous, and while they wear easily on rolling surfaces they are exceedingly durable upon level areas. Some of the clayey soils are refractory, and require to be broken in the fall, so that they may be ameliorated by the winter freezing. The bluff loam, owing to its large content of sandy material, as well as the deep, black, sandy soils that prevail in the bottoms, is always in fine tilth when well broken, and seldom compacts so closely as to diminish the vigor of vegetable life, and owing to its powdery condition it readily supplies to the plant the food with which it is so freely charged. By far the largest proportion of the tobacco crop of the state is grown upon this loam and upon alluviums derived, in part or in whole, from its erosion.

Very little land is turned out as old fields and abandoned in Missouri, but a few spots here and there may be seen on abrupt declivities, where the surface soil has been removed by heavy rainfalls.

VARIETIES GROWN IN THE HEAVY TOBACCO DISTRICT.

CHARITON AND CARROLL COUNTIES.—Previous to 1880 Yellow, Silky, and Blue Pryors were grown more extensively in these counties than any others. A small percentage of Shoestring and One-sucker was planted, and some Orinoco, Little Vick, and Frederick. The Shoestring variety is less liable to be broken by heavy winds, and is therefore preferred for prairie lands. Shipping leaf is mostly made of the Blue Pryor, manufacturing fillers of the Yellow and Silky Pryors, and stemming tobacco of the Orinoco and Frederick, the two latter having very wide leaves. The White Burley was extensively planted in 1880.

HOWARD COUNTY.—Orinoco is largely planted on white-oak hill lands, Blue Pryor on bottom lands, the White Burley on clover lands and on lands freshly cleared, and the Shoestring on open prairie.

RANDOLPH COUNTY.—All the varieties which are grown in Chariton county, with the addition of Medley Pryor and Red Burley, are produced in this county. The last-named variety is used for making cutters, and is grown for the most part on freshly-cleared white-oak lands. The Medley Pryor makes a good shipping leaf, and finds its most congenial soil on creek bottoms and on old manured lots.

The varieties grown in the remaining counties of the district do not differ from those already given.

VARIETIES GROWN IN MANUFACTURING DISTRICT.

CALLAWAY COUNTY.—Golden Pemberton, Tomahawk, Silky Pryor, and White Burley are most generally cultivated in this country. The first resembles both the Orinoco and the Yellow Pryor, and is supposed to be a sub-variety from cross-fertilization of the two varieties. Its habit of growth is like the Orinoco, but it cures to a bright-yellow color much more easily. It is sweeter and heavier than the Yellow Pryor, and colors like it, but in general appearance, weight of leaf, and sweetness of flavor it is like the Orinoco. It is a great favorite among growers for making yellow wrappers and smokers. The Tomahawk resembles the Golden Pemberton, but has a quicker growth. It is the sweetest and most easily cured to a bright yellow of any variety yet produced in the state, but its leaf is too short to make the highest-priced wrappers. The Silky Pryor is thought to equal the Tomahawk in its growing and curing qualities, having sufficient length of leaf, but lacking sweetness of flavor. The White Burley, up to 1880, had not been tested here sufficiently to justify an opinion as to its merits. A few who occupy farms on the river and creek bottoms plant the Orinoco, Brittle-stem, and Blue Pryor, and make a good quality of shipping leaf. The first three varieties mentioned are held in high repute by manufacturers, and are grown upon a light sandy soil with a yellow-clay subsoil. If planted upon the more fertile black soils they approximate the shipping varieties in general coarseness of appearance, but without the richness or size of the shipping leaf. Only the white-oak ridge lands of the county supply soils well adapted to the growth of the yellow tobacco. The cigar varieties, when tried, failed in quality, and they are not planted to any extent.

PIKE COUNTY.—A variety called Yellow Orinoco is grown in this county in addition to the kinds already mentioned as growing in Callaway county. This is said to have a long, large leaf, and varies very much in color and in quality upon different soils. The variety known as the Golden Pemberton, already described as growing in Callaway county, when grown upon the soils of Pike county has a thin, light leaf, curing with a considerable variation in color, and is unsatisfactory when employed for manufacturing purposes. In this county the yellow Orinoco is preferred because of its richness, sweetness, and delicacy of flavor. Here, as in Callaway county, the finest tobacco, and that which commands the highest price, is grown on white-oak ridges, while that grown on elm and hickory land is coarse in structure and strong to the taste.

LINCOLN COUNTY.—Two kinds of Orinoco are grown; one suited for making heavy shipping tobacco, and the other, doubtless the Yellow Orinoco, suitable for manufacturing purposes. The first is planted on the elm and hickory lands, and the last on white-oak lands. The White Burley does not succeed well except on rich river and creek bottoms, and the Yellow Pryor, which is grown to some extent, is light and trashy.

All the other counties in the district raise the same varieties, some farmers preferring one and some another, according to the soils and the purposes for which the tobacco is grown.

Of the counties included in the manufacturing district Callaway, Pike, Osage, and Franklin attempt to grow tobacco for manufacturing purposes exclusively, while Montgomery, Lincoln, and Warren grow both manufacturing and shipping tobacco. In the first group of counties the proportion of types, as compared with 1869, is as follows:

Type.	1879.	1869.
	Per cent.	*Per cent.*
Dark shipping	20	40
Fillers	40	20
Bright wrappers and smokers.	20	....
Cutting	10	....
Nondescript	10	40

It will be seen that the advance has been very rapid from low types of shipping leaf and nondescript to fillers and bright wrappers and smokers.

In the second group of counties a comparison of the proportion of types for the same period shows:

Type.	1879.	1869.
	Per cent.	*Per cent.*
Dark shipping	35	35
Fillers	35	25
Bright wrappers and smokers.	20	20
Nondescript	10	20

These are merely approximations, but they indicate that there is a general tendency to abandon the cultivation of the heavier export types and grow such varieties as may be used most profitably in domestic manufacture. The same may be said of the region known as the heavy shipping district, where the change is going on with much greater rapidity, as the following will indicate:

Type.	1879.	1869.
	Per cent.	*Per cent.*
Dark shipping	33	60
Fillers	30	10
Bright wrappers and smokers.	17	....
Nondescript	20	30

It was estimated that fully half the crop of 1880 would be suitable for the domestic manufacturer. The quality of shipping and stemming sorts is gradually deteriorating under the discouragement of the low prices. On the other hand, there is a decided improvement in the quality of the sorts suitable for manufacturing, some of the worst and some of the best types of tobacco being grown side by side on soils identical in character, productive capacity, and exposure.

PLANTING, CULTIVATION, CURING, AND HANDLING OF THE TOBACCO CROP.

In the cultivation of the crop in Missouri, especially in the heavy tobacco district, fertilizers are rarely used. Most of the land is freshly cleared, which, after growing three or four crops of tobacco successively, is devoted to the production of corn, wheat, or hay. When grown upon old land, the crop is rotated with wheat and clover. Of the land planted in tobacco one-sixth is virgin soil, one-fourth has borne one crop, one-fourth two crops, one-fourth three crops, and one-twelfth is old manured land. The tobacco of the second year on fresh land is the heaviest, and there is a deterioration of 10 per cent. in quality and quantity after that time.

The time for sowing seed-beds is the first week in March, and the transplanting is generally done from the 1st to the 20th of June. Beds are protected from the fly by a covering of muslin, and also by sprinkling them with a diluted preparation of *aqua ammoniæ*.

The land intended for tobacco is turned to the depth of 6 or 8 inches, sometimes in the fall, but generally in March, and again in May. After the last breaking it is well harrowed two or more times, is then laid off $3\frac{1}{2}$ feet each way, and hills made at the points of intersection. Sometimes two furrows are thrown upon the first, making a ridge. The top of this is cut off and patted at intervals of $2\frac{1}{2}$ to $3\frac{1}{2}$ feet, and the plants are set out at these places. In the preparation of virgin soil the leaves and trash which remain after the wood and brush are taken away or burned up are raked in piles and burned. A jumping colter is then used for breaking, going over the land twice, the last plowing crossing the first. It is then harrowed, rebroken with a turning-plow, and again harrowed. The roots are removed, the land is laid off in rows $3\frac{1}{2}$ feet apart one way, and the plants are set on the edge of the furrow, $2\frac{1}{2}$ feet apart.

The amount of cultivation which the crop receives depends more upon the time at the planter's command than upon anything else. Each one, however, endeavors to plow the crop sufficiently often to keep down the weeds and grass, which, upon all land except virgin soils, is about three times, following the plows each time with hoes and cutting away any grass or weeds which may be left. On virgin soils the cultivation is much less, being restricted to about two plowings, only one being given when it is desired to make a very fine article of tobacco.

Some good growers do not prime the tobacco plant; others pull off five or six of the lower leaves at the time of topping, which takes place when a sufficient number of leaves has developed on the stalk, generally when the button makes its appearance. If the planting be early, and a heavy article of tobacco is desired, the plant is topped to ten leaves, and to a less number as the season advances. On virgin soils the plant is topped to twelve or fourteen leaves; the White Burley variety usually to fourteen or sixteen leaves. This latter variety is only suckered twice, while the heavier varieties are suckered three or four times before ripening. The usual time between topping and cutting is from four to six weeks, the shorter time being sufficient to mature the White Burley. The cutting season begins September 1, and continues throughout the month, sometimes running into October. The only difference to be observed in the method of cutting tobacco in this district and in the Lower Green River district of Kentucky is that in the latter district the plants are split with a knife before they are severed and afterward straddled over a stick, while in Missouri the practice is to sever the stalk with a knife, chisel, or hatchet, and spear the plants upon a stick, as is done in Maryland and in the seed-leaf districts. Of plants of ordinary size, eight are put on a stick 4½ feet long, but of the White Burley variety only six.

In the heavy tobacco district ninety-nine hundredths of the crop is air-cured. A very few planters use log fires, and still fewer have adopted flues. When cut, the tobacco is scaffolded in the field until partially cured, when it is removed to open barns, generally built of logs, 20 feet square. Sometimes these barns are studded with hip-rafters (*vide* cut in chapter on Tennessee), but are always so constructed that the air can have free circulation. The damage done the crop by pole-sweating varies greatly with the season, being always greatest in a hot, damp season. From four to six weeks are required for the tobacco to cure fully by the natural process of evaporation. A very small part of the crop is sun-cured on scaffolds, which process gives it great sweetness.

In the manufacturing district about 5 per cent. of the area cultivated receives a slight application of stable manure. The deterioration of the productive capacity of the soil in this district is much more rapid than in the heavy shipping district, and fertilizing or rotation of crops becomes a necessity. The rotation most generally practiced is: First year, tobacco; second, wheat and clover; third and fourth, clover; and fifth, tobacco. This rotation results in remunerative crops, not only of tobacco, but of grain and of clover.

It must be borne in mind that there is not such a difference in the constitution of the soils of the two districts as the statement above would seem to imply. In the heavy shipping district the very best soils are planted in tobacco, and they can be kept in tobacco for several years in succession. In the manufacturing district the thin white-oak soils, naturally poor and with but little strength of constitution, are utilized in the growing of the crop, and are adapted to the production of the finest types of tobacco. The time required to ripen is longer than in the heavy tobacco district, running from five to eight weeks; in fact, the plants are allowed to stand upon the hill until they turn yellow and begin to waste. The cutting begins about September 10, and continues until frost. When air-cured, it is allowed to remain on scaffolds in the fields for several days, and is then taken to the barns, and the same is done when cured with wood; but when cured by charcoal or by flues it is the usual practice to take it at once to the curing-houses and arrange it properly on the tiers. The processes of curing by charcoal and by flues are elaborately given in the chapter on North Carolina. That portion of the crop cured with wood fires is generally placed in the shipping grades. It is estimated that three-tenths of the product of the district is sun- or air-cured, three-tenths cured with wood fires, one-third with charcoal, and one-fifteenth by flues. Flues are often constructed of brick, at a cost of $30, and old steamboat-boiler flues are sometimes utilized for curing the crop, being elevated above the floors of the barn 6 or 8 inches. The flues most generally used are made by digging trenches in the floors of the barns and covering them with sheet-iron, and have apertures on the outside of the barns for firing and for the discharge of the smoke.

In the shipping district farmers usually make two grades, lugs and leaf, and sell to redriers, who assort into long bright and short bright, long dark and short dark, bright and dark lugs, and nondescript. Occasionally a farmer will pack his crop in casks. He then makes three grades: lugs, long leaf, and short leaf.

In the manufacturing district the assorting is much more tedious, for the yellow tobacco is usually put into three or four grades, in addition to the grades already named in which tobacco is assorted in the heavy shipping district. The crop is usually prized from May until July.

The market prices for the various types and varieties of the crop are about as follows: Flue-cured yellow leaf, per one hundred pounds, $10 to $60 for selections; White Burley, well handled, $6 to $10 for the whole crop; manufacturing fillers, air-cured, $5 to $7 for the whole crop; shipping leaf, air-cured, $3 50 to $6 for the whole crop. About one-ninetieth of the crop is yellow wrapper. Where a division is made in the crop of lugs and leaf air-cured shipping will bring, for lugs, from $1 to $2; leaf, from $4 to $7 per hundred pounds.

Where the crop is sold loose to dealers it is tied in very large bundles, containing from thirty to forty leaves each, and when it is to be prized each bundle contains only eight or ten leaves. Loose tobacco is delivered to dealers in very damp condition, and they redry, reassort, and retie it. It is then bulked down, each grade being kept separate, and allowed to go through the process of sweating or fermentation.

The casks used for packing are 42 inches in diameter and 56 inches in length, and the number of pounds packed in a cask varies with the grade of tobacco, as follows: Shipping leaf, 1,300 to 1,400 pounds; lugs, 1,600 to 1,800; fillers, 1,000 to 1,200. Wrappers are packed usually in tubs 3 feet in diameter and 2 feet high, each of which contains from 50 to 150 pounds. Sometimes they are packed in boxes weighing from 200 to 400 pounds. The staves for hogsheads are sawed, and cost $1 per hundred feet. Sixty-five feet, board measure, will make one hogshead, and 25 feet additional for two heads. Hoop-poles cost 3 cents each, delivered. Nails and cooperage make up the cost of hogsheads to $1 90 each.

TOBACCO STRIPS.

No strips for exportation were made in the state for the year beginning June 1, 1879, and ending May 31, 1880. Previous to 1860 a very large proportion of the product of the heavy tobacco district was stemmed, the large and leafy character grown, with its great absorptive capacity, making it well adapted for that purpose.

COST OF GROWING TOBACCO.

The great fertility of the virgin soils of Missouri, their adaptation to the growth of the tobacco plant, and the small amount of cultivation required to produce the crop, reduce the cost of production to a minimum upon the richer soils. Taking as an illustration Chariton county, which occupies a central position in the heavy tobacco district, the best tobacco lands, cleared and inclosed, are worth in the market $20 per acre, and they have the capacity to produce from 1,000 to 1,800 pounds of tobacco to the acre, varying with a favorable or unfavorable season. Assuming the average to be 1,400 pounds to the acre for best soils, we have:

DR.	
Hire of one man for four months, at $12 50	$50 00
Board of hand	20 00
Use of horse and feed for same	12 25
Use of plows, wagon, barn, etc	10 00
Use of three acres land (interest on price)	3 60
	95 85

CR.	
By 4,200 pounds of tobacco, at 4½ cents	189 00
Profit on best lands, per acre	31 05
Profit on each hand employed	93 15
Cost of production, $2 28 per hundred pounds.	

This, it must be remembered, is for the best soils and under the most favorable conditions of culture and development. There are thin soils planted in tobacco that will not make over 650 pounds per acre, but the growth upon such soils commands a much higher price, and in this there is often a compensation for the loss in the quantity produced. The average yield per acre for Chariton county in 1879 was 937 pounds, and on this basis, taking the average price of the crop at 4½ cents per pound, the expense of labor, tools, and land remaining the same, we shall have:

Average profit per acre	$10 21
Profit on each hand employed	30 63
Cost of production per 100 pounds	3 41

A gentleman residing in Boone county writes that he raised 40 acres of tobacco a few years since entirely with hired labor and kept an accurate account of the cost up to the time the crop was delivered at the factory. The entire product was 42,000 pounds, and the total cost of production was $3 35 per hundred pounds. The profits arising from the cultivation of the White Burley, at an average price of 8 cents per pound (prices vary from 6 to 10 cents, crops round) and an average yield of 1,200 pounds per acre, will be: Per acre, $64 15; per hand, $192 15; cost of production per hundred pounds, $2 66.

The following statement comes from a trustworthy source in Callaway county, in the manufacturing district: The price of the best tobacco lands per acre varies from $5 to $8 per acre. Two crops are usually given tenants for clearing and fencing the land, and some tobacco is grown on "shares". The price of labor varies from $12 to

$15 per month for men, and from 50 to 75 cents by the day. Half these prices are paid for women, who, when well trained, are excellent workers in tobacco. The cost of cultivating an acre in fancy tobacco is given as follows:

Cost of seed-bed for one acre	$1 00
Cost of seed	25
Weeding and attention to bed	1 00
Rent of land (interest on price)	50
Cost of breaking one acre twice	3 00
Harrowing, lining, and hilling	4 50
Drawing and setting out plants	2 25
Cultivating	5 50
Topping, worming, and suckering	5 00
Harvesting and curing with charcoal	20 00
Taking down, assorting, and stripping	10 00
Bulking and prizing	5 00
Use of horse, wagon, laths, etc	10 00
Delivering to market	2 00
	70 00

The average yield is 500 pounds; value in market, at 20 cents per pound, $100; profit per acre, $30; cost of production, 14 cents per pound. The enumerator's returns of the crop of 1879 in Callaway county show an average yield of 485 pounds per acre.

Planters and dealers who pack their tobacco in this district aim to get the wrappers on the market while in the sweat, and the smokers and fillers just after they have passed through that process.

An estimate given by a gentleman in Stoddard county places the total cost of production per acre at $30 50. The yield on good soils is not far from 800 pounds per acre, though the average for the county in 1879 was only 686 pounds. Taking the highest yield, and the cost amounts to $3 81 per hundred pounds; with the average yield it amounts to $4 44. The price of labor in this division of the state is much lower than in other tobacco-growing sections. Good men are hired at $10 a month and board, and excellent tobacco lands can be bought at $5 per acre.

The following are the estimates of value per pound for the crops of the various counties reporting:

BOLLINGER.—But little sold; 10 cents.

BOONE.—Average value, 7.7 cents; cutting and Burley tobacco, 10 cents; shipping leaf, 5 cents.

BUTLER.—Average value, 5 cents.

CARROLL.—Average value, 5 cents; lugs, 2 cents; shipping leaf, 4½ to 5 cents; fillers, 7 to 7½ cents; wrappers, bright and mahogany, 10 to 25 cents.

CALLAWAY.—Average value, 8¼ cents; lugs, 2½ cents; shipping leaf, 5 cents; fillers, 7 to 9 cents; wrappers, 10 to 60 cents.

CHARITON.—Average value, 4½ cents; lugs, shipping, 1 to 2 cents; leaf, shipping, 4 to 6 cents; fillers, manufacturing, 5 to 7 cents; White Burley, crop round, 6 to 10 cents; bright wrappers, 10 to 60 cents.

FRANKLIN.—Average value, 8 cents; dark shipping, crops round, 5 cents; fillers, for manufacturing, 5 to 6 cents; bright wrappers, first grade, 50 to 70 cents; second grade, 40 to 50 cents; third grade, 17 to 28 cents; fourth grade, 7 to 15 cents.

HOWARD.—Average value, 4¾ cents; trash, 2 cents; medium shipping, 3½ cents; good shipping, 4½ cents; bright tobacco, 5 to 8 cents; White Burley, 5 to 10 cents.

LINCOLN.—Average value, 6½ cents; lugs, 2 to 4½ cents; fillers, 6 to 9 cents; wrappers, 12 to 20 cents.

LACLEDE.—Average value, 5 cents.

MACON.—Average value, 4½ cents.

OSAGE.—Average value, 8 cents; shipping leaf, 4 cents; fillers, 7 cents; wrappers, 10 to 30 cents.

PIKE.—Average value, 7 cents; shipping tobacco, crop round, 4½ cents; air-cured manufacturing fillers, 7 cents; bright wrappers, 10 to 27 cents.

RANDOLPH.—Average value, 4½ cents; lugs, shipping, 1 to 2 cents; leaf, 4 to 6 cents; fillers, 5 to 6 cents; wrappers, 10 to 15 cents; White Burley, 7 cents.

SALINE.—Average value, 4 cents; lugs, 1 to 2 cents; leaf, shipping, 4 to 5½ cents; fillers, air-cured, 5 to 6 cents.

STODDARD.—Average value, 5 cents; best heavy shipping, 8 cents; lugs of same, 3 to 4 cents; good air-cured fillers, 9½ cents; wrappers, 13 cents; trash and nondescript, 1 to 3 cents.

SULLIVAN.—Average price, 4 cents.

WARREN.—Average value, 7 cents; common heavy lugs, 2 cents; low leaf, 3 cents; fillers, manufacturing, 4 to 5 cents; wrappers, common, 6 to 7 cents; wrappers, fine, 8 to 15 cents.

Chapter XI.

CULTURE AND CURING OF TOBACCO IN NEW YORK.

The culture of tobacco in New York began in Marcellus township, Onondaga county, in 1845, where it was introduced by Chester Moses and Nathan Grimes. In 1846 Mars Reading, of Salina township, raised 10 acres, and others were engaged in its culture in different parts of the county. In 1855 the county raised 554,987 pounds, or about 1,178 pounds to the acre. In 1856, or about that time, agencies for New York houses were established at Syracuse, and by 1863 the culture of tobacco had grown to large proportions in several counties.

During the early years of its culture the product was put up in boxes of various sizes, usually dry-goods or shoe cases, purchased second hand. There was no system, and neither grower nor buyer knew what kind or how much of any grade of tobacco each box contained. In the absence of inspection, buyers were compelled to rely each upon his own judgment as to grades and values, and few farmers had the knowledge of what was required for proper curing. The industry was a new one, the character of the product uncertain, and the profits of its culture were more frequently realized by the trader than by the farmer. Many new varieties have now been introduced, including Cuban and Spanish tobacco, together with some hybrids of considerable value, and the product of the New York tobacco districts now approximates that of the Connecticut valley.

Between 1845 and 1863 prices were subject to great fluctuations, often 5 or 6 cents per pound during the season. No statistics have been kept as to either price or production for those eighteen years, but prices ranged from 5 to 30 cents, the market sympathizing with the values in the Connecticut markets, and it is estimated that by the year 1863 the production had increased to about 6,000 cases of 400 pounds, net, each. The great bulk of the crops up to this time had been sold to local speculators and to manufacturers at from 5 to 18 cents, and sometimes, when the market was excited or cigar tobacco was scarce, as high as 20 to 30 cents.

In 1862-'63-'64 tobacco was very high, 30 cents being paid for some, while 25 cents was not uncommon. In 1863 prices fluctuated violently, falling at one time to 8 and 10 cents, and from 1864 to 1870 prices varied from 5 to 25 cents. In 1870 tobacco was sold as high as 30 cents, and much of the product was sold from second hands at from 27 to 35 cents. The crop of that year was excellent.

The crops of 1872 and 1873, being large, brought low prices. In 1872 prices ranged from 7 to 19 cents, but most of the crops were sold at from 10 to 12 cents. The crop of 1873 brought from 5 to 12 cents. Since that year prices have varied considerably, ranging from 4½ to 20 cents.

The quantity of tobacco produced is increasing, and is of a better quality. In 1879 prices ranged from 5 to 16 cents for Big Flats Seed-Leaf, while domestic Havana brought from 10 to 18 cents. The quantity produced in 1879 was about 6,000 cases on Big Flats and vicinity, and 10,000 cases elsewhere in the state. The product of the Big Flats district from 1858 to 1863 is estimated to have been from 1,000 to 2,000 cases; from 1863 to 1866, from 2,500 to 3,000 cases; and from 1866 to 1878, from 3,500 to 4,000 cases.

The prices paid for Big Flats tobacco have been higher than those paid in Onondaga county, except for domestic Havana, which is not raised on Big Flats. New York raises only seed-leaf and the foreign or domestic Cuba tobacco, used mainly for cigars.

The chief tobacco regions are fifteen townships in Onondaga county, eight in Cayuga, seven in Oswego, five in Madison, three in Tompkins, seven in Chemung, three in Steuben, two in Schuyler, one in Monroe, one in Genesee, three in Wayne, four in Tioga, and several in Orleans, with the eastern tobacco region of New York, which forms part of the Housatonic valley, and is described with Connecticut.

CLIMATE.

The temperature at Ithaca during a period of over fourteen years of observation showed a mean of 48.2 degrees, and the average annual rainfall during eight years was 30 inches. The prevailing winds during June, July, August, September, October, and November for the same period were from the northwest. The mean average temperature of Cayuga for ten years was 48.93 degrees, and the average range 88. The prevailing winds in June, July, August, September, October, and November were from the south. The mean average rainfall was 32.50 inches. Cayuga is 447 feet above tide-water. The town of Hamilton, in Madison county, from the record of eighteen years, showed a mean temperature of 44.89 degrees, and for fourteen years had an average annual rainfall of 35.77 inches. The prevailing winds for June and July were from the west, and those of August, September, October, and November were from the northwest. The average mean temperature of Onondaga for sixteen years was 47.18 degrees, the average rainfall for the same time 31.40 inches, and the prevailing winds were from the west. At Rochester the mean temperature of fourteen years was 46.54 degrees, and the average fall of rain 39.95 inches. During May, June, July, August, September, October, and November the prevailing winds were northwest. Rochester is 506 feet above tide-water. The summer climate of interior New York is tempered by the numerous lakes which are inclosed in its bounds. The city of Albany, on near the same latitude as the places named, had a mean average temperature for twenty years, covering the same periods before cited, of 48.26 degrees. The average quantity of rain which fell was 40.80 inches, and the prevailing winds were from the south.

COMPARISON OF RECENT TOBACCO CROPS.

The tobacco area of 1879 was greater than that of 1878 by 35 per cent., greater than that of 1877 by 50 per cent., and about equal to that of 1876, and the yield per acre is reported as about the same for the different years. The quality in 1879 did not differ from that of 1878, but was better than that of 1877, and was about the same as that of 1876, being sound, of good quality, and thick in leaf.

VARIETIES OF TOBACCO.

A great many varieties are grown, as the Connecticut Broad Leaf, Ohio Broad Leaf, Connecticut Long and Narrow Leaf, Belknap Broad Leaf, Wellington Leaf, Deer's Ear, Duck Island, Wilson's Hybrid or domestic Havana, Spanish, Cuba, and Maryland Broad Leaf. The seed-leaf is raised more than any other. Of this variety all the kinds mentioned are represented, the Connecticut being perhaps the most extensively cultivated. The domestic Havanas come next, and both kinds are almost exclusively used for cigar fillers and wrappers, while the lower grades of seed-leaf are quite largely exported. The Glessner and Pennsylvania Broad Leaf are most highly commended in the reports, and are beginning to equal the Connecticut Seed-Leaf in general cultivation. The seed-leaf varieties are, in general, large, drooping, and tall, but with much difference in the length and breadth of leaf. The Havana grows tall and slender, with leaves erect, short and round, and far apart on the stalk. There are many varieties of the Cuban tobacco, and the nomenclature is in inextricable confusion—one being called Cuba, another "Havana", and another Domestic Havana. The Havana is raised mostly in Clay township, Onondaga county, and is there said to come nearest to the true Cuban flavor. The distinction between these tobaccos is not difficult to point out. The seed-leaf is native, and then there are the foreign or Cuban varieties, all more or less changed by soil and by climate. The hybrids are supposed to be crosses between the Cuban varieties and the seed-leaf, and tend to supersede the foreign varieties, because, with as fine flavor, they will produce more. The Wilson Hybrid grows erect, with broad, well-formed leaves, glossy, thin, and fine in texture. It is delicately organized, with veins and stems small and the ribs of moderate size. Mr. Wilson, who has experimented for thirty years in tobacco, tried the Cuban with moderate success, and from a western seed-leaf and Havana seed from the Vuelta Abajo district he obtained a cross which is the Wilson Hybrid. He claims a high rank for its flavor, color, and the excellence of the cigars made from it, its erect habit and tenacity of life under adverse circumstances, and affirms that it does not require as strong land as the seed-leaf. He frankly admits that it is yet an experiment, and the question is whether it will deteriorate and lose its flavor. Until 1880 it was raised only by three or four farmers beside Mr. Wilson, and by them only for two years; but in 1880 it was largely raised, with growing favor, in Onondaga and adjoining counties.

Haynes' Hybrid is similar, but darker in color, with the leaves thicker and broader. This variety has been raised for several years, although by a few growers only until recently. Within two years its cultivation has been widely extended. Both this and the Wilson will raise from 1,200 to 1,500 pounds per acre, although larger crops can be grown. Mr. Wilson raised 10 tons from 10 acres in 1878. More than three-fourths of the crop of 1881 will be of these two varieties. Both stand without injury the second sweat which the cigar manufacturers give their tobacco.

Much attention is now paid to cross-fertilization. Successful experiments with strawberries and other plants stimulated the same line of experiment with tobacco, and Mr. Wilson's is about the first systematic attempt to improve tobacco, although chance has developed some excellent varieties.

GRADES OF TOBACCO.

In 1879 the grades of the product were reported as follows: Seed-leaf wrappers, 65 per cent.; binders, 25 per cent.; fillers, 10 per cent; in 1869, wrappers, 50 per cent.; binders, 30 per cent.; fillers, 20 per cent. Havana tobacco being newly introduced, no data can be given.

The reasons for the increase of higher grades in the decade are better culture, handling, and assorting. The quality of the leaf is reported improved in burning qualities, the ash being whiter. Great care is exercised now in selecting soil adapted to produce a free-burning white-ash tobacco. Tobacco is grown much darker than ten years ago, the dark color being as much a desideratum as a light color in North Carolina.

TOBACCO SOILS.

A sandy or gravelly loam, with soil deep, dark, and rich, is preferred, for seed-leaf especially. The timber growth of the lands most in use is beech, maple, pine, and chestnut. Where the growth is beech and maple the soils produce a very fine, dark, rich tobacco, but the growth is not so fine as when the soil is a very fertile, sandy loam, with a growth of chestnut and pine. No new land is used, and the product is not valuable. The soils cultivated in tobacco are generally of limestone or drift derivation. Clay and peat or muck soils are not adapted to the growth of tobacco of a good quality, and the light, friable, porous, sandy loams, well drained, dry, and warm, grow the best leaf. On these a rapid growth and early maturity can be secured. The pine and chestnut soils are from

6 to 20 inches in depth, and will bear plowing from 6 to 10 inches deep. While the best crops are raised on the fertile, sandy loams, very fine crops are also raised on the beech and maple lands, with basswood or linden and elm intermixed.

Much the larger portion of Onondaga, which is the chief and a fairly typical tobacco county, is on a limestone formation. The leaf grown on the sandy loams of the pine and chestnut regions and that grown on the strictly limestone soils, with a loose, friable loam and a growth of beech and maple, burn freely with a white ash, and has an excellent flavor, is rich in color, is of fine texture, and has a good body. The muck or peat-swamp lands and stiff clay soils produce a slow-growing tobacco, which lacks free-burning qualities, and the leaves are a dark ash. The sandy lands, dark and light, and the limestone soils, are those mostly cultivated in tobacco. The clays are stiff, moist, cold, and hard to work, the product often full of white veins, stiff and harsh, and burns poorly. About one-half of the soil suited to tobacco in Onondaga county is now occupied. Of the woodlands of this county most of the upland is adapted to its growth.

The underlying rocks in Onondaga, Madison, and portions of Oswego are blue limestone. In Manlius township, Onondaga county, there are large deposits of gypsum and water-cement limestone. Excellent free-burning tobacco is produced on the gypsum formations. Gypsum is used freely on tobacco lands with good effect. Red sandstone crops out in portions of Onondaga, but the lands on this formation are but little used for tobacco. The great salt belt also runs through the tobacco region. This belt has an underlying formation of red, soft shale, or "marking stone", upon which tobacco is grown with success. Much the larger portion of the crop of New York is grown upon limestone soils.

The soil of the Chemung Flats and of the Big Flats is a rich, deep, dark loam, sometimes mixed with fine gravel, and admirably suited to tobacco. These soils are made up of alluvial deposits, and differ in that respect from those of Onondaga.

TOBACCO MANURES.

Manures of various kinds are used on between 50 and 80 per cent. of the tobacco raised, and phosphates and guano are sometimes applied in the hill, about 200 pounds to the acre, at a cost of $4 per acre. Tobacco-growers, however, are only beginning to experiment with commercial fertilizers. Generally fifteen or twenty, and often as much as forty loads of stable, barn-yard, and hog-pen manures are applied per acre, and the cost is estimated at from $5 to $40 per acre, a good authority placing the average at $15. The improvement in quantity is estimated at from 25 to 75 per cent. in actual practice, according to the kind and quantity used, with an improvement in quality of from 40 to 60 per cent. The coarser portions of barn-yard manures are scattered on the field and plowed in, but the more valuable portions are made into composts, with ashes, lime, gypsum, and potash, to be applied in the hill, a handful being covered 2 or 3 inches deep in the center and the plant set in this. When it can be bought at all, stable manure is sold at the barn for about $1 a load.

Bone dust, plaster, and lime have been used to some extent, but the concentrated fertilizers very little. These are sold at from $25 to $45 a ton. Many growers consider them hurtful to the burning qualities of tobacco, to the flavor, and, in any excess, to the growth of the plant; but there is a substantially unanimous opinion that well-rotted barn-yard and stable manures are the best fertilizers. Some planters have reported excellent results from commercial fertilizers, and adverse reports are to be taken with the allowance that growers have had but little experience with them. Lands, when manured, may be cultivated indefinitely in tobacco; without it, the best lands will be exhausted in three or four years.

For rotation the best crops of tobacco are raised after clover. Wheat usually follows tobacco after the second or third year, though often after the first. Clover is sown on the wheat and plowed under in June of its second year's growth, and the land is immediately planted in tobacco. The tobacco crop is also made to follow wheat, corn, potatoes, and other crops.

TRANSPLANTING OF TOBACCO.

When the leaves of the plants are of the size of a silver half-dollar, if a rainy season comes they are set out; but if the weather is dry, a season is sometimes made by making with a stick a hole in the hill about 4 inches deep, which is filled with water. Plants thus set out will stand any ordinary spring drought and grow at once. In general, farmers wait for a natural season, and, if it can be avoided, weak or spindling plants from a crowded bed are never set out. Plants are set in rows, 3 feet 4 inches apart and 18 to 22 inches in the rows. The soil is thoroughly manured in March and April, and plowed twice, once in April or May, and a second time in June or July, just before planting. The cultivator and the harrow are used after the second plowing to level and pulverize the soil. Six thousand plants of Connecticut Seed-Leaf are planted to the acre, the same number of Pennsylvania Broad Leaf, and eight thousand plants of Cuban tobacco. Transplanting begins about the 10th of June, and continues to the 10th of July.

CULTIVATION OF TOBACCO.

The cultivation of tobacco is performed with a cultivator between the rows twice or three times during the season, and each time the rows are carefully hoed out. The cultivator is started as soon as the plants have fairly taken root and commenced to grow. The plants are not hilled up, growers preferring flat culture. The hoe. however, is used to loosen the soil around them and to destroy weeds.

TOPPING AND SUCKERING OF TOBACCO.

The best growers top low at from ten to fourteen leaves, estimating the gain from low topping at 25 per cent., and is commenced as soon as the blossom buds make their appearance. If the season is late, or the plant weak, a smaller number is left. Topping is now done much lower than formerly. Many, however, still top to as high as twenty leaves, and the result is late maturity, with small, imperfect top leaves. Seed-Leaf is topped fourteen days before cutting, but domestic Havana is allowed to stand thirty to forty days after topping. The time is varied as to both, however, by the season. Cutting is done from August 15 to October 10.

The suckers are kept carefully pulled out as soon as they are long enough to remove, and this is done as often as they appear. Worming is done at the same time.

CUTTING OF TOBACCO.

Knives are generally used in cutting, though several appliances for cutting without injuring the plant have been tried. Many use a long-handled hatchet with a thin blade. Bending the plants, they are cut off with a stroke. The best time for cutting depends on the weather, and if very hot and dry this should be done after four o'clock in the afternoon. During the night they will have wilted sufficiently to haul to the shed by nine or ten o'clock the next morning. In mild or cloudy weather the plants may be cut at any hour. Most growers haul to the shed and then string on laths, and the latter method is growing in favor. A "horse" is made of scantling, 5 by 4 inches, and 6 or 7 feet long, one end on the ground, the other raised $2\frac{1}{2}$ or 3 feet on two legs. In the raised end a slot receives one end of the tobacco lath, the other projecting forward. A knife, 5 to 7 inches long, sharply pointed and edged, with a socket at one end, is placed on the end of the lath, and by means of the sharp point from six to ten plants are placed on the stick. (*a*) The stick is then removed, and the knife serves for the whole crop. Laths cost $1 75 per thousand, and with proper care will last several years. The sticks are generally removed from the "horse" at once to the wagon and placed on the rack. The rack is made the full width of the wagon, and as long as is convenient, and in width is 4 feet, or the length of a stick, and as high as the longest plants. The rear end is left open for convenience in loading. This is the most convenient and economical way of hauling, and exposes the plant to the least danger of injury.

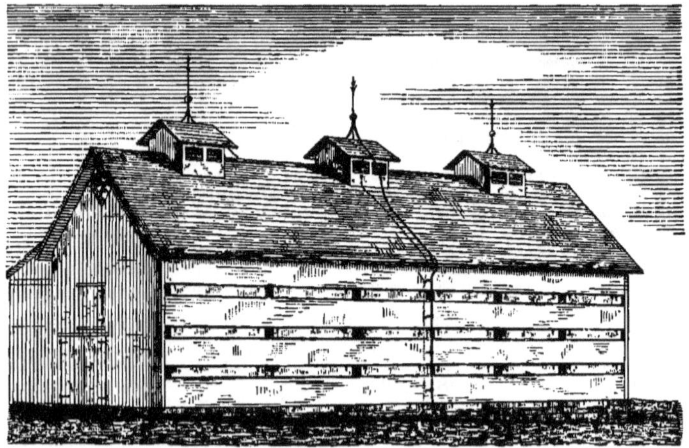

TOBACCO-SHEDS.

A description of one of the best barns or sheds in Onondaga will answer for a number of its class. It is built with well-laid stone foundation walls, with windows 4 feet long and 15 inches wide for ventilation and lap doors. On this foundation the building is erected, 24 by 80, or 28 by 100 feet, and 20 to 24 feet high, with tiers 5 feet apart.

a A cut in the chapter on Maryland, p. 91, shows a device for the same purpose.

This barn is built with gable roof, which sometimes contains ventilators, and doors are made in each end large enough for the entrance of a wagon and team. Side or ventilating doors are made horizontal, and not vertical,

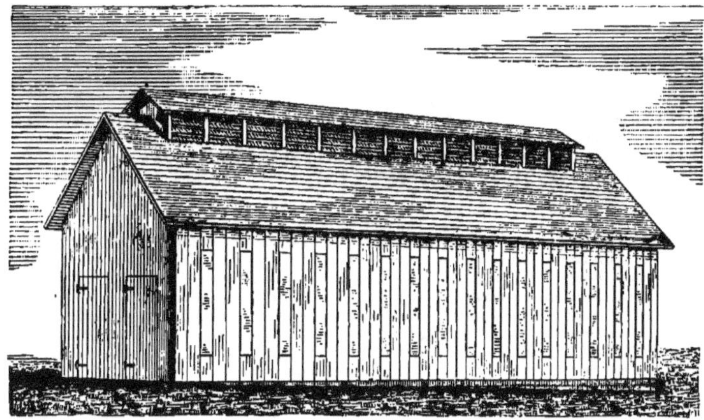

and are hung with strap-hinges, so as to be raised and hooked up. The siding is made of a good quality of pine timber and painted. Blocks and tackle are arranged in the top, supporting a platform, on which the laths are placed and hoisted to the tiers, generally by horse-power, the horse being hitched to the end of a rope. A room is built in one corner, 12 by 14 feet, for stripping and assorting. This room is ceiled tightly and floored, and contains a stove, on which a vessel of water is placed, to preserve a proper moisture in the air. Plenty of light and ample ventilation are secured by doors and windows in the end and sides of the room. This barn cost about $600, and the regulation of its admirable ventilation is entirely within the control of the owner. The medium shed in general use costs less, and is often merely a common farm barn altered to a tobacco-barn, and when not occupied with tobacco is used for sheep and cattle. It is without a stripping and assorting room, and is a rude structure of unplaned boards. The ventilating doors are vertical and hook back into staples. Sometimes these sheds are used for hay and grain, and are often half full of hay and grain when a crop of tobacco is stored in the top for curing. One-third or one-half of the sheds in Onondaga and Big Flats are of inferior or medium class, and their average cost is from $200 to $300. They are too diversified in structure to be described.

Sheds of a third class, of poor construction and badly adapted for the housing and curing of even a small quantity of tobacco, are found in large numbers throughout the district, but a description of these is unnecessary.

In such a barn as the first described, 28 by 80, with 24-feet posts and five tiers, four acres of 6,000 plants to the acre can be housed. The best sheds are ventilated in the top, so the ascending moist air from the green plants can be liberated and a free current circulated through the tobacco from bottom to top. Experience alone can teach when this is needed in the process of curing.

CURING OF TOBACCO.

Seed-Leaf raised upon some soils cannot be cured dark, while other soils will grow a plant which, with any ordinary care, will make a dark tobacco. The curer can do a great deal to regulate the process and secure the color desired if the shed is properly constructed, so that the ventilation can be perfectly controlled. It must be kept closed in hot, dry weather, or the rays of the sun will bleach the leaves, and neither light nor air should be admitted. Sometimes moisture is lacking, and it is necessary to place straw on the ground, and to keep it moist. One of the most experienced growers, however, declares that tobacco must never be cured over a plank floor or over straw, but, if necessary, the earthen floor must be moistened. When the crop is first housed, or when the weather is very moist and warm, the ventilators are kept open, and with continual watchfulness and proper regulation of them extremes of dryness and dampness may be avoided. During and after curing great care is necessary to obtain and preserve the colors of a good leaf, to avoid pole-sweat and stem-rot, and, while there is much badly-cured tobacco, it is almost all found to come from poorly-constructed, badly-ventilated sheds. Insufficient or badly-managed ventilation is the chief cause of bad curing. The part of the crop next the door is often bleached by too much air or sunshine, and other parts show house-burned spots or "fat stem". Stem-rot is indicated by a moldy, wet stem, with incipient decay in the leaf adjoining, and is sometimes caused by early frost, when the curing has not gone far enough to prevent freezing of moisture in the stem. When crops are planted so as to be cut and cured before frost and sheds are well ventilated pole-sweat, house-burn, or stem-rot is the result of negligence.

AFTER CURING.

When cured, the crop is taken down from November to May; perhaps more in November than in any other month, and nearly all by the 1st of February. Tobacco is taken down when the wind is southerly and the weather moist and rainy, so as to handle the leaf without breaking, as can be done when it is soft and the stem hard. More than half the planters strip as soon as the crop is taken from the poles, placing the leaves in bundles of five or six. These bundles are then bulked or "ranked" in some secure place to cure out thoroughly before assorting. Others take down the crop, stalks and all, laying them in heaps until they are ready to strip. The plan of stripping and afterward assorting in the assorting-room is generally preferred, as assorting is then done less hastily and more carefully, and the cured leaf is not exposed to danger of partial injury in bulk from possibly damp stalks.

ASSORTING OF TOBACCO.

Formerly tobacco was assorted into two grades; now growers assort into three or four, and sometimes five grades—as many as the crop requires. When graded into three sorts, they are designated A, B, C, wrappers, binders, and fillers; if into five sorts, AA, long wrappers; A, short wrappers; BB, long binders; B, short binders; and C, fillers. The leaves in each grade are made, as nearly as possible, of the same length.

Uniformity adds greatly to the appearance and value of the product. From fifteen to seventeen leaves are placed in the "hands", and each is neatly straightened and bulked down. After lying several weeks, each kind is packed in a box by itself, in quantities varying from 350 to 400 pounds. The amount to go in each box is carefully weighed out, and the weight is marked on the box. Packing is now done lengthwise of the box by most growers, although a few adhere to the old method of packing crosswise. The screw or lever press is used to prize lightly, and the character of the leaf determines the amount to be packed in a box. Thick, heavy leaves of good body will stand a heavy sweat, and may be packed closely and prized heavily, while light, flimsy ones must be packed lightly. Mixed cases are allowable when there is not enough left of a kind to fill a box, but the weight of each kind should be carefully marked on the mixed box.

Tobacco packed lengthwise can be more neatly arranged, looks better when opened, is more easily examined, and prevents fraud in packing, and the best growers keep memoranda of weights and boxes, contents and qualities, which are often valuable to both grower and buyer. Packing is usually done from January 1 to April 1.

BOXES.

Cases for tobacco are made of pine, 50 feet to each, including cross-pieces, which are of seasoned hemlock, costing about $12 or $14 per thousand. The box complete costs about $1, and, if planed inside, $1 05 to $1 10. It is 3 feet 6 inches long, and in each of the other two dimensions 2 feet 6 inches, measures being from outside to outside. In packing many use one-inch head-boards, which are slipped in loose, even with and on the inside of the ends. The tobacco is packed against these, after which they are withdrawn, leaving a space of one inch between the tobacco and the ends of the box for the circulation of air. This prevents rot, which sometimes occurs when the butts touch the ends of the cases. These cases are sometimes made with a crack one-fourth of an inch wide between the two boards of which the ends are formed.

RANGE IN PRICES OF TOBACCO.

The variation of prices is wide. One crop, well managed, sold in 1879 for 15 cents per pound; another, fairly managed, for 6 cents. There is sometimes a difference of 50 per cent. when it is hard to fix the cause, whether in the soil, the culture, the handling, or the curing.

VALUE OF THE LAST TOBACCO CROP.

The value of the crop of 1879, per pound, is thus reported by one: Seed, 6 to 9 cents; Domestic Havana or Hybrid, 9 to 18 cents. Value of different grades: Seed-Leaf—1, 13 cents; 2, 6 cents; 3, 3 cents. Wilson's Hybrid—1, 28 cents; 2, 12 cents; 3, 6 cents. Another gives 9 cents average for Seed-Leaf; shipping or export grades, 6 to 8 cents. These are all estimated, since tobacco is usually sold at a round price, which renders it difficult to distribute the price to the different grades.

SELLING OF TOBACCO.

Tobacco is sold on the pole, in the field, or in the assorting-room, and more frequently assorted and in lumps, or in the cases. Fully one-half is sold in cases. If it is not packed, the grower sells, to be delivered to the buyer in good merchantable condition, at so much per pound. In the main, however, growers do their own packing, and haul to market, usually in March, April, or May, before it has gone through the sweat, in order to avoid loss of weight, and it is often sold to dealers at a certain price for each quality. The buyer frequently makes an estimate of the amount of each grade, and "averaging up", as it is called, offers the average round; for instance, 3 cents for C's, 4, 5, or 6 cents for B's, and 20 cents for A's, averaging 12 cents. The following example shows the method:

2,000 A's, at 20 cents	$400
1,500 Short A's, at 14 cents	210
2,500 B's, at 5 cents	125
800 C's, at 3 cents	24
6,800 pounds	759

The average will be $11 16 per hundred pounds. Tobacco is delivered at some convenient point, but usually at buyers' warehouses, and cash is paid on delivery. After tobacco is sold to the buyer, it is usually left in the warehouse until the following August, or even until January, when it is sampled by New York samplers, although sometimes shipped without being sampled. It is now generally sold from second hands by sample. This method greatly facilitates sales, and is growing in favor each year. Many home manufacturers of domestic cigars come from surrounding states, and often from Canada, to buy leaf, and frequently make their purchases directly from the grower.

WHERE SOLD.

New York leaf is sold largely in the United States and Canada for cigar-making. Very little is used for cutting into smoking- or chewing-tobacco, although some is so used, and is mixed with and sold as genuine southern leaf. Domestic cigar manufacturers furnish the great market, although considerable quantities are sold in Bremen and in some other foreign markets.

SWEATING AND SHRINKAGE OF TOBACCO.

When tobacco is stored for sweating the cases are placed on the sides, so that the moisture, when fermentation takes place, will condense on the sides of the case. It is also said that when thus stored it comes out more easily when the boxes are stripped off than when stored top up. The product is of no use to the cigar manufacturer until it has gone through the sweat or fermentation. This begins with warm weather, generally in May, although when it once begins cold weather will not cause it to cease, and unless disturbed it will continue until October or November. Sometimes crops are seriously injured by growers becoming alarmed and interrupting the sweat.

Manufacturers generally practice artificial sweating, especially when the natural process has been interrupted. This is done in sweating-rooms with steam-heating pipes. The temperature is raised from 125° to 140° F., and steam is let into the room in proper quantities, but not excessively. A second fermentation sets in, which lasts about forty days. This artificial process is found to be perfectly satisfactory. Tobacco shrinks about 10 per cent. in one year in the natural sweat.

SAMPLING OF TOBACCO.

A licensed sampler, regarded as fair and impartial, is procured, and the boxes are placed in position in the warehouse. The covers are removed, and a "stripping jacket" is used to remove the case from the tobacco. This is placed over the top of the box, and two men, one at each end, take hold of the handles, turn the box bottom upward, and lift it from the tobacco, leaving it exposed. The sampler takes six hands from different places, at either end or at both ends, usually one or two in a place, and in order to draw them easily two strippers "break" the mass in different parts, so that the sampler can get at its real condition. The case is replaced over the tobacco, and the box reversed and closed up as before. The boxes are weighed before and after stripping, to ascertain the net weight, the tares and gross weights being placed on the ends, and each box is numbered from 1 up, according to the number sampled. Sometimes the cases are also marked, according to the fancy of the owner, ⟨A⟩ or ⟨P⟩, or some other mark. The six samples from each box are tied tightly together with strong cord, and a card is attached by a tape, over which a seal is affixed by the sampler. This card contains the number of the box, the gross weight, the tare, and the date of sampling, all corresponding with the case-marks. The sample is then ready for examination by buyers, and the cases may be sold from these samples in any part of the world, the tobacco remaining in the warehouse of the owner. The cases are generally forwarded after a sale by sample.

PRICE OF LANDS, ETC.

Lands in the Big Flats and in the valleys are worth from $75 to $150 per acre, according to location and improvements. On the hills in the vicinity of the bottoms the lands are cheap, running from $15 to $35 an acre; but in Onondaga, Cayuga, and Oswego counties the prices vary according to location and soil, the best farms selling at from $75 to $175 an acre, and the great majority may be set down as ranging from $10 to $75 per acre. The farmers in these counties generally have fair buildings and most of the modern conveniences. The average cost of production is estimated to be about 8 cents per pound for the state.

LABOR.

Men receive on tobacco farms from $14 to $20 per month for six or eight months, with board and washing; day hands from $1 to 10 shillings per day during the summer, and are generally boarded at these prices. In winter, in assorting season, wages are low when board is included, ranging from 50 to 75 cents per day. Labor is abundant in winter, and is not very scarce in summer.

DISEASES OF TOBACCO.

Except some trouble with the horn-worm, the gray cut-worm, and the wire-worm, injury from diseases and insects is very slight. The flea-beetle is hardly accounted at all, and white-firing, brown-rust, and kindred wet and dry weather diseases are reported as of small moment. The horn-worm is more injurious to cigar tobacco than to that grown for other uses.

The following statement shows the production, acreage, yield per acre, value of the crop in farmers' hands or in primary markets, the value per pound, and the value per acre of the tobacco crops of the state of New York for the years 1876, 1877, 1878, and 1879. The figures for the first three years are estimates from the best data attainable, those for 1879 being made up from returns of enumerators and from schedules returned to this office:

Year.	Production.	Acreage.	Yield per acre.	Value in primary markets.	Value per pound.	Value per acre.
	Pounds.		*Pounds.*		*Cents.*	
1876	6,297,600	4,920	1,280	$503,808	8.00	$102 40
1877	4,368,901	3,292	1,327	393,201	9.00	119 44
1878	4,805,700	3,669	1,310	576,695	12.00	157 18
1879	6,481,431	4,937	1,313	721,059	11.12	146 05

CHAPTER XII.

CULTURE AND CURING OF TOBACCO IN NORTH CAROLINA.

The development of the fine-tobacco interest in North Carolina exhibits one of the most remarkable transitions in the annals of agriculture. Its growth was first begun in this state by two brothers, Eli and Elisha Slade, of Caswell county, upon a ridge between two small tributaries of the Dan river. The soil was thin and sandy, and, in comparison with the river bottoms, was of little value. About 1852 or 1853 the Slades grew, by chance, as they supposed, a small crop of yellow tobacco. As it grew year after year its peculiarities were attributed to special methods of culture and curing. They communicated their methods to all inquirers, and it was soon found that soil was the chief element, although care in the modes of cultivation and curing was also found to be necessary to the production of the best qualities.

From the plantation of the Slades its growth extended over Caswell county, and along the same ridge into Pittsylvania county, Virginia. This covered almost the entire area of yellow-tobacco culture before the civil war, when the production of tobacco was almost entirely suspended. The war increased the manufacture of tobacco in the North, where no tobacco suitable for plug or wrappers was grown, and at its close attention was called to the fitness of the North Carolina yellow leaf for this purpose. The price rose with the demand, and the production extended to other counties, especially to Person, Granville, and Rockingham. Granville outstrips all competitors, although many other counties have entered the lists, from Buncombe and Madison, in the west, where it is grown on the slope of the Alleghanies, 3,000 feet above sea-level, to the coast belt about Goldsboro', 200 feet above the sea—a vertical range of 2,800 feet, and a climatic range equivalent to about eight and a half degrees of latitude. While yellow leaf may have been raised in Virginia in small quantities, this may be taken as an accurate sketch of the origin and spread of the new product in North Carolina and in the contiguous counties of Virginia.

After the war the cheap and abundant production of shipping tobacco in the West and the reduction of the price below the cost of production in North Carolina coincided, with the demand for fine tobacco, to diminish the growth of the heavy tobacco and to extend widely the production of fancy leaf.

There are, broadly and generally stated, two varieties of soil in North Carolina: a gray, sandy, light soil, with a yellow, sandy-clay subsoil, suited to yellow leaf and the various types of fine tobacco, and a dark loam, a rich, unctuous, heavy soil, with a red-clay subsoil, suited especially to the cereals and to a heavy dark or red tobacco.

The change in the growth of tobacco has been from one of these to the other. Shipping leaf is still grown, however, both as an industry, upon soil selected for it, and as an incident to attempts to raise fine tobacco upon lands not suited to its production. Sometimes a part of the same field will offer both kinds of soil and grow both fine and heavy tobacco. The production of shipping leaf is not regarded as profitable, and planters generally endeavor to raise the fine leaf, so that this is the only branch of tobacco culture worthy of especial notice.

Alongside the decline in wealth in old areas of prosperity there are other instances in the South of the growth of thrift and wealth in communities which were poor before the war, but no other section presents such wonderful changes. Comfortable farm-houses have taken the places of rude log-cabins, excellent and convenient barns and outhouses exhibit the new thrift, and new life has been infused into all classes and into both races. The distinctive feature of this phenomenon is that it has brought into requisition, as most profitable, the poorest soils in the state, and wrought its improvements on the poorest farming classes. It has also enhanced the value of such lands until they actually sell for more than the most fertile bottom lands, and the spectacle has actually been witnessed of a contention between counties as to which could show the most poor land. The effect of this is practically to increase largely the wealth-producing power of the state, breaking down the ordinary economic distinctions between sterile and fertile lands. The amount of this enhancement cannot be given with even approximate accuracy, because nothing definite can yet be known as to the area of fine tobacco lands, the continued value of poor lands depending also on the stability of the demand for such tobacco.

The population of Winston, Forsyth county, in 1870 was 443. The leaf market opened in 1872, and one small factory was built, making 40,000 pounds. There are now fourteen plug factories in operation, and one smoking-tobacco factory not in operation. The plug factories make 3,880,000 pounds. Population in 1880, 2,854.

Reidville, Rockingham county, had, in 1870, no corporate existence. In 1880 it had 1,316 inhabitants and nine plug and two smoking-tobacco factories, with a capacity of 3,000,000 pounds of plug and twist.

Lands worth from $1 to $3 per acre in 1860 now bring from $20 to $100, and old fields, worn out fifty years ago and grown up in pines—fields which would scarcely produce a bushel of corn to the acre—are now often sold for $50 per acre.

PROGRESS OF THE TOBACCO INDUSTRY.

The area of tobacco has been enlarged in most of the counties reporting, showing a gradual growth from 1876 to 1879, Clay, Guilford, and Warren alone reporting a decreased area.

As to quality, the crop of 1879 is generally reported better than that of the three years preceding, only two counties reporting deterioration in quality by comparison with 1876–'77–'78, and the care directed to the production of quality rather than quantity renders the exhibit as to the yield per acre apparently more unfavorable, nearly half the schedules reporting a decreased yield per acre, two counties about the same, and one-half an increased yield for 1879, as compared with 1876–'77–'78. If the comparison were with the years when shipping leaf was raised, the diminution would be general; but this comparison is only in fine-tobacco culture. It is worthy of notice here that the counties where the industry is older show increased yield. The most experienced planters have learned to combine body and weight with quality, and the production of different grades in the crop, in comparison between 1879 and 1869, shows the rapid change in the character of the product. In 1869 the shipping leaf averaged 36 per cent.; in 1879, 15 per cent.; while the proportion of fine tobacco, wrappers, fillers, and smokers, was enormously increased in all the counties. In many localities fine tobacco has only been grown since 1869.

The chief reason given for the great change in the character of the tobacco grown is the decline in price for shipping leaf, coinciding with the demand for fancy leaf at high prices.

The deterioration of quality in certain localities is attributed to the following causes: High prices have led many to undertake the culture of fine tobacco without experience and on unsuitable lands; others have been induced to plant more than could be perfectly cultivated; and hasty and careless handling and curing have been the faults of still others; all these resulting in the production of much light, chaffy tobacco. This deterioration is reported at from 1 to 5 per cent. in Granville, which is the best fine-tobacco county. The general product of this county is, in the main, of improved character, better cultivated, and handled with increasing care and skill; but the average of quality has been somewhat lowered by the numbers of inexperienced and unskillful men who have rushed into the business of growing fine tobacco.

VARIETIES OF TOBACCO.

Slight differences in nomenclature, local names, and the uncertain use of descriptive adjectives make it difficult to reach absolute accuracy in treating of the varieties of tobacco cultivated.

The Orinoco, popularly called in some localities "Iron Oak", is a widely grown plant, of which at least three varieties are reported—the Yellow, the White-stem, and the Little or Sweet Orinoco. The Yellow Orinoco is early, matures well, becomes bright on the hill, and has a broad, heavy leaf of a fine, silky texture. The White-stem Orinoco grows brighter and whiter on the hill than most varieties, and is more easily cured the desired color. The fiber is also white. Silky Pryor has a long, sharp-pointed leaf, and grows thin on the stalk, with a leaf very tough and pliant when cured, which can be handled drier than any other variety. The Bullock has a broad, smooth leaf, with no ruffle on the stem. It stands heat well in curing. The leaves are far apart on the stalk, and it bears few suckers, often not more than four or five to the plant; nor do suckers start from below the surface of the hill. On account of the space between the leaves, a hand can sucker one-third more of this variety than of any other. The Cary makes a good sample, has a round leaf, and yellows well on the hill. Virginia Seed-Leaf and Tally are also grown to some extent. The Yellow Orinoco has largely the preference among planters, the Gooch and the Bull-face coming next, and perhaps the Yellow Pryor next to them, and the Little or Sweet Orinoco, the Blue Pryor, the Adcock, the Mann, and the Cunningham, described under "Varieties", chapter II, are extensively cultivated. One general truth is established: that soil adapted to coarse shipping tobacco will not produce fine tobacco with any variety, and *vice versa*.

All varieties cure dark brown or red when grown on red-clay soils with heavy dark or brown top soil, but incline to brighter and lighter hues on sandy, gray soil, with yellowish subsoil, and cure from bright red to mahogany and fine yellow. On all fresh lands, except the very best fancy-tobacco soils, all varieties are somewhat lighter and brighter than on old lands. This is especially the case with those lands which will only produce shipping leaf after the first or second year.

Such is the effect of soils, that the purity of any variety can only be preserved by procuring seed from the soil which produces its original and most perfect type. This is a rule, however, of very little practical value until experiments shall have determined the entire subject of adaptability, and even then the purity of any given variety can only be maintained by great care. The seed-plants must be remote from any other variety to avoid the intermixture of pollen by insects, and the seed is to be selected from the crown, that alone reproducing the same plant. Seeds from the lower and side shoots grow plants resembling those coming from seeds of suckers; indeed, the side shoots are but suckers.

TOBACCO SOILS.

In determining the question as to what constitutes fine tobacco lands, or what element is fatal to the growth of yellow leaf, the inquiry must embrace the important matter of drainage. Tobacco is a plant which delights in a dry, warm soil, requiring comparatively little moisture, and in no respect do these lands differ more widely from others than in thorough drainage. While such lands are very miry in wet weather, so that it is difficult to drive a wagon or even to ride over them, the top soil is always dry and warm.

There is a difference of opinion as to new lands. In the western counties, where the growth of tobacco is quite recent, new land is almost altogether planted, but in the older tobacco counties planters have learned to conserve their old lands and to raise upon them tobacco of the best quality by the judicious use of fertilizers, and no longer depend upon clearing. All agree, however, that a very fine quality of leaf is grown on new lands. Some lands will produce a fair fancy wrapper one or two seasons, and never after. It is also generally agreed that the first crop is very fine and most easily cured, but lacks the body and uniformity of texture and color of the second year's growth on the best tobacco lands.

Fertilizers are applied upon new as well as upon old lands. In the older tobacco counties cases are given where tobacco has been grown upon land for twenty years in succession without decrease in yield or deterioration in quality, but always with the aid of manure. Such lands appear to possess permanent qualities, which need only the addition of fertilizers and manures, and it is believed that with proper care and rotation most of them can be kept up indefinitely. (*a*)

Old fields of the proper soil, which have been worn out and abandoned, make, when cleared of their new growth, the best tobacco lands. They are generally overgrown with pines, with an undergrowth of whortleberry, chincapins, and other bushes, the pines growing to 2 feet in diameter in about twenty-five years. About fifteen or twenty years are required for the resuscitation of old, worn-out lands. One field was planted in corn in 1850, and the yield was so poor that the fence was removed. In 1876 it was cleared of its pine growth and planted in tobacco, which brought 50 cents a pound for the whole crop. This field has been cultivated in tobacco for five successive years, and the last crop was better than the first. The land was treated the first year with 200 pounds of a commercial fertilizer, and has since received yearly applications of stable manure and fertilizer in the drill. A great many farmers are of opinion, however, that the lands are exhaustible and require years of rest, and assert that, although the first crops on old fields reclaimed are better than when first cleared, a great falling off occurs after the second crop, the soil wearing out much more rapidly than in the first instance.

These old pine fields, when they have a gray, sandy soil and a yellow subsoil, are the best of tobacco lands. A man selected a few acres which had grown up in "bald-faced Spanish oaks", scrub hickory, chincapin, and sourwood, all indicative of very poor lands, and the crop raised sold for 50 cents a pound at the barn door. When the soil is of the right kind, old fields which have lain for years in "broom-sedge" or broom-grass (*Andropogon scoparius*) grow the very finest tobacco, while they are almost worthless for other crops. This "sedge" is turned under in the fall before frost, and tobacco is planted the next spring.

A southern exposure is generally sought for fine tobacco. This soil is drier and warmer, and the plant matures earlier. The rich, black soils of northern slopes will not produce fine tobacco, while a few yards off, on the other slope, the finest may be grown.

---

a It is unquestionably true that the mechanical condition of the soil and the absence of certain inorganic elements have more to do with the production of fine tobacco than a supply of plant food. This soil is, indeed, a sponge, which receives and retains just fertilizers enough to bring the plant to the proper size, when they become exhausted, and the plant goes into a gradual decline, growing more and more yellow and more and more delicate in tissue, until it is cut. Too much manure will destroy the fine qualities of the leaf, impairing its color and increasing its coarseness.

Reports show a general average of 33 per cent. of preferred tobacco soils cultivated, and the proportion of new lands is reported at 45 per cent. In Buncombe and Madison counties, in the west, where tobacco culture has been recently introduced, the proportion of new lands is 80 per cent., and the general average proportion of uncleared lands adapted to the plant is given as 58 per cent. Since fine tobacco lands are precisely those which farmers would avoid clearing for other crops, this is probably too low rather than too high an estimate.

THE TIMBER GROWTH.

The forest growths are found upon soils of such diverse character, and coincide over such wide areas, that it can only be said generally that hickories, white oaks, the tulip-tree, walnuts, maples, sugar maples, and beeches are indications of good land, and post oak, scrub oak, black-jack, chestnut, chincapin, pine, and whortleberry are indications of poor land; but either of these growths may be found upon lands better suited to the other to such a large extent that one must judge by the predominance of species and by the character rather than by the kind of growth, and especially by the undergrowth. The timber test for land is of little use to the inexperienced, while it is of great value to the experienced eye.

ROLLING AND LEVEL LANDS.

With regard to the "lay of the land", planters generally report no difference between rolling and level lands, provided the latter are well drained. If not well drained, the level land makes a heavier product, which does not ripen so well or so early, on account of excess of moisture.

PREPARATION OF THE SOIL.

In the preparation of tobacco lands methods vary with the character of the soils, old "sedge" lands, clover fallows, and stubble lands requiring more plowing than land last cultivated in corn or tobacco.

New ground is coltered twice or oftener, and is cleared of roots and trash; lot lands are plowed in autumn or in early winter, to obtain the help of the winter frosts in reducing the soil to fine tilth, are again plowed early in the spring, and a third time before planting. Turning-plows are used to a depth of from 2 to 5 inches, the object being to invert the upper soil as deeply as possible without exposing the subsoil.

If the land is trashy, or not in thorough tilth, it is dragged with a heavy harrow after the last plowing. It is then bedded up by throwing from two to four furrows together with a turning-plow, and the hills are laid off from $2\frac{1}{2}$ to 3 feet 3 inches apart and patted on the top, so as to compact the soil where the plant is to be set. Hilling is strongly recommended by the best planters, especially in wet seasons, affording better drainage and protection against all the wet-weather diseases of tobacco. Hills present a flat surface of from 10 to 15 inches in diameter, and are made when the ground is in good order for working. If too dry, it will require too much rain to moisten them sufficiently; if too wet, they will bake. In new ground the hills may be made in March or April; in old ground they are to be made late enough to avoid danger of growing up in weeds and grass before planting, not earlier than the first of May. Listing or bedding up by 3 or 4 furrows of a turning-plow saves labor in making hills.

There is a wide difference of opinion and of practice as to the proper distance between plants, varying from $2\frac{1}{2}$ by 2 feet 3 inches to 3 feet 3 inches by 3 feet 3 inches. Many hold that nothing is gained in aggregate weight, while something is lost in length, breadth, and body by crowding closer than 3 feet 3 inches apart each way. Hills are generally made by measuring or stepping off one row and placing the hills of the next opposite the center of the space between those in the first, and so on, in quincunx order.

TOBACCO FERTILIZERS.

Both commercial fertilizers and home-made manures are used: of the former, special tobacco fertilizers and Peruvian guano; of the latter, chiefly stable manure. Stable manure is used in connection with numerous commercial fertilizers—guano, superphosphates, and special compounds prepared for tobacco.

In the eastern tobacco counties no attempt is made to raise tobacco without fertilizers and manures; in the western counties planters are farming a virgin soil and using very little manure; and the policy of clearing new to replace old lands promises to go on until it has wrought the ruin it has elsewhere. It is generally agreed that upon most lands in the west two crops can be raised without manure, and this is generally the limit.

The use of fertilizers is said to yellow the crop in the hill as well as to increase the yield, and they are applied broadcast in the hill and in drills. The practice of placing them in the drills possesses advantages every way. The most approved method is to apply stable manure in the winter. A furrow is opened, in which it is placed, according to the character of the soil, and a furrow is thrown over it. In the spring the center of this is divided with a bull-tongue or shovel-plow, and the commercial fertilizer is placed in the new furrow with the stable manure, a bed being thrown over this by three or four furrows with a turning-plow. In this way the soil of the bed becomes thoroughly permeated by the fertilizer and manure, and upon this bed the hills are made at the proper time, the object being to place both the manure and the fertilizer so that the plant will receive the stimulus from the very start. Both commercial fertilizers and barn-yard manures are applied according to the soil, and this must be done, after long experience, with great care and judgment. Too much will injure the quality and the texture or may cause firing; too little may leave the plant small, lean, and poor; the object being to use enough to make eight or ten plants yield a pound of fine tobacco when cured. Quantities applied are variously reported, as from 50 to 500 pounds per acre, and when no home-made manure is used the amount of commercial fertilizer is very nearly doubled. Peruvian guano has been generally abandoned in raising fine tobacco. Most of the fertilizers used are manufactured especially for fine tobacco under various names and brands, and most of them are said to be rich in ammonia, soluble phosphates, and potash.

Much attention has been paid to home-made manures, stable manure being generally used and preferred to all others, and giving best results when used in combination with commercial fertilizers—the latter starting the plant and giving quick growth; the former finishing the growth, giving body and maturity. Size may be attained without manure by the use of fertilizers alone, but not body. Some planters make their own fertilizers by treating bone dust with sulphuric acid, and composts are also made of muck and stable manure. Ashes are also used, and by some guano is considered especially applicable to new land.

Reports from various counties show an average increase of yield per acre of 70 per cent. by the use of fertilizers, with a considerable improvement in quality; but the cost varies so much with the amount used and the distance from market that it is hardly necessary to give it when intelligent planters report it as ranging from $1 50 to $15 per acre, the area of their use being of more importance, as exhibiting progress in careful culture. The area of tobacco land on which fertilizers and manures are used is reported as follows: Granville, 90 per cent.; Rockingham, 95; Guilford, 98; Warren, 75; Alamance, 75; Forsyth, 95; Yadkin, 25; Wilkes, 10; Buncombe, 5; Madison, 2; Cary, Randolph, and Haywood, none. The counties using the least quantity are those in which fresh soils are mainly employed for the production of tobacco.

ROTATION.

The rotations practiced in connection with manuring for the preservation of the soil vary somewhat, but wheat is almost unanimously regarded as the best crop to follow tobacco, both to allow the land time to recuperate its exhausted tobacco-producing qualities, and because the clean cultivation necessary for tobacco and the unconsumed manures and fertilizers make an excellent preparation for wheat. Wheat is followed by pease, one bushel to the acre, the growth of which is turned under in the fall when just beginning to ripen and followed by wheat or corn. What is called green-manuring is not practiced, except in the use of pease. A succession of tobacco two seasons, then wheat, followed by corn, is a common course; after which the land is often allowed to lie idle one season. On account of wire-worms it is almost impossible to obtain a stand of tobacco after clover or grass; hence they are not used to any great extent as rotating crops. Some of the best planters report planting for several successive years in tobacco, with yearly improvement in quality and in quantity. Soil may have something to do with this, but it is in the main due to superior care and diligence and to the judicious use of proper fertilizers. Some planters follow tobacco with wheat and clover for two years, followed by rye or wheat, and then tobacco. As a rule, when wheat stubble land is intended for tobacco, it is plowed early in the fall or winter, to receive thorough freezing and to destroy the cut-worms, and cross-plowed in the spring, thoroughly harrowed and pulverized, and cleared of trash and unrotted stubble. Corn is not regarded as a good crop to rotate directly with tobacco.

SEED-BEDS.

The soil selected for the seed-bed is as fine as flour, with the least possible admixture of coarse sand and gravel, inclined to be moist, but not wet, and thoroughly drained. The sowing is done sometimes as early as December 1, and again as late as the 15th of April, but January and February are preferred.

Usually the plants appear about the 1st of March if the sowing has been timely, and are sufficiently well grown for transplanting by the first week in May.

Plants are ready for setting out when the leaves are about 3 inches long and the width of three fingers, but for old ground the plants should be larger, and the leaves 5 or 6 inches long.

TRANSPLANTING TOBACCO.

Planters generally agree that the 10th of May is soon enough to begin transplanting, and that successive plantings are desirable, in order that the crop may not all mature at once. Later than the 10th of June is not looked upon with favor by the best planters. Planting is sometimes done as late as the 1st of August, but never with expectation of more than very moderate returns. If set out too early, the plants are likely to be damaged by cold, and to be deprived of the dews of August and September; if too late, they may not mature properly before frost.

In general, planters wait for rain in order to transplant, though crops of seventy acres have been successfully planted by making artificial seasons.

CULTIVATION OF TOBACCO.

As soon as the plant has rooted and begun to grow, which is shown by the color, and is usually within five or six days, the turn-plow is run, with the bar next the plant, thus "barring" off the soil. The hill is then cleared of weeds with a hoe, and a little fresh earth is drawn to the plant. An excellent authority opposes the use of the plow unless the rows have become very foul, and recommends breaking the crust of the hill with the hoe and drawing loose earth around the plant until it has covered the hill to a breadth of 12 inches. This is probably the better way, but it is too tedious and costly for general practice.

About a week after the first plowing the earth is thrown to the plant by the plow, and a broad, flat hill is made with the hoe. A third plowing is given before topping, and the hoe hands follow, hilling up well with a high hill. Unless grass and weeds are very prolific this will be cultivation enough. Both the turning-plow and the bull-tongue are used, the former being preferred when the rows are foul. The cultivation is shallow, and the subsoil is but little stirred, and cultivation is avoided after topping unless the weeds and grass require the hoe.

The plowing is often done with a cotton sweep, which is growing in favor, and cultivation is pushed rapidly by the best planters. In shipping leaf cultivation is continued until August, but in fine tobacco, beginning with plow or hoe when the plant has commenced growing, it is continued about once in ten days until the 10th or 15th of July.

PRIMING, TOPPING, AND SUCKERING OF TOBACCO.

At the last hoeing, as a general rule, the bottom leaves are primed off. When it is possible, all plants for fine tobacco are topped by the last of July, or at latest by the 10th of August. There is, however, the greatest diversity of opinion as to both priming and topping. The general rule as to priming, however, is from 4 to 6 inches, while the range in topping up to the last of July is usually from ten to fourteen leaves. Ten may be taken, however, as the number approved most widely, as measuring that which can be easily matured with the greatest weight and desired texture and color. Planters who adopt a standard of ten top as high as twelve leaves when the plant is gross, or go below that if it appear that ten cannot be properly matured. Topping is usually done at intervals of a week, and at each successive topping fewer leaves are left, so as to make all plants set out at the same time ripen together. The season and the character of the plant have much to do with the topping, but the best authorities assert that those who are tempted to go beyond ten leaves, except with very gross plants, lose in body, oil, and toughness, and gain nothing in weight, texture, or color. Some planters top even as high as twenty leaves on strong land, holding that low topping makes the plant coarse and the fibers large.

One planter advises topping high in dry weather and low in wet weather, on the ground that if the plant be topped low in dry weather and rains follow it will be surfeited with moisture and the top leaves will grow large and the bottom leaves fall off. If dry weather succeeds wet, the plant having been topped high and the supply of moisture ceasing, the growth is checked, the plant is not filled out, and the leaf grows thin and papery. Perhaps the best rule given us to priming is to allow the tips of the bottom leaves at maturity to hang well clear of the ground.

Suckers are pulled off when 2 or 3 inches long, and every week, as they appear, until the plant is cut, usually from three to four times. There are two weeks between successive crops of suckers.

The usual time between planting and topping is about six weeks, but this is so dependent on the season that the time may be from forty to sixty days. The time between topping and cutting is from six to ten weeks, varying according to season and according to soil, gray lands maturing the plant earlier than red lands. The variation on account of soil is given at as much as four weeks, and the plant will stand longer on strong than on thin land. The method of cultivation also has an influence on the time, shallow culture ripening the plant earlier than deep culture. The time of maturing is also affected by the quality and the quantity of fertilizer used, and the variation in time of planting finds a corresponding variation in the time of cutting, from the last of August to the 15th of October.

RIPENING TOBACCO.

Ripening is indicated by the leaf becoming sleek, the fuzz disappearing, and the appearance of dappled yellow spots, called "graining". Dappled leaves make a mahogany leaf when cured; uniform grayish-green color (melon-apple green), when cut, indicates the finest leaf. Poor tobacco, without body, has a smooth, lifeless yellow, improper ripening, due to wet seasons, rendering it almost impossible to attain the desired color. The plant will not ripen well in wet seasons, especially when rain follows drought, but it is not injured by rain after it is ripe. It may begin a new growth, but will ripen again in a few days. Cool nights and heavy dews thicken the plant, and cause it to mature rapidly, with good body.

CUTTING OF TOBACCO.

Tobacco is always cut thoroughly ripe, unless it is necessary to sacrifice quality to escape total loss from frost. There is a difference of opinion as to the effect of rain or dew, almost all asserting that it does no harm to cut even when wet with rain or dew; yet one of the best authorities on the subject declares that the least water on the leaf spoils the color in drying.

When the plants are fully ripe each cutter takes two rows, a stick-carrier walking between two cutters, holding a stick. The plants are split down the center of the stalk and cut, and six to eight plants are placed astride the stick; another hand takes two sticks at a time to the wagon; and a third hand keeps the stick-carrier supplied. The plants are assorted in the field, so that those only of a uniform color and ripeness shall be cut and cured together, and the tobacco is placed at once in the wagon, if possible, without exposure to the sun, and without allowing it to wilt or to lie upon the ground. It is desirable that the plants shall be stiff and open, so that the hot air can circulate freely among the leaves, and is never scaffolded before housing.

Cutting is done on Monday and Tuesday, so as to cure by Saturday, or it is cut on Friday and Saturday, postponing the curing till Monday, from the rigid regard for the Sabbath and its universal observance by all classes, although the planters suffer serious inconvenience and expense in the cutting season when the weather on Monday is unfavorable for outdoor work.

Twelve hands will fill a barn of 600 pounds' capacity in two days; but this is excellent work, and the last loads will not be gotten in until after nightfall.

The sticks are 4½ feet long, and are placed at a distance of from 8 to 10 inches apart on the tier poles, but never less than 8 inches, for fear of sweating or "house-burn".

TOBACCO-BARNS.

For fine tobacco curing barns are built of logs, small and tight, from 16 to 22 feet square. The larger size has the merit of economy, while 16-foot barns have the approval of the larger number of planters. The comparative housing capacity is about as 4 to 7, the smaller holding 352 sticks, the larger 650, one foot apart. If 16 feet, the barn is divided by five sets of tier poles into four equal compartments; if 20 feet square, six sets of tier poles divide the barn, including, in both cases, the joists, and exclusive of the collar beams. A slope to the east is used, if possible, that the furnace may open on that side, prevailing winds being from the west in the curing season.

When, as is generally the case, more than one barn is needed the barns are grouped together for convenience, but not nearer than 100 feet, on account of danger from fire. An inclination of 2 feet in 20 will be found advantageous in arranging the furnaces. The reason assigned for the use of log instead of frame barns is that the latter, even though they be ceiled, cannot be heated sufficiently. The ground sills are of oak, well underpinned, and on these the pen, 20 feet square, is built of logs about 6 inches in diameter, notched down closely. At the height of 5 feet a set of six tier poles, generally of pine, and 4 inches in diameter, is laid horizontally, resting upon the northern and southern walls, the two outside poles lying against the east and west walls. The first tier is only used in hanging and hoisting; the next is laid on in the same way, three logs above; and so on to the top, when the sixth is laid, serving also as joists, and resting upon the plates. If the roof is framed, the rafters are raised directly above and in line with the joists or last tier, and the collar beams are nailed to the rafters, giving one and a half more tiers in the roof. Cabin roofs are usually built; that is, each gable is built up with logs of decreasing length, with their ends beveled, the long side down, to the last and shortest, which is notched in the center for the ridge pole of the roof. Each end of the gable log is laid upon a roof pole, which extends the full length of the barn, and by the shortening of these logs the roof poles form on both sides the slant of the roof, which is crowned by the ridge pole. Into these roof poles the collar beams are let in the cabin roof. The walls for a barn 20 feet square, when completed, contain about twenty logs each, plates included, and are about 16 feet high. The cracks are then closely chinked and daubed with mud, to which lime enough has been added to make it adhere well, and doors 4 feet square are cut in the north or south side and are provided with very closely-fitting shutters.

THE FLUES.

The Smith patent is the one most commonly used. Furnaces are built, if the barn is properly located, on the east side; and if the ground is rightly inclined only one log need be sawed out, which is done 4 inches from the corner next to both the north and the south walls. The arch is of brick or fire-proof stone, 5 feet long, projecting externally 18 inches. The walls are built of brick, two bricks thick, and 2 feet apart, 18 inches high, 4 inches from the walls of the barn, the space being filled with dry earth, and the space between the two carefully filled up to the first log. A covering is then made over the external arch, running the length of the barn, and an ash-bed is dug out in front of the opening of each arch. The iron flue pipes are let in about 6 inches from the floors of the arches, and the cracks are stopped with clay. In order to give the greatest heating capacity the flues are built one foot from the north, the west, and the south walls, and, as a protection against fire, when this is done a thin wall is built between the pipes and the ground sills, running from where the pipe joins the furnace 6 feet along the flue, the distance to which the pipes are heated red. The pipes are made of No. 24 iron, except the two joints that enter the furnaces, which are of 18-inch iron, and are from 12 to 15 inches in diameter. The pipe is elevated gradually about 1 inch in 2 feet, and runs continuously from both flues along the north and south walls and the west wall. In the center of the pipe, along the west wall, which lies horizontal, and 1 foot from the wall, the return pipe makes a T, and conducts the draught through the center of the barn back to the east wall, rising gradually, so as to make the perpendicular distance between the points where the pipes leave the furnaces and that where the return pipe comes out through the wall about 18 inches. A short elbow joint in a small chimney receives the return pipe on the outside.

From two to three cords of dry wood suffices for one curing. Barns thus constructed, with flues complete, cost from $50 to $75 each; packing-houses, about $200 each. With barn and flues properly constructed fires are always the result of carelessness, and yet about one barn in twenty is reported as lost by fire.

CURING OF TOBACCO.

The process of curing tobacco by fire is the most difficult and delicate in the whole course. Experience alone will make a curer of fine tobacco, and that only of one who possesses nice judgment, excellent powers of observation, and care. A trifling inattention may, at a critical moment, reduce a barn of the finest yellow tobacco to the lower grades. If the fires are allowed to die out or decline after the leaf is cured, sap remaining in the stalks or stems will diffuse itself through the leaf and mar the color irremediably in twenty-four hours; and, on the other hand, too much heat will cause sweating, which will, unless checked by speedy ventilation, both injure the color and impair the body and texture. In order to prevent this it is necessary to use a thermometer, hung level with the tails of the plants on the lowest tier, and, to guard the degree of heat by constant care, to watch day and night, with frequent inspection of the plants, generally selecting some one plant as a guide, but not by any means omitting general inspection.

CURING TOBACCO BY CHARCOAL.

In curing by charcoal, as soon as the crop is housed in a barn 20 by 20 feet square four rows of fires are built, four fires in a row, 1½ bushels to the sixteen fires. The entire process requires from three to four entire days. About 100 bushels of charcoal, at 4 cents per bushel, are allowed to 800 pounds of tobacco.

FLUE-CURING.

Since curing by flues promises very soon to supersede all other methods this process is more particularly described. The only difference between that and charcoal-curing is in the manner of applying heat. Two distinct stages are recognized in curing: yellowing with a damp heat at a low temperature, which is generally 90°, or, when the tobacco is very light and yellow, 100°; but if the weather is very cool, 80°. The second is the drying, which may be divided into curing the leaf and curing the stalk.

A few examples of curing will illustrate the variations in the process. The first is from a *Manual of Tobacco Culture*, by R. B. Davis, a successful planter of Catawba county:

YELLOWING.—This is done at 90°, or at 80° if the weather be cool, in from eighteen to thirty-six hours, until the desired color is attained.

DRYING OR CURING is then effected by the following management of temperature: 95° for two hours, 100° for two hours, 105° for two hours, 110° for two hours, 115° for two hours, 120° for six hours, 130° for two hours, 140° for two hours, 150° for two hours, and 160° for twenty-four hours, the last temperature being kept up until the stalks and stems are dried. This table is for tobacco not gross and very yellow when cut, and to be modified with judgment. If the tobacco is gross and of a gray color, four hours instead of two should be taken to each stage from 100° to 120°.

THE RAGLAND METHOD.—This method is for medium tobacco. Ripe tobacco only is to be cut, and is then placed five to seven plants on a stick 4 feet long and from 10 to 12 inches apart on the tier poles. Steaming or yellowing is done at 90° from eighteen to forty-eight hours, according to character of tobacco. When yellowed, the heat is raised from 90° to 95° in from one to two hours, from 95° to 100° in two hours, from 100° to 105° in two hours, from 105° to 110° in from one to three hours, from 110° to 115° in two hours, and from 115° to 120° in two hours, at which the leaf is cured in from four to eight hours. The stalk is cured by a temperature advancing from 120° to 175°, at about 5° an hour, keeping the temperature at 175° until the stalk is thoroughly cured.

These two curings, from the *Border Review*, are based on records made at the barn door:

No. 1. The barn was 18 feet square, four firing tiers high; 450 sticks, grown on old-field land, bright yellow on the hill, leaf long, but thin and light, due to light cultivation. The fires were started and run up to 90° in six hours; then to 100° in six hours; then to 110° in six hours; leaf thoroughly yellowed at the end of eighteen hours. The temperature was then advanced to 120° in six hours; to 125° in six hours more; to 130° in six hours; to 140° in three hours, at which it was allowed to remain six hours; at the end of which time the leaf was about cured. The temperature was then run up to 150° in three hours, and held at that for three hours; then to 175° in twelve hours, where it stood twelve hours, until the stalk was dry—a perfect cure, a bright lemon color, within seventy-five hours.

No. 2. The barn was of the same size, with the same kind of flues, same number of sticks of tobacco, grown upon the same character of land, but of larger and thicker leaf. The fires were started and run up to 95° in eight hours; to 100° in six hours; to 110° in ten hours, when the leaf was yellowed. The temperature was then advanced to 120° in eight hours; to 130° in six hours; to 140° in six hours; from 140° to 150° in eighteen hours; from 150° to 175° in six hours, where it was held twelve hours; at the expiration of which time leaf, stem, and stalk were fully cured a bright lemon—all in eighty hours. The difference in time was due to the difference in size and grossness.

THE GROWTH OF FLUE-CURING.

Air-curing was practiced in many counties until the demand for fine leaf required better results. with more certainty. Charcoal-curing was the first step forward. This was found expensive, difficult to regulate, soiling the plant with dust and soot, and often giving it a bad flavor. The first flues were of stone or brick, or were trenches covered with sheet-iron, running through the barn. The flue has been gradually growing into use from about 1867 or 1868, a general adoption dating from about 1872. Twenty reports give but nine counties where air-curing was practiced at all in 1879, and only three in which more than 10 per cent. of the crop was thus cured. Fourteen counties report an average of 56 per cent. flue-cured and 34 per cent. charcoal-cured. As the flue is comparatively recent, this shows that it is rapidly superseding other means of curing. These flues are constructed of brick, stone, and iron, preference being expressed for brick, as being more durable and safer and giving better results, although costing more. The iron flues are cheapest, and the heat can be regulated with the utmost nicety, rapidly raised with dry wood and as rapidly lowered by drawing fires, but requiring greater care and vigilance. Iron flues cost from $15 to $20.

TREATMENT OF TOBACCO AFTER CURING.

When the stalk is cured thoroughly dry the fires are allowed to die out. There is a wide difference of opinion as to the after treatment. It is agreed that the plants cannot be safely stripped in the moist, warm weather which follows the curing season, because of the danger of loss of color. The plant comes from the drying barn always with a little greenish tinge. In the after treatment this fades away, and it takes on a solid bright yellow, uniform throughout. The crop is allowed to remain with fires out and doors open for thirty-six hours, until it can be handled. Some, however, recommend throwing wet straw on the flues, which is kept moist, and the tobacco thus is steamed at a safe temperature, to bring it at once into "order" for removal. It is then "bulked down" in the packing-house on the sticks, butts out, in square piles. This improves the color and straightens out the leaves, rendering them smooth and neat in appearance. Many farmers allow it to lie in bulk for only three or four days and then rehang it, crowding very closely, to prevent injury to the color from atmospheric changes. On the other hand, the best opinion favors more permanent bulking down, in such order that it can be handled without breaking, the leaf soft and stem hard. Those who thus bulk down rehang, to come in order for stripping. After it is stripped, it is tied in hands of six to twelve leaves: bright wrappers, six; fillers, eight; smokers, ten to twelve, when it is by some rehung and crowded closely, but, according to the best practice, it is bulked down on sticks, heads out, each grade by itself, and carefully covered with carpets, to exclude light, the colors being very sensitive to light as well as to air. In this condition the color is fixed, and after two months in bulk it is no longer subject to change.

Fine tobacco is packed in tierces of from 350 to 800 pounds, each grade by itself, or it is sold loose at the barn or carried loose to market, where it is placed in piles and sold at auction. Dealers buy enough of each grade to fill a cask, when they prize lightly and ship to the various markets.

It is sometimes necessary in very small crops to sell loose, because the quantity of each grade is not sufficient to fill a cask; but to pack in casks or boxes before taking to market avoids risks in handling. Sometimes, though rarely, it is put up by farmers in casks or boxes, being usually packed by mere hand pressure.

The period for stripping, assorting, packing, and marketing is generally from October to August, and the unstripped crop of one year may be on hand until the next. May is probably the season most favored. The spring sweat comes in May if bulked or packed; if not, it will come later, after which it is bulked down and packed. This sweat sweetens the tobacco, if its condition is dry; if too moist, it is injured in flavor and in color, and has the effect to redden a bright tobacco and brighten a dark leaf. If the tobacco is very moist and the sweat excessive, "funking" to some extent occurs, the injury being estimated at about 5 per cent., which can only be avoided by bulking in good order. Natural seasons are used for stripping and packing. Some experiments have been made with steam or warm air, but not enough as yet to determine their value.

ASSORTING TOBACCO.

When the tobacco is kept bulked down on the stalk until the stripping season it is necessary to hang up as much as can be stripped in a day to "order" for stripping, that is, to absorb humidity enough to handle without breakage; but, to avoid the danger of a possible change of color, it is not allowed to become too soft. An assorter then strips off from each plant one or two leaves, to be tied by a boy as lugs or common smokers, and from one to three of the next leaves for smooth lugs or fancy smokers. These are tied into hands of eight or ten leaves by the assorter. The remainder of the leaves is then cast together in a pile, to be assorted into the various higher grades of leaf and tips. All the leaves of each grade must be uniform, and every bruised, worm-eaten, or injured leaf excluded from the best grades. So particular are the best planters, that the assorting-houses are constructed with a window to the north, that a uniform light may fall upon the leaf all day, increase or decrease in the intensity of the light making it very difficult to keep up the narrow line between the finer grades.

GRADES OF TOBACCO.

Fine tobacco is variously graded by different planters and in different counties in from four to ten grades. The best average prices round are obtained by those who exercise most fully a delicate discrimination, which results, when the crop presents a great variety, in a large number of grades. The attempt to make fine carry coarse and inferior leaves results in loss to the planter and benefits only the rehandler. It is to be understood, however, that the grading is to be determined by the character of the crop. When assorted into six grades the proportion of the various grades in each crop is about as follows: 1st, one-thirteenth; 2d, one-tenth; 3d, two-sevenths bright mahogany; 4th, two-tenths dark mahogany; 5th, one-fifteenth bright lugs; 6th, rest of the crop.

Bright wrappers are sometimes classed in grades 1, 2, 3, and 4, beside tips, which are sometimes suitable for wrappers. Lugs are generally divided into two grades: sand lugs and smooth, clean lugs. Sometimes a third grade is made, called wrapping lugs, composed of larger and better leaves than the other two, and made of inferior wrapping leaf and the best lugs. First-grade wrappers are used on the best brands of chewing-tobacco, and the rest on lower brands, and are bought by all the best manufacturers in the United States and Canada. Tips are thicker, have more body, and make first-class fillers. Tobacco commanding the highest price has a very large leaf, bright yellow and mahogany or a clear, whitish yellow, of good body, with fine texture, toughness, and elasticity, an oily appearance, small stems and fibers, and no holes or spots. Body, size, and color are indispensable for the very best. Thin, papery tobacco, easily torn, brittle, inelastic, and lifeless, will not bring the best prices, no matter how fine the color.

DISEASES OF TOBACCO.

"Firing", known in New England as "brown rust", "frenching", "walloon", or "waterloon", and "hollow stalk", all make their appearance when soil conditions, bad weather, or inferior cultivation invite their attacks. No great amount of loss or damage by diseases of any sort is reported.

INSECT ENEMIES.

The flea-beetle is the dreaded enemy of the plant-bed, and the gray cut-worm is sometimes very destructive to newly-set plants. The horn-worm is more injurious than all other insects and all diseases combined.

HAILSTORMS.

Hailstorms are local, of narrow breadth, and the damage from such storms is of little consequence, being placed at from 2 to 5 per cent.

AVERAGE VALUE OF TOBACCO.

The average value of the product is thus reported by various counties from all parts of the tobacco region: Buncombe, 15 cents; Madison, 15 cents; Haywood, 20 cents; Warren, 10 cents; Rockingham, 15 cents; Alamance, 15 cents; Caswell, 16 cents; Granville, 14 cents; Forsyth, 11 cents; Yadkin, 7 cents; Wilkes, 6 cents; Randolph, 12½ cents; Guilford, 8 cents; Person, 15 cents.

VALUE OF DIFFERENT GRADES IN 1879.

Reports from a number of counties are given—in some cases two from one county—as the best way to illustrate the wide range in the prices. These are for 100 pounds, except where otherwise stated:

MADISON.—Average around, $8 to $20.

BUNCOMBE.—Common lugs, $6 to $8; medium lugs, $8 to $10; good fillers, $8 to $10; common wrappers, $10 to $15; medium wrappers, $15 to $25; fine wrappers, $25 to $50; extra wrappers, $50 to $80; small lots, exceedingly fine, $2 50 per pound.

WILKES.—Common lugs, $2 to $4; good lugs, $4 to $6; bright wrappers, $15 to $40.

YADKIN.—Fillers, $3; smokers, $6; dark wrappers, $10; bright wrappers, $16; nondescript, $2.

FORSYTH.—Sixth grade, lug fillers, $2 to $7; fifth grade, bright smoking lugs, $8 to $20; fourth grade, lower grade fillers, $5 to $7; third grade, best fillers, $10 to $15; second grade, wrappers, $25 to $40; first grade, best bright wrappers, $40 to $80.

WARREN.—Shipping lugs, $2 to $4; dark nondescript, $4; shipping leaf, $5 to $6; dark wrappers, $10; bright fillers, $8; sweet sun-cured fillers, $10; bright smokers, $12; bright wrappers, $30; fancy wrappers, $80 to $100.

ALAMANCE.—Dark lugs, $4 to $6; dark fillers, $4 to $7; good fillers, $7 to $18; good red wrappers, $18 to $30; common smokers, $6 to $8; good smokers, $8 to $12; fancy smokers, $12 to $25; common yellow, $15 to $25; good yellow, $25 to $50; fancy yellow, $50 to $75; extra yellow, $80 to $90; extra fine, $90 to $150; small choice lots, $3 per pound.

HAYWOOD.—First grade, $100 to $200; second, $50; third, $30; fourth, $20; fifth, $10; sixth, $5; seventh, $4; eighth, $3.

ROCKINGHAM.—Common grades, $3 to $6; good fillers, $6 to $12; bright leaf, $15 to $30; fine wrappers, $30 to $80. From the same county: First grade, $50 to $70; second, $30 to $40; third, $12 to $20; fourth, $8 to $10; fifth, $6 to $8; sixth, $4 to $6.

GRANVILLE.—Trash, $3 to $10; good lugs, $10 to $16; green tips, $8 to $15; dark mahogany, $10 to $15; bright mahogany, $25 to $50; bright tips, $25 to $50; fourth grade, $30 to $75; third grade, $60 to $75; second grade, $60 to $80; first grade, $90 to $100.

VALUE OF LANDS—COST OF PRODUCTION—MARKETING THE TOBACCO CROP.

Granville and Rockingham counties may be taken as fairly typical as to the character of the product, value of lands, cost of production, etc. Want of transportation facilities, nearness or remoteness of markets, and the cost of fertilizers as affected by freights, would alter some of the figures given if applied to other counties.

GRANVILLE COUNTY.—The price of the best lands is about an average of $42 per acre; yield, 600 pounds. Inferior lands are worth $5 to $7; yield, 500 pounds of inferior tobacco. The rental value is one-fourth of the crop, or, for best lands, $25 in money per acre. Wages, by the day, for field hands, 50 cents and board; by the year, $100 to $150 without board, or $80 with board. Estimated cost on the best soils, $10 to $12 50 per hundred pounds. In the northern part of this county a considerable amount of red, coarse shipping tobacco is raised, which greatly reduces the average price for the county.

Estimate of crop of fine tobacco for one man, careful, skillful, and intelligent:

Rent, 2 acres	$20 00
Laborer, six months	50 00
Board of laborer, six months	42 00
Horse and feed	10 00
Use of wagon and plow	3 50
Use of barn and packing-house	3 00
Firing-wood, 9 loads, at $1	9 00
Fertilizers	15 00
Hauling to market	2 00
Total cost for 2 acres	154 50
Product, 1,200 ponuds, at 35 cents	420 00
Profit	265 50
Cost per hundred ponuds	12 87½
Profit per hundred pounds	22 12½

Inspection and selling cost $1 to $1 50 per 100 pounds. When sold loose, the crop is placed in piles of separate grades upon the floor of the warehouse and sold by auction, and 2½ per cent. commission and 25 cents a pile, auctioneer's fee, are charged. The piles in weight range from 8 or 10 pounds to 300 or more. The following accounts of sales show the cost of marketing in Granville, as well as the proportions of grades and range of prices in a good crop:

Sales of 311 pounds.

30 pounds, at 46 cents	$13 80
32 pounds, at 60 cents	19 20
194 pounds, at 38 cents	73 72
55 pounds, at 13¾ cents	7 55
	114 27
Charges	4 77
Net proceeds	109 50

Sales of 1,127 pounds.

54 pounds, at 88 cents	$47 52
149 pounds, at 67½ cents	100 57
97 pounds, at 80 cents	77 60
228 pounds, at 67½ cents	153 90
90 pounds, at 60 cents	54 00
34 pounds, at 51½ cents	17 51
167 pounds, at 34½ cents	57 61
308 pounds, at 40 cents	123 20
	631 91
Charges	22 31
Net proceeds	609 60

The usual average in Granville does not exceed $150 to the hand, but there are frequent instances of profits of $500 or more. From two to two and a half acres are planted to the hand, and the cost of production is diminished by such increase of crop as will employ a full set of tools and keep the team busy.

ROCKINGHAM COUNTY.—Price of good tobacco lands, $10 to $25 per acre; yield of such lands with manure, 500 pounds. Inferior lands are worth $5 to $7, and yield with manure 500 pounds of inferior tobacco. The rental is one-fourth of the crop. Wages by the day: Men, 40 cents; women, 25 cents, with board. Skillful tobacco hands command from $15 to $24 per annum more than ordinary farm laborers, and double what they could get in the shipping-tobacco regions. The following is the estimated cost of raising two acres of tobacco in Rockingham county:

Hire of hand and board, deducting time employed on other crops	$75 00
Horse and feed while employed in crop	20 00
Use of plow, harness, and wagon	3 00
Fertilizers	10 00
Use of barn and fixtures	2 00
Hauling to market	2 00
Cost of two acres	112 00

Product, 1,200 pounds; cost per 100 pounds, $9 33.

The cost of production decreases going west, and this may be regarded as about the average cost of growing tobacco in North Carolina. An account of sales of a small crop is given, which shows the proportion of grades, range of prices, and cost of marketing fine tobacco in this county:

152 pounds, at 10½ cents		$15 96
224 pounds, at 12 cents		26 88
286 pounds, at 30 cents		85 80
37 pounds, at 53 cents		19 61
699		148 25
Charges:		
Warehouse	$0 70	
Auction fees	85	
Commission, 2½ per cent	3 70	
		5 25
Net proceeds		143 00

The following statement shows the production, acreage, yield per acre, value of the crop in farmers' hands or in primary markets, value per pound, and value per acre of the tobacco crops of North Carolina for the years 1876 to 1879, inclusive, only the figures for 1879 being from the census returns:

Year.	Production.	Acreage.	Yield per acre.	Value in farmers' hands.	Value per pound.	Value per acre.
	Pounds.		*Pounds.*		*Cents.*	
1876	20,351,152	43,672	466	$2,840,161	14.00	$65 24
1877	22,819,790	46,571	490	2,567,226	11.25	55 12
1878	21,861,525	46,885	465	3,270,220	15.00	69 75
1879	26,986,213	57,208	472	3,805,056	14.10	66 51

It will be observed that the quantity produced each year varies less than in most of the states producing tobacco. This is due, in part, to the practice among farmers of making artificial "seasons" by watering the hills when the weather continues dry at planting time. In this way they never fail to get a crop planted.

It will also be observed that the value per acre is very low. This arises from the fact that fully three-fifths of the product is of a very inferior brown nondescript leaf, bringing very low prices. No idea can be gained from this tabular statement of the profits of growing yellow tobacco on soils well adapted to its production. The value of the product upon suitable soils often reaches $250 to $400 per acre.

It is possible that the average price returned in the schedules is too high; but the average of all grades in the market at Danville for the year ending September 30, 1880, was $11 38 per hundred pounds, and it is generally conceded that the finest tobacco, and that which brings the highest prices in that market, is grown in North Carolina. It is therefore believed that the prices given in the schedules are very nearly correct.

GEOLOGY AND SOILS OF THE TOBACCO REGION.

The appended report, by the state geologist of North Carolina, discusses fully the geology and the soils of the tobacco regions of the state.

REPORT ON THE GEOLOGY AND THE SOILS OF THE TOBACCO REGION OF NORTH CAROLINA, BY PROFESSOR KERR, STATE GEOLOGIST.

Until very recently the area of bright-tobacco production was confined to less than half a dozen counties—Granville, Person, and Caswell, in North Carolina, and Pittsylvania and Halifax, in Virginia—and in these counties the industry was limited to a few supposed favored spots or patches of a few farms, or, at most, to a few square miles of territory here and there. But within half a dozen years it has been ascertained that the area of soils capable of producing it under proper management embraces not only a considerable portion of the territory of the counties above named, but also includes two or three tiers of counties in North Carolina and two in Virginia, and in the former state it has pushed up under the flanks of the Blue ridge and crossed over and occupied several counties on the French Broad and Nolichucky rivers. Beside this rapid lengthening and widening of the territory proper, experiments set on foot within one, two, and three years in the heart of the cotton section, and in several counties within a hundred miles of the sea, have demonstrated that nearly the whole of that section of the state is equally adapted to this industry, so that now this tobacco is actually produced this year through a range of territory more than 250 miles long and nearly 100 in width, including thirty counties in North Carolina (nearly one-third of the whole) and five in Virginia. While the experiments made in the middle of the eastern (cotton) section have shown that the cotton soils generally of that region are adapted to the production of the bright tobacco, the experiments made on a much larger scale in the Midland, Piedmont, and Mountain sections have demonstrated the practicability of extending the culture over the whole of those sections, the result being the conviction that this grade of tobacco may be produced in every county of the state, the controlling and determinant condition of its successful and profitable production being found in the character and texture of the soil, and being quite independent of climate within this wide range. In the discussion of these soils the natural and obvious geographical division of the territory may be adopted. This will give us: First, the Champaign district of the east, embracing parts of three counties, as may be seen on the map; second, the Midland district, embracing seventeen counties, fifteen in North Carolina and two in Virginia; third, the Piedmont district, twelve counties, nine in North Carolina and three in Virginia; fourth, the Mountain district, three counties. The first has an altitude (above sea-level) of from 50 to 120 feet, and lies under the isotherm of 60°; the second has an altitude of from 400 to 800 feet, isotherm 58°; the third, an altitude of from 1,000 to 1,500 feet, isotherm 57°; and the fourth an altitude of from 2,000 to 2,500 feet, isotherm 54°. The rainfall does not differ greatly for the several districts, being a little less for the Midland and Mountain districts, and a little more than the average for the Eastern, the average being a little above 50 inches per annum. If the geology of the several districts is considered, there is a notable uniformity through them all, except the Eastern. This last lies in the region occupied by the latest formation, the post-Tertiary or Quaternary; the other three occupy the other geological extreme, the Archæan, with the exception of two narrow interrupting zones of Triassic rocks in the Midland district.

THE CHAMPAIGN OR EASTERN DISTRICT.—The Quaternary formation in North Carolina consists of nearly horizontal, uncompacted strata of sand, sandy clay, clay and gravel, the latter often irregularly stratified and false bedded. The thickness of this formation varies from a few feet to 20 and 30 feet, and occasionally reaches 50 feet and more. It forms comparatively a very thin covering of the underlying Tertiary marls, clays, and sands, which often come to the surface, especially along the bluffs and flats of the water-courses. The surface of the region is nearly level, or only slightly undulating, except along the borders of the streams, where it is channeled into hills and bluffs.

The subsoil is generally a yellow, sometimes gray (occasionally brownish or red) sandy (occasionally clayey) loam, and is covered by a few inches of sandy, gray soil, often dark-colored, from the presence of vegetable matter when freshly cleared, but bleaching in the course of a few years' cultivation. The growth is a mixture of long-leaf and short-leaf pine (*Pinus australis* and *P. mitis*), sometimes the one predominating and sometimes the other; in either case a subordinate growth of oaks of various species, post oak, white oak, black oak, red oak, black-jack, and hickory, and an undergrowth or scrub of gum, dogwood, huckleberry, honeysuckle (*Azalia*), etc. On the slopes of the hills in the neighborhood of streams, and occasionally where there is a larger percentage of clay in the soil and in the river bottoms, the pines become the subordinate and the oaks the chief forest growth.

There is no occasion to describe here all the varieties of soil and forest growth of the region, the extensive tracts of river bottoms, or the swampy, peaty soils, with the growth peculiar to such lands, on the one hand, nor, on the other, the sandy "pine barrens", as they are called, or "sand-hills", with their open, glade-like forests of long-leaf pine exclusively, or pine and black-jack, as these soils are not adapted to tobacco culture or not yet used for this purpose. The features which are common to soils of this section on which the bright-yellow tobacco has been successfully grown are of an open, sandy texture and light-gray color, with a gray or yellow sandy subsoil, *i. e.*, permeable and naturally drained, with a mixed growth of pine (long and short straw) and oaks, chiefly post oak and white oak, with undergrowth as above described. These are, of course, not fertile soils. They belong to the medium and poorer class of upland or ridge cotton soils, that produce not more than 300 pounds of seed-cotton to the acre. This district includes as yet only three counties—Wayne, Lenoir, and Sampson—although it might extend itself over the whole cotton belt of the two states. In fact, a number of sporadic experiments, even as far east as the county of Gates, have demonstrated its feasibility.

Let it be noted that, geologically, these are drift soils, and belong to Professor Johnson's class of "transported soils"; that the materials of the decomposed and comminuted rocks in the up country have been transported, generally by full and rapid glacial currents, and have been effectually sifted and sorted; and that most of the finer particles, the clay and the iron oxide, have been washed out and carried seaward, leaving generally only the heavier, coarser, sandy, and gravelly materials, with but little adhering and intermingled clayey matter. The conditions which determine their adaptability to the production of the bright-yellow variety of tobacco seem to be these: First, thorough drainage and consequent warmth; and second, a very small proportion of clay, iron, and humus.

A very notable peculiarity of the growth of the tobacco of this district is its early ripening. The golden yellow hue which indicates maturity anticipates the beginning of August, and the crop is gathered and cured before the first cuttings are made in the more westerly districts, and it is essential to the success of this crop in all the districts that it shall acquire the proper golden hue, *i. e.*, ripen on the hill, before being cut. This gives an advantage of a full month and more in the matter of liability to damage from drought and from excess of rain.

Another peculiarity of this district is worthy of mention, viz, that a much larger proportion of its territory is adapted to the culture of this crop than in any of the other districts, amounting probably to fully one-half the area of the cotton region of both states. Another advantage hitherto found in this district is the comparative freedom from the ravages of worms, two hands being able to "worm" 25 acres.

THE MIDLAND DISTRICT.—This is the most extensive and important of the four divisions, as it is also the oldest; the one in which this industry took its rise and reached an extended development before being transplanted to other regions. This division is strongly contrasted in several of its physiographical features with the one already described: in its topography, in the geological origin of its soils, in some of their physical characters, and in their indigenous forest growth. This region is generally hilly, and is often described as the hill country, the streams having cut their way down through the decaying and easily abraded strata to the depth of 50, 100, and often more than 200 feet below the water-sheds or summits of the intervening ridges.

The bright-tobacco soils are very irregularly distributed, forming, even in the most favored counties, a small proportion of the whole area, and even of the tobacco-growing area. So controlling is the constitution of the soil that a part of the same farm, and even of the same field, may produce the finest brands known in the market, and another part be wholly incapable of making anything better than the commonest article. The quality of the tobacco is determined absolutely in the field before the cutting, and no manipulation in the handling or curing will make a "fancy-bright" tobacco out of a plant of inferior texture and color of leaf, although, of course, the best grades may fail and be spoiled in the curing. As a general statement, the bright-tobacco patches and belts of land are found on the ridges and benches, the divides between the water-courses. Wherever there is found on these ridges a subsoil of a gray or yellowish, gravelly, or sandy loam, covered with a gray, sandy, or gravelly soil, the bright tobacco may be grown. These favorable conditions of soil are always indicated by the native growth, and are readily recognized by the experienced tobacco raiser; and even in riding over a region for the first time he can with unerring certainty point out the best bright-tobacco tracts. The most noted sections of the district, which have obtained the highest prices for their product, are commonly described as pea ridges, chincapin ridges, and huckleberry ridges. The forest growth is usually of stunted oaks, chiefly post oak and white oak, generally mingled with pines (*Pinus mitis*), and sometimes with an admixture of dogwood, hickory, black-jack, or sourwood (*Oxydendron*). All these characteristics of the best bright-yellow tobacco soils are obviously also those of leanness and infertility. In fact, such soils are generally nearly worthless for wheat or corn, or for any other of the ordinary crops of the country, and until this new industry developed their capacity they were valued at $2 or $3 per acre, whereas they are now the most valuable lands of the district, most eagerly sought after, and are valued at $10, $15, $25, and often more, per acre. Here, as in the eastern district, the distinctive features of these favored soils are, first, an open texture of soil and subsoil, securing drainage and warmth; and second, the absence or low percentage of humus, of clay, and of iron oxide, with the same (consequent) unproductiveness as to other crops. In the former case these conditions were found to be dependent on the geological origin of the soils, the constituents which would have made a more fertile soil having been eliminated by the mechanical and the chemical agencies by which it was found. In the Midland district the geological conditions are very different. The soils here are of the other class of "sedentary soils", formed by the decomposition and disintegration of the underlying rock *in situ;* so that whatever this rock contains is in general to be found in the soil. This carries us directly to the question of the relation of geology to the origin and distribution of these bright-tobacco soils, and suggests the important inquiry: What are the favorable conditions of geological formation and structure under which such soils may be expected to occur?

As already stated, the rocks of the Midland district belong to the oldest formation, the Archæan, and consist of granites, gneisses, schists, and slates of various structure and composition, indicated even to the casual and uninstructed observer by difference of color, bedding, texture, and other obvious physical characters. These differences of physical characters indicate profounder differences of lithological and chemical structure and composition. A little observation suffices to show that wherever the rocks consist of light-colored feldspathic, binary granites, as about Oxford, in Granville county, or of light-colored feldspathic and quartzose gneisses and slates, as in the eastern part of Granville, the northwestern corner of Person, the southeastern corner of Caswell, the northwestern part of Alamance, and much of the northern half of Guilford, the middle of Rockingham, about Reidville, eastward and westward, for example, and the section of Pittsylvania, in Virginia, lying north of Danville for several miles—wherever this geological condition is observed, we have exceptionally good bright-tobacco soils. The mineralogical elements are wanting (or present in small percentage) in these rocks, which give rise by their oxidation and decomposition, to the rich, red-clay soils, on which are the large oak forests, the black and red oaks and hickories.

These latter soils are found overlying gray or dark-colored granites, syenites, greenstones, hornblende, and chlorite schists, and the like, and to their lithological constitution the derived soils owe their distinctive characters. Again, the bright-tobacco soils are found prevalent on the ridges, benches, and higher levels, as already stated, and for two reasons: first, the feldspathic (and quartzose) granites and slates are less readily decomposed and abraded than the more complex hornblende and chloritic rocks of the red soils, and hence the valleys are chiefly hewn out of these; second, on account of their situation and open texture, they are subjected to a continual leaching process by meteoric waters charged with organic acids, which dissolve and wash out, and thus continually diminish the percentage of clay mechanically, and of iron chemically. In addition, owing to their situation, they are older, that is, have been subjected to this leaching, improving process longer, than the soils on the slopes and hillsides, which are subjected to a greater amount of abrasion, and the consequent continual exposure of new surfaces.

This genetic relation of the soil to the underlying rock explains the obvious fact that the irregular patches and zones of bright-tobacco soils have generally their longer dimension in a northeast and southwest direction. This is the direction of the outcrops of the rocks, which has evidently exercised a marked influence upon the topography of the district, determining in some and modifying in many cases the direction of the streams and valleys, and so the trend of the ridges. Herein also is found the cause why no considerable area produces bright tobacco exclusively, not often even an entire farm of much extent; and also of the other equally familiar fact, that in regions and on isolated farms outside of the recognized bright-tobacco areas not unfrequently some of the best crops are produced, and beds and patches and ledges of the rocks adapted to the production of the proper soils are intercalated here and there among masses of unfavorable composition, and *vice versa*.

Such are some of the conclusions to which we are conducted by a general study of the more obtrusive facts connected with the culture of the bright tobacco of this district.

But one important feature of the district remains to be considered. Two tracts of quite exceptional character occur within the limits of the district, very nearly bounding it, in fact, on the northwest and on the southeast. Topographically, these tracts are notable as basins or troughs, whose trend is northeast and southwest. They are marked almost everywhere by a considerable depression below the general level of the surrounding country. They are notable also as furnishing the channel-ways of many streams, and when the course of a stream lies across their track they commonly end by changing that course to conform to that of these troughs. Geologically, they will be noted on the map as narrow ribbons of Triassic rocks. Lithologically considered, they consist of alternating beds of sandstones, sandy-clay slates, and shales, sometimes indurated, generally soft and little compacted, and readily yielding to the erosive agencies of a climate characterized by a heavy rainfall. It will be observed that nearly the whole of these tracts is included in the bright-tobacco territory, and most of them in the choicest areas, as, for example, Granville and Pittsylvania conspicuously. This is due to the obvious fact that these rocks, by their decomposition, usually give rise to light, sandy soils, with subsoils of corresponding open sandy texture, and furnish in general the class of soils already described as especially favorable to the growth of the bright-tobacco plants. These rocks furnish a much larger proportion of such soils than the granites, gneisses, and schists of the older formations, and are comparable in this respect to the Quaternary rocks of the first district. These zones of Triassic soils, it hardly need be said, are everywhere recognizable, even when the rocks are concealed by the forest and undergrowth already described as characteristic of the bright-tobacco soils, the pine being an almost invariable element, the white oaks, black-jacks, gum, sourwood, etc., being very prevalent. Of course, there are exceptional areas of very different soils, often of high fertility; but the general fact remains conspicuous that these Triassic soils are generally better adapted than those of older formations to the special industry under consideration.

The soils of many of the counties southward are just as well adapted to this industry as those included.

PIEDMONT DISTRICT.—The bright-yellow tobacco culture has been extended gradually during the last eight or ten years into this region, receiving an earlier and larger expansion in the counties of the district lying in Virginia than in those of North Carolina. Specimens of the product of this region (Wilkes county) were taken to Vienna in 1873 as part of the exhibit made by the geological survey of North Carolina, and were pronounced by experts to be equal to the best from any part of the world. Buyers in Reidville, Lynchburg, and elsewhere place the best product of this region with the corresponding brand from the older sections.

The description of the soils which produce this tobacco in the third district would be a mere repetition of that for the second. The rocks which give origin and character to the soils are of the same age and description. The characteristic growths are also the same, with the exception that the chestnut and chestnut oak are to be added. A peculiarity of the product of several of the counties of this district, mostly in Virginia, is a substitution in large part of the bright yellow by the mahogany tobacco. This is notably true of the eastern part of Henry and most of Franklin, except the southeast, and a considerable part of Patrick, and to a smaller extent of the adjacent counties of North Carolina. The most common variety, the Orinoco (popularly Iron Oak), and to some extent the Flannigan, is grown, especially in Henry county. This mahogany tobacco bears as good a price (and finds as ready sale) as the average of the bright-yellow tobaccos, and is preferred to those by most of the manufacturers of these counties, although they do not reach the fancy prices of the brights. Henry county is the chief producer of this tobacco, Franklin coming next, but making also a considerable quantity of the brighter brand, chiefly in the southeastern section of the county. Patrick county produces also a mahogany, but inferior to that of the eastern half of Henry. The soils which produce this quality of plant are very similar to those of the bright-yellow district, but the subsoil is brown to reddish, and the forests contain a greater variety of oaks, black and Spanish, replacing in part and mingling with the white oak, black-jack, chestnut, etc. There is a less proportion of feldspathic and quartzose gneisses in these counties than is found generally in the second district, and less than in several of the counties of the third in North Carolina.

MOUNTAIN DISTRICT.—The culture of tobacco for market is of very recent introduction into this district. About five years ago the subject began to attract attention in Madison county, on the French Broad river, and in 1878 the tobacco product of that county was sold for some $50,000; that of 1880 is estimated at $225,000, which means about 1,000,000 pounds. The bright-yellow tobacco from this new quarter grades, both in texture and in color, in

Lynchburg and elsewhere with the best from the Midland district. A description of the soils and rocks of this region would be a mere repetition of that of the two districts preceding.

In Mitchell county this industry, as in the counties of the first district, at the other end of the state, is only three years old, but the success has been complete and the expansion enormously rapid, and a large proportion of the area of the county, as well as of the district, and of all the counties of it, is adapted to this culture. A very large part of Henderson county, and nearly as much of Transylvania, are to be added to the productive area. A few tentative experiments have already been made in these counties, more than sufficient to corroborate the conclusion suggested by the geology and the character of the soils.

It seems best to make a distinction between the bright-yellow tobacco region proper and that section of the Piedmont district, which, while entitled to be placed within the area of "bright-yellow" production, is especially characterized by its "mahoghany tobacco".

SOIL ANALYSES.

	1.	2.	3.	4.	5.	6.
Silica, soluble......	2.67	1.24	4.85	1.10	0.67	3.84
Silica, insoluble....	89.00	91.96	90.85	96.10	76.69	77.06
Alumina............	2.40	1.24	1.22	0.71	12.46	6.97
Oxide of iron	0.24	0.52	0.42	0.65	8.57	4.07
Lime...............	0.23	0.08	0.20	0.13	0.51	0.10
Magnesia...........	0.10	0.09	0.76	0.14	0.39	0.29
Potash	0.04	0.06	0.06	0.07	0.16	0.11
Soda...............	0.60	0.00	0.00	0.00	0.45	0.00
Phosphoric acid....	0.04	0.04	Trace.	Trace.	0.00	0.05
Sulphuric acid......	0.01	0.03	Trace.	Trace.	0.02	Trace.
Chlorine	0.02	0.01	0.02	0.01	Trace.	0.00
Organic matter.....	4.90	4.10	2.60	2.40	4.60	6.65
Water..............	0.40	0.80	0.30	0.20	1.07	1.10

The first three of these represent the bright-tobacco soils of the first district, the first from Sampson county, the second from Wilson, and the third from Columbus. They are all just such soils as are described in the remarks on the Champaign district as producing the bright-yellow tobacco, and represent a large proportion of the lands of the district. No. 4 is from one of the most famous of all the bright-yellow tobacco localities in the southeast corner of Person county. The sample was taken from a farm part of whose product was sold at $2 per pound. It was taken one foot deep (as all the others) in the forest adjoining the field where the fine "fancy bright" had been raised. The growth is post oak and white oak of moderate size, hickory, dogwood, sourwood, and a few pines. The soil is sandy and gravelly, of a light-gray color, and the subsoil is of the same texture, but yellowish in color. The rock is quartzose, feldspathic, slaty gneiss.

No. 5 is from the bright-tobacco section of Catawba county, in the Piedmont district, in the town of Hickory. The growth is medium to small-sized oak, black-jack, sourwood, and pine; the soil yellowish gray, a little sandy; the subsoil yellowish brown, sandy.

No. 6 is from Mitchell county. It does not represent the precise variety of soils on which the fine tobacco of that county is produced. It is very much like the last in color and texture, but is much poorer. The growth is chestnut, Spanish oak, post oak, sourwood, and laurel (*kalmia*). These last two soils resemble more the mahogany-tobacco soils of Henry and Franklin counties, in Virginia.

These are all virgin soils, and therefore contain a much higher percentage of humus than ordinary cultivated bright-tobacco soils, this element being subject to very rapid diminution on account of the sandy and porous texture of the soil, and of course but a small percentage of it is in an available condition.

All of these soils would be classed as poor from the analysis. The low percentage of clay and of iron is also notable, except in the last two, which are not bright-tobacco soils.

Chapter XIII.

CULTURE AND CURING OF TOBACCO IN OHIO.

A gentle, ridge-like elevation, whose slopes are scarcely perceptible, stretches diagonally across this state from Trumbull county, in the northeast, to Mercer and Darke counties, in the west, forming the "divide" in the hydrography of the state. The general elevation of the state is from 800 to 1,100 feet above the sea. The highest point, a spot in Logan county, is 1,540 feet above sea-level, and the lowest 433 feet, the latter being low-water mark of the Ohio river near Cincinnati. The streams which flow southward from the "divide" have cut out many wide and fertile valleys, which are not excelled in natural fertility by any on the continent. The southern slopes of the water-shed are well adapted to the production of the cereals, while the northern slopes furnish grazing lands of a very high order.

CLIMATE.

The climate of Ohio is one of considerable extremes, being very cold, as low as —16° in winter, and very hot, from 94° to 100° in summer, the thermometer marking an extreme range of 116°.

The annual mean temperature for ten years at Cleveland (latitude 41° 30′, elevation 660 feet above the sea) is 49.77 degrees. The annual mean for January, the coldest month, for the same period was 27.36 degrees; for the hottest month, July, 72.57. This will give the mean annual range of the thermometer 45.21 degrees.

Observations taken at Cincinnati (latitude 39° 6′) for sixteen years by George W. Harper show the average annual mean temperature to be 54.67 degrees; the mean for the coldest month, January, 31.20, and for the hottest, July, 78.61. The greatest annual precipitation for the same period was 49.17 inches, in 1858, and the lowest 28.03 inches, in 1870. The highest average for any one month was for May, 4.12 inches, and the lowest, February, 2.33 inches.

For Cleveland, observations for ten years, taken by G. A. Hyde, show the average annual rainfall to be 35.59 inches. The greatest rainfall was in 1866, which reached 48.91 inches, and the lowest in 1863, which was 30.76 inches.

The amount of precipitation varies greatly in different portions of the state. The following table has been compiled from the geological survey of the state and from other sources:

Place.	Latitude.	Length of period of observation.		Average annual amount of precipitation.
		Y.	*M.*	*Inches.*
Portsmouth	38° 45′	26	0	38.83
Cincinnati	39° 06′	31	0	44.87
Marietta	39° 25′	47	11	42.70
Urbana	40° 06′	11	0	40.31
Cleveland	41° 30′	11	8	37.61
Kelley's Island	41° 36′	7	6	33.24
Hudson	41° 15′	11	4	35.26
Toledo	41° 39′	6	0*	39.46

GEOLOGY.

The geological formations of the state are mainly horizontal. An arch or slight anticlinal extends from lake Erie through Cincinnati into Kentucky and Tennessee. From this arch there is a slight dip westward to the Illinois coal-fields and eastward to the Appalachian range. The principal formations are the Lower Silurian, the Upper Silurian, Devonian, Carboniferous, and Glacial. The Silurian forms a belt from Cincinnati northward to the lake; the Devonian is found in the northwestern corner of the state, and also in a belt running through the state from north to south, separating the Silurian from the Carboniferous in the southeast. The eastern part of Ohio, constituting nearly one-third of the state, belongs to the Carboniferous era, the northern and western to the Devonian, the center to the Upper Silurian, and the southwestern to the Lower Silurian. The bed-rock of this region is the Cincinnati group of limestones, the blue limestone of the Trenton period being the chief; but for the greater portion of this latter area this limestone is covered by drift.

There are three well-defined tobacco-growing districts in Ohio. These districts may be called, for the sake of description: 1, the Burley district; 2, the Seed-Leaf district; 3, the Spangled Tobacco district.

BURLEY DISTRICT.

The first, or the Burley district, is confined mainly to three counties, lying on the Ohio river, viz: Adams, Brown, and Clermont. These counties commercially belong with the great Burley tobacco-growing district of Kentucky.

It is not ascertained at what period tobacco began to be grown in these three counties. Unquestionably its culture has been carried on to a greater or less extent for half a century, but the type has been changed from a shipping leaf to an article suited to domestic manufacture. The following table exhibits the production in the district for each census year from 1840 to 1880, inclusive:

	1840.	1850.	1860.	1870.	1880.
	Pounds.	*Pounds.*	*Pounds.*	*Pounds.*	*Pounds.*
The district	131,338	1,483,518	2,482,836	4,009,978	10,823,163
Adams	88	20,500	43,060	102,473	1,054,076
Brown	63,200	1,279,510	1,808,840	2,687,743	6,244,036
Clermont	68,050	184,508	630,930	1,219,762	3,524,151

From 1840 to 1850 there was an increase of 1,036 per cent.; from 1850 to 1860, the next decade, an increase of 66 per cent.; for the ten years ending in 1870 an increase of over 61 per cent.; and the decade ending in 1880 shows a still further increase in ten years of 170 per cent.

This rapid growth of the tobacco interest in these three counties is due to two causes: one, a fortunate development of a variety, and the other, the change in the demand of manufacturers and consumers for a milder type, in place of the heavier grades which thirty years ago were employed in making plug. Up to 1866 the farmers of the Burley district raised what is now known as Red Burley. This variety cured up a reddish or cinnamon color, was very light and chaffy and almost destitute of gum, and for that reason was used for cutting into fine shreds and making a particular brand of chewing-tobacco, being a mild, pleasant product. The White Burley had its origin in Brown county. A farmer named George Webb, living near Higginsport, in that county, in the year 1864 sowed his seed-bed with Red Burley seed, which is said to have come from the farm of Joseph W. Barkley, of Bracken county, Kentucky. The plants came up and except in one particular spot were very healthy. Here they had a whitish, sickly appearance, and when the time came for setting out his crop these were left in the bed, as they were thought to be worthless. Finding, however, that he still lacked enough to set two rows, he returned to his seed-bed and drew out the sickly-looking plants and used them, rather than go to a neighbor for a quantity sufficient to finish his crop. For two or three weeks the white plants seemed to grow but little, but when they became well rooted they grew with greater rapidity, and the tobacco grew rapidly to fine size, retaining all its creamy richness of color, and ripening two weeks earlier than any other tobacco in the field. When cured in the ordinary way, by atmospheric influences, it was discovered that on the under-side of the leaf there was a whitish tinge, while the upper side was of a beautiful golden yellow. A few plants were cut and cured which measured near 6 feet in length, and were put on exhibition in the Bodeman warehouse, in Cincinnati. Buyers gave encouragement to its further cultivation, and the next year (1865) the gentleman on whose farm it originated planted 10 acres, from which 11,000 pounds of tobacco were gathered, which was very handsome and silky, and had all the characteristic marks in coloring which the sample of the previous year had displayed. This tobacco, when put on the market, brought from 25 to 45 cents per pound, and a premium of $300 was awarded, in addition to this large price, to the successful grower. From this beginning the White Burley has gained the position noted in the description of other states, especially in that of Kentucky.

The district consists of a river valley, fringed by bluffs of modified drift, rising to the height of 500 feet above the low water of the Ohio river. These bluffs run off into a plateau, sometimes deeply gashed by numerous tributaries of the Ohio and the Little Miami, but generally the erosion has not been deep, and frequent instances occur where small streams meander through broad valleys. Broad stretches of level land are found, sometimes so flat that in times of excessive rains they overflow and form temporary inland lakes. The main axis of the Cincinnati group passes through Clermont county.

The limestones are even bedded, and vary in color from a dark-blue to a buff. These beds have a gentle dip to the north, as well as to the east or to the west, the latter especially in Clermont county, and many beds appear along the river, which lie below low-water mark at Cincinnati. Some of these beds are full of fossils, and analysis shows that potash, soda, and phosphoric acid enter largely into their composition.

The drift deposits are extensive, and contribute mainly to the formation of the soil. Every part of the district, except the slopes of the hills that border the streams and the more recent drifts of the Ohio river bottoms, is covered with them. It is a fact well established that the drift formations of this region contain much less imbedded gravel than the region on the Miami river and districts further north. This drift is composed largely of clays, and its thickness varies from 10 to 50 feet. Its usual thickness, however, is about 20 feet, and it is composed for the most part, according to a recent geological survey, of the following materials, beginning at the surface and descending:

1. Surface clays, generally white, sometimes darkened by an accumulation of humus, especially in swamps or basins.

2. Yellow clays, abounding with limestone gravel, forming the surface where the first has been carried away by denudation.

3. Forest bed, a dark carbonaceous clay, abounding in the remains of vegetable matter; often peaty; generally resting upon a bed of bog-iron ore 1 or 2 feet in thickness.

4. Hard-pan, a blue, compact, putty-like mass, with occasional layers of intercalated sand. This last generally rests upon the bed-rocks. This clay contains pebbles and bowlders, mostly of limestone.

The soils of the district may be divided into four classes, viz: 1, native soils, formed from the disintegration of the bed-rocks of the country; 2, drift soils of the uplands; 3, black soils of swampy places; 4, alluvial of the river bottoms.

The soils of the first class are not widespread, but are confined to the slopes of the streams. Some of them abound in vegetable humus, and are dark in color, very friable, and exceeding fertile. When the soil is deficient in vegetable matter, it is of a reddish hue, though always fertile. This fertility is derived from the large amount of carbonate of lime, potash, soda, and phosphoric acid which often abound in the limestone rocks; and their fertility is still further increased by the arenaceous character of the limestone, which makes them open and light. They wash easily, however, on account of their slight depth and the general unevenness of the surface where they exist, but are preferred for tobacco. The chief trees are sugar maple and walnut.

The drift soils may be further subdivided into yellow clays and white clays.

The yellow-clay soil is derived from the weathering of the drift, which is largely composed of limestone pebbles. These soils contain occasional seams of sand and gravel. The surface, however, is made up of one or two feet of whitish, fine-grained clay, comparatively free from gravel, which is due in part to the decay of vegetable matter and in part to the work of earth-worms and animals, which bring up the fine particles from beneath.

The white-clay soil is identical in character with the last described, except as to its origin, and changes to a yellowish hue under the surface. Analysis shows a considerable amount of potash and soda in its composition, as well as phosphate and carbonate of lime and carbonate of magnesia. It also contains over 6 per cent. of the sesquioxide of iron.

The black soils of the swamps are for the most part composed of humus in a greater or less degree of decay, and when sweetened by aeration are very durable and highly productive.

The alluvial soils of the streams partake of the nature of the region whence their material has been derived, sometimes being very sandy, sometimes gravelly, and at other times highly argillaceous and stiff, but generally very productive; but the soils on the smaller streams are not generally so sandy as those on the Ohio river.

COMPARISON OF RECENT TOBACCO CROPS.

In Clermont county the increase in the acreage of tobacco has been very rapid. It was 20 per cent. greater in 1879 than in the previous three years, and the yield also is reported to have been 10 per cent. greater.

In Brown county the area planted in tobacco was 20 per cent. greater in 1879 than in 1878, 12 per cent. greater than in 1877, and 20 per cent. greater than in 1876. The yield for the census year is reported as 5 per cent. less than in 1878 and 8 per cent. less than in 1877, but 12 per cent. greater than in 1876. The crop of 1879 was greatly inferior in quality to that grown for the two years preceding, because of damage in curing, the season being a very unfavorable one. It was characterized by large stems and thin web or fiber, and lacked body, and was very much like the crop of 1876, though not of such a thin, flimsy character.

In Adams county the acreage was 20 per cent. greater in the census year than in the year previous, 25 per cent. greater than in 1877, and 50 per cent. greater than in 1876. The yield also was 5 per cent. greater for 1879 than for either of the two previous years.

Taking the whole district, it is safe to say that within four years the average of the crop has been increased by 25 per cent.

VARIETIES OF TOBACCO GROWN.

The White Burley, the only variety grown to any extent, is of medium size, the leaves usually attaining a length of about 24 inches, sometimes, however, on heavily-manured lots, reaching a length of 42 inches. It has generally in growing cream-colored leaves, but these run into various shades of green; so that a field shows a great variety of colors, from a milky white to a deep sea-green.

The Red Burley, which produces a greater number of pounds to a given area, is planted to some extent; but the quality is not so fine, nor does it command such ready sale as the white variety.

The White Burley is losing some of its distinctive features. At first the stalk and leaves were white, but each successive year shows a larger proportion of green. The original White Burley, when cured, had a golden surface; but this golden color is giving place to a yellowish-brown or red, and each successive crop shows a nearer approach to the Red Burley.

Nine-tenths of this product is taken for the home trade. It is used for making fine-cut, for plug fillers, for smokers, and very recently it has been used in the place of mahogany wrappers for plug, and these are said not to blacken under pressure, as many of the fine wrappers of the West do.

When this variety of tobacco is planted on bottom lands with a large admixture of sand it cures up bright in color, but is not so heavy in body as when grown upon a clayey, calcareous soil; but when planted upon a hillside it has a good body, a fine stem, a more delicate fiber, and a better flavor. The soils of the maple swamps, when cleared and well drained, are said to grow a very superior quality of tobacco, noted for its beauty and for its fineness of leaf. On strong limestone soils it grows heavy and cures a dark color, and this color can be improved by planting more closely, but it will have less body. Newly-cleared land, with a good proportion of clay, makes the most valuable leaf, but does not produce so many pounds to the acre.

In 1869 all the tobacco grown in this district was graded as cutting leaf and dark shipping, the latter constituting one-third of the crop. The grades for 1879 show a marked change, and are variable in different parts of the district, the extremes being as follows: Dark shipping, 0 to 10 per cent.; fillers for plug, 5 to 33⅓ per cent.; smokers, 16 to 25 per cent.; and cutting, 20 to 66 per cent. The average of the crop would probably be: Dark shipping, 3 per cent.; fillers, 30 per cent.; smokers, 17 per cent.; and cutting, 50 per cent.

Since 1869 the dark shipping has been reduced to almost nothing, and whatever of this grade is now produced results from accident, rather than from design. There were no fillers for plug in 1869. These constitute now 30 per cent. of the crop, and the demand for them is increasing so rapidly that much tobacco graded as cutting leaf is sold for fillers. The nondescript is wanting entirely, all suitable for that grade in other varieties being placed with the smokers, to which the significant name of "trash" is given.

The improvement in quality of the product of the same grade has not been very marked in the past ten years, though there is a better demand for the tobacco grown in the district, because it is used for more purposes than it was in 1869. The best crops of White Burley were grown in 1877 and 1878. Probably the change in the relative quantity of cutting leaf and fillers will amount within the past three years to 10 per cent., the fillers increasing and the cutting leaf diminishing. Nor is this the result entirely of natural changes. A few years ago, when there was a very limited demand for fillers, the object of the planter was to increase the proportion of cutting leaf and to diminish the quantity of fillers. Tobacco was planted thickly and topped high, so that the thin and gumless leaves, suitable for cutting, might be in excess. Now a wider space is given the plants, and they are topped much lower; and the consequence is that the growth has more gum, body, and sweetness, and is far preferable for fillers. Nine-tenths of all the Burley tobacco grown is taken at high prices in the United States. A little trash is exported, because it is needed in making bright smokers, and brings as much in the market as the good leaf of heavy export tobacco. There is no lack of inquiry abroad for the White Burley or the Red Burley, but the American manufacturers will pay higher prices for tobacco than the buyers of any other country will pay here.

The alluvial soils, both sandy and clayey, are cultivated extensively in tobacco. On the Ohio river the alluvial soils, in their primitive condition, are covered with sycamore, red maple, hickory, Spanish oak (*Q. palustris*), white oak (*Q. alba*), and burr oak (*Q. macrocarpa*). On the bottoms of the smaller streams are found sugar-tree, buckeye, beech, hickory, and various species of oaks. The northwestern slopes, characterized by a rich, black soil and a growth of walnut, linden, and sugar-tree, with an undergrowth of papaw and grape-vines, are often planted. The northeastern slopes have soils not so dark in color, but they are clothed with the same forest trees as the northwestern slopes, with the addition of ash and black locust. Both of these situations are selected for the growth of tobacco, but the latter is preferred. Of the crop planted in 1879, at least 15 per cent. was grown on freshly-cleared lands, which produce a brighter, smoother, lighter-colored leaf than the old lands, of a much finer fiber, and which will bring a higher price by 10 per cent. for like grades. The tobacco grown on level lands is generally coarser and of a darker color than that grown on rolling lands, and in seasons of extreme humidity it frequently suffers from "sunstroke" and "sore shin". These flat lands were originally maple swamps, and great care is necessary to secure good drainage.

While the soils of the Ohio bottoms produce excellent tobacco, the rolling lands are preferred, on account of their freedom from overflows of the river in summer and fall. For the Red Burley the bottoms are most suitable, but the white variety does best on uplands.

It is a source of solicitude that, though this district was at one time considered equal in fertility to any portion of the upland districts of the state, the diminution in the yield of staple crops within the past twenty-five years has been from 25 to 50 per cent. This is the more alarming because very few farmers even now pay any attention to the fertilization or the preservation of their lands. In many places the sides of the hills are scarred and ribbed with deepening gullies, which form channels, down which the rich plant food is carried by every rain. From the testimony at hand, even in the cultivation of tobacco—a crop which is well known to be a voracious feeder—not one farmer in twenty in Brown county considers it necessary to apply fertilizers to restore or to preserve the fertility of the soil. In Clermont county one farmer in five makes use of fertilizers in the growing of the crop, and in Adams county the number is so small as to be inappreciable.

The general practice with new lands is to plant two or three crops of tobacco in succession, the third crop showing a decrease in the yield of from 200 to 300 pounds per acre. If the land is able to endure this first heavy draft upon it, wheat follows tobacco in the fall of the second or the third year, and in the spring clover is sown on the wheat. The more thoughtful farmers will permit it to remain in clover for the two years following, when corn succeeds; many, however, only leave the clover for one year, when it is put in corn or in tobacco, at the convenience of the farmer. Tobacco grown on clover lands is coarse and heavy, and is greatly inferior to that grown upon fresh lands, or even after corn.

When fertilizers are applied in liberal quantities on the thin soils a very marked effect is produced in the yield, especially if the season is favorable, making it from one-fourth to one-half larger. The quality of the leaf, however, is coarser, but heavier even than upon river bottoms without fertilizers.

Rye is considered a good crop to rotate with tobacco and to prevent rapid exhaustion of the soil. In the succeeding spring clover is sown on the rye, and is allowed to stand one or two years, and it is said that on lands so treated a good crop of tobacco may be produced every third or fourth year. A few sow rye in the fall and turn it under just before planting the tobacco crop in the succeeding spring, and this practice is said to be very beneficial.

With the very small attention given to fertilizing it is not surprising that farmers complain that the average production per acre is rapidly declining. Ten years ago from 1,200 to 1,500 pounds per acre was thought to be a fair average crop. Enumerators' returns make the average yield per acre for 1879 only 961 pounds. This statement will probably correctly represent the deterioration in the productive capacity of the soils, and even this low estimate would be still further reduced but for the almost universal practice of planting from 10 to 20 per cent. of the crop on virgin soils each year.

SEED-BEDS.

The management of seed-beds is mainly as described in chapter III. As soon as the land becomes dry enough in the spring—from the middle of February to the middle of April—a spot is selected in the woods on the northeastern slope of a hill and cleared. If no such slope can be had, any good moist (not wet) soil in or near the woods will do, but virgin land is preferred. In this part of the state the land is burned with wood or brush.

The extreme limit of transplanting is from the 15th of May to the 4th of July. Very little, however, is set out so early as the first date given or so late as the last, and the bulk of the crop is planted between June 1 and June 15.

PREPARATION OF SOIL AND PLANTING.

The soil for tobacco is prepared by reversing the soil, either in the fall or early spring, with a turning-plow, going to the depth of 6 or 8 inches. Just before the plants are large enough to transplant the soil is again broken with a shovel-plow, usually so as not to reverse the soil, and by frequent harrowings afterward it is reduced to a fine tilth. The distance between the rows is variable, some farmers laying them off $2\frac{1}{2}$ feet, others 3, others $3\frac{1}{2}$, and many others 4 feet apart. The latter distance is preferred when tobacco of good body is desired, but when a cutting leaf only is to be produced the shorter distances are adopted. When the field has been marked off, hills are made in the furrow, sometimes 2 feet apart, but generally 30 inches. The plants are usually set out after a shower, but in dry seasons, when they are liable to become overgrown in the seed beds, they are set in hills artificially watered. This is generally done in the cool of the evening, and when done properly very few of the plants perish.

The amount of cultivation which the tobacco receives varies much with the weather. The land should always be stirred after every rain as soon as it is in proper condition to work, either with a shovel, turning-plow, or with a cultivator, and the dirt should be drawn up to the tobacco with hoes at least twice, so as to make a broad, flat hill. Two or three plowings and as many hoeings are always sufficient to bring it to the period of topping.

TOPPING TOBACCO.

This is done when the blossom buds appear, which, on new land, is in about forty days, and upon old land from forty to fifty days, after transplanting. The number of leaves left to the plant is determined by the fertility of the soil, the time at which it is topped, and the character of the tobacco which the planter desires to produce. If the season is early, and the land very fertile, to make the best cutting tobacco from sixteen to eighteen leaves should be left to the plant, but if the season is advanced it becomes necessary to top low, in order that the tobacco may ripen before killing frosts. If the planter, however, wishes to make tobacco of good body, best suited for fillers, no more than ten or twelve leaves should be left to the stalk, however early the plant may come in top, and this number must be decreased as the season advances.

No "priming" is done, and when cut and cured the lower leaves, often half burned by the parching heat of the ground, are put in the trash grade

SUCKERING, CUTTING, AND CURING OF TOBACCO.

After the process of cultivation has been finished and the field topped the suckers are carefully removed from the plants as they appear and the horn-worms are diligently sought and killed. This is kept up until the tobacco is ready to be harvested, which varies from four to seven weeks after topping, the time being governed by the season, kind of soil, number of leaves left on each plant, and the character of tobacco desired. A large proportion is cut within six weeks from the time it is topped, but on new land it will ripen sooner. Sandy soils will mature the plant a week or two earlier than clayey soils.

The cutting is done with a knife, the blade of which is placed at right angles to the upper two leaves, and a split is made down through the middle of the stalk to within 4 inches of the ground. The knife is then withdrawn and inserted under the lower leaves and the stalk severed. When cut, it is straddled over a stick stuck in the ground, conveniently placed for the person cutting. From five to seven plants are put upon each stick, the number being regulated by the size of the plants. When the plants have wilted sufficiently to handle without breaking they are taken to the barns and arranged on the tier poles, so as to permit the free circulation of air. A great many planters scaffold in the field, and when the weather is open and bright it facilitates the curing process greatly and economizes barn room, for after remaining on a scaffold for four or five days a third more may be hung with safety in the same space. Scaffolds are made with round poles and forks, the latter being driven in the ground and the poles placed on them 4 feet apart, and upon these the sticks are hung 5 or 6 inches apart.

The time of day preferred for cutting is the afternoon, as at this time there is no risk of sun-burning; and by the following morning the tobacco will be wilted sufficiently to be handled with safety.

In seasons of great humidity two causes conspire to make the curing of tobacco without fire very difficult. Though well ripened, in long continued wet weather the tobacco will become full of sap, and after it is put in the barn it requires a much longer time to effect a cure, even though the weather should be favorable.

The barns, many of them constructed of rough logs, with the spaces between left open, are too little secured against the invasion of dampness to make successful cures in very bad weather without resort to artificial heat, and this is only used as a preventive of house-burn or mildew, and not for curing. The cost of the largest and best barns in the district does not exceed $500 or $600, and the majority not even $100 each.

A certain amount of dampness is desirable, in order that the plant may attain its highest perfection of color. Whatever the cause, if the leaf is entirely cured without becoming pliant during the process it becomes harsh.

During the past decade there have been two years in which the planters have had great difficulty in curing their crops. One of these was 1876, and the other 1879. Much "house-burned" tobacco was placed on the market, and much that was mildewed and "funked", estimated to equal one-fourth of the crop. House-burned tobacco is easily recognized by its rigid, lifeless appearance, never coming in condition even in the warmest and dampest weather. It retains only the form of the leaf, with all the valuable properties destroyed.

A large majority of the farmers in this district sell their tobacco loose to dealers at a stated price through, and it is delivered to them in hands, each one containing eight or ten leaves. The tobacco is stripped as early after the process of curing is finished as possible, and is hung up closely in the barns, where it remains until the weather is suitable, when the sticks containing it are put wider apart, to bring it into condition for packing in bulk.

Tobacco should remain in bulk several weeks, for nothing else improves the flavor and equalizes its condition so much. If it should go through the sweat while in bulk, so much the better, as it can be watched, and all danger from excessive fermentation can be avoided.

Farmers, as a rule, do not grade their tobacco very closely in stripping. A few who understand the best grading find their profits quite as great in handling, packing, and "prizing" the crop as in growing it.

Dealers and the best informed planters usually assort into five grades. The first grade consists of the bright perfect leaves of the crop; the second of the red perfect leaves. The third grade consists of the tips or top leaves of the plant, which, though perfect in form, have a greenish tinge, and are generally immature when the plant is cut. This grade is greatly lessened by low topping. The fourth grade is the worm-eaten and slightly damaged leaves; and the fifth grade, or trash, is made up of ground leaves. The second, third, fourth, and fifth grades are often thrown together.

After the tobacco has been properly assorted and has remained in bulk for a sufficient length of time it is taken up and packed in casks, 52 inches high and from 42 to 44 inches across the head. Some 500 or 600 pounds are first packed in the hogshead, when it is placed under a screw press, worked by hand with levers or sweeps, much like a cotton-press, and pressed down to about half the space it first occupied. The hogshead is again filled and pressed, and this process is continued until about 1,000 or 1,200 pounds are put in the hogshead. It is then headed up and sent to market. These hogsheads cost from $1 75 to $2 each.

The average price of the crop for the district in 1879, sold loose to dealers, was about $12 per hundred pounds through. This, divided into grades, would give about 5 cents for trash, 10 cents for red fillers, and 18 cents for fine leaf. Local markets are established at every convenient shipping place, Higginsport and Ripley being the principal points.

COST OF TOBACCO PRODUCTION.

Good tobacco soils are rated very high in the Burley district. Lands capable of producing 1,500 pounds to the acre readily bring from $75 to $100 per acre, and inferior soils, those that will yield from 500 to 800 pounds per acre, are worth $25. Wages by the year for field-hands range from $12 to $20 per month; by the day, in summer, from $1 to $1 50, the highest prices in both cases being paid for hands skilled in the cultivation and management of tobacco. A good hand can easily manage from 4 to 5 acres when the horn-worms are not troublesome.

To cultivate 5 acres and prepare it for market will require the constant work of a good man for twelve months. This quantity of land will make 7,000 pounds. The following estimate of the cost of growing tobacco on the best soils was made by four tobacco-growers of Brown county:

Dr.	
Hire of hand, twelve months	$200
Board of same	108
Use of team for breaking land and feed	15
Use of team, harrowing, preparing for planting, etc	15
Use of team for three plowings	7
Use of tools, wagon, barns, etc	5
Rent of land, general price	40
	390

Cr.	
By 7,000 pounds tobacco, at 12 cents	840
Profit on 5 acres	450
Cost per hundred pounds, $5 57.	

725

This estimate indicates a profit of $90 per acre; but the average yield of the district is only 961 pounds per acre. At the same outlay for cost of production as that above given the cost per hundred pounds would be $8 12. This estimate, however, is for a first-class crop, upon good land, and with best cultivation. The reduced yield is probably produced at less expense for labor, rent of land, etc., with a corresponding reduction in cost of harvesting and preparing for market—say 5 per cent.; making the average cost of production about $7 70 per hundred pounds.

Dealers estimate the expense of prizing and marketing tobacco, including freight, insurance, inspection fees, and warehouse charges, at from 1½ to 2 cents per pound. The cost of selling is 1 per cent.; warehouse charges, $2 upon every hogshead; inspection fee, 35 cents per hogshead; insurance, one-third of 1 per cent.

There is at Cincinnati, the principal market for Burley tobacco, a tobacco association chartered by the state of Ohio. A board is elected, one of whose duties is the election of an inspector. This inspector appoints a weigher for each warehouse, but such appointments must be confirmed by the board. A commission of reclamation is also appointed by the directors. This commission assesses all damages where the samples drawn by the inspector fail to represent the quality of the tobacco in the hogshead. These damages are paid by the inspector, who has recourse upon the dealer or planter who sells the tobacco. The last has the privilege of rejecting all bids within a limited time, so that, should the sample be inferior to the tobacco in the hogshead, he can have another taken. These checks and balances are happily adjusted to protect every interest, and but few complaints of unfair dealing are made by either buyers or sellers.

The following statement shows the production, acreage, yield per acre, value of crop in farmer's hands, value per pound, and value per acre of the tobacco crops of the White Burley district of Ohio for the years 1876 to 1879, inclusive. The figures for 1879 are from census returns; for the other years they are from state assessors' returns:

Year.	Production.	Acreage.	Yield per acre.	Value of crop in farmers' hands.	Value per pound.	Value per acre.
	Pounds.		*Pounds.*		*Cents.*	
1876	7,900,683	9,085	870	$632,055	8	$69 57
1877	9,590,696	9,772	982	671,706	7	68 74
1878	8,874,751	9,281	956	976,223	11	105 18
1879	10,826,983	11,255	962	1,299,202	12	115 43

SEED-LEAF DISTRICT.

The Seed-Leaf district occupies the largest portion of the two Miami valleys, and embraces the northern parts of Butler and Warren, a small area in the northwestern corner of Clinton, the western halves of Greene and Clarke (in the southern part of Greene, extending eastward so as to include New Jasper and Painterville), the southwestern corner of Champaign, the southern part of Shelby, and all of Darke, Preble, Montgomery, and Miami counties. Several adjoining counties in Indiana belong commercially to this district. Seed-Leaf is also grown to a limited extent in Wayne and Medina counties, in Chippewa valley, and in Defiance and in small parts of other counties in the Maumee valley.

HISTORY OF TOBACCO CULTURE IN THE MIAMI VALLEY.

About the year 1838 Mr. Thomas Pomeroy, from Suffield, Connecticut, moved to the valley, carrying with him some tobacco-seed from his native place. He planted a small crop in Miami township, Montgomery county, and its cultivation gradually spread to the neighboring farms. The only tobacco, however, reported for the census of 1840 from the present Miami valley district was 75 pounds from Clarke county.

The cultivation of the Seed-Leaf was confined to Montgomery county until 1850, when some farmers in the neighborhood of Alpha, in Greene county, began to grow it, the first persons engaging in its cultivation being George and Solomon Glatfelter. In 1851 a small quantity was raised in Butler county, in Dick's Creek valley. Within the next three or four years the cultivation of the Seed-Leaf extended successively into Warren, Preble, and Miami counties, and a few patches were grown in several of the counties from Virginia seed for domestic use previous to 1850. The census of that year reports 2,500 pounds for Butler, 1,460 pounds for Clinton, 135 for Champaign, 7,132 for Darke, 2,500 for Miami, 50 for Preble, and 2,601 for Warren. Montgomery county for the same year reported 196,971 pounds, or about 500 cases, which shows that its culture as a standard crop was becoming fixed.

The crops grown in Miami valley in 1850 and 1851 were estimated each year to amount to 2,000 cases, or 800,000 pounds. The crop in the succeeding year was largely increased, reaching 4,000 cases, or 1,600,000 pounds: an increase of 100 per cent. in a single year. All of these crops were marketed in New York. That grown in 1850 brought from 9 to 10 cents per pound, but that grown in 1851 only brought an average of 4½ cents.

The following statement of the crops grown in the valley up to 1880 was furnished by Mr. A. H. Nixon, of Dayton, Ohio, who has been a successful dealer in the valley for thirty years, and has kept memoranda of each crop:

Crops.	Planters' price.	Amount.	Remarks.
	Cents.	*Cases.*	
1852	9	4,000	
1853	5	7,500	
1854	4 to 8	2,500	Very poor crop.
1855	4 to 7	3,500	Beautiful and silky.
1856	12 to 18	4,700	Much pole-sweat.
1857	5 to 6	7,500	
1858	8	9,000	Over-sweated.
1859	6 to 7	12,000	
1860	5 to 6	13,000	
1861	5 to 6	1,400	Result of the civil war.
1862	5 to 6	1,400	Do.
1863	12½	40,000	High prices caused by scarcity.
1864	4 to 5	18,000	Tax and poor crop diminished production and price.
1865	5 to 6	20,000	
1866	7 to 8	13,000	Very good.
1867	5	13,500	White stem.
1868	10 to 13	15,000	
1869	8 to 9	18,000	
1870	12½	33,000	Quality medium.
1871	8½	36,000	Quality fair.
1872	6	20,000	Quality poor.
1873	8	40,000	Quality fair.
1874	6	25,000	Quality poor; want of body.
1875	5	25,000	Do.
1876	7	35,000	House-burned or pole-rotted.
1877	5½	35,000	Quality medium; some flea-bitten.
1878	8	30,000	Quality good.
1879	6	32,000	Quality common.
1880	....	40,000	Quality common; some flea-bitten.

AREA, GEOLOGICAL FORMATIONS, AND SOILS.

The counties and parts of counties in Ohio which have their drainage in the Great and the Little Miami rivers comprise an area of about 7,500 square miles. The total length of the valley is not far from 150 miles, and its greatest width 60 miles. The Great and the Little Miami flow nearly parallel, and their valleys are often united. The Great Miami is navigable for a considerable distance, and the Miami canal runs along the river for a distance of 70 miles, furnishing an easy outlet for the products of the soil. Beside these means of transportation, several lines of railroad have been constructed, which pass through the very heart of the valley.

Almost the entire region is covered with the drift formation, ancient or modified. The underlying bed-rock of all the lower valley is the Cincinnati group of the Lower Silurian. Farther up the Clinton and the Niagara rocks of the Upper Silurian form the rocky bed. The soils, with a few local exceptions, are formed from the weathering of the drift formation, and vary in fertility in proportion to the commingling of the sands, clay, and gravel and the amount of accumulated humus. A few places occur where a fine-grained clay, impermeable to water, forms the surface. Such places have physical defects that render the accumulation of humus impossible, and they form the most sterile soils in the lands adjoining the valley. These places occur on the sloping ridges, and are characterized by a deficiency of limestone pebbles.

The lands adjoining the river in the lower part of the valley are usually divided into three classes: 1, the alluvial bottoms; 2, the second bottoms; and 3, the gravel beds, or third bottoms.

The alluvial bottoms owe their origin to causes now in operation. They are formed of the sedimentary sands, clays, gravel, silt, and decayed vegetable matter gathered by the surface waters from the second and third bottoms and deposited in times of overflow upon the present flood plain. These various materials are deposited sometimes very irregularly, making sandy bottoms, loamy bottoms, clay beds, or gravelly bottoms, the manner of deposit being governed by the swiftness or the gentleness of the stream and by the currents and counter-currents produced by interfering obstacles. Most frequently, however, all the ingredients are mingled so as to form a very fruitful soil, and the regularly recurring deposits keep up a high fertility. Land shells are very common on this soil.

The second bottoms form a terrace about 30 feet above the first bottoms. The widespread plains of this terrace are the very best farming lands of the valley, and here are found the best tobacco and wheat soils of the region. The soil is loamy, and is characterized by the growth of sugar maple, walnut, oaks of various kinds, ash, hickory, mulberry, buckberry, elm, locust, buckeye, linn, soft maple, sycamore, tulip-tree, cherry, cottonwood, ironwood, white walnut, gum, and beech.

Rising above these second bottoms by gentle slopes, in which remains of the gravel beds appear, are the uplands, which are in the main highly productive, but have not the original strength of constitution of the soils of the first and second bottoms. Sometimes these lands are stubborn, and when there is a predominance of clay they are sterile. Bowlders lie scattered in considerable quantities even upon the highest points, and in such abundance in some places as to preclude cultivation. The yellow, gravelly clays often form the main element of the drift, and are regularly stratified. There are also beds of blue clay underlying these, as well as the forest beds, 20 feet below the surface, in which stumps of ancient trees are still found, with roots firmly fixed in the hard pan.

Near the "divide", in the upper part of the valley, the soils are divided into—

1. Clayey soils, well adapted to the production of wheat and tobacco. This is the soil of the uplands and higher portions of the region. Its color varies from yellow to red and brown, but upon the water-sheds it is almost white. Free and porous usually, it is sometimes compact, tenacious, and difficult of tillage. The physical condition of the darker soils makes them produce more kindly, but they are not more durable than the white soils of the ridges.

2. The second class of soils is alluvial, generally confined to the river basins. Greenville and Stillwater creeks are bounded by wide stretches of these soils. They are usually dark in color, very loamy and friable, on account of the large admixture of sand or gravelly deposits, are rich in vegetable mold, and produce very large crops of corn.

3. A third class is ashen in color, light and friable, with a clayey subsoil. This soil is generally found in well-drained, low situations. Its excellence results from the character of the subsoil and from the large amount of decayed vegetable matter which has been incorporated with the clay by the untiring industry of insect life. Though limited in extent, this peculiar soil is held in very high esteem for the production of wheat, tobacco, hay, and corn. It will probably produce a greater diversity of crops than any other in this section.

4. The peat deposits are enumerated as constituting a fourth class of soils. They occupy depressions supposed to be the beds of marshes or ancient lakes, and the half-decayed vegetable remains, when well drained and aerated, become highly productive. Tobacco is sometimes planted upon these peat beds, but never until they have been relieved of superfluous water, when it is said to grow well and to exhibit qualities of high excellence. The material which makes up the peat beds is often used as a fertilizer, and when properly combined with stable manure it acts with readiness on all standard crops.

The soils in Shelby county are composed largely of vegetable matter, and are not all alluvium. Mr. John Hussey, of the geological survey, asserts that in some of the tributaries of the Miami the width of the bottoms is disproportioned to the size of the streams, the latter being very small and the former very wide. He attributes the width and the exuberant fertility of the lowlands to the fact that before the clearing away of the forests, owing to the very slight fall toward the streams, the water was impeded by rubbish and underbrush and stood on the ground for at least a portion of the year. The consequence was a large accumulation of vegetable mold, the vegetation which produced it growing up in swamps and along the sluggish courses of the streams. This soil is very fertile and very durable.

There are two classes of upland soil: first, the black soil, composed of the clay of the drift, intermingled with vegetable matter in a state of decay; and, second, the light-colored, thin soil, with but little vegetable material in its composition. The dark soils are of a kindred nature with the bottom soils, and result from the accumulation of vegetable matter in low places. In due course of time the vegetable matter became intermixed with the clay, and formed a rich, dark-brown loam. The clay of the light-colored, thin soils is very compact, is composed of a fine-grained material, which sheds water readily, and is deficient both in limestone pebbles and in greenstone bowlders.

Montgomery county is the center of the tobacco interest of the district, and Miamisburg and Dayton furnish the largest primary markets, much of the tobacco produced in adjoining counties finding its way to these markets.

Probably the proportion of the clayey uplands and gravelly soils is somewhat less than in several of the counties of the valley lying near the "divide" between the waters of lake Erie and the Ohio river, with a corresponding larger proportion of second bottoms and black upland soils. The yellow and the black loamy soils are preferred for tobacco, and when in good tilth, and not partially exhausted by overcropping, they are very friable and produce kindly. A large preponderance of clay, unless ameliorated by turning under green crops, clovering, or high manuring, makes the soil too stiff, and, though some crops are grown with success on such soils, tobacco proves a comparative failure.

The timber trees, named in the order of their predominance, are sugar-tree, hickory, white ash, white oak, red oak, burr oak, walnut, beech, elm, blue ash, poplar, hackberry, linn, red maple, sycamore, butternut, dogwood, ironwood, and buckeye, all denoting a very high fertility; indeed, it is to be doubted if any other equal area can be found in the United States where so many kinds of trees grow, all indicative of the very best soils.

We find in the drift almost every variety of hard rock to be found on the continent, and a metamorphic series—feldspar, hornblende, diorites, schists, quartz, sandstones, and limestones, argillaceous clays tinged with the protoxide and the peroxide of iron—mingled in a thousand varying proportions, form the base of the soils. To these the leaves and decayed trunks and branches of a myriad generation of deciduous trees have been added, making a combination filled with all the elements of plant food.

Under excessive and long continued cultivation the yellow upland soils become white and poverty-stricken. The black upland soils differ from the last only in the fact that they occupy more favorable positions for catching and retaining vegetable humus. This renders them light, friable, productive, and easy to work. They are always found in depressions, and are excellent corn and tobacco soils. Some analyses made of the various soils by Professor Wormley for the geological survey are here tabulated:

	Bottom soils.	White clay—unproductive.	Yellow clay, or common upland soils.	Upland black prairie soils.
Soluble in hydrochloric acid	**60.84**	**5.20**	**4.80**	**13.20**
Organic matter and water	3.53	0.80	1.13	5.18
Silicic acid	0.23	0.06	0.08	0.08
Iron, sesquioxide	1.80	2.80	2.09	2.50
Alumina	0.90	0.50	0.02	1.65
Manganese	Trace.	0.09	0.02	Trace.
Lime, phosphate	0.24	0.07	0.10	0.21
Lime, carbonate	50.87	0.21	0.35	2.48
Magnesia, carbonate	2.39	0.29	0.29	0.83
Soda and potash	0.53	0.10	0.10	0.10
Sulphuric acid	0.12	0.03	Trace.	0.06
Soluble matter found	60.67	4.95	4.18	12.79
Insoluble in hydrochloric acid	**39.16**	**94.80**	**95.11**	**86.80**
Organic matter	6.03	2.05	2.02	8.02
Silicic acid	20.05	85.52	80.12	64.12
Alumina and traces of iron	4.23	2.43	8.91	10.76
Manganese	Trace.	0.32	Trace.	Trace.
Lime	0.92	0.79	0.91	0.59
Magnesia	0.34	0.63	0.20	0.45
Soda and potash	1.40	2.62	2.84	8.00
Phosphoric acid	0.34	0.18	0.02	0.13
Insoluble matter found	39.31	94.54	95.62	87.07
Soluble matter found	60.67	4.95	4.41	12.79
Total matter found	99.98	99.49	99.80	99.86

The hills which surround the Chippewa valley reach a height of 1,200 feet above the sea. These great rolling hills rise up in gentle slopes. Their tops are supposed to indicate the surface of an original table land, which has been deeply eroded and cut into ravines and valleys, giving a wonderful diversity to the surface. The soils are clayey and adhesive, and are more suited to grazing than to tillage. The soil of the Chippewa valley is a very fertile sandy loam, exceedingly friable and generous, and is from 10 to 20 inches deep. It has a dark ashen color, and in consistency is rather fine-grained, though mellow. The trees indigenous to the valleys are elm, ash, beech, white oak, and sugar-tree. The second bottoms are the soils preferred for tobacco, being free from the dangers of overflow, and generally warm and dry. Some gravelly lands in Medina county are cultivated, but not with the best results.

COMPARISON OF CROPS.

The seed-leaf crop of Ohio was about 10 per cent. greater in 1879 than in 1878, and less by 12 per cent. than the crop of 1877, and 5 per cent. less than that of 1876, and the quality was greatly inferior to that of the two years previous. It was planted late, grew badly, had a greenish smell when cured, with but little gum, and in appearance looked as though it had been drenched in water. The crops of 1878 and 1877 were not only of large growth, but of excellent quality, ranking with the best ever grown in the state. The growth of the year 1876 was good, but the weather was unfavorable for curing, and much of the crop pole-sweated in the houses. Indeed, so excessive was the moisture, that in order to prevent an almost total destruction of the crop after it was harvested many planters during the curing season of that year had to resort to light firing.

VARIETIES OF TOBACCO GROWN.

Many varieties of tobacco are cultivated in Miami valley, the principal being the long-leaf Baltimore Cuba; Connecticut Seed-Leaf, five or six varieties, including Pennsylvania Seed-Leaf; Washington or Zimmer Seed-Leaf, probably the Baltimore Cuba, or a modification of that variety. All those mentioned are large and leafy. The Baltimore Cuba is generally preferred, because it yields well, sweats a uniform dark color, has a fine, silky texture, is tough, and has a good body. The Connecticut Seed-Leaf, while everything that could be desired as to size and delicacy of texture, does not cure up so readily with the dark color most desired by manufacturers, nor does it yield so much per acre as the Baltimore Cuba. The seed of the latter variety was grown by Sinclair & Son and sold to the Department of Agriculture, from which it was distributed. Still another variety was sent out by this department, called the Graham. This has a good body, but on account of its narrow leaf is not so much liked by the manufacturers. By the farmers, however, it is regarded with much favor, because it will bear rough handling, wilts quickly when cut, and is not so liable to house-burn or pole-sweat. Little Dutch, a sweet-scented variety, grown principally around Miamisburg, was introduced into the valley by Mr. Rayendorf, who brought the seed from Germany. It has a narrow leaf, grows small and short, but is very popular with cigar manufacturers for fillers and binders, making a cigar with a flavor highly pleasant and odorous, resembling the Yarrow more than any other tobacco grown in the United States, and usually commands a very high price, selling for nearly one-third more per pound than the other varieties. The yield is not so great as that of the Baltimore Cuba by one-half. The chief reason assigned for raising it is that it is always in active demand. It requires great care in sweating, the leaf being very thin and easily damaged by that process. The production does not exceed 500 cases. There are probably thirty or forty local names produced by the interfertilization of these leading varieties, but they all resemble the parent plants in some leading characteristic. The most noted of these sub-varieties is known as the Black Leaf, but within the past two or three years the Spanish variety has been introduced from Wisconsin, and promises well.

Nearly all the tobacco grown in the Miami, Maumee, and Chippewa valleys is employed in the manufacture of cigars, and a considerable proportion is exported to Bremen and to Amsterdam, it being preferred to any other seed-leaf tobacco grown in the United States for exportation, because it retains a smaller proportion of water in its composition, and will bear the ocean sweat with less injury.

PREFERRED TOBACCO SOILS.

Tobacco grown upon the sandy soils of the first bottoms will attain fine size, but the leaves are rough and wanting in tenacity and fineness. Nor does it sweat well, coming out of that trying process brittle, with a dead lifeless appearance. When grown upon second bottoms or upon the yellow uplands it attains its highest perfection, being fine fibered, well bodied, elastic, and with good sweating qualities. It is exceedingly important that the soil be warm, dry, and well drained. · Where it is very fertile, black, and charged with organic matter, tobacco sometimes fires, especially in a dry summer, and is apt to be coarse. There must be a fair proportion of clay in the composition of the soil, enough to give a certain degree of plasticity. This gives fineness to the tobacco. The soil preferred is a clayey loam, mulatto or yellowish in color, either upon the second bottoms or upon the uplands, where the original forest growth was, in the main, sugar-tree, walnut, and tulip-tree. When grown upon freshly-cleared lands, before the vegetable matter has been thoroughly incorporated with the soil, tobacco is fine but flimsy, and wanting in gum and toughness. Herein appears the difference in soil required for the best Burley tobacco and for the best seed-leaf. New soils, other things being equal, will always produce tobacco that will cure of a brighter color than that grown on old. The plug manufacturers using the Burley type demand a bright leaf, with but little substance, and the grower selects new land as best adapted to meet the wants of his customers; but the cigar manufacturer requires a leaf dark in color and strong enough to withstand the strain of rolling. The farmer, to supply this want, must take old land, clayey loam, highly manured if possible, and the larger the application of manure the better the seed-leaf becomes adapted to the purposes for which it is grown.

Rolling lands grow a finer leaf than level lands, for the latter, having oftentimes tenacious clays, are compacted by heavy rains to such a degree as to check the growth of the plant.

In the best seed-leaf crops grown there will be about two-thirds wrappers and one-third fillers and binders; but these proportions vary greatly with the variety planted.

Whether the quality of the tobacco produced now is equal to what it was twenty years ago is a mooted question among dealers and planters, and some believe that the quality has deteriorated in consequence of planting the same land so often in the crop. This has caused a decrease in the amount of gum, and a consequent want of body; so that the transfusion of the juices through the pores of the leaves is not so perfect as formerly, and the glossiness, suppleness, and finish of leaf have given place to a harsher, "shucky" feel. There is, in other words, a comparative lack of oily substance in its composition. In its greatest perfection the seed-leaf has the appearance of a dark-colored sand-paper, the minute pellicles covering thickly the entire upper surface. These globulous pellicles are charged with the gums and oils that give pliability, glossiness, "stretchiness," and life to the leaf. When these are imperfectly developed, or where they are wanting in resinous compounds, the tobacco becomes brittle, and cannot withstand the heat of the sweating process. Others among the growers and dealers of the valley maintain with a considerable show of reason that the quality has been gradually improving; that there has been no deterioration of quality, but that the sharp competition has raised the standard. They assert that every appliance for the handling of tobacco is better than it was twenty years ago; the barns are better; the varieties grown are better; the farmers better understand its culture and management; and that, so far as the soil is concerned, though the amount produced per acre may not be increasing, the virgin soils, which were then chiefly planted in tobacco, were so rank that the product was large, coarse, and bony. It is probable that the real truth lies between the two. In some sections of the valley very little attention is paid to fertilizing tobacco lands, and each successive crop shows a deterioration in quality.

Scattered here and there a few tobacco-houses may be seen well adapted to their purposes. The great majority, however, are temporary structures, with posts set in the ground, sides more or less open, often leaning to one side or to the other, and entirely out of keeping with the other buildings of the farm. Oftentimes a vacant space in a stock-barn, corn-crib, or chicken-house is the only provision made by the planter for harvesting his crop; and it cannot be expected that the profits, under such circumstances, will always be satisfactory. Indeed, the wonder is that so much excellent tobacco should be marketed from a district where so little preparation is made for properly curing and handling the crop.

The best farmers of the seed-leaf district pay great attention to fertilizing tobacco lands, and from twenty to forty loads for a two-horse wagon are frequently applied in the spring to every acre to be planted in tobacco. Occasionally, but rarely, some stimulating fertilizer is applied, to give the plant a good start; and it is estimated that the yield of tobacco is increased, even on lands of good fertility, fully one-third by a free use of manure. But an equal profit comes from the superiority of the tobacco produced, it being much richer, tougher, and of better body. It is a rule long established by experience that the quicker seed-leaf is grown, the soil and situation being the same, the better the quality; and in this is observed another marked contrast in growing this type and in growing the heavy shipping leaf. The best qualities of the latter are made by long but healthy growth. It must stand until the secretory glands have developed the globular structure of the plant to its utmost capacity, filling the vesicles with gums and other proximate elements. The value of export tobacco often depends upon its strength, as it is largely used for mixing with the inferior and milder kinds. The practice of fertilizing is, however, not universal. Two-thirds of the number growing tobacco fertilize but little, and many not at all. The greatest amount of manure is applied in Montgomery and Miami counties, where also the largest quantity of good tobacco is grown.

It is customary in the Miami valley, where land has been freshly opened, to grow tobacco five or six years in succession, and so great is the inherent fertility and strength of the soil that no perceptible difference is seen in the yield for three or four years; in fact, there is a positive improvement in the quality of leaf produced up to the fourth year. Upon old lands it is generally rotated with other crops in the following order: Tobacco, wheat, clover, corn, and tobacco. Clover is sometimes allowed to remain two years before the land is put in corn. Tobacco rarely succeeds clover, as damage from the cut-worm is more decided after clover than after any other crop.

PREPARATION OF LAND FOR PLANTING AND CULTIVATION OF THE TOBACCO CROP.

Usually the land intended for tobacco is broken up the preceding fall with two horses to the depth of 8 or 10 inches. Manure, if used at all, is applied broadcast in the spring, when the land is rebroken, and all the tobacco stalks on hand are cut up fine and placed on the land at this time, along with the other fertilizers. Sometimes the manure is plowed in, and again it is put on after the second breaking and harrowed in. Should the weeds grow very luxuriantly on the land intended for tobacco, or should heavy rains occur after the second breaking, it becomes necessary to break a third time.

After the last breaking, and just before the plants are large enough to set, the land is harrowed and marked off in rows, 3 or 3½ feet apart. The furrows are sometimes thrown on these, making a bed, and the hills made on the beds—if for the larger varieties, 3 feet apart; if for the smaller varieties, 2½ feet. Sometimes the hills are made in the furrow, the plant, when set out, being level with the general surface of the field. In dry seasons this, perhaps, is the better method, but in wet seasons it is better to have the plant elevated somewhat above the general level.

When the leaves of the plant are 3 inches long they are sufficiently large to transplant, and this generally takes place from the 1st to the 20th of June. If the weather is very dry, the hills are watered artificially; but on new lands this is not necessary, as the moist condition of fresh land is generally sufficient to insure the vitality of the plants, especially if the hills have been freshly made.

The amount of cultivation which the crop receives is sufficient to keep the land mellow and clean. A cultivator, a small harrow, or a double shovel is run between the rows three or four times, followed each time with the hoe, by means of which a small amount of dirt is pulled up to the plant.

No priming is done in the district, and the plant is topped in from fifty to sixty days after it is transplanted, when the blossom bud appears; but some wait until it blossoms, under the impression that it will ripen sooner. From twelve to eighteen leaves are left to the plant, and in a week the suckers are long enough to pull off. It is again suckered just before cutting, which for the seed-leaf varieties is from two to three weeks after it is topped; but the Little Dutch and the Spanish varieties improve in flavor by standing a week longer. The worming is constant, and a good tobacco-raiser never ceases to hunt for the worms from the time they appear until the tobacco is safely harvested in the shed. It is thought that when the seed-leaf stands too long upon the hill it is more liable to be injured by the presence of white veins, for which no satisfactory cause has yet been assigned.

The crop is cut from the 15th of August to the 20th of September. No bad effects result from rains just before cutting; in fact, it is thought by some to be advantageous in washing off any dust that may have settled upon the leaves. Heavy dews are also desired, not so much to thicken the leaves as to keep the tobacco from ripening too rapidly. The seed-leaf is never permitted to ripen fully, but when yellowish spots begin to appear on the leaves, shading away into a ground of green, it is thought to be ripe enough to cut. When it ripens more fully, the color, after being cured, is too bright for wrappers, and the leaves are too thick.

The cutting in the seed-leaf district is done with a hatchet or a corn-knife, and sometimes with a saw, the stalk being severed near the ground and the plant laid back on the row. Here it lies until it wilts sufficiently to be handled without breaking, being carefully watched to prevent sun-burn. It is then speared on the laths in the same manner as in Connecticut, from six to ten plants being put on each lath, and after this it is carried to the sheds and hung upon the tier poles, the laths being placed 6 or 8 inches apart on the tiers, and the plants being evenly distributed on every lath as it is put in position.

A few planters still adhere to the old method of tying the plants with twine alternately on each side of the tier poles, a full description and drawing of which method is given in the article on Connecticut valley.

Whether scaffolding in the field is, on the whole, an advantage or a disadvantage depends entirely upon the weather and upon the quantity of available shed room. Where the latter is ample, it is thought best to carry the tobacco directly to the shed and place it in position; but if, on the other hand, a planter has a large crop and but little shed room he is compelled to resort to scaffolding or run great risk of damage from pole-sweat.

When the shed has been filled, the doors are kept open day and night, until the plants, by evaporation, have become thoroughly wilted and yellow; after which they are closed during the day and opened at night, so as to check the process of curing. Curing too rapidly injures the quality of the tobacco, and for this reason frequent rains are desired, so that the plants may come in condition and a transfusion of the juices through every portion of the leaf may take place. It is said to be a favorable sign in the process of curing when a delicate purplish color appears on each side of the midrib, and indicates that the land upon which the tobacco grew was well manured, and dealers who go through the country to inspect the crops during the curing process look to this as the most favorable sign by which to judge of its future quality.

In 1876 nearly one-fourth of the crop was lost by pole-sweat or house-burn after it was harvested. This was caused by overcrowding in the sheds and by continuous damp weather. Thorough ventilation, or drying of the atmosphere by artificial means, is the only effective preventive.

The best tobacco-houses in the district are built four tiers high, the tiers being placed 4½ feet apart, and the largest are probably 200 feet long and 32 feet wide, with a capacity of 20,000 pounds. The bents are from 14 to 18 feet apart. The roof is covered with shingles, and vertical doors are constructed to open on the sides and ends. By far the largest proportion of the crop of tobacco is cured in open sheds; but it does not cure so well, and is liable to be weather-beaten and mildewed. Beside, the tobacco is not within the control of the grower. In dry seasons the evaporation is too rapid, and the circulation of the juices from the stem and stalk to the leaves is checked, and in very wet seasons it pole-sweats. Many of the essential oils are also wasted by being first extracted from the leaves by the excessive moisture and then lost by dripping or by evaporation.

It is believed that the more frequently the tobacco goes in and out of condition during the process of curing, other things being equal, the better will be the quality, and this has given rise to the custom of closing the doors of the sheds during the day and opening them at night; but it should never become so damp as to drip. The warm sun shining upon the roof and sides of the shed during the day will dry the tobacco out slowly, while the process is reversed when the doors are opened at night.

The changing conditions of the weather and of the plant itself make curing one of the most troublesome operations connected with the tobacco industry, and a little mismanagement may result in the almost total loss of the crop.

When the tobacco has hung in the sheds until well cured, which requires about eight or ten weeks, it is taken down in damp weather, when it is pliant, and assorted into grades, stripped and tied into bundles or hands, from twelve to twenty leaves being put in each hand, and carefully assorted into four grades, viz: long wrappers, short wrappers, binders, and fillers. After being tied in bundles, each grade kept to itself, it is packed in bulk, as illustrated in the chapter on New England.

The tobacco, while in the bulks, grows sweet, the heads dry out, fat stems disappear, and after remaining for a month or two it is sold to dealers or packed in cases; and it often happens that dealers take the tobacco as fast as it is stripped, and the trouble of bulking is obviated. About one-fourth of the whole crop is packed by the farmers. This is usually done in February and March, in boxes 42 inches long, 30 inches wide, and 30 inches deep. The amount packed in each box is 400 pounds, and a lever press, such as is described in the chapter on the Connecticut valley, is required to get this quantity into the box.

When the crop has been tied in bundles or packed it is usually sold to dealers at a fixed price through. These prices are variable, depending both on the character of the leaf as to color and substance and on the relative amount of wrappers. The range for the crop of 1879 was from 4 to 10 cents through. Of the inferior crops, when the grades were sold separately, wrappers brought from 7 to 8 cents, binders 3 to 4 cents, and fillers 2 to 3 cents, and wrappers of the better crops brought from 12 to 15 cents. The range in prices for fillers and binders is very small; the average is put at from 6 to 7 cents through.

Dealers buy the crop, after inspection, while growing and curing, and about three-fourths of it is bought and packed by them.

May, June, July, and August are the months in which tobacco goes into sweat or fermentation, and during this process it grows very warm, reaching a temperature of from 100° to 140° F. It remains in this condition from two to three months, but it can be artificially sweated in a much shorter time by placing the boxes on their sides in a close room and keeping up the heat of the room to 100° or more. The loss by sweating is 12 per cent. for Ohio Seed-Leaf.

A few strips are put up in Miami valley for European consumption, amounting, however, to only about fifty cases. This is the only instance reported in which strips are made of the seed-leaf varieties.

COST OF GROWING AND MARKETING SEED-LEAF TOBACCO.

The price of the best lands for tobacco in the Miami valley ranges from $80 to $100 per acre, and rent readily at from $10 to $20 the acre, the prices varying with the comparative fertility and nearness to market. The crop is often cultivated on what is known as the "share system". Land owners agree to plow the land and cultivate the crop, furnishing sheds, laths, etc. The cropper does the remainder of the work, and the proceeds of the crop are equally divided between them. Sometimes the cropper agrees to furnish the tools and team and feed, and he then gets three-fifths of the crop. It is estimated that one man can cultivate 4 acres. The price of farm labor (men) varies from $15 to $20 a month and board; by the day, in summer, the prices are $1 and $1 25 and board.

The cost of cultivating and marketing one acre of tobacco is given by Mr. Jacob Zimmer as follows:

Cost of making seed-bed for one acre	$1 00
Weeding and attention to seed-bed	1 00
Rent of land (interest on price)	6 00
Stable manure, $10; cost of applying same, $5	15 00
Breaking one acre twice	3 00
Harrowing, lining out, ridging, and hilling	3 00
Drawing and setting out plants	2 00
Cultivating and hoeing	4 00
Topping, worming, and suckering	5 00
Harvesting	10 00
Taking down, assorting, and shipping	5 00
Bulking	1 50
Use of barn, laths, etc	2 00
Hauling to market	1 50
Total cost	60 00

The best average yield on the very best soils of the valley is 1,800 pounds per acre. This would make the cost of producing and marketing the crop $3 33 per hundred pounds. The average yield is 1,124 pounds, which, at the same cost per acre as stated above, would show a cost of $5 34 per hundred pounds; and other estimates, without giving details, put it at $5 per hundred pounds.

The yield of the different varieties on the best land is about as follows: Baltimore Cuba, 1,500 to 2,000 pounds; Connecticut Seed-Leaf, 1,200 to 1,800 pounds; Little Dutch, 800 to 1,000 pounds. The Spanish varieties yield about 1,000 or 1,500 pounds.

In Chippewa valley the prices of the best tobacco soils vary from $100 to $250 per acre, and are capable of producing from 1,800 to 2,400 pounds per acre. The clay uplands are rated from 25 to 50 per cent. lower in price, and the yield is so much lower on them that the average of the district does not exceed 1,200 pounds per acre.

Two to three acres are considered as much as a good man can cultivate well. The rate of wages paid for farm hands by the year ranges from $150 to $200 and board for common to good hands; by the day, in summer, the price is from $1 to $1 25. Crops cultivated on shares are equally divided between landlord and tenant.

Six dollars per hundred, as given by others, is about the average cost of raising tobacco, taking all qualities of soil into consideration. It will be observed that much more expense is incurred in making and taking care of seed-beds in the Medina district than in the Miami valley, and also that the quantity of manure applied per acre is much larger, while the average yield is somewhat greater. The quality of the growth, however, would seem to justify a larger outlay; for while the average price of the crop in the Miami valley is reported to be 6 cents per pound, its average price in the Medina district is from 7 to 8 cents per pound, and when put in casks and sweated it will average from 10 to 15 cents. It is thought that the cost per pound decreases considerably in a large crop, and that 12 acres, cultivated by three men, working together, can be produced at 10 per cent. less cost than for each man to work separately upon 4 acres. The reason assigned is that three men are a necessary group in the cultivation of the crop. When the tobacco is transplanted, one person is required to drop the plants for two to set; and when it is harvested, the wagon can be loaded proportionally much sooner for one to place the laths on the frame, while two others bring them to the wagon. So, in putting up in the shed, two men in the shed and one on the wagon can place the tobacco in position in one-fifth the time required for one man to do it alone. The same rule holds good in stripping, assorting, and bulking.

Inspectors' fees are 25 cents per case. The method of inspecting is very simple. The top of the box is taken off, and the box containing the tobacco is turned upside down. It is then gently lifted up, leaving the tobacco exposed of the size and form of the box. Six bundles are then pulled out, each bundle being drawn from a different place. These are carefully tied and labeled, and the tobacco is sold from the sample so drawn, the inspector in every case guaranteeing the sample to represent correctly the quality and condition of the tobacco in the box. The cost of cases varies from 90 cents to $1 50; tobacco presses, from $10 to $50.

As to the quality of Ohio Seed-Leaf, as compared with that grown in other states, Mr. E. H. Griest, an extensive dealer in Cincinnati, says:

In the markets of the world the Ohio Seed-Leaf takes about the third rank as to quality. Just at present (1880), on account of its dark colors, Pennsylvania is ranking first, Connecticut, notwithstanding its light colors, coming second. In burning qualities Ohio Seed-Leaf is entitled to stand in the first rank, but it is not equal to the other two in uniformity and desirableness of color. Ohio Seed-Leaf is a favorite for export to Germany, and a small quantity is taken experimentally in France. The average export amounts to between 20,000 and 30,000 cases, and it has happened, when there has been an accumulation of stocks, that 70,000 cases have been exported in a single year.

The following will give the comparative prices for the different grades of the principal growths of seed-leaf when put in casks and sweated and sold in open market:

States.	Best wrappers.	Common wrappers.	Best binders.	Best fillers.
	Cents.	*Cents.*	*Cents.*	*Cents.*
Ohio	18	12	7	5
Pennsylvania	30	20	14	10
Connecticut	25	18	10	7
Wisconsin	15	10	5	4

Little Dutch, a small tobacco, probably from the Baden seed of Germany, is growing in favor, notwithstanding its tendency to produce white veins. This variety burns well, but is easily injured in fermentation, and must be stripped and put in bulks until the butts of the leaves are thoroughly cured. When packed in boxes before the butts are well cured it butt-rots, and is greatly damaged. It brings one-third more than the same grades of seed-leaf.

Tobacco dealers claim that the handsomest tobacco grown in Ohio is raised in the Chippewa valley, but it is not so well sweated, and consequently does not burn well. The appearance of the leaf is perfect in length, breadth, and texture, but the color is too bright at present for cigar purposes. It very much resembles the leaf of the Connecticut valley, and, having gum enough to give elasticity, in this respect it is much superior to that grown in some other portions of the state.

The following statement shows the production, acreage, yield per acre, value of crop in farmers' hands, value per pound, and value per acre of the seed-leaf tobacco grown in Ohio for the four years from 1876 to 1879, inclusive:

Year.	Production.	Acreage.	Yield per acre.	Value of crop in farmers' hands.	Value per pound.	Value per acre.
	Pounds.		*Pounds.*		*Cents.*	
1876	18,231,402	16,010	1,140	$1,277,508	7	$70 80
1877	19,964,695	16,499	1,210	1,098,058	5½	66 55
1878	15,702,574	13,240	1,190	1,261,000	8	95 20
1879	17,580,512	15,870	1,108	1,054,830	6	66 47

Of the total amount of seed-leaf tobacco grown in Ohio in 1879 the acreage and production of the several districts are as follows:

District.	Acreage.	Pounds.
Miami valley	15,017	16,879,520
Maumee valley	204	182,411
Chippewa valley	96	120,846
Eastern Ohio	143	120,000
Detached districts	410	277,720

The amount grown in forty-three counties in various parts of the state—small crops of a fraction of an acre to three or more acres—is embraced in the above statement. This product, although of no special type, is usually of the seed-leaf or Cuba varieties, and is most properly included in this statement. Most of it is retained by farmers for home consumption, though a small proportion may find its way to market in near-by cities or towns. Only the figures for 1879 are from census returns.

SPANGLED, OR EASTERN TOBACCO DISTRICT.

The counties and parts of counties embraced in this district are the southern part of Harrison, eastern part of Athens, eastern part of Gallia, the southeastern half of Guernsey, the eastern part of Morgan, and all of Belmont, Monroe, Noble, and Washington. Vinton and Lawrence are also referred to this district.

GEOLOGY AND SOILS.

Nearly the entire region of the Eastern Ohio tobacco district belongs geologically to the Carboniferous period. Its surface is high and rolling, and contains a very small proportion of level lands, confined, for the most part, to the alluviums of the river basins. The highest lands attain an elevation of nearly 1,200 feet above the sea.

The rocks of the region are sandstones, shales, and limestones, and in their dissolution give rise to soils of varying fertility. Whenever the underlying rocks are of limestone, the soil is dark in color, with a yellowish subsoil, and sugar maple, walnut, and white oak are the prevailing timber growth. Where the underlying rocks are sandy shales or sandstones, the soil is thin, but kind, and is well suited for pasturage, but washes very rapidly when cultivated, and chestnut, chestnut oak, and in places yellow pine are the predominating trees. Where the limestones and sandstones both have, by weathering, produced the soil, it is very friable and productive, and probably is better for growing tobacco than any other soils in the region. In such places the timber growth is much more varied, and indicates great fertility. The alluvial bottoms on the larger streams, as on the Muskingum and Ohio, will equal in fertility any lands in the state. The second bottoms, or gravel terraces, on these larger streams have a warm, rich soil, but are not so durable as the lower bottoms.

The rolling surface of the country adapts it better for grazing than for tillage, and it is estimated that at least two-thirds of the improved lands are devoted to the production of grasses, either for hay or for pasturage. The tobacco crop is usually grown upon freshly-cleared lands on the slopes of the hills. The sandy soils are said to produce the finest leaf, but the argillaceous, loamy soils are better adapted to the growth of a heavy leaf, and will yield more pounds to the acre. On preferred tobacco soils the timber growth is chestnut oak, hickory, and maple.

The soils may, for convenience, be divided into: 1, alluvial; 2, black soil, with sugar-tree and walnut; 3, white oak, sandy soil; and 4, white oak, clayey soil. The alluvial soils are composed of varying proportions of sand, clay, and vegetable matter, and are enriched by the washings of the adjacent hills. They are very deep and durable, and some of them have been cultivated in regular succession for over half a century without showing the least signs of exhaustion. They rest for the most part on a substratum of gravel, clay, and sand, intermingled oftentimes with fragments of limestone and sandstone. The black soil is highly calcareous, and has been derived from the crumbling down of the limestones, which make up a large part of the rocky structure of the country. This soil shades off into lighter colors, and may be taken as the best type of the calcareous soils, which abound in almost every part of the district. It rests generally upon a yellowish clay, and, though strong in constitution, its occurrence on slopes makes it liable to be carried away by heavy rains to the lower alluvials. This black soil generally occurs on the eastern sides of hills, and for the growing of heavy tobacco is preferred above any other. The third class of soils results from the disintegration of the argillaceous shales and limestones, and, though stiff, is fertile. They are characterized by a dense growth of white oak, and are often cultivated in tobacco. The fourth class is only a modification of the last, the sandstones taking the place of the limestones. These are more friable than the last named, and occur on the tops and slopes of hills, where the underlying rocks are sandstone and shales. These lands will produce from 1,000 to 1,200 pounds of tobacco per acre when freshly cleared.

The southwestern part of Belmont county constitutes the principal tobacco area of the district, and the principal crops are corn, wheat, and grass. The prevailing timber is oak, sugar tree, and beech, though hickory, walnut, ash, gum, poplar, and locust grow in considerable abundance, and sycamore is found near the streams. The district is likely to be rapidly denuded of its forests wherever the soil is suitable for growing tobacco. Fresh lands are greatly preferred for making the high-priced spangled leaf, which is sought for by the nobility of Russia.

Tobacco is cultivated on the tops of the hills and on the eastern slopes mainly. Wherever there is a mixture of sand and clay and calcareous deposits, into which has been incorporated vegetable matter, the soil will produce tobacco of excellent quality, the white oak and chestnut lands being selected for growing a fine leaf, the sugar-tree lands for growing a heavy leaf. The sugar tree is generally associated with beech, ash, walnut, poplar, hickory, and sometimes buckeye. The soil of such lands is black, deep, friable, of great strength of constitution, but unfortunately situated for constant tillage, being liable to be swept away to a greater or less extent by every heavy rain. These black soils often produce 2,000 pounds of tobacco per acre without manure. The sandy calcareous white-oak lands will yield 1,200 pounds, and the sandy chestnut and white-oak lands, where there is a deficiency of calcareous matter, will yield, when fresh, from 800 to 1,000 pounds of very fine tobacco.

HISTORY OF TOBACCO CULTURE IN THE DISTRICT.

Tobacco as a staple was cultivated in the Eastern Ohio tobacco region as early as 1825. At that period it was all cured on the stalk and handled by the planters, as is now the practice in many parts of Virginia, Tennessee, and Kentucky. The prices received by the planters from 1825 to 1840 ranged from 4 to 7 cents per pound, but in 1841 the average price was 3½ cents per pound. From 1842 to 1846 the price ranged from 3½ to 6 cents per pound. After 1846 farmers ceased to prepare their tobacco for market, but sold in the leaf to dealers, who assorted, packed, pressed, and shipped it to Baltimore.

The following statement, taken from the books of Mr. John Bradford, of Barnesville, Belmont county, an old dealer, will give the prices paid for loose crops since 1845. The quantity produced in the district was furnished by Messrs. Gierke & Niemann, tobacco merchants in Baltimore:

Year inspected.	Amount of crop in hogsheads.	Average price paid farmers for loose tobacco.	Average price in Baltimore market, gold.	Premium on gold.	Year inspected.	Amount of crop in hogsheads.	Average price paid farmers for loose tobacco.	Average price in Baltimore market, gold.	Premium on gold.
		Cents.	*Cents.*				*Cents.*	*Cents.*	
1845.......	28,700	4 to 5	....	....	1863.......	17,000	6 to 8	7½	$1 37
1846.......	29,000	4	....	....	1864.......	22,000	7 to 14	7½	1 56
1847.......	9,700	2½ to 4	....	....	1865.......	15,500	6 to 10	7	2 02
1848.......	13,600	3½ to 6½	....	....	1866.......	15,500	4 to 7	6¼	1 41
1849.......	13,900	3½ to 6	....	....	1867.......	21,500	5 to 12	6½	1 41
1850.......	10,800	3 to 5	....	....	1868.......	9,500	5 to 12	7½	1 40
1851.......	17,700	3½ to 5	....	....	1869.......	15,500	5 to 7	5¾	1 39
1852.......	17,000	3 to 4	....	....	1870.......	13,500	4½ to 8	6¾	1 23
1853.......	10,300	3½ to 5	....	....	1871.......	14,500	5 to 7	7¾	1 12
1854.......	10,100	4½ to 6	....	....	1872.......	16,500	5 to 7	8 1/16	1 13
1855.......	12,900	3½ to 6	....	....	1873.......	24,000	3½ to 5½	7	1 16
1856.......	13,000	3 to 6	7	....	1874.......	29,000	6 to 10	7	1 12
1857.......	7,500	4 to 8	11	....	1875.......	6,000	5 to 8½	8	1 15
1858.......	22,000	3½ to 7	7½	....	1876.......	17,500	4½ to 8	6½	1 12
1859.......	15,000	3 to 5	6¾	....	1877.......	23,000	3 to 6½	5¾	1 06
1860.......	28,000	3½ to 5	6	....	1878.......	15,500	3½ to 8½	5½	....
1861.......	14,000	3½ to 6	6½	....	1879.......	16,500	4 to 8½	6½	....
1862.......	13,500	5 to 8	7	$1 02	1880.......	8,000	3 to 8	6	....

In the above table is included all the eastern Ohio and West Virginia tobacco inspected and sold in Baltimore for the years named, the proportion of West Virginia tobacco being estimated at a yearly average of 1,000 hogsheads. The table represents, not the year the tobacco was grown, but the year in which it was inspected, the inspection generally comprising the crop of the previous year.

About the year 1875 the White Burley was introduced into this district, and it has extended until it has become the principal variety grown in Belmont and in the counties immediately surrounding. About 300 cases of Connecticut Seed-Leaf are produced annually, but the culture of this variety is not extending rapidly. On the Muskingum the Peartree tobacco is principally grown. There are three sub-varieties of this, namely: the White Stem, the Yellow Stem, and the Large Peartree. The first two get their names from the color of the stem while growing. These varieties are characterized by a wider space between the leaves than in the Burley or other compact varieties, resembling more the Connecticut Seed-Leaf in their habits of growth. The White and Yellow Peartree, when planted upon sandy white-oak soils, will make yellow tobacco, but the Large Peartree produces a heavy red leaf. In Vinton county the Maryland Thickset is principally grown. It grows a large, heavy leaf of fine texture. In Athens county the Four Stem is the favorite. This variety is said to be thick set, leaves close on the stalk, large and slender, and is preferred because of weight.

Of the varieties now planted in the district the White Burley is preferred on account of its tendency to cure fairer and more easily than the older ones. It yields from 1,000 to 2,000 pounds per acre when well cultivated, newly-cleared lands producing the finest colors and quality.

The tobacco grown upon heavy limestone soils is mostly "red" and "brown"; but on the clay soils it makes finer colors, such as go in the grades known as "bright reds", "yellow spangles," and "fine yellows", the latter being the highest grade made in the district.

The Connecticut Seed-Leaf is planted only to a limited extent, and, being cut before fully ripe, cures a dark brown and goes into a separate classification, the grades being wrappers, fillers, and binders.

The crops of 1874 and 1879 were the smallest that have been grown for twenty-five years. That of 1874 failed for want of plants, which were destroyed by frost in April, and by the ravages of the flea-beetle, but the comparative failure of the crop in 1879 resulted from the extreme drought that prevailed during the planting season. The knowledge gained as to the influence of particular soils and exposures has aided in improving the quality, and no one would now attempt to grow a fine leaf on bottom lands. The gradual substitution of air-curing for fire has modified many grades, and made them more suitable for domestic manufacture, rather than for export trade.

Fertilizers are applied upon old soils to a larger extent than formerly, and the size and body of the leaf have been greatly improved. The question of fertilization is one, however, that demands more attention than it is receiving, for a wise policy ought to restrict the further cutting away of timber for growing tobacco.

PREPARATION OF THE SOIL.

It is well understood by the best tobacco-growers that thorough preparatory work is essential to the growing of a heavy crop of tobacco. The more the soil is pulverized by frequent plowings and harrowings the more rapid will be the growth of the plants when transplanted. In old land a turning-plow is used, which reverses the soil to the depth of 6 or 8 inches. Frequently the plowing is done in the fall, and one or more plowings are given in the spring, so as to keep the soil loose and free from grass. On new lands a "gopher-plow" is considered best for breaking and preparing the soil, and frequent harrowings are necessary to pulverize the new soil sufficiently to induce an even and rapid growth. Winter breaking is necessary on soils which have a large admixture of clay, in order that the frosts may ameliorate their physical condition. Stable manure is applied broadcast on old land in the spring, and is either plowed or harrowed in at the last working before the soil is prepared for the plants. New lands are not manured, and the quantity of manure applied to old lands is governed by the supply made at home. Commercial fertilizers, as a general rule, are not applied. After the preparation of the soil, it is lined out 3 feet apart, and no hills are made to receive the plants, which are set on the sides of the furrows, 2 feet asunder. In this practice, which must be called a slovenly one, the farmers of this district stand almost alone. If the plants are large enough, they are set out after the first rain that falls after the land is prepared. The scarcity of plants often retards the planting, and many crops have been curtailed by the failure of the planters to provide a sufficient number of seed-beds. When plants are abundant, the best can be selected and the delicate ones rejected, and a crop set out with strong, thrifty plants will come on rapidly, mature early, and have a much larger proportion of those colors which command the highest prices. As soon as the young plants are well rooted and begin to grow the soil should be stirred often. The tobacco plant is a great absorber of moisture, and, while an excess of humidity is fatal to its vitality, the moisture brought to the roots by capillary attraction is exceedingly important to its healthy growth. On hard, lumpy soils the plant shows its starving condition by turning yellow, and if a drought should then occur it will bloom, after putting out six or eight leaves. When the land is kept loose and light and free from grass and weeds the plants will not suffer greatly even in a drought, for the condition of the soil not only brings up moisture by capillary attraction from below, but condenses moisture in its infinity of pores from the atmosphere. The farmers having the greatest success in growing the crop work it often, and do not cease until the plants are large enough to top. After this it is difficult to work it without breaking the leaves.

TOPPING AND SUCKERING TOBACCO.

On new land from six to seven weeks, and on old land from seven to eight weeks, are required for tobacco to come into top. The time preferred for topping is when the bud appears, but before it blooms. As to the number of leaves that should be left to the plant there is a great diversity of opinion. When the purpose is to make heavy tobacco fewer leaves are left, say from ten to fourteen; but if a light leaf is wanted, from sixteen to twenty are left to the stalk. The suckers are pulled off generally in about a week after the plant is topped, and about the same time, sometimes before, the first gathering of leaves is made. The method of harvesting tobacco in eastern Ohio is practiced in but few other places in the United States: around Gadsden, Florida, in some parts of North Carolina, and among the Kite-Foot growers of Indiana. The harvest begins by pulling from the plant four or five of the lower leaves after they are fully ripe. This is done in the morning after the dew is off, and the leaves are strung in the field and put upon scaffolds or taken immediately to the curing-house and strung. The work of stringing is done by girls or women. A needle with a strong thread, somewhat longer than the lath or stick upon which the tobacco is to be hung, is employed. Two leaves are then pierced in the midrib, about an inch from the end, and slipped down on the thread to the point where it is fastened to the lath. These two are hung on one side of the stick. Two more are then strung in the same manner, and hung on the opposite side of the stick, and so on, two being placed alternately on each side of the stick, until it is full. The other end of the thread is then fastened, and the stick is ready to be hung up.

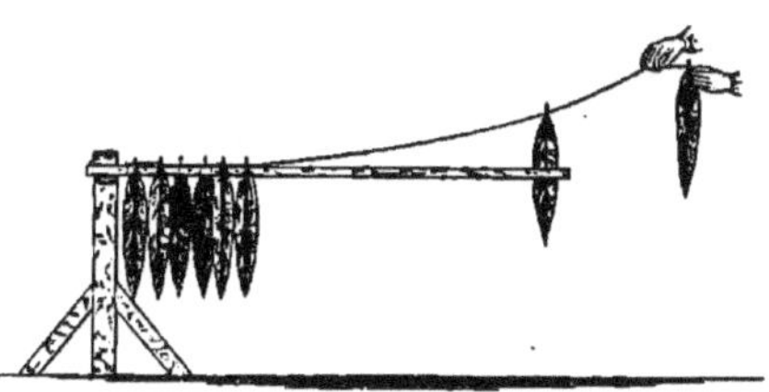

From seventy to one hundred leaves are strung on a stick, the number being regulated by their size. The usual weight of a stick of tobacco after it is cured is 1½ pounds, though with some of the heavier varieties it has been known to weigh 4 pounds. These sticks are placed upon the tier-poles of the barn 10 or 12 inches apart; but if tobacco has been scaffolded in the fields for two or three days a less distance is required, 6 to 8 inches being ample. In about ten days after the first gathering five or six leaves more are plucked and strung in the same manner. Usually about four gatherings are made, from a week to two weeks apart, before all the leaves are harvested, the object being to give every leaf time to ripen well. The first plucking makes inferior lugs and trash, the leaves being more or less soiled with dirt and punctured with holes, and sometimes half burned up by the heat of the ground. The last plucking, which embraces the tops, is the next inferior, curing up a dingy green if the leaves are harvested late in the season. The best portion of the crop comes from the second and third gatherings. Tobacco planted upon newly-cleared lands ripens about two weeks in advance of that planted upon lands long cleared. The occurrence of bad weather during the period of gathering induces a second growth, filling the leaves with fresh sap, which militates greatly against the production of fancy colors. Heavy dews, however, stimulate the secretory glands, and assist in the formation of the gums and oils that give elasticity, flavor, and other desirable qualities to the leaf.

The growers in this district claim many advantages from gathering the leaves instead of cutting the stalk. No leaves are plucked until they are fully ripe, and this insures a larger number of pounds per acre. The different qualities are kept separate, and the comparative quantity of each grade can be estimated, so that less time is required to prepare it for market. The crop is cured in a much shorter space of time, less fuel being required, and the risk of burning the barns is greatly reduced. There is great economy in the saving of barn room, the same height required for four tiers when the plants are housed making six when the leaves only are harvested, and all the trouble of stripping after it is cured is saved. Cheaper labor can be employed in harvesting, and girls, who would be of little service in the housing of a crop in the ordinary way, are by this method of more service than men, since they are more dextrous in the use of the needle.

CURING THE TOBACCO CROP.

It is estimated that about one-third of the crop of the district is air-cured, and the proportion is regularly increasing every year with the introduction of the White Burley. About half of this variety is now cured by fire, and a fine, bright leaf is made; but the use of fire unfits it for American consumption.

To cure red tobacco slow fires are kept up for four days. The heat is then gently raised for three or four days more, but at no time exceeds 125° F. This is kept up until the leafy part is cured, and the product is thought to be of a little better quality when the fires are drawn before the stem is fully cured. To make yellow tobacco slow fires are kept up for a day or two, and the heat thereafter is increased more rapidly and carried to a higher degree than in the case of red tobacco. The leaf and the stem are thoroughly cured, and as soon as the tobacco comes in condition it is taken down to prevent the running of the sap.

TOBACCO-HOUSES.

The log-pen "tobacco-houses" of the Eastern tobacco region of Ohio are erected at a cost not exceeding $25 each, and are made of round logs, most frequently with the rough bark left on them. They are from 14 to 20 feet square, four to five tiers high, and are daubed with clay on the outside. Some of them are open. Their capacity is from 500 to 1,000 pounds. It is impossible, in badly constructed buildings, to prevent injury to the crop, even after it has been cured, and farmers are obliged to hurry it off to market, whether the prices prevailing are satisfactory or not.

In Vinton county and parts of Gallia and Noble the largest proportion of the crop is packed in hogsheads by the farmers themselves.

In almost every part of the district, except the section above named, the farmers prefer to sell loose to dealers without assorting. It is taken down, the ends of the strings are cut, and the leaves from two sticks, with the strings, are rolled up, packed in wagons, and thus taken to market. Dealers assort it into all the grades mentioned, and it is by them pressed into hogsheads and shipped to Baltimore, and thence distributed to markets in the Old World. Of the fancy-bright tobacco from 600 to 750 pounds net are packed in a hogshead 50 inches high and 40 inches in diameter; of the darker tobacco the number of pounds varies from 800 to 900. The rule is, the brighter the tobacco the less the number of pounds to the hogshead. One-fourth of the whole crop grown in the district is put up at or shipped from Barnesville, in Belmont county; the remainder, with the exception of a small quantity of air-cured White Burley that goes to Cincinnati, is shipped by the Ohio river to Parkersburg, and thence by railroad to Baltimore. Hogsheads cost $1 each. The commission for selling is 2½ per cent., and an additional sum of 20 cents per hogshead is paid for insurance.

The average crop of the district is about 16,000 hogsheads, of which 1,000 should be credited to West Virginia. In stripping it is graded carefully, about one hogshead in a thousand being fancy yellow tobacco. The Yellow Spangled has generally a red edge and red and yellow colors, interlacing one with another in the central parts of the leaf, and usually makes 5 per cent. of the crop; the Red Spangled has the red predominating in the center of the leaf, relieved by frequent yellow spots, and embraces 10 per cent. of the crop. Spotted Red is a grade in which the general color is red, with occasional spots of yellow. This grade constitutes 10 per cent. of the crop. Fine and medium reds are made from the middle leaves of the plant without blemish. The color is a bright brown or red, and the proportion in an average crop is 10 per cent. Brown and unripe old-ground tobacco and nondescript make 18 per cent. of the crop; green and brown tips, made from the undeveloped and partly green leaves of the top, make 20 per cent. The remainder of the crop, classed as ground leaves, being imperfect, trashy red and spangled leaves, will make 27 per cent. of an average crop.

PRICES OF TOBACCO.

The bright crops, containing a fair proportion of yellow and yellow-spangled brights, brought in the winter of 1879–'80 from $6 to $8 50 per hundred pounds, loose, through; red and red-spangled crops, from $5 to $6 per hundred pounds; common and unripe crops, $3 50 to $4 50. The average value of the crop in farmers' hands for Belmont, Harrison, Guernsey, Noble, Monroe, Washington, Morgan, and Gallia counties is estimated to be: For 1879–'80, $5 50 per hundred pounds; in Athens county, from $3 to $6; in Vinton county, $4. The quotations in Baltimore in June, 1880, for the various grades were as follows:

	Cents.
Fine spangled to yellow	10 to 18
Common to medium spangled	6½ to 9
Medium to fine red	7 to 10
Greenish and brown	5½ to 7
Inferior ground leaves to common	3½ to 5½

USES OF TOBACCO.

The bulk of the tobacco grown in this district is used for smoking, while a small quantity raised from White Burley seed and air-cured is manufactured into chewing-tobacco in the United States, and a few hogsheads are occasionally used for cigar wrappers. The Connecticut Seed-Leaf, amounting to about 300 cases, is used also for cigar wrappers and fillers. The demand for the main distinctive type, however, is from France, for 5,000 hogsheads; from Germany, for 7,000 hogsheads; from Austria, for 500 hogsheads; from Italy and Spain, for 1,000 hogsheads, irregularly; and in the United States, 2,000 hogsheads. The fine yellow and yellow-spangled are taken in Bremen, where most of it is rehandled and put into lighter casks for the Russian markets. Part of the yellow and yellow-spangled is taken in Austria and in England, which take also the red-spangled, and England also takes some of the fine red. Germany takes all grades, except the fine yellow and the leafy dark-brown colors, and France and Italy take the leafy brown and red grades. The unsound and nondescript are often bought for Spain. Scraps or trash are used in this country for making smoking-tobacco.

COST OF PRODUCTION.

The cost of raising tobacco in the Eastern Ohio district is variously estimated, and depends so much on the original fertility of the soil and the difference in the amount of preparation required for the different soils that it is a very difficult task to give an estimate that may not in some portions of the district be fairly criticised. After a comparison of several estimates, however, the following may be considered approximately correct for well manured old land. The price of old land adapted to the growth of tobacco has in the district a range of from $30 to $75 per acre. The rental value is more uniform, being about $5 per acre, and the average yield for such lands is not far from 1,200 pounds per acre. On this basis the following estimate of the cost of raising one acre of tobacco is given:

Dr.	
Making seed-bed	$1 00
Plowing one acre	2 50
Manure, and spreading same	20 00
Harrowing and lining out	1 25
Planting	2 00
Plowing and hoeing three times	5 00
Topping, suckering, and worming	5 00
Harvesting	8 00
Wood for curing	1 50
Attention while curing	2 00
Taking down and rolling	1 50
Carrying to market	1 50
Rent of land	5 00
	56 25
Cr.	
By 1,200 pounds of tobacco, at 5½ cents	66 00
Profit	9 75

Cost to produce, $4 69 per hundred pounds.

The profits increase very rapidly as the yield per acre is increased. Putting the yield at 2,000 pounds, the profit would be $53 75, and the cost of production per hundred would be reduced to $2 81. This virtually agrees with the statement of Mr. John Bradford, a large planter and dealer, who thinks the cost on old land will vary from 4 to 5 cents per pound.

In Vinton county, where good tobacco soils, that will make from 1,000 to 1,200 pounds to the acre without manure, may be bought for $25 per acre, the cost may come within the estimate made by Mr. J. N. Randall, of McArthur, of from $2 to $3 per hundred pounds.

The estimated cost of production for newly-cleared lands is from $5 to $7 per hundred. This arises from the fact that, independent of the cost of clearing, which should not be charged alone to the first crop grown, the labor of preparing the land for planting is greatly increased. There is a compensation, however, in the larger proportion of high grades in such a crop.

WAGES.

Men are hired at $15 per month and board from spring until autumn; sometimes the price is as high as $20 or as low as $12. In harvesting tobacco boys are paid from 50 to 75 cents per day for plucking off the green leaves, and girls are paid half a cent per stick for stringing them. It is considered a fair day's work to string 100 sticks. Dealers pay for assorting and tying 50 cents per hundred pounds, and the price paid for receiving, weighing, "ordering," packing in hogsheads, and pressing varies from 37 to 40 cents per hundred pounds. Packers are sometimes paid $1 per day. Renters furnish tools and teams, and pay to the landlord from one-third to two-fifths of the product, delivered in market.

The dealers are generally provided with comfortable rooms, in which the work of assorting, tying, and bulking goes on all winter. About the 1st of March the packing season begins, and continues until the whole amount in the dealers' hands is pressed and shipped or sold.

One item in relation to the method of bulking deserves notice. In bulking seed-leaf, shipping leaf, and almost every other leading type grown in the United States the bundles are passed through the hands and made cylindrical in shape. Those of leading grades in this district are flattened out when bulked, and even when packed in hogsheads, so that when drawn they are fan-shaped, and this form displays all the gaudy colors peculiar to the tobacco.

The farmers of the Eastern Ohio district raise a great diversity of crops, so that a failure in the tobacco crop is not felt to the same degree as in some other tobacco districts. It is rather an extra crop, and extra hands are employed to work it. Frequently a farmer having in his employ two grown men, with families of children, will plant 8 or 10 acres in tobacco. The wives and daughters are employed in stringing the leaves for a month or two in the summer, and the small boys strip the leaves from the stalks. When plucked from the stalks, they are put in bunches in the middle of the rows. These are gathered up by other boys and put on sleds or wagons, and are taken to the barns and strung in the manner already described. So the raising of tobacco may be considered profitable in so far as it furnishes a certain class with employment who otherwise would probably be idle.

The following statement shows the production, acreage, yield per acre, value of crop in farmers' hands or in primary markets, value per pound, and value per acre of the tobacco crops of the Eastern Ohio (Spangled) district for the four years from 1876 to 1879, inclusive. One hundred and twenty thousand pounds of seed-leaf tobacco, grown upon 143 acres in this district, are not included in this statement, having been already embraced in the statement for the Seed-Leaf district. Only the figures for 1879 are from census returns:

Year.	Production.	Acreage.	Yield per acre.	Value of crop in farmers' hands.	Value per pound.	Value per acre.
	Pounds.		*Pounds.*		*Cents.*	
1876	19,967,289	16,329	1,224	$849,400	4¼	$52 05
1877	13,173,297	12,534	1,051	658,665	5	52 55
1878	14,081,953	13,260	1,062	774,507	5½	58 41
1879	6,328,040	7,551	838	316,402	5	41 90

INSECT ENEMIES AND DISEASES.

The horn-worms are more numerous some seasons than others, and in 1877 and 1878 about one-third of the crop was very much damaged by them. Tobacco-growers, especially those of the Miami valley, are usually industrious and energetic enough to prevent serious injury to their crops, but now and then their vigilance is severely taxed.

In the Burley district seed-beds are protected from the flea-beetle by covering with canvas, and plants are rarely wanting to set out the crop in good time.

"Frenching" occurs during wet seasons in crops planted on cold, stiff uplands, having a stiff clay subsoil.

"Red speck" or field-fire prevails on the black lands of the Miami valley during hot, dry weather, and "white speck" or "frog-eye" appears occasionally, but the injury from this cause is small.

"Walloon" is of very common occurrence. The best preventive for this disease is good drainage of both soil and subsoil.

"Scab", or "brown rust", said to be produced by hot weather, at certain stages of the growth of the plant is reported as sometimes appearing in the White Burley district. This appears to be the result of soil and atmospheric conditions acting unfavorably at the same time.

"Frog-eye" or "white speck" sometimes occurs in tobacco thoroughly ripe. This disease is, however, much less injurious than "scab". No "fire" or "white speck" is reported from the Eastern Ohio district.

The following statement shows the production, acreage, yield per acre, value of crop in farmers' hands or in primary markets, value per pound, and value per acre of the tobacco crops of Ohio for the four years from 1876 to 1879, inclusive. The figures for the first three years are made up from the most reliable data to be obtained, and are believed to approximate the actual results very closely. For 1879 the statement is made up from the returns of the census enumerators:

Year.	Production.	Acreage.	Yield per acre.	Value of crop in farmers' hands.	Value per pound.	Value per acre.
	Pounds.		*Pounds.*		*Cents.*	
1876	40,139,374	41,424	1,114	$2,750,113	5.98	$66 60
1877	42,734,686	38,805	1,101	2,428,492	5.68	62 56
1878	38,719,279	35,787	1,082	3,011,736	7.77	84 10
1879	34,735,235	34,676	1,002	2,670,434	7.68	77 00

CHAPTER XIV.

CULTURE AND CURING OF TOBACCO IN PENNSYLVANIA.

ITS CULTIVATION IN COLONIAL TIMES.

The colonists brought over by Penn early engaged in tobacco culture, and as early as 1689, only seven years after the proprietor came over, no less than fourteen cargoes of tobacco were exported from the colony to the mother country. It is impossible to say what the tonnage of the vessels was, or how many pounds of tobacco were grown in the youthful colony, but we may safely conclude it was no inconsiderable amount.

In time, however, tobacco ceased to be extensively grown in Pennsylvania. Some doubtless was grown for home consumption, but not as an article of export.

ITS CULTIVATION IN RECENT YEARS.

There are men still living who grew tobacco as early as 1828 in Lancaster county, in the vicinity of Ephrata. An old grower asserts that it was planted in those days about the season of haymaking, or about the middle of June. The ground was prepared very much as it is now, and a second crop was sometimes raised when the season was favorable, the later product being exclusively used as fillers. The planters had a portion of it made up into cigars for their own use, and if there was a surplus the cigars they were sold or exchanged at the country stores, as was the practice also in Connecticut. These cigars were of a very common kind, and were generally retailed at the rate of four and five for a cent.

In 1840 the total production returned for the state was 325,018 pounds, of which York county produced 162,748 pounds, Lancaster county 48,860 pounds, and Dauphin county 46,730 pounds.

The culture began to extend more rapidly in 1845, but the occurrence of the Mexican war the following year made the production of wheat far more remunerative, while the prices for tobacco declined, until it was no longer a profitable crop. The census of 1850 did not report a pound for Lancaster county. The amount grown for the state reached 912,651 pounds; a result due, no doubt, to the partial inflation of prices immediately after the close of the Mexican war. York county took the lead in the census of 1850, reporting its production at 418,555 pounds, or over 45 per cent. of the whole. Lawrence county is credited with 378,050 pounds, and Dauphin county with 50,200 pounds.

A very rapid increase in production took place between 1849 and 1859, the returns for the latter year showing for the state 3,181,586 pounds, or an increase of over 248 per cent. in ten years, while Lancaster county rose from nothing in 1849 to 2,001,547 in 1859, making about 63 per cent. of the whole production of the state. In the same year York county produced 695,405 pounds, each of the other counties in the state falling below a production of 40,000 pounds.

The next ten years show an inconsiderable increase, due to two causes mainly: the high prices which prevailed for breadstuffs and provisions, and the heavy draft made upon the laboring population for army purposes. The increase in production was very rapid from 1866 to 1870, the amount reported in the census of 1870 exceeding that reported in any previous year, reaching for the state 3,467,539 pounds; for Lancaster county, 2,602,584 pounds; for York, 527,808 pounds; and for Bucks, 151,372 pounds.

Since 1870 the acreage has gradually increased, and the limits of tobacco culture have extended until nearly half the counties now grow it as a staple crop. All varieties have been abandoned for the seed-leaf and domestic Havana, and Pennsylvania has reached the third rank as a tobacco-producing state.

The census of 1880 shows a production of 36,943,272 pounds, an increase of 965 per cent. in ten years.

PHYSICAL AND GEOLOGICAL FEATURES.

The surface of the state is generally level in the southeast, the level areas being wide and often separated by flanking hills or ridges, which rise 200 feet or more above the river basins. In the interior the surface is mountainous, but in the west it is generally broken or rolling. The southeastern counties, in their cultivated portions, are but little elevated above tide-water, but in going westward and northward several parallel ridges, running northeast and southwest, reach an elevation of 1,500 feet and upward, forming the Appalachian range.

The geological formations of the state are confined to three of the principal divisions of rocks. In the southeast are found the Eozoic rocks, which form a belt having a general course northeast and southwest, along which, on the eastern side mainly, in a belt 20 to 30 miles wide, lie the Mesozoic. The Paleozoic series come next, including the Carboniferous, in the western third of the state, extending north nearly to the state line, the Devonian rocks running east and west all along this line, and the Silurian, with alternating belts of Devonian, between the Eozoic and the Carboniferous rocks. The drift covers the north and northwest tiers of counties, and gradually thins out in going south, and it is even wanting on the table lands along the middle portion of the northern boundary of the state. The gneissoid rocks are mainly confined to the southeastern counties. They are succeeded on the northwest by a belt of metamorphic limestones of the Silurian age, after which come the red sandstones of the Mesozoic.

The principal tobacco area from north to south rests first upon the Devonian rocks, covered with their beds of drift on the lowlands, then on a small arm of the Carboniferous rocks, these two occupying a third of the distance across the state. Next succeed the Silurian rocks for a distance of 75 miles, giving place 35 miles south of Harrisburg to the Mesozoic and Eozoic rocks, which supply the best tobacco soils in the state.

The soils of the state are very fertile, except where the face of the country is rugged, and where sandstones or shales alone abound. The best soils of Lancaster county rest mainly upon limestone and chloritic slates, and are noted for their great strength and durability. In the counties south and east the abundance of limestone assures a high productiveness for the soils. Limestones abound in the mountain valleys, and give rise to good soils. On the upper Susquehanna, in the northeast, the soils are rich, but they are poor and thin and cold on the highlands in the central counties of the north, and become fertile in the northwest.

The counties of the state that produce 100,000 pounds of tobacco and upward each are Bradford, Tioga, Clinton, Lycoming, Union, Northumberland, Snyder, Dauphin, Cumberland, York, Lebanon, Lancaster, Chester, Berks, and Bucks. The eastern edges of Adams, Perry, Juniata, Mifflin, and Centre also produce some tobacco. The tobacco counties form a belt from north to south across the state. Midway north and south the belt is about 40 miles wide, and the Susquehanna divides the lower half. That portion of the belt lying east of the Susquehanna produces over 75 per cent. of the entire amount of tobacco grown in the state; and that portion extending from the center of the state southward, on both sides of the Susquehanna, will be found to produce over 90 per cent. of the whole. Lancaster county is the producing center, making two-thirds of the whole product of the state, taking the first rank in 1879 among all the counties of the United States.

CLIMATE.

The climate of Pennsylvania is very hot during summer in the southeastern part of the state, but cool and pleasant in the mountainous region. Observations continued by the signal service for nearly ten years show that the average temperature of the spring months at Philadelphia is 50.1 degrees; summer, 74; autumn, 57.7; winter, 33.3. The greatest difference between the highest and the lowest temperature recorded in any one year during the period of observation was 100 degrees; the average yearly fluctuations in temperature, 44.8. For the same period the mean annual precipitation was 42.95 inches, and the mean of the prevailing winds was northwest.

The deep, wide gorges through which the Susquehanna and its tributaries flow, and the slight elevation of the valleys above tide-water, make the summer very severe at times, the temperature ranging from 90° to 100°. The summer heat is prolonged late into autumn in southeastern Pennsylvania, and frosts rarely occur before October, giving ample time for the tobacco to come to maturity, even though planted as late as the 1st of July. The seasons are shorter in the northern parts of the state, due both to increased elevation and to latitude. In this section the tobacco crop must be harvested ordinarily before the 25th of September.

LANCASTER COUNTY.

In Lancaster county there is constant improvement in the fertility of the soil, notwithstanding the heavy drafts that have been made upon it. This improvement is shown by a comparison of the yields of the crop within the past five years with the five years previous. The increase has been fully 12 per cent.

The methods of managing the crop in Lancaster county furnish a guide which other counties follow more or less closely, and there is a gradual improvement throughout the state, Lancaster county taking the lead.

SITUATION AND EXTENT.

Lancaster county is situated in the southeastern part of the state, the Susquehanna river forming its southern and western boundaries. The area of the county is 970 square miles, or 620,800 acres. The extreme length of the county is 33 miles, and its greatest width 28 miles. Its central latitude is 40° 3′ north. Its surface is diversified, its soils good, and abundantly watered by small streams.

GEOLOGICAL FEATURES.

The surface of the country presents three separate and prominent geological features. The northern portion belongs to the Triassic or new red sandstone formation, and this extends along the entire northern boundary. It gives evidence of once having covered much of the surface, from which it is now entirely eroded. In the heart of this formation, and entirely inclosed by it, are several basins of limestone. Along the margins of these basins, as indeed over the great part of the new red sandstone, the beds are broken up into what is called "gravel" by the country people, or small angular fragments of hydro-mica schists.

The next formation, and the one to which Lancaster county may be said to owe its great agricultural importance, is the limestone belt, which traverses the county from east to west, covering more than 300 square miles of territory. This limestone has great masses of hydro-mica schists, argillites, rhomboidal slates, and other rocks associated with it. In many places it is shivered, which contributes largely to give the soil an excellent drainage, and renders it dry and warm.

The last and lowest of the formations found in the county is the Eozoic, taking in the mica-schist and gneiss belt running through the southern part and bordering on the Susquehanna. Blocks of quartzite are found loosely imbedded, and argillite or roofing slate also occurs. Quartzite is also found within the limestone belt, but generally only in blocks and fragments. Both within the limits of the limestone and gneissic belts vast deposits of iron are found, sometimes in beds, and again loosely scattered through the soil. There are also extensive trap dikes, and some serpentine ridges, carrying chrome ores.

The general surface of the country is rolling, and is diversified by several timbered ridges, the principal ones being the Conewago hills in the north, the Martic hills in the south, and the Welsh mountains in the eastern part of the county. The average elevation of Lancaster city is 359 feet above the mean level of the ocean, although portions of the county rise to the height of 611 feet.

There is a wide range in the temperature, the readings of the thermometer running from 100° F. during the heats of summer to 10 or more degrees below zero in winter. The rainfall is generally pretty evenly distributed throughout the year, the annual average being about 38 inches.

The entire surface of the county was at one time densely wooded with hickory, various kinds of oak, chestnut, and other timber. These have been nearly all cut away on the Martic hills and Conewago hills. On the Welsh mountains there is still an abundance of chestnut timber, which begins to renew itself as often as it is cut down. Most farmers still have small patches of woodland on their farms, which have been carefully preserved, but even these are gradually disappearing.

THE SOIL.

In the limestone region the prevailing colors of the soils are gray and grayish brown, while in the sandstone districts red prevails. The soil varies in depth from a few inches on the hillsides to as many feet in the alluvial bottoms along the streams. Whatever its depth or general character, it responds freely to manurial applications, whether natural or artificial, and whatever its character, it is everywhere throughout the county adapted to the cultivation of tobacco. There is a current belief that the soil embraced within the limestone belt will grow a better and finer article of tobacco than any other portion of the county, and the product, it is alleged, when made into cigars, will burn with a white-ash residuum. There are reasons for believing this to be a mistake. The soil, as a rule, is richer within the limestone limits than out of them, but this is largely the result of careful farming. The sandstone soil is generally thin, but where it is as heavily manured as in the best limestone sections the results compare favorably with those of the latter. This has been notably the case during the present year (1880), when the sandstone districts had the finest crops in the county, while in limestone townships of the highest reputation it was comparatively inferior. This is, however, a matter that will bear further investigation, and perhaps it is too soon to pronounce authoritatively on the question. At the present time the light, gravelly soils are not so highly esteemed, and they bring much smaller prices.

It is indisputable that the islands in the Susquehanna and the alluvial lands along the banks of that stream, as indeed along those of most other rivers and streams in the county, are naturally the best tobacco lands, as the silt of which these islands are mainly formed is exceedingly rich and the soil has a fine and sandy composition. No doubt the moister atmosphere that prevails in the immediate vicinity of such a large water-course, the more numerous fogs, and the low-lying situation all contribute their share to the general result. Another advantage is their greater exemption from frosts in both the spring and the fall, which naturally results from the presence of so large a body of water. Island lands that are cultivated command large prices.

VARIETIES OF TOBACCO CULTIVATED.

So many kinds of tobacco have from time to time been tried by the growers that perhaps no single variety is grown in its purity. Every farmer has his favorite, which is now one kind and then another. There are what is known as the Pennsylvania Seed-Leaf, the Glessner, the Connecticut Seed-Leaf, and others named after the individuals who claim to have originated them; in fact, nearly all the varieties cultivated in the seed-leaf districts have been tried. Whatever the kinds cultivated, unless renewed with fresh seed every few years they seem to lose their distinctive features and eventually to become hardly distinguishable from what is known as Pennsylvania Seed-Leaf.

Cuba tobacco has been tried frequently, but the inferior yield in pounds has always more than counterbalanced the increased price received for it. Latterly it has not been grown to any extent. In a few years it loses its distinctive features and some of the qualities that give it the most value. A few acres grown by Mr. Fendrich near Columbia, Pennsylvania, in 1879 attained a development of leaf that was astonishing, some measuring 18 by 40 inches.

At the present time the Glessner is the principal favorite. It develops a very large and handsome leaf, and yields more pounds to the acre than the others. The great size and weight of the leaves sometimes cause them to break when blown about by a strong wind.

Seed is constantly brought from other parts, and growers make frequent changes. Where a foreign variety is cultivated, this is no doubt necessary; but some of the old growers believe that changes in domestic kinds are not necessary. They hold that all the plants intended for seed should be standing near each other, instead of being scattered here and there over the field. In that way they fertilize each other and bear prolific seed true to the original variety. A few of the more advanced growers are in the habit of removing one-half or more of the seed pods from each stalk left for seed.

THE SEED-BED.

A southern or southeastern exposure is always preferred for the seed-bed, and the same plant-bed is used for several years in succession. Very few farmers burn over the seed-bed, the frosts of winter, heavy manuring, and the most careful preparation of the soil being relied upon to secure a good stand of plants, free from the intrusion of weeds.

The bed is prepared for seeding in the latter part of March or the beginning of April, and the seed is sown immediately upon the freshly-prepared soil. Under favorable circumstances, the seedlings are ready for transplanting about the middle of May, and the planting is usually completed by the 1st of June. Plants set as late as the middle of June generally mature well and make a fair crop, but early planting is the rule.

There is a current belief that early-cut tobacco cures into a lighter color, because the juices dry out more rapidly, and it is thought the late cut cures darker, because it cures more slowly. For this reason some growers do not plant till about the 10th of June. Their tobacco will then be ready to cut in September and cure in moderately cool weather.

PREPARATION OF TOBACCO GROUND.

As a rule, any land that will grow a good crop of corn or wheat will produce a good crop of tobacco. It is not necessary that any particular system of rotation should be followed. Grass lands are generally selected, although some growers prefer fields planted in corn the previous year, as when planted on sod trouble from the dreaded cut-worm is always expected, and the tedious and wearisome task of replanting is sure to be necessary.

It is customary to turn the ground in the fall, and manure should be put on at that time. This is especially desirable when it is sod or clayey soil. A sandy loam is preferable to a stiffer soil, and it is an axiom with the tobacco-growers of Lancaster county that tobacco ground cannot be made too rich. The amount of manure which farmers can afford to put on an acre varies with individual cases. From eight to twenty loads is the customary amount. Colonel James Young, who is one of the largest growers in the county, in 1879 drew 100 six-horse loads on a seven-acre field. The ground was more than covered, but the results justified the expenditure. Well-rotted barn-yard manure is preferred to all other fertilizers, tobacco-growers not taking kindly to artificial fertilizers. There are several reasons for this. In the first place, such fertilizers require a large outlay of money; and secondly, their use is discouraged by the tobacco buyers, who assert that tobacco raised by means of artificial fertilizers, when made up into cigars, does not burn with a pure white ash, which fashion at present demands, and which stable manure yields; and they further declare that the flavor of the cured leaf is also inferior. The fact that the tobacco raised in Lancaster county is preferred to any other grown in the state would seem to lend color to these views.

Thorough preparation of the ground having been made, the earth is thrown up into hills or into ridges, the latter being almost universally the practice. The ridges are 3½ or 4 feet apart; when the ground is rich the latter distance, although the former is thought sufficient on thin soils. Along the ridges indentations are cut. The distance between these varies with the different planters, generally from 22 to 28 inches being allowed between the plants. In a good season the latter is not too much. The indentations are not cut down to the general level of the field, as in that case the plant might be flooded during heavy rains. The ground is never marked out two ways or checked, the after cultivation being sufficiently thorough to render this unnecessary.

SETTING OUT THE PLANTS.

The field should be ready to receive the plants when the latter have put forth four leaves and are about 4 inches across. There is diversity of opinion as to planting in dry weather, some being in favor of planting just so soon as the plants are of the proper size, whether the ground is wet or dry, while a large majority prefer to wait days, and even a week or more, for rainy weather. When plants are set in dry ground the work is tedious and costly, and great care is required in every detail of the operation. The water-cart accompanies the planters, and water is poured about the plants when set out, this being repeated a number of times in dry seasons, the inevitable consequence of which is that the ground about the tender plants becomes hardened and the surface baked, retarding growth and delaying cultivation. Set out in moist soil, under favorable conditions the plants grow off quickly and are soon out of danger from the cut-worm; less replanting is necessary, an even stand is more surely obtained, and cultivation can be commenced much sooner.

In order that the plants should have a good start great care is exercised in setting them in the ground. Formerly a pointed stick was used to punch a hole in the ground, into which the roots of the plants were crowded without order or arrangement. Now, however, more attention is given to this matter. The roots are spread out into their natural position, and then covered with earth, which is gently pressed down upon them. A few successful planters in dry seasons put about half a pint of water on the ground where the plant is to be set, and when this has well soaked into the ground the plant is put in place. No second watering is necessary. This method seems to possess very decided advantages over that of watering simply after the plants are put in position.

A hot sun, long continued, often renders some artificial covering for the plants necessary. Small pieces of paper are generally used, as being most convenient and easily obtainable. The leaves of other plants or pieces of shingles are also frequently called into service. This is continued until the plants are well set and in no further danger from this source. Plants are very often set out while still too small, but nothing is gained by such a course. They will make more growth in the seed-bed in two days than in a week after transplanting, and a large, strong plant not only has more chances of growing in the field, but will grow faster.

FIELD CULTIVATION.

The cut-worms in some seasons destroy many plants, and these must be replaced. In 1879 many planters were compelled to replant their fields three times, owing to the ravages of these destroyers, they being far more numerous in some years than in others. Any sickly-looking plant is also removed, or another one is set by its side to supply its place in case it should die. The search for the cut-worm is continued until the plant is too large to be injured by it.

The cultivator or the shovel-plow is run twice through each space between rows, and care is taken that the earth is not thrown upon the plant. The hoe is used in making nearer approaches to the plant, as well as to pulverize the large lumps of earth that may be lying near it. All the weeds are carefully cut down, and particular care is taken to keep the ground around the plant loose and in good order.

These earliest stages of the life of the plant are regarded as requiring the utmost care. The hoe and the cultivator are kept going constantly, and destroy the weeds so effectually that they give no trouble later in the season; and, beside, the looser and finer the soil is, the more moisture it will absorb from the atmosphere, which in dry seasons is a consideration of no little importance. This cultivation continues until the great size of the leaves finally puts an end to it.

WORMING THE TOBACCO.

When the danger from the cut-worm has been passed successfully attention is directed to its immediate successor, the tobacco-worm, as, if left undisturbed, it will soon ruin the most promising field. Pennsylvania tobacco being used almost entirely for cigar-making, defective leaves, unfit for wrappers, materially depreciate the value of a crop. The earlier worms appear about the 1st of July, and it is well understood that thorough work at this period secures comparative exemption from them later in the season. The plants are examined two or three times a week, so that the eggs of the moth may be found before the worm is hatched out or the young worms killed before inflicting any injury upon the leaf. Various devices are employed for killing or entrapping the moth, some of which have proved fairly successful; but no plan has been devised so certain and reliable as hand-picking. The use of poisons, mixed with sweetened waters and dropped into the blooms of the Jamestown weed, planted for the purpose, is more or less practiced; but, as bees are kept by many farmers, this method is regarded as somewhat hazardous.

TOPPING AND SUCKERING.

The hunt for worms continues until the day the tobacco is carried from the field. Topping is a matter into which so many considerations enter that every man makes a rule for himself, modified by the several kinds of tobacco, the varying soils, the season, and the condition of the crop. The custom is to top about the time the blossom bud makes its appearance, which in Pennsylvania is about the 1st of August in an average season; others top when the desired number of leaves has appeared. Where the soil is thin and the plants backward, or when the season is dry, low topping becomes a necessity. From eight to ten leaves are left on the plant under these circumstances, the top being pinched out, not cut, thus causing less bleeding of the plant. When the soil is rich, the growth strong, and the season favorable, from twelve to fourteen leaves are allowed to each plant. This growth is generally so unequal that all cannot be topped at the same time; but if plants of the same size are set out at the same time the period of topping will not vary much in a field. This is a great advantage, as the crop will mature more evenly, and the color be more uniform.

Dry weather is most unwelcome as topping time comes on. When such weather occurs, topping is deferred a short time. Some growers wait until the last possible moment, preferring rather to let the lower leaves drop off than to top in a period of drought. By deferring topping ripening is retarded, which under the circumstances is a very important advantage. The cupidity of the grower too often leads him to top too high, leaving more leaves on the stalk than it is able to mature. When this is done, and a season of drought comes on, the tobacco is apt to ripen prematurely and cure up a bad color—"foxy," as it is termed. Topping after a warm, soaking rain is of much advantage.

Close upon the operation of topping follows the first crop of suckers. These are removed when they attain a length of 3 or 4 inches. It is believed that the sooner they are removed after they make their appearance the better.

CUTTING THE CROP.

Some years ago the tendency was to let the plants become fully ripe, and in many cases overripe. The careful grower has several ways of determining maturity. The time selected by some is when the lowest leaves send out suckers of good size. A far better evidence of maturity is when the leaves assume different shades of color and become brittle, and if, when they are doubled over, they show a tendency to break, the sooner they are cut the better. Of late years, however, planters have been accustomed to harvest their crop before it is ripe, just when it is on the point of ripening. Experience has demonstrated that if cut at this juncture the color will be darker and more acceptable to manufacturers, fashion at the present time running almost entirely in that direction. Beside, such early cutting places the crop beyond the reach of hailstorms, heavy rains, and early frost. It is deemed unadvisable to cut immediately after a rain, as the gum or resin secreted by the numerous hair-like glands of the leaf is dissolved and, in a measure, washed off. A few days' sunshine restores this gum, and the tobacco may then be cut.

THE FIELD SCAFFOLD.

The proper time for cutting having arrived, from twenty to thirty days after the process of topping, some transfer the tobacco at once from the field to the barn; but the custom of scaffolding in the field is almost universally practiced. It is conceded that scaffolding in the field is not so important to early-cut tobacco as to the later harvested, because the weather being warm at that time it is not likely to suffer danger in the barns. As the later cut dries much less rapidly, it is in more danger from pole-burn or from freezing. There are those, however, who, when they have ample storage-room, scaffold neither the late nor the early tobacco.

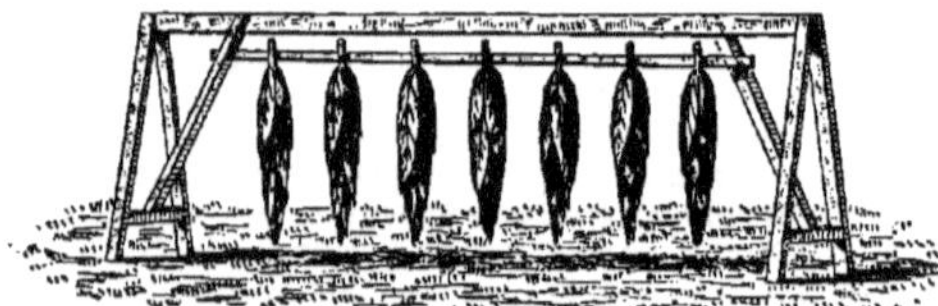

The accompanying cut gives a representation of the field scaffold, and shows how it looks when loaded with tobacco. Sometimes it is made of ordinary fence posts, sunk in the ground, with common rails inserted in the holes of the posts. In other cases large trestles are made, across which timbers of the proper size are laid. A spot shaded by trees is generally chosen for it. The engraving represents the latter kind. They can easily be preserved from one season to another. Both side and end views are exhibited.

CUTTING OFF AND PLACING ON LATHS.

The tobacco plants are either cut off carefully with a sharp hatchet or sawed off with a short, sharp saw. The morning and the evening are chosen for this work; generally the latter. When cut in the morning, the dew, and, if it has rained, the rain water, are first allowed to dry from the plants, the valuable qualities of the leaf, it is believed, being best secured by this method. The plants being cut off, they are laid down carefully to prevent injury to the leaves. A short time to wilt is usually given, but sunburn must be guarded against by turning the plants when there is danger of it.

When sufficiently wilted to be handled without injury the stalks are speared on the laths, as illustrated in the chapter on Maryland, and, when small, six and seven plants are strung on a single lath, while not more than five are put on when the plants are large. When the tobacco is left on the scaffold for some time it can be more crowded than when taken from the field direct to the barn.

NEW METHOD OF HANGING TOBACCO ON LATHS.

During the past three or four years several new methods of attaching the tobacco stalks to the laths have come into use which possess many advantages over the method of spearing them. Laths of a heavier size than those ordinarily employed are used for this purpose. This size is three-fourths of an inch thick and 1½ or 2 inches wide, made out of pine, poplar, or some other light wood, and is of the usual length, 4 feet. Into this stout lath six iron or wire hooks are driven, resembling this shape: ——˩, three on each side, the first one 4 inches from the end, the next one 16 inches from the first, and the third 16 inches from the second, leaving a space of 12 inches from the last to the end of the lath. Hooks are driven at points midway between those on the opposite side of the lath, thus giving room for six large stalks, 8 inches apart from side to side, hanging alternately on one side or on the other. In this way they do not interfere with each other, and can be hung much more closely, for there is no waste of space, the alternate hanging filling up not only all the space on the same lath, but also between all the laths when they are hung up in the barn. The hooks are clenched on the opposite side to prevent their drawing out. In several cases wire hooks, shaped like the letter **S**, were used, but they did not give satisfaction, as the laths that were used were the ordinary laths, and could not stand the strain at the ends, and were often broken; beside, the hooks being loose, required frequent adjustment. There were several objections to these hooks, which have prevented their general introduction. They were too expensive for the majority of tobacco farmers, costing about $22 per acre. The principle, however, is so excellent that growers were not long in finding out a substitute equally effective and far cheaper. The following cut explains the entire process.

Laths of the same size, ¾ by 1½ inches, are used, but instead of iron hooks or wire five- or six-penny nails are used. These are driven through the laths at alternate intervals on both sides, with a slight upward inclination, to prevent the tobacco from falling off readily. This method is far cheaper and equally efficacious, and no one who has ever tried it thoroughly will be likely to give it up; indeed, many of the most careful tobacco-growers take it up every year more and more.

The advantages possessed by this system over that of spearing are as follows:

1. The large hole made in the tobacco stalk by the spear has a tendency to dry out the stalk too rapidly at that point, and the more slowly the stalk dries the better and more uniform the color of the leaf is likely to be. The leaves nearest the spear hole are generally "off-color".

2. Tobacco can be hung on hooks or nails much more quickly than speared upon laths. At least nine stalks can be hung on nails while six are strung on laths, thereby causing a great saving in time.

3. It is far easier to fix the stalks on nails than on laths. The tobacco stalk is not hard, and a slight pressure will drive the nail through it. A boy can easily do this, whereas spearing tobacco is man's work.

4. The tobacco is preserved in far better condition by the new than by the old method. The spear so very often comes into contact with one or two of the leaves where the orifice is made that they are ruined as wrappers, which cannot occur with ordinary care by the new method.

5. The tobacco is far more easily removed when stripping time comes, hardly an effort being required to remove it from the nails, which is not the case when it is withdrawn from the laths.

6. When once hung on the nails no further adjustment of the stalks is required. Their places are definitely fixed, and they cannot get out of place, which is by no means the case when hung on laths, for then the utmost care must be observed that they are at their proper places when finally hung up in the tobacco-barns to cure. This also is a saving of time and labor.

7. It has led to the invention of several other devices which have a tendency to preserve the leaves from damage.

Some farmers have a place on the tobacco-wagon, commonly an arrangement beneath the hind axle, where the empty laths are carried. At the rear end of the wagon-scaffold are iron hooks or other contrivances, upon which the lath is hung and firmly held while the stalks are attached to the nails. As fast as a lath is filled it is removed to the usual place on the tobacco-wagon, and another is placed on the hooks, to be filled in turn. In this way the tobacco need be handled but once, and is not thrown on the ground at all, to the great damage of the leaves. Where it is not desirable, or when it is impossible to take the tobacco-wagon through the field, another contrivance, in the form of a tripod, with arms above the point of junction as well as toward the ground, is called into requisition. This is about 4 feet high, and at the top of the upper arms are attached iron hooks, to hold the laths firmly in place while the tobacco is hung upon them. A boy can take the stalk from the man who cuts it off and place it where it belongs on the lath. The tripod holds three laths. In driving the nails into the laths a measure is used which indicates where they are to go, so the work can be done regularly and rapidly.

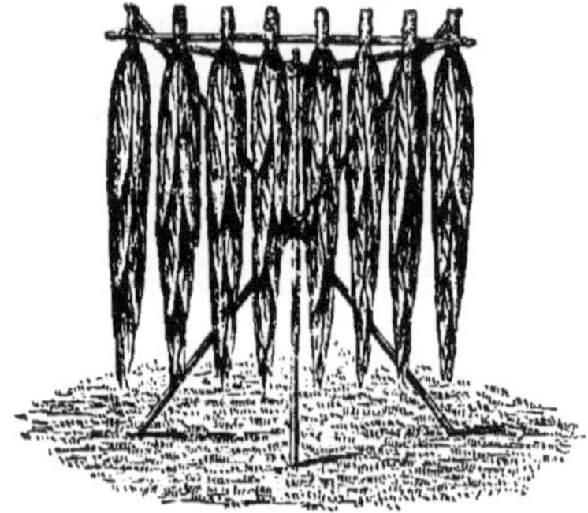

A small trestle is sometimes used in the field for the same purpose as the tripod already described, which, although intended for a single lath, answers the purpose admirably.

There is no special period during which the tobacco is allowed to hang on the scaffolds, but from three to ten days is the usual time. While on the scaffold the access of air on all sides effectually prevents injury to the crop. The removal from the scaffold to the barn was a few years ago accomplished in any way the farmers found most convenient, but the exigencies of the situation have led to the production of a wagon specially adapted to this work. A frame, 18 feet long and a little narrower than the length of the laths, the upper rails of the frame having a cleat nailed or bolted on the outer edges and projecting above them an inch or more to prevent the laths shifting endwise, is placed upon a low-wheeled wagon, and the laths are transferred from the scaffold to the wagon and hung upon the framework, and are easily removed to the shed or barn without injury to the plants. The illustration gives a good idea of this tobacco-wagon.

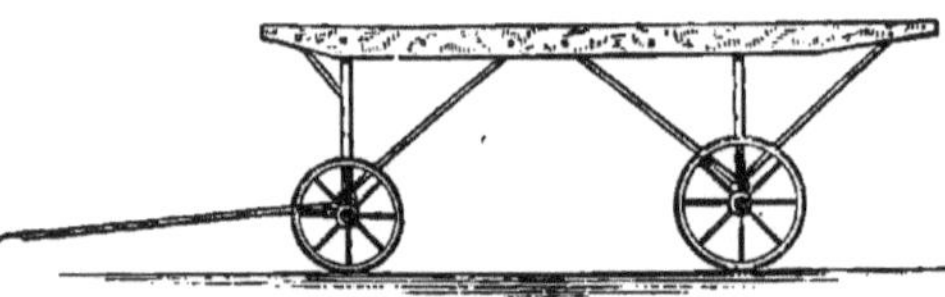

When the tobacco is taken from the field it is at once hung in the barn. The barn is filled from the top downward in sections; that is, a certain space, 10, 12, or 16 feet long, and as wide as the barn, is filled up at a time. The wagon is drawn into this section, and directly beneath the place where the tobacco is to be hung. By an arrangement of ropes and a pulley the laths are hauled to their places at the top of the barn (which may be 40 feet high) and carefully put on the cross-pieces arranged for that purpose. The careful planter observes, before the lath is fixed in its place, that the leaves do not adhere, but that they are well separated, in order that each individual leaf shall receive its due share of ventilation. A final adjustment of the plants on the laths is also made, as they may not have been originally so carefully placed as they should, or they may have been moved out of place during the subsequent stages of removal. Placing the laths at proper distances is also important. If too close, "pole-burn" will result, and much may be destroyed; or, if discovered in time, it often necessitates the removal from the barn for a time and the rehanging of the crop. The size of the plants, other things being equal, governs the distance at which they are placed, usually from 6 to 8 inches. In the process of curing proper ventilation is the all-important factor. The barn must be capable of being closed tightly when need be, and of affording thorough ventilation to all the tobacco in it, as rapid drying is not desirable. The plan generally adopted is to keep it closed during the day and to open it at night. Especially should it be kept closed on damp, foggy days, in order to exclude the moisture, although a few thorough dampenings from this cause are by no means objectionable, but are believed by some to be beneficial in fixing the color.

STRIPPING AND BULKING.

Under favorable circumstances tobacco cures rapidly. During the year 1880 some that was cut unusually early was stripped on the 1st of September, but generally very little tobacco is stripped until the middle of December, by which time the stems are thoroughly dried out and the tobacco is cured. Advantage is taken of wet, damp weather, when the laths are lowered into the cellar under the barn and the work of stripping begins. If there should happen to be no damp days when it is desired to strip, a few days in the cellar will impart the necessary moisture. Perhaps as many as three-fourths of all the growers assort their crops into three kinds, known, respectively, as "fillers", "seconds," and "wrappers". This is done not because it is the most profitable, but because it entails far less labor than when several additional grades are made. Sometimes the wrappers are reassorted into two kinds as to length, and these again as to evenness of color. This, however, is rare. Such lots command high figures, as the buyer sees at a glance the full character of the crop. The leaves are tied into what are called "hands", from ten to twelve being put into each. More attention is given each succeeding year in tying up these hands carefully, and the more neatly and systematically the work is done the more attractive the hands look and the more salable they are. After the stripping has been finished, bulking comes next in order, for which a platform is made in the tobacco cellar about 4 feet or less in width and slightly raised from the ground, to prevent mold and undue dampness. If bulked in warm weather, say in October or November, it is apt to undergo the sweating process. This produces no bad results, but care must be taken that the bulks are not disturbed during the sweat. If not bulked until cold weather has set in, the tobacco is not likely to sweat until the warm weather of spring begins.

TOBACCO-BARNS.

However well the soil of Lancaster county may be adapted to the growth of good tobacco, it may well be doubted whether the product would ever have reached its present excellence except for the careful handling it receives after being taken from the field. In the early days of tobacco culture in this county, while it was still regarded as an irregular crop, little attention was given to proper buildings for its storage; in fact, few knew what was really needed. After being cut, it was hung up wherever there was any room, any vacant place in the barn, the poultry-

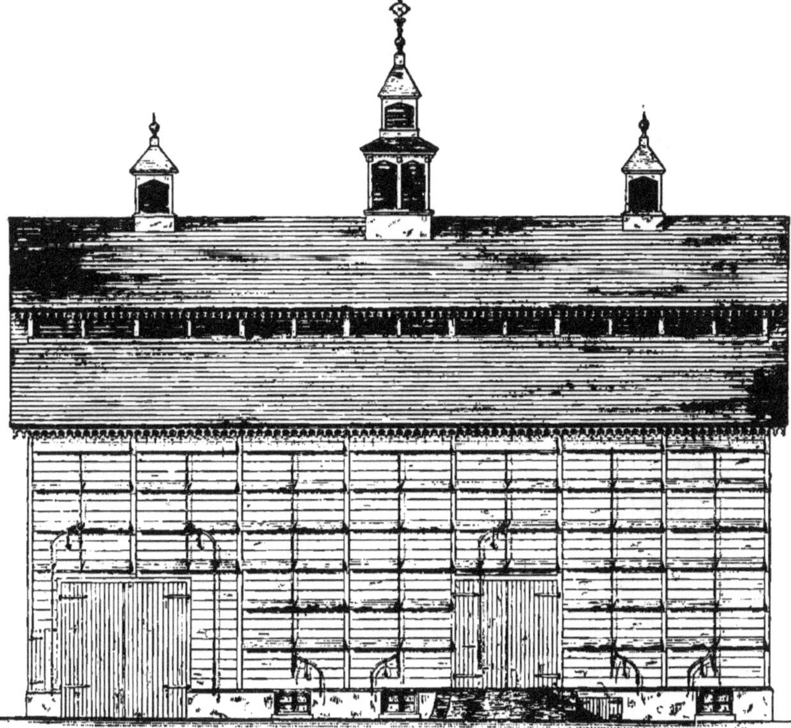

No. 1.

house, and the garret, or unused rooms in the dwelling, being utilized for this purpose. But as the crop grew in importance these make-shift conveniences were found to be totally inadequate, and common wooden sheds were built, without any particular reference to anything except their capacity to house the crop. Ventilation was very imperfectly understood, and was provided for by hanging some of the vertical boards of the building at certain intervals upon hinges, which left continuous openings from the bottom to the top, with no place above for the hot air to escape. Cellars underneath the structure were unthought of, and when stripping time came it was necessary to wait until the needed wet weather to make stripping possible.

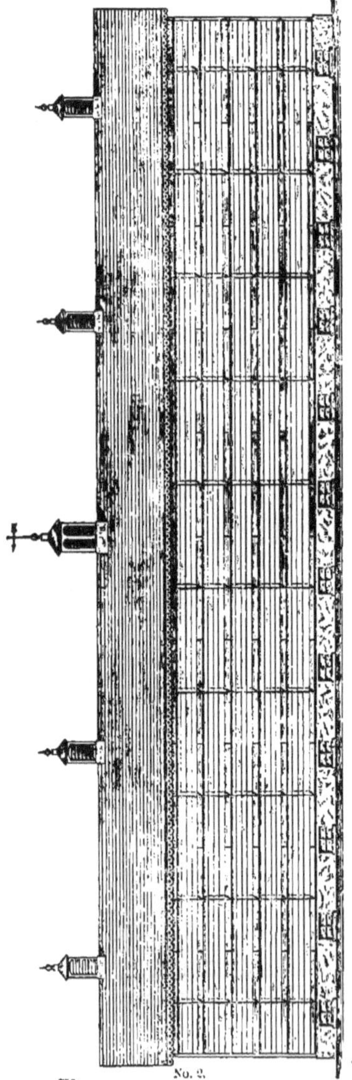
No. 2.

As a knowledge of tobacco-growing spread among the farmers improved buildings began to be erected everywhere, with an eye to better results. Cellars were found to play so important a part in the preparation of the product for market that all good tobacco-barns were built with them, but now almost every farmer has his improved tobacco-barn. These are of all sizes, from 20 feet square to 40 feet wide and 150 feet long, but a well-proportioned tobacco-barn is thought to be one that is 36 feet wide by 72 or 80 feet long. Some of these are model structures of the kind, and present a fine appearance. The cost varies with the size. From $500 to $1,500 may be considered the ruling figures, but some of the more elaborate structures cost twice the latter sum; and barns costing in the aggregate about $200,000 were erected in the year 1877. With prudent foresight the farmers have built them so that should the time come when tobacco-growing shall cease to be desirable these structures can be utilized for general farm purposes. The cut No. 1 shows what is perhaps the finest structure of the kind in the state. It stands on the farm of B. J. McGrann, who owns 145 acres immediately outside the eastern limits of the city of Lancaster, and who has recently purchased 70 additional acres adjoining, at $300 per acre. Mr. McGrann some years ago built the tobacco-barn marked No. 2, 28 feet wide and 150 feet long; but having increased the size of his tobacco-field to 28 acres during the present year, the old barn was unequal to the demand made upon it, and the erection of another (No. 1) was begun and completed during the past fall.

The plans and several elevations give an excellent idea of what these barns are, but only a written description can do full justice to their model arrangement. Beginning with the cellar of No. 1, it will be seen that the excavation extends beneath the whole length and width of the building, 41 by 84 feet. This is divided by a partition into two apartments of unequal size. The larger of the two is used as a dampening room, into which the tobacco is lowered through trap-doors in the floor. Here it is also bulked after being stripped. The second and smaller apartment is used exclusively as a stripping room. Arranged around its four sides are permanent tables or counters, with a raised wooden floor immediately behind them, on which the men engaged in stripping stand. Elsewhere throughout the whole cellar the floor is of earth. The stripping room communicates with the larger room by a door, while a second door communicates with the outside. There are seven windows, affording all the light desired. There is also a smoke-flue running to the top of the building, and a stove to keep the place comfortable in cold weather. The cellar is 9 feet high in the clear. Upon this is erected a wooden superstructure, 29 feet high from the floor to the square or eaves. This space is so divided that seven tiers of tobacco can be hung one above the other, while the central portion of the building, being considerably higher, furnishes accommodations to three additional tiers, making ten in all. The ventilation is provided at the sides, at the gables, and also at the roof. At intervals of 4 feet there are horizontal openings along the entire building, the lowest one being at the floor and the rest above it, each one opening just where the tier of tobacco begins. These openings are about a foot wide, and are operated by a series of vertical levers, running from the floor to the eaves, across a space of 12 feet, each one acting independently. The slatted openings along the roof, and those in the cupolas, give a draught, which insures a steady supply of fresh air, and will prevent any damage to the tobacco near the roof. The patent levers work so easily that a boy can work them, closing all the openings in one section at a single operation. At one end of the building arrangements have been made for a corn-crib, which, however, can at any time be utilized for tobacco-curing purposes. The building is somewhat embellished with ornamental work, and the outside has received three coats of paint. The cost of this barn was $4,000.

Barn No. 2, while it combines most of the features of No. 1, is not so well ventilated, having no ventilation in the roof proper, but only through the slatted cupolas. It is less elaborate throughout in its appointments, and cost about $1,500. Barn No. 1 combines in itself every valuable feature so far developed among the planters of Lancaster county as successful aids to tobacco culture and curing.

The tobacco-growers have not yet secured the best ventilation possible in their tobacco-barns. The plan of admitting the air through the horizontal openings is almost universally adopted, but every one who studies the principles of ventilation must see that unless some means are provided at the apex of the roof for the escape of the heated air the circulation throughout the building must needs be imperfect. Of late a modification of this plan has been introduced, which promises better results. But two openings are provided on the sides of the building, one at the floor and the other at the eaves, but these openings are three or more feet wide, and admit a large volume of air, which the opening at the eaves at once induces to rise and escape at that point. A series of slatted openings along the comb of the roof will divert a portion of the current in that direction, and a better ventilation than by the more numerous narrow openings would seem to be assured.

It is possible to secure better and more satisfactory results by another method, as yet untried by growers. By admission of a current of air directly beneath the hanging tobacco, instead of at the sides, this could easily be done. With the cellar so far out of the ground as to admit of windows several feet high on every side the floor above could be provided with numerous trap-doors, instead of the one or two now allowed, while ventilators could be placed in sufficient numbers at regular intervals upon the roof, running from the eaves to the comb; or, instead of trap-doors in the floor, the floor might be laid with strips a few inches wide, with open spaces of equal width between. When the cellar windows are thrown open the air from without would enter, pass directly beneath every plant in the barn, rise through every tier, and make its escape at the openings in the roof. There being no openings at the sides, there would be nothing to interfere with the ascent of a steady current. By the present system the outside air is driven against the sides of the outer leaves, instead of coming into contact with each one of them, as it should do, to secure uniform curing and color throughout the whole crop. This would also prevent the beating in of rain, as sometimes happens, or the ingress of heavy winds to break the dry leaves.

MARKETING THE CROP.

It is only when growers are unable to sell the crop at what they believe it to be worth that they pack it in cases themselves. The planters prefer to be clear of the old crop before they begin with the new, and probably not one case out of every hundred raised is packed by the growers. There is no particular time for the purchasing season to begin. Buying is done altogether by sample. Farmers take advantage of favorable weather at any time after October to prepare their goods for market. Buyers begin their operations generally in November, but often not until December. They congregate in Lancaster, thirty and forty at one time, and come from all parts of the country: from Baltimore, Saint Louis, Philadelphia, and San Francisco, but principally from New York. There is beside, a large number of local buyers and packers, and during the season these men visit every out-of-the-way nook and corner and search out every lot of tobacco in the county. Many packing-houses send their agents to spy out the ground while the tobacco is still in the fields and mark choice lots. If the price is agreed upon, a contract in duplicate is drawn up, the buyer retaining a copy and the grower receiving the other. At the time specified, or, if none is specified, when the grower is ready to deliver the crop, it is taken to the packing-house of the purchaser and done up in bales of varying sizes, generally of 100 pounds' weight, and it is there weighed and paid for on the spot. Occasionally, however, the packers do not wait until the crop is stripped before they begin purchasing. If the crop is a very desirable one, they begin operations before the farmers are ready to sell, or before their tobacco is ready for the market. This was notably the case in 1879, when the season opened before the growers had commenced to strip, and while the tobacco still hung in the barns. It was examined while still on the poles, and much of it was bought in that condition. This method does not always result satisfactorily. Sometimes the buyer is deceived by the crop as it hangs in the barn and offers more for it than it afterward proves to be worth, in which case there is likely to be dissatisfaction and dispute. The planters, as a rule, prefer to sell their crops after they are stripped and fully ready for the market.

PACKING TOBACCO.

There are upward of fifty firms engaged in packing stationed at Lancaster, or with agents there to represent them. The cost of buying, receiving, assorting, casing, and storing tobacco, including the cases themselves, may be put down at from 1½ to 2 cents per pound. The shooks for the cases come from the pine regions of Michigan, although many are made in the lumber regions of Pennsylvania. The cost of cases is about $1 05 each at the present time (1880); the size is 2 feet 6 inches high, 2 feet 6 inches wide, and 3 feet long, and will easily hold 400 pounds of tobacco. Generally only about 375 pounds of fine wrappers are packed in a case, close packing being considered objectionable to that part of the crop, while rather more than 400 pounds are packed into a case of the other grades. Some packers, however, put in exactly 400 pounds. The loss on tobacco incurred by the sweating process after it is cured is from 9 to 15 per cent. Sometimes the tobacco is sold at the marked weight, that is, at the weight of the tobacco at the time it was cased, at which time the weight of case and tobacco are plainly marked on the box; and sometimes by reweight, that is, with the loss from the sweating deducted. The cost of sampling, including labor for handling, opening, and shutting of cases, is 50 cents per case. The average wages of hands engaged during the winter season to receive, handle, assort, and pack the tobacco is $9 per week; the foreman gets about $12. The only tax (*a*) packers are required to pay is the government tax of $25 as dealers, irrespective of the quantity bought and sold.

TOBACCO WAREHOUSES.

The warehouses and packing establishments are brick structures from 75 to 150 feet long and of corresponding width, and from two to three stories high, and their capacity runs from 500 to 5,000 cases. On one short street in the eastern part of the city of Lancaster there are six of these structures standing side by side. This street is appropriately named Tobacco avenue. Often the adjoining streets for several blocks are crowded with double rows of vehicles of all descriptions, from the wagon with a single horse to the "Conestoga wagon" with its six magnificent horses. Teams that have twenty or more miles to come leave their homes on the previous evening, and as early as one o'clock the train of wagons begins to pour in, each driver being anxious to be the first comer, in order to secure a favorable place, and, consequently, an early discharge of his load. During the receiving season from ten to eighty hands are constantly employed, and sometimes a night gang is taken on in addition. As many as 1,000,000 pounds have been received by the packing-houses in Lancaster in a single day, while as much as $175,000 has been paid to the growers in the same time by the packers. A single firm has purchased $400,000 worth of tobacco in a season, while many buy to the value of $100,000 each.

DOES TOBACCO IMPOVERISH THE SOIL?

Tobacco is a voracious feeder and makes heavy drafts on the soil, but the growers in Pennsylvania do not believe it is harder on the soil than the ordinary farm crops. For more than thirty years it has been continuously grown on their fields, and yet there is not a single acre in the county that has been worn out from this cause. Under the system of cultivation practiced in Lancaster county the tobacco lands are growing richer, instead of becoming impoverished. It will be observed that one of the gentlemen who have furnished estimates of the profit on an acre of tobacco, Mr. H. G. Rush, claims a credit of $25 because of the increased fertility of the soil. That should settle this matter very effectually so far as Lancaster county is concerned.

Where careless farming prevails the case would, no doubt, be very different. To crop tobacco year after year without returning an ample equivalent to the soil can, of course, have only one ending. All the money realized from the tobacco crop remains in the farmers' hands, and they are at little expense, except for labor. Few artificial fertilizers are purchased, the great aim being to produce as much home-made manure as possible. No straw, hay, or corn is sold by the best farmers; all is fed on the farm. Large numbers of stock cattle are purchased in the fall, fattened during the winter, and if the farmer only realizes a fair price for the corn fed them he looks for no other profit for his trouble, well aware that the increased size of his manure pile will make him ample amends, and that the fertility of his farm will be maintained.

Another fact must not be forgotten. Great care is exercised in the amount of land set out in tobacco. While there are three or four persons who have planted as many as 50 acres in a single year, a few only plant as many as 10, while by far the greater number grow only from 1 to 5 acres each. In 1879 the acreage which a farmer might safely plant was discussed at a meeting of the county agricultural society, and, an expression of opinion being taken, the limit was placed at 5 per cent. of the tillable acres of the farm, but a large minority of the members thought 3 per cent. enough. As the farms run from 75 to 100 acres, it will be seen that the danger of ruining the farms through tobacco-growing is not a contingency that gives much alarm.

LABOR AND WAGES.

It cannot be said that there is any appreciable difference between the cost of labor employed in tobacco culture and that paid for ordinary farm work. This rule holds good throughout the state. On page 159 is given the ordinary wages paid to farm laborers, which will represent the cost of hands employed in tobacco culture. Most farms of the average size employ at least one hand throughout the entire year, and when such labor is employed only during

a More recently a modification of this law has been made, so that by paying a tax of $5 a merchant may buy tobacco to the amount of 25,000 pounds.

the summer the wages are but very slightly higher. Most farm laborers prefer to contract their services for the entire twelve months, rather than for a shorter period. The following are the rates that have prevailed during the past four years:

	By the month for the whole year.	By the month for the summer months.
1877	$12 39	$15 10
1878	11 24	14 50
1879	10 58	13 40
1880	11 79	14 90

There has been a growing tendency in some places to hire help who will board themselves, although the custom cannot be said to be at all general. In such cases the rates averaged as follows:

	Whole year.	Summer months.
1877	$20 97	$26 07
1878	18 41	24 07
1879	17 44	21 25
1880	18 32	22 35

Transient labor during the same period, harvest time excepted, has been as follows per day:

	With board.	Without board.
1877	$0 80	$1 15
1878	75	90
1879	63	88
1880	71	98

Board on an average is estimated at about 30 cents per day.

COST AND PROFIT OF TOBACCO-GROWING IN LANCASTER COUNTY.

Tobacco has proved to be the most profitable of all Lancaster county farm crops, and, although generally considered a precarious one, it has proved quite as certain as any other grown during the past twenty years.

The high-priced lands of the county, and the labor bestowed upon the tobacco crop, require not only that a heavy crop be grown on the land, but that a good price be obtained when it is marketed. Both these conditions have been realized for a long series of years. The average price of good farm land is about $200 per acre; sometimes the price is not higher than $175, but it frequently runs up to $250. To get at the true cost of growing an acre of tobacco four of the best known and most successful growers were invited to make estimates, which are here given. It will be observed there is considerable difference in some of the estimated items.

The estimate of Mr. J. M. Frantz, of Wabank, is as follows:

Dr.		
Making seed-bed and attending plants		$1 00
Plowing one acre of ground		1 50
Manure		50 00
Preparing ground for planting		2 00
Planting		2 00
Cultivating and hoeing after planting		5 00
Topping, worming, and suckering		10 00
Harvesting, cutting, spearing, and housing		5 00
Use of shed, laths, wagon, etc. (interest on cost)		5 00
Stripping, bulking, and preparing for market		12 00
Rent of land (interest on value of)		10 00
Hauling to market		2 00
		105 50
Cr.		
1,000 pounds tobacco, at 25 cents	$250 00	
500 pounds tobacco, at 10 cents	50 00	
300 pounds tobacco, at 5 cents	15 00	
		315 00
Net profit		209 50

Cost per pound, 5.86 cents.

Mr. Frantz further says that in his opinion an additional expenditure of $50 for manure would give this result:

Dr.		
For labor, manure, and interest on investment		$155 50
Cr.		
1,500 pounds of tobacco, at 25 cents	$375 00	
500 pounds of tobacco, at 15 cents	75 00	
		450 00
Net profit		294 50

Cost per pound, 7.77 cents.

The latter estimate, moreover, favors the idea that it is far more profitable to cultivate fewer acres, cultivating them more highly, making more pounds and a better article, a larger gain being the result.

Mr. H. G. Rush makes the following estimate:

DR.

Making seed-bed and care of plants		$5 00
Plowing one acre twice		4 00
Manure and cost of application		50 00
Harrowing and preparing the ground		3 00
Planting and replanting		5 00
Harrowing and hoeing three times, each $2		6 00
Topping, suckering, and worming		12 00
Harvesting		10 00
Use of barn, laths, etc. (interest on cost)		6 00
Taking down and stripping		18 00
Rent of land (interest on value)		12 00
Taking to market		2 00
		133 00

CR.

1,200 pounds of tobacco, at 20 cents	$240 00	
200 pounds of tobacco, at 8 cents	16 00	
400 pounds of tobacco, at 3 cents	12 00	
Value of stalks as manure	2 00	
Increased fertility of the soil	25 00	
		295 00
Net profit		162 00

Cost per pound, 7.39 cents.

Mr. Rush adds the following remarks:

On the debit side it will be observed that $68 apply to the farmer as owner and $65 as cultivator. The cost of labor is rated at $2 per day for a man and team, and $1 for other labor, board included. The ordinary cost of cultivation is not nearly so high, as much of the work is done by hired help at lower rates, and by children; but then it is also claimed that the credit side is somewhat above the average. I think, for the kind of tobacco sure to command the prices given, the expenses are not much too high. It may not be amiss to say that efforts to curtail expenses would almost certainly result in a triple reduction on the credit side of the account; a saving of $10 loses $20, and not seldom $100.

Joseph F. Hershey, president of the Lancaster County Agricultural Society, makes this estimate:

DR.

Making seed-bed and care of plants		$8 00
Plowing ground twice		4 50
Manure		30 00
Preparing the ground		3 00
Planting		3 00
Harrowing and hoeing		12 00
Worming, topping, and suckering		15 00
Harvesting		5 00
Rent of barn, wagon, laths, etc. (interest on value)		20 00
Taking down and stripping		20 00
Rent of land (interest on value)		9 00
Marketing		6 00
		135 50

CR.

1,400 pounds of tobacco, at 20 cents	$280 00	
200 pounds of tobacco, at 10 cents	20 00	
400 pounds of tobacco, at 5 cents	20 00	
		320 00
Net profit		184 50

Cost per pound, 6.77 cents.

Or, for a poor crop, 800 pounds of tobacco, at 16 cents	128 00
150 pounds of tobacco, at 8 cents	12 00
250 pounds of tobacco, at 3 cents	7 50
	147 50
Deduct expenses	135 50
Leaving a profit of only	12 00

And costing 11.29 cents per pound.

The fourth and last estimate is made by Mr. M. D. Kendig, of Creswell, and is as follows:

DR.		
Making seed-bed and care of plants		$3 00
Plowing one acre twice		5 00
Manure, 15 tons, at $4 per ton		60 00
Harrowing and preparing the ground		4 00
Planting		4 00
Harrowing and hoeing three times		8 00
Topping, worming, and suckering		9 00
Harvesting		5 00
Use of barn, wagon, laths, etc. (interest on value)		15 00
Taking down and stripping		17 50
Rent of land (interest on value)		12 00
Taking to market		3 00
		145 50
CR.		
1,300 pounds of tobacco, at 20 cents	$260 00	
150 pounds of tobacco, at 8 cents	12 00	
300 pounds of tobacco, at 4 cents	12 00	
		284 00
Net profit		138 50

Cost per pound, 6.3 cents.

Taking the foregoing estimates and grouping them as the basis of a calculation, and including the poor crop, we find that the cost of growing a pound of tobacco in this county is 7.68 cents. It is considerably less in other portions of the state, as a reference to the other counties will show. This is owing to the cheaper lands, cheaper barns, and various other items that enter into the general account. None of the foregoing calculations give an idea of the amount of money that has in a favorable season been realized from an acre of Lancaster county seed-leaf tobacco. In 1879, when the crop was unusually heavy and the prices were very high, $300 was no unusual sum to be realized from a single acre. The best result heard of was from 15,800 plants, set out on 3 acres of ground, which produced 7,681 pounds of merchantable tobacco, or nearly half a pound to the stalk. This crop was sold at 25 cents through, the fortunate owner receiving $1,920 25, or $640 08 per acre. The expenses of growing it are not known, but the net profits could hardly have been less than $450 per acre. This certainly shows high farming.

THE YIELD PER ACRE.

The average yield of 1879 per acre, as shown by enumerators' returns, was 1,409 pounds. From 1,800 to 2,400 pounds were grown to the acre by many planters, while 2,000 pounds was not regarded as a very heavy crop among good planters. At the present rate of production, Lancaster county, if its whole area was planted with tobacco, would grow nearly double the entire crop of the United States.

The crop of 1879 was good as well as large. Although there was an extraordinary development of leaf—40 to 50 inches in length having been common—its rapid growth toward the close of the season resulted in giving it that soft, pliable, silky character so much sought for by cigar manufacturers. The average price realized by the growers was also large, having been about 15 cents. All this is the more surprising, as the early part of the season was very unfavorable on account of drought, and several hailstorms did damage in some parts later in the season.

INSPECTION OF TOBACCO.

All tobacco is sold strictly upon its merits. No public system of inspection is desired at the present time, but there is a system of voluntary inspection, which has been found to work admirably. After the work of casing the crop is done the tobacco is carefully stowed away in the large packing establishments, where it is allowed to undergo the final process of sweating. When that operation is completed, which is in August and September, experts are brought out from New York, who perform the work of sampling. Every case is opened, and a number of "hands" are drawn from it, from which a fair average is selected. The samples are marked with the number of the case, and the sampler's signature is attached, and nearly all transactions are made on that basis. These samplers receive 35 cents per case for such service, and when a case of tobacco is found not to correspond with the sample he is held responsible for any damage or loss that may be sustained.

STALKS AS FERTILIZERS.

Tobacco stalks are considered an excellent fertilizer. They are cut into short pieces, and then either thrown on the manure pile or plowed under. Lard scraps are also used by some. In 1878 General Simon Cameron and his neighbor, Colonel Duffey, both large tobacco-growers, used 50 tons of lard scraps on their tobacco lands with satisfactory results. A few planters are accustomed to throw a handful of hen droppings wherever a plant is set. It is found, however, that chicken manure, when applied uncomposted to seed-beds, has frequently a tendency to burn the tender plants.

BLACK-ROOT.

In some years the plants, both in the seed-bed and after being set out, are affected by a disease known as the "black-root". The plants so affected do not die, but after standing comparatively still for a long time revive later in the season, but do not make a good quality of tobacco. It is not known what the agencies are in producing this disease, nor has there been a remedy discovered for it. By some it is believed to be the result of sowing seed continuously in old seed-beds. Seed-beds in newly-cleared ground are said to be entirely free from it.

FOXY TOBACCO.

Loose, sandy soil is the kind where "foxy" tobacco is most found, but all soils and localities, uplands and bottoms, occasionally develop it. Some think it more likely to be the result of drought, accompanied by very warm weather, rather than a matter of soils and situation. This disease is known as "walloon" in the southern states.

RAPID GROWTH DESIRABLE.

Rapid growth during the last two weeks the tobacco remains in the field is highly desirable, and the quality of the leaf is always superior when such is the case. The growth which tobacco will make under favorable circumstances is wonderful, leaves 42 by 30 inches and 47 by 27½ inches in size having been grown in sixty days from the time they were set out. Connecticut Seed-Leaf planted in Lancaster county has, under favorable circumstances, produced leaves 26 by 14 inches in twenty-one days.

TIMBER LAND OF THE COUNTY.

Probably only 12 or 15 per cent. of the area of Lancaster county is now in timber, and during recent years the cultivation of tobacco has contributed much to reduce the timber area. Newly-cleared lands are the best for tobacco culture. A virgin soil seems to contain all the elements required by this voracious feeder, and no old lands are comparable with them.

BY WHOM TOBACCO IS CULTIVATED.

When only a few acres of tobacco are planted by a farmer he and the hired help on the farm attend to it, in addition to the other farm crops; but when a larger area is planted, say from 10 to 30 acres, it is generally given out to croppers on shares, the farmer furnishing the land and the barn and the cropper providing all the labor. The labor being light, much of it is performed by the women and children of the family; so that there is really little or no expenditure in cash on the part of the cropper. Land is seldom rented outright for tobacco-growing, but a few cases of this kind do occur. The rental of land for this purpose is about $60 per acre, and when the season is a good one even this large sum leaves a handsome profit to the renter. In many cases laboring men who have given their attention to tobacco-growing have bought a few acres, for which a single successful season has enabled them to pay.

SECOND TOBACCO CROP.

A second crop is rarely grown. Although this might be done in favorable seasons, when the main crop is cut very early, farmers are content with housing the first growth in good condition. Fields are frequently seen late in the fall, upon which the second growth has been left to take care of itself, that look almost as if no tobacco had been cut from them. This second crop is turned under by good farmers, for the double purpose of enriching the soil and to destroy the numerous insects that feed upon the plant at that time.

SOWING TOBACCO SEED IN THE FALL.

It is the general practice to sow tobacco seed in the spring; but some farmers have tried late fall sowing with excellent results, the plants being stronger and better than spring-grown plants set in the same field. In 1879 a grower neglected to gather all his seed, and that from several plants was scattered by the winter winds. In the spring they came up well, and produced better plants than any he grew in the regular way.

INSURANCE OF TOBACCO-BARNS AND CROPS.

Insurance is as readily effected on tobacco-barns, warehouses, and buildings in which tobacco is handled as on property of a like kind used for other purposes. A company was organized in 1879 to insure tobacco in the field, and a considerable amount was thus insured, the association taking a risk of $150 per acre.

WIDE OR CLOSE PLANTING.

The merits of wide and close planting have been much debated, but very few have taken the trouble to determine the question by experiments carefully conducted and continued for a series of years. So far as is known, Mr. John F. Charles, living near Washington borough, on the banks of the Susquehanna, is the only tobacco planter who has persevered in experiments in this direction. His first experiment was made in 1876. He set out 16,000 plants in rows 3½ feet apart and 33 inches apart in the row. The result was 7,505 pounds of cured tobacco, which he sold at 22 cents per pound through.

The second experiment was with the crop of 1877. The rows were 3½ feet apart, but the plants were set somewhat closer, 18,000 being put upon the same piece of land. The result was 6,580 pounds of marketable tobacco, which sold at 5 cents for fillers, 8 cents for seconds, and 20 cents for wrappers.

The third experiment was made in 1878. As in 1876, the rows were marked out 3½ feet apart, and the plants set out in them at intervals of 33 inches, 16,000 being again planted. The season was far from favorable, and the result gave 5,620 pounds. The price for which it was sold is unknown.

In 1879 the fourth experiment was made, with rows 3½ feet apart and the plants also 3½ feet apart in the rows, planting 16,000 plants. The product was 7,690 pounds.

These results seem to show that wide planting, even when carried to the extreme, as was done in 1879, gives the most favorable results.

The methods practiced in tobacco culture in Lancaster county, with slight variations, are equally applicable to all the counties in the state producing this staple. A brief notice of the soils and the varieties of tobacco planted elsewhere in the state will therefore suffice.

BERKS COUNTY.

This county is greatly diversified in its topographical features, and it has many wide and fertile valleys bounded by rough ridges and mountains. The new red sandstone passes through it, while the soils are very similar to those of Lancaster county. About one-third of the area of the county is underlaid with limestone, but in the southern portion red shales predominate. For the production of tobacco a clayey loam is selected, in preference to a sandy one. The surface soil is brownish in color, with a subsoil of yellow clay, and is warm and dry. Every part of the county, except steep hills, is adapted to the growth of tobacco, and the crop is managed as in Lancaster county, though less skillfully. Reading is the principal tobacco market, and has three or four packing-houses. Good tobacco lands are worth $150 per acre, and such lands will yield 1,500 pounds to the acre. Hands for working in tobacco are rarely employed by the year, but they are paid 80 cents a day, without board, and strippers get 1 cent per pound.

BRADFORD COUNTY.

This is one of the northern counties in the tobacco belt of the state. The surface of the county is uneven, being broken by numerous ridges of high hills. The Susquehanna has numerous feeders within this county, and near the mouths of these are many flats, which are rich and productive. On the highlands the soils are heavier, having a larger content of argillaceous material. The mean summer temperature is much less than in Lancaster and other counties south, being 63° F., and the mean winter temperature approaches 23° F. The average rainfall is 40 inches. A large portion of the county is underlaid with the Chemung and Catskill groups of rocks, consisting of red and blue shales and sandstones, with some limestones. In the river bottoms the soil is a dark chocolate-colored, sandy loam, and on the first bench of the uplands it is of a light brown color generally, often gravelly, varying in color from a light gray to a dark brown. It has a gravelly subsoil of porous yellow clay, which is light and warm. The latter soils are preferred for tobacco. On the river bottoms the leaf grows thick and heavy, and is altogether inferior. Nor does tobacco do well on the heavy soils of the highlands, there being a difference of a week or ten days in the growth and ripening of tobacco on the warm, light soils and on the heavy soils of the highlands. In harvesting the crop the plants are fastened to poles with twine, thirty-six plants being placed on a 12-foot pole. A few growers drive a wire hook in the butt of each plant and hang six plants on a stick four feet long. Tobacco is not scaffolded before housing. The best tobacco soils are worth from $150 to $200 the acre, and with good manuring will yield 2,000 pounds per acre. Wages are $8 to $14 per month, with board, for boys and men; by the day, 50 cents to $1. Cases for packing cost $1 each. The estimated cost of production on best soils is $100 per acre, and the value of the product is $200, or a profit of $100. Profit on thinner tobacco soils, $66 per acre.

BUCKS COUNTY.

This county began to grow tobacco in 1856, since which time there has been an annual increase in acreage. The general surface of the county is undulating, but the ridges of South mountain and the Lehigh hills, in the northern part, encroach upon the Delaware. In the southwestern part of the county the rocks are gneiss, mica-schists, and hornblende, producing a soil of moderate fertility generally, but near the Delaware river it is very productive. The red shales and sandstones, accompanied by conglomerates and limestones, occupy a large portion of the county, making excellent soils. Trap and gneissoid rocks also abound in the ridgy parts of the county, where there are many fertile limestone valleys. The soil preferred for tobacco is what is known as isinglass soil—a light loam on rolling lands, in which particles of mica are abundant. The texture of the tobacco grown on rolling lands is finer than that grown on level lands. Five townships in the southern part of the county are well adapted to the growth of tobacco. The acreage has increased 25 per cent. since 1876, and the quality is much finer, improving with the experience of the farmers. Duck island, in the Delaware river, is noted for its excellent tobacco. Stable manure yields on sandy loams the best results in the culture of tobacco, and about 16 tons of horse manure, at a cost of from $2 50 to $4 per ton, are applied with three or four hundred weight of artificial fertilizers to the acre. Rotation: wheat, grass, corn, tobacco. The quality of the tobacco made is rank. Tobacco plants are set on ridges raised 3 inches above the general level. These ridges are 4 feet apart, and one plant is set at every 30 inches. In 1879 the crop was badly damaged by pole-sweat, at least 50 per cent. having been injured. The tobacco-houses are greatly inferior to those of Lancaster county. There are two packing establishments near Tullytown. The cost of growing one acre, producing 1,500 pounds, is estimated at $125, including manure, which costs $40 per acre; value of product in the barns, 12 cents per pound, or $180 per acre; net profit, $55. Another report gives the cost of labor alone at $100; other expenses, including $65 for manure, at $81; making a total cost per acre of $181. The crop is credited with 1,800 pounds of tobacco, at 14 cents through, or $252, which would give a net profit of $71 per acre.

CHESTER COUNTY.

This county adjoins Lancaster on the east, and partakes largely of its general character in surface and soil features. The Welsh mountains, a sandstone chain, run along its northwestern boundary. South of that lies a wide belt of red shale and sandstone and a considerable area of gneissoid rocks. Chester valley is based on metamorphosed limestone and forms a distinguishing feature in the county. South of the valley lies a belt of Eozoic rocks, consisting of gneiss and mica slates. In this belt serpentine hornblende, trap and feldspar, chrome-iron ore, kaolin, and corundum occur. Tobacco is principally grown in those townships adjoining Lancaster county, and sandy loams are preferred, though limestone and slaty soils are employed in its production. Tobacco culture has increased very rapidly. In 1878 but little more than 100 acres were planted; in 1879 the returns show 487 acres, yielding 633,632 pounds. The crop of 1879 far exceeded any other in quantity as well as in quality, the varieties planted being the same as those grown in Lancaster county. Tobacco-barns are of a poor character, mere temporary make-shifts. The market for tobacco is Lancaster. The cost of producing an acre is variously estimated at from $50 to $67, which would indicate light manuring; the yield per acre is 1,301 pounds.

CLINTON COUNTY.

The west branch of the Susquehanna flows through Clinton county for a distance of 50 miles. As in other counties in central Pennsylvania, the surface is varied by mountains, hills, and valleys, and the timber growth is pine, oak, chestnut, walnut, and hickory. Limestones and sandstones prevail generally throughout the county, but the latter are more common. The soil, both on the uplands and in the valleys, is mostly a sandy loam, this being especially the case along the streams; indeed, there is scarcely an acre in the upper west branch region that is not more or less strewn with broken fragments of sandstone. Yet this soil is generous and kind, and even elevated farms produce crops of all kinds. Limestone is found in nearly every township, but the northwestern portion of the county lies within the limits of the Clearfield coal-basin. The culture of tobacco was begun in this county as early as 1854, some say ten years earlier, but the census of 1850 does not report tobacco among the productions. The crop is now cultivated mainly east of the center of the county. The best tobacco soil is a dark sandy loam, light, warm, and loose, with a red-clay subsoil, and in preparing it it is plowed only once in the fall and again in the spring. Large applications of barn-yard manures are made after plowing and are harrowed in, and the soil is said to increase in productiveness every year, so large is the quantity of manure used. The crop is managed generally as in the southern counties, only that in the preparation of seed-beds the land is frequently burned. In harvesting the plants are speared on laths, and no hooks or twine are used. The tobacco-barns in this county are from 24 to 32 feet wide and of any desired length, and are made as tight as rough boards will make them, and it is estimated that a barn 24 feet wide, 20 feet long, and fourteen tiers high, with a short one under the roof, is sufficient to house one acre of good large tobacco. A barn 24 feet wide and 100 feet long will cost $500. Scaffolds are used in the fields, but it is believed that the color of the tobacco is improved if carried to the barn as soon as cut. Contrary to the usual rule, in assorting and classifying tobacco only two grades are made, wrappers and fillers. Rarely is the third grade, seconds or binders, separated. The growers sell to local dealers, who pack it in boxes 40 inches long, 28 inches wide, and 30 inches deep. The best lands in the county for growing tobacco are rated at $200 to $250 per acre. These lands will grow in a favorable season from 1,800 to 2,000 pounds of tobacco. Inferior tobacco lands, with a capacity for growing 1,000 to 1,200 pounds to the acre, are worth from $100 to $150 an acre. When rented, the best lands bring from $25 to $30 an acre. For working a tobacco crop labor is hired by the day at from 75 cents to $1. The estimated cost of growing an acre in tobacco is $60; average yield on best lands, 1,600 pounds; average price, 8⅓ cents; profit per acre, $73 33. From 2 to 3 acres are generally allotted to the hand. Artificial curing with charcoal, costing 25 cents per bushel, is sometimes practiced in very damp weather.

CUMBERLAND COUNTY.

This county lies in the southeastern portion of the state, directly west of the Susquehanna river, which forms its eastern boundary. Its natural boundary on the north is the Blue mountain, and on the south the South mountain. The surface of the county is comparatively level, especially in the limestone sections, but the slate region is uneven and hilly. Along the South mountain there are numerous tracts which are composed principally of hard, white sandstone. There is also a detached bed of limestone in this portion of the county, although further to the north nearly the entire formation is of this stone. The county is unusually well watered, and the wood is principally oak, hickory, and walnut. Tobacco is grown on limestone loam with clay subsoil, and some on black and yellow slate, but the former is the preferred soil. The eastern half of the county only is well adapted to tobacco culture, and the larger portion of the crop is grown in the central portion of the eastern half—a strip about 16 miles long and 10 wide. As long ago as 1862–'63 a few small lots of tobacco were grown in this county, and little attention was afterward given to it until about 1876, since which time the growth in acreage has been rapid. The increase in product is due, for the most part, to the fact that growers are better informed as to the requirements of the crop in the matter of preparing the soil, kinds of soil, manures, planting, cultivation, and general handling. The product has steadily increased in quality as well as in quantity. About 10 per cent. of the crop is grown on newly-cleared lands, and it may be stated that, in round numbers, about 40 per cent. of the timbered area of the county is adapted to the growth of tobacco. Freshly-cleared lands are always preferred, and there is no perceptible difference between the product of level and that of rolling lands, in case both are equally manured. No artificial fertilizers are used, but stable manure is applied at the rate of from 20 to 40 tons to the acre, at a cost of from $25 to $50, increasing the yield largely, and at the same time improving the quality; and a neglect to use it in the growing of the crop is at once indicated by a loss of from 25 to 50 per cent. of its quantity and value. Wheat generally follows tobacco in the rotation of crops, after which the fields are left in grass for several years, when they are again plowed. In some cases the manure is plowed under, while in others the application is made to the surface and mixed with the soil by means of thorough surface cultivation. The cultivation of the crop and the varieties planted are the same as in Lancaster county. The schedules report the following prices: 20 cents per pound for wrappers, 10 cents for seconds, and 5 cents for fillers, making an average of about 14 cents per pound. The houses in which the tobacco is cured have been mostly built for this special purpose, and some of them are very large. The tobacco is mostly sold at home to dealers from New York and elsewhere. There are two packing establishments in this county, located at Mechanicsburg. The cost of growing an acre of tobacco is estimated at $75.

DAUPHIN COUNTY.

Rocks: Limestones and hills of slate; timber: hickory, oak, ash, walnut, and chestnut. Tobacco is cultivated mainly in the lowlands along the eastern side of the Susquehanna, and on the numerous islands with which that wide stream is everywhere dotted. The crop has greatly increased since 1876, that of 1878 being a very fine one, much better than any of the preceding ones. The varieties grown are the Connecticut Seed-Leaf, Glessner, Mud Island, and Pennsylvania Seed-Leaf. The soil preferred for tobacco is a rich loam, known as bottom lands, and it is said that the first and second crops grown on freshly-cleared bottom lands are superior to any grown subsequently. Twenty four-horse loads of barn-yard manure, the value of which is from $75 to $100, are often applied per acre, the crop being doubled in quantity and greatly improved in quality by such applications. Lime is freely applied to the soil, as much as 100 bushels being used every five years. It takes from fourteen to twenty-one days for tobacco to ripen after being topped, and the average value of the crop through is 7½ cents, fillers bringing 2 to 3 cents, seconds 4 cents, and wrappers 7 to 10 cents. There are packing-houses at Middletown and Conewago.

LEBANON COUNTY.

The best tobacco soils in this county are found along the line where the sandstone and limestone belts join, the preference being given to those on the limestone side, especially in the bottom lands, where water stones or small, round bowlders prevail, but all parts of the county, except the northern portion, are adapted to its growth. Plaster and gypsum are occasionally applied to the hill. Five thousand four hundred plants are usually set to the acre. Transplanting may be done as late as July 5, and forty-five days elapse between planting and topping. The plants are topped to from eight to fourteen leaves, and the time between topping and cutting is about twenty-five days. The plants mature earlier on rich soils than on thin ones, and when ripe are cut with a corn-knife, a saw, or with tobacco shears. There are but few houses built expressly for curing tobacco, and the crop of the county is sold loose at Lancaster and at Lebanon. The best tobacco lands are worth $200 per acre, and will yield in good seasons as high as 2,000 pounds per acre when well manured and properly managed. Inferior lands cost $60, and yield 600 pounds per acre. Good laborers cost $1 25 and board per day during summer, and 75 cents per day, with board, at other seasons of the year, and strippers are paid 1 cent per pound. The cost of growing 100 pounds of tobacco on the best land is $7 94; on the worst lands, $19 28. The quantity of land generally planted to the hand is 2 acres. Three per cent. of the tillable land of the county is planted in tobacco. The following is the cost of growing an acre of tobacco on the best lands in this county:

Dr.		
Making seed-bed		$1 00
Plowing one acre twice		3 00
Manure		52 00
Harrowing and preparing ground		3 00
Planting		2 00
Harrowing and hoeing three times		9 00
Topping, suckering, and worming		10 00
Harvesting		5 00
Use of barn, wagon, laths, etc. (interest on value of)		15 00
Taking down and stripping		20 00
Rent of land (interest on value of)		10 00
Taking to market		5 00
		135 00
Cr.		
1,100 pounds tobacco, at 18 cents	$198 00	
200 pounds tobacco, at 8 cents	16 00	
400 pounds tobacco, at 4 cents	16 00	
		230 00
Estimated profit		95 00

TIOGA COUNTY.

This county adjoins on the north the state of New York, and lies within a belt where there is more than the average rainfall for the state. The surface is rolling, often hilly, and much of the land is rough and mountainous, the ridges being separated from one another by broad valleys, underlaid by the Devonian rocks of the Chemung and Catskill series. Agricultural industry is confined to the valleys, while the steep mountain sides are covered with hemlock, birch, pine, and maple. Angular blocks of conglomerate often cover the mountain slopes, the coal measures a considerable portion of the county, and there are numerous patches of red slate. The siliceous soils predominate. There are large bodies of alluvial, sandy soil, but clayey loams are met with, and the color varies from a dark brown to a yellow. The subsoil is chiefly a red and yellow clay resting on a gravelly bed slightly cemented in places. Stable manure is largely used in the production of the tobacco crop, and cold frames, with glass, are sometimes used in growing plants. The plants are set in ridges, made 3½ feet apart. About 7,000 are considered sufficient for one acre. The crop is suckered generally but once, and that just before harvesting. The plants at harvesting are cut with a hatchet or with a flat piece of thin steel, with a handle and two edges, the instrument being about 6 inches wide and 7 inches long. Sticks with wire hooks are used to some extent in hanging tobacco, but generally the plants are tied to poles with twine. The tobacco-houses are of ordinary character, framed and battened, from 28 to 30 feet wide and from 60 to 250 feet long. The crop throughout is cultivated, handled, and marketed more after the methods pursued in New York than after those usually practiced in Pennsylvania. Wages for good farm hands vary from $120 to $170 a year and board. The erection of tobacco-sheds costs from $2 to $2 50 per lineal foot of barn 4 feet wide. Tobacco culture is a new industry in this county. It was first cultivated near the junction of the Tioga and Cowanesque rivers, and its culture has increased with great rapidity. No tobacco was reported for this county in the census of 1870; but it now reports 292,198 pounds, grown on 234 acres, showing an average yield of 1,249 pounds per acre. The nearest packing establishments are at Elmira, New York.

WESTMORELAND COUNTY.

In this county, lying in the western part of the state, tobacco was first grown in 1878, and the reported production for 1879 was 62,096 pounds, grown upon 54 acres. Limestone soils are preferred for its growth, but the sandy loams of the river bottoms and black-walnut clearings are considered excellent. Fully 75 per cent. of the wooded lands of the county are adapted to the growth of tobacco, and it is said that the quality grown on newly-cleared lands is much superior to that grown on old lands. No fertilizers are used, yet about 1,150 pounds per acre is the reported yield, which would indicate an unusual adaptation of the soil for tobacco. The crop of 1879 sold for 14 cents per pound, a high average. The market for the crop is at Latrobe.

YORK COUNTY.

York is separated from Lancaster county by the Susquehanna river, and in physical characteristics, soils, and geological formations resembles it very much. The conveniences for handling and taking care of the crop are not so extensive as in Lancaster, and as a consequence the prices received are lower by several cents per pound. The lack of experience by those who have recently entered upon the cultivation of tobacco is another reason assigned for the difference in price of the product of the two counties. Improvement in these respects, however, is made every year, and there are already twelve packing-houses established in the county. Tobacco is marketed somewhat later than the crop of Lancaster county, and is generally bought by the same packers. The average price of the crop of 1879 was 10 cents, but the range of prices was from 5 to 15 cents, depending on the skill exercised in curing and handling. This crop has increased from 10 to 25 per cent. annually for four years. The varieties planted are the Connecticut Narrow Leaf, the Connecticut Broad Leaf, Hoover Leaf, Brooklyn Leaf, Valley Green, Kill Island, Glessner, and Pennsylvania Seed-Leaf. The sandy soils require more fertilization, but produce a finer type of tobacco. The tobacco grown on limestone lands is inclined to be rank.

The following table shows the production, acreage, yield per acre, and value in primary markets or farmers' hands of the tobacco crop of Pennsylvania from 1876 to 1879, both inclusive, only the figures for 1879 being from the census returns:

Year.	Production.	Acreage.	Yield per acre.	Value in primary markets.	Value per pound.	Value per acre.
	Pounds.		*Pounds.*		*Cents.*	
1876..................	13,634,744	9,880	1,380	$1,227,126	9.00	$124 20
1877..................	21,630,000	15,450	1,400	1,946,700	9.00	126 00
1878..................	23,550,922	19,625	1,200	2,355,092	10.00	120 00
1879..................	36,943,272	27,566	1,340	4,636,380	12.55	168 19

Chapter XV.

CULTURE AND CURING OF TOBACCO IN TENNESSEE.

The cultivation of tobacco in Tennessee began with the settlement of the state. The early pioneers, those who settled in the fertile valleys of the Watauga, Nolachucky, the Holston, and the French Broad rivers, raised it for their own consumption, and those who planted colonies on the Cumberland river during the last two decades of the eighteenth century brought the seed from the tobacco-growing districts of Virginia and North Carolina. Though grown for many years in a small way, it was not until about the year 1810 that tobacco began to form one of the great staples of the state, the comparatively easy access to the seaboard by the Cumberland, the Ohio, and the Mississippi rivers, and the dependence of the population on New Orleans as a market for their surplus productions, soon awakening a general interest all along the Cumberland river in the production of a crop which occupied less room in their small flatboats and keelboats, in proportion to its value, than any other which could be produced. Montgomery and Smith counties, with portions of Sumner, entered vigorously into its cultivation, and by 1820 several thousand hogsheads were annually carried out in flatboats to New Orleans and exchanged for coffee, sugar, salt, and other commodities. The extinguishment of the Indian titles in western Tennessee, and the throwing of a wide domain into market in 1819, added immensely to the available area for the cultivation of the crop. Experience had demonstrated also that the tobacco grown in the state possessed those qualities most sought after in the European markets. Prices were generally low, but the cost of production was scarcely appreciable, as the acreage in other crops was not decreased in consequence of the tobacco crop, requiring, as it did, the largest amount of attention at a time when the other crops required the least, and the rich, fertile soils, freshly cleared, could in no other way be so well prepared for the growth of corn, oats, and wheat as by planting them for a year or two in tobacco. Probably during the decade between 1820 and 1830 the actual cost of growing tobacco did not exceed $1 per 100 pounds. Most farmers owned their labor, and, even when hired, $50 and board was considered a fair average price for good men during the cropping season, which lasted from March 1 to November 1. From 1830 to 1840 the culture of the crop was widely extended. Henry county, in western Tennessee, headed the list, and in 1840 reported a yield of 9,479,065 pounds, 1,212,604 pounds more than any county grows at the present time. Smith county came next, reporting 3,017,012 pounds; and then in regular order came Sumner, 2,615,100 pounds; Montgomery, 2,549,984 pounds; Wilson, 2,313,000 pounds; Robertson, 1,168,833 pounds; Williamson, 1,126,982 pounds; and Rutherford, 1,089,000 pounds. Stewart, Jackson, and Davidson produced, respectively, 993,495, 859,336, and 334,394 pounds.

The prices which prevailed in 1837 were very low, and many planters who shipped their crops to New Orleans during that year were brought in debt for freight and charges. An account of sales of four hogsheads of tobacco in New Orleans in 1837 makes return of the net proceeds as $22 01, or about $5 50 for a hogshead weighing, net, 1,550 pounds, and another account shows that two hogsheads of tobacco netted $7 04, or $3 52 each, scarcely enough to pay for the casks in which the tobacco was pressed. The two years succeeding, however, show a marked increase in price, and from 4 to 10 cents were frequently paid for ordinary crops. The year 1839 is noted for the high prices paid, but in the succeeding year prices again fell very low, good crops bringing from 2 to 5 cents per pound. In 1841 prices rose, and the crop proved remunerative to the planters. From that period until 1846 prices for good crops, pressed in hogsheads, ranged from 2 to 8 cents. The last-mentioned year was a disastrous one to many dealers, the occurrence of the Mexican war reducing prices to a very low point, from $1 to $3 being generally paid round for crops loose, and planters were glad to dispose of their crops at almost any price. It was not until 1850 that fair prices again prevailed.

About the year 1834 dealers began to put up factories in Clarksville and to purchase loose tobacco. Several establishments for making strips sprang up shortly thereafter, and in 1840 the number of stemmeries had considerably increased. The erection of these stripping establishments gave great animation to this industry, millions of pounds of tobacco being annually brought to Clarksville and prepared for the English trade, and in 1860 there were sixteen of these factories in operation, handling over 2,000,000 pounds of tobacco.

The first effort to establish a market for the sale of tobacco in casks was made in the same place in 1842; but it was a difficult thing to persuade such planters as still adhered to the practice of pressing and shipping their tobacco to New Orleans, influenced also by the agents of the New Orleans houses, to consent to sell in Clarksville. It was not until February, 1845, that warehouses were open for the inspection and sale of tobacco in casks, and from September 1, 1844, to September 1, 1845, there were reported as sold on inspection 900 hogsheads. Encouragement was given to these sales by the merchants and business men of the place, who attended and swelled the list of buyers. Three or four of these warehouses were opened by 1846, and since that period they have been increased, both in size and in number. With the single exception of Louisville, Clarksville opened the first inspection warehouses in the West. A warehouse was opened at Trice's Landing, a point across Red river from Clarksville, in 1847, and at this place the rich product from southern Kentucky was sold, and the sales continued to increase until the opening of the line of railroad to Louisville, in 1860, when a large portion of the production of southern Kentucky found its way to the latter city. The occurrence of the civil war paralyzed the market at New Orleans and Clarksville, and Saint Louis and Louisville swelled into the largest tobacco markets in the West, a position they have maintained to the present time.

Nashville also was a point where some business was done in tobacco as early as 1835. In 1840 the receipts amounted to 4,000 hogsheads, but the hogsheads were then light as compared with those of the present day, and until 1850 they remained about stationary, varying from 4,000 to 5,000 hogsheads annually. About 1850 two tobacco stemmeries were put up, which prepared from 125 to 150 hogsheads of strips and put up leaf for the New Orleans market, the tobacco being bought loose, and being grown principally in Williamson county, with small quantities from Wilson, Maury, and Robertson counties. During the decade between 1850 and 1860 the trade increased considerably, reaching between 7,000 and 8,000 hogsheads annually, the weight of the hogsheads having been increased about 20 per cent, and the handling of the crop being greatly improved through the influence of the local market. Mr. A. Hamilton established the first regular sales warehouse about the year 1851, which stimulated the trade at this point, and the great losses resulting from shipments to New Orleans made the opening of local markets much easier. The sales of tobacco in Nashville closed in 1861, and the receipts were very light, dropping from 7,000 to 500 hogsheads. A great part of it was kept in the country, and during the war dealers from Louisville and from other places bought it up on speculation. The business did not greatly revive until 1872.

In the territory tributary to Nashville the crops of 1878 and 1879 were small. About three-fifths of the total receipts of this market come from the Upper Cumberland River district, one-fifth from western Tennessee, and the remainder from the Clarksville district.

There are at Paris, in Henry county, six tobacco factories, only three of which are in operation. These factories buy annually about 400,000 pounds of tobacco, paying from 3 to 8 cents per pound for fillers and from 10 to 15 cents for wrappers. One hundred and sixty hogsheads of strips, or 208,000 pounds, were put up in the county during the season of 1879-'80.

In Clarksville, while the annual sales of leaf tobacco in hogsheads vary considerably with the success or the partial failure of each crop, there is always a considerable amount sold loose to factories for the manufacture of strips. In 1879 the number of hogsheads of strips was less than for many years. In that year five factories in operation in and around the town reported an aggregate make of strips of 544 hogsheads, weighing 1,250 pounds net, a total of 680,000 pounds. The usual number of hogsheads put up varies from 800 to 2,000.

The following were the shipments from Clarksville—mainly from planters' hands—for eight years, 1873 to 1880, inclusive: 1873, 15,607 hogsheads; 1874, 15,161; 1875, 4,245; 1876, 16,737; 1877, 11,233; 1878, 22,554; 1879, 14,434; 1880, 16,566.

TOPOGRAPHY, GEOLOGY, AND SOILS OF TENNESSEE.

In natural facilities for transportation Tennessee is unsurpassed, the Mississippi river washing the western boundary, and the Cumberland and the Tennessee, with their sources in other states, sweep in concentric curves through the fairest agricultural and mineral districts of the state. The state has eight well-marked topographical divisions:

1. The Unaka mountains, on the east, swelling in great ridge-like masses, some of which attain an elevation of more than 6,000 feet above the sea, upon the summits of which the flora of Canada is found. This division has an area of 2,000 square miles

2. The valley of eastern Tennessee, lying between the Unaka mountains on the east and the Cumberland mountains on the west, a succession of minor ridges and valleys running northeast and southwest—a great fluted trough, where inequalities of surface, when viewed from the high elevations on either side, melt into a common plain. This valley has an average elevation of 1,000 feet above the sea, and covers an area of 9,200 square miles.

3. Next in order going west is the Cumberland table-land, a high plateau that rises abruptly 1,000 feet from the valley of eastern Tennessee. Its eastern edge presents a formidable, bold, cliff-lined rampart, but its western edge is everywhere jagged in outline, notched and scalloped by deep indentations, and shooting many bold spurs and outlines far out into the western plain at its foot. It is generally higher at its southern termination, and covers 5,100 square miles.

4. Resting against the last division on the east, and extending to the Tennessee river in its reflex course across the state, are the terrace lands, or rim lands, which have an average elevation of 900 feet, the surface, however, tilting toward the northwest, so as to reach a depression of not more than 500 feet above tide-water. This division is a plain, which has been cut and eroded by numberless streams until its once level surface presents generally a highly diversified character. Its area, not including the central limestone basin, is 9,300 square miles, and furnishes by far the most important tobacco district of the state.

5. In the center of the last division, and surrounded by it, is the great limestone central basin of the state, elliptical in form, the major axis running northeast and southwest, and depressed about 300 feet below the rim lands that surround it. This is the garden of Tennessee, comprising an area of 5,450 square miles, and is the center of population, wealth, and influence. It produces every crop grown in the state.

6. The Tennessee river, in its regular course across the state, has hewn out a narrow valley, with spurs from the rim lands at places running down to the river, but sending out subordinate valleys, sometimes 20 or 25 miles in length, before they are lost in the rim lands. The surface is broken and hilly, and marshy spots, often covered by cypress forests, occur at intervals along the river. This valley has an area of 1,200 square miles, and an elevation above the sea of 350 feet.

7. West of the Tennessee river is a great plain, gently undulating, which slopes toward the Mississippi river. No hard rocks appear, except here and there a sandstone bowlder. The streams, cutting through low, muddy banks, wind on their tortuous courses with feeble currents through the district, and find an outlet into the Mississippi with only one or two exceptions—the largest tributary of the Tennessee from the west side being the Big Sandy river. Frequently furrowed with wide river valleys, the plain has an average width of 84 miles, and abruptly terminates in a series of rockless bluffs, that overlook the Mississippi and its lowlands. In superficial extent this division covers 8,850 square miles, with an average elevation of 500 feet above the sea.

8. The last division of the state is confined to the low alluvial bottoms of the Mississippi river. It is often dotted with lakes, marshes, cypress forests, and canebrakes, and, as is usual with the bottoms of the Mississippi, a chain of lakes and marshes lies back from the river a few miles, the best drained soils being those lying upon its immediate banks.

The tobacco area is, for the most part, confined to a belt beginning at the bluffs overlooking the Mississippi river and extending along the northern boundary of the state easterly to a point in Pickett county, 12 miles east of where the Cumberland river first crosses the line between Kentucky and Tennessee. The southern limit of this belt is very irregular. Beginning at the southern boundary of Dyer county, it runs nearly east until it strikes the Benton county line, where it dips to the south for a few miles, inclining northeastward after it crosses the river, so as to include Charlotte, in Dickson county; then on by Ashland City, in Cheatham county, taking in the whole of Robertson and the northern part of Sumner county. Just after passing the eastern limit of Sumner county it turns south, so as to embrace Trousdale county and the northeastern corner of Wilson, and thence through Smith, Putnam, Jackson, Overton, and Clay counties, six or eight miles south and east of the Cumberland river, to the Kentucky line, the whole district embracing about 5,550 square miles. To this may be added the southern and eastern parts of Williamson county and a limited area in eastern Tennessee. Unicoi and Hawkins counties produce the largest crops of tobacco grown in eastern Tennessee, but neither of them reach 100,000 pounds.

It must not be inferred that the soils in the other portions of the state are not suited to the production of tobacco, although it is grown as a staple crop mainly within the limits mentioned, as it can be cultivated profitably in nearly every county in the state, and experiments made on the sandy soils of the Cumberland plateau have shown that even there a fine manufacturing leaf may be produced.

The soils in Obion and Dyer counties adapted to the growth of tobacco are calcareo-siliceous in character, often of an ashen color and consistence, sometimes of a reddish cast, occasionally black, and now and then mulatto-colored. These soils are soft, light, and very loose when first cleared, and contain a large amount of calcareous matter, which occurs in nodules or concretions of carbonate of lime. The subsoil is usually of yellowish clay, the humus is deep, and the arboreal growth dense and large. These soils are very durable, and, when the seasons are favorable, yield larger crops than any others in the state. Three kinds of soils, according to the nomenclature of the farmers, prevail in Dyer and Obion counties, viz, the black, the ash-colored, and the mulatto. The black is deep, with an open subsoil, through which the water percolates rapidly, and is very productive. The native growth is gum, tulip tree, box-elder, elm, linn, cypress, hackberry, and occasionally black oak and walnut. The proportion of this soil is estimated to be one-sixth, and it is more highly prized for corn, small grain, and the grasses than any other, but some farmers prefer it for tobacco, though tobacco grown upon it is large, coarse, and bony. The ash-colored soil, though lying at a higher elevation than the black, is close, compact, and often water-soaked, the native growth being hornbeam, tupello gum, and pin oak. Properly subsoiled and underdrained, this soil produces herds' grass luxuriantly, and when aerated will grow the cereals well, as well as tobacco of good quality. Usually, however, it is avoided for the growth of tobacco and wheat, because if not well drained tobacco will "french", and wheat will be injured, if not destroyed, by rust. This soil occupies about one-tenth of the area of the two counties. The mulatto land, occupying the highest elevation, is grayish on the top and mulatto below, and prevails to a much larger extent than both of the others. The native growth is tulip tree, white ash, sugar-tree, elm, white and red oak, black gum, black and white walnut, mulberry, honey locust, and coffee-nut, with an undergrowth of papaw, red-bud, dogwood, and sometimes hazel-nut. This, for all purposes, is regarded as the most valuable soil in the two counties under consideration. It occupies a rolling surface, which rises sometimes into hills 100 feet high, in the western part of the counties of Dyer and Obion. By a large majority of farmers this soil is preferred for tobacco, wheat, and cotton. The mulatto soil pulverizes more finely than the black, does not become so wet or so dry, and forms the bulk of the farming lands in the two counties. The black occupies a more level surface, and, it is said, will stand more constant cropping than the ash-colored, and does not wash, in consequence of the level surface upon which it rests. The tobacco of Obion and Dyer counties is noted for its large size, wide leaves, uniform brown color, and fitness for making strips.

In Weakley county the soils vary greatly in productive capacity, the western portion of the county being generally fertile and the timber large. The principal growth is black oak, interspersed with white oak, post oak, hickory, black gum, ash, and dogwood, with but few tulip trees. In other places the tulip tree predominates, associated with white oak, sweet gum, hickory, post oak, black gum, and dogwood. The lands presenting the best growth are generally level, are of a mulatto color, sometimes dark brown, and are especially adapted to the growth of corn, tobacco, and wheat. The soils east of Dresden are called "the barrens", and are divided into "hickory barrens", on which the hickory tree predominates, interspersed with dogwood and black gum; "black-jack barrens," which have a thin soil; and "post-oak and hickory barrens", in which the soil is intermediate in character between the two previously mentioned. All the "barren" lands are well adapted to the production of a fine quality of tobacco. The soil, composed mostly of decayed vegetable matter, is incumbent on a red clay, beneath which is a reddish sand, and when properly cared for is of great durability. The best tobacco lands in Weakley county lie between the northern and middle forks of the Obion river, and include about 170 square miles. Three classes of soils are recognized by the farmers as suited to tobacco: the tulip-tree lands, the black-jack lands, and the bottom lands. The first makes a very leafy tobacco, that cures a brown and piebald color, and makes a wrapper suitable for navy or common plug. The tobacco grown on old black-jack lands usually cures up a dark brown, sometimes of a yellowish piebald color. The brown makes a good German shipper, and the bright tobacco is mainly used in the manufacture of plug. Tobacco grown on freshly cleared black-jack lands always cures up a bright color, and the leaf is oily, compact, elastic, and of small fiber; that grown upon bottom lands is large, coarse, dark in color, very porous, and is only suited for making strips for the English market.

In the barrens the black-jack is dying out and the red oak is taking its place. The black-jack is fed upon the top-dressing of potash left by the annual fires, and in every state in which inquiries have been instituted it grows with vigor upon suitable soils, only where fires annually consume the dead grasses, and it dwindles into feeble vitality as these conflagrations grow less frequent, it having long been known that no tree of the forest is richer in potash, and the failure of this food soon produces decay and death.

The same character of barren soil, characterized by the same forest growth, prevails in the northern part of Carroll county, where tobacco is grown. On Givens' creek the soil is of singular excellence, the timber growth being tulip tree, red oak, white oak, beech, black gum, sweet gum, hackberry, and catalpa. This is a favorite soil for the growth of tobacco, making an article with all the fineness of fiber of the black-jack lands and all the leafiness of the tulip-tree lands. On the low ridges bounding the streams black-jack, post oak, and chestnut abound, and the soil is of the same general character as that in the barrens of Weakley county, and is well adapted to the growth of tobacco. It is a black, sandy loam, with a deep red clay subsoil, which, however, is sometimes sandy. The bottom lands were once boggy, but during the past twenty-five years they have been filled up by the washings from the adjacent hills, and partake of the same general character as the hillside soils, but are more durable, and produce excellent tobacco. On the road leading from Huntingdon to Paris there is a sandy soil, resembling that which prevails in the northern part of Henry county, upon which some of the finest yellow tobacco of the West is grown.

In Benton county black-jack and post-oak soils prevail in the southwest, where are found limestone and sandstone. These are the first hard rocks *in situ* met with in going east. The soils in the northern part of the county are dark in color, with a reddish subsoil, and are characterized by a growth of the tulip tree, white oak, hickory, and red oak. In the eastern part of the county many high cherty ridges prevail, and the soil has a large amount of angular cherty gravel in its composition, being very much like the soils of Montgomery and adjoining counties, hereafter described.

The geological formations of Henry county will indicate the character of the soils. All that part of the county lying west of a line drawn north and south through Paris, the county-seat, belongs to the La Grange sands of the Tertiary. In this part of the county the soils are mellow and siliceous, loamy, working kindly, but very easily washed, and are very much of the same character as those already described as lying in the eastern part of Weakley county. They are excellent for tobacco, wheat, and cotton. The subsoil is reddish in color, and inclined to be sandy, rather than clayey. A belt lying parallel with this, on the east, belongs to the flatwoods of the Tertiary, in which there are local accumulations of white clay, which make the soil in places wet, and scarcely arable without drainage. Then comes a belt, six miles wide, known as the Ripley sands of the Cretaceous formation, and the soil of this belt is very kind and productive. Many of the hills are capped by a ferruginous sandstone, which is generally disintegrated into a friable, easily-cultivated soil. This soil, with the formations already mentioned, is mainly great strata of sands and laminated clays, covered with a thick bed of humus. The remains of the drift formation, or, as locally called, orange sand, are found over all this portion of the county. The eastern line of this belt marks the termination of the more recent formations of western Tennessee. Between this and the Tennessee river is a ridge, considerably elevated, known as Tennessee ridge, which divides the waters of the Tennessee from those of the Mississippi. Here appear the Upper Silurian rocks, and the character of the soil changes altogether, sandy and clayey accumulations giving place to cherty hills, and the soil, though fertile, is filled with masses of angular gravel. Some of the sub-Carboniferous rocks also appear. East of the ridge the surface soon becomes level or gently rolling, and is underlaid with red clay, more or less intermingled with gravel. The timber growth of the county is much diversified, elm, ash, beech, maple, locust, mulberry, hornbeam, dogwood, white oak, post oak, and red oak being found in great abundance, some white oaks being 6 feet in diameter. Several varieties of soil are recognized, among others a gray, gravelly soil; a stiff, red, clayey soil; a black loam with clayey subsoil; a red loam, clayey or sandy, and a grayish sandy loam, the last and the first being preferred for growing the yellow tobacco, the second and third for shipping tobacco, and the red sandy loam for a light manufacturing leaf. The soil in the northern part of the county is noted for its capacity for growing the finest yellow tobacco raised in the state, and in all the other parts of the county a large leafy tobacco is grown, which is used largely for making strips for the European markets.

Passing now across the Tennessee river, we enter upon a group of counties which, in geological and topographical features and in the character of the soil, very much resemble each other. These counties are Humphreys, Dickson, Houston, Stewart, Cheatham, Montgomery, Robertson, the northern part of Sumner, Macon, Clay, and a part of Jackson. They all belong to that division of the state known as the rim lands, and are referred to the sub-Carboniferous formation. The soils of these counties, though similar, may be divided into several sub-varieties: 1. Calcareo-siliceous soils; 2. Barren soils; 3. White clayey soils; and 4. Alluvial soils.

The calcareo-siliceous soils occupy nearly all the northern part of Stewart county, a part of Dickson and Cheatham, and nearly the whole of Montgomery and Robertson counties, the northern part of Sumner, a part of Macon, and nearly all of Clay county. It forms the soil of what is known as the Lithostrotion bed, and is composed for the most part of variable proportions of humus, commingled with silica, alumina, and carbonate of lime, the quantity of oxide of iron being so large that it gives a deep red color to the subsoil. After being brought into cultivation, the dark loam of the surface, by being intermingled with the red subsoil, changes to a chocolate color. Stiffer than other calcareous soils, it is not so liable to wash when the surface is moderately broken, having generally underlying it cherty beds, which alternate with beds of clay and supply a natural drainage. In wet weather these beds take off the superfluous moisture, and in dry weather the thick beds of tenacious clay beneath supply moisture to the growing crops. The soil is strong and durable, and never fails to produce fair crops when well cultivated, whether the seasons be wet or dry. The surface of the country is usually broken, and hopper-shaped sink-holes and wide, circular, pond-like depressions are nearly everywhere met with; not so frequently, however, as seriously to impair the value of the land for cultivation. The characteristic timber is red oak, black-jack, hickory, tulip tree, white oak, and, near the streams, walnut, black gum, ash, elm, sycamore, and beech. This soil has long been recognized as the very best in the state for tobacco, the quality grown upon it being fine, yet rich and oily, resembling the softness and pliancy of a kid glove, and for years it stood at the head of all classes of export tobacco. Outside of the counties under consideration and a few lying contiguous in Kentucky this peculiar type of tobacco is grown nowhere else in the Mississippi valley. For many years it was a great favorite in the market; but the recent change in the taste of consumers has diminished its popularity and restricted its use. Clarksville, the center of this district, was long famous in the tobacco marts of the world.

The second character of soil in this group of counties is light in color, with a porous, yellowish clayey subsoil, in which a large amount of whitish chert is intermingled. It is usually fine grained and infertile; nevertheless, when first cleared, it produces tobacco which, though small, is very fine.

This white clayey soil is interspersed without any regularity, a considerable body being found in the eastern part of Stewart county, the northern part of Cheatham, the southeastern part of Montgomery, the southern part of Robertson, and a large portion of Macon. This soil is close, compact, water-soaked, difficult to till, and is characterized by the growth of sweet gum and water oaks. The surface is usually a dead level, and wherever elevations occur within the boundaries of such places the soil is open and productive, but it lacks drainage, and is deficient in humus. In a few places, where well drained, it has been known to produce a fine type of tobacco.

Some of the alluvial soils, when well drained, grow a very fine type of tobacco, especially the lowlands on Dry creek, in Stewart county; on Red river, in Montgomery and Robertson counties; and on Buzzard creek, Sulphur fork, and Miller's creek, in the last-mentioned county. Generally, however, the rich uplands in all the counties under consideration are preferred for tobacco.

The remaining counties in the tobacco belt of the state, viz, Trousdale, Wilson, Smith, and the river basins of Jackson and Clay, have a rich calcareous soil, derived from the crumbling down of the limestones belonging to the Cincinnati group of the Lower Silurian formation. This soil is dark-brown in color, very loose, and very fertile; has often intermingled with it limestone gravel, and sometimes chert; is generally thirsty, and will not stand a drought as well as the calcareo-siliceous soils of the rim lands. Nevertheless, if the season is sufficiently wet, it will yield larger crops than any other soil in middle Tennessee. The subsoil is pale yellow, and is inclined to be porous. The surface is generally broken into large, mound-like protuberances, which, though fertile to the top, are liable to be denuded of their soil by heavy rain-storms. Though employed for the production of tobacco, this soil does not usually produce a fine leaf, being large but bony, with thin web and large fibers, lacks oil, and when cured often resembles a lifeless oak leaf. This region is admirably suited to the growth of blue-grass and to the breeding and raising of cattle.

It only remains to note the character of the soil that prevails in two detached areas in the state in which tobacco is grown for market, viz: A part of Williamson county, and a portion of Unicoi and other counties in eastern Tennessee. The soil of Williamson county is of the same character as that last described, and needs no further mention, while that in Unicoi is a micaceous, sandy soil, often clayey, and varies greatly with the formation. Where the dolomite limestones in eastern Tennessee form the foundation rock the soil is highly calcareous and magnesian in its character, and sometimes a chert, which is associated with the dolomite, preponderates. The soil then is thin and inclined to be gravelly or sandy. Sandstones belonging to the Potsdam age also abound, and the soil derived from its disintegration is very infertile. In the coves a commingling frequently of all these constituents gives a very loose, mellow, and productive soil. The soils in the metamorphic areas are generally good, being derived from the gneiss and trap rocks of the district. These soils very much resemble those about Asheville, North Carolina, where a considerable amount of fine yellow tobacco is grown; and the recent culture of tobacco in Unicoi county has been stimulated by the prices paid for the tobacco grown in the adjoining counties of North Carolina, with which its tobacco culture is identical.

CLIMATE.

Tennessee has a climate neither very wet nor very dry. The heat is not extreme in summer, nor is the cold in winter so intense as to interfere with the ordinary occupations of its inhabitants. The average degree of cold in winter is indicated by the limit of domestic ice-houses, which would be a line east and west through the center of the state. North of this line it rarely happens that the cold of winter is not severe enough to make a bountiful supply of ice, while south of it the ice seasons are so infrequent that it is not considered profitable to construct ice-houses, and in all the tobacco-growing districts of the state the winter frosts are sufficient to ameliorate the soil. Along the median line which marks the southern limit of ice-houses the mean temperature of the year is about 57° in the valley of eastern Tennessee, 58° in middle, and 59° in western Tennessee, a range, in traversing the state from east to west, of 3°, partly due to elevation. Along the southern boundary of the state the annual mean is about 1° higher than on the corresponding longitude of the middle parallel, while on the northern boundary it will be found as much lower, thus giving an approximate range from south to north of 3°, especially in the valley of eastern Tennessee.

From observations made by the Signal Service at Knoxville, extending from January 1, 1871, to October 31, 1880, the mean spring temperature is 57°.4; summer 75°.2; autumn, 56°.8; winter, 39°.6. The greatest difference between the lowest and the highest temperature recorded in any one year was 109°. The highest recorded temperature was 100°, and the lowest −14°. The prevailing winds were from the southwest. The mean annual precipitation for the same period was 53.54 inches.

In Memphis the period of observation extended from February 28, 1871, to October 31, 1880, and the mean annual temperature of spring was 61°.4; summer, 79°.4; autumn, 60°.2; winter, 42°.7. Extreme range of the thermometer any one year, 97°; highest recorded temperature, 101°.5; lowest, —2°; mean annual precipitation, 53.98 inches; prevailing winds, southwest.

Near Clarksville, Professor William M. Stewart made meteorological observations for the Smithsonian Institution for nearly a quarter of a century. From these observations it appears that January is the coldest month, the mean for that month being 34°.08; then December, 38°.54; February, 41°; November, 46°.45; March, 47°.30; October, 57°.17; April, 57°.84; May, 64°.98; September, 69°; June, 72°.14; August, 74°.85; July, 76°.32, being the hottest month in the year. The number of days between killing frosts varied within this period from 173 to 228, the average being 189. The mean of the rainfall for twenty-one years was 45.712 inches, the lowest being 33.8, and the highest 60 inches. Within this period the thermometer did not reach a higher point than 99°, and the lowest was —8°.

TOBACCO DISTRICTS OF TENNESSEE.

Tennessee has three well-defined tobacco districts, as recognized by the trade, each producing types more or less distinct:

1. West Tennessee tobacco district.
2. Clarksville tobacco district.
3. Upper Cumberland River tobacco district.

THE WEST TENNESSEE DISTRICT.

This district embraces all the tobacco-growing area lying between the Mississippi river on the west and the Tennessee river on the east. This region is well adapted to the growth of cotton, fluctuating in cultivation between that staple and tobacco. When cotton is high and tobacco low a comparatively small amount of tobacco is grown, and when tobacco is high and cotton is low the acreage of the latter crop is largely decreased. When both staples bear good prices, it is no uncommon sight to see large fields of both cotton and tobacco on the same farm.

VARIETIES OF TOBACCO PLANTED.

A large number of varieties of the tobacco-plant are grown in western Tennessee, prominent among them being the White Stem, Orinoco, Yellow Pryor, Blue Pryor, Kentucky Bull Face, One Sucker, Little Yellow, Nimblewill, Thickset, Sleek Stem, Twistbud, and many others with local names.

The White Stem has a long, narrow leaf, which cures up with good body and of a dark-brown color usually, but the stem is very large and out of proportion to the leaf. It is probably not identical with the White Stem of Virginia, which has weeping leaves. The leaf is of bad shape for wrappers, but is not ruffled about the base of the stem. The Orinoco grows better on thin soils than the other varieties, ripens about two weeks earlier than the Yellow Pryor, and is preferred by many on account of its peculiar sweetness. The Yellow Pryor will stand on the hill longer, resisting field-fire, and will ripen more perfectly than any other variety planted in western Tennessee. The Blue Pryor is probably more extensively cultivated in Weakley county than in any other. It breaks but little in handling, and resembles very much the Yellow Pryor, but makes more pounds to the acre. The Kentucky Bull Face is very valuable for making strips. The One Sucker is the "lazy man's pride", because its vitality is so feeble that it sends out only one crop of suckers after being topped. It has, however, a very long, narrow leaf, coarse in texture, and is suited for scarcely any purposes of manufacturing. This variety sunburns easily when cut, and when growing every leaf extends downward until it touches the ground, making "luggy" tails, the only redeeming quality being its weight and usually large yield. It is called by some Lizard-tail. Little Yellow makes a nice wrapper. It has a well-shaped leaf, drooping from the top and widening for about one-third of its length, and then gradually coming to a wide, well-rounded point. Grown upon suitable soils, it cures up a bright yellow, which commands a high price; but when planted upon a rich, clayey loam, it develops a rich, heavy shipping tobacco. Nimblewill has a leaf of the same shape as the White Stem, but is coarser in texture, and is not popular. The Twistbud, so named from the habit which the plant has of developing a screw-shaped bud with the terminal leaves twisted, has narrow leaves, growing close together, and is chiefly commended for its hardiness and its disposition to grow very heavy. The Thickset is but little cultivated. The Sleek Stem makes a valuable "shipper". The Yellow Pryor, Blue Pryor, Little Yellow, Orinoco, and Sleek Stem are generally preferred, some in one county and some in another. The tendency is now largely toward the White Burley.

SOILS PREFERRED FOR TOBACCO.

It is universally true throughout western Tennessee that rich upland soils with a clayey subsoil will produce a leaf much finer in texture than the alluvial soils, and with much better body, but not so large. When the same variety of tobacco is planted upon these different soils the quality differs so materially that it can rarely be used for the same purposes. The following will approximate the proportions of grades for the several counties in western Tennessee:

Counties.	Bright wrappers.	Dark shipping.	Fillers.	Nondescript.
	Per cent.	Per cent.	Per cent.	Per cent.
Dyer	....	50	25	25
Obion	....	50	30	20
Weakley	....	50	20	30
Benton	....	50	....	50
Henry, northern part	20	5	50	25
Henry, western part	40	30	20	10
Henry, eastern and southern parts	5	30	10	55

The improvement during the past decade has been very marked in Henry county, the proportion of bright wrapper having been greatly increased, owing to the local demand of manufacturers; and while there has been a disposition on the part of farmers living in the southern and eastern parts of the county to curtail production, the disposition among those living in the northern and western portions has been equally as pronounced in extending the cultivation. Tobacco for domestic consumption pays a handsome profit, but raising tobacco for export scarcely pays expenses. In the northern and western sections tobacco suited for domestic manufacture can be grown, but in the southern and eastern portions only a heavy export tobacco for the most part is raised. In Dyer, Obion, Weakley, and Benton counties, where heavy tobacco only is made, the tendency toward diminished production is apparent. In these counties there has been no improvement in the quality for ten years or more.

Tobacco in western Tennessee, on freshly-cleared lands, is not so rich or oily, or of such good body, as on old lands, but is larger and brighter in color and finer in texture, the finer qualities being produced upon rolling lands. It is estimated that fully one-third of the crop planted each year is upon newly-cleared lands. For the production of the finer grades the soils should be well drained and not too rich.

FERTILIZATION AND ROTATION OF TOBACCO.

The returns show that in a few localities, as in Benton county, 50 per cent. of the old lands planted in tobacco are well treated with stable manure, one correspondent being of the opinion that three-fourths of the area planted has an application of from one to one and a half tons of stable manure per acre, at a cost of $10. This is an exception, however, to the general practice, for in Dyer county one-fourth only of the area cultivated is fertilized and in Obion county not 10 per cent.; in Henry county, from 1 per cent. on the Tennessee river to 50 per cent. in the northern and western portions. In Weakley county not 5 per cent. of the tobacco area is fertilized, and but a very small quantity of manure is hauled out, only such fertilizers as accumulate about the barnyards being generally carried out in the spring and scattered upon the old lands intended for tobacco, and sometimes manure is put into the hills. Newly cleared lands are never manured. All concur in the statement that the yield, even on good lands, will be increased 20 per cent. and the quality improved in weight and body by manuring.

In the more westerly counties three successive crops of tobacco can be taken from freshly-cleared soils without any apparent diminution in their fertility; but in Henry, Benton, and Carroll, and the eastern parts of Weakley, soil deterioration progresses at the rate of 20 per cent. per annum in the absence of fertilizers, except on rich bottom lands, which may be cultivated for many years without any perceptible decrease in yield.

In Henry county clover and stock pease are largely used to renovate such lands as have been impoverished by the cultivation of tobacco. In Benton county also stock pease, turned under when green, have proved to be very effective in reclaiming the soil. In the more westerly counties the general rotation is tobacco, wheat, and clover, and this is kept up indefinitely on tobacco lands.

The following statement shows the production, acreage, yield per acre, value of crops in farmers' hands or in primary markets, value per pound, and the value per acre of the tobacco crops of western Tennessee for the years 1876 to 1879, inclusive, only the figures for 1879 being from census returns:

Year.	Production.	Acreage.	Yield per acre.	Value of crop in farmers' hands.	Value per pound.	Value per acre.
	Pounds.		*Pounds.*		*Cents.*	
1876......	13,837,150	18,055	730.00	$890,414	6.50	$47 45
1877......	9,505,210	13,294	715.00	570,312	6.00	42 90
1878......	9,535,240	13,336	715.00	476,762	5.00	35 75
1879......	7,655,346	10,666	717.73	401,140	5.24	37 61

These estimates will all show larger crops than are reported in the commercial transactions of the country, because a considerable part of the product is retained at home for domestic consumption. In that portion of this district producing tobacco as a staple, embracing the six counties of Benton, Carroll, Dyer, Henry, Obion, and Weakley, the product of 1879 was 7,294,411 pounds, grown upon 9,781 acres, an average of 746 pounds per acre, and the remaining fourteen counties during the same year produced 360,935 pounds on 885 acres, an average of 408 pounds. A very small portion of this product, which is grown upon small patches, ever finds its way even to primary markets.

CLARKSVILLE DISTRICT.

This district comprises Montgomery, Robertson, Cheatham, Humphreys, Dickson, Houston, and Stewart counties, in Tennessee, and several adjoining counties in Kentucky, which are described in the chapter on Kentucky. It was the well-deserved fame of the Clarksville leaf which first induced European buyers to leave the seaboard for the interior.

The acreage of tobacco in the district in 1879 was about 10 per cent. greater than in 1878, but 30 per cent. less than in 1877 and 50 per cent. greater than in 1876. The yield per acre in the census year was about equal to that of 1878, 15 per cent. less than in 1877, and 20 per cent. greater than in 1876, and the quality of the crop of 1879 was 10 per cent. better than in 1878, 10 per cent. worse than in 1877, and 5 per cent. better than in 1876.

VARIETIES OF TOBACCO GROWN.

The varieties of tobacco planted are numerous, and correspond closely to those in the Kentucky part of the district, most prominent among them being the Orinoco, Yellow Pryor, Blue Pryor, Yellow Mammoth, and Morrow. The Yellow Mammoth, when grown upon rich soils, is inclined to be coarse and harsh, but when planted on the thin whitish soils which prevail in some portions of the district it makes a very fine Swiss wrapper. This variety has a large, broad leaf, and stands long on the hill after it is fully ripe, becoming more yellow and better up to the time of cutting. The tobacco of this district, under the name of "Clarksville Leaf", is tough and strong, large, fine fibered, silky and oily, is of a blackish brown or chestnut color, retaining well its strength and elasticity after passing through the sweat, making it specially useful for cigar and spinning purposes, and is consumed mainly in Germany, Austria, Switzerland, England, Italy, and France, as indicated in the description of the part of the Clarksville district lying in Kentucky. There are many variations of this standard raised in various portions of the district having a general likeness, and too distinct from any other growth of the West to be classed as anything else than "Clarksville".

The African leaf, which goes to the Guinea coast, is used in a singular way. The negroes dip the bundles into a pot of boiling lard and then hang them up to drip and dry, and the leaf is then made into huge cigars, a foot or more long. A circle is then made, the cigar passed from hand to hand, and the smoke swallowed, until, one by one, the smokers fall back insensible from tobacco drunkenness.

SOILS ADAPTED TO THE GROWTH OF TOBACCO IN THE CLARKSVILLE DISTRICT.

On heavy clay soils, long cleared and heavily manured, the tobacco leaf is very thick, heavy, and fatty, and cures up a dark or blackish-brown color. Grown on thin land and poor ridges, the tobacco is light and thin. A slight admixture of sand and gravel in the soil is no disadvantage, but when in excess the plant blisters in the hot sun before it ripens and the product is much damaged. A soil with an excess of vegetable matter produces an overgrown, coarse article, and the tobacco ripens too rapidly to insure the requisite amount of gum. For this reason alluvial lands on the streams are not so well adapted to its growth as uplands, where the soil, though thin, is fertile. Some of the finest tobacco grown in the Clarksville district is raised upon soils not three inches deep, where the prevailing timber is black-jack and hickory. When grown upon such soils it has a fine, smooth, silky texture, small stem and fibers, and a lively, rich brown color, and is very elastic, oily, and soft. Rich, heavy shipping leaf may be grown upon river and creek bottoms when well drained, and when the alluvial deposits have not an excess of vegetable matter. The best tobacco lands in the district, or rather those which grow the quality which has given character to the region, are characterized by a brownish loam, resting upon a deep red subsoil, and underneath the latter a stratum of chert, which, alternating with clayey beds, rests finally upon limestone at a greater or less depth. Such a soil as this is made warmer in the spring by the excellent drainage induced by the cherty beds, and is kept cool in summer by the constant but gradual evaporation from the underlying clay. Three good effects result from the peculiar physical condition of the soil: 1. The earth being warm in spring, the plants get an early start. 2. The plants are guarded against the blistering heats of the sun by the coolness produced by evaporation. 3. The plants stand long on the hill, ripening, thickening, mellowing, and secreting the gums and oils that have given to this tobacco a world-wide character.

The subsoil of these best tobacco lands is remarkable for its tenacity, unctuousness, and peculiar red color, due to the presence of oxide of iron. In the early settlement of the state these lands were called "barrens", because they were destitute of timber, and it was the universal custom of the aborigines and early settlers to burn off the dead grass from these lands annually. In this way a large amount of potash, so necessary to the growth of the tobacco-plant, was accumulated in the soil. The presence of this constituent gave rise to harsh forests of black-jacks, with a bark thick enough to resist the heat of the fires, and following these came the scrub hickory, which was known to the early settlers as "grub hickory", so named because a sprout an inch in diameter often has a root 6 or 8 inches through. As soon as fires were interdicted hazle bushes, dogwood, and black gum shot up, and what was once a wide expanse of prairie or open woods became a tangled mass of thick underbrush, above which towered the black-jack, oak, and hickory. In the course of years the black-jack gave place, in large part, to red oak in swales and on rich hillsides, and to post oak on rocky hills. The lands here described are *par excellence* the tobacco lands of the Clarksville district.

Wild cherry, black walnut, tulip tree, ash, and beech, with an undergrowth of dogwood, papaw, and blackberry bushes, are indications of a most desirable soil for the growth of the cereals and grasses, but it is not suitable for tobacco, which would acquire its growth too rapidly and begin to waste early. Such a soil will grow large, leafy tobacco, and sometimes it will be very showy in its brilliant colors after being cured, but it will be wanting in quality.

When tobacco is planted upon freshly-cleared land, it grows off rapidly and matures early; but when cured, it is apt to be light, thin, and is usually of a mahogany or piebald color. For chewing tobacco it is preferred, because it is milder and sweeter. Grown upon land gently undulating or level, tobacco is heavier-bodied than when grown upon hilly lands. All the wooded lands of the district, except where too rough for cultivation, as near the margins of streams and where a few marshy areas occur, are well adapted to its production, and it is estimated that about one-tenth of the area planted now is freshly cleared, though this proportion has been gradually reduced since the first settlement of the country. At one time it was the general practice to plant at least half the crop on newly cleared lands and the other half on lands cleared the year before, but the growing scarcity of timber has made farmers resort more and more to well-manured lots. The usual rotation is tobacco, wheat, and clover one or two years, and then tobacco again, and this is kept up, on what are called tobacco lots, for many years. Some few alternate corn with tobacco every third or fourth year, but this is by no means general. Usually, when lands are once planted in corn, the rotation becomes corn, oats or wheat, and clover one or two years. Those farmers who practice the biennial rotation with clover keep their lands in a high state of productiveness. With clover one year in the rotation, the land requires to be supplemented by liberal applications of manures to retain its productive capacity. About 60 per cent. of the area cultivated in tobacco is fertilized with barnyard manures and commercial fertilizers, the latter being usually applied to the hill, about 200 pounds being required for one acre. The barnyard manures are used according to domestic supply, some farmers making every effort to increase the quantity, while others are totally indifferent. Leached ashes are an excellent manure for tobacco, and are carefully saved after soap-making and applied broadcast, or in the hills. Ground raw bone has also been experimented with, but without satisfactory results, and Patapsco guano, though used only to a limited extent, has proved an efficient manure for the tobacco-plant. The science of manuring to increase, as well as to preserve, fertility is but little understood, however, by the great majority of the farmers of the district, the idea being to apply only enough to meet barely the requirements of the crop to be grown. In the past thirty years the average yield of all crops per acre has been largely decreased, and it is a rare thing at the present day to harvest over 1,000 pounds of tobacco to the acre planted, while within the memory of planters yet in the vigor of manhood a product of 1,500 pounds per acre was by no means uncommon. It may be safely stated, however, that were the application of fertilizers increased the yield would be augmented from 10 to 60 per cent., according to management and season. When land is freshly cleared, the crop improves on good soil for the first three years, but the fourth year, without manuring, would probably show a depreciation of about 30 per cent. This rapid decline in fertility is owing, probably, as much to the surface configuration of the district as to the partial exhaustion of the soil. In all the Lithostrotion bed of the Lower Carboniferous formation there are underground caverns or streams, and in very many places the surface above these caverns or streams drops down, forming within a short time hopper-shaped sink-holes. Sometimes these drops determine the contour of the surface around for one or two hundred yards. When these slopes are continuously cultivated for a number of years a great quantity of surface soil is swept from the surrounding rims to the bottom of the sinks, reducing very rapidly the producing capacity of the slopes without adding to the fruitfulness of the bottoms. Indeed, the bottoms of these wide sinks are very uncertain for the production of crops, as after heavy rains the water is liable to stand sufficiently long to kill out any crop that may be planted. Great skill and care are required in the management of these lands to preserve their fertility. In large areas of the Clarksville tobacco district, however, the surface is comparatively level, and in these the lands are easily preserved.

The grades of tobacco grown in this district vary somewhat with seasons, but in an average good crop the following proportions are about correct: Dark shipping, 40 per cent.; fillers for European cigars, 30 per cent.; bright wrappers, 5 per cent.; nondescript, 25 per cent.; cutting (American), none.

There has been no special change in the proportion of grades for many years; but, in the main, the crop has depreciated in good qualities and dark colors, brought about by careless cultivation and inattention to the details of curing and handling, the deterioration, as compared with the crop twenty years ago, being probably 30 per cent. in dark, fat German tobacco, the production of this grade being in much smaller proportion than formerly.

The following is the statement of production, acreage, yield per acre, value of crop in farmers' hands or in primary markets, value per pound, and value per acre of the tobacco crop of the Clarksville district for the years 1876, 1877, 1878, and 1879, only the figures for 1879 being from census returns:

Year.	Production.	Acreage.	Yield per acre.	Value in primary markets.	Value per pound.	Value per acre.
	Pounds.		*Pounds.*		*Cents.*	
1876......	8,081,700	13,275	588.00	$673,627	7.5	$44 10
1877......	27,111,042	32,604	830.00	1,762,217	6.5	53 95
1878......	14,788,500	22,051	670.00	813,372	5.5	36 85
1879......	16,157,934	22,912	705.22	888,687	5.5	38 79

UPPER CUMBERLAND RIVER DISTRICT.

This district comprises the northern part of Sumner, the northern and eastern parts of Wilson, all of Smith, Trousdale, Macon, Clay, Jackson, and Putnam, and a small part of Overton county.

In the western part of Sumner county the tobacco is of a finer texture than that grown in the eastern part, and closely approximates the Clarksville type. In portions of Macon and Wilson counties the type produced is of a much higher character than the general product of the district, and would, with the same care and attention, closely approximate the best types of the Clarksville district. This finer quality of tobacco is grown on the hills and uplands, where the soil is much of the same character as that of the uplands of Montgomery county, that grown on bottom lands, and where the Cincinnati limestone crops out, being coarse in texture, more porous, and deficient in gum.

Sumner and Trousdale counties report a decrease in acreage in 1879, as compared with 1878, of from 5 to 20 per cent. in different localities, and from 30 to 50 per cent. as compared with 1876 and 1877. In all the other counties of this district the decrease was about in the same proportion. The estimate for the whole district is that the production of 1879 was 5 per cent. less than that of 1878, 33 per cent. less than in 1877, and 20 per cent. less than in 1876. The quality of the crop of 1879, with the exception of some injury by mold after curing, was much better than that of the two crops preceding, and equally as good as that of 1876.

VARIETIES OF TOBACCO CULTIVATED.

The varieties most cultivated are the Lovelady, the Shoestring, Big Hester, Little Hester, Yellow Pryor, White Stem, and Zollicoffer. The Big Hester has a large, heavy leaf, stands wet or dry weather well, is not so subject to disease as other varieties, and cures a fine bright color when properly managed. The White Stem is the same as that known under that name in western Tennessee, but does not tally with the description of the White Stem of Virginia. The Lovelady is a very popular variety, grows well, has a medium leaf, is easily handled, cures up a beautiful color, and produces great weight to the acre, but is not desirable for export. The Zollicoffer is large, but subject to spot, and is preferred for the African market, being very long. The Hester and the Lovelady make good wrappers, as also a fine shipping leaf. Twistbud and Orinoco are also grown in Jackson county. New land will make a light chaffy article, very much like the Burley, often used for a cutting leaf. It is used principally for smokers. Old lands produce heavy, dark tobacco, and beech lands are preferred for growing the finest grades. Where the soil is thin, the Lovelady is the best variety to plant, as upon such soils it will attain a greater size and make a better quality than any of the other varieties. In Trousdale county the southwestern slopes of the hills are preferred for growing fine tobacco, while the northern slopes grow a coarse article, very much like that produced on the flat lands.

With the exception of Sumner, Wilson, Trousdale, Smith, Putnam, and Overton counties, it may be said that three-fourths of the tobacco in this district is raised on creek and river bottoms, on rich, loamy alluvial soils, the plant in consequence growing very large, and the texture being rough and coarse. It is very spongy, and has the capacity of absorbing and holding large quantities of water, the large stem, however, with the consequent heavy loss in weight when it is taken out, depriving it in a large degree of its usefulness for the manufacture of strips. The tobacco grown in Putnam and Overton counties is planted principally on uplands, which have a thin soil, grows small, is generally of an inferior character, and is taken mostly for the Spanish market. Some fine tobacco is occasionally grown on hickory land. A portion of the product of these counties is also grown on creek bottoms, the soil and the product being of the same character as that heretofore described. Wilson county now produces the best tobacco grown in the district. It is cured more thoroughly, the stem and fibers are not so large, and it is taken for purposes for which the tobacco of the other counties cannot be used, as, for instance, an occasional crop suited for Germany or Italy, and now and then a crop suited for plug work and for manufacturing wrappers. The crop of this district generally is suited for export on the Regie contracts of France and Spain, which countries pay the lowest prices for tobacco, a small quantity being taken as fillers for the manufacture of plug tobacco, and not an inconsiderable portion for the African market through Boston.

As a general rule, the district is poorly provided with barns for the curing of the crop, most of it being air-cured in log or rail pens, exposed to the beating rains. Some improvement in this respect has been made within a year or two, yet the truth must be confessed that in no other portion of the United States is tobacco handled more roughly, or less pains taken in its preparation for market. Since the establishment of sale warehouses in Nashville, to which point a large proportion of the tobacco of this district finds its way, a free intercourse between planters and buyers has resulted in a more earnest effort to improve, not only the quality of the tobacco grown, but the methods of curing and handling. Already in some of the counties on the upper Cumberland in Kentucky the White Burley has been introduced, and promises to make a good cutting leaf for domestic manufacture. The Morrow tobacco, on good uplands, topped to ten or twelve leaves, frequently makes an excellent cutting leaf. On good bottom lands most of the varieties named will yield an average of one thousand pounds to the acre.

The tobacco grown in this district may be divided into the following grades: Dark shipping, 25 per cent.; fillers, 20 per cent.; bright wrappers and smokers, 15 per cent.; cutting, 5 per cent.; nondescript, 35 per cent.

Ten years ago there was very little effort made to cure tobacco of bright colors, the only sorts raised being large, dark, heavy grades, for export, and size and weight constituting the sole aim of the planter; but since a demand has sprung up for a better quality a few farmers here and there are very successful with the tobacco grown on uplands and second bottoms. The low prices which have prevailed have also caused many to abandon its cultivation altogether. The idea is gradually being received that this whole region is well adapted to the production of a type of tobacco suited to domestic consumption.

The following statement shows the production, acreage, yield per acre, value in farmers' hands or primary markets, value per pound, and value per acre of the tobacco crop of the Upper Cumberland River district for the years 1876, 1877, 1878, and 1879, only the figures for 1879 being from the census returns:

Year.	Production.	Acreage.	Yield per acre.	Value in primary markets.	Value per pound.	Value per acre.
	Pounds.		*Pounds.*		*Cents.*	
1876......	5,644,826	7,447	758.00	$366,913	6.50	$49.27
1877......	6,800,148	9,308	731.00	306,411	4.50	32.89
1878......	4,829,685	6,571	735.00	217,335	4.50	33.07
1879......	4,576,452	5,885	777.65	217,381	4.75	36.94

PREPARATION OF TOBACCO SOIL AND PLANTING.

Old lands, whenever it is possible, are broken with a turn-plow in the fall, not close but deep, 8 to 10 inches not being unusual, the object in not plowing closely being to leave the land in ridges during the winter, so as to expose as large a surface as possible. In February, if the soil be too thin, the land is cross-plowed with care, in order that too much clay may not be brought to the surface and the best soil be buried too deep beneath it. It is thought to be the better plan at the second plowing to turn only a shallow furrow and follow with a subsoil plow; but the latter implement is rarely used. If not subsoil, the furrow slices are cut very narrow, so that the plow does not reverse them, but leaves them on edge or turned but half-way over.

If it is the purpose of the farmer to plant tobacco upon a clover sod, it is very important to break it in mid-summer or early in the fall, and again as early after New Year as the condition of the land will permit. This has the effect of destroying the cut-worms, which are always numerous upon clover lands. Dead grass, plowed under in the late fall or midwinter without time to rot thoroughly before spring, is a serious disadvantage to the tobacco crop.

If the plowing is deferred until the advent of freezing weather, more fruitful results will follow if the grass is burned off. It is not only better for the soil, but the larvæ of the cut-worm, and of other insects injurious to tobacco, are destroyed. About the 1st of May all the stable manure, leached ashes, scrapings from stock yards, and manures from hog pens and other places are scattered over the land, and are plowed in immediately to the depth of three or four inches. After the expiration of a week or two, when the manure has had sufficient time to become incorporated with the soil, the land is well harrowed and laid off into rows, generally 42 inches wide. Upon this two furrows are thrown with a turning-plow drawn by one horse, and then crossed with furrows the same distance apart. This leaves the ridges in broken hills, the tops of which are cut off with a hoe and patted, when they are ready for the reception of the plants.

If the farmer should wish to apply fertilizers to the hill, no ridges are made; but the land is laid off both ways, and the manure is placed at the points where the furrows intersect one another. Upon the manure thus applied a small hill is made with the hoe.

While 3½ feet apart each way is the usual distance of setting the plants, the distances are greatly varied in different localities, in western Tennessee, where the tobacco grows very large, 3 feet by 4 being preferred, as the wider distance will allow passing between the rows with less danger of breaking the leaves. On thin soils the rows are often laid off 3 by 3 feet; others prefer 3 feet 3 inches by 3 feet 3 inches; and a few set out the plants 3½ by 2½ feet. On the strong bottom lands of the upper Cumberland the rows are frequently laid off 3 by 4 feet. The practice of manuring tobacco in the hill is heartily condemned by many good farmers, because in very dry weather the tobacco is more subject to field-fire; but in a wet season the results are often very satisfactory, the object of manuring in the hill being to make a small quantity of manure go as far as possible. Commercial fertilizers, at the rate of about 200 pounds to the acre, are always applied in the hill.

An excellent manure for tobacco is made by composting leached ashes with well-rotted stable manure. When placed in a heap this mass soon decomposes, and is in excellent condition for putting in the hill.

The method of preparing the soils, as given, is applicable only to those that are loose and mellow; and the land should be plowed and replowed and frequently harrowed until it is brought to this condition, it being the generally received opinion among farmers that a thorough preparation of the soil is equal in its effects upon the crop as all its subsequent cultivation.

TRANSPLANTING TOBACCO.

When the lower leaves of the plants are as broad as three fingers they are of sufficient size for transplanting, this being usually done immediately after a rain. A gentle rain, in which the water is soaked into the earth as fast as it falls, is much preferred. The transplanting should not be done while the ground is wet enough to be compacted by pressure against the roots, for this gives a check to the plant in its new situation. The plants are carefully drawn, one at a time, and placed straight, with the heads all in one direction. After this is finished they are picked up and laid straight in baskets or in a wagon-bed and taken to the field. Transplanting is done by means of a wooden peg, 6 inches long and an inch and a half thick, gradually sloped at one end to a point, and a good man may set out 5,000 plants in a day, though to set 3,000 properly is considered a fair day's work. An acre, when the rows are 3½ feet apart each way, will contain 3,555 hills, so that two acres, with one person to drop plants for every two engaged in setting, may be considered a satisfactory day's work for three hands, including the drawing of plants.

The manner of transplanting is this: A dropper, with a basket of convenient size filled with plants, takes two rows, dropping a plant on each hill. Two transplanters follow, each with an extra plant in his hand, called a "hand-plant". With the peg described he makes a hole in the center of the hill, two or three inches deep, depending upon the size and length of the plant. The roots are thrust into this hole to the bottom, and a gentle pressure is made downward upon one side of the plant, while the dirt on the other side is supported by the fingers of the left hand. The plant dropped upon this hill is picked up and carried to the next, and while passing from one hill to the other the person transplanting has time to adjust it in his hand ready for setting. The use of the "hand-plant" greatly facilitates the work. When the supervening weather turns off dry and hot, many plants will perish, and to prevent this it is the practice among some farmers to put lumps of dirt, either upon the plant or on the southern side of it, in order to screen it from the blasting rays of the sun. This is very troublesome, and rarely pays for the time and labor expended. Others draw the dirt up closely to the leaves of the plant, so that the bud, enfolded in the leaves, will be just beneath the surface of the soil. This is found to be much more effective and less troublesome.

The usual period of planting tobacco is from the 20th of May until the 10th of June, though very often a considerable quantity is planted during the first week in May and as late as the 4th of July; but it rarely happens that a good crop is made when the plants are set out later than the 15th or 20th of June. Some plants are always destroyed in the field, either by cut-worms, grasshoppers, or dry weather. The replanting is carried on as late as the middle of July. The eagerness among planters to have their crops planted at as early a day as possible induces many to set out plants before they are large enough.

CULTIVATION OF THE TOBACCO CROP.

The cultivation of tobacco among the best farmers is continuous, no sprig of grass being permitted to interfere with its growth. As soon as the plants have become well rooted, it is the practice with many farmers to run a turning-plow, drawn by one horse, twice between the rows, with the bar next to the plants. This wraps up all the grass in the center of the row, and leaves the plants standing on a narrow ridge. Hoes are then brought into requisition, and all the grass is scraped away from the plants and a little fresh dirt is put about them. In a week thereafter a cross-plowing is given in the same way, followed again with the hoes, and in about four weeks after the plants have been set a third plowing is given, this time the mold-board being turned toward the plants, the dirt thrown up about them, and the "middles" split out. With many farmers this ends the cultivation, while others will use the plow once or twice more, always throwing the dirt to the plants after they are large enough.

Within a few years past cultivators have been largely used in working the crop. These are run through the rows every week for five or six weeks, the hoes following, when necessary, to cut out any grass or weeds that may not have been reached by the cultivator.

Just before the third plowing, when the plants have attained a height of eight or ten inches, three or four of the lower leaves next the ground are generally plucked off, in order that the dirt may be thrown against the stalk and wrap up any grass that may have come up in proximity to the plant. Some excellent farmers, however, maintain that the tobacco-plant is greatly injured by this operation, and that if the lower leaves are permitted to remain the plant will be much healthier, the crop heavier, and there will be a smaller proportion of lugs, the two lower leaves acting as a protection for the others against the spattering of mud in rainy weather. The object in throwing the dirt to the plant is to give it such lateral support that it will not be readily blown down by the winds. It was once a very common practice, after the last plowing, to go over the field with hoes and make a large broad hill about the plant. These hills give the appearance of a higher and more careful culture, and may have the effect of preserving the ends of a few of the larger leaves which would otherwise rest upon the top of the ridge made by the plow, but the saving in this particular will scarcely compensate for the increased labor, and it is by no means improbable that the plants may suffer more from drought by breaking the continuity of the ridge into separate hills; at all events, the practice has been well-nigh discontinued. In cultivating tobacco farmers avoid working the land when it is too wet. Clayey soil worked when wet will bake, and the injury done the crop is vastly more than the presence of grass can effect. Even upon sandy soil no good results follow.

TOPPING, WORMING, AND SUCKERING TOBACCO.

In from six to seven weeks, during a favorable season, the "button", or blossom-bud, begins to peer out above the topmost leaves, when it should be topped. The usual method of topping is, after "priming", so as to leave the stalk bare six inches above the surface of the ground, to pinch out the top, leaving usually ten leaves, more rarely twelve, and sometimes but eight. The almost universal custom once was to leave from twelve to sixteen leaves on each plant; but experience has demonstrated that the maximum yield, and a better quality, can be obtained by leaving fewer leaves. For a long time ten leaves were believed to produce the highest results, but recent experiments have favored the idea that the highest production may be reached by leaving only eight leaves to the plant. As the season advances the number of leaves is decreased, and the general practice is to have every plant in the field topped by the 1st of September, even though it be so small that it will furnish only four leaves. The first topping, when the crop has been set out in May, will usually occur about the 4th of July, and every week thereafter the field is gone over until the whole is topped.

An important experiment was made in Montgomery county to test the difference between topping to eight leaves and topping to a higher number, and while one such experiment is not conclusive, it accords fully with the convictions of the most intelligent growers of the county. The land selected was a highland basin, in which the soil was a dark brown loam, with a few nodules of chert intermingled. The subsoil was a ferruginous clay, unctuous and highly retentive of moisture, though well drained by the underlying beds of chert. The land had been in cultivation for half a century, and was well preserved. Two lots of four acres each were selected, both receiving applications of stable manure. No. 1 was set out, 3½ feet each way, in the latter part of May, was well cultivated, and the tobacco topped to eight leaves. No. 2 was set out about the same time at the same distance apart, and was cultivated in all particulars like No. 1, and topped to ten leaves. The tobacco on No. 1 ripened first, but was permitted to stand fully two weeks after it was apparently ready for the knife. It was not cut, however, until the tobacco on No. 2 was well ripened, and both pieces were housed about the same time. Hot fires were employed in the curing of both. The tobacco grown on No. 1 was a long, rich, black wrapper, very oily and elastic, fully 30 inches in length, and very heavy; that grown on No. 2 was lighter in color, but poorer in quality, and was deficient in gum and elasticity. A prominent New York dealer called at the barn after both lots had been stripped and packed down, preparatory to pressing, and offered 17 cents for that grown on No. 1, but only 12 cents for that grown on No. 2. But this was not all. Lot No. 1 yielded 1,200 pounds, and lot No. 2 only 900 pounds per acre. The tobacco grown on lot No. 1 was far less expensive in suckering and stripping, for the number of suckers was less, and the number of leaves to be stripped from the stalk was one-fifth less, as compared with No. 2. The entire gain, considering the saving in labor, the difference in price, the excess in weight of the tobacco grown on No. 1 over No. 2, was fully 50 per cent. There was no apparent cause for the difference, except that the tobacco on one lot was topped to eight leaves and allowed to stand a considerable time after it was ripe, and on the other topped to ten leaves and cut as soon as it was thought to be mature.

Generally about two weeks before the plants are large enough to top the worms begin to make their appearance in sufficient numbers to demand attention, and from this time until it is harvested the war against them is continued.

There are usually two heavy "showers" of worms, the first coming on just before the period of topping, and the second about the middle of August, or rather during the time of full moon in that month. The last influx of worms is the most destructive and the one most dreaded by the farmers, because it comes at a time when the suckers are troublesome, and they furnish a hiding-place for many worms which are thrown on the ground with the suckers, and, not being destroyed, crawl up on the plant and are unmolested in their depredations until the planter has another opportunity to go over his crop.

In the experience of the most observant planters, if the first influx or "shower" of worms is diligently destroyed the second brood is much lessened, for it is believed that the moths, the mothers of the second brood, come from the first worms. In some years the number is astonishingly great, as many as one hundred worms having been taken from a single plant during its period of growth. Such a large number, however, is exceptional. They are thought to be very numerous when there is one to the leaf, but generally there are from two to three to the plant. If the previous summer and autumn have been dry, with the ground hard, very few worms may be expected; but if the previous season has been a wet one, followed by a mild winter, they are apt to prove very troublesome. When the worms are in excess, there is no time for idleness with the planters. All the extra help which can be secured is employed, it being often the case that a good, active man is not able to keep one acre well wormed. Early and late, through bad weather and good, a constant warfare is waged against these insects, and neglect or inattention at this time may so depreciate the crop that it will be unfit for any except the lowest grades. Taking a number of years in succession, three acres have been found to be about equal to the ability of one man to keep properly free from worms, upon which basis crops are arranged. The worms appear in great numbers about one year in five.

Various schemes have been devised to destroy the tobacco moth. One enterprising tobacco firm in Clarksville a few years ago offered a premium of $50 in gold to the boy who should kill the greatest number of flies. This aroused exertion among the lads throughout the counties of that district, and many thousand moths were destroyed.

The poisoned artificial Jamestown-weed bloom, described in chapter XXI, has been favorably tried, and in very rare cases reliance is placed upon droves of turkeys for suppressing the horn-worms; but the safest and surest means for the destruction of this great enemy of the tobacco-plant is in the employment of a sufficient number of good, steady, trustworthy hands. When as many as five hands are engaged in the work, it is found profitable for the employer or his manager to follow behind them and catch what worms they may leave. This active supervision will insure the attention of each laborer, and a rivalry springs up as to which one shall leave the smallest number. Suckers, as a usual thing, are pulled off at least once a week, and cease to be troublesome after they have been broken off twice from the same place.

As the plants ripen they become more brittle, and greater care is necessary to prevent breaking the leaves in passing through worming and suckering. The worming process also becomes more difficult, for in raising the leaves to look for worms on the under surfaces they are apt to break off. At this stage winds often invert half of the leaf, folding it over on the other half. Such leaves should be carefully turned back, as the heat of the sun soon impairs their value by blistering or burning the under surfaces.

TOBACCO-HOUSES.

In the early history of tobacco culture in the state the tobacco-houses were simply pens, built with rough logs. Afterward an improvement was made by hewing the logs on two sides, so as to have an evenness of surface on both the outside and the inside. As good, straight building logs became scarce and dear, frame barns were substituted; yet at the present day fully three-fourths of the barns in the state are built of logs, and there are many excellent farmers who prefer them for curing tobacco. They are usually built from 20 to 24 feet square and four or five firing-tiers in height. Two of these pens are sometimes built so as to leave a passage between, as in the illustration. Others are shedded around with hip rafters, so as to have three firing-tiers in the shed. The shed is usually constructed from 12 to 15 feet wide. Such a barn (see engraving) has the capacity of housing and curing 10,000 pounds of tobacco.

Sometimes, when more curing space is needed, a room is added to each end of the log barn, 10 or 15 feet in length, the walls of the same height as the log pens, the roof being continuous; and side sheds are added, if desired. Such an addition, while no more expensive, is more easily constructed, and is much more roomy than hip-rafter sheds built on the four sides of an ordinary barn.

In building a log barn, the pen is raised to the height of about 9 feet, when a set of tier poles, 4 feet apart, is put across and notched down. About every 3 feet in height thereafter another set is put in, until the barn is raised as high as is desired. Two or more sets of tiers are framed on the rafters, giving additional room in the roof. A barn five tiers high in the body and 20 feet square on the inside will hold 1,000 sticks, each stick containing 7 plants, or will house and cure two acres of tobacco.

Frame barns are constructed in a variety of ways. The diagrams on page 182 will serve to show the details in the construction of a frame barn 40 feet square, with a capacity of holding seven acres of well-grown tobacco.

A represents a wagon-way 13 feet wide, the posts on each side of which are framed into sills. The posts on each side, on the lines marked B and C, are 21 feet high, capped with a stout plate 4 by 6 inches. At the height of 9 feet from the sills the first set of streamers is let in the posts, parallel with the passage, and three other sets above these, 3 feet apart, which, with the plates 3 feet above the last set, make fine foundations for tier poles put at right angles and extending over the passage-way. These tier poles are put 4 feet apart, every alternate one resting against the posts on each side. The posts in the lines marked D and E are 15 feet high, with two sets of girders or streamers let in from the outside, the first set 9 feet from the ground sill, so as to be on a level with the

first set in the passage-way. A plate rests on top of the posts, 3 feet above the last set of girders. Tier poles extend from the girders on the outside posts to the girders on the central line of posts. The accompanying section will give a better idea than a written description, the cross-pieces representing tier poles, the girders supposed to be perpendicular to the plane of the paper.

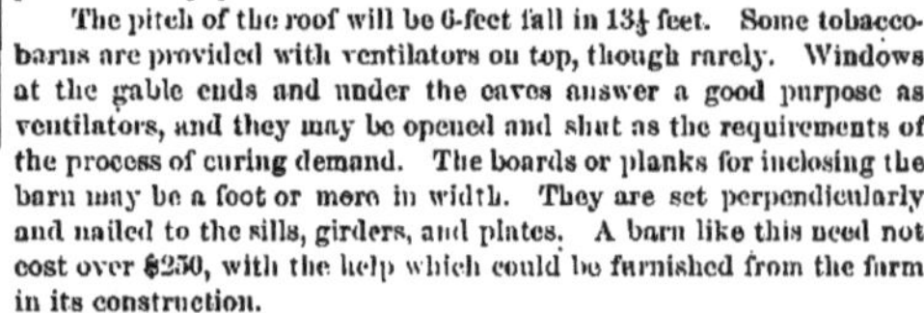

The pitch of the roof will be 6-feet fall in 13½ feet. Some tobacco-barns are provided with ventilators on top, though rarely. Windows at the gable ends and under the eaves answer a good purpose as ventilators, and they may be opened and shut as the requirements of the process of curing demand. The boards or planks for inclosing the barn may be a foot or more in width. They are set perpendicularly and nailed to the sills, girders, and plates. A barn like this need not cost over $250, with the help which could be furnished from the farm in its construction.

When the tobacco in the field is fully ripe, it should be cut immediately, or it will waste rapidly. When there is an insufficiency of barn room the cured tobacco has to be crowded. In this crowded condition the stems, which are rarely cured up entirely, often rot, and not only is the leaf near the stem injured, but every leaf which touches the rotting stem is damaged. House-burned tobacco is, in fact, nothing more than tobacco that has rotted for want of air. In crowded houses, where the fires are kept in such low condition as to induce an accumulation of moisture or "sweat" on the leaves, there is always more or less house-burned tobacco. Such tobacco is lifeless, is of a dark-brown color, breaks easily, and seldom comes in case for stripping.

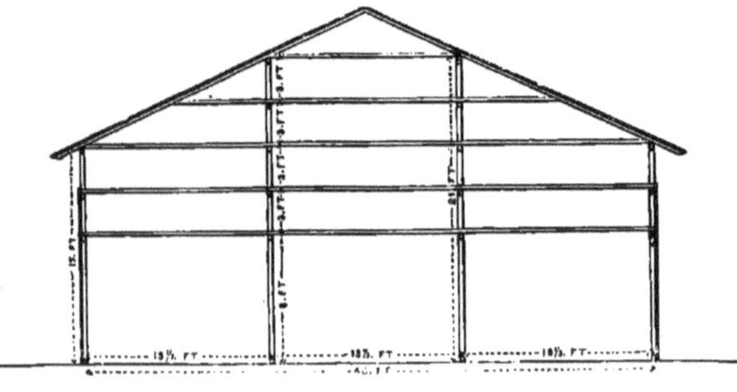

The only furniture needed in a curing barn is plenty of good sticks, rived from hickory or oak, 4 feet 6 inches long by 1½ inches wide and 1¼ inches thick. Thoughtful farmers always have these well-seasoned before they are used. Green sticks are apt to sag under the strong heat required for curing tobacco.

In portions of western Tennessee, notably in Henry county, the schedules returned to this office mention flues as among the means used for curing tobacco. These are especially valuable in curing the bright tobacco, but Dr. R. G. Tuck, who first introduced flues for the curing of tobacco in Virginia, and subsequently removed to the Clarksville tobacco district, was of opinion that they were not well adapted to curing the rich, heavy leaf of that district, and therefore abandoned their use. A few, however, are used in Montgomery county and in some of the counties of the Upper Cumberland River district. They are by no means common, however, in any portion of the state.

Almost every extensive planter, in addition to his curing barns, has a stripping barn and a "prizing" room, where the tobacco is pressed in hogsheads.

CUTTING AND HARVESTING THE TOBACCO CROP.

There has been little change in the method of cutting and housing since tobacco began to be cultivated in the state, the class of laborers employed not adapting themselves readily to new plans.

In the state of Tennessee the tobacco harvest usually begins about the 10th of September and lasts until the first week in October. Occasionally crops are cut earlier, and sometimes later. Generally, with favorable weather, about six weeks intervene between topping and cutting. By that time the leaves droop, become thick, and assume a yellowish mottled color. When the upper surface of the leaves is carefully examined, it has an oily, granulated appearance, and when examined through a magnifying glass semi-globular excrescences are thickly distributed, with depressions between them. The leaves also become more rigid, breaking easily. These are indications of maturity. Cut in this condition, the tobacco-plant, when cured, will reach its maximum in weight and quality; but if the cutting be deferred a few days, rusty spots will begin to appear on the leaves, and the quality is rapidly impaired. It rarely happens that all the plants in a field will ripen at the same time. To do this there must be a remarkable homogeneity in the soil and a uniformity of surface exposure, and all the plants must be topped about the same time. Newly-cleared land will ripen the plants several days earlier than old land originally of the same character, and in general, whatever hastens the growth, whether a southern exposure, a rocky soil, which catches and retains the heat of the sun, stimulating manures, or a dark soil, is calculated to bring the plant to an early development and maturity. It is not considered best, however, for tobacco to mature too rapidly. In such a case it will be comparatively deficient in the oils and gums that give it strength and flavor.

Generally the first cutting will take about half the plants in a field, and these are carefully selected, leaving the unripe ones. If the number of green plants be inconsiderable, say not more than an eighth of the whole, it is thought by the best planters to be profitable to cut the whole, as the time lost in going over a considerable field to gather up a few plants will cost more than the difference between the matured and immatured plants is worth. As the season advances and dangers from frosts are feared, planters are always disposed to cut a field clean, for a green plant is greatly preferred to a frost-bitten one. When cut late, the custom is to bring the plants together and stack them in what is known as "frost piles", and this must be done when the plants are cool; for if put in such piles, when warmed by the sun the plants will "coddle" or scald from the heat generated. These frost piles are made by setting the plants bottom side uppermost in a round pile, the leaves resting on the ground and the butts sticking upward. When put into such piles properly, it will become of a bright golden color in three or four days, when it may be strung upon sticks and carried immediately to the curing barn. As a general rule, however, it is better, in the heavy styles of shipping tobacco, to allow the plants to stand a little too long than to cut them when green, because thoroughly ripe tobacco is much heavier and sweeter. The leaf usually attains its full size in three or four weeks after being topped. After this it thickens and becomes fat, under the combined influence of copious cool dews and hot suns. There is as much difference between the fragrance of ripe and that of green tobacco, after being cured, as between the taste of a rich, ripe, luscious peach and that of a green one.

Three or four days, if possible, are allowed to intervene between heavy rains and the next cutting, for during this time the gums washed by rains are secreted in as large quantity as ever. Nor is it the practice to cut tobacco when a shower of rain is imminent, for if caught in a rain it will be bespattered with dirt and sand, which detract largely from its value. Should the rain continue for a day or more after the plants are cut, the tobacco absorbs the moisture and gets in a "strut", in which condition it cannot be handled without great breakage. When the dew is on the leaves, it is considered injurious to cut tobacco, for when laid on the ground a considerable amount of dirt will adhere, stop the pores, and prevent successful curing. Nor is it cut in the morning, even after the dew is off, if the day promises to be a hot one, because it will be liable to sunburn before it can be taken to the scaffold or the barn. The most approved time for cutting tobacco is in the afternoon, when the rays of the declining sun have been tempered sufficiently to prevent sunburn, but not enough to keep the plants from wilting properly, from three to four o'clock being the best time.

The instrument employed for cutting tobacco is a butcher-knife of medium size, with a thin and sharp blade of about six inches in length. The handle of the knife is wrapped with old rags, in order to relieve the pressure on the hand. The person who cuts stands over the plant, places the blade of the knife nearly at right angles to the two upper leaves, and splits the stalk from the top to within a few inches of the lower leaves. Withdrawing the knife and grasping the plant with the left hand, he bends it slightly from him and severs the stalk an inch or two below the lowest leaves. The plant is then inverted and set up in the middle of the row, or over the stub, care being taken not to let any of the leaves be perforated by the stub. In this condition it stands until it wilts, which on a warm day, with tobacco of medium size, will require half an hour.

The management of the plants after they wilt varies with different planters, but the most common course is to put them in piles of six or eight, or as many as may be deemed sufficient to put on a stick. These piles are made with the heads of the plants turned toward the sun, and the tails of the leaves carefully tucked under. The plants of two rows are put in one row of piles, and the pile rows are arranged in groups of two; that is to say, the plants from four rows are piled on the two central rows. This leaves room for a wagon to pass without danger of running over the piles, and facilitates the dropping of the sticks, one of which is put beside each pile. The next thing is to hang or straddle the tobacco over the sticks. For this purpose the stick is set firmly in the ground at an angle of about 45 degrees with the surface of the ground, the stick leaning away from the sun. The plants are now taken, one by one, and straddled over the stick, with heads toward the sun. The subjoined engraving will illustrate what has been described.

When all the plants are strung, careful planters tuck the tails of the leaves under them. The tobacco is now ready to go to the scaffold or the barn. If the tobacco is very heavy, and the barns are at an inconvenient distance from the fields, planters usually prefer to scaffold until the tobacco is lightened by evaporation and dessication, when much larger loads may be carried and a large amount of labor saved. When tobacco is to be air-cured, the scaffold is almost always employed for a week or more. If the weather foreshadows rain, it is desirable that the tobacco be put under shelter as soon as possible. The points of practice are: 1. To keep the rain from catching it while on the ground after it is cut; 2. To keep it from being caught by rains while on the sticks; and 3. To keep it free from rain while on the scaffolds. The amount of damage which the tobacco will sustain by rains will be very great in the first case, less in the second, and least of all in the third.

Some farmers prefer to carry the plants directly to the barn when they are well wilted and before they are hung, and in such cases it has been found convenient to carry them in low sleds, when they are immediately hung up. Two sleds are usually employed, and a part of the force is kept busy loading one sled in the field, while the other part is engaged in hanging the tobacco from the sled in the barn. Scaffolds are built with poles four or five inches through and as long as they can be conveniently handled. These are supported four feet above the ground by forks at one end, the other resting upon the bed pole, which is placed at right angles to the tier poles. One end of this is usually placed on a high stump, or on the corner of a fence, and the other supported by stout forks.

When first put upon scaffolds, the usual plan is to crowd the sticks together, for tobacco soon wilts and lightens by evaporation, so that there is ample space between the sticks for the circulation of air. In from three to five days it is carried to the barns and arranged upon the tier poles, the sticks being placed six inches apart.

When tobacco is carried directly from the field to the barns without scaffolding, more space is required upon the tier poles, or there will be danger from pole-sweat. Each stick then occupies a space of eight inches. When carried to the barn on sticks, a long frame is frequently employed, four feet deep, four feet wide, and open on the sides, and the tobacco is placed on the frame in the same manner as that in which it is put on the tier poles, only it is crowded as closely as possible. The saving in hauling is about one-third when the tobacco has been on a scaffold for a few days. Many farmers haul on an ordinary wagon body, or on one made for hauling wood, a few planks being put in the bottom, and the tobacco being laid flat, in "coops", the sticks being placed parallel with the frame of the wagon. These are laid right and left, with the butts of the tobacco out and tails overlapping in the middle, and is piled up in two or three "coops" to the height of four or five feet, the "coops" being supported by long standards on the sides of the frame. This method of hauling tobacco is objectionable because the lower plants are liable to bruise by the superincumbent weight. It is considered a fair day's work for one hand to cut and house one hundred sticks.

CURING TOBACCO.

At one time in the Clarksville region great efforts were made to cure the crop dark, and for this purpose fires were kindled under the tobacco as soon as it was taken to the barn from the field, without waiting for it to yellow or even to wilt well. The consequence was the production of a bluish color, answering the purposes of no market, and classed as *nondescript*.

There are two methods of curing pursued by the best planters. One is to scaffold in the field for four or five days, until the tobacco is well yellowed, then haul to the barns and apply heat by means of good seasoned wood, placed in trenches dug in an earthen floor. Two logs are placed side by side in these trenches, and fires are kindled all along their points of contact. If the bottom of the trench be made sloping, the logs will remain pressed up against each other. Sometimes it is necessary to lay a small stick of wood over the line of contact, in order to keep the fires steady. Seasoned hickory wood is preferred, as it gives out less smoke and burns readily, and, when once on fire, it will burn steadily until wholly consumed. The only objection to this kind of wood is its tendency to sparkle, which, under some circumstances, might endanger the barn by fire. The heat is kept at about 90° for the first day and 120° for the second, afterward increased to 150°, and is kept at this point, or above it, day and night until the leaf is wholly cured, with the exception of half the stem. The fires are then put out; but should damp weather supervene, small fires are kindled in the barns every morning, so as to prevent the tobacco from being injured by the "running" of the half cured stems. If the weather, however, is bright, the doors of the barn are usually left open for a few days, when all danger from the green stems will be gone.

Another method of curing is to take the tobacco directly to the barns from the field and arrange it, already strung on sticks, on the tier poles, the sticks being put eight or ten inches apart. In this condition it remains for about three days—longer if the weather is cool. Slow fires are then put under it, and a gentle heat is kept up until the tails begin to curl, when the heat is increased to about 150°, and kept at that point until the tobacco is cured, with the exception of the stalk and the upper half of the stem. Good planters are very careful in keeping the heat gentle for a day or two, for tobacco, when very green, may be permanently injured by too much heat, which gives it a "coddled", lifeless appearance.

After the fires are once kindled, it is thought to be important to keep them in full blast day and night until the tobacco is cured. No injury, however, is apt to result, if the weather is clear and dry, by suspending the fires at any time.

In the Clarksville region at least 90 per cent. of the crop is cured by fires; in western Tennessee, about 75 per cent.; and in the Upper Cumberland district only about 25 per cent., the remainder being air-cured.

In air-curing, the tobacco is left upon the scaffolds for four or five days, and is then hung up in open barns where there is good ventilation. Air-cured tobacco, if ripe, is always brown in color when cut, and to prevent its piebald or yellow colors from changing to a brown it must be kept excluded from a damp atmosphere, either by packing it down or by kindling small fires under it whenever moist weather occurs.

The price of tobacco depends very much upon the manner in which it is cured, a fancy article often bringing on the market three or four times as much as the same tobacco cured a dingy brown. A rich black color is always in demand for black wrappers, but this color is more the result of the soil upon which it is grown than of the methods of curing. A heavy, rich manured lot is more likely to grow tobacco that will cure dark than a clover or grass sod. The tendency, when grown on rich, new oak lands, is to cure a bright brown; on fresh lands, where the tulip tree grows, a rich piebald; on hickory lands, a golden yellow. One correspondent from Henry county, in speaking of the advantages derived from skill in curing, says:

> Mr. Jackson Wimberly, one of the most skillful curers in the county, realized $12 50 per hundred pounds for his entire crop in 1878, and Mr. William Gulledge $10 per hundred for a part of his crop grown in 1879. Others grow as good tobacco as either of these gentlemen, but, lacking skill to cure it properly, they readily took $5 per hundred, showing a difference of from 100 to 140 per cent. in favor of the skillful curer.

ASSORTING, STRIPPING, AND PREPARING TOBACCO FOR MARKET.

Good planters always put their most careful hands to the work of assorting. The various qualities and colors are first separated, and these are afterward arranged into various grades. In the same crop there are often bright and dark tobacco, heavy and light, rich and poor, long and short, the product of different plantings, of diversified soils, and of freshly cleared lands. Much can be done in the way of assorting when the tobacco is cut. It is the practice with tobacco-growers to keep that grown on freshly-cleared lands separated from that grown on old manured lots, the long from the short, the ripe from the green or frosted, and each kind is put in a different barn, or on different tiers of the same barn. This is considered a great help when the season for stripping and preparing it for market comes on. The stripping rarely begins until November, for in all the tobacco districts of the state the month of October is usually consumed in sowing wheat, and the tobacco is not then considered sufficiently well cured to strip. During the warm, soft days in November, when the leaves are pliant but the stems dry enough to crack when bent, a large portion of the product is taken from the sticks and packed in bulks. These bulks are covered with planks or sticks, and are sometimes surrounded with wheat straw, to keep the exposed heads in a damp condition. The stripping may then be performed during the winter months, especially if a room heated by a stove is provided. If the weather is severely cold, tobacco cannot be handled without injury outside of such a room; and it is not taken down by the best planters in cold weather, for though it may appear to be in proper condition, it will quickly sour should warm weather supervene.

Many planters prefer to take down their tobacco only as they strip and assort it, because the leaves, not having been compacted in a bulk, are much more easily examined, and less time is required in separating the various grades. The chief advantages of having tobacco in bulk are:

1. That it is always in condition, and gives employment in bad weather oftentimes when that left hanging in the barn is not in proper condition.

2. If taken down in a good season, and in right case, it need not be hung up again.

3. That it suffers no damage from high winds, and from the frequency with which it will go out of and come in "case", if left hanging in the barns.

Supposing the tobacco to have been taken down in proper condition for handling without breakage, it is put upon a platform and every leaf is carefully scrutinized, and all the imperfect, much injured, and badly worm-eaten and sunburned leaves are taken first from the stalk and tied by themselves. These constitute planters' lugs. In the vocabulary of tobacco dealers, all the product except lugs is termed "leaf". The leaves which are but slightly eaten or injured make what is called low leaf, or seconds, which are kept separate from the lugs, the remaining leaves being termed good. There are various grades of good, viz.: Medium, which may be short, or poor, or of bad color; good leaf, which may be long and poor, or short and rich, or of excellent color without being either long or very rich; fine leaf, which has nearly all the desirable qualities, lacking in only one or two; selections, which combine all the qualities of length, richness, good color, small stem and fine fiber, silkiness, body, elasticity, gum, and fatness. The basic idea in assorting is that there shall be a uniformity in length, color, and quality, and this uniformity should be preserved in all the leaves which enter a bundle, and the bundles themselves should be classified in the same manner.

In stripping tobacco, the leaves are pulled from the stalks and tied in bundles. The size of the bundles is considered a very important matter. If the tobacco is to be sold loose to a dealer for the purpose of stemming, the usual practice is to tie into hands as large as one's arm, or even larger; but if the tobacco is to be packed and pressed into hogsheads and offered for sale by samples after inspection, the bundles are made to contain not more than five or six leaves. In the management of this peculiar type of tobacco neatness in tying the hands is considered of prime importance. A rough, shabby tie will injure the sale 10 per cent. The leaf selected to tie with is usually small. This is smoothed out at the tail and doubled over, so as to make a band an inch wide. This band, with the stem downward, is wrapped tightly around the head of the stems, and is then tucked between the leaves. Careful handlers pass each bundle through the hands as it is tied, so as to press the leaves together. It is then laid back in its proper place on the stripping pile. If the tobacco is in proper order for packing in hogsheads, it may be put in immediately; but the more common way is to bulk it down.

Tobacco for bulking having been laid in piles before the platform, is taken up, two bundles at a time, and passed through a succession of hands, each person through whose hands it passes straightening, pulling, and squeezing the bundles from the heads to the tails, so as to make a cylindrical roll, the last person passing the bundles to the bulker, who lays them down side by side, keeping the heads in contact and even with the outer edge of the platform and the tails drawn closely together, pointing to the middle of the platform. A similar course is run on the other side of the platform; then two courses in the center, the heads of the bundles resting midway the first and second courses and tails overlapping in the center. These four courses form the first layer of the bulk, and this operation is continued until the bulk is finished. The bulker, on his knees, packs before him, keeping the bundles laid flat and pulled up closely meanwhile with his right hand and forefinger, placing the leaves of each two bundles, as he puts them down, separate, and not suffering them to spread out, fan-like, over the other bundles. The bulk is thus built up like a solid wall of masonry. Sometimes the center of the bulk builds up too rapidly; then one of the middle courses is left out. It is very necessary to keep the top of the bulk level, as otherwise, when the tobacco is taken up, the bundles will be bent. When finished, it is covered and weighted.

There are two ways in which tobacco is packed in hogsheads, both of which have their advocates among good planters. One of these, called the "square pack", is made by running two courses across the bottom of the hogshead, the heads of the central bundles in a course being about eight inches from the staves, as indicated in the accompanying diagram.

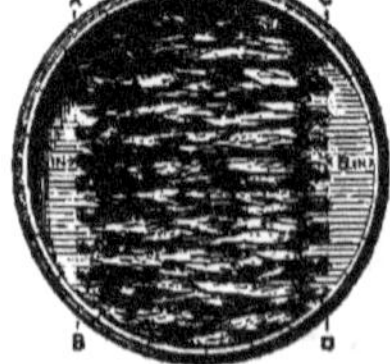

A course is run from A to B, the bundles being placed at right angles to this line, and a second is run from D to C, the tails of the bundles overlapping the first course. The third course will cross these at right angles, the heads of the bundles resting on a line drawn from A to C. The heads of the bundles, forming a fourth course, will rest on a line drawn from B to D, and overlapping the third course. In every case the courses must be run out to fill the round of the hogshead. These four courses are called a layer.

The second method of packing is to run two courses, as in the first instance, and then two more with the bundles in the same direction as in the first two, but with the heads jammed against the rounds of the hogshead, as shown in the diagram on page 187.

These bundles are usually put in one at a time and pulled up close to each other, and when pressed properly come out of the hogsheads straight and firm, but open easily. It is the habit of some planters, particularly of those residing in the Upper Cumberland River district, to press their tobacco very heavily; and it is said by New York dealers that the heaviest hogsheads received in that market come from this district, some of them weighing as much as 3,000 pounds each, the tobacco being so bruised by the heavy pressure that in many cases it can only be used by snuff-makers. In the Clarksville district from 1,400 to 1,700 pounds are considered about the average weights for fine tobacco and lugs, but within recent years the tendency has been to make lighter hogsheads, for nearly all the European markets prefer tobacco that will open freely when it comes from the hogshead.

False packing, or "nesting", is when inferior or short tobacco is packed in next to the staves, where inspectors are least likely to observe it. This practice is made an indictable offense by the laws of Tennessee. The practice observed by all honest planters, when there is not enough of any one grade to fill a hogshead, is to put in all of one kind first, and then fill up with another, but not to mix the two grades in one layer.

All rich or moderately rich leaves of uniform color, 26 inches in length and over, are tied neatly and packed in hogsheads made to weigh about 1,400 pounds. This is called a Liverpool African, and is shipped through Liverpool to the African market. When the tobacco is 30 inches long and over, and pressed as above, it is called a Boston African. Both these grades also make what is called a good English shipper. When dark brown and silky, it may be classed as a Swiss wrapper; when of a mottled and light brown color, with good body, it may be classed as a German saucer.

Short, rich tobacco makes good shippers for Germany and for Great Britain, and such tobacco is usually pressed into casks which are made to weigh about 1,600 pounds. Heavy, bad lugs are more heavily pressed, a hogshead weighing sometimes 1,800 to 2,000 pounds; but if the lugs are of good body, and not much worm-eaten, nor blistered, nor dirty, but are suitable for fillers, the hogsheads should not weigh more than 1,500 or 1,600 pounds net. Light, fancy yellow tobacco is prized more lightly, 800 to 1,000 pounds sometimes being sufficient to put in a hogshead.

The casks vary greatly in size in the different portions of the state. In western Tennessee they are 56 inches high and 44 inches in diameter; in the Clarksville region, 56 inches high and 42 inches in diameter, sometimes 54 inches high and 40 inches in diameter; in the Upper Cumberland River district, 60 inches high and 42 inches across the head. Very often, however, they are much larger, some of them being 6 feet high and 50 inches across the head.

The casks or hogsheads are usually made of red-oak staves, rived and drawn, but sometimes they are sawed and are strongly bound with flat hoops made of young white oak, though small hickory poles, divided in halves, are occasionally employed. Staves sawed from the wood of the tulip tree are used to a considerable extent in the Upper Cumberland district, though rarely in the other parts of the state. When sold with two heads, hogsheads cost from $2 to $2 25 each. Planters sometimes prefer to furnish one head themselves, and in that case the cost of the hogshead is $1 75. Sticks cost 25 cents per hundred. Tobacco is very rarely packed in boxes, and when these are employed for the purpose they are procured at second-hand from the merchants.

TOBACCO PRIZES AND THEIR CONSTRUCTION.

What are known as the beam and lever prizes have three "swords", two movable, but the third dovetailed into the ground sill upon which the hogshead stands. This sill passes through a mortise in an upright post, which is set four feet in the ground. The beam which brings the pressure on the tobacco in the hogshead is also mortised into this post about six feet from the surface of the ground. When the beam (C) is thrown up by the small sword (D) a pen of stout blocks is built upon a loosely fitting head that lies upon the tobacco in the hogshead. The lever (G) being raised, a pin is put through a hole in the first movable sword (F) above the beam and the lever is pulled down. This has

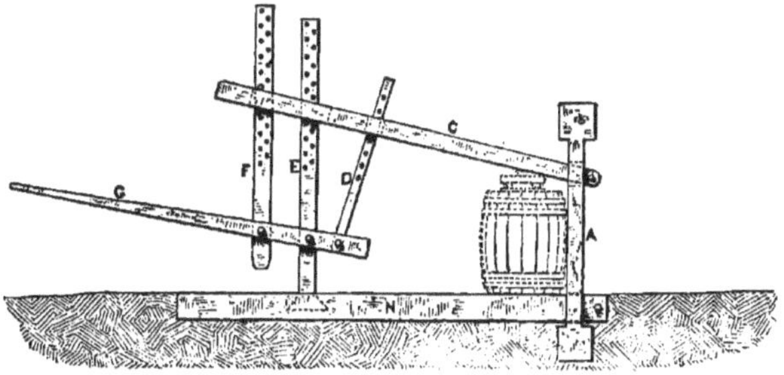

the effect of drawing down the beam (C) on the tobacco, and it is kept down by the insertion of a pin above it in the fixed sword (E). This process is repeated until the beam is brought to a level. If the tobacco in the cask should not be pressed sufficiently hard, the pins are worked out by a reverse process, the beam thrown up and more blocks put under, and it is then again worked down. The illustration on the preceding page represents the beam and lever prize, and the dimensions of each piece are given, so that any carpenter can erect one.

A is an upright post, 18 by 6 inches, with mortises 6 feet apart for beam and undersill. The size of the mortises is 10 by 3 inches. This post is set in the ground to the depth of 4 feet. N is a ground sill 18 inches thick, of which the top surface only is hewn. This is placed level with the surface of the earth, and forms a foundation for the hogshead to rest upon. This sill is let into the upright post by a mortise. C is the prize beam, 11 by 9 inches, tapering to 9 by 7, and 15 feet long. It has two mortises, the first 9 feet from the post (A), 5 by 3 inches, for the uplifting sword (D); the second one foot from the smaller end of the beam, and 4 by 20 inches. Through this both the movable sword (F) and the fixed sword (E) are put. E is a fixed sword, 12 feet long, 7 by 2 inches, dovetailed into the ground sill. F is a movable sword, 10 feet long, 7 by 2 inches, and is moved up and down by the lever G, which is 24 feet long, with mortises for E and F and a half mortise for D. The size of the lever is 7 by 7 at the larger end, tapering to 3 inches at the smaller end.

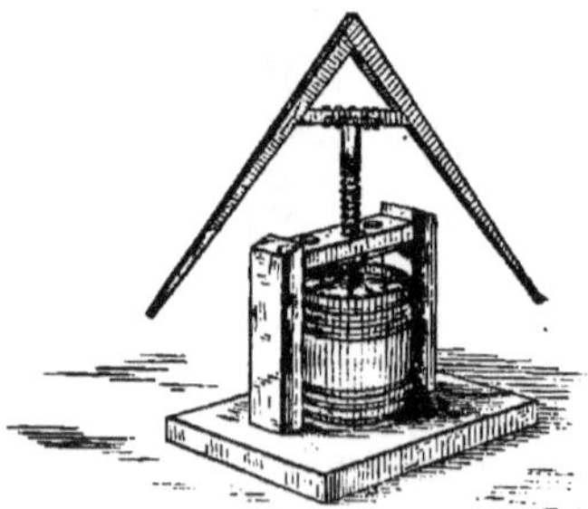

This prize, with one even more simple in construction, has been used by the average planter in Tennessee for nearly half a century. With two such, filling up the casks alternately under each one, thereby giving time for the tobacco to be fixed in its pressed condition, three good hands may prize a hogshead weighing 1,000 pounds every day.

More recently screws of various kinds have been introduced, all of which are convenient and efficient. The accompanying illustration represents one of the best, which sells at from $40 to $60.

MARKETING THE TOBACCO CROP.

When tobacco is sold loose to dealers, it is usually tied up in hands of from twenty to thirty leaves, and sometimes it is sold in small bundles of five to six leaves to local dealers, who prize and ship it without stemming. The usual time of selling and delivering loose tobacco is from November to April. When tobacco is prized and put on the market the season for delivery extends from February to October; but more or less is delivered to the warehouses every month in the year.

From 15 to 25 per cent. of the crop of the Clarksville district is sold loose to dealers, generally at a specified price for the crop round, though sometimes definite prices for different grades are agreed upon. In almost all contracts it is stipulated that the tobacco shall be in good keeping order, and that only a certain proportion, generally 25 per cent., shall belong to the lower grades.

In the Upper Cumberland River district and in western Tennessee fully four-fifths of the crop is prized by the planters, except in Henry county, where probably half the product is sold loose to dealers for making strips and for manufacturing purposes.

When tobacco is sold at auction on the market, samples are drawn from four or more places, the cask being first stripped from the tobacco. These samples are drawn by inspectors, who are the warehousemen themselves or their deputies. The state laws permit any citizen to open a warehouse under certain conditions and regulations. Among other regulations, the warehouseman is required to keep good and sufficient scales for weighing tobacco, which shall be tested at the beginning of each tobacco year, and every three months thereafter, by the keeper and sealer of weights and measures for the county, and at any other time when written application is made by two or more planters or burghers. He is required to keep the necessary breaking-irons for the proper inspection of tobacco, and screws for proper cooperage and return of loose tobacco to the hogshead after inspection. By the law he is created inspector of tobacco, and is required to take an oath for the faithful performance of his duty. He is also empowered to appoint deputy inspectors or samplers, for whose acts he is responsible. This inspector, or one of his deputies, is required to inspect the uncasing or breaking of any tobacco for inspection and to examine and classify the same according to law; to break each hogshead for inspection in at least four different places, drawing from each break at least four bundles from different courses or layers, so as to get a fair and just representation of the quality and condition of the tobacco; to place these bundles together in one sample, stamp it "state tobacco inspection", and mark with ink upon the label of the sample the name of the warehouse, the planter's name, the warehouse number, its approximate gross weight, date of inspection, and the name of the inspector who drew the sample. These samples he is required to mark "A" or "Admitted", if sound, well-assorted leaf tobacco, clear of lugs or trash, and in good keeping order, but to mark all lugs or trash, or clean leaf tobacco if not in good keeping order, with an "R", for "Refused". If the hogshead is insecure, or is made of green timber, he is required by law to condemn it and have it put in proper merchantable order at the cost of the owner, and if the tobacco be damaged so that the sample does not show the character and extent of the damage, he is required to mark it "Damaged" on the label. If any hogshead of tobacco is falsely or fraudulently packed with intent to deceive, it is made the duty of the inspector to refuse to classify the same, and, when called upon for the facts, to give information to the grand jury about such hogshead from his books.

The compensation of warehousemen for receiving, storing, inspecting, coopering, and selling tobacco is regulated by law, as follows: For each hogshead of tobacco received and weighed, 50 cents; storage, 50 cents; inspection and cooperage, $1; reweighing, 25 cents; auctioneer's fee, 25 cents; for selling, rendering an account of sales, collecting the money, and paying it over, $1, and 1 per cent. commission on proceeds of sales—the whole cost of selling being $3 50 per hogshead and commission. Warehousemen are also permitted to charge $1 per hogshead for storage for one year or less, which is to be paid by the purchaser of the tobacco. Any warehouse keeper who shall charge more than is allowed by law subjects himself to a penalty of $10, and is declared guilty of a misdemeanor.

Planters are protected by being allowed to reject any bid offered, but in that case they are charged with the fees. A lien is given on the tobacco to the warehouse keeper for fees and charges; but no planter is prohibited from selling his tobacco at private sale, with or without inspection, though stored at a licensed warehouse.

Tobacco goes into "the sweat", or fermentation, with the advent of warm weather, from the middle of April to the middle of August, according to the weather and the order in which it has been prized. If in good order, this sweating process ripens it and improves its color and flavor; but if too damp, it comes out with mold, and is very tender. This applies more particularly to the tobacco grown in western Tennessee and in the Clarksville district, that grown in the Upper Cumberland district being generally injured by becoming harsh, dry, and lifeless. Mr. Wallace, a high authority on tobacco in New York, is of opinion that the tobacco grown in the latter district ought to be used before going into the sweat. But damage is not always confined to this tobacco, fully 50 per cent. of that opened in the Clarksville market in the year 1880 being injured by mold; but this was exceptional, the season having been very unpropitious for prizing tobacco. The usual proportion injured is about 15 per cent.

COST OF RAISING TOBACCO.

All definite estimates of profits in any industry are liable to be fallacious, the difference in the soils and the seasons, the degree of attention given, the reliability and capacity of the labor employed, and the quality of the the article produced, all being important but variable factors in the solution of the problem.

The following represents the cost of improved lands, and their capacity for production in the several tobacco districts of the state:

Districts.	Price of best soils per acre.	Price of inferior soils per acre.	Yield per acre on best soils.	Yield per acre on inferior soils.	Rent per acre of best soils.	Rent per acre of inferior soils.
			Pounds.	*Pounds.*		
West Tennessee	$15	$5	1,200	600	$5	$2
Clarksville district	35	10	1,200	600	10	3
Upper Cumberland district	20	10	1,200	500	5	3

The range in prices for different qualities of land in the Upper Cumberland district is far less than in the other portions of the state. The prices paid for labor in the different districts are given below:

Districts.	Wages of men by the year, with board.	Wages of men by the year, without board.	Wages of men by the day, with board.	Wages of boys and girls of 14 years of age by the year, with board.	Wages of boys and girls of 14 years of age by the day, with board.
					Cents.
West Tennessee	$125@$150	$150@$175	$1 00	$60@$70	40
Clarksville district	130@ 160	150@ 200	75@1 00	60@ 80	40
Upper Cumberland district	100@ 110	140	75	40@ 50	30

Experts in curing tobacco frequently command much better wages than ordinary hands, especially in those districts where attempts are made to produce fine tobacco, as in Henry county, western Tennessee, and Montgomery and Robertson counties, in the Clarksville district. In all other portions of the state laborers in tobacco are paid the same prices as those engaged in the production of other crops, but in all the tobacco-growing counties labor is employed, for the most part, winter and summer, and wages are from 15 to 20 per cent. higher than in the stock-growing and cotton-producing counties.

For stemming tobacco the price paid is 50 cents per hundred pounds of strips made, and when men are employed at the factories in prizing tobacco they are paid from $1 to $1 25 per day, without board.

The estimated cost of the production of tobacco in the three divisions of the state, in detail, is subjoined. In western Tennessee, on the best soils, one hand can cultivate 3½ acres, and this will require his time for five months of the twelve; so that we have:

DR.

Five months' labor, including board		$72 91
Rent of land, 3½ acres, at $5		17 50
Use of team, wagons, barns, and manure		20 00
Hauling to market		7 50
		117 91

CR.

By 4,200 pounds of tobacco, at $5		$210 00
Profit on 3½ acres	$92 09	
Cost per acre	33 69	
Cost per pound to produce on best soils, 2.8 cents.		

Should the production fall below 674 pounds to the acre, there would be a positive loss, unless the quality of the tobacco is such as to command a higher price. At $6 per hundred, the cost of production can be met with 562 pounds to the acre; at $10 per hundred, a yield of 337 pounds will pay all expenses incurred in production.

In the Clarksville district, the quality of the crops produced and the yield per acre are variable quantities, there being localities where 1,200 or more pounds can be produced to the acre, which will bring on the market, prized, from 6 to 12 cents per pound. In other places the yield is not more than 500 pounds to the acre, and the quality of the tobacco is such that it will not bring on the market over 5 cents per pound. Taking the best soils, however, the estimate will be as follows:

DR.

Five months' labor, including board	$83 33
Use of team, wagon, and manure	20 00
Rent of land, 3½ acres, at $10	35 00
Hauling to market	7 50
Cost of growing 3½ acres	145 83
Cost of growing 1 acre	41 66

CR.

By 4,200 pounds of tobacco, at $6		$252 00
Profit on 3½ acres	$106 17	
Cost per pound to produce, 3.47 cents.		

It must be borne in mind, however, that this estimate is for the very best soils and the best labor. Taking the average yield for the district, which in favorable years is about 800 pounds per acre, and the average price 6 cents per pound, which is a full one, the whole amount realized from the work of one man, cultivating 3½ acres, will be $144, or a loss on every hand employed of $1 83. Unfortunately this estimate is too often the true one, and it will hardly be otherwise until the farmers of the district learn that heavy manuring of the land and the production of a superior article are the principal factors in the creation of profits. With manure to the value of $25 applied to every acre the yield can be made to exceed 1,000 pounds.

Still more variable are the profits in the Upper Cumberland River district. Where a fine type is grown and good prices are obtained there are evident signs of prosperity, but no progress is visible where the planters grow a poor leaf, which brings only 3 or 4 cents per pound. The average price of the best soils in Smith, Trousdale, and Jackson counties is not far from $25 per acre, and the rental value $5 per acre. Labor is worth, with board, $100 per annum; without board, $140 per annum. The yield of tobacco on best soils is about 1,200 pounds per acre, and the average yield, according to the returns of the enumerators, 819 pounds per acre. Taking the maximum yield and basing an estimate upon it, and assuming the amount cultivated by each grown man to be 3 acres, we shall have:

Five months' wages of one man, with board	$58 33
Use of team, wagon, and manure	18 00
Rent of three acres of land, at $5	15 00
Hauling to market	6 00
Total	97 33
By 3,600 pounds of tobacco, at 4 cents per pound, the average of all the counties in this district	144 00
Profit on 3 acres	46 67

Cost per acre, $32 44; cost to produce, per pound, 2.7 cents.

When the average yield per acre is only 707 pounds (the average for the state, as shown by the enumerators' returns) the cost of production is just about balanced by the amount received from the crop. Disregarding the amount raised for home consumption, the cost of that produced for market may be put at $4 50 per hundred pounds.

It will be observed that where the price of land is very low rents are disproportionately high, amounting often to over 25 per cent. of its value. Labor in 1879 was abundant and cheap. The relation between the price of rents and the value of lands depends mainly upon the supply of labor, and, as a rule, throughout the southern states the cheaper and more abundant the labor the higher the rents and the lower the lands, and *vice versa*. In some districts the rental value of the land for one year is half what the land would bring if sold in open market.

Throughout the state tobacco is, to a considerable extent, cultivated on the "share system". The chief objection urged against this system is that the land is apt to be run down, and the fencing is not kept up so well as when the labor is employed at a definite price. The saving and application of manure are neglected, and the steady habits of industry, so much needed to make farming profitable, are seriously interfered with. The "new and old field system"—that is, the clearing up of new lands and the abandonment of worn-out fields—has run its natural course in Tennessee. The next step will be one of renovation and restitution.

PRICES OF TOBACCO.

The following table, compiled from the schedules returned to this office, shows the price received by growers in the different counties of each district for the crop of 1879. The proportion of lugs in each crop will average from 25 to 30 per cent. Farmers usually classify into four grades, viz: Lugs, medium, good, and bright, the latter in localities where bright tobacco is produced:

Counties.	Average crop round.	Lugs.	Medium.	Good.	Bright and selections.
	Cents.	*Cents.*	*Cents.*	*Cents.*	*Cents.*
WEST TENNESSEE DISTRICT.					
Benton	4½	2	4	5	8
Dyer	5	2½	5	6 to 7	....
Henry	5½	2½ to 4	4 to 5	6 to 8	10 to 15
Weakley	5	2 to 4	4 to 6	6 to 8	....
CLARKSVILLE DISTRICT.					
Cheatham	5	1½ to 3	3 to 5	6 to 8	....
Dickson	4	2	3	5	6 to 7
Houston	4½	1 to 3	3 to 4	5 to 7	8 to 16
Montgomery	6	3	5	7	10 to 15
Robertson	5½	2½ to 3½	4 to 5	5½ to 6½	6 to 12
Stewart	5	2 to 3	4 to 5	5½ to 6½	8 to 11
UPPER CUMBERLAND RIVER DISTRICT.					
Jackson	4	1 to 2½	3½ to 4	6	7
Macon	3½	1 to 3	3½ to 4½	5	....
Smith	4½	2 to 3	3½ to 4½	5	7
Sumner	6	2 to 3	3½ to 4	5 to 5½	....
Trousdale	4½	2 to 3	3 to 4	5 to 6	....
Wilson	5	2 to 3	3½ to 4½	5	7

A small amount of tobacco is grown in Scott county, on the Cumberland plateau, a region of great attractiveness on account of its elevation, its fine freestone water, its magnificent scenery, and its salubrious climate, but one whose soil is deemed by many as sterile. This tobacco, however, commands a very high price, reaching an average of 14 cents per pound, the finest grade of the crop of 1879, as reported on the schedules, bringing 18 cents. In no other portion of the state, except Unicoi county, does the average price exceed 6 cents. It may be that these sandstone soils will yet prove very profitable in the production of cigar tobacco, the samples exhibited from the Cumberland plateau showing great delicacy of structure and a wide wrapping leaf, mild and pleasant to the taste, and free from acrid bitterness.

In McMinn, Knox, and other counties of eastern Tennessee tobacco has been grown in years past, and is raised to a very small extent at the present time, but never with great profit, and on some of the slopes of the Unaka range a fine yellow wrapper is produced in limited quantities.

The soils of White, Coffee, Rutherford, De Kalb, Warren, Franklin, Lawrence, Wayne, Lewis, Perry, Hardin, and Hickman counties are identical in character with those of the best tobacco-growing counties of middle Tennessee, and the small patches raised for domestic consumption show the adaptability of the soils to its growth.

TOTAL TOBACCO PRODUCTION, ACREAGE, YIELD, AND VALUE.

Taking the production, acreage, yield, and value of the crops of the three tobacco districts of the state for the four years ending with 1879, and combining them, adding the production of the territory not attached to either of the districts, we have the following result, only the figures for 1879 being from census returns:

Year.	Production.	Acreage.	Yield per acre.	Value in primary markets.	Value per pound.	Value per acre.
	Pounds.		*Pounds.*		*Cents.*	
1876......	28,463,676	41,677	683	$1,941,222	6.82	$46 59
1877......	43,425,400	55,266	780	2,635,921	6.07	47 71
1878......	28,900,362	42,058	677	1,445,010	5.00	33 85
1879......	29,365,052	41,532	707	1,598,287	5.34	37 05

EXPERIMENTS WITH CUBAN TOBACCO.

A few experiments have been made with Havana tobacco grown from seed imported from Cuba. One of these was made by Mr. W. B. Bryan, sr., near Clarksville, who says:

As requested, I give you an account of the manner of growing, handling, and curing tobacco grown by me in 1868 from fresh Cuba seed. The seed and special instructions were furnished by a friend who was a resident of New Orleans, but the owner of a large tobacco plantation in the province of Vuelta Abajo, in Cuba. I first soaked the seed in fresh milk forty-eight hours, keeping them in a warm room. Without allowing them to dry, they were mixed with ashes and sown on a bed prepared in the usual way by burning. I selected rather gravelly hillside land of good quality, prepared it well, and cast it up into ridges three feet apart. The ridge was cut through with a hoe, taking off about one-half of it at spaces as near twenty inches apart as could be done. The plants were set out and kept well worked, allowing them to run up until the blossom bud shot out, which I pinched off, but did not prime the plant. I let the suckers grow to about two inches in length; turned out one of the most vigorous next the ground for a second crop; broke down from one side all the rest, taking care not to break them entirely off, but leaving them hanging by the skin on one side. I had no more suckers to trouble me or draw the sap from the growing plant. I found many of the suckers struggling for life when my tobacco was ripe. The same plan succeeds well with our heavy tobacco. The plants were allowed to stand until thoroughly ripe, which is of great importance. The leaves are then stripped from the stalk as is fodder from corn. The stalk was cut above the sucker, and the latter was worked and treated in every respect like the first crop. This second crop was somewhat smaller, but was much finer, richer tobacco, and ripened about the 10th of October. When the crop was ripe and stripped from the stalk, I dug a pit long enough and two feet deep, just as though I was preparing to barbecue meat, filled it up with sound hard wood, which I set on fire. When the wood burned down, I carefully raked off all coals. I had freshly-cut crab grass ready, clear of weeds, with which I lined the bottom, sides, and ends of my pit, and packed the freshly-stripped tobacco smoothly and closely down and covered it over with about four inches of crab grass, and then put on eight or ten inches of earth, being particular to leave no part uncovered to allow the steam to escape. It remained in this condition about forty hours. I then stripped off the covering and took out the tobacco. The water was streaming from a black, unsightly, and, as I thought, ruined mass. Still I obeyed instructions, tied the leaves into small hands, put them on sticks, and hung them up in the open shed of my barn. I was so sure that my trouble and labor had been thrown away I felt no anxiety to look at it. The fourth day I was riding by the barn and happened to pass on the windward side. I caught a whiff that brought me to the ground immediately. I threw open the door of the shed and was saluted by a perfect billow of rich, real Havana aroma filling the entire barn. My tobacco was as dry as snuff and perfectly cured. The first damp day brought the leaf in order, when I packed it in a large dry-goods box, nailed it up, and stored it in a dry room. I did not open it for one year. None but a connoisseur can imagine what a luxury I enjoyed in return for my perseverance. The tobacco was very dark, almost black, and was equal to the best cured Havana tobacco.

CHAPTER XVI.

CULTURE AND CURING OF TOBACCO IN VIRGINIA.

A SHORT HISTORY OF THE TYPES OF TOBACCO PRODUCED IN VIRGINIA AND MARYLAND

The original standard type with the planters of Virginia and Maryland was what is now termed the dark export type. For a long series of years the laws regulating production, especially those passed by the colonial assembly of Virginia, requiring all of the product that failed to come up to the legal exactions of quality and soundness to be burned, were rigidly executed. Tobacco was all raised for export, then the only market, and the price being uniform, whether for sale or as a circulating medium, it was necessary to institute an inspection to compel uniformity of grade.

With a virgin soil of great fertility, the planter who did his work well had reasonable assurance that his crop would "pass".(a) Its cultivation was commenced by the colonists in the historic town of Jamestown, in James City county, and John Rolfe produced the first tobacco exported from the colony.

a A word used by inspectors to brand all hogsheads of tobacco fit for export.

Captain John Smith describes the soil of tidewater Virginia as he saw it in 1607: "The vesture of the earth in most places doth manifestly prove the nature of the soyle to be lusty and very rich."

The culture of tobacco rapidly spread as the colonists built houses and cleared lands, the tobacco-patch often taking precedence of the corn-field, and its production being carried to such an excess as seriously to threaten subsistence of the colonists, the colonial legislatures of Virginia and Maryland passed sumptuary laws that "every person planting one acre of tobacco shall plant and tend two acres of corn". As tobacco grows better on new soil than corn or other crops, it was the first to utilize the fresh cleared land. New soil produces a finer and better flavored article than old land; therefore thousands of acres of forest were annually cleared. Thus extensive areas in Virginia and Maryland were early denuded of forest growth, and the continued cultivation of tobacco for many years on the same lands without manure greatly impoverished the soil; for a Virginian never thinks of reinstating or manuring his land with economy until he can find no more new land to exhaust or wear out" (William Tatham, *Historical Essay on the Culture of Tobacco:* London, 1800).

Tobacco raised on cow-penned land was considered of only second quality, and was sold accordingly. Tatham states that tobacco at first was cultivated continuously for twenty years on the same land, and describes the spots selected for seed-beds as those preferred at the present day—"rich, moist, fine soils, with sunny exposure." The "fly" was a trouble then, as now; and the remedy then practiced was "to sow mustard around the border of the plant-bed, and as the fly prefers the mustard to the tobacco plants the latter will escape injury". But of late years this irrepressible insect takes more kindly to the tender tobacco plants, and planters find it hard work to coax or to drive them off.

The primitive mode of harvesting tobacco in Virginia was "to pull the leaves from the stalks as they ripen and hang them on cords, to be dried in the sun and air" (Rev. Hugh Jones, *Present State of Virginia,* 1724). In after time they split the stalks and hung the plants astraddle of sticks, as is now generally practiced in Virginia.

The early planters cured their crops mostly in the sun and air. "In March or April the tobacco was conveyed to the storehouse and dried with fire. * * * Salt was used in passing tobacco through the sweat." In time "smoke was considered a prime agent in keeping tobacco sound. * * * Small, smothered fires were used, made of bark and rotten wood". The fires were increased from year to year until log fires were built in three rows upon the barn floors, which dried out the green tobacco in from three to five days. The firing process prevailed generally in both Virginia and Maryland, and was kept up for a long series of years. Maryland finally abandoned it; but in the dark shipping district of Virginia it is still the mode practiced, except that less fire is now used than formerly.

After the close of the war of 1812–'14 the demand for colored tobacco for export caused a change in the process of curing in both Virginia and Maryland. After being cut and hung upon sticks, the tobacco was either placed upon scaffolds in the sun to yellow and then housed, or it remained several days in the house, without fire, until it had yellowed sufficiently to receive the heat without curing dark. Many planters in the two states learned to cure a beautiful piebald or spangled leaf, which commanded high prices in Richmond and in Baltimore. In the former city it was called "piebald"; in the latter, "spangled."

Open wood fires constituted the only mode of curing by artificial heat until about the year 1828 or 1829, when flues were first used in Virginia, Dr. Davis G. Tuck, of Halifax county, being the originator of the flue constructed inside the barn, for which he obtained a patent. This plan, however, was adopted by but few planters, and soon fell into disuse.

About this time began the use of charcoal as fuel for curing tobacco, enterprising planters in Halifax and Pittsylvania counties, Virginia, and in Caswell county, North Carolina, being among the first to substitute it for wood. The results were such as to induce others to adopt the new process, and thus it spread from farm to farm throughout neighborhoods, and afterward from state to state, until it has extended over a wide area of the tobacco belt.

Meanwhile improvements were made upon flues, mainly since 1865, which justified their substitution for charcoal open fires in the yellow tobacco belt of Virginia and North Carolina. Charcoal is now but little used. Flues are constructed either of brick, stone, or mud walls, or by digging ditches in the floor of the barn, and some are wholly of iron, furnaces and pipes, and these are generally patented.

A diagram of a cheap, efficient, and durable flue is given in Plate I, showing the ground plan of a tobacco barn 20 by 20 feet and the arrangement of the flues therein. Plate II shows the elevation.

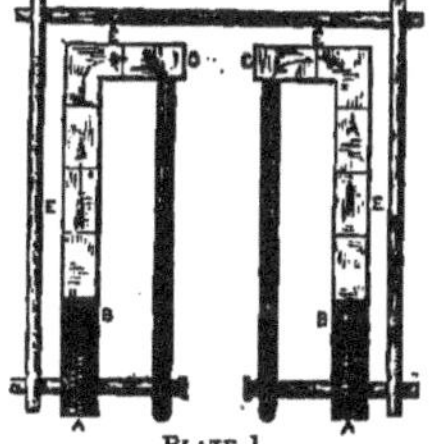

PLATE I.

To construct flues on the plan given, it is first necessary to cut out two or three logs from the end of the barn; then build the walls of the flues 12 or 13 inches distant from the sills or walls of the barn, as at EEEE, in Plate I, and projecting outside the walls at AA 18 inches. Build the walls of flues 18 inches apart, and 18 to 20 inches in height at the openings AA, decreasing in height as they run back to 14 inches at CC. Put in sheet-iron pipes at CC, 10 or 12 inches in diameter, equidistant from the flues and from each other, and carry them through the body of the barn, out at DD, with the ends elevated at DD 3 feet higher than at CC. The flues should be arched with brick or covered with flat fire-proof stone for about 5 feet—from AA to BB; then cover the flues from BB to CC with sheet-iron. Use No. 16 iron nearest the fire, commencing at BB, and thinner iron, No. 18 or 20, for the remainder of the covering.

PLATE II.

A number of patent flues are used, some of which greatly economize fuel and perform admirably, and where the saving of fuel is an object they are to be preferred.

A cheap flue is constructed by cutting ditches in the floor of the barn from 15 to 18 inches wide and as deep as necessary and covering them with sheet-iron, as recommended for the stone or brick flue. A better one is made of mud walls, covered with sheet-iron. The mud walls are built by placing two wide boards from 12 to 14 inches apart and packing moist clay between them, beating it down hard, in position and arrangement similar to the walls of stone, and covering with sheet-iron. Upon firing the flues the boards are burned away and the dirt walls are hardened. If the clay is of proper quality, such as is fit for making tolerably good bricks, these walls will last a long time. It is necessary with the ditch or mud-wall flue to attach furnaces of stone, brick, or iron.

QUALITY OF TOBACCO IN VIRGINIA.

There are five distinct qualities of tobacco produced in Virginia, viz: Dark Shipping, Red and Colored Shipping, Sun- and Air-cured Fillers, Bright Yellow Wrappers, Smokers and Fillers, and Orange and Mahogany Flue-cured Manufacturing. These are severally characterized by peculiarities of color, quality, body, and flavor, the result of soil influence and variety, modified by curing and management.

DARK SHIPPING.—Of this there are four grades of leaf and two of lugs, classed as follows: 1. Dark, rich waxy leaf, English; 2. Nutmeg and mahogany leaf, English and Continental; 3. Dark red leaf, English and Continental; 4. Dull red leaf; 5. Long lugs; 6. Short lugs.

Dark Shipping tobacco is generally raised on rich lots, and is cured with open wood fires. The English, French, Germans, Spanish, and Italians take the bulk of this tobacco, with a growing preference for that cured without smoke. It is produced more or less all over the tobacco belt of Virginia, but the bulk of it is raised south of the James river and east of the Blue Ridge.

RED AND COLORED SHIPPING.—Like the foregoing, this tobacco is produced more or less all over the tobacco region of the state. The region producing most of it is colored red on the type map, and contains the following: Northeast of the region just described, Dinwiddie, Chesterfield, Goochland, and Fluvanna, with Rockbridge and all the counties west of the Blue Ridge down to the Kentucky and Tennessee lines, except Montgomery, which is classed in the yellow district.

This tobacco is divided into three grades: 1. Bright spangled; 2. Mahogany; 3. Cherry red; and is generally cured with open wood fires, a method which greatly detracts from its worth. The red and mahogany wrappers of this and the dark tobacco, if fine, sell well, notwithstanding the smell of smoke.

SUN- AND AIR-CURED FILLERS.—These include all that is cured without artificial heat, whether by the sun or by air, or by both. The counties raising this tobacco mainly are Caroline, Hanover, Louisa, and Spotsylvania. Their product is eagerly sought after by manufacturers, is never in oversupply, and those long accustomed to its use prefer it to all others, even to the White Burley.

BRIGHT YELLOW has many grades, the finest, smoothest, and brightest leaves being rated as wrappers: 1. Fancy; 2. Fine; 3. Medium, running 0, 00, 000, etc., according to quality and color; 4. Fillers, several grades. Lugs are graded as follows: Fancy Smokers, Fine Smokers, Medium Smokers, Common Smokers, Bright Lug Fillers, and Common Lug Fillers.

Instances are on record of its first grades having been sold for $3 and $4 per pound, and to sell at the highest average, or to obtain the highest price, is an honor sought by the best planters of the yellow belt.

FLUE-CURED FILLERS.—These are known as Henry county fillers, being produced mainly in Henry county and in portions of Franklin and Patrick counties. This tobacco is divided into fillers and wrappers, according to size, color, and quality, and is mostly manufactured into plug chewing. It is characterized by its tough, rich, silky leaf, and sweet flavor, due to the soil, the varieties cultivated (Sweet Orinoco and Flannagan), and the peculiar mode of curing by flues, both walls and tops of stone, and slow firing until the leaf is dried.

CLIMATE.

The climatic conditions most favorable to the growth and maturity of the Virginia tobaccos are in localities where the mean temperature ranges between 52° and 60°.

The mean temperature of Lynchburg, situate about the center of the tobacco belt east of the Blue Ridge mountains, is as follows (Hotchkiss' *Summary of Virginia*, p. 53):

	1869-'70.	1870-'71.
Spring	54.3	55.0
Summer	76.1	76.1
Autumn	54.5	58.8
Winter	42.1	40.5
Yearly mean	56.7	58.0

According to the *Statistical Atlas of the United States*, temperature chart, Plate VII, the isotherm, or mean annual temperature line, of 60° runs through Eastville, on the eastern shore, and then southwest, by Hickford, to Weldon, in North Carolina, and thence on to Montgomery, Alabama. The region southeast of this line, in Virginia, is in the cotton-producing zone.

The isotherm of 56° enters Virginia near Alexandria and runs southwest between Middle and Piedmont, passing through Lynchburg and a little west of Danville, thence through Greensboro', North Carolina, on to Atlanta, Georgia. The country between this line of 56° and that of 60°, before described, is the tobacco zone proper of the state.

The country west of the isotherm of 56°, on to 52°, includes all of Piedmont, the less elevated portions of the valley, and much of Appalachia, that portion included between 56° and 54° producing tobacco of fine quality, unsurpassed by that of similar type grown in any other portion of the United States.

The tobacco zone proper of Virginia lies between the isothermal lines of 58° and 54°, in a temperature where the frosts of winter penetrate to the depth of several inches, breaking the cohesion of the soil, forcing its particles asunder, and causing it to fall loose and mellow from the mold-board; where spring opens and vegetation puts forth early in the month of April; where the summer's sun shines with a warmth sufficient to expand and ripen without burning the tender leaves; and where autumnal frosts are delayed until the crop is matured.

The average rainfall is plentiful, and rarely excessive, throughout the tobacco zone.

The following table shows the average precipitation of rain and melted snow over the main tobacco belt of Virginia, the averages of 1869-'70 and 1870-'71 being calculated from tables in Hotchkiss' *Summary of Virginia*, pages 57, 58:

	Middle.	Piedmont.	Valley.
Spring	13.90	15.90	12.14
Summer	13.90	10.85	11.81
Autumn	8.50	12.65	17.70
Winter	10.30	7.70	9.20

The rain-chart in the *United States Statistical Atlas*, Plate V, shows that Virginia lies principally in the belt where the annual amount of precipitation is from 32 to 44 inches. The moist spring hastens the growth of the plants in the beds and facilitates their transplanting and promotes growth, a dry summer matures the leaves and mellows the juices, and a dry autumn gives body, gum, and oil to the product, and permits the gathering of the crop in good condition.

The tobacco belt proper has a dry climate, with a medium temperature, except for a short term of excessively hot weather.

The Virginia tobacco requires from 90 to 100 days after transplanting to mature well. Plants grown in the open air ought to be ready for transplanting on an average by the 20th of May east of the mountains, and by the 1st of June west of the mountains. If a propitious season follows, and the tobacco is properly cultivated, it will rarely fail to ripen before frost in either locality.

STORMS.

All of Virginia, except Tidewater—the country east of the tobacco belt—lies in the zone of the lowest number of storms (*United States Statistical Atlas*, Plate VI). The rain and wind storms, which usually do most damage to the tobacco crop, occur about the autumnal equinox, when the plant, from its size, is most easily damaged. The tier of counties on the eastern edge of middle Virginia, and bordering on Tidewater, suffer most, as the coast storms often extend inland.

VIRGINIA SOILS.

The soils of Virginia are as varied as the rocks they overlie. A geological survey of the state was made by Professor William B. Rogers in the years from 1835 to 1840. It is necessary to notice carefully only the soils of the tobacco area.

THE TIDEWATER REGION.—This is Tertiary, and its soils are principally alluvials—sand and clay. Tobacco was once cultivated over the greater part of this district, but it has long ago given place to crops more suited to its soils or to the choice of their owners.

THE MIDDLE COUNTRY.—This is the great tobacco-producing area of the state, bounded on the north by the Rappahannock, on the east by Tidewater, on the south by North Carolina, and on the west by Piedmont. It is an extended rolling plain, greatly diversified by hills and vales, forests and streams. Its geology is primary; its rocks Azoic, many containing mineral elements that by decomposing greatly enrich the soil, such as granite, gneiss, syenite, hornblende, mica schist, micaceous, talcose, and argillaceous slates and shales, and the sedimentary rocks of the Jurassic and Triassic formations. The soil varies in depth on the hills and plains from 2 to 8 inches, while along the rivers and creeks they are much deeper, in some places practically inexhaustible. The usual depth of forest soils is from 4 to 5 inches, with a subsoil rich in mineral elements. The tobacco soils proper are the rich bottoms and clay-loam lots for shipping, and thin, gray, light soils, fertilized, for manufacturing. This district produces about seven-eighths of the tobacco of the state, and of every grade heretofore described, except the flue-cured manufacturing grown in Henry and adjoining counties.

PIEDMONT.—Like the Middle division, this is in the primary region; but here the metamorphic rocks differ considerably from those of middle Virginia. The gneiss is coarser and darker in color. The hornblende and iron pyrites form large belts of red soil, called the "red-land district". Here is found more greenstone (epidote), and where this abounds the soil is richer, but is not better adapted to the manufacturing grades of tobacco. The belts of limestone which traverse portions of this district are overlaid by soils rich and admirably suited to grasses and the cereals, but they produce a coarse staple of tobacco, not much in demand, even at low prices. The tobacco soils of this division are the low grounds and red-clay lots for shipping, and the gray uplands, sandy and slaty, for manufacturing. The chief tobacco-producing counties of this district form a line along the eastern slope of the Blue Ridge southward from Madison, and include Henry county.

BLUE RIDGE.—This district forms the border between the Transition and Fossiliferous, and partakes somewhat of the character of both. Gneissoid sandstones, epidote, granite, syenite, slates, and shales abound in the east, while the western flank of the Blue Ridge is composed of the rocks of the Cambrian, Potsdam, Sandstone, and Primal. The abundance of epidote accounts for the great fertility of the soils of this division.

The gray sandy slopes and ridges are the best tobacco lands. The tobacco counties of this district are Floyd, Carroll, and Grayson.

THE VALLEY AND APPALACHIA.—In this district are included all the remaining counties of the state west of the Blue Ridge, southwest from Rockbridge, in the northeast, some of these counties producing but little, but all capable of growing, to more or less extent, a good type of tobacco. The lighter soils are the better, but the arenaceous soils of the mountain slopes and foothills are preferred. The limestone belt is an extensive one, rich and well adapted to general farming. The poorer siliceous soils, notably in Poor Valley, in Washington and Lee counties, are growing a fine article of brights, but the south and southeastern slopes of the mountains also produce desirable manufacturing grades.

While the above are classed in the red and yellow shipping district, there are extensive areas in most of these counties well adapted to produce the bright yellow type, as is being demonstrated by individual planters every year.

SURFACE ROCKS OF THE TOBACCO REGION.

In a narrow section of Albemarle county limestone suitable for burning is found in abundance; in other parts iron pyrites are found in large quantity, and large tracts are covered with quartz. Such lands are quite poor. Slates and shales are found in many neighborhoods. Where feldspathic, gneissoid, and hornblendic rocks come out the best tobacco soils are found.

Greene, Madison, Nelson, Amherst, Bedford, and a portion of Franklin exhibit the same surface rocks as Albemarle, except that there are less iron pyrites in some of the counties, less limestone, and more of the Azoic rocks cropping out and on the surface.

Buckingham, Cumberland, Amelia, Prince Edward, Charlotte, Nottoway, Lunenburg, Dinwiddie, Brunswick, Mecklenburg, Campbell, and a portion of Halifax counties, of the Middle division, south of James river, may be classed together as generally of like formation. This group, like that portion of Piedmont above described, belongs to the Eozoic or Primary formation. Here the rocks which most commonly come to the surface are granite, syenite, gneiss, and quartz, micaceous, talcose, and hornblendic slates, and occasionally argillaceous slates, sandstone, steatite, serpentine, etc.

The counties of Chesterfield, Powhatan, and Goochland, being largely on the Jurassic and Triassic formations, the rocks in places are sandstones; in others, granites.

Hanover, Louisa, Caroline, Fluvanna, and Spotsylvania—the air-curing district—are for the most part on the same formations (Primary, running through the Triassic and Jurassic), and differ somewhat from the last group mentioned in the underlying and the surface rocks, as also in the soils. The gneissoid rocks of western Hanover and Caroline pass into the micaceous and hornblendic in Louisa, Spotsylvania, and Fluvanna, constituting the best tobacco soils of this famous sweet-filler section.

Pittsylvania, Henry, Patrick, and portions of Halifax and Franklin counties—the yellow tobacco district east of the Blue Ridge mountains—may be classed together, as mainly of the same geologic formation, the outcropping rocks being principally quartz, syenite, feldspathic and hornblendic, mixed often and largely with mica, slate, etc.

Rockbridge, Botetourt, Roanoke, Craig, Montgomery, Giles, Bland, Tazewell, Russell, Scott, and Washington counties are principally on the Cambrian, Silurian, and Devonian, the rocks being mainly limestone, sandstone, Potsdam shales, slates, greenstone, epidote, and hornblende. The soils vary from very poor to very rich. The siliceous soils are best adapted to tobacco, limestone soils producing a strong, bony tobacco, of inferior quality.

CONDITION OF TOBACCO SOILS.

The soils of the Middle and Piedmont districts best suited to tobacco are generally of easy tillage. The stiff red clays are refractory if plowed out of condition; but if well broken in the fall, turning under vegetable matter, they become friable in the spring, are readily brought into fine tilth, and, if properly handled, work easily all through cultivation. A soggy blue clay never works easily, and should never be planted to tobacco.

All the light gray soils, sandy or slaty, are easily worked; and these are the preferred soils for fine tobacco. Many counties abound in a rich, flat soil, too wet for any crop, and hundreds of thousands of acres of valuable land lie idle for want of drainage. Little progress has been made in reclaiming these lands. Some good soils in the mountain region are hard to cultivate, owing to the steepness of the hills and the abundance of bowlders and loose stones on the surface.

The soils of Virginia east of the mountains are generally tender, as the galled and gullied surface over large areas too plainly indicate. For generations the mode of culture has been of the shallowest and most imperfect character, followed by its inevitable results—an impoverished soil and fields abandoned, because no longer capable of yielding a return for labor. Many good farmers are improving their lands by deeper plowing on all lands cultivated and by adopting the horizontal system on hilly lands, so as to dispose of surface water without cutting the soil into gullies.

Of the gray soils, the gneissoid and micaceous are the most tender, the syenitic, hornblendic, feldspathic, and argillaceous being less liable to wash.

The valley and mountain soils are generally of close texture, and are not liable to wash, except on some of the sandstone spurs of the mountains.

Nearly every foot of land in the Middle and Piedmont divisions west of longitude 77° 30′ and south of latitude 38°, now in old fields, occupied by pines, broom-straw, briers, and sassafras, produced while under tillage one or more crops of tobacco. Thousands of acres of such lands are capable, with a little help, of producing tobacco again, in some cases of a better type than the first grown upon them. No reliable estimate can be made of the number of acres turned out as old fields, or of the proportion such lands bear to the area once cleared; but a careful analysis of reports justifies the opinion that of the lands turned out more than three-fourths are in an improving condition, ready to furnish large supplies of fuel, compensating in some measure for the destruction of the original forest. In some sections, especially of the Middle district, there are now more "old fields" than arable lands, while in others these rarely occur. The exhausted lands, gullied and washed until there is none of the original soil left, are for all practical purposes worthless, and are likely to remain so for a long time.

Lands in the tobacco belt east of the mountains, when worn and turned out, grow up first either in "poverty grass" (often called "hen's nest") or in broom-sedge, according to the amount of fertility left in the soil when it ceases to be cropped. If very poor, the poverty grass first takes possession, then broom-sedge, and afterward pines. The length of time it takes these worn soils to recuperate depends largely upon their original fertility and the nature of the subsoil, and if the underlying rocks are of the character to disintegrate slowly under the action of the atmosphere, rains, heat and frost, recuperation will be faster than where such agencies are wanting, the softer rocks, micaceous and feldspathic, yielding more readily to the action of the elements than the harder ones of the gneissoid, hornblendic, and granitic group. About ten years' growth of pines and other plants will restore these old fields to a moderate condition of fertility, if this growth is cut down and allowed to rot on the land.

Requiring clean culture, this crop exposes the soil for a long period to drenching rains, which injure the land, one year with another, fully as much as the abstraction of fertility by the tobacco plants. Nevertheless, with proper care, lands can be readily improved by a rotation of tobacco, wheat, clover, etc. Wheat succeeds better after tobacco than after corn, even when the manuring and cultivation of the preceding crop are the same. It is the received opinion that tobacco is less exhaustive than corn, much less than sorghum, and about as exhaustive as cabbage, beets and potatoes.

VARIETIES OF TOBACCO.

The types and grades for which any given district or section is especially noted depend not so much upon variety as upon peculiarities of soil, methods of cultivation, and subsequent management in the curing processes.

MIDDLE DIVISION.

GOOCHLAND.—The variety mostly planted is Orinoco, making the finest grades. White stem is also grown, which is not so liable to be eaten by the horn-worms, because it is coarser and tougher, but does not sell so high as the Orinoco.

HANOVER.—The varieties generally cultivated are the Broad and Narrow Orinocos—the latter noted for its small fibers and delicate flavor. The Narrow Orinoco is probably the same as is known elsewhere in the sun- and air-curing district as Little or Sweet Orinoco. The Johnson-Green is also grown to some extent; it is stronger in flavor than the Orinocos, and is preferred when the product is intended for strips or shipping leaf. Single leaves of this variety have been known to weigh two ounces when cured.

BUCKINGHAM.—The Broad and the Narrow Orinocos are used for both shipping and manufacturing. One peculiarity of the White Stem is its difficulty of curing to a uniform color, it being liable to have green streaks if cured too hastily, or white stems and fibers if cured too slowly. The Medley Pryor is preferable for rich lands, and being a late variety, it does not always ripen, but when well matured it is sought by purchasers for manufacturing. Nicely handled, it makes the finest bright shipping, and brings high prices.

CUMBERLAND.—The planters raise Orinoco, White Stem, Frederick, dark, rich and heavy, and Medley Pryor. The dark tobaccos, which are mostly cultivated in this county, are intended for export.

AMELIA.—Formerly the White Stem was almost universally planted. The leaves are long and fibrous, of rapid growth; top leaves sweeping the ground, and, for that reason, often ragged at the ends. Recently the Medley Pryor has been preferred.

APPOMATTOX.—Orinoco and White Stem are the principal varieties.

DINWIDDIE.—Orinoco is now generally grown. White Stem and Long Green are grown for quantity rather than for quality, and are popular with rough managers. Blue Pryor and Silky Pryor are favorites with careful planters, the latter variety being disposed to cure bright.

CHARLOTTE.—The Yellow and the Medley Pryor are cultivated for the continental market; the Big and Little Orinocos for the home trade principally, for fillers and wrappers; Long Green for English shipping. The Yellow Pryor is capable of filling a greater variety of uses than any other kind, readily adapting itself to variations of soil and of cultivation, and will make bright wrappers as well as the best grades of dark and mahogany wrappers for the Austrian and Italian markets. Long Green makes a coarse, heavy, rich tobacco, and yields more to the acre than the others.

LUNENBURG.—Planters raise Blue Pryor, Yellow Pryor, Orinoco, Medley Long Leaf (a very broad leaf, but late) for shipping and dark wrappers; Wells (short, broad leaf, early), for wrappers; One Sucker, Spread Eagle (large, broad leaf, resembling, though not identical with Blue Pryor), Caswell (leaf medium size, and cures a bright color, and used for bright wrappers and smokers), and White Stem.

PITTSYLVANIA.—The Little and the Big Orinocos are most cultivated. Spotted Pryor is raised by some, grows rather larger than Orinoco, is of fine quality, yellows well on the hill, but is several weeks later in maturing than the Orinocos, and is therefore not desirable except for early plantings. Gourd Leaf, a new variety, is rapidly coming into favor. This variety has a large, fine, silky leaf, broad but short, yellows on the hill better, and is more easily cured than any other variety. White Stem, Bull-face, Scruggs, Gray Pryor, and Frederick are also grown for shipping.

HALIFAX.—For fancy wrappers and smokers Yellow Orinoco, Gooch, Gold-Leaf, and White Stem are grown. Little Orinoco is best for plug fillers; Medley Pryor, Big Orinoco, and White Stem for export.

MECKLENBURG.—This county produces Orinoco, Pryor, and Gooch.

BRUNSWICK.—Orinoco, Blue Pryor, Long Green, and White Stem are preferred. Most of the tobacco grown in this county is for export.

GREENSVILLE.—Orinoco is generally preferred. Cotton and peanuts are taking the place of tobacco in this county, very little of the latter being now cultivated.

PIEDMONT DIVISION.

ALBEMARLE.—Orinoco and Pryor are preferred for new grounds and the lighter soils, upon which they produce fine grades of light-colored tobacco. White Stem is generally planted.

GREENE.—Orinoco, Green, Frederick (elsewhere known as Bull-face), Pryor, and Long Green are all planted.

AMHERST.—Pryor, Orinoco, White Stem, and Bull-face are grown.

BEDFORD.—Broad Orinoco and Little or Narrow Orinoco are the varieties produced.

HENRY.—In this county there are two varieties in general cultivation: Broad Leaf or Big Orinoco, and Narrow Leaf or Little Orinoco, sometimes called Brittle Stem, and by some Flannagan, the favorite with the manufacturers of plug chewing. Though very much like the Little Orinoco of the Middle division, the Flannagan is evidently a distinct variety, produced possibly by hybridizing the Little Orinoco, or changed in habit and character by selection and culture. The leaf is broader and the fiber finer than the Little Orinoco, while it is equally as sweet, silky, and tough as that old favorite. White Stem is not much grown. This is evidently not the White Stem of the dark shipping district, but probably a hybrid Orinoco, called in some places White-stem Orinoco.

BLUE RIDGE DIVISION.

FLOYD.—The only variety produced is Yellow Pryor.

VALLEY AND APPALACHIA DIVISION.

ROCKBRIDGE.—Orinoco, White Stem, Blue Pryor, Bull-face, Cotton Boll (a large, heavy-leafed tobacco of vigorous growth, a favorite for export), Gray Pryor, and Yellow Pryor are raised.

BOTETOURT.—Bull-face, for which the local name Little Frederick is a synonym, Yellow Pryor, and Orinoco.

GILES.—Yellow Pryor, Brittle Stem, White Stem, and Orinoco are produced in the county.

CROSS-FERTILIZATION.

The Johnson-Green variety is a hybrid of Orinoco and White Stem. The White Stem itself is a hybrid; so is the Gold Leaf, a cross of the Yellow Orinoco and the Yellow Pryor. The Gooch, Flannagan, and Mayo are all hybrids of more than ordinary merit, and are said to be superior in many respects to most of the old varieties. The Medley Pryor originated in Halifax county sixty or seventy years ago with Mr. Isaac Medley, a successful and observing planter, and is a cross of the old Blue Pryor on the Orinoco, partaking both of the symmetrical habit of the Pryor and of the fine texture and body of the Orinoco. In the estimation of some of the best planters in Virginia, this hybrid has no equal in the production of a first-class export leaf or dark wrapper. Some attempts have been made here and there to obtain new and better varieties by crossing such as possess desirable characteristics, and generally much care is taken to maintain the purity of the seeds of favorite sorts.

INFLUENCES OF SOILS UPON THE QUALITY OF THE TOBACCO PRODUCT.

Soils have a material influence on the quality and color of most varieties of tobacco, gray soils being best suited to the yellow varieties, and dark, rich soils to the shipping. In general, the color of the soil is indicative of the color of the product, its fertility being indicative of the quality of the crop grown thereon. Rich clays of any color will produce a heavy, waxy leaf, if planted to a suitable variety—one that has a tendency to grow thick, leathery, and large. Gray, porous soils will develop a thinner but finer leaf, particularly if planted to those varieties that have grown on such soils for a long series of years and have been kept pure.

Varieties which produce an excellent quality of tobacco on soils to which they are suited fail entirely when planted on lands of a decidedly different character. For instance, the White Stem, which in Buckingham county produces a grade desirable for stemming and English shipping, on new lands in Albemarle county produces a large plant, with long and broad leaf, but so deficient in body, texture, and waxiness as to bring it under the nondescript class. Yellow Pryor and Orinoco, grown upon rich old lands, especially if manured, will yield a strong, dark tobacco, while upon light, new lands the product of the same varieties is yellow, fine-flavored, and sweet.

If tobacco of the same variety be planted on lands contiguous, of the same formation and character, as nearly of the same topography and fertility as possible, one field freshly cleared from the forest, the other long cleared but well preserved, the product of the first will be brighter in color when cured with artificial heat or by the sun and air, finer in texture and sweeter in flavor, and have less nicotine than that produced on the old land. This applies to the manufacturing grades and types. If both the new and the old land be planted in Medley Pryor, and cultivated, cured, and managed for dark shipping, that produced on the old land will be richer, heavier, darker, and stronger than that from the new land, and will sell higher in the market.

The product of new or fresh lands, if planted to the variety best suited thereto and properly cured and managed, commands more money generally; but if these new lands are red, and otherwise unsuited to the manufacturing types, the product of old rich lots makes the more desirable staple. To get the best returns from both the planter must choose the variety suited to the soil according to the type in demand, and cure and manage accordingly.

Some varieties grow to perfection on certain localities; while others, possessing a wider adaptability, succeed well on both rolling and level lands.

The Orinocos, Gold Leaf, Gooch, Mayo, and other yellow varieties grow to highest excellence only on rolling lands, requiring a dry, warm, quick soil, a porous subsoil, and thorough drainage.

Lands nearly level can be better plowed and cultivated, hold manure better, and can more easily be made rich. On such the Medley Pryor, White Stem, Frederick, Bull-face, and other dark varieties succeed best. The same varieties on rolling lands are finer in texture and brighter in color than when raised on level fields.

Tobacco of first-rate quality may be raised on lands so hilly and steep that they cannot be plowed, and where the hand-hoe alone can be used to cultivate the crop. As an economical method to bring such lands into cultivation and to get them seeded down to grass nothing excels tobacco as a first and a second crop to kill out the remains of forest growth; for any crop which the soil is capable of producing will do well after tobacco.

The adaptation of soils to certain varieties is not well understood. The yellow varieties are grown to greatest perfection on the feldspathic, micaceous, and slaty soils, all siliceous, gray in color at the surface, and yellow, running to red, in the subsoil. The dark varieties do best on rich, black alluvials, or heavy clays.

PRESENT QUALITY OF VIRGINIA TOBACCO.

As compared with the product ten years ago, the tobacco grown in most sections of this state has deteriorated in quality, but in a few counties there has been a marked improvement.

The agricultural depression, low prices, and the scarcity of skilled labor have discouraged farmers; less fertilizers are used; less pains are taken, and the condition of the soil has been steadily declining for several years. The old "hands", trained in the operations of priming, topping, assorting, and the various details of cultivation and management, are dying out, and the younger generation is decidedly inferior to the old as trained and skilled laborers.

The prices received for a few years past have been scarcely sufficient to meet the cost of production, while the area of production has been reduced. The endeavor has been to reduce the cost of production rather than to increase the value of the product.

In Goochland, Caroline, Louisa, and Hanover counties of the Middle division, north of the James river, there has been a general improvement of quality, farmers having been stimulated by the wide difference in prices between the low and the high grades. In some portions of Hanover county the quality has depreciated, especially the product of the sandy plateau, but in Louisa county some of the colored planters are raising the finest sun- and air-cured tobacco.

In Buckingham, Cumberland, Amelia, Appomattox, Charlotte, Mecklenburg, Brunswick, and Greensville, all south-side counties, the quality of the general product has materially deteriorated, although the most careful planters are raising a better article than formerly. Too much poor land is put in tobacco, and there is too much disposition to rely upon commercial fertilizers, to the neglect of yard and stable manures. Tenants, the majority of whom are negroes, raise, as a rule, an inferior grade, which is forced into market through local dealers in an unfit condition. In Lunenburg tobacco raised by experienced farmers has increased in quantity per acre and improved very much in quality. The bulk of the crop of this county, however, is grown by colored people, inexperienced and unskilled, who pay but little attention to the management of their tobacco. In Dinwiddie the quality of the crop has improved. Farmers are making more domestic manures, and are studying more carefully the needs of the tobacco-plant, and there exists a spirited rivalry among a large number of planters as to who shall raise the finest tobacco and get the best prices. In Pittsylvania the quality has greatly improved in the last ten years, owing to improved methods of handling and curing, as well as to better cultivation and management of the crop in the field. In Halifax county there has been considerable falling off in the quantity and in the quality of dark shipping grades; but now planters are attempting, with fair success, the production of bright grades.

In Greene, Franklin, and Henry counties of the Piedmont district the quality of the general product has improved, the curing being better on account of improved processes, and planters are stimulated to attempt the production of the finer grades by the higher prices. In Amherst and Bedford counties quality appears to vary to some extent with the seasons. If prices are good and the seasons favorable, there is a disposition to overcrop, resulting in an inferior quality from want of proper care: prices decline; there is a falling off in production; a shorter crop, more care, a better grade, and better prices. The tobacco buyers of Lynchburg claim that the quality of Bedford county tobacco has deteriorated very much, and express the opinion that this is caused by the use of commercial fertilizers. Although the tobacco is large and leafy, it is said to be light and chaffy as compared with the former product.

In Floyd and the other counties of the Blue Ridge district the product has improved.

In Rockbridge, Botetourt, Craig, and Roanoke counties, of the Valley and Appalachia districts, there has been some improvement in quality, and more attention is paid to curing, assorting, sizing, packing, etc. The tobacco of Montgomery county has improved. In Giles, Pulaski, Bland, Tazewell, Russell, Scott, and Washington counties the culture of tobacco is comparatively a new industry.

PROPORTIONAL ACREAGE IN TOBACCO.

In the Middle and Piedmont districts about 6 per cent. of the arable soil of the tobacco district is planted in tobacco; a larger percentage on the small farms and smaller on the large farms. A farm with 100 acres or less of cleared land may have from 5 to 10 acres in tobacco, while it is not uncommon to find one of 1,000 acres near by with only 30 to 50 acres planted to that crop.

The percentage is larger in the yellow than in the dark belt. In the yellow belt planters sometimes make a specialty of tobacco and raise but small crops of the cereals, devoting their efforts mainly to the money crop. A majority, however, attempt to make their farms self-sustaining by raising enough of home supplies.

In the Valley counties, extending from Rockbridge to Washington, tobacco is not a staple crop, except in Rockbridge, Botetourt, Roanoke, and Montgomery. In these counties the area occupied varies from 2 to 5 per cent. of the cleared land. This section is just beginning to develop the capability of its soils to produce a staple of high grade.

Of freshly-cleared land the proportion planted to tobacco in the dark or shipping belt varies from 10 to 40 per cent.; in the bright yellow belt, from 15 to 50, with occasional instances of 100 per cent.; in the Valley, from 8 to 30 in the eastern to 75 per cent. in the southwestern section.

South Middle and Piedmont Virginia still retain much original forest. Of these wooded lands fully nine-tenths is adapted to the production of tobacco. Beside the forests, there are in this territory large tracts grown up in old-field pines and brush, capable, when cleared, of making the finest kinds of tobacco, especially the yellow and the filler types.

The varieties of forest growth on preferred tobacco soils differ somewhat in the several belts. In the dark belt, hickory, dogwood, red-bud, poplar, walnut, beech, and oaks indicate a good rich soil; in the yellow belt, white and post oaks, hickory, dogwood, pine, maple, chestnut, whortleberry, etc., are found on lands adapted to the manufacturing types; and in Montgomery county an isolated section, covered with pine, sugar maple, beech, hickory, buckeye, etc., is well suited to the yellow types. The forests on the mountain slopes of the Valley consist for the most part of pine, oaks, maple, and hickory; on the lower and limestone lands, of walnut, varieties of the oak, poplar, buckeye, etc. In this portion of Virginia a much larger proportion of original forest is standing, but owing to the rugged and mountainous character of large tracts of land not more than three-fourths of the uncleared soils are adapted to the culture of tobacco.

During the past ten years the yield per acre has not materially decreased or increased in the greater portion of the tobacco belt. A decreased product per acre is general in the south-side counties of the Middle division, except in Buckingham and Dinwiddie, where the average yield has been somewhat increased by improved culture and more liberal manuring. In Piedmont the quantity produced per acre has increased to a considerable extent, in Greene county especially, the more careful planters having improved their lands by judicious rotation, in which clover is an important factor, and by a liberal use of fertilizers. In Botetourt county, of the Valley district, the increased yield has been from 20 to 30 per cent., mainly due, as is claimed, to the use of commercial manures of good quality.

Various rotations in connection with green-manuring and other fertilizing are practiced, with a view to recuperate worn soils and maintain the productiveness of the lands. Throughout the dark-shipping and air-curing districts the mode usually practiced by the most successful farmers is to sow wheat after tobacco and follow with clover, to stand one or two years; then rotate as before, applying domestic or commercial fertilizers, or both, to the tobacco crop, which helps the succeeding wheat and rarely fails to secure a good crop of clover. This is called the "lot system", and is the prevailing one. Another rotation is tobacco, wheat, and clover two years; then corn, followed by wheat or oats; then clover again.

Clover, following close after a tobacco crop, properly manured, thrives on most of the soils of the Middle and Piedmont divisions, and the acreage of this best of all plants for green-manuring is annually increasing.

In the Valley district substantially the same rotation is followed—the grasses, sometimes alone and sometimes mixed with clover, following wheat, preceded by tobacco.

Green fallowing is but little practiced in the yellow tobacco district, a green clover fallow, beside bringing an unwelcome army of cut-worms, being unsuited to the production of this variety of tobacco, the plant being too coarse and ripening with too green a color, and being, therefore, difficult to cure properly. This is true also of tobacco grown after wheat, as only on fresh gray lands and old fields, or following corn, will the product possess the requisites for the yellow type.

An application of ashes and plaster, at slight cost, will produce a luxuriant growth of pea-vines on land so poor that it will not yield five bushels of inferior corn per acre. Yellow tobacco may be grown on a pea-fallow to great advantage by the use of commercial fertilizers without detriment to color.

THE USE OF FERTILIZERS: HOW APPLIED—QUANTITY AND COST PER ACRE.

The use of commercial fertilizers has largely increased since 1870, and in every neighborhood of all the counties of Middle and Piedmont Virginia manufactured manures or guanos are purchased annually by tobacco planters, often by those who seem to be utterly careless of the home-made article. The ease and rapidity with which these fertilizers are put into the soil is strong recommendation for their use; and, when honestly compounded, they return a fair profit upon the amount invested in their purchase In Goochland and Louisa counties from 70 to 80 per cent. of the tobacco crops are fertilized with special manures, using from 150 to 300 pounds, either in the hill or in drills, at a cost of from $3 to $9 per acre. In Caroline more farm manures are used in connection with the commercial fertilizers. In Hanover it is the practice of some excellent farmers to plow in 12 to 15 cords of yard and stable manure and use in the hills or drills about 150 pounds of one of the tobacco compounds, this preparation of the soil costing not much less than $15 per acre. These farmers think that commercial fertilizers alone do not produce perfect tobacco.

In all the tobacco districts of south-side Virginia the use of commercial fertilizers is general. In some of these counties no special efforts seem to be made to save and utilize the bulky but valuable accumulations of the farm-yard and stables, and too much reliance is placed upon the numerous special manures sold as tobacco fertilizers. In Halifax home-made manures from the stables, hog-pens, farm-yards, hen-house, etc., are hauled on the land in the spring and plowed in at the rate of from five to twenty wagon-loads per acre, according to the quality and kind of manure. This goes over from one-half to two-thirds of the land to be planted, the balance being supplied with commercial fertilizers, at a cost of from $3 to $10 per acre. In the remainder of the south-side counties this practice is followed more or less. From three-fourths to nine-tenths of the lands planted in tobacco are manured with either domestic or commercial fertilizers, at a cost varying from $3 to $12 per acre.

In Piedmont substantially the same practice is general. Superphosphates, ammoniated superphosphates, bone meal, kainit, guanos, and numerous "tobacco compounds" are used in hills or drills, and sometimes broadcast, as the experience or the fancy of the farmer may direct; sometimes alone, but usually as an addition to a previous application of home manures, and, more rarely, composted with stable manure. The quantity of commercial fertilizers used varies from 150 to 500 pounds per acre.

In the tobacco counties of the Middle division north of the James River the increase of yield, where commercial fertilizers alone are used, is from 20 to 50 per cent., and in combination with a liberal dressing of farm manures the increase is from 25 to 80 per cent.; but on the poor sandy soils of Hanover tobacco cannot be raised without the help of guanos or other nitrogenous fertilizers. It is the common opinion in this section that the use of commercial manures has not improved the quality of the product.

In the south-side counties, where the use of commercial manures is general, the quantity of the product is increased from 25 to 200 per cent., according to the soil, its previous condition, and the greater or less quantity of such manure applied. Many of the "tobacco compounds", containing, as the manufacturers claim, certain constituents especially adapted to the needs of the tobacco-plant, prove of little value, either because of insufficient quantity, injudicious application, bad management, unfavorable seasons, or the want of real value in the fertilizer itself.

In the Piedmont counties the use of fertilizers in generous quantities has increased the yield from 25 to 100 per cent.; but the quality of the product is somewhat inferior. As fertilized crops ripen earlier, some advantage is thus obtained.

In the Blue Ridge district, and in Botetourt, Roanoke, and Montgomery counties, of the Valley, commercial fertilizers are found to increase the yield quite as much as elsewhere—from 25 to 75 per cent.—and it is claimed that the quality of the tobacco is improved from 10 to 20 per cent. by their use. In the other counties of the Valley very little tobacco is grown, the small amount planted being usually on new lands, rich enough to produce good crops without manures.

As a general thing, concentrated fertilizers of real merit pay better in the yellow belt than anywhere else. They hasten growth and ripening, and contribute, when of the right materials, toward yellowing the plants as they mature on the hills. For heavy, rich, dark tobacco, no manures have met the requirements so completely as that of the farm-yard and stable.

DETERIORATION OF TOBACCO SOILS.

North of the James river fresh soils sufficiently fertile to produce one good crop of tobacco will produce a second of fair quantity; but if further cropped will deteriorate rapidly, and soon fail to repay cultivation. The usual plan is to follow the second crop of tobacco, grown on new land, by wheat, seeded to clover, under which system the land improves. Old lands planted to tobacco are always manured.

In south-side Virginia heavy alluvials withstand the effects of repeated cropping in tobacco for some years without great loss of productive capacity; but the light, gray soils, so well adapted to the growing of bright yellow tobacco, deteriorate rapidly unless fertilized every year.

In Piedmont the deterioration of tobacco lands is estimated as high as 15 per cent. per annum, especially the light soils on the rolling uplands and slopes. This damage is more than half the result of surface washing, and can be prevented, in great measure, by careful tillage.

PREPARATION OF LAND FOR TOBACCO.

The usual mode in preparing old land for tobacco is to turn the soil with two-horse plows 5 to 8 inches deep in the fall or winter; but this work is done from September to April, as opportunity permits. New land is first cleared of all brush, grubs, and trash, making the surface as clean and free from obstructions as possible, and is either broken with the turn-plow, if practicable, or plowed closely with the common colter, or with the implement known as a "jumping colter". Subsequent plowings are various, as the condition of the land or the implements at hand will allow. For tobacco, perhaps more than for any other field crop, thorough pulverization of the soil is absolutely necessary, not only to make the subsequent cultivation rapid and easy, but to bring the whole body of soil into such condition that plant food can be readily appropriated by the fibrous roots of the plants.

Subsoiling is practiced to some extent, with varying results, in all portions of the tobacco region, the successes and failures being of nearly equal number; but there is no record of injury to the land where the subsoil plow has been used with judgment.

Experience has demonstrated clearly the benefit of subsoiling on red lands underlaid with stiff clay. The ground, when this operation is in progress, should be so dry that the subsoil can be readily pulverized; and the work should be so managed that the stratum of subsoil subjected to the operation shall be thoroughly broken, but be left in its original position. If two or three inches or less of clay subsoil be thrown to the surface by an improper use of the turn-plow, the field so treated must lie some years before it is restored to its former productiveness.

The tobacco-fields, having been broken the preceding fall or winter, are again plowed as early in the spring as the condition of the soil will permit, a third and sometimes a fourth plowing being necessary to put the land in first-class order. These spring plowings are usually done with the double-shovel or other cultivating implement, and frequently it is necessary to use the harrow, or a drag of some form, to break down the clods and fit the soil for subsequent operations. When farm manure is applied, the most approved plan is to haul it upon the land previously broken during the months of March and April, broadcasting it upon the surface, so that it may be thoroughly incorporated with the soil by the repeated plowings and harrowings which precede the immediate preparations for planting.

When the farmer has failed to break tobacco land until spring the various operations of plowing, manuring, replowing, and cultivating follow in the same order; but there is greater difficulty in securing fine tilth. In some instances, upon old clay lands, it has been found best to break in the fall with colters, running close, but without turning under the surface soil. This method is also adopted by many good planters in the preparation of newly-cleared lands, where there is but little sod.

If the farm-yard manures applied in the early spring are finely broken, so as to be readily and evenly distributed upon the surface, the double-shovel, or some form of cultivator, is used. Should the manure be coarse, strawy, and lumpy, repeated harrowing or dragging is necessary to prepare the surface soil for subsequent cultivation.

In May, when the plants are ready, the soil is prepared for planting, the methods differing as required by the condition, locality, or situation of the land. In Hanover, Spotsylvania, and adjoining counties it is the practice to mark off the land with a shovel-plow, drill the fertilizer in the furrow, "list" by two furrows of a turn-plow, rub down the ridge with a block or board, and plant. The usual distance between the rows is 3 feet 6 inches, with the plants set at the same distance in the row; but this varies with the fertility of the soil and the variety of tobacco to be grown. In Buckingham and other south-side counties it is usual to bed upon the fertilized drill and make flat hills with the hand-hoe, chopping the earth finely and marking the position of the plant by a pat of the hoe; but in Henry county the approved plan is to cultivate just before planting, "check" the land, and make a small, flat hill in each check. This plan admits of plowing both ways, and is preferable on rolling lands, the direction of the rows, and the choice between the two methods of simple rows or planting in checks, being determined by the locality and the greater or less liability of the soil to wash.

SEED-BEDS.

It is the practice of many careful planters to select beds for forward plants on the hillsides and suitable localities on low or flat land to secure a continued supply of plants.

The time of sowing tobacco-seed south of the James river, in middle Virginia, is January and February; north of the James river, in February and March. On the upper south-side, in the yellow belt, many planters commence sowing in December, especially in the counties of Halifax and Pittsylvania, and in the Valley the sowing rarely begins until after the middle of February. The date of transplanting depends upon locality, and upon the supply of plants and the season. The south-side planters commence about the 10th of May; on the north side, from the 15th to 20th of May; in the Valley, near the 1st of June, if the plants are in supply and the hills are sufficiently moist.

Most planters prefer large plants for old land, and for late planting, on any soil, large stocky plants, with good roots, are best. Small plants, set early in the season, generally do better than larger ones set late. As new lands are better adapted to the manufacturing types, they are generally prepared sooner than the old lands, and small plants are used by preference. There is an old adage, "A bud in May is worth a plant in June."

The plants are set in hills or drills, as suits the convenience of the planter, at the rate of from 4,000 to 5,000 plants to the acre, and sometimes as many as 6,000. Planters in the shipping belt give most distance between the plants, those in the yellow belt, preferring fineness of leaf to body, planting closer.

The general practice is to plant after a rain; but when the season is growing late, and plants are getting overgrown in the beds, the hills are watered and planted. This is more extensively done than formerly, especially on lots convenient to water. When necessary to do this, a sharpened stake, 3½ or 4 feet long and 2 inches in diameter, is thrust into the hill 3 or 4 inches deep. Two or three quarts of water are poured into each hole, and as soon as the water settles the plant is stuck, the earth closed around the roots, and the plant shaded with leaves, grass, weeds, or by a clod. This is a tedious and costly work.

CULTIVATION OF TOBACCO.

As soon as the plants are well established the work of cultivation is begun, and the usual method is to run a light furrow with a small turn-plow or light shovel on each side of the row, throwing the earth from the plants. The hills are then scraped down or "skimmed" with the hoe, this being followed immediately by a close, deep plowing with a colter and slight hilling with the hoe. The middles of the rows are then thrown out with a one-horse turn-plow, and the hills again dressed by pulling up a little more earth about the plant, these operations being so timed as to keep ahead of the grass. One deep plowing about the time the leaves are as large as the hand is considered of prime importance, especially upon old and rather heavy lands.

In some localities in the valley of the upper James river the land is not ridged or "listed"—merely harrowed and leveled. The field is then rolled, marked, and planted, the after culture being level, with little need for hand work. This method is not admissible except on dry, porous soils. The tobacco-plant is impatient of an excess of moisture about the roots, and is quickly injured thereby.

When tobacco has been planted on the check system the cultivation is as follows: First, run cultivators each way as soon as plants are rooted, chopping around the plants with hand-hoes; second, run shovel-plow three times in the row, the last furrow in the middle, following with hoes, and putting a small hill to the plant; third, run turning-plows two furrows to the row, throwing earth toward the plants, finishing with a shovel furrow in the middle, and again hill up plants with hoes. Usually three plowings and as many workings with the hand-hoe complete the cultivation, and when the work is done at the proper time and in a thorough manner this is quite enough; but the labor is often much increased by suffering the grass and weeds to get the start of cultivation.

Old lands require more cultivation than new with both the plow and the hoe, and the shipping more than the manufacturing types.

TOPPING, PRIMING, AND SUCKERING OF TOBACCO.

Tobacco planted from the 20th of May to the 10th of June usually grows off promptly, and is ready for topping in from 35 to 50 days after transplanting, according to soil. Planted very early or very late, the intervening time is longer—from 40 to 60 days.

At each hand-working the "baby leaves", as the plant-bed leaves are called, and all other poor bottom leaves, are taken off. The final priming is done when the plant has formed at least eight thrifty leaves. Then the small bottom leaves are primed off, and the terminal bud, or "button", is broken out. In Hanover county the best farmers top to eight leaves, suckering beginning immediately after topping, and being continued until the tobacco is ripe.

In Amelia, Appomattox, and other south-side counties priming is commenced as soon as the plant will allow the ground leaves to be pulled off, so as to strip the stalk six or eight inches above the top of the hill or bed; then it is topped to eight, ten, or twelve leaves, according to strength of soil. If topped late, fewer leaves are left on the plant. It is the usual practice to top to ten leaves up to the 15th of July; after that date to eight leaves for shipping tobacco. For yellow manufacturing the plants are not topped until the "buttons" make their appearance, the custom being to prime high and top to twelve or fourteen leaves early, lessening the number as the season advances down to six leaves on very late plants.

It is a good rule not to commence topping in a field of tobacco until enough can be topped on the same day to fill a barn when ripe for harvesting.

In some parts of south-side Virginia, in Pittsylvania county particularly, some good planters do not prime, claiming that the lower and inferior leaves protect the crop leaves and secure a larger out-turn of cleaner and more salable tobacco.

Aside from the advantage of increased product (for it must be admitted that unprimed plants make greater weight), the advanced price paid for a clean staple of the best grade, made from the upper leaves, appears to decide this question in favor of those who do not prime.

In Piedmont priming and topping are usually done at the same time; but occasionally the topping is deferred a few days until the requisite number of leaves can be obtained, the number left on the plant differing with the type of tobacco to be produced—a greater number being left for bright manufacturing and a less number for shipping.

In priming, topping, and suckering great care is necessary to avoid bruising or breaking the leaves, especially those at the top of the plant.

CUTTING, HANGING, AND HOUSING OF TOBACCO.

In from forty to fifty-five days after priming and topping tobacco is ripe enough to cut, this interval between topping and ripening varying with locality, climatic conditions, character of the soil, healthiness and vigor of the plants and the peculiar management of the growing crop.

In the north-side counties of middle Virginia cutting begins about the 10th of September and continues until danger of frost, or about the 5th of October. A few planters think that tobacco is more pliant and works smoother when not quite ripe, but the majority of growers in this section prefer to cut when well ripened.

In Buckingham, Cumberland, and other upper south-side counties cutting begins about the 10th of September and continues until October 10 or thereabout.

In Pittsylvania, Halifax, and other counties near the North Carolina line tobacco is ready for cutting from the 20th of August to the 10th of October, from five to eight weeks after topping, according to season and other circumstances. The forward plantings are cut when fully ripe; the later, when the leaves are nicely yellowed. The finest wrappers from this section are from plants cut barely ripe, but for the smoking tobacco the well-ripened plants afford the best quality.

In Henry county (Piedmont) cutting begins about the 10th of September and continues until the danger of frost compels the finishing of the harvest. Tobacco cut fully ripe is not so bright, but makes a sweeter and better chew. In other counties of Piedmont, the Blue Ridge and Valley districts, the custom is to cut as soon as ripe, as the product is easier handled, and is esteemed of better quality, than when suffered to become too brittle by over ripeness.

As tobacco approaches the period of maturity, cool nights, without dew, retard growth and otherwise injuriously affect the plant; but when accompanied by heavy dews cool nights greatly aid in maturing the plant. Dews benefit the shipping much more than the manufacturing types.

If the sun is hot, and the tobacco heavy, cutting can be done safely after four o'clock p. m. At an earlier hour there is danger of sunburn while the plant is wilting, or of "coddling" after it is piled. On a hot, dry day, from eleven o'clock a. m. to four p. m., it is almost impossible to prevent sunburn. Tobacco should not be cut in the morning till the dew is off; but in cloudy weather, when there has been no dew, cutting can be continued all day with great advantage. Medium-sized plants can be cut during the greater part of a bright warm day if a little extra care be exercised in the handling and conveying to the scaffold or barn.

It is the common practice of Virginia tobacco-growers to split the stalk in cutting and harvesting the plants, the instrument most used being the ordinary tobacco-knife, resembling a small butcher-knife, with a blade about 5 inches long and 1½ inches broad, riveted into a wooden handle 4½ inches long; but knives of various shapes are used, the common shoe-knife being one. A patent knife, having a curved blade, and resembling a pruning-knife, with an exaggerated hook, made so as to sever the plants by a pulling cut, was introduced some years ago, but, being rather a dangerous tool, it has never been extensively used.

All tobacco split in cutting is hung upon sticks, varying in length to suit the distance between the tier poles of the barns in which it is to be housed, the usual length being 4½ feet, a majority of tobacco-houses having tier poles 4 feet apart. Three inches catch at each end of the stick is sufficient.

The Shelton hanger is used by a few planters, who pull off the leaves without cutting the stalk and string them on this hanger. This is constructed by passing a No. 15 wire through the middle of an ordinary tobacco-stick, twisting the wire twice on the upper edge of the stick and extending the ends of the wire to each end of the stick, the leaves being strung so as to hang alternately on either side of the stick, the latter thus supporting the wire and its load of leaves. By the use of this hanger more tobacco can be housed in the barn, the sticks can be placed closer together, and, if cured by artificial heat, less fuel is needed, and the process is completed in less time than when tobacco is cured on the stalks. It is used to great advantage in harvesting the ground leaves, but planters generally claim that the old process is the more expeditious for the main crop.

The number of plants placed upon a stick of the usual length, 4½ feet, varies with the size and type. For shipping, from five to ten plants, according to their size, are enough, if the planter desires to give plenty of room and not crowd the barn.

In the sun-curing belt the plants are not so large as in the shipping belt, but as no artificial heat is employed for this type it is always safest not to crowd too many on a stick. Eight medium-sized plants are enough; of large plants fewer; of small ones more may be placed upon each stick.

In the yellow belt only about six plants of medium size are put on each stick, and more or less as they are smaller or larger.

In the sun-curing district the tobacco, placed first upon scaffolds for from five to seven days, or longer, if the weather is favorable, is then placed in the barn. It is not fired if it can be avoided, but is allowed to cure by air alone. The best arranged barns for such curing are constructed with adjustable ventilators, to be opened in fair and closed in damp or rainy weather.

In the yellow district the practice varies. Some place the tobacco in the barn as soon as it is cut and hung, the two operations going on at the same time if the force is adequate. The sticks are placed well apart on the tiers, regulating the plants on each stick as placed in position, so as to secure free circulation of the heat and prevent sweating and house-burn. The curing process is usually commenced as soon as the barn is filled, but some planters wait a few days before applying heat. Another practice, more rarely adopted, is to place the tobacco on scaffolds first. Still another mode is followed by a few planters, who place the tobacco in the barn as soon as it is cut and crowd it close on the tier poles, thus to remain two or three days to yellow, when it is opened. The sticks are placed at a suitable distance apart, and heat is applied. While each of the plans above described has its advocates, a majority of the most skillful and successful growers claim that the desired color can be more readily and certainly obtained on tobacco to which heat is applied as soon as cut.

In the dark tobacco district the harvest is conducted as follows: Two cutters cut two rows each, placing the plants, top down, upon the ground, the upper leaves forming a base upon which the reversed plant stands erect. A third man gathers the cut plants, placing the requisite number in piles for each stick. A boy follows the gatherer, dropping a stick at each pile. Two men complete this part of the work by hanging the plants upon the sticks, which are immediately carried to the scaffold or barn by carriers or on a wagon.

In the yellow belt a "stick-holder" follows two cutters, from whom the holder receives the plants as cut, places them upon the stick, which is passed, when filled, to a "carrier", who places it upon a wagon. For want of the necessary number of hands the sticks, when filled, are sometimes carefully laid upon the ground by the stick-holder, and the "cutting-team" assists in housing or scaffolding. When the force is adequate, and the tobacco is carried direct from the cutter to the scaffold, there is perfect immunity from sunburn, and the leaves are kept clean. When distance makes it necessary to haul from the field to the barn, crates, so constructed as to carry two tiers of sticks with the tobacco hanging at full length, are placed upon the wagons, by which means there need be no breaking nor bruising in handling.

Rough and careless handling prevails to a large extent, often causing damage to fully one-half the value of the product.

The broken leaves, of which there are very many in the heavy shipping tobacco, are either split with knives or are pierced with short, sharpened sticks, and strung upon ordinary sticks for hanging. A few use the Shelton hanger, already described. Some tie eight or ten of the green leaves closely with small willow withes, imbedding the tie deep into the pulpy butt stems, so that they may not fall apart when dried—an expeditious and economical method.

Frames of peculiar construction, on which tobacco hung upon sticks is carried to the barn and hoisted therein, so as to be rapidly placed upon the tier poles, have been patented, and are used to a very limited extent.

TOBACCO-HOUSES.

Most of these tobacco-houses are built of logs from 16 to 24 feet long. In the shipping belt there may be found many large and costly framed barns, while in the yellow district the houses are small, and are rarely built of other material than hewn logs.

A barn 20 by 20 feet, with five firing tiers, one above the other, in the body of the house, with additional tiers in the roof space, will hold from 700 to 800 sticks of shipping, or 600 to 700 sticks of tobacco to be cured by the air, or with flues, or charcoal fires. Such a house, 20 feet high in the body, built of good oak logs, hewn on the outside, boarded at the gables with heart weatherboarding, and covered with heart shingles, will cost from $80 to $110, according to locality and workmanship.

Framed barns are from 20 feet square to 30 by 60 feet, and their cost depends upon local cost of materials and labor. These barns are now being provided with flues, and are used successfully in curing both shipping and yellow manufacturing tobacco.

The small planters, among whom are found the most successful producers of the finest grades, prefer small houses, 16 to 18 feet square. These small barns can be quickly filled by a small working force; and it is claimed, with good reason, that the color can be fixed more readily in a small than in a large barn.

TOBACCO CURING.

The process of curing to be adopted by the planter depends upon the character of the tobacco as it comes to the knife. If of medium size, thoroughly ripe, of a yellowish green color, grown upon gray sandy or gravelly land, it will suit for fillers, and ought to be cured by sun and air; if of fine texture, smooth or dappled yellow on the hill when ripe or nearly ripe, properly cured with flues or charcoal, it will command good prices for wrappers and smokers.

The north-side counties (Caroline, Spotsylvania, Hanover, and Louisa) produce mainly sun- and air-cured fillers. After being scaffolded until the leaf is nearly cured, generally in from four to seven days, the tobacco is then removed to the house, where it hangs until cured. In unfavorable weather the tobacco sometimes gets but little sun, when especial care is given to prevent crowding, the sticks being placed far enough apart to keep it from touching, and dried without fire, unless in very damp weather, when it is fired very gently, to keep off mold. For dark shipping tobacco the plants are carried to the house and hung as soon as cut, and, when the house is filled, slow fires are started. To cure red shipping the tobacco is allowed to yellow for a few days, either on the scaffold or in the house. That which has yellowed on the scaffold will require but two or three days of firing when housed; but that put immediately into the barn remains two or three days to yellow without fire, is then fired, and is cured in four or five days. Where the yellow manufacturing type is the principal product, flues and charcoal fires are used to cure nearly all the better grades.

Where heavy shipping tobacco is the leading product, with a small proportion of manufacturing tobacco, the shipping is mostly cured with open wood fires, and the new-ground manufacturing with charcoal. In firing with wood two logs of seasoned hickory or other hard wood are placed side by side under each tier, the fires kindled along between the logs, using small bits of wood to get the fires started.

In Albemarle, Greene, Amherst, and Bedford, counties of Piedmont, wood fires are mostly used in curing.

For curing bright yellow tobacco two modes are in use: one with charcoal, and the other with flues. The process is minutely described in the chapter on North Carolina, and is known as the Ragland method.

A barn containing 700 sticks of green tobacco, six medium plants on each stick, holds, along with the tobacco, from 4,500 to 5,000 pounds of water, which must be expelled in from eighty-five to one hundred hours.

Charcoal produces an open, dry heat, well suited for the purpose; but it is a costly fuel, its use tedious, dirty, and laborious, and it deposits a black dust on the leaf. With properly constructed flues of stone or of brick, covered with sheet-iron, or with furnaces and cast-iron pipes, wood is burned at little cost, the tobacco being cured free of dust, and having a sweeter flavor.

The following table shows the proportions of the product of the several counties, air-dried or cured by artificial heat, and the proportion of that cured by heat with open wood fires, or by charcoal and flues:

Counties.	Air-dried.	Cured with artificial heat.	Cured by artificial heat.		Counties.	Air-dried.	Cured with artificial heat.	Cured by artificial heat.	
			With open wood fires.	With charcoal and flues.				With open wood fires.	With charcoal and flues.
	Per cent.	Per cent.	Per cent.	Per cent.		Per cent.	Per cent.	Per cent.	Per cent.
Goochland	25	75	72	3	Powhatan	5	95	95	....
Hanover	90	10	10	....	Campbell	10	90	75	15
Caroline	90	10	5	5	Prince Edward	10	90	85	5
Louisa	95	5	5	....	Albemarle	40	60	50	10
Fluvanna	40	60	36	4	Amherst	10	90	75	15
Amelia	50	50	40	10	Bedford	10	90	74	16
Appomattox	8	92	70	22	Greene	70	30	30	....
Buckingham	5	95	92	3	Nelson	10	90	80	10
Brunswick	5	95	95	....	Franklin	15	85	15	70
Cumberland	7	93	88	5	Henry	....	100	....	100
Charlotte	9	91	87	4	Patrick	8	92	12	80
Dinwiddie	25	75	70	5	Floyd	10	90	5	85
Greensville	20	80	80	....	Giles	10	90	30	60
Mecklenburg	40	60	55	5	Botetourt	10	90	70	20
Lunenburg	12	88	82	6	Roanoke	8	92	70	22
Nottoway	10	90	85	5	Rockbridge	3	97	87	10
Halifax	25	75	30	45	Montgomery	8	92	12	80
Pittsylvania	8	92	15	77					

Planters who use charcoal burn it on their farms, if suitable wood can be had; others buy from parties who make a business of charcoal burning. The old-field pine makes a prime article of coal, gives off but little smoke in burning, and does not taint the tobacco with the taste of creosote, as does charcoal from many kinds of wood. Good charcoal sells at four to five cents per bushel, and is often delivered at the barn for the latter price. A barn 20 feet square, with five main firing tiers, filled with tobacco, will require from 120 to 130 bushels to cure the contents thoroughly. Many planters continue the use of charcoal, and claim for it certain advantages over the flue—that it cures better, and is safe—this opinion being probably formed by comparison with imperfect and wrongly-constructed flues, or those which have been ignorantly managed. Charcoal-cured tobacco holds its color well, possibly better than flue-cured; but this does not compensate for the extra cost.

LOSSES BY FIRE AND RATES OF INSURANCE OF TOBACCO-BARNS.

In the air-curing district the number of tobacco-houses burned annually is less than 1 per cent. of the whole; in the open wood-fire district, from 2 to 3 per cent.; and in the charcoal and flue-curing district, from 3 to 5 per cent.

In the shipping district, where open wood fires are used, the temperature of the house rarely exceeds 90°. Brights require very hot fires at certain stages of the curing processes, but nevertheless the larger proportion of losses by fire in flued barns is due more to defective construction and careless management than to the necessarily greater heat. Now and then a planter, in order to cure quickly and make room for another filling, raises the heat unnecessarily high—to 200° or more—at which high temperature a spark is all that is needed to bring sudden disaster.

Responsible companies, home and foreign, are taking risks upon tobacco-houses, along with other farm buildings, but at higher rates, the average charge being 4 per cent. per annum; but for shorter time, higher rates, from 1 to 2 per cent. a month, are charged.

POLE-SWEAT.

Pole-sweat rarely occurs in the yellow belt, the mode of curing by flues or charcoal dispelling the excess of moisture. The free application of heat remedies the ill-effects of overcrowding to a great extent, but at the same time there is danger of scalding tobacco so crowded, darkening and deadening the leaf, making it almost worthless, and entailing much loss every year. Crowded tobacco requires slower firing, at a lower temperature, and can never be cured as bright as if placed far enough apart to permit free circulation of heat and air. In firing with flues or with charcoal a draft is kept up as long as the leaf is green by leaving openings over the furnaces, or by making vents in the walls of the house.

In the air-curing district lack of house room induces planters to crowd the barns too full, resulting in serious damage if the weather should be damp and warm during the curing season.

MANAGEMENT OF CURED TOBACCO BEFORE STRIPPING.

The curing process completed, tobacco is allowed to hang until both stems and stalks are thoroughly dry. When in the right condition, it is either crowded close upon the main tiers or into the roof of the barn, there to remain until taken down to be sold or stripped, or the tobacco is taken down, pulled from the sticks, and packed away in bulk. This bulk is built upon the floor of the barn, or other suitable place, upon a bed of tobacco-sticks. In some instances tobacco is bulked without removing it from the sticks, but not unless it is thoroughly cured, as otherwise there is serious danger of damage. It is of prime importance that yellow tobacco shall be kept from light, and in a dry place, to prevent loss of color.

MANAGEMENT OF STRIPPED TOBACCO.

Tobacco is often damaged after the processes of curing and stripping while hanging in the barn. In long-continued wet weather a fungous mold makes its appearance, mostly upon the bottom and outside tiers, especially in barns with defective walls or damp floors. There are two kinds of mold produced by excessive moisture in warm weather, commonly known as "white" and "yellow" mold, really only different stages of the same disease. White mold is the incipiency of decay, and yellow mold is an evidence that the tobacco is no longer fit for any grade but "nondescript". The white mold, if rubbed off as soon as it appears (and it comes off easily if taken in time), rarely leaves any disagreeable smell to the leaf; but the yellow mold cannot be rubbed off, and taints the leaf with an unpleasant flavor.

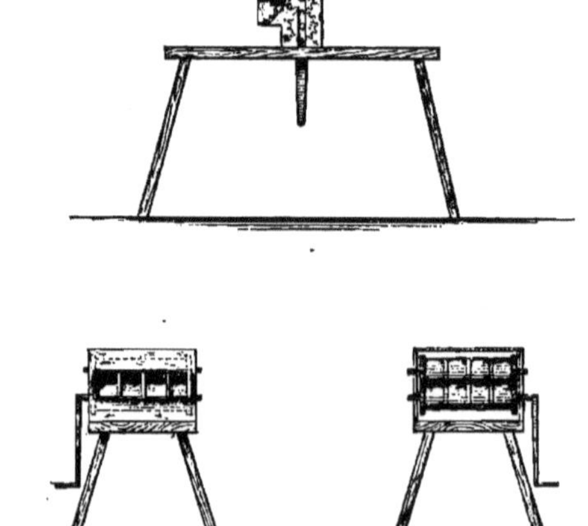

When sold in winter order, as is usual in some districts, tobacco is bulked down as it is stripped; but if it gets too "high" or soft in bulk, or if it is desired to sell it in shipping order, it is hung until spring, when it is again put in order for prizing or is bulked in good keeping order on a close floor, usually of a width to accommodate two courses of the kind of tobacco to be packed, long, short, or lugs. In some cases, if the tobacco is to be prized, it is hung up to dry thoroughly, and is then ordered for prizing, taken down, bulked on a platform 3 to 4 feet wide, laying three or four courses of bundles, and heavily weighted.

Shipping tobacco is generally hung up to dry out after being stripped and reordered before bulking for prizing. Manufacturing is largely sold loose, and most of this type is bulked as stripped, and either sold in "winter order" or hung up again and ordered to keep until sold. The safest way to bulk tobacco when stripped in winter or early spring is to "tail down" two rows with heads outward, tails slightly lapping.

In Henry county stripped tobacco is sometimes bulked down as stripped, but the general practice is to hang up. If bulked down, it is packed in parallelograms 5 by 10 feet, putting the darkest tobacco at the bottom, fine in the middle, and lugs on top.

A machine for straightening tobacco, invented by a citizen of Albemarle county, has been used to great advantage. This machine consists of a bench, supporting at its middle an iron frame containing two iron cylinders, working upon each other by cogs, with a crank handle fixed on one end of the lower cylinder. In each cylinder are four grooves an inch or more in width, completely filled with gutta-percha; also an iron funnel or hopper, with four partitions, through which the bundles of tobacco to be straightened are fed to the rolls, the bundles being delivered from the rolls perfectly straightened and flattened out. This machine saves much labor in bulking and rebulking tobacco, the only objectionable feature being the liability of the gutta-percha filling to wear out too quickly, and the consequent difficulty and expense of replacing it. (See illustration on page 208.)

Tobacco usually remains in bulk at least four weeks in the shipping district, where most of the product is bulked. In the yellow district much the larger part of the crop is sold loose, and it is bulked only for the purpose of keeping it in order for ready sale, as convenience, necessity, or interest may prompt.

BEST SEASON FOR PRIZING TOBACCO.

The summer months are best and safest for prizing tobacco; for then the warmth liquefies the vegetable oil in the leaf and it comes into "order"—a supple, pliant condition—without absorbing much moisture. Some of the very best "ordering" seasons come without a drop of rain, and a warm, humid south wind, condensing moisture upon the colder rocks during the night or early morning, brings an excellent ordering season, experienced planters, when they see the "rocks sweating", accepting it as a sign of a favorable time to take down their tobacco. A "coming" season is better than a "going out" season. The condition of the tobacco indicates to the practiced eye at a glance the one or the other, as in a "coming" or "quick" season the leaf is pliant, while the stem is dry and brittle, but in a "going out" or protracted season the tobacco shows that moisture has been absorbed by the stems, which are as pliant as the leaves. As it is important that the leaf should be pliant and the stem dry enough to crack full half way from the large end to be in *safe* order, the tobacco should be watched and taken down in that condition. Any slight moisture will then be absorbed by the drier stems, and fermentation in bulk or in the package be impossible.

If there are moisture and heat enough in the atmosphere, tobacco bulked or prized will go into "sweat". Thoroughly dry tobacco never sweats; nor can sweat be induced without heat. Some heat is developed in sweating, and if this is only to a slight degree the bulk will "sweat sweet"; if the heat is excessive, the tobacco is either ruined or greatly damaged. The duration of the sweating process depends upon the condition of the tobacco when bulked or packed, the temperature, and the type. Tobacco remaining in bulk through a second summer undergoes the same process of sweating, but to a less extent.

PREPARATION OF TOBACCO FOR MARKET.

When stripped from the stalk, tobacco is assorted into three grades: lugs, short leaf, and long leaf. It is then tied into bundles of from five to eight leaves of the better grades and eight to twelve leaves of lugs, bulked down and heavily weighted, is often rebulked twice, and finally it is prized into hogsheads, to weigh from 1,000 to 1,500 pounds of shipping or 700 to 1,000 pounds of manufacturing. In some counties a large proportion of the crop is taken to market loose.

Much attention is given by successful growers to the stripping, assorting, and packing processes; and it is not unusual to find bulks of tobacco in some of the finest dwellings in the region where the best grades of bright tobacco are produced.

The product of Albemarle, Amelia, Buckingham, a portion of Appomattox, Cumberland, Charlotte, Mecklenburg, Lunenburg, Hanover, Caroline, and some other counties, when prized for shipment, is mostly sold in Richmond; that of Amherst, Bedford, a considerable part of Appomattox, and the shipping tobacco of the Valley and Blue Ridge counties, is marketed at Lynchburg. A large part of the crop is sold loose in the various market towns of the sections in which it is raised, and finds its way thence either to the manufacturers or to the large markets, where it is assorted and prized for shipment. Of Henry county tobacco, about one-half is manufactured in the county and the remainder is marketed at Danville.

Tobacco hogsheads are about 54 inches in length, and from 38 to 44 inches across the head, and the price varies, according to the cost of lumber, from \$1 25 to \$2.

Half-hogsheads and tierces are more used in the yellow district. These are of all sizes, holding from 300 to 800 pounds, the cost varying with the size, material, and workmanship.

Dark shipping tobacco is prized to weigh from 1,200 to 1,600 pounds of leaf and from 1,400 to 1,800 pounds of lugs, and air-cured from 800 to 1,200 pounds. Yellow is always packed lightly. It injures the sale of this grade to prize so tightly as to stick the leaves together, as they should shake out loosely when opened.

In colonial days, and until 1800, or later, Virginia planters delivered their crops in market and sold before Christmas. From 1810 to 1830 the common practice was to prize and sell in the early spring or summer; but after that period, and until 1860, the greater part of the crop was sold during the summer months. Since 1865 an entire change in the time and manner of marketing has taken place, planters now selling their tobacco at any time during the year, as necessity may compel or prices induce. Most of the loose tobacco sales are made early in the spring, unless prices are very low.

Loose tobacco is sold in Richmond and in Petersburg during the winter, and in March and April; prized tobaccos are sent to these markets in the summer and fall.

In the up-country markets planters commence selling in a small way as soon as the tobacco is cured, disposing of lugs, primings, and poor leaf first and the better grades afterward.

Farmers in Henry, Franklin, and Patrick counties sell mostly to country manufacturers, who purchase for cash "at the barn door". What local manufacturers do not require is shipped or hauled to the nearest market.

LOOSE TOBACCO—HOW SOLD.

Warehouses for the sale of loose tobacco are of recent origin. In construction, arrangement, and fixtures they are very different from those in which prized tobacco is inspected and sold, being generally spacious structures, with ample floor room, abundantly lighted on either side and above, having covered ways for unloading tobacco from wagons, and most of them have accommodations for the teams and the drivers of the farmers' wagons.

On the arrival of a wagon loaded with tobacco it is driven upon the covered way, some three feet lower than the adjoining warehouse floor, and the tobacco is taken from it by the warehouse employés, assisted by the driver or owner, and is placed upon trucks in round piles, heads outward and tails to the center, until the truck is filled or all of any one grade is placed thereon. The loaded truck is run upon a scale platform and weighed, and thence to the proper place on the floor, where the tobacco is skillfully dumped, without disturbing the symmetrical packing of the pile. A card, with the appropriate warehouse number, name of owner or seller, and weight of the lot, is put into the cleft of a stick thrust into the pile, and as far as possible each grade, according to size, color, and quality, is placed in separate piles.

When the piles have been arranged upon the warehouse floor, at a given hour an auctioneer proceeds to sell at public outcry, beginning at the end of one of the rows of piles and disposing of each lot in turn until all are sold. The regulations in all such warehouses allow the owner to "take in" his tobacco if the price is not satisfactory, and he may again offer it at public sale or sell privately, at his option.

The charges for handling, selling, and delivering loose tobacco in the several markets of Virginia are: For receiving and weighing, per pile or lot, 10 to 15 cents; auction fee for selling under 100 pounds, 10 to 15 cents; over 100 pounds, 25 cents; commission for selling, 2½ per cent. In some warehouses a charge of 5 to 10 cents is made for delivering.

The buyers remove the tobacco from the warehouse as soon as the sale is over, large, flat-bottomed baskets, holding from 200 to 300 pounds, being used for this purpose, and care is taken to keep the several lots, as sold, separate, each lot retaining its appropriate ticket. This precaution is to prevent disputes if there should be any cause for reclamation.

In the up-country markets, when tobacco is received by rail or otherwise, in hogsheads, tierces, boxes, or crates, the packages are broken and the tobacco is sold loose in the same way as above described.

PRIZED TOBACCO—HOW SOLD.

In Richmond and Petersburg, where there are regular inspection warehouses, the hogsheads or other packages are first stripped off, the tobacco broken in three or more places, and samples are drawn from each break. The samples from each package are tied together, sealed, and stamped with the name of warehouse, number, owners' name, weight (gross, tare, and net), and date of inspection, and the tobacco is then sold, either at auction, on 'change, or at private sale.

The system of state warehouses, under the control of inspectors appointed by the governor, which existed for two hundred years has recently given place to free inspection, under rules and regulations adopted by trade boards or associations.

The average charges, to be paid by the seller, are: Storage, four months, per hogshead, $1; after four months, per month, 10 cents; inspection, 75 cents to $1; review, $1 50; commission for selling, 2½ per cent.; payable by the purchaser is a charge for outage of $1 per hogshead. The samples are guaranteed by the inspectors, and reclamations for non-conformity of package with sample are settled by committees of arbitration elected or appointed by the boards of trade.

With the construction of better barns, the introduction of flues or other means of applying artificial heat, and a better understanding of the processes of curing and handling, the quality of Virginia tobacco has been improved. In Pittsylvania county, for instance, tobacco skillfully cured with flues brings from \$20 to \$30 per hundred pounds, crop round; the same tobacco cured with charcoal, and with equal skill, sells for \$15 to \$25; while that cured with open wood fires in the old way, supplies a demand for lower quality at \$4 to \$10.

A still greater range of prices is found in the sales of manufacturing and smoking tobaccos, market values ranging from \$5 to \$75 per hundred pounds, this difference of prices being due almost entirely to different skill in curing and handling.

TOBACCO STRIPS.

Strips are not put up by tobacco growers, but by dealers and manufacturers in Richmond, Petersburg, Lynchburg, and Farmville. Some parties make this a special business, and the larger manufacturers make strips of such portion of their stock as is better suited for that purpose than for their own special line of goods.

Formerly only long, dark mahogany or red leaf was selected for strips; but the demand of late years for other types to suit the various export markets has greatly diversified the character of leaf used.

In making strips the loss of weight by drying is from 8 to 12 per cent.; by removal of stems, 18 to 20 per cent., and about 5 per cent. by waste—a total loss of weight of about 31 per cent. of dark leaf and 36 per cent. of bright tobacco, that purchased in winter order losing by drying much more than that bought after March.

Making strips is a large industry in Lynchburg. An account of the methods there employed will fairly describe those followed elsewhere.

Loose tobacco is taken to the factory and placed upon the floor of a room adjoining that in which the work of stemming is done, each lot or pilebeing kept separate as purchased, or, if want of space makes it necessary, several lots of the same grade, style, and quality are bulked together. The number of pounds of leaf needed to make a hogshead or a tierce of strips of a given grade is carried from the storage-room into the stemming apartment, sprinkled with water to soften, and heated in a steam-box, a few basketsful at a time. The bundles are then ready for the stemmers, the leaves being supple, pliant, and in such condition that the stems may be quickly removed without tearing the strips.

Stemming is mostly done by negro women, who are very dexterous at the work. They are assisted by children, who untie the bundles and place them ready for the stemmer, and straighten and tie up the stems. The stemmers tie the strips in bundles of moderate thickness, and are paid 50 cents per hundred pounds, weighed at the close of the day's work, thus earning from \$2 to \$4 per week. After the weighing is done, the stemmers are required to put the bundles of strips upon sticks (in which work they are assisted by their children) and to carry them to the drying-room to be hung up. Each lot intended for the filling of a hogshead or other package is hung by itself, the time required for drying varying from eight to twelve hours, according to the quality of the tobacco. The bundles dry more slowly at the ties, and care is necessary to insure perfect dryness throughout.

When the tobacco is thoroughly dry, the windows of the drying-room are opened to let it cool off—usually all night. They are then closed again, and soft steam is turned into the room through perforated pipes, so managed as to render the tobacco fit for handling. It is then carefully laid upon the floor in "coops"—one stick with tobacco overlapping another—and built up straight to a height of five feet or more, each coop containing one tierce, or two to make one hogshead. Here it remains two days, to cool off and toughen, when it is ready for packing. In the work of packing steam is again used to soften the tobacco, six or eight sticks of bundles at a time being carefully placed within the steam-box, the door of which is slightly closed, and soft steam being turned on for one or two minutes. The sticks are then carried to the packing table, opened, the bundles shaken out and straightened, and neatly packed with the least possible delay.

DISEASES OF TOBACCO AND INSECT ENEMIES.

The damage from diseases is rarely very great; still there is more or less loss every year, principally because of what is known as "red-fire". "Frenching," "walloon," "hollow stalk," and "white speck", all occur when soil or atmospheric conditions favor their development.

There are but two insect enemies whose depredations are seriously dreaded by the tobacco-planter—the flea-beetle, which attacks the seedling in the plant-bed, and the horn-worm. Cut-worms are sometimes troublesome upon sod lands, or upon clover leas planted in tobacco.

COST OF RAISING AND MARKETING TOBACCO.

The average value per acre of farms in the tobacco region may be estimated at \$12. A good rich lot, suitable for tobacco growing, will sell for \$25 to \$40 per acre; but such lots are very rarely purchasable separate from the adjoining lands. The best soils will produce from 800 to 1,500 pounds, according to variety, cultivation, and management. Inferior lands are worth from \$5 to \$10, and produce from 300 to 500 pounds of tobacco per acre.

Lands are usually rented for one-fourth of the gross crops of all kinds produced thereon. In the few instances in which tobacco lots are rented for money the best soils bring from $10 to $15, and ordinary lots $5 per acre. Lots rented for one-fourth the crop of tobacco, in districts which produce the best grades, sometimes yield a rental of $100, and very often $25 per acre. Farms which contain a fair acreage of good tobacco soil are rented at from $3 to $5; ordinary farms at from $1 to $3 per acre, the rent paid depending upon the condition of the land, the fences, barns, etc., and the distance from market, as well as upon the productive capacity of the soil.

Field workers in tobacco are paid from $5 to $10 per month, with board; and by the day, in summer, from 40 to 60 cents, with board. Laborers hired by the year, or even by the day during the active season, are not employed exclusively in the tobacco-fields, and are not paid no higher wages than ordinary farm hands. Experienced curers, assorters, prizers, etc., are paid extra wages; but usually the farmer himself supervises the more important processes.

The cost per hundred pounds of tobacco, cured and ready for market, is variously estimated at from $5 to $8 for an average yield per acre. A poor crop costs proportionately more—often much more than the market value of the product. An estimate of the cost of producing yellow tobacco and flue-cured fillers may be stated as follows, the prices for labor and other expenses being the averages for the state:

Cost of seed-beds and seed, per acre to be planted	$1 00
Weeding, etc., plants in bed	1 00
Interest and taxes on land, $25 value	1 60
Twice breaking, at $1 50	3 00
Harrowing, marking, and hilling	3 25
Drawing and setting plants	2 00
Cultivating, three plowings, two hoeings	5 25
Topping, worming, and suckering	6 50
Harvesting and curing, with charcoal or flues	20 00
Taking down, assorting, stripping, etc	9 00
Bulking and prizing	4 50
Use of horse, wagon, tools, and implements	10 00
Delivery to merchant	2 25
Total cost per acre	69 35

This estimate covers the outlay for the production of a good crop upon good land with all the needed appliances for cultivation, harvesting, and preparation for market. The cost of ordinary cultivation may be reduced to as small an amount as $40 per acre; and that this sort of economy is much practiced is evidenced by the fact that the average yield for the state in 1879, as shown by the census, was only 572 pounds per acre.

Much the larger part of the tobacco produced in Virginia is cultivated on the "share" system, in some instances the proprietor furnishing the land, teams, feed for teams, implements, and house and firewood for the laborer and family, and receiving from one-half to three-fourths of the crop made, the proportion varying with the fertility of the land, variety grown, cost of curing, appliances, etc. If the tenant furnishes teams, implements, etc., the landlord gets from one-fourth to one-third of the crop. Sometimes "croppers" are employed by tenants, who receive for their labor one-half of the residue after the rental is paid. When fertilizers are used upon crops grown by tenants or croppers, the cost of such manures is deducted before the division into shares is made.

From two to three acres, 8,000 to 12,000 hills, can be cultivated by each full hand. Large areas of tobacco can be grown at less cost per acre only by the closest attention and careful supervision on the part of the planter; and, as a rule, small crops, well handled, are much more profitable, proportionately, than large ones.

There are no authoritative and reliable data from which to estimate the production, acreage, and value of the tobacco crops of the state during the three years preceding the census year.

A SUCCINCT ACCOUNT OF TOBACCO IN VIRGINIA,

HISTORICAL, AGRICULTURAL, AND STATISTICAL, 1607-1790, WITH SOME MENTION INCIDENTALLY OF ITS HISTORY IN MARYLAND, PREPARED FOR THE TENTH CENSUS OF THE UNITED STATES BY R. A. BROCK.

It is an unquestioned fact that tobacco reigns supreme among artificial stimulants in popular estimation. No sooner were its peculiar qualities made known than it was sought after with the greatest avidity, until now, after a lapse of a little more than three centuries since its introduction into civilized Europe, its use has become universal, the world yielding to its fascinations in one or more of the forms of its use, either as smokers, chewers, or snuffers. As many as forty varieties of the tobacco-plant have been noted by botanists, but one of them alone claims here our attention in its connection with our narrative, that designated by Linnæus as *Nicotiana tabacum*, and common to Virginia, to the material prosperity of which it has held the most important relation as a staple product from the first settlement as a colony. Among the aborigines of the continent of America, according to Sir Hans Sloane (*a*) it was known as *pætum*, while those who inhabited the islands called it *yoli*. Its several present modes of use were subjects of early observation. In November, 1492, the natives of Cuba were seen smoking it by the companions of Columbus during his first voyage to America, and in the narrative of the second voyage, in 1494, Roman Pane, the friar who accompanied it, examples the use of tobacco in snuff-taking. He uses the name *cogiaba* for the plant, which was its Hispaniolan name, but by other travelers it was spelled *cohiba*. It was known as *pëtun* in Brazil, and as *piecelt* in Mexico. Its use in chewing was observed by the Spaniards upon landing in Paraguay in 1503, the natives coming forth to oppose them beating drums, throwing water, "chewing herbs, and spitting the juice toward them." In 1519 tobacco is said to have been discovered near Tobasco, but the event is assigned to the next year. (*b*) In 1535 the negroes had already habituated themselves to its use, and had cultivated it on the plantations of their masters. Europeans likewise smoked it, and its use in Canada is mentioned by Cartier. In 1559 it was introduced from Saint Domingo into Europe by Hernandez de Toledo, a Spanish gentleman, who brought a small quantity into Spain and Portugal, and in the same year Jean Nicot, envoy from the court of France to Portugal, first transmitted thence to Paris, to Queen Catharine de Medicis, seeds of the tobacco-plant, and from this circumstance it was called *Herba Regina*, and, in honor of him, *Nicotiana*. In 1565 Conrad Gesner became acquainted with tobacco, and several botanists cultivated it in their gardens; the same year Sir John Hawkins carried it from Florida to England. (*c*) Hariot, who was with the expedition of Sir Richard Grenville, undertaken under the auspices of Sir Walter Raleigh, in 1584, and which resulted in the discovery of Virginia in 1585, makes this mention of tobacco:

> There is a herbe which is sowed by itselfe, and is called by the inhabitants *uppowoc*. In the West Indies it hath divers names, according to the severall countries where it groweth and is used; the Spaniards generally called it *Tobacco*. The leaves thereof being dried and brought to powder, they used to take the fume or smoke thereof, by sucking it through pipes made of clay, into their stomache and head.—*A Briefe and True Report of the New Found Land of Virginia*, London, 1588, p. 16.

William Strachey, the first secretary of the colony, wrote *circa* 1610:

> Here is a great store of tobacco which the salvages call *apooke*, howbeit, it is not of the best kind; it is but poor and weake; and of a byting taste; it grows not fully a yard above ground, bearing a little yellow flower like to henbane; the leaves are short and thicke, somewhat round at the upper end; whereas the best tobacco of Trynidado and the Orinoqno, is large, sharpe, and growing two or three yards from the ground, bearing a flower of the breadth of our bell-flowers in England; the salvages here dry the leaves of the *apooke* over the fier, and sometimes in the sun, and crumble it into powder—stalks, leaves and all—taking the same in pipes of earth, which they very ingeniously can make.—*The Historie of Travel into Virginia Britannia*, London, 1849, pp. 121, 122.

Beverley states as to the Indian care of tobacco:

> I am informed that they used to let it all run to seed, only succoring the leaves to keep the sprouts from growing upon and starving them; and when it was ripe they pulled off the leaves, cured them in the sun, and laid them up for use.—*History of Virginia*, edition of 1722, pp. 227, 228.

The common mode of curing it, however, as we find it stated by other annalists, was to hang it up in their habitations, to be dried by the heat and smoke of their fires. Both Sir Richard Grenville, on his return to England, in 1585, and Sir Ralph Lane (who was sent out by Sir Walter Raleigh as the first governor of the colony), in 1586, on his return home, carried with them pipes and tobacco. So between them, and not with Sir Walter Raleigh, as popularly accredited, lies the honor, it appears, of the introduction of tobacco into England. According to Hamor, (*d*) the meed of inaugurating, in 1612, the cultivation of tobacco systematically in the colony is due to John Rolfe, the husband of Pocahontas. (*e*) In 1616, under the stimulus and fostering care of Sir George Yeardley, the deputy governor, the attention of the colonists was engaged in its planting for profit, which speedily became so alluring that they forsook for it all other occupations. When, in 1617, Captain Samuel Argall arrived in the colony as its governor, "he found all the Publick Works and Buildings in James-Town fallen to Decay, and not above five or six Houses fit to be inhabited; the Market Place, Streets, and all other Spare Places planted with Tobacco; and the Colony dispersed all about, as every man could find the properest place and best Conveniency for planting" (Stith, p. 146).

---

a *Natural History of Jamaica.*

b *Précis sur l'Amérique*, p. 116.

c Fairholt, *History of Tobacco*, p. 51, quoting from Taylor, the water poet.

d *Raphe Hamor's True Discourse*, 1614. London, 1615, p. 24.

e John Rolfe was clearly a man of sagacity, as well as enterprise, as is evinced in his further interest in and management of tobacco. He wrote in 1616: "Tobacco, though an esteemed weed, is very commodious, which thence thriveth so well that no doubt but after a little more trial and expense in the curing thereof, it will compare with the best West Indies" ("Relation of Virginia," printed in the *Virginia Historical Register*, vol. I, p. 505).

In 1617 one "Mr. Lambert made a great discovery in the trade of planting, for the method of curing tobacco was then in heaps; but this gentleman found out that it cured better upon lines; and therefore the governor wrote to the company to send over lines for that purpose" (Stith's *History of Virginia*, p. 147).

According to the journal of Glover (time of Sir William Berkeley) lines had then fallen into disuse. We quote from this author (whose work we have not at hand) from the paper prepared in 1876 by Mr. John Ott, secretary of the Southern Fertilizing Company, Richmond, Virginia, as follows: "They drive into the stalk of each plant a peg, and as fast as they are pegged they hang them upon tobacco-sticks, so nigh each other that they just touch much after the manner they hang herrings in Yarmouth. When the plant hath put out so many leaves as the ground will nourish to a substance and largeness that will render them merchantable they take off the top of the plant. If the ground be very rich, they let a plant put out a dozen or sixteen leaves before they top it; if mean, then not

The result is exhibited in the shipment to England, in June, 1619, of 20,000 pounds, the crop of the preceding year. This year is noted also as that in which the royal pedant, James I, fulminated his furious *Counterblast to Tobacco*. Although by letters-patent dated the 23d of May, 1609, the Virginia Company of London had been granted "freedom from all Custom and Subsidy for twenty-one years, excepting only five per cent. upon all such Goods and Merchandize as should be imported into England or any other of his Majesty's Dominions", the tobacco of Virginia growth was now subjected to a most onerous and disproportionate taxation, comparing its relative value with that of foreign production, for "upon a general rate made of Tobacco, both *Spanish* and *Virginia*, at ten shillings the pound" there was demanded "sixpence a pound equally upon all; although *Spanish* tobacco was usually sold at eighteen shillings a pound, and sometimes more, and Virginia would seldom bear above three or four shillings." (*a*)

To induce a permanent residence of the colonists, who were chiefly young and unmarried men, the company, in 1620, sent over in two shipments ninety young women of respectability, to supply them with wives, they being chargeable with the cost of transportation, which was first 120, and afterward 150 pounds of tobacco each. In this year also there was exported to England 40,000 pounds of tobacco, of which, however, owing to the little care observed as to quality and the onerous taxation imposed, "the better halfe" did not yield eight-pence per pound, and "the rest not above" two shillings. (*b*) The large production of tobacco at the sacrifice of other crops was not only to the disadvantage of the planter, but occasioned great dissatisfaction with the Virginia Company, as is evidenced in their communications. August 12, 1621, they wrote to the governor and council, "We desire you to give notice to the Collony that after this yeare they expect no further supply of any necessaries to be exchanged with them for their darling tobacco," (*c*) and on September 11, following, the wish is expressed that there would be made "some provision for the burninge of all base and rotten stuff, and not suffer any but very good to be cured, at least sent home whereby these would certainly be more advanced in the price uppon lesse in the quantity". (*d*)

The governor and council were obedient to the wishes of the company, as is exhibited by a communication dated January, 1621–'22:

> It is a thinge very well liked of here that you have left the Price of Tobacco at libertie since it is of such an uncertaine valew by reason of the great difference thereof * * * * For the drawinge of the people from the excefsive plantinge of Tobacco we have by consent of the Generall Assemblie restrayned them to one hundred plantes ye headd, uppon eache of wch plantes there are to be left butt nyne leaves wch pportions as near as could be guessed was generally conceaved would be agreeable with the hundred waight you have allowed. By wch means as also by the course we have taken for the keeping of every man to his trade, we doubt nott but very much prevent the immoderate Plantinge of Tobacco.—Neill's *History of the Virginia Company of London*, p. 282.

This restriction was but badly observed; for in 1628 it was allowed to take 12 leaves "instead of 25 or 30, as heretofore"; and in 1629 to raise 3,000 plants per poll, and 1,000 each for women and children. The next year (1630) this was reduced to 2,000, and in 1631 "no seconds were to be tended".

It was further desired by the colonists that seven shillings per bushel should be established as a merchantable rate for the corn produced, to be paid for by bills of exchange on England "or in commodities to be delivered here at 25 per centum." (*e*) Governor Wyatt was instructed that the colonists were "not to plant above one hundred pounds of tobacco per head", (*f*) and that their attention should be directed instead to the planting of corn. Section 21 of the acts of assembly, March, 1623–'24, also provided "that there be some men in every plantation to censure tobacco". (*g*) Notwithstanding the attempts made to divert the people from the cultivation of tobacco, so profitable had it become through the increased productiveness under improved tillage with the spade and the augmentation

---

above nine or ten, and so according to the strength of the soil" (p. 10). In connection with so exhausting a product as tobacco it is interesting to note the opinion of doughty John Smith of the bountiful lands of Virginia as presented to him: "The verdure of the earth in most cases doth manifestly prove the nature of the soyle to be lusty and very rich. * * * For the most part it is a black sandy mold, in some places a fat, slimy clay, in other places, a very barren gravel. But the best ground is known by the vesture it beareth, as by the greatness of the trees, or abundance of weeds, &c. * * * All the varieties of fruits may be there in great plenty by the industry of men" (Smith's *History of Virginia*, etc., Richmond ed., 1819, i, p. 115).

Beverley says of their tobacco-houses and mode of curing: "Their tobacco-houses are all built of wood, as open and airy as is consistent with keeping out the rain; which sort of building is most convenient for the curing of their tobacco" (*History of Virginia*, edition of 1722, p. 251).

The tobacco put up by the colonists for export was in bundles of leaf, as at present; that from the West Indies was in balls, in the preparation of which molasses was used. They made use of manures from their cow-pens and stables, and also of "white and blue fossil marl. * * * Under the government of Sir George Yeardley in 1619, and by the aid of it, they obtained wheat at the rate of 30 bushels per acre" ("Mineral Resources of Virginia"), by G. W. Featherstonehaugh, article in the *Farmer's Register*, vol. I, No. 9, p. 521 (February, 1834).

Much additional of value as to the agriculture of the period may be found in the pamphlet *Early History of Agriculture in Virginia*, 8vo., by N. F. Cabell, esq., of "Washington", Virginia.

a Stith, p. 168.

b Neill's *History of the Virginia Company of London*, p. 243.

c *Ibid.*, p. 238.

d *Ibid.*, p. 244.

e *Ibid.*, p. 282.

f Neill's *History of the Virginia Company of London*, p. 482.

g Hening's *Statutes at Large*, i, p. 115.

of price and consumption in Europe that in 1621 storehouses and factories were established at Middleburgh and Flushing, and 55,000 pounds were exported to Holland, but none to England, because of the excessive impost already mentioned. In 1622 the crop was 60,000 pounds. (*a*) James I had, as stated, in extorting a revenue from the sale of tobacco, violated the charter granted the Virginia Company (which was revoked in 1624 and the company dissolved). His successor, Charles I, with narrow selfishness and an utter disregard of the interests of the colonists, went farther, and proposed that a monopoly should be granted him, to which the colonial assembly entered their protest, and by act passed March 26, 1628, offered to contract with the king for all their tobacco at 3*s.* 6*d.* per pound, delivered in Virginia free of freight or customs, or 4*s.* if delivered in London, its good quality to be insured by an examination by sworn inspectors after being cured. They also requested the king to take annually at least 500,000 pounds weight at the prices stated, and if he should not be disposed to take the overplus, if there should be any, that they be permitted to ship it to the Low Countries, Ireland, Turkey, or elsewhere. They offered to contract for seven years, with the request that, if the consumption of England, with the quantity above stipulated, should exceed the supply from the lower islands, it might be proportionably increased; and in the event of the king's acceding to these terms, they requested that the importation of Spanish tobacco be prohibited. (*b*) It was stated that they had ordered a proclamation to be made requiring the plants to be set 4½ feet apart, (*c*) and twelve leaves only to be gathered, instead of twenty-five or thirty, as had been the custom, great care to be taken also not to burn it in sweating, and they had reduced the quantity to be planted as low as they could, considering the population of the colony and a due regard to the culture of corn. In March, 1629, increased production was allowed in the admission of "2,000 pounds for every head" in a family, "including women and children," but "bad or ill-conditioned tobacco" was required to be burnt under the penalty of being debarred from planting until readmitted by an act of the assembly. (*d*) In February, 1631–'32, in consideration of the low price of tobacco, the poll-tax, which had been 5 pounds, was increased to 10 pounds of tobacco, with the addition of a bushel of corn, (*e*) the price of tobacco in barter being fixed at 6*d.* per pound. (*f*) It was also enacted that "noe person should tend over fourteen leaves, nor gather over nine leaves upon a plant of tobacco, nor tend any slips of old stalks, or any of the second crop" upon forfeiture of the whole crop raised, (*g*) and "all tobacco was to be taken down before the end of November, or else not to be adjudged or accounted merchantable". (*h*) By act passed February, 1632–'33, it was provided that "five storehouses be appointed severally at James City, Shirley Hundred, Denbeigh, Southampton river in Elizabeth City, and Kiskyoke", and the planters were obliged to bring in all of their tobacco to the same before the last day of December, where it was to be repacked, viewed, and tried by sworn men appointed for the purpose, the quantity entered to the several accounts of the planters, and then all payments of debts were to be made at these storehouses, in the presence of the keeper. No tobacco was to be "made upp in rolle", except between the first day of August and the last day of October, (*i*) "and no other tobacco to be made up at all." (*j*) It was directed also that "the planters shall endeavor themselves to plant and sowe those kindes of the long sortes, and all other sortes the next yeare shall be quite left off and given over". (*k*)

a Hening's *Statutes at Large*, i, p. 126. Bishop (*History of American Manufactures*, i, p. 30) says 66,000 pounds.

b Hening, i, pp. 134–'5, "Mr. Edward Bennet, a citizen of London, was presented with the freedom of the company, because he had written a treatise, setting forth, in a clear and lively manner, the great inconvenience and damage to the nation from this cause" (Stith, p. 199).

c In the time of Glover the distance was reduced to 4 feet, and in that of Smyth, the English traveler, who visited Virginia in 1773, to 3 feet (see *Virginia Historical Register*, vi, 81), which is the distance at the present time. Smyth adds that "the produce of an acre in the culture of tobacco, in the best land, is about 1,600 pounds; on the worst, about 500 pounds. (*Ibid.*, p. 132.) Beverley states that in his day (1722) a dozen hands would produce 16,000 pounds of "sweet-scented" and sometimes more (p. 212).

d Hening, i, p. 152.

e *Ibid.*, p. 159.

f *Ibid.*, p. 162.

g *Ibid.*, p. 164.

h *Ibid.*, p. 165.

i The time was afterward extended to the last day of December.

j Hening, i, pp. 204–205.

k *Ibid.*, p. 205, Clayton (*Force's Tracts*, vol. iii, No. 12, p. 18) says: "There are not only the two distinct sorts of sweet-scented and Aranoka; but of each of these there be several sorts much different, the seeds whereof are known by distinct names, they having been given the names of those gentlemen most famed for such sort of tobacco, as 'Pryor' seed, etc. Nay, the same sort of seed in different earths will produce tobacco much different as to goodness. The richer the ground, the better it is for Aranoka tobacco, whose scent is not much minded, their only aim being to have it spacious, large, and to procure it of a bright color." To insure an early setting of the plants, he steeped the seed in an infusion of stable manure and soot. In sowing the seed he mixed them with ashes. Of the varieties of tobacco, Jones writes: "There are two sorts of tobacco, viz, the Oroonoko, the stronger; and sweet-scented, the milder; the first with a sharper leaf, like a fox's ear, and the other rounder and with finer fibers; but each of them is varied into several sorts. * * * The land in the latitude between James and York rivers seems most nicely adapted for sweet-scented, or the finest tobacco; for it is observed that the goodness decreaseth the further you go northward of the one and the southward of the other. But this may be, I believe, attributed in some measure to the seed and management, as well as to the land and latitude; for on York river, in a small tract of land called *Digges' Neck* [from Edward Digges, who was governor in 1655], which is poorer than a great deal of other land in the same latitude, by a particular seed and management is made the famous crop known by the name of 'E Dees', remarkable for its mild taste and fine smell" (*The Present State of Virginia*, Hugh Jones, 1724, pp. 34–39).

In *Mair's Bookkeeping*, Edinburgh, 1765 (pp. 231–234), the following lesser varieties are enumerated: Long-green, Thick-joint, Brazil,

In August, 1633, the price of tobacco in barter was fixed at 9*d.* per pound, (*a*) all accounts and contracts being required to be kept in money, (*b*) and the rate of freight was fixed at £3 per ton. (*c*) January 6, 1639, "tobacco, by reason of the excessive quantities made, being soe low that the planters could not subsist by it," was required to be inspected and the rotten and unmerchantable and half the good to be burnt, so that the whole quantity be reduced to 1,500,000 pounds, without stripping and smoothing, and for the two next years 170 pounds per poll, stripped and smoothed, was to be made, which would make in the whole about 1,300,000 pounds, "and all creditors are to take 40 pounds for the hundred," and "noe man to be obliged to perform above half his covenants about freighting tobacco in 1639". Debts were to be satisfied in tobacco at 3*d.* per pound, and merchants were only allowed to advance 30 per cent. on their goods. (*d*) A ton of tobacco was to consist of four hogsheads, and freight was fixed at £6 per ton. (*e*)

The tobacco made in 1640 was not to be sold under 12*d.*, and that made in 1641 not under 20*d.*, on forfeiture of the whole crop. (*f*) In 1646 the culture of tobacco was introduced into the Dutch colony of New York. In 1649 the quantity of tobacco had so increased that the price had fallen to 3*d.* a pound. (*g*) In 1652 the cultivation of tobacco was forbidden in England, and all plantations there were ordered to be destroyed. In 1655 the crop in Virginia failed through drought. In March, 1657–'58, by enactment, its planting after the 10th of July was forbidden under forfeiture of 2,000 pounds of tobacco, and a duty of 2*s.* per hogshead was levied on all tobacco exported, in lieu of the poll-tax. (*h*) Collectors were to be appointed for the several rivers, and fraudulent practices are manifested by the following provision:

In case anie person or persons whatsoever shall false pack anie tobacco, that is pack any ground leaves to the quantity of five pounds in a hogshead, among his top tobacco, it shall be lawful to give order for the burning it.—*Hening*, i, p. 492.

In March, 1659–'60, a duty of 10*s.* per hogshead was levied on all tobacco not discharged in the English dominions in Europe. (*i*)

In 1661 the price of tobacco in Maryland was fixed at 2*s.* per pound. (*j*) In March, 1661–'62, tobacco was forbidden to be planted after the last of June (*k*), and in 1662 its price in Virginia fell from 12*s.* to 10*s.* per hundred weight. (*l*) To the detriment of Virginia, it appears that the colonies of New York and Maryland were in this year also engaged in a secret trade in tobacco with the Dutch, and upon complaint Lord Baltimore gave his promise to the English board of admiralty that all such tobacco so discovered in the province of Maryland

---

Lazy, and Shoestrings, but it is stated that "all the tobacco in the country, when brought to the warehouses, comes under one of two denominations, viz, Aronoke and sweet-scented. The latter is distinguished by its scent and flavor, is most valued, and grows in greatest plenty in the lower parts of Virginia, viz. James river and York river, and begins now to be planted on Rappahannock and the south side of the Potomac. The planters used to strip a great deal of it, by taking the stem out of the leaf, which then gets the name of stemmed tobacco, as before the stripping it was called leaf. Aronoke, denominated by an Indian name, is generally planted up Chesapeake bay and the back settlements on all the rivers. It is the sort the merchants generally purchase; they do not deal much in the sweet-scented, and any of that sort they buy is commonly leaf. The planters seldom or never strip the Aronoke as they do the sweet-scented". The account in *Harris' Voyages* is to the same effect, both as regards the kinds and the excellence of the sweet-scented tobacco which grows on the York river (Ed. 1764, ii, p. 231). General Washington also recognizes the two great classes, and speaks of his own careful experiments to test the value of different kinds (*Sparks' Writings*, xii, pp. 253, 257, 258, 260). The Oroonoko is no longer confined to the richest soil, nor is it now thought to be less sweet-scented than its rivals. Some years ago the fresh, sandy highlands of Fluvanna—not more fertile than many others—produced it in high perfection, and, being a favorite with the manufacturers, the growers reaped unusual profits. The Pryor tobacco is still also cultivated largely on the south side of James river (*N. F. Cabell*, p. 21).

a Hening, I, p. 210.

b *Ibid.*, p. 216. This was not observed, for accounts of clerk's fees and other charges were kept chiefly in tobacco until 1754, as evidenced in the statutes.

c *Ibid.*, p. 217.

d The advance of the Virginia merchants upon the goods imported by them, as is exhibited by M. S. account books in our possession, varied from 25 to 50 per cent., and in some accounts against John Baylor, 1758–'70, the advance in 1758–'65 is 100 per cent., and in 1766–'70, 75 per cent. *Mair's Bookkeeping*, p. 334, states that in 1761 it was from 35 to 40 per cent. The pound, Virginia currency, rated with the pound sterling as two to three—the first being only worth two-thirds as much as the last, or decimally 3.33⅓ per cent. A valuable article on colonial exchange, entitled "Virginia Colonial Money, and Tobacco's Part Therein", was published by W. L. Royall, esq., now of New York city, in the *Virginia Law Journal* for August, 1877.

e Hening, i, pp. 224–225.

f *Ibid.*, p. 226.

g "A Perfect Description of Virginia", *Force's Tracts*, ii, No. 8, p. 4.

h Hening, i, p. 448.

i *Ibid.*, p. 536.

j Scharf's *History of Maryland*, ii, p. 35.

k Hening, ii, p. 30. From the *Diary of Colonel William Cabell, Sr.*, of Union Hill, (now) Amherst county, Virginia, kept prior to, during, and immediately after the revolutionary war, it appears that plant patches were generally burnt in January and the seed sowed for a succession in February and March, though in 1769 he drew and planted from a patch sowed by the 11th of April. He finished planting his crop June 20, 1774, from seed sown 7th of May. Tobacco seed were sown by him on the 9th of May, 1785, and tobacco hills were made in February and March, generally in new ground. Coltered planting commenced the first season (rain) in May and was generally finished by the last of June, though replanting is mentioned as late as 24th of July. The earliest planting mentioned is the 6th of May, 1787. Cutting commenced about the middle of August and ended about the last of September; but in 1770–'87–'88 and '90 tobacco was cut in July, "on account of its firing." The latest cutting mentioned is the 28th of October, 1786. Prizing commenced the last week in October, and sticking and stripping the first week in September.

l *A Letter to the Clergy of Virginia*, Richard Bland, 1760, p. 12.

should be seized. (*a*) The salary of Sir William Berkeley as governor of Virginia, which was paid out of the revenue from quit rents and the impost of 2*s.* per hogshead on tobacco, was £1,000 per annum. (*b*) In December, 1662, 30 pounds of tobacco per poll was levied for the building of James City. (*c*) In September, 1664, Maryland having refused to co-operate with Virginia in lessening the quantity of tobacco produced and thus advancing its value, all restrictions upon planting were rescinded. (*d*) In October, 1665, the impost of 10*s.* per hogshead on all tobacco exported elsewhere than to England was restored because of the competition of Maryland, which, under its proprietary charter, enjoyed rights of trade which were denied to Virginia, the latter being restricted in the importation of tobacco to England alone. (*e*) In June, 1666, it was recited that "whereas the quantity of tobacco made in this colony is become so great that all markets have become glutted with it, and the value so reduced as not to offer subsistence to the planter", and in consequence a cessation from planting for one year from February 1, 1666, to February 1, 1667, was proposed, subject to the ratification of the colonies of Maryland and North Carolina, with which commissioners were appointed to treat. (*f*) The conference was successful, for, by act of October, 1666, the preceding act was confirmed and made operative, the two colonies having assented to its provisions. (*g*) This had been a favorite scheme with the assembly, and conferences with the authorities of Maryland and North Carolina had previously been held in 1663-'64-'65.

In August, 1667, "there happened all over Virginia a gust or storm of wind and rain, which continued for three days with such violence * * * that above one-half of their crop of tobacco, which was then standing in the field, was blown away and torn to pieces, the tobacco-houses were blown down, and not one part in three saved of what was made that year." (*h*)

The customs collected in England in 1676 upon Virginia tobacco amounted to £120,000 sterling, while the whole custom duties in the reign of Queen Elizabeth (1590) amounted to only £50,000. (*i*) In April, 1679, the importation of all tobacco from North Carolina, save in payments of debts due, was prohibited, (*j*) and by act of June, 1680, tobacco was forbidden to be shipped before March 20 for two years ensuing, for the better enhancement of price and the lessening of freights. (*k*) In October, 1681, it was provided that after the 10th of September, 1682, all tobacco casks were required to be branded with the first two initial letters of the name of the owner, and the cask was to be allowed for at 30 pounds of tobacco. (*l*) In November, 1682, the price of tobacco was fixed at 10*s.* per hundred-weight. (*m*) During the disputes, in May, 1682, between the governor, Lord Culpepper, and the house of burgesses the inhabitants of the counties of Gloucester, New Kent, and Middlesex proceeded riotously to cut up the tobacco-plants in the beds, especially the sweet-scented, which was produced nowhere else, (*n*) and in October, 1686, the shipment of stalks from which the tobacco had been stripped was prohibited. (*o*) In 1687, the merchants of London petitioned the general assembly to prohibit the exportation of tobacco in bulk, and the statement was made that such as was sold at the mast at 1½*d.* and 2*d.* a pound had been sold to buyers in London at 6*d.* per pound, while sweet-scented in entire parcels sold for 7¾*d.* and 7½*d.* (*p*) According to the report of the receiver-general of the colony, Colonel William Byrd, the revenue of 2*s.* per hogshead and 5*s.* per ton for the year—24th July, 1688, to 24th July, 1689—was as follows:

	£	*s.*	*d.*
For Colonel William Cole's accompt of the lower district of James river	608	0	7¾
For Colonel Matthew Page's accompt of the upper district of James river	527	0	6¼
For Secretary Spencer's accompt of the Potomac district	458	4	3
For Colonel John Custis's accompt of the Accompt district	137	11	1
For Colonel Ralph Wormeley's accompt of the Rappahannock district	746	13	8¾
For Colonel Edmund Jenings's accompt of the York district	1,153	18	4
	3,631	8	6¼

a *Calendar of State Papers*, America and West Indies (1661-'68), August 25, No. 537.

b *Ibid.*, No. 368.

c Bland, p. 12.

d Hening, ii, p. 209.

e *Ibid.* The impost on tobacco in Maryland in 1671 was 2*s.* per hogshead.

f *Ibid.*, pp. 224-225.

g *Ibid.*, pp. 229-232.

h Postlethwayt's *Dictionary of Trade and Commerce*, 1757, vol. ii, art. Tobacco.

i Bishop, i, p. 322.

j Hening, ii, p. 425. From *The Revisal of the Laws of North Carolina*, printed by James Davis, Newbern, 1773, it appears that no inspection of tobacco was provided until 1768, when the requirements were made similar to those of Virginia. The weight of the hogshead was made 1,000 lbs. net, and all accounts, according to the statutes, were kept in pounds, shillings, and pence.

k Hening, ii, p. 479.

l *Ibid.*, p. 31.

m *Ibid.*, p. 506.

n Introduction by Charles Campbell to Beverley's *History of Virginia*, edition, Richmond, 1855, pp. 2-3.

o Hening, iii, p. 35.

p "Westover Papers", Wynne's Edition of 1866, *Essay on Bulk Tobacco*, vol. ii, p. 140, *et seq.* Colonel William Byrd wrote January 11, 1688, as to the crops of the preceding (1687): "We had ye most promising this year ever known, but it was generally spoiled by some thicke, close weather in S^br [Sept.] so that now tobacco is for ye greatest part either house burnt or hath sweat so much that its become (as you call it) husky, though I dare say y^t if mine * * will not pass you must expect none this year from Maryland or Virginia wch has made as bad tobacco this yeare as ever. They have had Assembly lately in Maryland about Bulke. To Perry & Lane, London."—MS. Letter-Book, 1682-'93, in *Collections Virginia Historical Society*.

which is the impost on 36,314 hogsheads at 2*s.* per hogshead. Computing the hogshead at the prevailing weight, 500 pounds, the export was 18,157,000 pounds. (*a*)

In October, 1686, tobacco hogsheads were required to be branded with the weight contained, as well as with the initials of the owner. (*b*) In April, 1695, their size was fixed, the staves to be 48 inches in length, "and noe more," and the diameter of head to be 30 inches. (*c*) The receipts of Receiver-General Byrd between April 25 and October 25, 1704, were:

	£	*s.*	*d.*
Upper district of James river	666	4	0
Lower district of James river	498	14	0
York district	1,297	11	6
Rappahannock district	754	2	4
Potomac district	442	11	9
	3,659	3	7

which is the impost on 36,590 hogsheads, which, at 500 pounds each, would be 18,295,000 pounds. (*d*)

An act passed by the general assembly, October, 1705, provided "that if any tobacco hereafter in any wise whatsoever shall be imported or brought from Carolina, or other parts without the capes, into this Colony and Dominion, in order to be here laid on shore, sold or shipped, the same shall thereby be forfeited and lost", one-half to go to the crown, the remainder to the informer. A further duty of 1*s.* 3*d.* English money per ton burden, according to gauge, was imposed to maintain the cost of the postal service, (*e*) but both this tax and that of 2*s.* per hogshead (now made for hogshead, or 500 pounds of bulk tobacco) were remitted to Virginia owners. (*f*) The abuse of the tobacco trade by smuggling, which the act above was intended to reach, was complained of also in the instructions from the president and masters of William and Mary College, dated August 10, 1723, to John Randolph, then about to depart for England. For the support of the college, their majesties, William and Mary, had in 1692 (O. S.) provided a revenue from a tax of 1*d.* per pound on all tobacco exported from Virginia and Maryland to other plantations. This, it was complained, had been reduced one-half from several causes, among which it was recited that the officers in the lower counties of Pennsylvania and North Carolina, instead of exacting good money, had taken currency of the country, that of North Carolina being little above one-fourth and that of Pennsylvania one half of the value of good money, as to the relative nominal values, which occasioned a greater export from those places. (*g*) It was also stated that there was no longer, as formerly, an officer maintained in Elizabeth river ("from which is the greater part of the exportation of tobacco to the plantations"), nor a searcher at Hampton, "both offices being sunk;" and that "vast frauds" were perpetrated, it being a common practice to carry out tobacco in barrels entered as beef or pork, to conceal it under corn, and to mark the hogshead with less than the real weight. (*h*) The average annual export of tobacco from Virginia and Maryland during the ten years ending in 1709 was 28,858,666 pounds, of which England consumed on an average 11,260,659 and the rest of Europe 17,598,007 pounds. (*i*) The authorities teem with accounts of the distress of the inhabitants of the colonies, of both Virginia and Maryland, at this period from the low price of tobacco, which had been occasioned by overproduction, and planters were unable, from lack of means, to clothe themselves, the practice having been to import their clothing from England and to pay for them with the proceeds of their sales. This is detailed by Governor Alexander Spotswood, together with a beneficial result, who wrote, in 1710, to the lords commissioners of the council of trade, London, as follows:

The great number of negroes imported here (so long as there remained any money or credit in the Colony to buy them), and solely employed in making tobacco, hath produced, for some years, an increase of the commodity far disproportionate to the consumption that could be made of it in all markets wch the war had left open, and, by a natural consequence, lowered the price to a great degree. This was first felt in those parts of the country whose tobacco is reputed mean, and the people being disappointed of the necessary supplys of clothing for their familys in return of their tobacco, (*j*) found themselves under the necessity of attempting to cloath themselves with their own Manufactures. And the market for tobacco still declining and few stores of goods brought in other parts of the country, through the like necessity have been forced in the same humour of planting cotton and sewing flax and by making the first with their wool, to supply the want of course clothing and Linnen. This is now become so universal that even in one of the best countys for tobacco I'm credibly informed that there has been made this last year above 4,000 yards of divers sorts of Woolen, Cotton and Linnen Cloth. (*k*)

---

a *Virginia Historical Register*, iii, pp. 187–188.

b Hening, iii, p. 135.

c *Ibid.*

d *Virginia Historical Register*, iii, p. 188.

e Governor Alexander Spotswood, in his letters of the period, makes frequent mention of the opposition of the planters to a tax for the postal service, which was quite as obnoxious to them as was the fateful stamp act afterward; which is interesting, as showing the early drift of political sentiment.—MS. Letter-Books of Governor Spottswood in the *Collections of the Virginia Historical Society.*

f Hening, iii, p. 553.

g This inequality of money values in the several American colonies or states continued during the eighteenth century, and is a constant source of complaint on the part of travelers.

h *Papers Relating to the History of the Church in Virginia*, A. D. 1650-1776. Ed. by Rt. Rev. Wm. Stevens Perry, D. D., p. 550.

i In 1697 the crop in Maryland was unusually small, and it was reported to the general assembly that the tobacco lands were worn out (Scharf's *History of Maryland*, ii, p. 198). In 1708 fines due in tobacco were commutable in the province of Maryland at 10*s.* per hundred-weight.

j "They have their clothing of all sorts from England, as Linen, Woolen, Silk, Hats and Leather."—Beverley's *History of Virginia*, Ed. 1722, p. 255.

k MS. Letter-Book of Alexander Spotswood in the *Collections of the Virginia Historical Society.*

An act was passed by the Virginia assembly at the session for October, 1710, for protection in the standard of tobacco hogsheads, from "cropping, cutting away of the bulge", "drawing the staves," etc., its violation being punishable with a fine of £5 sterling. (*a*) The income of the secretary of the colony at this period from his fees of office was about 110,000 pounds of tobacco. In October, 1712, rolling-houses (warehouses) were appointed for each county in the colony, (*b*) so called from the manner in which tobacco was then transported, the hogshead of tobacco being actually rolled to market on its own periphery through mud, mire, and stream. The cask was made of good oak staves, well hooped, and into this cask the tobacco was pressed, layer by layer, by a lever some 30 or 40 feet long, inserted in a mortise made in a large tree for the fulcrum, against which the hogshead was placed. When fully packed and headed, a wooden spike, some 2 feet long, was driven into the center of each head. The ends, projecting some inches, were rounded, and thus formed an axle-tree, to which shafts, made of a split sapling, were fitted. On these, in front of the cask, a few slabs were nailed, making a platform, which, with sides added, formed a box, in which were stowed provisions for man and horse, a frying-pan, a hoe, an ax, and a blanket. Attached to the rear was a contrivance for carrying fodder. If the distance was moderate, the hogshead was thus rolled on its hoops as tires; but when the distance was considerable (from 50 to 150 miles), rough fellies were spiked to each end about the quarter hoops, and these rude tires served to keep the cask out of the mud and prevent its being worn through. The tobacco-roller, as the driver (usually the owner) was called, never sought shelter on his journey—often of a week's duration—but camped at night by the roadside. This mode continued in vogue until after the beginning of the present century. Arrived at market, and after having had it inspected, the owner himself sold his tobacco, offering the note until he found a purchaser, often, by barter with the merchant, receiving in exchange domestic supplies. (*c*) The price of storage for every cask of tobacco, or its equivalent in bulk (500 pounds), was 12*d.* for the first day or first three months, and 6*d.* for every month afterward. In 1729 tobacco employed nearly three hundred sail of ships in its transportation from Virginia and Maryland, producing jointly over £600,000 worth, and yielding a revenue of £200,000 annually.

It was enacted by the Virginia assembly, November, 1720, that "whoever shall weed, top, hill, succour, house, cure, strip or pack any seconds, suckers or slips of tobacco, shall forfeit the same and pay a fine of 500 pounds of tobacco". (*d*) For the six years 1719-'24 the impost alone of 4*d.* per pound on tobacco yielded to Great Britain the sum of £59,529 7*s.* 2*d.* (*e*)

The abuse of the tobacco trade in North Carolina continued, as was set forth in an act of the assembly passed in 1726:

> Whereas the Act of the General Assembly now in force doth not effectually prevent the bringing of tobacco from North Carolina; and whereas since the making of the said act great numbers of people have, contrary to the repeated orders of this government, seated themselves on the lands between Wiccon's Creek and the line run from the mouth of Nottoway river to describe the boundaries in controversy between this Colony and the said province, and are there encouraged and protected, under pretense of being under the government of North Carolina, contrary to the agreement with that government that the said tract should remain unseated until the bounds should be determined; which persons, so seated as aforesaid, as well as those inhabiting within the province of North Carolina, being under no regulation in the manner of making and packing their tobacco, do, notwithstanding, make and transport in the colony, for traffic and sale, great quantities of tobacco of the growth and manufacture of Virginia to the great deceit of honest traders and the depreciating the staple commodity of this country. For the remedy whereof, a penalty was fixed of ten pounds fine for every hogshead, barrel, or parcel so brought in.—Hening, iv, pp. 175-177.

This grievance doubtless hastened the running of the dividing line between Virginia and North Carolina in 1728, of which Colonel William Byrd has left so interesting an account.

In May, 1730, it was enacted: "for the more effectual preventing the exportation of all trash, bad, unsound and unmerchantable tobacco," it was required after the 1st of August of that year "that all which shall be exported out of this Colony and Dominion to be brought to a public warehouse and inspected", an infringement of this requirement being made a felony. The inspectors at each warehouse were to be "three fit and able persons", two of whom were to act as inspectors, and the third was to be called in case of difference of judgment, (*f*) the tobacco, after being duly inspected and weighed, to be receipted for with notes, under the hands and seals of the inspectors of the warehouse, for the tobacco, specified as sweet-scented or Orinoco, stemmed or leaf, the same to be current and payable for all tobacco payments within the county where issued, or any county adjacent thereto. Thirty pounds was made the allowance for cask and 5*s.* as the price of the hogshead, well-lined and fit for shipping, and each hogshead was to contain not less than 800 pounds. (*g*) The allowance to the inspector for

---

a Hening, ii, p. 498.

b *Ibid.*, iv, pp. 32-36.

c Article, "Tobacco", by Samuel Mordecai, in the *Transactions of the Virginia State Agricultural Society*, vol. i, 1853, p. 57.

d Hening, iv, p. 87.

e Beawes, *Lex Mercatoria Rediviva*. London, 1773, p. 561.

f Hening, iv, pp. 247-271.

g The hogsheads, as first described, contained about 350 pounds, and were enlarged successively to the capacity of 500, 800, 850, 900 950, 1,000 (act of October, 1776), and 1,100 pounds, though they were often latterly much greater. In *Mair's Bookkeeping*, Edinburgh, 1765, it is stated (p. 334) that they were frequently 1,400 and even 1,800 pounds in weight. In the MS. Account Book of Thomas Stegge, auditor-general of the colony, of several hundred hogsheads received by him as dues and shipped in the years 1663-'66, the weights as enumerated by him range from 420 to 755 pounds.

"shrinking and wasting" was two pounds in every hundred if not paid away in two months, and one pound for every month afterward, the whole, however, not to exceed six per cent., and various allowances in different counties were provided in the weights of tobacco, to compensate for the expenses of transportation, according to their distance from market or points of shipment. Sheriffs and collectors were allowed 4 pounds in the hundred for all tobacco paid to government by inspector's notes. All tobacco shipped to Maryland was required to be inspected and stamped. All stemmed tobacco not laid straight, whether loose or in bundles, and all tobacco packed in hogsheads which exceed 48 inches in length of stave or 30 inches across the head within the cross, making reasonable allowance for prizing—not to exceed 2 inches above the gauge in the prizing head—was to be accounted unlawful tobacco, and not be passed or received, and was also to be repacked in sizable casks.

Refuse tobacco was to be burned in the presence of the inspectors, and overseers of plantations were made liable for such waste. All marks, numbers, weights (gross, net, and tare) were required to be entered in a book kept by the inspectors, as also the ship or ships upon which the tobacco was loaded, and they were required to make an annual report to the naval officer before the 1st of July; to make out and give bond with good security of £1,000 lawful money; to be fined if found guilty of receiving bribes; to be disabled from holding any other colonial office and not to be allowed to trade in tobacco, their salary being fixed at £60. (*a*) Forging tobacco notes was made a felony, and the penalty for taking unstamped tobacco on board a vessel was £25 and forfeiture of the tobacco.

In 1731 the price of tobacco in the province of Maryland was fixed at 6s. per hundred pounds. (*b*) In this year also the exports of tobacco from Virginia and Maryland was 60,000 hogsheads of 600 pounds each, which yielded £375,000, the net value of which to England was £180,000, which sum was paid in merchandise. The imposts upon tobacco by Great Britain became so onerous, and the abuse of the trade by the English factors in the extent and multiplicity of their charges so oppressive, that the colonists in 1732 published their grievances to the world in pamphlet form. (*c*) Nor were fraudulent practices confined to England, for an instance is cited of a dishonest shipper in Virginia, who, in loading a vessel with 310 hogsheads of tobacco in the year 1727, by a misrepresentation of weights (the original marks being erased) defrauded the crown of nearly one-seventh part of the duties. (*d*) The contrast of the prices obtained in Virginia and in England is exhibited in the statement that "in this present year tobacco has been sold to foreign buyers from twopence half-penny to threepence half-penny; * * * * yet at this juncture the best Oronoko tobacco is sold to buyers in London, for the home consumption, for sevenpence a pound", and the charges to which it was subject are evidenced by the fact that the price yielded to the planter was "not more than one penny half-penny, without the duty". (*e*)

Examples of the government duties and the merchants' charges are afforded by the following bills rendered of sales:

TEN HOGSHEADS OF TOBACCO.

Dr.	£.	s.	d.	Cr.	£.	s.	d.
Duties, freight, and other charges	165	15	7	Sold 5,237 pounds, at 1*d*	21	16	3
Commission, at 2½ per cent	3	16	4	Debentures and other allowances	131	19	2
					153	15	5
				The owner in debt	15	16	6
	169	11	11		169	11	11

FORTY-FOUR HOGSHEADS.

Dr.	£.	s.	d.	Cr.	£.	s.	d.
Duties, freight, and other charges	652	9	4	Allowance for damage	4	16	10
Commission, at 2½ per cent., on £694 4*s*. 7*d*	17	7	2	7 hogsheads, at 3*d*	46	10	10
Net proceeds	29	4	11	11 hogsheads, at 1*d*	23	9	9
				1 hogshead, at 1¼*d*	3	4	10
				5 hogsheads abroad	22	16	10
				1 hogshead, at 8¼*d*	14	19	3
				16 hogsheads, at 1½*d*	45	6	7
				3 hogsheads, at 1¾*d*	10	14	2
				Drawbacks, &c	527	2	4
	699	1	5		699	1	5

a Hening, iv, pp. 247–271.

b *The Case of the Planters of Tobacco in Virginia*, as represented by themselves; signed by the President of the Council and Speaker of the House of Burgesses, to which is added a vindication of the said representation. 8vo. London, 1733.

c *Case of the Planters*, etc., p. 23.

d *Ibid.*, p. 25.

e *Ibid.*, pp. 34, 35.

ONE HOGSHEAD OF TOBACCO. (a)

Dr.	£.	s.	d.	Cr.	Pounds.	£.	s.	d.
				Sold:				
Old subsidy of 739 pounds tobacco, at 1d. per pound, 25 per cent. deducted	2	6	2	Suttle	812			
Custom, at 5d., one-third per pound, 15 per cent. off	13	19	2	Tare	86			
				Damage	30			
				Draught and sample	8			
	16	5	4	Tret	26			
Entry, land waiters and bill money	0	1	0		— 150			
Freight	2	0	0					
Primage and petty charges	0	2	2		662 net, at 6¾d.	18	12	4
Cooperage and porterage	0	2	6	By the ship for 40 pounds damage		0	5	0
Cartage home	0	0	9	Certificate for allowance on do. at one-half penny per pound		0	1	8
Warehouse rent	0	2	6					
Brokerage	0	2	0			18	19	0
Impost and cocket	0	3	0	The planter in debt upon balance		0	11	9
Cutting	0	2	0					
Commissions, at 2½ per cent	0	9	6					
	19	10	9			19	10	9

An additional example is given, in which the net proceeds of six hogsheads of tobacco were only £15 2s. 8d., (b) and it is stated that from "an Account of the year 1694 * * * * all the small Charges upon a Hogshead of Tobacco amounted to no more than 3s. 6d.", and that "in all the Accounts of a Gentleman about Ten years ago [1719] no more than 7s. 8d." was "charged besides Bill Money". (c) The rate of interest charged the planters was seven per cent. (d) The practices cited continued until the Revolution, for in an account of sales in our possession, rendered in December, 1776, by John Norton & Son, of London, of twenty hogsheads of tobacco, for Savage & Norton, of Virginia, the charges and duties were £579 17s. 7d. and the commissions, etc., £87 12s. 5d., making a total of £667 10s., while the net proceeds were less than one-third of the amount, being only £207 6s. 4d. Of these practices Keith says:

As to the British merchants and the planters' interests, with respect to their conduct and management in carrying on the tobacco trade, they have each of them taken great pains to pursue that business in such a mysterious way as it is not easy for those who are not immediately concerned therein to trace; and in truth it must be owned that the multiplicity of duties, drawbacks, bonds, and other regulations of the customs wherewith the trade is perplexed, has, in a great manner, forced the merchants into many contrivances, which in all probability would otherwise never have been thought of.—*History of Virginia*, by Sir William Keith, London, 1738, p. 184.

The first manufactory of tobacco in Virginia of which we have found mention was that of a Major Woodford, on the Rappahannock river, described by Colonel Byrd, in his *Progress to the Mines* in 1732, as follows:

Major Woodford manufactures 60 hogsheads yearly, for which he gets 11d. a pound. * * * * The tobacco he cuts is long Green, which, according to its name, bears a very long leaf, and consequently each plant is heavier than common sweet-scented or Townsend tobacco. The worst of it is that the veins of the leaf are very large, so that it loses a great deal of its weight by stemming. This kind of tobacco is much the fashion in these parts, and Jonathan Forward (who has great interest here) gives a good price for it. This sort the Major cuts up. * * * * The Tobacco is stemmed clean in the first place, and then laid straight in a box, and pressed down hard by a press that goes with a Nut. This Box is shov'd forward towards the Knife by a screw receiving its motion from a Treadle, that the Engineer sets a going with his foot. Each motion pushes the Box the exact length which the Tobacco ought to be of, according to the saffron or oblong cut, which it seems to yield one penny in pound more at London than the square cut, tho' at Bristol they are both of equal price * * * * After the Tobacco is cut, it is sifted through a Sand Riddle and then thro' a Dust Riddle, till 'tis perfectly clean. Then 'tis put into a tight Hogshead and prest under the Nut, till it weighs about a Thousand Neat. One considerable benefit from planting long Green Tobacco is, that 'tis much hardyer and less subject to fire than other sweet-scented, tho' it smells not altogether so fragrant.—*Westover Papers*, Wynne's Edition, Richmond, 1866, ii, pp. 76–77.

Another manufactory, on a smaller scale, of no little note in its day, was set up by Colonel Cabaniss, of Mecklenburg county, about, or before, 1769. Mr. Custis, of Arlington, who has recorded this fact, professes to have divulged the before secret mode of management which gave its extraordinary popularity to "the weed" as it came from this first tobacco factory on the south side of the James river, where they are so numerous. (e) In 1731 there were owned in the province of Maryland sixty vessels of 2,000 tons burden, manned by 480 sailors, and by Great Britain one hundred and eighty more, of 10,000 tons burden, employing 3,000 men, which were employed in the tobacco trade. (f)

In 1732 tobacco was made a legal tender in Maryland at 1d. a pound, and in March of the same year it is recited in an act:

As by inspection tobacco is deemed one-fourth better than tobacco before the inspection took place, 12s. 6d. is now the rule and standard for the 100 pounds of tobacco.

In the following year, in the same province, all "trash tobacco" was ordered to be burned, and the tax upon every hogshead of tobacco was 1s. 3d. (g)

a *Case of the Planters*, etc., pp. 40, 41. b *Ibid.*, pp. 42, 43. c *Ibid.*, p. 50.
d *Ibid.*, p. 56; afterward reduced to five per cent. by some merchants at least.
e N. F. Cabell, in his *Early History of Agriculture in Virginia*, p. 21, quoting from *The Southern Planter*, iv, p. 165.
f Scharf's *History of Maryland*, ii, p. 14.
g Bisset's *Abridgment of the Laws of Maryland*, 1759, p. 169. Systematic inspection of tobacco was not provided in Maryland until 1748.

In August, 1734, by an act of the Virginia assembly, the salaries of inspectors were graded from £30 to £60.; (*a*) in 1736 they were prohibited from serving as burgesses, to be present at elections, or to meddle therewith, (*b*) and by the act of November, 1738, they were required to attend at the warehouses between November 10 and the last day of August. (*c*) In 1739 the church wardens of Henrico parish, Henrico county, were empowered to sell the parish tobacco at 12*s.* 6*d.* per hundred-weight. (*d*) In 1740 Maryland exported 30,000 hogsheads of tobacco of 900 pounds each. By act of the Virginia assembly, November 9, 1742, fraudulent delivery of tobacco was made a felony, (*e*) and in May of that year the several county courts were required to nominate inspectors. (*f*) In 1745, the weight of a transfer hogshead of tobacco was fixed at 950 pounds. (*g*) In 1744–'45–'46 the average annual export from the American colonies was 40,000,000 pounds, of which 7,000,000 pounds were consumed in Great Britain and 33,000,000 in other European countries, and in 1745 tobacco appears to have been current in Virginia at 14*s.* per hundred-weight. (*h*) The annual exports of tobacco from Virginia for twelve years, 1745 to 1756, were as follows: (*i*)

Exports.	1745.	1746.	1747.	1748.	1749.	1750.	1751.	1752.	1753.	1754.	1755.	1756.
	Hhds.	*Hhds.*	*Hhds.*	*Hhds.*	*Hhds.*	*Hhds.*	*Hhds.*	*Hhds.*	*Hhds.*	*Hhds.*	*Hhds.*	*Hhds.*
Upper district of James river	10,991	10,799	9,355	12,489	11,509	12,974	10,858	13,530	18,830	13,900	13,739	7,262
Lower district of James river	1,381	1,372	1,718	3,170	3,150	2,218	2,525	1,423	2,113	1,181	918	1,096
York River district	11,118	11,015	12,895	11,089	10,970	13,802	12,054	12,623	15,127	14,878	15,344	6,918
Rappahannock district	12,332	10,745	12,132	13,052	15,012	14,331	13,553	14,209	16,615	13,512	11,963	8,531
South Potomac district	6,659	6,311	5,704	6,983	7,346	5,242	7,713	6,505	6,959	7,332	5,723	4,645
Accomac, 3 barrels in 1753 and 11 in 1755	....	....	....	....	....	....	....	....	....	....	....	....
Total	42,481	40,242	41,804	46,783	47,987	48,507	46,703	48,380	59,844	50,803	47,687	28,452

In February, 1752, by an act of the Virginia assembly, no crop notes of an older date than eighteen months were allowed as a legal tender. (*j*) In 1747 and the two years previous there were annually exported from the American colonies 40,000,000 pounds of tobacco, of which 7,000,000 were consumed in England, yielding a revenue of £700,000.

In 1755, under the "option act", the clergy in Princess Anne and Norfolk counties, Virginia, were deprived of their tobacco (the fixed annual salary being 16,000 pounds) and were forced to accept a compensation in money. In those counties which yielded tobacco, the worst and meanest in the country did not sell for more than 8*s.* or 10*s.* per hundred-weight, and often under, the land not being suited to its culture. (*k*) The price in London this year was from 11*d.* to 12½*d.* per pound. In a communication from the clergy of Virginia to the Bishop of London, dated February 25, 1756, it is stated in complaint that the colonists "value our tobacco at 2*d.*, when 3*d.* is expected, if not 4*d.*, when the market is low, as has generally been the case since 1724". (*l*) The price in 1755 is stated not to have been under 10*s.* per hundred-weight. In a communication dated November 20, 1756, it is stated that the common crops are about 50,000 hogsheads, and the price from 12*s.* to 18*s.* per hundred-weight. (*m*) In 1758 the crop was short, only 24,500 hogsheads being made, and it is given in evidence that tobacco was purchased during this year by Humphrey Hill, merchant in King William county, at 50*s.* per hundred-weight. (*n*) "In 1757 many thousands of the people of Virginia did not make a pound of tobacco, and all made would not have been 200 pounds per tithable." (*o*) By an act of the Virginia assembly, passed November, 1759, fees due in tobacco were made payable in money at 16*s.* 8*d.* per hundred-weight. Burnaby, an English traveler who visited Virginia in 1759, stated that the annual export of tobacco from the colony was from 50,000 to 60,000 hogsheads of from 800 to 1,000 pounds weight each; (*p*) but in 1761 the governor and council of Maryland reported to the board of trade, London, that the annual export from that province was 28,000 hogsheads, valued at £140,000. (*q*) The price of tobacco in Virginia during the years 1761–'63 ranged from 18*s.* to 25*s.* per hundred-weight, the average price being 22*s.* 6*d.* (*r*) According to Mair, who writes in 1765, the yearly export of tobacco from Virginia and Maryland was 80,000 hogsheads, rather more than half of the quantity being from Virginia, the value to the planter being £5 sterling per hogshead, which made their yearly income £400,000, and, allowing the sale price at £9, the amount was £720,000. (*s*)

In 1765 a duty of 3*s.* per hogshead on all exports of tobacco (*t*) was levied by the Virginia assembly, and the weight of the hogshead was fixed at 950 pounds, that for transfer at 1,000 pounds. (*u*) The annual exportation

a Hening, iv, pp. 382–386.
b *Ibid.*, v, p. 482.
c *Ibid.*, v, p. 98.
d Vestry Book of Henrico parish, 1730–1773.
e *Ibid.*, v, pp. 10–16.
f *Ibid.*, v, pp. 124–160.
g *Ibid.*, v, pp. 367–369; edition by R. A. Brock, p. 52.
h MS. Minutes of the Society of Friends, Henrico county, Virginia, 1698–1756.
i *The Fairfaxes of England and America*, E. D. Neill, p. 225.
j Hening, vi, p. 225.
k Bland, p. 12.
l *Papers Relating to the History of the Church in Virginia*, A. D. 1650–1776; edition by W. Stevens Perry, D. D., p. 441.
m *Ibid.*, p. 465.
n *Ibid.*, p. 482.
o Bland, p. 16.
p Burnaby's Travels in Virginia, *Historical Register*, v, p. 87.
q Scharf, i, p. 520.
r MS. Account Book of Pettus Rayland, "Slasher," Hanover county (the weights of hogsheads given being from 1,000 to 1,350 pounds), and according to the Diary of Colonel William Cabell, of "Union Hill", the price of tobacco from 1760 to 1776 was from 20*s.* to 22*s.* per hundred-weight.
s Mair's *Bookkeeping*, Edinburgh, 1765, p. 336.
t Hening, viii, p. 73.
u *Ibid.*, p. 109.

from the American colonies from 1763 to 1770, both inclusive, was 66,780 hogsheads of about 1,000 pounds each, or 67,780,000 pounds. In 1770 Virginia and Maryland sold 110,000 hogsheads of tobacco to England, the share of Maryland in that to the port of Bristol alone being £300,000. (*a*) Tobacco was the great currency of Maryland until just before the Revolution.

As we have now approached the period when the exportation of tobacco arrived at a point from which it has vibrated (sometimes a little above or below it), we subjoin a statement of the exportation for the years 1772-'73-'74-'75 inclusive, which will furnish the remarkable fact that, compared with any succeeding four years since that period, the annual exportation of tobacco just before the Revolution was about the same that it has been at any time since, prior to 1840, in our most prosperous periods. For although 1790-'91-'92 were three years of very heavy exportation, they fell off in 1793 nearly one-half, making the annual average exportation not materially different from 1772-'73-'74-'75.—*Lex Mercatoria Redivira*, p. 56. (*b*)

The following statement shows the quantity of tobacco exported from the United Colonies from 1772 to 1775, inclusive: (*c*)

Year.	Pounds exported.	Pounds consumed or remaining on hand in Great Britain.	Pounds consumed or remaining on hand in other countries of Europe.
1772	97, 799, 263	97, 791, 805	7, 458
1773	100, 472, 007	3, 695, 564	96, 776, 443
1774	97, 375, 252	18, 698, 837	78, 678, 915
1775	101, 828, 617	27, 623, 451	74, 205, 166
Total	397, 475, 139	147, 809, 157	249, 665, 982

The inspection laws of Virginia expired by limitation October 1, 1775, and by act of December in that year it was provided that the quality of tobacco might be decided by the neighbors of the owner. (*d*) By act of October 7, 1776, the inspection laws were temporarily revived, the impost duties were abolished, and the exportation of tobacco to England was forbidden. (*e*)

We have now arrived at the period of the Revolution, and the following table will exhibit the exportation during that period:

Year.	Pounds exported.	Pounds consumed or on hand in Great Britain.	Pounds consumed or on hand in other countries in Europe.
1776	14, 498, 500	(*a*)	14, 498, 500
1777	2, 441, 214	(*b*)	2, 441, 214
1778	11, 961, 333	7, 520, 550	4, 440, 783
1779	17, 135, 907	10, 962, 909	6, 173, 008
1780	17, 424, 967	11, 474, 791	5, 950, 176
1781	13, 339, 168	7, 600, 296	5, 738, 872
1782	9, 828, 244	6, 364, 813	3, 463, 431
Totals	86, 649, 333	43, 943, 349	42, 705, 084

a This year Great Britain exported to the continent nearly 28,000,000 pounds of old stock.
b Great Britain exported this year to the continent 6,000,000 pounds of former stock.

The total exportation for the seven years was 86,649,333 pounds, or an annual average of 12,378,504 pounds. Of the total seven years' exportation, 33,974,944 pounds were captured by the British during the war. (*f*) J. H. Norton, of the firm of John Norton & Son, London, England, writing from thence under date of February 2, 1776, to Nathaniel Littleton, Virginia, says, speaking of the 5th of September preceding: "Tobacco was then selling at about 11 to 12 and 12½*s.* and likely to rise." And further on he says: "I have such expectations of a change in favor of the colonies, that I should like to speculate with you in a purchase of tobacco on the Eastern Shore if it could be purchased for about 10 or even 12*s.* 6*d.* current, per cwt." (*g*)

In October, 1777, by an act of the Virginia assembly, a duty of 10*s.* per hogshead was required to be paid on all tobacco exported, (*h*) and in May, 1779, it was increased to 30*s.* per hogshead, the inspection fees being fixed at

a Scharf's *History of Maryland*, ii, p. 47. According to Beawes, 100,000 hogsheads were exported yearly, employing between 300 and 400 ships, navigated by upward of 4,000 sailors; of these 60,000 hogsheads are re-exported to foreign ports, yielding £5 per hogshead, beside duties and drawbacks.

b According to the British *Annual Register* of 1775: "The imports into Great Britain before the war from Virginia and Maryland were 96,000 hogsheads of tobacco, of which 13,500 were consumed at home, and the duty on them, at £26 1*s.* each, amounted to £351,375. The remaining 82,500 were exported by our merchants to different parts of Europe. This single trade constantly employed 330 ships and 3,960 men." Jefferson says: "Before the war we exported *Communibus annis* Tobacco, 55,000 hhds. of 1,000 lbs., at 30 dollars per hhd., amounting to $1,650,000."—*Notes on Virginia*, edition of J. W. Randolph, Richmond, 1853, pp. 177-178.

c De Bow's *Southern States*, "Sugar, Tobacco, etc.," iii, p. 348.

d Hening, ix, p. 97. "While tobacco was largely grown on our principals below tide, and the market was wholly abroad, it was thought a hardship on such planters as could load a vessel from their own shores to compel them first to carry their crops to a distant warehouse to be inspected; and these clamors, after a few years, induced a repeal of the law. But its benefits had outweighed the inconvenience, and in time it was re-enacted; and as the culture of the plant spread westward the planters acquiesced in the arrangement, which improved the quality of their staple and presented numerous brands.—N. F. Cabell, p. 92.

e *Ibid.*, pp. 153-163. *f* De Bow, iii, p. 348. *g* *Calendar Papers of State of Virginia*, i, pp. 270, 271. *h* Hening, ix, p. 368.

8s. (a) In November, 1781, the charge allowed for storage was 2s., and for reprizing, 5s. per hogshead, (b) and tobacco fees were made payable in money at 12s. 6d. per hundred-weight. (c) In May, 1782, the export duty was 6s., (d) and in May, 1783, 4s. per hogshead, (e) and "Death without clergy" was made the penalty for forging tobacco notes. (f) In May, 1784, an additional 3s. per hogshead was imposed on all the tobacco exported. (g)

The following table exhibits the exports of tobacco from the United States for the years 1787–'88–'89, immediately preceding the adoption of the present constitution:

The following exhibits the depreciation of continental money rather than the true prices of tobacco. In 1777 it sold for 34s.; in 1778, for 70s.; in 1779, for 400s.; in 1780, for 1,000s.; in 1781, for 2,000s. per cwt. But the prices given in 1782–'83–'84–'85 as from 36 to 40s., and in 1786–'87–'88 as from 21 to 30s., were doubtless the actual values.—*MS. Diary of Colonel William Cabell.*

In the argument of counsel in *Doe, lessee of Baylor, v. Dejarnette* (reported in 13 Gothaux, p. 152), in some accounts adduced (p. 92), the net proceeds of sales of 60 hogsheads of tobacco made December, 1774, are given as £687 15s. sterling, and of sales of 73 hogsheads, March, 1776, net £1,710 14s. 10d. sterling. In 1780 the price of tobacco advanced at the Richmond warehouses from £30 per hogshead in January to £75 per hogshead in December.

Year.	Pounds exported.	Pounds consumed or remaining on hand in Great Britain.	Pounds consumed or remaining on hand in other countries in Europe.
1787	90,041,000	45,379,705	44,661,295
1788	88,595,590	39,600,404	48,995,186
1789	88,675,000	48,831,232	39,843,768
Total	267,311,590	133,811,431	133,500,159

In the progress of our task of compilation, the conviction has been enforced that it is invested with more importance than we had apprehended. It is manifest, from the detailed abuses and frauds which were practiced in the tobacco trade of the colony, that the accepted estimates of the extent of the product of Virginia, heretofore published, must have been largely assumptive, because of the necessary incompleteness of the records kept of the exports. This conclusion finds, too, strong additional basis in the varying figures presented by different writers for the same periods. It is evident from the records and from the concurrent testimony here adduced that the tobacco crop of Virginia for several decades prior to the Revolution, if not earlier, has been underestimated, the more especially when a comparative quantity has been assigned to her in the English records of the combined exports of Virginia and Maryland. Not only is it now established by authoritative figures and testimony that the proportion of Virginia in such published reports was greater than has been assumed, but it may be presumed also, from the greater latitude of exportation enjoyed under her proprietary rights by Maryland, that her apparent export was largely augmented by surreptitious and illegal shipments of the product of her sister colony, to the diminishing exhibit of the last.

It is feared that a complete record of the tobacco product of Virginia prior to the Revolution may not now be attainable, but the justice of our remarks is sufficiently established by the following array of facts which have been presented in the preceding pages:

A RECAPITULATION OF THE QUANTITY OF TOBACCO EXPORTED FROM VIRGINIA, AND OF THE PRICES, FROM 1619 TO 1775 (WITH INTERVALS), INCLUSIVE.

Year.	Crop.	Prices.		Year.	Crop.	Prices.		Year.	Crop.	Prices.	
	Pounds.	*Per pound.*	*Per cwt.*		*Pounds.*	*Per pound.*	*Per cwt.*		*Pounds.*	*Per pound.*	*Per cwt.*
1619	20,000	3s.		1666	(b)			1749	43,168,300		(f)
1620	40,000	8d. to 2s.		1667	(c)			1750	43,710,300		(f)
1621	55,000			1682			10s.	1751	42,032,700		(f)
1622	60,000			1687	(d)			1752	43,542,000		(f)
1628	500,000	3s. to 4s.		1688	18,157,000			1753	53,862,300		(f)
1632		6d.		1704	18,295,000	2d.		1754	45,722,700		(f)
1638		9d.		1729		2d.		1755	42,018,300	(g)	10s.
1639	1,500,000	3d.		1731	(e)			1756	25,806,800		
1640	1,300,000	12d.		1739			12s. 6d.	1757	(h)		
1641	1,300,000	20d.		1745	38,232,900		14s.	1758	22,050,000		50s.
1661			12s.	1746	38,217,800		(f)	1759			16s. 8d.
1662			10s.	1747	37,020,600		(f)	1760–1775	(i)		18s. to 25s.
1664		(a)		1748	42,104,700		(f)				

a 3d. to 3½d. per pound, the price in London.

b No crop made; planting prohibited.

c Two-thirds of the crop destroyed by a storm.

d Poor crop of bad quality. Price in London for bulk, 1½ to 2d., and for sweet-scented, 7¼ to 7½d. per pound, in packages.

e Exports of Virginia and Maryland *reported* as 30,000,000 pounds.

f Price current, at which estimated according to contemporaneous records, 1746–'64, was 2d. per pound.

g Price in London, 11d. to 12½d.

h A short crop made.

i The crop for the period 1760–'75, according to authoritative and concurrent testimony, was from 50,000 to 60,000 hogsheads, of 1,000 pounds each, annually, or an average at least of 55,000 pounds; of which the average price was 22s. 6d. per hundred-weight. The average price in London in 1775 was 12d. per pound. In 1769 the price in Antigua was from 5d. to 6d. per pound. In 1781 the price of tobacco in Virginia was fixed at 12s. 6d. per hundred-weight.

a Hening, x, p. 78. b *Ibid.*, p. 476. c *Ibid.*, p. 489. d *Ibid.*, xi, p. 95. e *Ibid.*, p. 201. f *Ibid.*, p. 241. g *Ibid.*, p. 394.

We have now brought our narrative to the period of the first national census, and our task has been, as it were, over a tangled and ungarnered field. With the limits as to length, scarce more than a bare recital of facts was admissible. We have been careful to omit nothing within the range of our acquirement which seemed essential, the authority for the statements being given in every instance. The matter presented has been laboriously gleaned from diverse, obscure, and unpublished sources, in some instances from manuscripts of which but single copies are in existence. The thorough and extended investigation already made secures a basis of reference that will be helpful to those who, in future years, may be able to extend the work to greater and more minute completeness. Tobacco has ever been the staple product of Virginia (the first settled of the English colonies in America) and its chief source of wealth. It is now one of the most prolific factors in the revenue of the general government. As has been demonstrated, it once permeated the entire fabric of society in Virginia. It directed the colonial laws, which consisted chiefly of regulations for its culture, quality, and sale. An attempt to make it yield a revenue for the sustenance of the postal service led to an expression of defiance anterior to the resistance to the stamp act by more than half a century. For two hundred and fifty years it was the principal currency of the colony and the basis of all values, and from its paramount profit its culture engrossed the attention of the colonists, and thus subordinated the entire remaining agricultural and manufacturing interests of Virginia.

Upon a careful examination of the whole subject, there is observed a kind of periodical fluctuation in the annual shipment of tobacco to foreign countries, as it appears that, when our exports of leaf tobacco for two or three successive years much exceed 100,000,000 pounds, for some succeeding years they are proportionately reduced below that standard. It is evident that the revolutionary war gave a check to the exportation of leaf tobacco from which it has never recovered; until that period the annual average exportations increased regularly and steadily. In other words, for the thirty-one years immediately preceding the Revolution our export of leaf tobacco annually increased, and for the sixty years since that period it has remained stationary, except when interrupted by wars or other commercial embarrassments. The reason is apparent. Before the Revolution all Europe depended on us for supplies of the article; but being cut off by the war, Europeans turned their attention to growing tobacco for themselves, and have continued to cultivate it all over the continent, while they have checked its consumption by the onerous taxation above indicated. (*a*)

According to the diary of Colonel William Cabell, senior, of Union Hill, tobacco in 1794 was worth in Richmond, Virginia, from 20*s*. to 24*s*. per hundred-weight. It appears also, from the same authority, that "Swan creek" tobacco of his section commonly commanded 1*s*. per hundred-weight more than that grown in other sections of Virginia.

According to the diary of Thomas Rutherford, an old and highly-respected merchant of Richmond, shipments of tobacco before the commencement of the war, and until 1814, in which he was interested, sold at that time in Dublin for 15*d*. per pound.

It will be remembered, in comparison of the tobacco production of recent years and the tobacco production of early years, that the Virginia of the early days included West Virginia, now erected into a separate state.

CHAPTER XVII.

CULTURE AND CURING OF TOBACCO IN WEST VIRGINIA.

Tobacco has been raised in West Virginia to a limited extent for more than a half century, and in 1860 the whole product of the state was only 2,046,452 pounds, many things having heretofore contributed to prevent large plantings of tobacco, the most important of which was the lack of facilities for transportation. This industry is growing rapidly of later years, as cheaper and quicker means of reaching market are afforded and the capabilities of the lands are becoming better known.

Formerly the bulk of the crop was produced in a few counties in the Great Kanawha valley and on the Ohio river, and was sold principally in Louisville and Baltimore; but Cincinnati is now the market for the greater part of this crop, which is mainly dark shipping tobacco.

Before 1853, and for some time afterward, the product of what is now West Virginia was all classed as "Western", and it has not yet received any distinctive name, the bright tobaccos being classed with the Virginia, and the dark with the Ohio crop.

QUALITY OF TOBACCO.

The tobacco produced in West Virginia may be divided into Dark Shipping, Red and Spangled, Bright Yellow, and White Burley, some counties producing two or more of these; but in the following description of the districts each county is classed according to the predominant quality of its crop, Tyler county, for instance, producing some of all four grades, and being classed in the Red and Spangled district.

DARK SHIPPING is produced in Kanawha, Putnam, and Mason counties, in the Great Kanawha valley; also in Jackson, Cabell, Wayne, and Wood counties, lying along the Ohio river.

a De Bow, iii, pp. 349-350.

RED AND SPANGLED.—There are many grades of this tobacco produced in Boone, Calhoun, Clay, Doddridge, Gilmer, Greenbrier, Harrison, Lewis, Roane, Ritchie, Tyler, Upshur, Wetzel, and Wirt counties.

BRIGHT YELLOW is the prevailing quality in Fayette, Raleigh, Monroe, Mercer, and Summers.

WHITE BURLEY.—This new variety has no fixed locality, but is principally grown in the Ohio river counties.

The tobacco produced in Kanawha, Putnam, and Mason counties is darker, heavier, and richer than the same type grown along the Ohio river, and might properly be classed separately. It more nearly resembles the dark Shipping of eastern Virginia than the product of the Ohio valley, which latter more nearly resembles the dark tobacco of eastern Ohio. This difference is partly the result of soil influences and partly the result of management. In the Kanawha district the leaves are cured on the stalks; in the Ohio river counties the bulk of the product is pulled from the stalks, and only the leaves are housed. The Kanawha tobacco is riper when cut, and is tougher and more waxy; the product of the river counties is thinner, more tender, and brighter in color. There are usually four grades of the dark tobacco: long leaf, short leaf, ground leaves, and tips; but in the best-assorted crops there are five grades, two of lugs, one of tips, and two of leaf.

Of the red and spangled tobacco there are numerous grades, there being several shades of red, running to black; several varieties of spangled, from a bright mottled yellow to a dark mahogany; colored sorts, from orange to cherry red; and some of a smooth yellow. All these are classed together, for convenience of illustration, and because they are all produced more or less in the same area, and sometimes on the same farm. Peculiarities of soil, different varieties, and varying modes of handling, curing, and management, produce the different colors.

Of the five counties classed in the Bright Yellow district, only one (Fayette) makes the production of this quality a specialty.

In several counties in the Red and Spangled district very good brights are produced by planters who have discarded the old plan of curing with open wood fires and have substituted therefor charcoal or flues. In Fayette county the production of fine yellow tobacco, begun twenty-five years ago by an immigrant from Amherst county, Virginia, has rapidly extended, the country from Cañon Hill to Oak Hill presenting a scene of thrift, enterprise, and prosperity—a suggestive picture of what skill and energy can accomplish in a rugged, and in many respects uninviting, region.

GEOLOGY AND SOILS.

West Virginia is in the Carboniferous Limestone and Great Coal groups, the counties of Mercer, Monroe, Summers, and Greenbrier being principally in the Carboniferous Limestone, while all the other tobacco counties are in the Great Coal group.

The soils of the Carboniferous Limestone group are varied: Limestones, sandstones, and slates are the prevailing rocks. The limestones are magnesian, siliceous, and carbonate. The sandstones and slates indicate the poorer soils.

The soils of the Great Coal group, except the alluvials on the rivers and creeks, are apparently very much alike, but are really unlike in constitution and character. Those of a dark color, approaching to red, where reddish sandstones occur, are generally the most fertile; the slaty and shaly mountain slopes the poorest; but with proper skill and management these latter soils produce the finest tobacco. The alluvials of the Great Kanawha and other rivers are generally dark, sandy loams, and are the most fertile of all. These produce the best shipping and Burley tobacco, those with most clay being best adapted for the first, and the more sandy soils for the latter.

The limestone soils are easy of tillage, retentive, not easily washed, and are susceptible of great improvement, and offer suitable lands for the production of the Burley type.

The soils of the Coal group, and those of the lower shale and sandstone formation, are not considered easy of tillage; for, aside from their closeness or adhesiveness, they are generally so hilly and steep as to make cultivation difficult and laborious to man and beast. They are not easily washed, except on some of the sandy ridges. The subsoil is generally porous, seldom soggy, and crops are rarely injured by excess of water in the soil, the natural drainage being perfect in much of the cultivated area. There are extensive areas of fresh lands awaiting development, and, from present indications, tobacco will be the first crop to utilize them.

CLIMATE.

Owing to the rugged and elevated character of three-fourths of the territory of West Virginia, the temperature, like that of all mountain regions, is variable, the isothermal lines making sharp and crooked curves, to correspond with elevation.

The *Statistical Atlas of the United States*, temperature chart, Plate VII, indicates that while a narrow belt of the most elevated portion of the state is in the zone of 48° to 52°, yet the main area is in the zone of 52° to 56°, and while there occur occasional extremes of low temperature, there are seldom seasons of extreme heat. The days are often hot in summer, but the nights are cool, affording just the most needful conditions to the tobacco-plant.

Early and late frosts, which may damage the young plants in the seed-bed or nip them before harvest in the fall, are most to be guarded against. The tobacco-plant, when quite young, will bear a low temperature—even below the freezing point—and live. Sheltered spots on southern slopes and hillsides and hot-beds will furnish the needed supply of plants, and by topping low they may ripen and be cut before the usual time for frost. Fertilizers expedite growth and maturity.

The average annual rainfall along the central zone is about 40 inches, and, as usually distributed over the tobacco belt, is admirably suited to this crop: gentle in spring, more in the growing season of early summer, and less in August and September, allowing the plant to ripen when excessive rains would do harm.

The lands everywhere in this region are richer than they seem, and produce crops beyond the expectation of those inexperienced in their capabilities. Green fields may be seen upon steep declivities and on rugged escarpments, even to the very tops of the mountains, proving that the soil on these apparently unfavorable and almost inaccessible localities may be made to yield abundantly.

West Virginia enjoys comparative immunity from storms, and the consequent damage therefrom, and the tobacco crops are rarely injured in the sheltered positions of the larger number of the fields, being protected by woods and hills from winds or driving rain-storms.

VARIETIES OF TOBACCO.

In the Kanawha valley the varieties mostly grown are Orinoco, Frederick, Pryor, Brittle Stem (Little Orinoco of Virginia), White Stem, and White Burley, one or the other being a favorite in different neighborhoods, according to the preference of the planters, or because of supposed adaptation to certain soils. The Burley has been recently introduced, and some farmers are pleased with it, while others are not. This variety is gradually growing into favor wherever the soil is suited to its proper development, and bids fair to succeed in the valley of the Kanawha, as well as in the Ohio river counties, where the soil is mellow and rich. Along the Ohio river the varieties in use are much the same as those grown in middle Virginia, with a sprinkling of Kentucky and Ohio names. Not much attention seems to be given to the selection of varieties, nor is there much care taken to keep desirable ones pure. As many as three varieties are sometimes seen growing in the same field promiscuously, showing that the planter had sown mixed seed, or had drawn his plants carelessly from beds sown with different varieties. In the Red and Spangled district there seem to be no fixed varieties. In Tyler county the Orinocos, White Stem, and Maryland Thickset are found. The "Yellow Spangled" is only another name for the Orinoco, and its product sells well—next in price to the bright yellow and a first-class Burley. The Burley, however, has not been successfully grown on the gray uplands of this state, such as produce a fine spangled or bright yellow leaf.

On old, rich, or highly-manured lands the growth is rank and the stalks and stems large, the leaves coarse, brittle, and full of sap when ripe, and consequently cure dark in color. On raw or fresh land, or on old land of medium fertility without manure, the plants are smaller, the texture of the leaves finer, the leaves ripen with less sap and of a yellower color on the hill, and cure brighter and with less body. Fresh land produces the finest tobacco, and that best suited for manufacturing purposes.

During the past ten years there has been a marked change from the dark to the colored types, the latter, bringing better prices, having increased in production, while the former has diminished. This is especially the case in the section south of the Chesapeake and Ohio railway, where most of the crops are now cured with charcoal, a few planters using flues, and the quality has greatly improved, due mainly to the better methods of curing. The same may be said of the counties growing the White Burley. The product is improved by the introduction of this variety, and the mode of curing it by air, without fire, is the cheapest of all. Where the crops are cured with open wood fires, there has been no improvement in quality, and lower prices have lessened the product.

In Mercer, Monroe, Fayette, and Raleigh counties the improvement in product, consequent upon the better modes of curing, has been more than a hundred per cent.

THE USE OF FERTILIZERS AND PRESERVATION OF TOBACCO SOILS.

Neither commercial fertilizers nor domestic manures are much used on the tobacco crop of this state, except in the Yellow district. In this district commercial manures have proved of great benefit, and their use is increasing. These are usually applied in the hill, as this is found to produce the greatest good at the least cost. These fertilizers increase the yield, hasten ripening, and improve the color; but opinions differ here, as elsewhere, whether or not there is any improvement in quality, different effects of fertilizers upon the quality of the cured product being attributed to the differing character of soils and the quantities of fertilizers used. Heavy applications contribute to the production of large, coarse leaves, particularly on some soils, and the product is unfitted for the finest types; but where applied in limited quantity, and on suitable soils, early growth and maturity without excessive stimulation is the result, and the product is increased without injury to the quality.

Usually two, and sometimes three, crops of tobacco are grown on newly cleared lands. The second crop is, in most instances, the best—larger in yield and of about the same quality as the first; and the third, when the land is not too poor, pays about as well as the first. Planted upon the same land for a series of years, without the application of manures in sufficient quantity, there is a heavy decrease of yield and a very marked falling off in quality, until the product ceases to be desirable to purchasers or profitable to the grower. In some counties there has been a decided increase in the product, the result of better cultivation, as well as of the extended use of fertilizers; in others, a decrease must be noted, due to exhaustion of the soils, inferior cultivation, and the neglect of manures.

On many farms, tobacco occupies the same fields for only two years after clearing, the land being then devoted to other uses, and new clearings being made for tobacco. No system of rotation, in connection with green-manuring or other fertilizing, for soil recuperation, is generally adopted; but a few of the more careful planters are beginning to follow tobacco with grass, to remain some years.

SEED-BEDS.

The general practice is to burn from January to March, and to sow the seed as soon as the beds are prepared.

PREPARATION OF TOBACCO LAND AND CULTIVATION.

New land is coltered or plowed, harrowed or shoveled over, marked, and hilled, the implements used varying with the condition of the "clearing"; but old land is broken usually with a two-horse turn-plow, harrowed or shoveled, furrowed off and hilled. The preparation is various—thorough by some; by the greater number, imperfect and in a slovenly manner.

The usual distance apart for the plants is 3 by 3 feet; for the larger varieties, upon stronger soils, 3½ feet each way. Planting is begun about the middle of May and completed by the first of July. No system of cultivation is adopted, even in any given neighborhood. Every farmer follows his own mode, as inclination or necessity prompts.

TOPPING AND PRIMING TOBACCO.

Topping commences as soon as the plants are large enough, some farmers waiting for the appearance of the "buttons", and others topping as soon as eight or ten leaves of good size are formed, the dark grades being topped to eight or ten leaves, the yellow to ten or twelve, and the Burley to twelve or sixteen.

In some localities all the tobacco is primed; in others no priming is done; and there is a growing disposition not to prime, especially where the Burley is grown.

CUTTING, HOUSING, AND CURING OF TOBACCO.

Most planters in West Virginia prefer to cut tobacco when fully ripe, so that the plants are not considered ready for harvest until thirty or forty days after topping. If, because of late planting, frosts threaten before the crop is ripe, the tobacco is cut before being fully matured. In some sections of the state the leaves are stripped from the stalk and are strung upon wires or twine to be cured; but for much the larger portion of the crop the stalks are split and the plants are straddled upon sticks, six to eight and sometimes eight to ten plants to the stick, according to size and type—a less number for the Burley and yellow, and more for the dark grades.

Nearly all the tobacco-houses are built of logs, are usually 20 feet square, with from four to five tiers in the body of the barn, and are covered with boards or shingles, the spaces between the logs being usually chinked and daubed with mud. The average capacity of these houses is from 4,000 to 6,000 plants. In the Yellow district the sticks of hung tobacco are placed well apart on the tiers. Where the curing is done with open wood fires the sticks can be placed closer together. The cost of an ordinary log barn, 20 feet square, 16 to 20 feet high, and covered with boards, is from $40 to $70.

The usual time of cutting is from September 1 to October 1. A few farmers scaffold tobacco, but the majority house it as soon as it is cut. A considerable part of the product of this state is cured with open wood fires—a method which makes a low-priced tobacco; but no tobacco grown in the state has sufficient richness and body to be properly cured in this way.

The Burley is air-cured, makes a salable product, and is growing in favor with manufacturers. This variety, as indeed all others intended for air-curing, should be cut dry, and either placed upon scaffolds or hung well apart in the house, not crowded upon the sticks nor on the tiers; and especial care is needed to maintain a free circulation of air to prevent pole-sweat, or house-burn as it is sometimes called. Some planters ruined their crops of Burley by failing to give room enough and by firing with wood. In Fayette and in Raleigh charcoal is principally used in curing brights, and the method of yellowing, fixing the color, and drying out the tobacco is substantially the same as practiced in Virginia and North Carolina. Flues are being introduced, to take the place of coal, and, where properly constructed, give satisfaction.

Hall's method of curing bright yellow, as practiced in Mercer county, is as follows: After housing, raise the heat to 100° F., to wilt the tobacco; then let it cool down. The following day raise the heat to 90° and cool down as before; repeat this every six hours until the tobacco is half yellowed; then raise the heat slowly to 120°, to dry the leaf. After the sweat is dried up raise the heat to 190°, and keep it there until stems and stalks are fully cured. Very fine tobacco is cured by this process. The directions above given can serve only as a guide, the condition of the tobacco when housed, the character of the house, the season, and the weather being all so variable as to make it impossible to lay down fixed rules for the curing of any desired color or quality. Skill is the reward of practice and close observation, and a certain amount of technical skill is absolutely necessary to success in curing fine tobacco of any type.

Some persons fix the color by burning sulphur, bran, and alum under the tobacco at what is considered the proper time; but this is of doubtful propriety or advantage. The heat, if properly regulated, will fix the color, and there is no disagreeable flavor, such as is often imparted by the fumes of sulphur, etc.

In the Yellow district it is the common practice to bulk down tobacco as soon as it is thoroughly cured, and some crowd the sticks together in the barn to preserve the color. In the Dark district it is left to hang as it was cured until a stripping season comes, when it is taken down, stripped, assorted, and tied in bundles or hands.

Very little damage to tobacco while hanging in the barns is reported. Mold sometimes injures air-cured tobacco, caused by long continued damp, warm weather, and sometimes late-cut tobacco is damaged by freezing in the barns before the sap is thoroughly dried out.

After being stripped, the tobacco is either bulked down, to be sold in winter order to country dealers, or is hung up, to be properly ordered for bulking or prizing. If bulked, it is permitted to remain from thirty to forty-five days to sweeten before being prized.

Most planters sell in prized packages; some sell loose to dealers. The wooden lever is generally used for prizing, but a few screws are found here and there. Ohio river planters ship to Cincinnati, all the Burley going there. Farmers within reach of the Baltimore and Ohio railway ship to Baltimore, and those near the line of the Chesapeake and Ohio find a market in Richmond, Virginia. The usual time of selling is from May till August, the larger part of the crop being marketed in June and July. The hogsheads of dark leaf vary in weight from 600 to 800 pounds for leaf to 1,000 and 1,400 pounds for seconds and lugs. Brights are usually packed in tierces weighing from 200 to 500 pounds.

DISEASES OF TOBACCO.

Except on the Kanawha and the Ohio rivers, where red-fire, speck, and hollow-stalk sometimes prevail to a limited extent, the tobacco of West Virginia is remarkably free from disease, and many of the interior counties report no disease.

COST OF RAISING TOBACCO, ETC.

In the region producing the dark types the price of the best tobacco lands varies from $15 to $30 per acre, and these produce, without manures, from 800 to 1,000 pounds of tobacco per acre. Inferior soils, producing from 500 to 600 pounds, are worth from $8 to $12 per acre. In the Yellow district, the best lands, producing from 600 to 900 pounds per acre, are worth about $10, inferior soils, producing from 500 to 700 pounds, being valued at from $4 to $7 per acre.

The approximate cost of raising tobacco in the Dark and Burley districts is estimated at $5 25 per hundred pounds; in the Yellow district, $7 75. These are approximations only, not one farmer in a hundred being able to make an accurate statement of the cost of production.

The average wages paid for field-hands is: for men, 50 cents per day, $10 per month, and from $100 to $120 per year, with board, and sometimes houses for their families, tobacco laborers being paid as common field-hands. Skilled curers and packers command better wages, proportioned to their special abilities.

Land is rarely rented by the acre. Where worked on shares, the cropper gets two-thirds and the landlord one-third—the latter furnishing only the land, barn, and barn fixtures. Where the land is to be newly cleared, the cropper gets a larger percentage of the product.

The number of acres planted to the hand varies widely, according to locality and peculiar circumstances. Where tobacco is one of several crops grown upon the farm, from 3 to 4 acres are planted for each full hand; where this is the main crop, or made a specialty, 5 to 6 acres per hand is not accounted too much. Extra labor must be employed, however, at certain times; for no one man can worm, sucker, cut, house, and cure 6 acres of tobacco without help.

Co-operative labor to a certain extent can produce tobacco more cheaply, and doubtless of better quality, than individual effort upon a limited area. When the number of workers is too small the work is performed at a disadvantage, and the planter is forced to rely upon assistance, which is not always obtained when needed, and not always skillful or reliable. On the other hand, when the working force is a large one, only the most careful and energetic supervision, with judicious management, will secure profitable results.

INSECT ENEMIES OF TOBACCO.

In West Virginia little damage by the cut-worm is reported, which is accounted for by the fact that most of the land cropped in tobacco is newly cleared.

The tobacco of the Ohio river counties bears evidence of a multiplicity of horn-worms, but in the interior counties they are not so numerous. The injury to the product along the Ohio, including the cost of hunting and killing the worms, is estimated at 15 per cent. of the entire crop.

CHAPTER XVIII.

CULTURE AND CURING OF TOBACCO IN WISCONSIN.

A line extending northwest from Milwaukee will nearly mark the limit between the small timber of the openings and the heavily timbered regions of the north, and the same line will almost mark the boundary between the agricultural and the lumbering districts.

The soils of central Wisconsin are divided, according to their origin, into drift, sandstone, limestone, and crystalline rock soils, and all partake of the character of the rocks from which they are derived. The Potsdam sandstone, which occupies a large district in central Wisconsin, gives a very poor, thin soil, and even where the material of the drift is of an arenaceous character the soil is often of the same nature.

If the drift material is of a calcareous and argillaceous character, though it may overlie sandstone, the soil is often good, as in the southern part of Adams and the eastern part of Waushara counties. Some few local areas of moderate fertility occur on the Potsdam formations, but they result from the accidental accumulation of other material, and are exceptions to the general rule.

A bed 30 feet thick, which rests above the lowest sandstone, is composed of a clayey or sandy magnesian limestone, called the Mendota limestone, and where the soil has been derived from this, as in portions of Columbia county, it is fertile. Upon this is another sandstone, with a thickness of from 30 or 40 feet, to which the name of Madison sandstone has been given. In its disintegration it makes a very poor soil, being nothing more than a bed of loose sand. This occurs in a part of Columbia county. The Lower Magnesian rests upon the Madison sandstone, and gives rise, by its crumbling, to a very fertile, durable soil. This limestone is from 8 to 200 feet in thickness, and is composed largely of siliceous and clayey matter. The elevated prairie belt of northern Dane and eastern Columbia carries this soil, and is one of the most productive regions in the state.

The Saint Peter sandstone rests upon the Lower Magnesian, but it rarely forms the surface rock, and is therefore of no importance as a soil-former. But few areas in central Wisconsin have soils derived from Trenton limestone or from the Galena.

The lead region embraces three of the most southwesterly counties of the state, viz: Grant, Iowa, and La Fayette. In the eastern part of La Fayette county the soil is sandy, owing to the disintegration of the calcareous sandy shales belonging to the Galena limestones.

South of the principal water-shed of the district the soils rest upon a strong, deep clay. These soils have been derived from the crumbling of the Galena limestones and the Cincinnati shales, and are remarkable for their fertility and strength. In other places, especially north of the water-shed, the soil abounds in flint on the higher points, derived from the Galena limestone.

TIMBER.

Nearly all the northern counties of Wisconsin abound in white pines, balsams, hemlocks, and other conifers. The widely extended prairies of western Illinois reach into several of the southern counties of Wisconsin, and between these prairies and the heavily timbered districts of the north are what are called "oak openings", in which the burr oak (*Quercus macrocarpa*) is the principal growth. Associated with this burr oak are the white oak (*Q. alba*), red oak (*Q. rubra*), and pin oak (*Q. palustris*). The chestnut oak (*Q. prinus*) occurs in the region around Janesville and Edgerton, the very center of the tobacco district.

CLIMATE.

In the southern and thickly-settled portion of the state the mean annual temperature varies from 45°.3, on the shores of lake Michigan, to 46°.9, on the Mississippi river, the average being about 46°.

For the tobacco-growing region around Janesville, Edgerton, and Madison the following table will give a fair idea of the prevailing meteorological changes:

	Latitude.	Longitude.	Height.	Spring.	Summer.	Autumn.	Winter.	Annual mean.
Edgerton	42.38	89.00	1,700	40.17	70.84	48.42	21.30	40.68
Janesville	42.41	89.00	780	44.73	70.43	48.25	20.84	46.07
Madison	43.15	89.24	1,088	43.47	69.11	48.20	20.84	45.40

The rainfall, including melted snow, averages for this region about 32 inches annually, of which about one-half falls in May, June, July, and August. The prevailing winds for the spring months are from the northeast; of summer, southwest; of autumn and winter, west. The mean of the prevailing winds for the region of the Mississippi river is south; for lake Michigan, northwest. The winters are usually cold, clear, and dry; springs, backward; summers, hot; and autumns, mild and pleasant.

HISTORY OF TOBACCO CULTURE IN WISCONSIN.

The census of 1850 reports the entire product of the state at 1,268 pounds. The first attempt to grow tobacco for market in Wisconsin was made near Madison by Ralph Pomeroy and by J. J. Heistand. There was not much, however, raised up to 1860, for the census returns show the whole amount grown in the state at that period to have reached only 87,340 pounds. Of this amount Walworth county produced 26,400 pounds, Rock 23,340 pounds, and Dane 8,968 pounds. An impression prevailed for many years that tobacco could not be profitably grown in high latitudes, and it was not until the value of the northern-grown leaf as a wrapper for Havana fillers was ascertained that it took a permanent place among the productions of the farm. The occurrence of the civil war, by making tobacco scarce and dear, gave a powerful impetus to its culture, and it was at this period that it began to claim the attention of some of the best farmers in Dane county; but its culture spread slowly, there being much prejudice existing with a large class of farmers against its production, and it was believed that it would quickly exhaust the fertility of the soil; that it was a useless product; that it ministered to a depraved appetite; and that the extension of its culture would be an unmixed evil. It gradually increased, however, in acreage, so that the census of 1870 showed a production of 960,813 pounds—an increase of just 1000 per cent. in ten years—Dane and Rock counties producing eight-ninths of the whole, the former 229,568 pounds, and the latter 645,508 pounds. Since that time its cultivation has spread over nearly the whole of Rock county, the southeastern portion of Dane, the eastern part of Greene, and the southwestern corner of Jefferson. In 1870 the production was very largely increased, and the crop that year, which was chiefly sold in Edgerton, was estimated to be worth $200,000, and that of 1871 between $300,000 and $400,000. Since that period it has formed a staple crop, and the farmers in Dane, Rock, and small portions of the adjoining counties rely upon it with more certainty as a money crop than upon any other staple grown, the production up to 1876 varying from 10,000 to 15,000 cases of about 400 pounds each.

THE TOBACCO DISTRICT OF WISCONSIN.

If one will take a map of Wisconsin and begin about three miles west of Madison, the state capital, on the shore of lake Mendota, and trace a line nearly south, so as to include the eastern half of the townships of Brooklyn, Albany, and Decatur, in Greene county, and the northeastern corner of Spring Grove township, in the same county, and then curving into Rock county, so as to exclude the southern half of the southern tier of townships in that county, passing north of Beloit about two miles, and striking the western limit of Walworth county near Allen's Grove, following the eastern boundary of Rock county north about two-thirds of its length, then turning to the northwest, so as to include lake Koshkonong, in Jefferson county, and from this point trace the line in a northeasterly direction to the very center of Jefferson county, and from the latter point in a line curving first north as high as Prairie, then southwesterly to the beginning, inclosing within the boundary something over 1,200 square miles, he will outline the limits of the tobacco-growing area of Wisconsin in 1879.

In the tobacco district of Wisconsin the area in 1879 was an increase of 17 per cent. over that of 1878, and of about 60 per cent. increase on that of 1877 and 1876. The yield was greater in 1879 than in 1878, but less than it was in the two years preceding. The quality of the crop, however, was inferior, having been very much injured by worms—a very rare occurrence—and in some local areas by hailstorms. The crops of 1878, 1877, and 1876 were very sound, and elevated the rank of the Wisconsin crop in the markets of the country. The main cause of the decrease in yield in the years 1878 and 1879, as compared with the two years preceding, was the extended culture of Spanish tobacco, a variety that always commands a ready sale, but does not yield as much per acre as the larger seed-leaf varieties. The Havana or Spanish varieties are exceedingly delicate in texture, with a peculiar aroma, and probably one-fourth of the whole amount grown in the state, and nearly one-half of the area planted, is of the latter varieties. While the yield does not exceed 1,000 pounds per acre, it sells readily for 11 cents per pound. The seed-leaf varieties, though yielding 1,600 pounds to the acre, do not bring in the local markets over 6½ cents through. The readier and earlier sales of the Spanish tobacco make it far less troublesome to the tobacco-growers, and it does not meet with such sharp competition in the markets as the seed-leaf.

Several varieties of the seed-leaf, however, are grown, among them being the Lancaster broad leaf, the Connecticut broad leaf, and the Vallandigham. The Lancaster broad leaf, generally preferred by the tobacco-growers of Jefferson county, has a delicate fiber and a silky appearance, and shows some slight modification, owing to the climate and soil, when compared with the same variety grown in Lancaster county, Pennsylvania. This variety loses in body but increases in fineness of leaf, and its capacity for moisture is increased 4 or 5 per cent.

The Connecticut broad leaf, or, as it is called by some, the East Hartford Connecticut leaf, is preferred by many on account of its superior yield. Though its color is inferior, being lighter than the Pennsylvania seed-leaf, it has a coarser fiber, but a very thin, delicate web. It has a drooping leaf in growing, while the Lancaster grows with an upright leaf, resembling in this particular the Cuba varieties, and the leaf is ruffled and corrugated. This is doubtless the same variety known in Pennsylvania as the Glessner, a variety highly prized for its excellence as a wrapper.

The Vallandigham is cultivated to a considerable extent in the neighborhood of Edgerton, Rock county, and has a large, pointed, smooth leaf, which makes it easy to worm.

All these varieties of seed-leaf are used for wrappers, fillers, and binders in cigar-making, the inferior grades being often mixed with southern leaf, in the proportion of one to four, for making fine-cut smoking tobacco.

The Cuba varieties, for the reasons already mentioned, are growing rapidly into favor. After three or four years' planting from seed originally brought from Cuba these varieties lose much of the aroma which distinguishes them the first year, but the size of the leaf is greatly increased, and enough of the sweet flavor is retained to make the product of great value; for as the amount of sweet fillers is decreased the ratio of wrappers to the whole is increased, and it is a question among growers whether the change is not, on the whole, a benefit rather than an injury—an improvement rather than a deterioration in the variety.

SOILS FOR TOBACCO.

Three classes of soils are recognized by the tobacco-growers in Wisconsin: 1. The calcareous sandy soil. 2. The clayey soils, light and heavy, mulatto in color. 3. The prairie soils.

The first is greatly preferred, not only because it is more easily tilled, but because the quality of tobacco grown upon it commands a higher price and readier sale. It produces a silky, elastic, glossy leaf, uniform in color, and the plant matures fully a week earlier than the clayey soil. The timber growth is chiefly white and burr oak, with hazel undergrowth. Sometimes this soil is found on the prairie lands. The clayey soils occupy more elevated areas, with open woods, the principal arboreal growth of which is white and burr oak, with maple on the heavier soils.

The tobacco grown on clayey soils is coarse, thick, not uniform in color, and is generally of an inferior quality in every way. The lighter the clay the better the tobacco.

The prairie soils are extremely variable in their adaptability to the growth of tobacco. Where there is a predominance of clay, and when these soils are of a black, waxy character, they are totally unfitted for the production of fine leaf, but with a suitable admixture of sand they belong really to the class first mentioned, and have the capacity of producing tobacco of a most desirable quality. The largest proportion of tobacco land in Jefferson county is prairie.

It has been ascertained by experience that the presence of gravel in a dry season is a great disadvantage to the tobacco-plant, but in a wet season it proves of benefit, inasmuch as it allows the superfluous water to drain off.

The slopes which run down to the shores of the lakes, and more especially the eastern slopes, in which there is a variable quantity of feldspathic, gneissoid, and limestone gravel, with sand in varying proportions, are found well adapted to the production of tobacco. Between the low bottoms on the streams and lakes and the elevated areas which rise up probably a hundred feet or more above the valleys are moderately undulating plains, in which, for the most part, the soils best suited for tobacco are found. Around Edgerton, which may be considered the center of the tobacco-growing region, there are many square miles occupying this medial topographical position, in which the light, marly clays and the calcareous, sandy loams abound. So also east and west of Janesville, for twelve or fifteen miles, the calcareous, sandy loams predominate. In the southwestern part of Jefferson, north and east of lake Koshkonong, the light, marly clays, well adapted to the growth of tobacco, abound; but the quality of the product grown upon these light clays is considered inferior to that grown on sandy loams or calcareous sands.

The prairie soils do not wash so easily as the more loose calcareous soils, the latter requiring considerable care in their cultivation, especially when the slopes are sharp, as they are liable to be damaged almost irreparably by heavy rain storms.

GRADES OF TOBACCO PRODUCT.

There are three grades of tobacco in Wisconsin: wrappers, fillers, and binders, the proportion of grades varying greatly with the seasons. If the season be entirely favorable, the proportion of wrappers will, in a good crop, reach 66 per cent. of the whole; but a very wet or a very dry summer will diminish this proportion to 50 per cent., or even less. Taking the average of crops and seasons, a fair estimate of the proportion of grades will be: wrappers, 50 per cent.; fillers, 25 per cent.; binders, 25 per cent. It is believed that the proportion of high grades has been very much increased during the past few years, and one reason given for such improvement. namely, that the tobacco is planted year after year upon the same land, is certainly an anomaly in agriculture.

The proportion of grades probably depends more upon the character of the soils than upon anything else. Tobacco grown upon new land, or land freshly cleared, has a harsh, woody, stiff leaf, but a pleasant flavor. Such tobacco furnishes a small proportion of wrappers, but a large amount of excellent fillers. It has but little gum, not enough to make it stand the sweating process well, and the color is light and the leaf thin. When the soil has been properly fertilized, there is an elasticity in the leaf which peculiarly fits it for wrapping purposes, and when tobacco is grown on such land the proportion of wrappers is largely increased and the inferior grades are reduced to a minimum. Level lands usually produce a much larger leaf than rolling lands, but it is not so fine, the tobacco grown on the latter commanding a higher price in market, while that grown on the former will make a heavier yield per acre. In many localities the seed-leaf is grown, for the most part, on level lands, and the Spanish varieties on rolling surfaces.

TOBACCO FERTILIZERS.

Fully four-fifths of the lands planted in tobacco are heavily fertilized with barn-yard manure, from ten to twenty loads being applied to every acre, at a cost varying from $10 to $20 per acre; and it not unfrequently occurs that the lands intended for other crops are robbed of their due proportion of manure in order that the tobacco lands may be enriched to their full capacity of production. This is plainly seen in the exuberant growth of the tobacco-plant and the scanty growth of some other crops. The tendency, however, is to a better preservation of the soil by increasing the manure piles and making use of the large deposits of muck which are so abundant in southern Wisconsin. Manure is applied broadcast, and is plowed or harrowed in a few weeks before the land is finally prepared for transplanting.

The effect of manures upon the yield and quality of the crop is very great, good, rich bottom-lands, without any recent application of manure, producing about 1,000 pounds of medium seed-leaf tobacco per acre; but with the application of ten loads of manure to the acre the yield is increased for the seed-leaf from 500 to 700 pounds, the quality being fully a third better, and the tobacco is darker, richer, and silkier. The increase in yield for the Spanish varieties is about 25 per cent., but manure does not appear to improve its quality to the same degree as with the heavier seed-leaf varieties. Instances are given where the same land has been planted in tobacco for a period of twenty-seven years in succession without any apparent diminution in its producing capacity. The land, however, has received heavy applications of manure every year. It is a very rare thing for any land, except that newly cleared, to be planted in tobacco without previously applying fertilizers. The few cases, however, reported show a decline in yield of at least 10 per cent. annually.

In the region immediately around Edgerton an increase in the yield of similar varieties is reported of 20 per cent. within the past ten years, but in Jefferson county a decrease of 10 per cent. within the same period is given. This difference is due to the fact that near the former place only heavily manured lots are planted in tobacco, while in the latter a larger proportion of newly-cleared lands is used for growing tobacco, and, as is probably the case, the best tobacco lands were the first cleared, leaving the inferior new lands to come in later. In Rock, Dane, and Greene counties the general practice among tobacco-growers is to keep the same field year after year in tobacco, the land receiving a heavy coating of manure every year; and in this way there is, so to speak, a cumulative strength given to the soil, no one crop being sufficient to exhaust the manure applied for its production. The soil, therefore, is constantly improved and enriched, and each successive crop shows a larger yield. In Jefferson county, on the contrary, the schedules show that the principle of rotation is practiced to a considerable extent. After tobacco comes wheat, followed by clover, and then corn, after which comes tobacco again. Notwithstanding the fact that the farmers in a large portion of the tobacco-growing district do not practice green-manuring or rotation, it is admitted that it would add to the friability of the soil and make it more retentive of moisture during the summer months.

Losses in the crop not unfrequently occur from "brown-rust" or firing, and a few days' delay in housing will sometimes reduce the quality of the tobacco fully one-half. "Brown-rust" is a disease resulting from the combined effects of hot weather and a superabundance of heat-producing manure in the soil.

All reports, however, concur in saying that the general quality of the crop during the past ten years has been greatly improved in consequence of increased care and attention in housing, curing, and assorting. The increased knowledge, too, among farmers has led to a better selection of soils, which, when once proved congenial to the growth of tobacco, are set apart for that purpose, and are kept up to a high degree of fertility.

Of the tobacco lands in cultivation probably two-thirds were originally prairie, with a calcareous, sandy loam; the remainder originally oak openings, with hazel undergrowth. Probably only 4 or 5 per cent. of the soils adapted to the growth of tobacco are occupied in its cultivation in the counties under consideration.

SEED-BEDS.

The seed-beds are burned lightly with brush, and a liberal supply of hen manure or horse dung is worked into the soil to the depth of 6 inches with a hoe or a spade. The work of preparation often begins in July, when the manure is applied. The bed is reworked in August and again in September, for the purpose of keeping down any weeds or grass that may spring up, and finally, in November, it is hoed and raked and prepared to receive the seed, which is either sown in the fall or early in the succeeding spring. When sown in the fall, the seed is not previously sprouted. After sowing, the bed is compacted by rolling, tramping, or clapping with a board. The plants are carefully nursed by liquid manuring, and by keeping the grass and weeds pulled out. By proper care, they will be large enough for transplanting in the field by the 1st of June.

PREPARATION OF TOBACCO SOIL.

The land for the succeeding crop is plowed in the fall, immediately after the tobacco is harvested. This checks the growth of suckers, which always shoot up from the old stubble, and are gross feeders, furnishing also a refuge for worms. The breaking is done with a two-horse turning or stubble plow to the depth of 5 or 6 inches. About the first of the succeeding May the soil is again broken with the same plow, and a third time about the first of June, or just before the plants are ready for transplanting. Manure may be applied at any time before either plowing. Coarse manures are better when applied in the fall, but fine, well-rotted manure is usually spread over the land just before the second or the third plowing. Some do not apply manure until after the third plowing, when it is harrowed or dragged in. After being thoroughly pulverized with a harrow or drag, the land is marked off: if for seed-leaf, 2½ by 3 feet, some preferring 4 by 2 feet; if for the Spanish varieties, 3 by 1½ feet. Hills are generally made with a hoe at the intersection of the lines and "patted" so as to compact the earth; but when only lined out one way, they are made on the line at proper distances. Sometimes no hills are made, but the plants are set out on the side of the lines. The plants are generally set out immediately after a shower of rain, but when water is convenient, and the plants are becoming overgrown in the beds, artificial watering is often resorted to. The planting is done from the 1st of June to the 4th of July, but these are extreme limits. The great bulk of the crop is set out from the 10th to the 20th of June.

By an easy calculation, it will be seen that, of seed-leaf, from 5,445 to 5,808 plants are set to the acre, and of the Spanish varieties 9,680 plants, a larger number to the acre than is planted in any other tobacco district in the United States. To this cause is no doubt due the exceeding tenuity and tenderness of the Wisconsin tobacco.

CULTIVATION OF THE TOBACCO CROP.

As soon as the soil is in proper condition to work after the plants have been set out a cultivator, with five teeth, is run between the rows, and this is kept up once or twice a week, until the field has been gone over five or six times. The crop is hoed twice, once after the cultivator is run through the first time. Very little dirt is put to the plant, level cultivation being preferred. In some portions of the district a horse-hoe is used in cultivating the crop, which, by its peculiar construction, enables the farmer to go very near the plant and stir every part of the soil. In very small patches the cultivation is done entirely with the hoe, which is kept up every week until the plants are so large that they cannot be worked without breaking the leaves.

TOPPING AND SUCKERING OF TOBACCO.

In about forty-eight or fifty days after the plants are set, if the crop has been well cultivated and the weather seasonable, the flower buds make their appearance, and are pinched out, leaving from fourteen to sixteen leaves on each plant. None of the bottom leaves are taken off, but all are left to mature or dry up, serving as a protection against the dirt. Fields, however, are often seen in full blossom before the tobacco is topped, and this results in great damage to the crop. Tobacco is suckered twice: once in about a week after it is topped, and again just before it is cut, which is generally about two weeks after topping.

As has been noted, tobacco is generally ready for harvesting in two weeks after being topped, and yet there is considerable variation in the time on different soils. On warm, sandy loams the plant will be as ripe in twelve days as it will be on heavy clayey soils in eighteen days. This is one of the reasons why the sandy loams are preferred.

TOBACCO INSECTS.

Fortunately for the tobacco-growers of Wisconsin, the horn-worm, the great enemy of the tobacco-plant in other states, has never appeared in great numbers, the farmers ascribing their immunity from them to the frequent plowings which they give the land before planting, thus disturbing them in their beds while in the chrysalis state, some of them being covered so deeply that they are not able to extricate themselves, while others are thrown to the surface and are devoured by fowls. The severity of the winters also destroys a considerable number. The farmers carefully search every leaf that indicates their presence. Grain is sometimes thinly scattered on the tobacco-fields and fowls are driven upon them, and while hunting for the grain they gather many of the worms. This mode is not reported from any other section.

CUTTING, HOUSING, AND CURING OF TOBACCO.

Harvesting begins early in August and continues without intermission into September. A large portion of the crop of 1880 was harvested during the first and second weeks in August. The time of day preferred for cutting is from two o'clock in the afternoon until nearly sundown, because at that time tobacco is less liable to be blistered by the heat of the sun. The instrument used for cutting is a hatchet, the plants being cut off nearly on a level with the ground and laid back on the rows to wilt. After wilting they are speared on laths. Of the large seed-leaf varieties only about six plants are put on a lath, but of the smaller Spanish or Havana varieties ten are not considered too many. After being speared on the laths, the latter are carefully put on a long wagon-frame, made for the purpose, and carried to the sheds, where they are arranged on the tier-poles, or racks, from 6 to 10 inches apart, according to the size of the plants, but never so close as to permit them to touch each other.

It requires six weeks to cure the Spanish varieties perfectly, and two months to cure the seed-leaf. If the weather is dry after the crop is housed, the doors are kept closed during the day and opened at night, but extreme care must be taken not to cure too rapidly. In muggy, sultry weather as much air as possible should be given, thorough ventilation being indispensable to prevent pole-sweat. Continuous damp weather or continuous dry weather are both to be feared. It is believed by many good growers that white veins are the result of a drought after the tobacco has been harvested, and it is said that no crop cured when there is plenty of rain is ever affected with them. Inferences of this kind, however, are too often drawn without considering a sufficient number of cases to warrant the enunciation of a general law. It is a well-established truth, however, deduced from the universal experience of the cultivation of seed-leaf tobacco in every state, that a crop cannot be well cured without the alternations of moist and dry atmosphere.

TOBACCO-HOUSES.

The tobacco-houses, or sheds, are generally very inexpensive frame buildings, 14 feet high, 28 feet wide, and long enough to harvest whatever number of acres the farmer may wish to raise. The height between the tiers is usually 4½ feet, which allows ample room for ventilation. The height of the shed gives three tiers from top to bottom, allowing half a foot between the tails of the tobacco hung on the lower tier and the ground. The capacity of these sheds varies from 2 to 12 acres, and many of them very rickety and open, and are totally unfit for the purpose. The tendency, however, is toward improvement, for observing farmers have discovered that to cure tobacco properly it is necessary to be able to control the conditions which surround it. The cost of the best sheds at present does not exceed $600.

PREPARATION OF TOBACCO FOR MARKET AND PRICES.

From the 15th of November to the 1st of January is the usual period for preparing the crop for market. The usual practice among farmers is first to strip the leaves from the stalks, tying them up in large bundles and assorting afterward. A few assort directly from the stalk, but "table assorting", or assorting after stripping, is preferred by the most painstaking farmers. After the tobacco has been carefully assorted into three or four grades, generally first wrappers, second wrappers, fillers, and binders, it is tied in "hands" of from eighteen to twenty leaves, securely wrapped with a leaf at the butt-end, and "bulked" or "banked" in piles, with the heads out and tails overlapping in the center of the bulk. Here it remains until the "fatty stems" are thoroughly cured, when it is ready for market, unless the grower prefers to pack it in boxes himself. The selling goes on all through the winter, and even up to May. In all the towns and villages of any considerable size in the tobacco-growing region there are established what are known as warehouses, where dealers buy, pack, and sweat the crop, preparatory to sending it to more distant markets. In the town of Edgerton there are thirteen of these warehouses, and it is estimated that during the year 1879 fully half a million dollars was disbursed among the farmers in the immediate vicinity for tobacco.

Stoughton has five warehouses, and the amount disbursed in 1879 in the purchase of tobacco was about $214,000. Janesville has one, which pays out $40,000, and Evansville one, where $25,000 was disbursed during the same year. Several other places, as Madison and Milton, have recently entered into the business of buying and packing tobacco, and there is no other crop grown in the state which gives such animation to trade, or which supplies the farmers so surely with ready money. The total expenditure in 1879 by local dealers in the state for tobacco delivered loose was estimated to exceed $890,000.

The following were average prices paid for crop through (that is, including all grades) for the product grown in the annexed years, but sold in the market the following years:

Year.	Seed-leaf.	Spanish.
	Cents.	*Cents.*
1875 (frosted)	4	None.
1876	6	8
1877	6½	8
1878	6½ to 7	9
1879	7	13

When sold by grades the following prices prevailed in 1879:

Grade.	Seed-leaf.	Spanish.
	Cents.	*Cents.*
Fillers	2 to 4	4
Binders	4 to 7	8
Wrappers	8 to 15	16

The crop of Spanish tobacco, when sold loose, averaged 11 cents round in 1879.

The crop of 1879 was damaged to some extent by winds and storms, and while the average price of the crop of seed-leaf did not exceed 7 cents per pound, the better crops readily brought from 8 to 10 cents.

LANDS, LABOR, AND COST OF TOBACCO PRODUCTION.

The price of tobacco lands in Wisconsin ranges from $35 to $75 per acre, the average being about $50. When rented, land commands $10 per acre, or one-half of the crop prepared for market, the landlord furnishing sheds and team, but not boarding the tenant. The price of labor is $30 a month for men, $1 25 per day, or $150 per year, board included. In such cases tobacco laborers command about $5 per month more than other field hands. Strippers of tobacco are paid $1 per day, and to strip from 150 to 250 pounds is considered a fair day's work. Packers are paid $1 25 per day. A good man, with help, during the season of harvest, can plant and cultivate five acres of tobacco.

The following detailed estimate of the cost of cultivating, curing, and marketing an acre of seed-leaf tobacco was made by Mr. Thomas Hutson, of Edgerton, one of the largest and most successful growers in Rock county:

DR.	
Cost of making seed-bed for one acre	$0 50
Cost of seed	50
Weeding and attention to seed-bed	1 00
Rent of land (interest on price, at 10 per cent.)	5 00
Stable manure, six cords, cost	6 00
Cost of applying same	6 00
Cost of breaking one acre three times	3 75
Harrowing, lining out, and hilling	1 50
Drawing and setting out plants	3 00
Cultivating and hoeing	7 00
Topping, 25 cents; worming, 50 cents; suckering, $2 50	3 25
Harvesting	5 00
Taking down, assorting, and stripping	12 00
Bulking	25
Use of barn, laths, wagon, etc	5 00
Delivering crop to market	1 50
Total cost	61 25
CR.	
By 1,600 pounds of tobacco, at 7 cents	$112 00
Profit	50 75
Cost, $3 83 per hundred pounds.	

It is believed that the cost will be reduced in a crop large enough to employ a full set of hands; that is, hands enough to handle the crop most expeditiously and to employ the team to its full capacity. As the Spanish varieties bring a much higher price, though not yielding so much per acre, it is probable that they pay as good if not a better profit than the seed-leaf. The estimated cost of production for the whole state may be stated as $4 95 per hundred pounds.

PECULIARITIES OF WISCONSIN TOBACCO.

The burning qualities of the Wisconsin tobacco are generally excellent, leaving as a residuum a whitish solid ash, much diminished in size from the original bulk. The tobacco is peculiar in holding more water than any other grown in America; is always limp, and retains its humid, flexible properties during the coldest weather, but loses from 18 to 20 per cent. during the sweating process. The Wisconsin tobacco has great uniformity in color, being a dark brown, but the leaf is extremely thin, and often lacks substance. When it has been resweated it very much resembles the Connecticut seed-leaf in texture, though somewhat darker in color. It then has a very fine finish, and but for its tenderness would take a very high rank among cigar manufacturers. The same humidity is observed in the Havana or Spanish leaf, and this excess of moisture often causes it to damage during the sweating process. It is probably owing to this excessive presence of water that the Wisconsin tobacco is so uniform in color.

MISCELLANEOUS.

Hailstorms are sometimes very destructive, one which occurred in 1878 destroying in the vicinity of Edgerton 10 per cent. of the crop. These storms occur more or less every year, but usually in narrow belts.

Cases 2½ by 2½ by 3½ feet, suitable for packing tobacco, cost $1 each, from 300 to 450 pounds being packed in a case. New York buyers pay local agents $1 per case for buying.

A day's labor is ten hours when the laborer is employed for one day only, but if he is employed by the month twelve hours are reckoned a day's work.

Artificial sweating is believed by some of the best dealers to be accompanied with less risk than sweating by the natural process, and the second stories of warehouses are sometimes prepared as sweating chambers by being plastered or closely ceiled. These are heated by furnaces, and the temperature of the rooms is kept at 110° to 140°. About forty-two days are required to complete the process, when the tobacco is ready for market.

Any one can become an inspector by guaranteeing the samples drawn from a case to represent correctly the quality of the tobacco and its condition in the case. These samples are, however, usually drawn by inspectors sent out from other places, or by agents representing houses in other cities.

The great bulk of the tobacco, after being cured and sweated, finds its way to New York, Philadelphia, Baltimore, Cincinnati, Saint Louis, Hartford, and other points where there is a regular demand for cigar tobacco, and is marketed at all times. Farmers, however, usually deliver the crop to local dealers in the winter and spring, and the latter usually keep a supply on hand throughout the year.

The tobacco product of Wisconsin is the tenderest of all the seed-leaf products, and in working must be handled with great care. In consequence of the great absorptive capacity of the leaf, much of it is damaged by extreme fermentation during wet, hot weather. Nor does it answer well for exportation, the sea sweat greatly damaging it.

The following statement will show the production, acreage, yield per acre, and value of the Wisconsin crop for the four years ending in 1879, the figures for the latter year being from the census returns:

Year.	Production.	Acreage.	Yield per acre.	Value in primary markets.	Value per pound.	Value per acre.
	Pounds.		*Pounds.*		*Cents.*	
1876......	7,572,302	5,568	1,360.00	$511,134	6.75	$91 80
1877......	7,265,602	5,504	1,320.00	506,502	7.00	92 40
1878......	9,082,002	7,506	1,210.00	653,904	7.20	87 12
1879......	10,608,423	8,810	1,204.18	690,118	6.47	101 99

CHAPTER XIX.

THE NEW ENGLAND TOBACCO-GROWING DISTRICT.

HISTORICAL NOTES.

The culture of tobacco in the Connecticut valley is almost coeval with its first settlement. As early as 1640 an act was passed restricting the use of tobacco to that grown in the colony, under a penalty of 5*s.* for every pound expended for imported tobacco, "except a license should first be obtained from the court." Under this restriction the culture, as well as its use, became general, and efforts were made by the colonists in 1646–'47 to curtail its consumption by a prohibitory law, which acted upon the consumer, but not upon the merchant, trader, or farmer. This law provided that no one under the age of twenty years, nor any other person who had not become addicted to the habit, should take any tobacco without a certificate from a physician that it would be beneficial to him. It also provided that tobacco should not be taken publicly upon the streets, under the penalty of sixpence for each offense.

In 1662 a duty of 25*s.* per hogshead, or 2*d.* per pound, was laid upon all tobacco brought into the colony. In 1753 inspectors were appointed to examine the tobacco for shipment abroad, and to take out all that was in any way injured by frost, heat, moisture, or in other manner, and to pack only the sound, well-ripened, well-cured tobacco, which should in every way be good and merchantable. For this service the owner was required to pay 5*d.* for every hundred-weight and 3*d.* per mile for travel of the inspector, and all tobacco sold without inspection was declared forfeited.

At no period previous to 1801 did the production of the Connecticut valley exceed 20,000 pounds, and it was shipped for the most part to the West Indies, being purchased at from $3 to $3 33 per hundred pounds by local merchants, by whom it was packed and exported.

About 1801–'2 tobacco was manufactured in a small way by individuals; but it was not until 1810 that cigar manufactories were established—one at East Windsor and another at Suffield, Connecticut. Spanish tobacco, imported from Cuba or the Brazils, was then for the first time employed in the fabrication of cigars, and these were peddled in wagons throughout the country.

The year 1825 marked a new era in the history of tobacco culture in the valley, and a packing-house was erected at Warehouse Point, about 3,200 pounds being packed and shipped to New York. This tobacco was packed in bales, inclosed with boards on four sides, leaving the ends exposed, and weighed about 100 pounds each. The cultivation was gradually extended, and in 1840 it was a general crop, though small, grown as regularly as any other in the valley.

Previous to the year 1833 a variety of tobacco, with a very narrow leaf, called the Shoestring, was cultivated, which, though strong and heavy, was not well adapted to the purposes for which Connecticut tobacco is now used. About this time a broad leaf variety was brought from Maryland, having a very delicate, thin, silky leaf, regular veins, comparatively tasteless, of fine finish, and very pliant. B. P. Barber, of East Windsor, Connecticut, has the credit of introducing this tobacco, which has, by skillful and intelligent management, established a reputation second to none grown in the United States.

Meanwhile factories were erected from time to time, until in 1856 about four hundred men and two hundred women found employment in making cigars at various points from Springfield, Massachusetts, to Middletown, Connecticut, the average wages earned by men being $6, and by women $4 per week.(*a*) In 1860 there were forty-five of these establishments, with a capital of $389,600, employing 731 persons, at an annual expenditure for wages of $274,911 and for material of $381,150, turning out an annual product estimated to be worth $914,500. In 1870 there were in Connecticut alone one hundred factories making cigars and manufacturing tobacco, employing 719 hands, with a capital amounting to $409,750, expending for wages $303,109, for material $441,663, and turning out a product valued at $1,133,665.

The demand for raw material created by these manufacturing establishments rapidly stimulated production, and the prices paid were highly remunerative, almost every farmer living within convenient distance for delivery, and who possessed lands suited to the growth of tobacco, endeavoring to supply the demand.

Mr. Henry A. Dyer is authority for saying that in 1840 1,800 cases, or about 720,000 pounds of tobacco, were packed in the Connecticut valley. The census for that year reports only 537,649 pounds for all New England, being the crop of 1839. In 1842 the estimated crop in Connecticut valley was 5,000 cases, or 2,000,000 pounds, and in 1845 the product of Connecticut alone was 3,467,940 pounds, as given in a state statistical report.

The first tobacco grown in the Housatonic valley for market was in 1845, in Kent, Litchfield county; the next was grown near New Milford; and in 1870 it became one of the leading products of the valley. Housatonic tobacco became very popular in 1876 for cigar wrappers, and thereafter the increase of product was very rapid.

TOBACCO PRODUCT.

The following table shows the production of New England for each of the census years from 1840:

States.	1840.	1850.	1860.	1870.	1880.
Connecticut	471,647	1,267,624	6,000,133	8,328,798	14,044,652
Massachusetts	64,955	138,246	3,233,198	7,312,885	5,369,436
New Hampshire	115	50	18,581	155,334	170,843
Vermont	585	....	12,245	72,071	131,432
Rhode Island	317	....	708	790	785
Maine	30	....	1,583	15	250
Total	537,649	1,405,920	9,268,448	15,870,409	19,717,898

Beginning with the year 1855, Massachusetts has taken a state census, intermediate between those taken by the general government. The state census makes the following showing for 1855:

Counties.	Acres.	Value.
Berkshire	2.0	$250 00
Franklin	93.5	12,403 00
Hampden	170.5	21,228 74
Hampshire	155.0	23,600 00
Total	421.0	57,481.74

It does not appear how many pounds per acre were produced during this year; but if it be estimated at 1,666 pounds, which was the yield per acre in 1865, the average value was $136 54 per acre, and $8 20 per hundred pounds.

In the year 1865 the following statement is given in the Massachusetts state census:

Counties.	Acres.	Pounds.	Value.
Barnstable	0.5	360	$90
Berkshire	160.0	198,800	29,277
Bristol	3.0	2,420	777
Dukes	0.5	809	150
Essex	5.0	4,850	1,076
Franklin	1,053.0	3,140,709	516,210
Hampden	1,087.0	1,509,643	308,445
Hampshire	2,400.0	4,394,925	751,654
Middlesex	5.0	3,405	732
Norfolk	0.5	775	248
Plymouth	2.0	1,646	701
Worcester	36.0	40,218	7,636
Total	5,617.5	9,361,641	1,616,396

a Connecticut Agricultural Report, 1856.

These figures show production per acre of 1,666 pounds; value per pound, 17.27 cents; value per acre, $287 74; an increase during the decade of 1,235 per cent. in total production, and an increase of value per pound of 9.07 cents, or 101 per cent.

The state census of 1875 shows the following acreage, production, and value:

Counties.	Acres.	Pounds.	Value.
Berkshire	69. 25	89, 600	$15, 148
Bristol	0. 25	530	78
Essex...........	0. 75	1, 000	80
Franklin	1, 210. 50	1. 897. 091	321, 815
Hampden........	808. 60	1, 224, 670	230, 475
Hampshire......	1, 652. 25	2, 655, 561	402, 956
Middlesex	0. 12	240	53
Plymouth	....	70	19
Worcester.......	10. 00	14, 895	1, 638
Total	3, 757. 62	5, 998, 606	1, 032, 262

This table shows production per acre, 1,595 pounds; value per pound, 17.22 cents; value per acre, $274 71; a decrease of production, as compared with 1865, of 36 per cent., and with 1870 of 18 per cent.

Previous to the year 1840 prices for the different grades ranged from $4 to $7 per hundred pounds. After that prices increased rapidly, and good wrappers were worth in 1857 $40 per hundred pounds.

The erection of numerous warehouses for packing tobacco finally resulted in making them sale houses as well as packing establishments. The custom has become general among farmers to sell their tobacco loose from wagons to the warehousemen at an agreed price for the crop through, the purchasers to assort, pack, and sweat the tobacco, shipping it for sale to such markets as offered the best net returns. Very few planters now assort and pack their own crop, as it is found to interfere very much with the production of another crop, requires more time than can be well spared from other farm work, and cannot be done as well nor as economically by the planter as by the dealer, who is provided with conveniently arranged houses and implements for the purpose.

SURFACE FEATURES.

Tobacco in New England is now cultivated in two well-defined regions: 1. The Connecticut valley. 2. The Housatonic valley.

The Connecticut valley is one of the finest regions in America, combining in an unusual degree a quiet beauty with great agricultural capabilities. The valley, so called, of the Connecticut river is about 300 miles in length, and is not far from 20 miles wide. The bounding hills are not, as a general thing, very symmetrical or rounded in outline, but have angular or irregular forms.

On the west the Connecticut valley is bounded by the Green mountain, the Hoosic mountain, and the great billowy plain which divides it from the Housatonic. On the east are the White mountains, culminating in Mount Washington, 6,428 feet above the sea. Mount Holyoke, 830 feet above the Connecticut river, which washes its base, and 900 feet above Boston harbor, is part of a greenstone range which, beginning with West Rock, near New Haven, runs northward across the state of Connecticut, entering Massachusetts between Springfield and Southwick, and at East Hampton, in Connecticut, it mounts into an elevation of over 1,000 feet, forming Mount Tom. The valleys on the north and west of Holyoke are very fertile.

GEOLOGICAL FORMATIONS AND SOILS.

A large area of the northern part of New Hampshire is covered by a series of greenstone or trap rocks, a compound of hornblende and feldspar. These occur in groups, and extend along the Connecticut river, through Massachusetts and Connecticut, to the sea-shore, and are believed to be metamorphosed sedimentary accumulations of the Silurian age. Although of a remarkable constancy in respect to their rock constituents and chemical composition, they frequently differ as to the relative proportions of these constituents, extensive granite and gneiss deposits, or sandstone, being frequently found in juxtaposition to the trap or greenstone, and in some instances limestones are found associated with feldspar and free quartz. In some granitoid rocks the feldspathic constituents predominate, in others the hornblende, and in others the mica, while apparently under less favorable conditions for metamorphosis the argillaceous sedimentary accumulations have retained to a considerable degree their original stratified amorphous character. Red sandstone ridges and trap rock also contribute largely in some parts of the valley to the striking beauty of the scenery along the river. The valley of the Connecticut river, like many of the New England valleys, has received extensive drift deposits, making thick beds of gravel, sand, clay, or fine silt, during the Champlain period. These drift deposits, composed for the most part of rounded pebbles, from the size of a goose egg to fine sand, are sometimes 100 feet or more in thickness, and show signs of stratification. In some places segregated beds of drifted sand appear, and in others beds of clay. These stratified and unstratified deposits have been modified by erosion.

The lands along the river rise on both sides quite frequently into terraces, and these level-topped elevations are the flood plains of the river, indicating distinct periods in the history of the erosion of the valley. The highest of these terraces extends over a wide area, and is cut here and there by the tributaries of the Connecticut river or disturbed by projecting hills. The lower terraces seldom extend over more than a mile or two, and on the opposite sides of the river these heights, unlike those of the highest terraces, are of different levels. The present flood plain is commonly known as meadows. The material which composes the highest plains is of a coarser character than that which contributes to the bottom lands or meadows; but before reaching Hartford these varying rocks have become ground into a fine material, and have commingled so thoroughly that all the elements find a lodgment in the soil; in fact, the areas covered by coarse material—due to immediate glacial action—are more extensive in the northern part of the valley than in the middle and southern portions. The superior physical condition of the soil upon the present flood plain of the Connecticut river is the principal cause of the high agricultural value of the lands along the river.

The more recent alluviums occur more or less in the valleys of all the streams, and form in the low depressions swamps and marshes. Sometimes the alluvium is composed of coarse material, very gravelly, and unsuited in a great degree for agricultural purposes; again it consists of very fine clayey or sandy loams; and when the sand and clay commingle in proper proportions the soil is generous in its fertility.

The tobacco area of the Housatonic valley is confined to Litchfield and Fairfield counties, spreading out westwardly so as to take in a small portion of the counties of Duchess and Putnam, in eastern New York. Only the northern part of Fairfield county, however, is embraced within this area, the southern part, as is the case with the southern part of Middlesex county, in the Connecticut valley, being, as is conjectured, too near salt water to produce tobacco of good burning qualities.

The Housatonic valley is narrow, and in many places can scarcely be said to have any bottom lands, resembling a deep gap cut through a high rolling region. Here and there small, semi-elliptical low fields or pockets are to be seen, covering a few acres, and these are succeeded by the plateaus of high terraces. These, in turn, are carved into so many fantastic shapes by ravines and small brooks as scarcely to be recognized as terraces. Beyond these, to the east and to the west, are long, sloping hills, irregular in outline, the sides of which are generally clothed with different species of the oak and the chestnut.

The soil of the country through which the Housatonic river flows is variable. What are called loamy soils in this valley are, for the most part, derived from the breaking down of the feldspathic and trappean rocks. These soils are very rich in potash, and are generally selected for growing tobacco. The alluvial soils vary much in quality, being at times white and argillaceous and very cold and tenacious, and at other times but little more than beds of gravel. When there is a proper commingling of these two the soil is very light, productive, and durable.

The soils of the tobacco-growing portion of New England may be divided generally into two classes:

1. Those formed from the crumbling of the rocks *in situ*.
2. Those which have been derived from transported material.

The soil derived from porphyritic rocks is a dark argillaceous loam, of excellent fertility, and is suitable for grain and for tobacco. The micaceous-ferruginous rocks supply a soil well adapted to the growth of grasses, and the rounded green hills attest the value of these lands for pasturage. It is a fine, light gray loam, works easily, and constitutes a considerable part of the soils of several counties.

The soils of the granitic rocks are inclined to be coarse in structure and arid, and where disintegration has been carried to a sufficient degree of fineness the soil is of moderate fertility. Slaty soils, from chloritic slates and mica-schist, are inclined to be cold and wet; yet, when sufficiently drained, they are strong, and will retain fertilizers well. They make a red clay or loamy soil. The red sandstones furnish a thin, poor soil, unless the sandstones are argillaceous, when a very good soil results. The trap rocks, by reason of the calcareous spar which is associated with them, often crumble into a very generous soil, and one that is durable in its constitution.

When there is a considerable amount of pebbles composed of carbonate of lime, commingled in suitable proportions with feldspathic and ferruginous-micaceous rocks, the drift soil is supplied with every inorganic element necessary to its fertility. On the other hand, when the drift is coarse, and is composed mainly of quartzose gravel, the soil has an original poverty of constitution and such porosity that heavy fertilization will have only a temporary effect upon its power of production.

The soils of the first terrace above the rivers are probably, for all purposes, the best, and on these, for the most part, the tobacco crop is grown, though some is planted on the meadow lands. These latter usually require draining, and must be protected from overflows. In some places in the Connecticut valley the soil is underlaid by a grayish clay, called "hard-pan", and when this is exposed to the atmosphere it crumbles very readily. In places it makes a spongy soil, in others a heavy clayey soil, but ill-suited for the growth of any crop except the coarse grasses.

As far as the mechanical and physical conditions are concerned, all stages, from a free pebbly mass to a retentive fine clayish soil, may be found in New England. The surface soil is in some cases deep, in others quite shallow. In the latter case, especially in the Connecticut valley, the subsoil is either hard-pan or stratified ferruginous sand deposits or gravel beds. In some localities the quartz sand is the predominating soil constituent; in others the hornblende, or the mica, or a ferruginous clay. The tobacco crop claims for its successful cultivation the best soils—well-drained, deep, mellow, clayey, or sandy loams—with a permeable subsoil. Such soil is the best protection against untimely dry or wet spells.

FOREST GROWTH.

The crests of the hills are usually covered with pines, oak, and chestnut. The hemlock (*Abies Canadensis*) is found in shaded ravines and on the rocky banks of the streams. The slopes of the hills and low plains are here and there covered with red oak (*Quercus rubra*), black oak (*Q. tinctoria*), white oak (*Q. alba*), burr oak (*Q. ilicifolia*). The sugar maple (*Acer saccharinum*) frequently occurs in groves more or less extensive. The exhausted pastures upon hills and along the slopes of the ridges are rapidly becoming covered with white birch (*Betula alba*, var. *populifolia*), in some places pines, in others junipers (*Juniperus communis*—*J. Virginiana*), and huckleberry (*Gaylussacia dumosa*). Upon elevated clay lands are found the ash (*Fraxinus Americana*) and the hickories (*Carya alba* and *C. porcina*). The original natural growth upon the river lands seem to be elm (*Ulmus Americana*), the pines (*Pinus strobus* and *P. rigida*), the red maple (*Acer rubrum*); in wet places the alder (*Alnus incana*), the poison sumac (*Rhus venenata*), several species of dogwood (*Cornus*), and various species of the order *Ericaceæ*, as rhododendrons, *Epigæa*, etc. The beech (*Fagus ferruginea*), the butternut (*Juglans cinerea*), and linden (*Tilia Americana*), and buttonwood (*Platanus occidentalis*) occur on some of the lower terrace lands where the soil is good.

CLIMATE.

The climate of the tobacco region of New England, though changeable, is remarkably mild and healthy for the latitude. Its severity is tempered by the proximity of the sea, and by the two large valleys, the Housatonic and the Connecticut, and the warm air from the ocean is drawn up into these channels and diffuses itself over the intermediate high lands.

At New Haven, observations extending from December 10, 1872, to October 31, 1880, show the mean temperature to be: Spring, 37°.3; summer, 71°.1; autumn, 53°; winter, 30°.8. The greatest difference between the highest and lowest thermometer in any one year was 105°; highest recorded temperature, 95°; the lowest, – 14°. The mean annual precipitation, 54.01 inches; mean of prevailing winds, south.

At Springfield, Massachusetts, the observations of the signal service bureau from July 19, 1873, to October 31, 1880, show the mean temperature to be: Spring, 47°.6; summer, 71°.2; autumn, 52°.1; winter, 29°. The greatest range of the thermometer in any one year was 102°.5; the highest recorded temperature, 94°.5; the lowest, – 10°. Mean annual precipatation, 47.74 inches; mean of prevailing winds, south. It will be seen that the temperature of the spring months is more than 10° lower at New Haven than at Springfield, though the latter is 48′ farther north.

LOCALITY OF TOBACCO PRODUCTION AND COMPARISON OF RECENT CROPS.

The production of tobacco in the Connecticut valley is confined for the most part to the following counties: Middlesex, Hartford, and Tolland, in the state of Connecticut; Hampden, Hampshire, and Franklin, in the state of Massachusetts; Windham, in the state of Vermont; and Cheshire and Sullivan, in the state of New Hampshire. In the Housatonic valley tobacco is cultivated in Fairfield and Litchfield counties, and to this valley belongs commercially the tobacco product of Duchess and Putnam counties, in eastern New York. New Haven county belongs in part to the Connecticut valley and in part to the Housatonic valley.

In acreage the crop of 1879 was in New Haven county 25 per cent. greater than in 1878, 20 per cent. greater than in 1877, and about equal to that of 1876. In Middlesex, Hartford, and Tolland counties the acreage for 1879 was about 5 per cent. greater than for each of the years 1878, 1877, and 1876. For the year 1879 the counties of the Housatonic valley report an increase in acreage of 10 per cent. as compared with 1878, and 5 per cent. as compared with 1877 and 1876. In Hampden county, Massachusetts, the area planted in 1879 was 5 per cent. greater than in 1878, 40 per cent. greater than in 1877, and 15 per cent. greater than in 1876. The acreage in Hampshire county, Massachusetts, has remained about the same for four years. On the other hand, there was a falling off in acreage in Cheshire county, New Hampshire, of 10 per cent. in the crop of 1879 as compared with that of 1878, the same as compared with the area of 1877, and a very great diminution, estimated at 50 per cent., as compared with the crop of 1876. In the yield per acre there was for New Haven county 10 per cent. decrease in 1879 as compared with 1878, 1877, and 1876; and Middlesex, Hartford, and Tolland show about the same. Hampden, as compared with 1877, shows 5 per cent. decrease, and with 1876, 10 per cent. decrease; Hampshire, 10 per cent. decrease as compared with 1878; Cheshire, as compared with 1878, 10 per cent. decrease, and the same rate of decrease for the years 1877 and 1876. The yield per acre in Housatonic valley in 1879 was 15 per cent. less than in 1878, and 10 per cent. less than in the years 1877 and 1876.

As to quality, the crop of 1879 in New Haven county was better than that of 1878, equal to that of 1877, and better than that of 1876. In Middlesex, Hartford, and Tolland counties the crop of 1879 was better than that of 1878 or that of 1877; and while the crop of 1876 was not so good as that of 1879, it was better than that of 1878, which was rather an inferior one. Hampden county, Massachusetts, reported the crop of 1879 as being better in every respect than those of the two years preceding, and as fully equal to the crop of 1876. The same may be said with reference to Hampshire county. On the other hand, the crop of New Hampshire in 1879 is said to be 20 per cent. worse than those of 1878 and of 1876, and equal to that of 1877. The same is true of the tobacco district in Vermont.

It may be assumed that in the tobacco-growing area of New England there has been a gradual extension of the area planted in tobacco, and the crop of 1879 shows throughout the seed-leaf district an increase of about 17 per cent. over the three years preceding, and that, compared with the crop of 1875, which was a very large one, there was a decrease.

The crop, though large in area in 1879, did not equal in yield per acre that of 1878 by 10 per cent., and the same may be said with reference to the years 1877 and 1876. The growth for the year 1878 was exceptionally large and the texture good, but a considerable portion of the crop was injured by white veins and pole-sweat. In 1879 a larger amount of Havana tobacco was grown in the counties of Massachusetts than usual, the entire crop of Seed Leaf and Havana being estimated to equal 10,000 cases, though the returns of enumerators would indicate 40 per cent. more. The crop of 1877 had a very large proportion of fine leaf, while that of 1876 was much below an average in quality. Cheshire county, New Hampshire, however, reports the crop of 1879 as 20 per cent. poorer in quality than that of 1878, about equal to that of 1877, and 10 per cent. worse than that of 1876. The crop of 1879 was good; on the whole, better than the crop of 1878, particularly the seconds, as there was not so much of it injured by white veins or pole-burn. The product of the Housatonic valley has gained popularity every year on account of its dark color.

For several years the wrappers of the Connecticut valley, though fine and silky in texture, broad in leaf, and well handled, have been too light, approaching a cinnamon color.

VARIETIES OF TOBACCO GROWN.

The several varieties of tobacco at present cultivated in Connecticut valley consist of Connecticut Seed Leaf, Connecticut Broad Leaf, Havana, Havana Seed, Belknap, and John Williams. The Connecticut Seed Leaf is broad, with small fibers, strong, thin, elastic, and silky, and the leaves are set closely upon the stalk. The best leaves of this variety are used for cigar wrappers and the poor ones for binders and fillers. The Seed Leaf is almost tasteless, and when used as wrappers for Havana fillers does not impair the flavor. The Broad Leaf is only a modification of the first, the leaves being broader in proportion to their length than the Connecticut Seed Leaf, and the fibers run out more at right angles to the midrib. The Havana Seed is grown to a considerable extent, especially in the valley counties lying within the state of Massachusetts. This variety has a very thin, fine leaf, is delicate in flavor, and yields more wrappers to the pound than any other variety planted. Grown in the Housatonic valley, this variety is noted for its fineness of texture and glossiness of leaf, which, after sweating well, has all the softness and brilliancy of a piece of silk; and as it cures a dark color, it is very popular with cigar manufacturers. It can be planted much closer than any other variety. Havana is that grown from imported seed; Havana Seed is that produced after four years. The principal objection to this variety is made by the farmers, who assert that, though the price is greater per pound than for the Seed Leaf, the small yield per acre does not make the crop so profitable, especially in those counties well adapted to the growth of the latter. This, no doubt, is the reason why Havana Seed Leaf is grown in larger proportions in the upper counties of the valley than in the lower ones. In the lower counties the soils produce a wrapping leaf unequaled in fineness by any other grown on the continent.

The Havana is grown to some extent in the upper part of the Housatonic valley for fillers. In answer to a letter addressed to him on the subject, Mr. Perry N. Hall, of New Milford, Connecticut, says of the Havana Seed:

> It is more generally known in market quotations as Connecticut Havana, and is produced in this way: Seed from the Vuelta Abajo district in Cuba is sown here three successive seasons, and the seed from the third and fourth years is laid up for future field cultivation. It is preferred, as being more leafy than other kinds of Cuba tobacco. The first year it grows small, producing little if any wrapper leaf, but makes a filler for cigars which retains some flavor. It is not used to any extent in field cultivation until the third or fourth year. It will retain its distinctive peculiarities for many years, provided the seed can be grown so as to entirely prevent its mixing with the Connecticut seed tobacco. As this is very difficult, on account of bees carrying the pollen from one plant to another, the plan of laying up and keeping the seed for a number of years is practiced. This tobacco produces fewer pounds per acre than the Connecticut Seed Leaf, but brings a somewhat larger price. It generally sweats to dark colors, and is easily cultivated and harvested.

The largest variety grown is said to be the Barber, a variety produced by making a careful selection of the earliest plants and carefully trimming the seed stalk of all late blooms. This variety is remarkable for the great size of its leaves, the smoothness of its texture, and the uniformity of its color, and it is highly esteemed for making wrappers. The Podunk has upright leaves, thickly disposed upon the stalk. Another variety of Seed Leaf, called Duck Island, is grown to a considerable extent in the Housatonic valley. It is medium in size, and very fine in texture and fiber. The other varieties mentioned are subvarieties of the Seed Leaf, and are distinguished from it only in the shape of the leaves, and not in the flavor, habits of growth, or uses.

The quality of these different varieties is greatly affected by the character of the soils upon which they grow. Where the soil is a heavy clay loam, the tobacco grows with more thickness of leaf, and has more gum in its tissues, cures a darker color, and will bear sweating better, but is not so well suited for wrappers, because of its comparative coarseness of texture. Upon light sandy soil the quality is very fine, but the color is light. By judicious sweating, tobacco can often be changed from a light cinnamon to a dark brown color, in which case it makes wrappers that command the highest prices. A quality of tobacco between the two is very popular, because it both sweats well and supplies a large proportion of wrappers.

Soils near the sea-coast, though in appearance having all the physical qualities required for the production of the finest leaf, yet often produce tobacco the burning qualities of which are imperfect. This doubtless arises from the existence of the chloride of sodium, or common salt, in the soil; for it is the result of long observation, both in Europe and in this country, that the use of salt, while it is thought to increase the crop, diminishes the burning qualities of tobacco. The soil preferred in the Housatonic valley is known as a ridgy loam, dark in color, with a small portion of sand. It is intermediate between a light sandy and a loamy clay soil, and is found on hill lands. The tobacco grown on this soil has all the fineness of texture of that grown upon a light sandy soil, and most of the body, and all the elasticity, strength, and sweating qualities, of that grown upon a clayey soil, and will supply more wrappers than if grown on either the light sandy or the heavy clay soils.

Of the tobacco raised in New England, the best crops will make 66 per cent. wrappers, 25 per cent. seconds or binders, and 9 per cent. fillers; but the inferior crops will show a reduced percentage in wrappers, and a corresponding increase in the other two grades.

It is the impression among many dealers and farmers that the quality of the tobacco has deteriorated during the past decade, but of this there is some doubt. Many maintain, with a good show of reason, that the crop is much better managed now than ever before, because buyers exercise more vigilance in the selection of good crops than formerly, and because the houses in which it is cured are better fitted for the purpose. There is a small area, about fifteen miles long and three miles broad, in which are included South Windsor, East Hartford, and Glastonbury, that is pre-eminently distinguished for its fine leaf. The soil is a light yellowish sandy loam, very mellow, made very fertile by the application of manures, moist and warm, and usually deep, but occasionally sandstones of the Triassic period appear above the surface, these sandstones being ferruginous, sometimes micaceous, and often conglomeritic. The fineness of the sedimentary deposits, the variety of the inorganic elements derived from the slates, traps, granitic, feldspathic, and hornblendic rocks that bound the valley, and the excellent drainage, all combine to make a soil perfectly adapted to the growth of the tobacco-plant. For the growing of tobacco a very small percentage of the land is employed; indeed, in a farm of one hundred acres, three or four acres may be considered the average amount planted.

ROTATION.

In the Connecticut valley all the soils cultivated in tobacco have been in careful and skillful tillage from one hundred to two hundred years or more. The rotation practiced in the valley is grass several years, after which succeeds tobacco for a number of years, two or three usually, but frequently four or five, after which the land is again seeded to grass. It is difficult to have any regular rotation, because the local variations in soil characteristics make some of it peculiarly adapted to the growth of tobacco, while other varieties are better suited to the production of hay, or corn, or buckwheat, or are found more profitable in permanent pasturage.

Grown upon rolling lands of the Housatonic valley, tobacco has a much darker and thicker leaf; but upon freshly-cleared lands it grows coarse, and is destitute of gum and elasticity. Probably one-third of the crop grown in this valley is planted on valley lands and the remainder on slopes and tops of ridges.

MANURES AND THEIR APPLICATION.

The original growth of the tobacco area is said to have been white oak, pine, red maple, birch, and chestnut, which would indicate soils of medium strength. In the raising of a tobacco crop especially manures always enter as much into the calculation of the cost of production as the labor employed, from five to ten loads of stable manure being applied to every acre intended for tobacco, and generally from 300 to 500 pounds of superphosphates or Peruvian guano. In the districts around Hartford the following are the kinds and the prices of the various fertilizers, as well as the amount used per acre:

Kinds.	Cost.	Amount applied per acre.
Stable manure	$6 to $8 per cord	5 to 15 cords.
Castor pomace	$22 per ton	When used exclusively, 2 tons; less quantity with other fertilizers.
Peruvian guano	$58 per ton	300 pounds, in connection with 5 cords of stable manure.
Superphosphates	$30 to $40 per ton	300 to 500 pounds, with from 5 to 9 cords of stable manure.
Bone meal	$32 to $40 per ton	Always used with other fertilizers; not a favorite with tobacco-growers.
Fish guano or scrap	Dry $35 to $38; half dry $18 to $20 per ton.	From 1,000 to 2,000 pounds per acre, always applied with other fertilizers; not a favorite manure.
Tobacco stalks	$10 to $14 per ton	When applied exclusively, from 1½ to 4 tons.
Lime	$1 50 to $2 per barrel of three bushels.	Two barrels, with other fertilizers.
Leached ashes	26 cents per bushel	Very popular with tobacco-growers; quantity applied very variable.
Newton marl	$3 to $8 per ton	Two tons; said to make tobacco of superior quality.
Stockbridge tobacco fertilizer		Used by some with good results; 500 pounds per acre.
Sheep manure	$8 to $10 per cord	All that can be obtained.

I. F. C. Allis, of East Whately, Massachusetts, in a letter to John L. Hayes, secretary of the National Board of Wool Manufacturers, says:

The cause for feeding so many sheep for their mutton in this valley is the high value of sheep manure for tobacco-growing, it having the effect on our light soil to produce a dark-colored silky leaf, of good burning quality, suitable for wrapping fine cigars. This tobacco burns white, and has a good sweet flavor, perhaps owing to the potash it derives from the manure. So valuable do we consider this sheep manure, that we have shipped, since 1870, from West Albany, from 50 to 60 cords, costing from $8 to $10 a cord, every spring. On our light soils, called pine lands, after raising crops of tobacco, 2,000 pounds to the acre, we have sown wheat, yielding 30 bushels, plump berry and heavy weight of straw, on land which, without this dressing of manure, is fit only for white beans. We of late years feed with our sweetest and finest hay, and mix with our corn one-third cottonseed meal. By so feeding, our sheep fatten more easily, being more hardy and better conditioned, beside increasing the value of the manure and rendering it more full of plant food.

There is a considerable contrariety of views expressed respecting the effects produced upon the quality of the tobacco by the application of the several fertilizers mentioned. In some of the schedules returned to this office from intelligent growers it is strongly stated that heavy manuring is not only necessary to grow heavy crops, but that in the heaviest crops is found the largest proportion of excellent leaf. Others claim that heavy fertilization, while it adds unquestionably to the quantity produced, yet affects the quality injuriously as to texture, strength, and silkiness. These contradictory statements can only be reconciled by the hypothesis that the soils in either case are radically different in chemical constitution. Says one schedule: "Fish guano makes tobacco heavy, rough, and scaly, with bad burning qualities." Others claim that fish-scrap is an excellent manure. The first statement accords fully with that made by Professor Johnson as to the widespread prejudice existing among tobacco-growers to the use of fish or fish guano on tobacco fields. Of the beneficial effects of Peruvian guano on tobacco soils there is no discordance of views.

In the Housatonic valley the land, whether sod or cultivated in a previous crop of tobacco, is treated to a heavy application of stable manure, running as high as thirty or forty cart-loads to the acre, at a cost of from $50 to $60. Cow-dung is said to have the best effect upon color, horse-dung, though making a good quality of tobacco, inducing lighter colors. Saltpeter also is applied to improve the quality. All fertilizers, except special manures, are spread broadcast over the land, and are plowed or harrowed in; and without their use it would be considered folly to plant a crop of tobacco, as the small size of the leaf and the deficiency in gum and other qualities would make the crop exceedingly unprofitable.

In Fairfield county the yield per acre has decreased considerably, but no cause for such decrease is assigned.

In Litchfield county the yield has slightly increased, owing to better cultivation than formerly and higher manuring. One fact in connection with tobacco culture in this county is significant: the tobacco lands have been enriched at the expense of the corn and grass lands, for all the manure made upon the farm is reserved for the tobacco crop. The hay, corn, and other crops have sadly fallen off in yield, and it is a mooted question whether, on the whole, the county has been benefited in an agricultural point of view by the production of tobacco. The breeding of cattle and sheep, the making of hay and butter, and the growing of wheat and oats, have all declined since tobacco has become a staple; and, though there is more money handled by the farmers than formerly, the farms are not generally kept up to such a high state of cultivation.

It may be remarked, however, in this connection, that the making and saving of manure all through New England is considered one of the most important operations of the farm. Barns are constructed with cellars, in which muck is spread, to collect and preserve the urine of the animals which feed above, and into this cellar are thrown all the droppings of horses and cows, which are worked over again and again by the swine that are permitted free access to the cellars. It being found impossible to make a sufficiency of manure for all the requirements of the farm, it is often imported from New York city at a cost varying from $10 to $15 the cord, a cord weighing about 4,500 pounds. Artificial fertilizers are largely used on the tobacco crop, more with a view of giving it an early start than as a safe reliance for carrying it to maturity. Peruvian guano is applied, as also the superphosphates, in connection with stable manure, which act as a stimulant to the tobacco-plant in its early growth, until its dense roots are able to reach out in tufted masses and appropriate the coarser material of stable and other barn-yard manures.

SEED-BEDS.

Burning as a preparation is rarely practiced, and then only for the purpose of destroying the seeds of weeds and grasses. The methods of growing tobacco-plants are like those given in Chapter XX of this report.

PREPARATION OF THE SOIL FOR TOBACCO.

The soil intended for tobacco is rarely broken in the fall, unless it is a heavy clay loam, which needs the ameliorating effects of freezing to make it crumble well. Upon sandy loams the work of preparation begins in the spring. The land receives a heavy coating of barn-yard manure, and is plowed with a turning-plow to the depth of from 7 to 12 inches. It is cross-plowed in May, harrowed, and smoothed. With a "ridger" beds are thrown up from 36 to 42 inches apart and 6 inches high. These are smoothed off at the top, and with a wheel prepared for the purpose are marked for planting at such distances as may be determined upon, these distances varying from 20 to 24 inches, and sometimes, but not always, hills are made at the points marked on the ridge for the plants. The longer distances given are for Connecticut Seed Leaf, the shorter ones for Havana Seed. When it is desired to supplement the application of stable manure with stimulating fertilizers the land is furrowed out 3 or 3½ feet apart and 300 pounds of guano or 500 pounds of superphosphates are strewn in the furrow. On this two other furrows are thrown, to make a bed, which, after being smoothed off, is marked for hills. The guano or superphosphates are sometimes sown broadcast over the land and harrowed in before it is marked off. The effect of fertilizers upon the crop is tersely expressed in one schedule as the "difference between a crop and no crop".

Dr. Riggs gives an account in the report of the Connecticut board of agriculture for 1871 in reference to the preparation of soil for his tobacco crop. After the tobacco is cut and housed in the fall the land is plowed lightly, and 1¼ bushels of rye are sown to the acre. This gets a good start before winter, and in the spring, when he wishes to plow for tobacco, it is 4 or 5 inches high. He then takes what he calls a "smoothing-iron", 4 feet square, made with 2-inch plank, spiked with railroad spikes to joists 3 by 4 inches, the front end and sides of the implement beveled so as not to carry the earth along with it. Two or three weeks before planting this is drawn over the rye to level it. The soil is fertilized with 300 pounds of guano, which, with the rye, is turned under to the depth of 12 inches. In this condition the land lies until it is nearly time to prepare it for the plants, when he applies about one-third of the quantity of barn-yard manure that would have been put on but for the rye and guano. This manure, with 400 pounds of additional guano, is spread over the land and harrowed in thoroughly. The "smoothing-iron" is then used until the whole field is as smooth as a floor. The land lies in this condition for a few days, until the guano and manure have become absorbed and incorporated into the soil; then the field is marked off into rows, and two furrows are thrown on each mark, making ridges which are 3½ feet apart. Hills are made on the ridges from 22 to 24 inches apart, and are planted after a shower of rain with plants the leaves of which are as large as the palm of the hand. The yield of his crop varied from 2,200 to 2,400 pounds per acre, although he applied two-thirds less stable manure than he would have done but for the rye which he plowed under.

In New Haven county, and probably in other counties, the rows for Connecticut Seed Leaf are sometimes made 4 feet apart, while the plants are set out 2 to 2½ feet in the row, the greater width being rendered necessary in seasons of vigorous growth to prevent breaking the leaves in passing through to destroy the worms and to pull off the suckers. It is also believed that wide spaces are favorable to a more thorough development of the leaves, air and light being necessary to insure a uniform growth and a uniform ripening of all the leaves.

The small area planted in tobacco by each farmer in New England enables him to plant his crop whenever the plants are large enough to transplant. This is done from the 1st to the 20th of June, sometimes earlier, whether timely rains make the ground moist or drying winds exhaust the moisture. In the former case, the plants are set rapidly; in the latter, every hill is moistened by artificial means, and each plant is protected from the scorching rays of the sun at midday by tufts of grass or in some other manner. It is considered very important to get a good "stand" at first planting, so that all the plants may grow evenly; otherwise the fields have a ragged look, some plants being small, while others tower above them. The topping and cutting are also made irregular, the first plants requiring to be topped and cut several days or weeks before those replanted, and in some years fully 25 per cent. of the first planting is cut off and destroyed by cut-worms. The younger or replanted stalks are often topped to a less number of leaves, in order that they may ripen with the first; but in this case there is a disparity in growth, and often a deterioration in the quality. Under very favorable circumstances the transplanting may be continued until July 4. After the plants have been in their places four or five days they begin to grow, when the earth should be loosened about them and the surface of the ground kept soft and fine. At least three plowings and as many hoeings are given the plants before they are ready to be topped, which is within from forty-five to fifty days after they are transplanted.

TOPPING, PRIMING, SUCKERING, AND WORMING TOBACCO.

In reference to topping there is the usual diversity of views. All, however, agree that the plants should be topped as soon as the flower buds generally appear over the field. If the soil has been well pulverized, the blossom bud will not show itself until the plant has developed a large number of leaves; but in dry weather it appears when the plant has comparatively few leaves. In topping on rich soils, from twelve to sixteen leaves are left on each plant, and on the Havana Seed variety a much larger number of leaves is left, sometimes as many as twenty or twenty-five; but on thin soils, or on soils not well manured, in very dry weather, only ten or twelve leaves are left on each plant. It is the experience of all good planters that a larger proportion of good wrappers is obtained by topping low, so that every leaf may become of a uniform size. When too many leaves are left to the stalk the top leaves rarely ever attain their full growth, and all will be deficient in gum and elasticity. No priming is done. Dr. Riggs maintains that "priming", or pulling off a few lower leaves, is a great advantage to the plant. The lower leaves are always classed with the inferior grades, being generally ragged, earth-burned, worm-eaten, and bespattered with dirt or sand. Beside, their presence on the stalk prevents the working of the soil near the plant, which is necessary to obtain the best results. Dr. Riggs' practice, which is a very successful one in results, is to top down to a good healthy leaf, and to top low enough so that the top leaves will attain an equal size with the best of the others. From eight to ten leaves in the most fertile fields, and less in a crop that does not grow so heavily, is the rule of guidance which he lays down. Nevertheless, but few planters adopt this suggestion, and the general average is from twelve to sixteen leaves for Connecticut Seed Leaf, and from sixteen to twenty four for Havana tobacco. The suckers are pulled off as they appear, the best growers rarely permitting them to attain a length of 4 inches. This operation is performed generally twice before cutting, first a week after the plant is topped, and again just before it is cut. A few pull off the suckers once only. The work of destroying the worms is done every day, if possible, as no tobacco is so much injured in quality by worm holes as the cigar wrapper. The moths are caught or beaten down with a wisp of fine brush at evening. A few farmers plow their land in the fall, in the belief that by exposing the worms in their chrysalis state to the frosts of winter they will be killed. The worms are destroyed by hand-picking, and sometimes, but not often, by gangs of turkeys.

After the Connecticut Seed Leaf has been topped from two to three weeks, by a careful inspection of the top surface of the leaf irregular yellow spots, shading off into the general green of the leaf, will be seen. A grainy appearance also becomes visible on the surface, and the leaf becomes somewhat crisp, and will break by doubling. Though not fully ripe, it is in the proper condition to make leaves best suited for wrappers, and to permit it to remain longer in the field would thicken them. Rains at this period injure the leaf by washing away the resinous substances that give it a satin-like face after it is cured and sweated. Heavy dews and cool nights are favorable for the development of these resinous compounds.

When the Connecticut Seed Leaf was first grown in the Connecticut valley it was the custom among farmers to let it ripen fully; but experience has taught them that its highest perfection is reached about the time the upper leaves attain their full size. In other words, the time most propitious for cutting tobacco is when the process of expansion ceases and that of granulation fairly begins. This is not the case, however, with the Havana Seed; for unless this variety is permitted to remain until the sweet gums are secreted the aroma for which it is prized and its glossiness will be lacking, and it will not occupy no higher standard than a small, thin, wrapping leaf, unequal in size and inferior to the Connecticut Seed Leaf. On this account it is allowed to stand for three or four weeks after being topped.

CUTTING AND CURING OF TOBACCO.

The cutting of tobacco usually begins in the second week of August, and continues through that month and often as late as the 10th of September. When planted upon warm, sandy soils, tobacco will mature from one to two weeks earlier than when planted on a clayey loam. While the latter will not mature so rapidly, it has more body and will cure up darker in color—a thing very much desired by the tobacco planters for two or three years past. The time selected for cutting is when the dew is off the leaf and the sun not too hot, from three to six o'clock in the afternoon being considered the best time. If cut when the dew is on, it breaks more easily, and dirt will adhere to the surface of the leaves that come in contact with the ground. A sunburned leaf, it may be well to add, is one whose juices have been dried out, in whole or in part, by the heat of the sun. Although perfectly green in color, it will crumble to the touch, and though it may become pliant, the green of the leaf never disappears if put in the shed. One method only will remedy in part this evil, and that is to let the sunburned plant take the dews for several successive nights.

The instrument employed for cutting is a hatchet, a hay-knife, or a saw, the latter being preferred, because, like the hatchet, it does not jar the plant. The plants are grasped about the center of the stalk with the left hand, and with the saw, hatchet, or knife in the right hand they are severed within an inch or two of the surface and laid back upon the row, and, after they are somewhat wilted, are taken by other hands and speared about 6 inches from the butt on a lath. From four to six plants are put upon each lath, unless they are very small, when a larger number may be put on. For this purpose a "horse" is used, represented in the following cut:

The spear has a socket, by which it can be fastened to the lath; and as fast as the laths are filled they are hung upon a frame on a wagon and are hauled to the curing shed, or, as is the practice with many, are put upon scaffolds in the fields, constructed with carpenters' trestles, as shown in the illustration. If taken to the sheds at once, the doors are left open until the tobacco is thoroughly wilted and the leaves hang perpendicularly. Before the laths are put in place on the tiers in the shed the plants are carefully arranged on them, giving to each plant an equal amount of space. These are then put upon the tiers, 6 or 8 inches apart, filling the top tiers of the shed first, and working downward until the whole shed is filled. The tobacco is carried to the barn on wagons having a frame nearly 4 feet wide, or just wide enough to catch the ends of the laths, and high enough so that when a stick of tobacco is hung on the frame the tails may not touch the bottom of the wagon bed. These laths are 1¼ inches wide and five-eighths of an inch thick. It was a practice, pretty generally followed in the Connecticut valley a few years ago, to tie the plants to poles with twine, these poles being 12 feet long. The plants were tied on alternate sides, from 9 to 12 inches apart on a side, making from twenty-four to thirty-two to the pole, as illustrated.

Some few farmers still adhere to this method of housing, and discard the lath and spear altogether. While it may require a little more time to harvest tobacco in this way, it is asserted that the number of leaves damaged is not so great. It is also said that the amount of tobacco injured from pole sweat is less, as each plant, when tied to the pole, has its distance distinctly marked, and, as the poles are put from a foot to 15 inches apart, currents of air can circulate more freely between them. Hanging in this manner, however, is a very tedious process, and though it may have some advantages over the spear and lath system, the greater care and the longer time demanded, at a period when time is most valuable to the tobacco-grower, has to a considerable extent brought it into disuse.

The character of the sheds or barns has been very greatly improved within the last decade. For a long time tobacco-growers utilized the stock barns, cattle-sheds, and other outhouses for curing tobacco; but much of it was injured by winds and undue exposure in damp, rainy weather, and in other ways. Judicious economy suggested the building of houses for the curing and handling of the crop, the usual size of these houses being 24 feet wide, from three to four tiers high, and as long as the necessities of the crop might demand. To hang an acre of tobacco requires a house 24 feet wide, 30 feet long, and three tiers high, or the same width, 24 feet long, and four tiers high. It is easy to estimate from this the length of the building required to house a crop of tobacco. The distance between tiers varies from 4 to 5 feet.

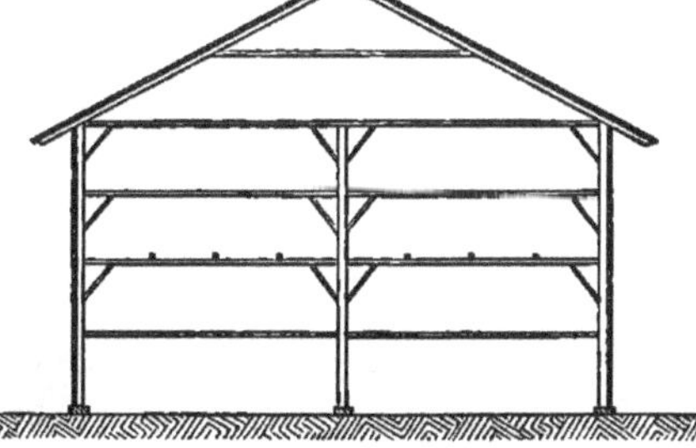

Havana Seed tobacco may be safely housed, with tiers 3½ feet apart, in perpendicular distance. There are two ways of constructing these sheds, one by a series of bents placed 12 feet apart. The accompanying illustration will show the manner in which these bents are constructed.

The posts rest upon low rock pillars, in place of sills, and the lower girders are movable, so that they may be taken out for the passage of a wagon.

A few barns are constructed 36 feet in width; but they are objectionable, from the fact that the middle range is not so well ventilated, and there is greater danger of pole-burn.

Many sheds are two or three hundred feet long, the length being always regulated by the size of the crop.

The poles upon which the tobacco is hung are put from bent to bent. If the tobacco is tied to the poles, a greater number will be required; but if laths are used, seven poles only are necessary between each two girders connecting the posts in a shed 24 feet wide, the lateral girders connecting the bents supplying two others.

The other method of constructing sheds is to frame two or three girders, according to height, into the posts on all sides of the building, the first 5 feet above the ground, the second 9½ feet, and the third 14 feet, the latter on the sides being used also to support the rafters. This gives a space of 4½ feet for each tier, but this distance should probably be increased to 5 feet for very long tobacco. Upon a line of posts along the center of the building, parallel with and 12 feet from the sides, are framed girders, corresponding with those on the sides, for the poles, 12 feet in length, to rest upon, one end on these, and the other on the corresponding girders on the sides. Ventilators are put upon the top of the roof. Better results are said to be obtained by having a monitor roof extending the whole length of the building.

In the case of a monitor roof, the building is raised a foot or more above the ground, and drop-doors are made for the openings below and for the monitor roof above. When these are opened a constant draught of air passes from bottom to top, and the tobacco is cured with a much smaller proportion of house-burn than when perpendicular air-openings are provided.

Cellars to the best sheds are now prepared to be used as stripping-rooms and for bringing and retaining the tobacco in proper condition. Sheds which have recently been erected cost from $300 to $1,000; sticks, $3 per thousand.

The following is the elevation of a model barn or shed for tobacco, erected by G. W. Mitchell, of South Britain, Connecticut. This barn is 60 feet long, 32 feet wide, and 27 feet in height, and holds six tiers of tobacco, beside a small tier in the ridge of the building:

CURING TOBACCO.

The dampness arising from the ground is supposed to exercise a beneficial influence in the curing process, and for this reason many prefer sheds with dirt floors. At every three or four feet vertical doors are made in the sides of the sheds, and these are opened or shut, as the necessities of the tobacco require. The rule governing this matter is that the tobacco shall become damp at least once a week. If the weather is very moist, the doors are closed to prevent pole-sweating; if it is very dry, so as to cure the tobacco too rapidly, the doors are closed and the floors dampened. The periodical dampenings cause the juices to permeate the leaf and insure a uniform color; but if subjected to too much moisture, there is a tendency to mold, and the texture of the leaf is impaired by the excessive absorption of water, which, when it evaporates, carries away the oils that give it softness and silkiness. The most difficult problem in wet weather is how to prevent injury from these sources without the use of fire, the practice being to close the sheds securely and keep out as much moisture as possible.

G. W. Mitchell, of New Haven county, says in relation to the ventilation and curing of tobacco:

The openings should be made at the top of each tier of tobacco horizontally, instead of perpendicularly, as the old style is. The usual method has been to put a pair of strap-hinges at the top of the door, one foot wide, and open at the lower end; but a much better plan is to have the doors open lengthwise of the building, so that the air will pass through between the tiers of tobacco. They should also open at the bottom and have a ventilation at the top, so as to have a circulation from bottom to top. The building should be so constructed as to be shut up tight in very dry or windy weather. Give plenty of air for two or three weeks after it is first housed, then let it cure slowly by closing the doors during the day and opening them at night, so that the tobacco may receive moisture. This will give a uniform color.

Some prefer to keep doors open day and night for two weeks after hanging, that the dampness of the night may better equalize the dryness from day opening only.

The course pursued in curing has been changed to a considerable degree during the past three or four years. When light wrappers were in demand the doors of the sheds were thrown open during the day and closed at night, but since dark wrappers have come into fashion the doors are opened at night and shut during the heat of the day; for it is a generally accepted opinion that light and heat, by accelerating the process, make a leaf light in color. Peruvian guano is thought to favor the making of dark colors, and has been extensively employed in the production of the crop, and gypsum, sprinkled on the plant while growing, will darken the colors. Tobacco, when thick, always cures up a darker color. Thin leaves, very fine and delicate, are always inclined to cure up light colors, and require from ten to twelve weeks for the tobacco to cure fully. The existence of white veins in the leaf occurs under circumstances sometimes seemingly opposite. By some they are believed to be caused by long continued dry weather before and after cutting; by others, as due to any check in the growth of the plant, whether from lack of manure, or cultivation, or drought, or too much water; and some think they are caused by the lack of some organic or inorganic substance in the soil. All that can be said with certainty is that they do occur, very much to the injury of the leaf for wrapping purposes. As a general rule, the product from a field well prepared, well fertilized, and well cultivated, planted in good season, the plants properly topped and kept free of suckers, will show, when cured, very few white stems.

POLE-SWEAT.

Damage from pole-sweat during a favorable season for curing is very small; but the years 1872 and 1878 are memorable among the tobacco-growers of New England from the large amount of tobacco injured in this way. The weather throughout the curing season of those years was damp and foggy, and the buildings, as a general thing, were not constructed so as to have the tobacco under control. The consequence was that a large proportion of the crop was lost, or was so badly damaged that the price was greatly reduced.

The best protection against pole-sweat in wet weather is tight sheds and plenty of room, frequent airing during dry weather, and the sheds closed tightly during long seasons of wet weather. In the Seed Leaf district pole-sweated leaves are thrown away or are used as a fertilizer.

ASSORTING, HANDLING, AND PREPARING TOBACCO FOR MARKET.

When the leaves and stalks are completely cured, so that no green is visible, the tobacco is taken from the laths, and the leaves are stripped off and are either tied into hands of 12 to 20 leaves or bound with twine into bundles weighing from 10 to 40 pounds. In this condition it is delivered to dealers, who pay a certain price agreed upon for the crop through.

Dark tobacco, made so in the curing process, will command, crop through, from 3 to 5 cents per pound more than crops of light color, though the latter may have the same texture, fiber, and length. Local dealers, who buy direct from the farmers, carefully assort the tobacco, classify it, pack, sweat, and sell it to jobbers.

The quality of the crop is determined by the wrappers. If the proportion of wrappers as compared with other grades is large, the price will be correspondingly high, the quality, size, texture, and color of the wrapper determining its price. A large, coarse wrapper is not so desirable as a smaller, but fine one; nor is a fine wrapper of bad color prized as highly as one coarse in texture but of a uniform color. The best wrappers are characterized by fineness of fiber, largeness of leaf, uniformity of color, and a satin finish, are free from white veins, and have an elasticity and strength of leaf sufficient to bear the tension required in wrapping cigars; the seconds are leaves slightly injured, but may be used for the inside wrappers of cigars. Mutilated, worm-eaten, and pole-sweated leaves, and those injured by fat stems, are used for fillers. In a good crop, well cured, there will be about the following proportion of each grade: Wrappers, 60 per cent.; seconds, 28 per cent.; fillers, 12 per cent.

The proportion of long and short wrappers is variable. If the crop is planted at the same time upon land of uniform fertility, there will be only one grade of wrappers; when, however, the crop is planted at different times, or upon soils of unequal fertility, the wrappers are put into two grades. At the time of assorting, the tobacco, unless already tied into hands by the farmers, is made into bundles of from 18 to 24 leaves each and bulked down in two courses, the heads being turned outward and the tails overlapping about 6 inches in the middle, the idea being to expose the heads so that they can dry out. The ends of the bulk are usually protected by boards nailed to upright pieces, as represented in the diagram on page 254. Bulks are made on a temporary platform raised a few inches above the ground, so that the air can circulate under them, are 4 to 5 feet wide, and of any length desired, the layers of tobacco alternating on each side, and are built up to any height desired, usually, however, about 4 feet. Two bundles are laid down, one at a time, heads out, until a course is run on one side of the platform. A similar course is run on the other side, the tails lapping from 4 to 6 inches, to equalize the height in the middle of the bulk. When bulked, the tobacco is in a moist and pliant condition. The completed bulk is covered with blankets and weighted down for a few days, when it is ready to be packed in boxes.

A cord of rich tobacco, well packed and weighted, will make a ton. Sometimes the planter, when he desires to put the tobacco in casks, assorts and ties up in hands of suitable size as fast as the leaves are picked from the stalk, the inferior or filler leaves being taken off first, the binders next, and lastly the wrappers.

Dealers examine the crop very thoroughly before buying, and even when it is growing agents ride from farm to farm to examine the crops in the fields, the culture, size, amount of worm-eaten, rust, regularity or irregularity of the crops being all noted. When the crops are housed, these agents visit the sheds to see that there is no pole-sweated, wind-shaken, or weather-beaten tobacco, and also to examine the uniformity or diversity of the color; and

after the leaves are picked from the stalks there is frequently another examination, to note its condition, so that by the time the crops are ready for market the dealers are as familiar with their quality as the farmers themselves. This vigilance on the part of dealers has had a good effect in stimulating planters to handle their crops with greater care.

It is exceedingly important to have the tobacco in a proper degree of pliability when it is packed; for if too dry, great damage is done to the leaves by breakage. The best wrappers may be reduced to the grade of fillers by handling when dry. On the other hand, too much humidity in the leaf will produce a fermentation so excessive as to destroy the vitality of the tobacco and induce a mold, which imparts to it a disagreeable odor. Good judgment is required in this stage. If bulked in very cold weather, the amount of humidity in the leaf is often greatly under-estimated, and if warm weather supervenes will endanger the tobacco. The plan adopted by the best managers is to see first that the stems or midribs are fully cured; that they do not hold a disproportionate amount of moisture as compared with the leaf. Should the leafy part be very dry and the stem very moist, there is more danger of injury from excessive fermentation than if the conditions of the leaf and midrib were reversed. The proper condition is to have the leaf soft and pliant, and the midrib just sufficiently moist to handle without breaking.

The usual date of delivering tobacco to dealers is from December 1 to April. A very small proportion of the crop is now packed by the planters, and damp days, or at least days in which drying winds do not prevail, are selected for delivering the crop.

For wrappers, the boxes are 3 feet 8 inches long and 28 inches square at the head; for seconds, 3 feet 3 inches long and the same size at the head as for wrappers; for fillers, 3 feet long and 28 inches at the head. These boxes are made of white pine. Boxes for wrappers cost $1 25; for seconds, $1 20; for fillers, $1 10 each. In these boxes the tobacco is packed with heads resting against the ends. The quantity of each grade packed in a box is:

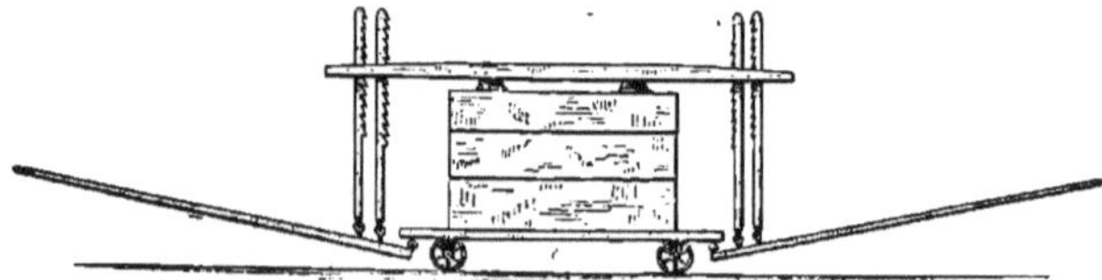

wrappers, 400 pounds; seconds, 350 pounds; fillers, 300 pounds; and it requires some pressure on the tobacco to get the quantity mentioned in the boxes. This pressure is generally applied by a double-lever press with a platform resting upon wheels, so that it can be readily moved to different parts of the building. A yoke crosses the case and works in racks, two on a side, which are attached to the levers. The accompanying cut will give a good idea of this simple press.

About 200 pounds are first packed in a box and pressed down; then the box is again filled and pressed, and this is continued until the requisite number of pounds have been put in each box.

SWEATING TOBACCO.

After being properly packed, the tobacco is ready to go into the "sweat", or fermentation, which begins as the weather grows warm and continues for many weeks, and during this period the tobacco becomes warm, reaching a temperature of 100° F., and sometimes more. All cases are marked with the weight, quality, the name of grower, etc. During the process of sweating the boxes are piled on one another, generally on their sides, but are never exposed to the rays of the sun. A well-plastered or ceiled room is prepared for this purpose, the heat generated being at times so great in the sweating rooms as seriously to affect plastered walls. The process of sweating is to tobacco what fermentation is to wine. It ripens it and prepares it for use. It perfects it in color, improves the flavor, subdues the acrid or pungent taste, increases its burning qualities, and gives it a shining, oily surface, which is called "satin face". All tobacco, however, does not go through this process well, as all wines do not ferment well. Some of it comes out with a lifeless appearance. Whether this is due to the want of essential oils, or arises from the improper condition in which it is packed, is a question not fully determined. Tobacco, like wine, will often go through a second fermentation the ensuing year with an improvement of quality. No artificial means further than "spraying" are used for "ordering" the tobacco before packing. The amount injured by oversweating is small, and will not exceed 1 per cent. The greatest loss is in weight, which amounts to ten or fifteen pounds in a hundred, varying with the lightness or heaviness of the tobacco. After it has gone through the sweat securely, which takes from three to four months, the ends of the boxes are opened, and samples are drawn from different layers in the boxes by inspectors, who, for a fee of 35 or 40 cents per case, varying with localities, guarantee the samples to represent the average quality of the box. A dealer may sample his own goods by giving a guarantee that the samples are a fair average. These samples are labeled and carefully packed in boxes, and all sales are made by them. There are many towns where warehouses are erected and some business is done; indeed, almost every village in the tobacco-growing districts does more or less business in tobacco.

PRICES OF TOBACCO.

The average price of the crop of 1879 in the several counties and districts was as follows: New Haven county, Connecticut, 14 cents; Middlesex, Hartford, and Tolland counties, Connecticut, 16 cents; for the Housatonic valley, 15 cents; Hampden county, Massachusetts, 9 cents; Cheshire county, New Hampshire, 9 cents. For the different grades the following prices prevailed:

Counties.	Wrappers.	Seconds.	Fillers.
	Cents.	*Cents.*	*Cents.*
New Haven, Connecticut	15 to 25	8	5
Middlesex, Hartford, and Tolland, Connecticut	15 to 25	5 to 6	3 to 4
Hampden, Massachusetts	15	8	4
Hampshire, Massachusetts	18	5	5
Cheshire, New Hampshire	13	5	5
Housatonic valley	15 to 25	6 to 8	4 to 5

It will be seen that the average price of the product in Middlesex, Hartford, and Tolland counties is higher than in any other counties in the Connecticut valley, and yet the price of wrappers is no higher than in New Haven county, and for inferior grades hardly equals the upper counties of the valley. This apparent anomaly is, however, of easy explanation. The three counties of which Hartford forms the center have a much larger proportion of fine wrappers, amounting to 66 per cent. of the crop, while the other counties have a larger proportion of inferior grades. This would make the average of the crop in the first district named greater. Beside, in the upper part of the valley, a larger proportion of Havana is raised, the seconds and fillers of which bring a much higher price in the market than the seconds and fillers of the Connecticut Seed Leaf.

As a general thing, the tobacco of the same variety grown in Massachusetts, New Hampshire, and Vermont does not sell as high by 25 per cent. as that grown in the Hartford district.

The prices paid farmers for crop through of Connecticut Seed Leaf in the Housatonic valley from 1870 to 1879 are as follows:

Year.	Worst crops.	Best crops.
	Cents.	*Cents.*
1870	10	30
1871	5	20
1872	5	25
1873	5	12
1874	10	25
1875	5	13
1876	5	15
1877	5	15
1878	5	16
1870	5	20

Havana began to be planted in the Housatonic valley about the year 1875, and the increased inquiry for it in 1877 induced a considerable planting, the farmers who had poor, thin soils finding it to be much more profitable than the Connecticut Seed Leaf; but upon soils of marked fertility, generally, but not always, the latter variety is preferred.

COST OF TOBACCO PRODUCTION.

In the Hartford district, composed of the counties of Middlesex, Hartford, and Tolland, the price of the best tobacco lands will average $200 per acre. The rate of wages during the active farming season, usually from the middle of March to the middle of November, is $15 per month for men; by the day, in summer, from $1 25 to $1 50. At the period when the ravages of the horn-worm are most destructive it is frequently necessary to employ extra hands, and it is always necessary to do so in harvesting. The following estimate of the cost of cultivating, handling, etc., one acre in East Hartford will be found very nearly correct:

Making seed-bed	$2 50
Seed	25
Weeding and attention to plant-bed	1 50
Rent of land (interest on value)	12 00
Stable manure, six cords, at $8	48 00
Three hundred pounds guano, at $56 per ton	8 40
Cost of applying manure	4 00
Plowing land twice	4 00
Harrowing and ridging	3 00
Making hills	1 50
Drawing and setting plants	4 00
Cultivating and hoeing three times, each $3	9 00
Topping, worming, and suckering	15 00
Harvesting	12 00
Taking down, assorting, and stripping	20 00
Bulking	1 00
Use of barn, laths, wagon, etc	12 00
Delivering to market	3 00
Total	161 15

A plan very generally adopted by the planters of the Connecticut valley is to contract to pay 3 cents per pound to the laborer for all the work necessary to be done in cultivating and handling the crop until ready for market, the landlord furnishing land, team, implements, barns, etc., and delivering the crop to market. The use of team, implements, etc., is estimated to be worth 1 cent per pound. The cost of producing a crop of one acre on the basis of this contract is:

Labor for one acre	$60 00
Use of team and implements	20 00
Manure (average amount), six cords, at $8	48 00
Three hundred pounds guano, at $56 per ton	8 40
Use of sheds and laths	12 00
Rent of land (interest on investment)	12 00
Delivering crop to market	3 00
Total	163 40

When twine is used, $1 should be added to the cost. This makes the cost about the same, whether the labor is employed by the pound or in the ordinary way. Both these estimates have been made on the basis of a yield of 2,000 pounds per acre, which is understood to be the yield of the best crops for the best portion of the Connecticut valley. The first estimate makes the cost $8 06 per hundred pounds, and the second $8 17. Assuming the average yield per acre of the Connecticut valley to be as the Tenth Census indicates, 1,620 pounds, the cost per hundred pounds to produce it would be, on the basis of the first estimate, $9 95, and on the basis of the second estimate $10 09. The average value per acre for the whole of New England being $217 19, from which deduct cost, $162 27, would leave a net profit per acre of $54 92.

In the Housatonic valley the cost of raising tobacco does not vary much from the cost in the Connecticut valley. Labor costs from 3 to 3½ cents per pound. The whole expense for an acre of Connecticut Seed Leaf grown in the Housatonic valley is given as follows:

Dr.	
Labor	$60 00
Manure	50 00
Use of land (interest on investment)	12 00
Use of team and tools	20 00
Use of barn and laths	10 00
	152 00

Cr.	
By 2,000 pounds of tobacco, divided as follows:	
1,200 pounds, at 25 cents	$300 00
666 pounds, at 10 cents	66 60
134 pounds, at 5 cents	6 70
	373 30
Deduct cost	152 00
Profit	221 30

Cost to produce, per 100 pounds, $7 60.

The Havana tobacco, though requiring the same amount of expenditure per acre for manure, rent of land, etc., would probably require 16⅔ per cent. more labor to cultivate, in consequence of the increased number of plants to the acre. Connecticut Seed Leaf, set in rows 3½ feet apart and the plants 2½ feet asunder, will give nearly 5,000 plants (4,978 accurately) to the acre. Havana is set in rows 3 feet apart, and the plants at the distance of 2 feet in the rows, which gives 7,260 plants to the acre, or 2,282 plants in excess of an acre planted in Seed Leaf. It involves as much labor to set, worm, sucker, cut, and spear a small plant as a large one, and the estimate of 16⅔ per cent. of labor additional does not appear too great. On this basis the cost of growing Havana tobacco will be as follows:

Dr.	
Labor for one acre	$70 00
Other expenses, as above	92 00
Total cost	162 00

Cr.	
By 1,350 pounds of tobacco, divided as follows:	
810 pounds, at 40 cents (extreme price)	$324 00
450 pounds, at 12 cents (extreme price)	54 00
90 pounds, at 7 cents (extreme price)	6 30
Total value	384 30
Deduct cost	162 00
Profit	222 30

Cost per pound, 12 cents.

Averaging the cost of production per hundred pounds of the two varieties, and it will be $9 80; but in both the estimates of yield the best tobacco soils only are considered. Taking the average yield of the whole valley at 1,328 pounds and the average price at 16 cents, the money value for each acre cultivated would be $212 48, from which deduct the average cost of production, and it would leave an average profit of $82 34 per acre.

It has not been satisfactorily settled which variety is the most profitable to plant on good soils. The Connecticut Seed Leaf always grows well, and the Havana always meets with ready sale, often at prices greatly beyond expectation; but the raising of Connecticut Seed Leaf appears to be accompanied with less uncertainty, the yield per acre and the prices received for the product being more uniform. The average number of acres allowed to a hand is from 2½ to 3.

Good tobacco lands in the Housatonic valley are worth from $50 to $200 per acre, according to the distance from railroads, and sometimes, when convenient to transportation, they will rent for $50 per acre for a single year, the landlord agreeing, however, to furnish the manure for the tobacco crop. Labor commands from $18 to $20 and board per month. From $1 to $1 25 and board is paid for men by the day in summer. Dealers pay for best packers $2 per day, and give 1 cent per pound for assorting tobacco and tying it into hands ready for the packer.

In Hampden county, Massachusetts, the prices of the best tobacco farms are put at $150, $200, and $250 per acre, according to location and improvements on the farm. These lands rent for $50 per acre, or one-half the crop, the landlord in the latter case furnishing everything except labor. Stable manure is worth from $5 to $8 per cord. The wages of labor are from $15 to $18 and board per month. The following estimate of the cost of growing a good crop of tobacco was made by Charles F. Fowler, of Westfield, Hampden county, Massachusetts:

Dr.	
Cost of making seed-bed	$2 00
Weeding and attention to seed-bed	2 00
Rent of land (interest on price)	12 00
Stable manure per acre	60 00
Guano or superphosphates	15 00
Cost of applying fertilizers	12 00
Cost of breaking one acre twice	4 00
Harrowing, lining out, ridging, and hilling	4 00
Drawing and setting out plants	4 50
Cultivating and hoeing	12 00
Topping, worming, and suckering	12 00
Harvesting	15 00
Taking down, assorting, and stripping	25 00
Bulking	2 00
Use of barn, laths, wagon, etc	10 00
Delivering crop to market	3 00
	194 50

Cr.	
2,000 pounds tobacco, at 14 cents	$280 00
Deduct cost	194 50
Net profit	85 50

847

This will make the cost per hundred pounds of Seed Leaf $9 72. Mr. Fowler, who made this estimate, says in conclusion:

This is not intended as an estimate for an average crop, but for a good crop. By the application of less manure, the cost and also the profits would have been reduced.

He further says: "It requires from sixty to seventy days in most favorable weather to cure the crop." This county reports the largest yield per acre for 1879 of any county in the United States, it being a little over 2,127 pounds.

George H. Gaylord, of Hampshire county, Massachusetts, estimates the value of good tobacco farms at $300 per acre; value of stable manure in winter, $8 per cord; in spring, $10 to $12. The wages of labor are $25 per month without board, or $1 25 per day. Contracts are sometimes made to pay a laborer $80 per acre for doing all the work required on a crop of from 2½ to 3 acres of tobacco, or the crop is divided, the landlord being at all expense, except labor. The itemized statement of the cost of producing an acre of tobacco is as follows:

DR.	
Cost of making seed-bed	$0 50
Weeding and attention to seed-bed	3 00
Rent of land (interest on price)	18 00
Stable manure applied per acre	80 00
Cost of applying same	20 00
Cost of breaking land twice	3 00
Harrowing, lining out, ridging, and hilling	3 00
Drawing and setting out plants	5 00
Cultivating and hoeing	10 00
Topping, worming, and suckering	6 00
Harvesting	10 00
Taking down and stripping	8 00
Bulking	1 50
Use of barns, wagon, etc	15 00
Delivering crop to market	2 10
	185 10

CR.	
By 1,700 pounds, at 15 cents	$255 00
Deduct cost	185 10
Net profit	69 90

Cost per pound, 10.9 cents.

It will be observed that in two items, that of making seed-bed and that of taking down and stripping the crop, there is a wide difference in the two estimates. This discrepancy is easily reconciled, for doubtless in the estimate made by Mr. Fowler the land for the seed-bed was burned over, which involved some expense, and this appears further from the fact that in the item for weeding and taking care of the bed the charge is much less in his statement than in that of Mr. Gaylord's, thus making the cost of seed-beds approximately equal. The wide difference in the cost of stripping arises from the fact that in the latter case it was tied up in large bundles without assorting or tying in hands. The other items approximate as closely as could be expected.

In Cheshire county, New Hampshire, $100 per acre is the price for the best tobacco farms. Stable manure costs $1 50 per cart-load, twenty cart-loads making seven cords, or about $4 30 per cord. Labor is worth $20 per month and board. The cost of cultivating and marketing an acre of tobacco, as estimated by George H. Gilbert, of Keene, is as follows:

DR.	
Cost of making seed-bed	$1 00
Cost of seed	25
Weeding and attention	1 00
Rent of land (interest on price)	7 00
Stable manure, per acre	30 00
Guano or superphosphates	12 00
Cost of applying fertilizers	10 00
Cost of breaking an acre twice	5 00
Harrowing, lining out, and hilling	5 00
Drawing and setting out plants	5 00
Cultivation and hoeing	10 00
Topping, worming, and suckering	5 00
Harvesting	10 00
Taking down, assorting, and stripping	8 00
Bulking	4 00
Use of barn, laths, wagon, etc	6 00
Delivering crop to market	4 00
	123 25

Cr.

2,000 pounds at 12 cents	$240 00
Deduct cost	123 25
Net profit	116 75

Cost per pound, 6.16 cents.

Some of the returned schedules put the cost of production at from $10 to $12 50 per hundred pounds, which is probably a little higher than the facts would justify for the Connecticut Seed Leaf. It comes, however, very near the true cost of growing the Havana Seed variety, which yields only from 1,200 to 1,500 pounds to the acre.

Sometimes tobacco is cultivated on the so-called "share system". Those contracts are varied sometimes by the landlord's agreeing to feed the team and to furnish implements, the laborer feeding himself, or paying board in all cases where he works on "halves". The quantity which one man can successfully manage is estimated to be 2½ acres.

In the warehouses the price paid assorters is $2 per day; packers, $1 50 per day, both being classed among skilled laborers. A competent assorter must have an eye for color and a knowledge of grades, which can only come from long experience. The packer should be acquainted with the proper condition in which to pack tobacco, so that it may go through the sweat with safety, and should be able so to dispose the bundles in the boxes that when drawn they may come out straight, with smooth leaves. As a general thing, laborers who know how to manage a tobacco crop successfully command higher wages than ordinary farm hands.

In consequence of the increased skill exercised in the management of the crop, the proportion injured by pole-sweat and excessive sweating is becoming less and less each year, and the last may be said even now to be inappreciable. The former is becoming more rare as the sheds are improved and new methods of ventilation are adopted.

QUALITY OF TOBACCO GROWN.

The quality of the tobacco grown in the Connecticut valley near East Hartford stood for many years without a rival as a wrapper. It is a very handsome, showy tobacco, and is very attractive when new. More recently, however, its light color has reduced its rank; but its fine burning qualities and sweetness of taste, added to its silkiness of leaf, still make it a formidable competitor in the markets.

"New England tobacco," or that grown in Massachusetts, Vermont, and New Hampshire, is heavy, with, comparatively coarse stems and fiber, and is altogether of a lower class when compared with the best Connecticut leaf or the Pennsylvania tobacco. It is deficient in oily substance, and does not sweat to a good rich color.

The points around which the finest Connecticut Valley tobacco grows are East Hartford, Windsor, Suffield, and Warehouse Point. There is a marked difference observed between the tobacco grown on the east and the west sides of the Connecticut river, the former growing a light-colored, fine tobacco; the latter, a tobacco of more substance, but not so delicate in fiber. Sandy soils are more common on the east; clayey soils on the west.

It is generally conceded, both by dealers and by manufacturers, that the finest tobacco for cigar wrappers comes from the Housatonic valley, having all the silkiness of texture and burning qualities of the Connecticut Valley leaf and all the desirableness of color of the Pennsylvania Seed Leaf. In elasticity of leaf, in fineness of face, and richness of color it stands unrivaled, and brings a higher price in the market than any other seed leaf grown in the United States. The tobacco of the Connecticut valley is of fine fiber, has admirable burning qualities, and is of good size, but the color is generally too light to suit the present requirements of the market. The Connecticut Valley tobacco has a delicate, sweetish taste, and burns with a solid, yellowish ash, which presents an oölitic surface, considerably reduced in size from the original cigar. The tobacco grown in the Housatonic valley also leaves a pleasant taste, and burns with a similar ash.

The following statement shows the production, acreage, yield per acre, value of crop in farmers' hands or in primary markets, value per pound, and value per acre, of the tobacco crops of New England for the years 1876 1877, 1878, and 1879, only the figures for the latter year being from census returns:

Year.	Production.	Acreage.	Yield per acre.	Value in primary markets.	Value per pound.	Value per acre.
	Pounds.		*Pounds.*		*Cents.*	
1876	18,709,106	10,834	1,727	$1,904,456	10.50	$181 33
1877	18,458,573	10,650	1,727	2,030,443	11.00	189 07
1878	18,309,175	10,725	1,707	2,059,782	11.25	192 04
1879	19,717,398	12,100	1,616	2,649,982	13.44	217 19

All the tobacco grown in New England does not enter into the commerce of the country, a small portion being taken by local manufacturers, and another small part of it being retained for home consumption. This will account for the discrepancy between the receipts at the principal markets and the returns of the census enumerators.

CHAPTER XX.

GENERAL INFORMATION NOT SPECIALLY GIVEN IN THE REPORTS ON THE CULTURE AND CURING OF TOBACCO IN THE SEVERAL STATES.

SEED-BEDS.

In Virginia, Kentucky, Tennessee, and in other southern tobacco-growing states, the methods of preparation are substantially the same, such variations from the general plan as do exist depending altogether upon local conditions.

The site for a plant-bed most usually preferred is that having a southern or southeastern exposure, that it may have the genial and fructifying warmth of the sun in early spring, so that the plants may be set out before the hot weather of summer. If the bed can be located near a stream, fogs will quicken the germination of the seed and the growth of the plants. Probably the best possible location is on a gently-sloping hill on the north side of a running stream, but sufficiently elevated to be above any danger from overflows. In such situations plants are often two weeks in advance of those in beds prepared on level land. The timber growth may be of any kind that denotes fertility of soil.

In Virginia, Kentucky, and Tennessee a dark-colored, almost a black, soil is preferred, because it is more readily warmed by the rays of the sun, and retains the heat much longer than light-colored soils. For the same reason a slight intermixture of gravel will be of advantage. In North Carolina, although many planters prefer a black soil, free from sand or gravel, the majority of fine-tobacco growers choose a sandy soil, such as that in which the plant is to be grown to maturity.

In Virginia, except where wood for the purpose is scarce, in North Carolina, Kentucky, Tennessee, Missouri, and in many tobacco districts in other states, the practice of burning over the seed-beds is general. The burning is not slight, as in the Connecticut valley, where this appears to be done simply to destroy the seeds of weeds and grass, but the soil is burnt until it shows a reddish tinge. Several methods of burning are practiced. In all cases the wild growth is first cut off with an ax and not dug up. Leaves and trash are carefully raked off from the bed space. If the intention is to burn with logs, skids or poles are laid down four feet apart and a layer of logs and smaller wood, four or five feet wide, is built upon the skids, the object being to keep the wood from resting on the ground, so that the heat may have full play upon the surface of the soil. The fires being set, they are kept burning for two hours or more, when the whole layer is moved forward by hooks, so as to cover another space of the intended seed-bed; and this is kept up until a plat is burned as large as desired. Another method is to lay down brush and bits of wood at one end of the bed space until the pile is five or six feet high. Against this pile brush from tree-tops is placed in a position nearly vertical, inclining against the foundation sufficiently to prevent its falling back on the bed; and this is continued until the full space intended for the plant-bed is covered. A platform of wood is then put on top of the brush, and the fire set on the windward side. Still another plan is sometimes adopted, which saves the hard labor of covering the brush with heavy wood. After a width of eight feet of the bed space has been covered with brush placed in a nearly vertical position, logs or sticks of wood eight feet long are set on end, leaning against the brush. Eight feet more of brush is followed by another layer of wood, and so on until the whole space is covered. When fired the brush burns out quickly, but not before it has set the wood on fire, which, falling all in one direction, covers the whole surface with hotly-burning wood. Old broken rails, thrown aside in resetting fences, and old logs from dilapidated buildings are preferred, because they are thoroughly seasoned and burn freely.

When the bed has cooled off it is generally dug up with grub hoes or worked lightly and closely with a colter plow. The ashes should be left on the bed, and in working the soil it should be reversed as little as possible. All grubs, roots, and large stones should be removed, and the surface soil should be worked several times with hoes or rakes until it is perfectly light and mellow. When in proper condition, marks are made four feet apart to regulate the sowing of the seed. About one large heaping tablespoonful is enough to sow one hundred square yards. The seed is mixed with ashes or plaster, one-half of the mixture being sown as evenly as possible over the entire bed, when the other half is sown in the same way. This is in order to secure a more equal distribution of the seed. The bed is then tramped or rolled, and finally covered with light brush—the smaller branches of dogwood, oak, gum, or sassafras—not thick enough to exclude the sunlight, but sufficient to protect the plants from frosts and the chilling and drying effects of the March winds. The brush also serves to keep the bed moist. Some care is required to put the brush upon the bed properly. The butt ends of the first layer should be laid on the ground outside the bed, the soft brush resting upon the bed, those of the second layer resting upon the bushy part of the first, and so on until the bed is covered by successive layers. In this way the thick, heavy ends, which would interfere seriously with the growth of the young plants, are kept above the surface of the bed. A covering of this kind will protect the plants against very hard freezing. In Wisconsin and in northern Illinois marsh or prairie hay is used, just enough to mitigate the severity of the rays of the sun and prevent the drying of the surface by winds until the plants start to grow, which requires a period of two or three weeks, when the hay is removed.

The covering of brush is generally allowed to remain upon the bed until the plants are nearly large enough to set out, but it may be necessary to remove it temporarily, in order to pick off any leaves or other trash which the winds are apt to drive upon the beds. To prevent the accumulation of leaves upon a bed prepared in or near a forest wicker fences, built of brush interwoven between sticks driven into the ground, have been found very efficient.

Trenches dug across the upper end of the bed and along the sides prevent flood-water from sweeping over the surface. Heavy rains are sometimes very injurious, washing the seeds from a portion of the surface and depositing them in depressions.

It is the usual custom to defer manurial applications until the plants are up and well started. Liquid manures are frequently used at this stage. A tight barrel, half filled with cow dung, is placed near the bed, water is added to fill the barrel, the mixture is stirred until it is a semi-liquid mass, and this is sprinkled on the bed with an old broom. Some prefer a solution of guano, a gallon of this fertilizer being mixed with a barrel of water and sprinkled upon the plants. These applications may be repeated one or more times with decidedly good results. Land plaster has proven to be a good application, giving a deep green color to the plants, indicating vigorous and healthy growth.

A hundred methods are practiced or suggested to prevent the ravages of the flea-beetle, but only one plan has proven really effective—to cover the bed closely with canvas or unbleached cotton cloth. A frame is first made around the bed of planks 8 or 10 inches high, care being taken to close every crevice between the planks and the ground. A few wires may be stretched across, the better to hold up the cloth, which is stretched over the frame and closely tacked upon the edges. In place of the wires, a small quantity of light brush thrown upon the bed will help sustain the weight of the cloth. A better plan would be to construct a number of smaller frames, of proper width and not more than 6 or 8 feet in length, upon which the cloth may be stretched and neatly fastened, a sufficient number of these frames being provided to cover the intended plant-bed. Such frames, with their covering, could be removed when no longer needed and stored for future use. If the cloth is treated with a single coat of white lead and oil, such as is used for the first coat of outside work on wood, it will last several seasons with ordinary care. Still another plan may be found more economical. The frames may be made and properly braced by cross-pieces let in flush with the upper edges of the planks. The cloth or canvas may be some three inches longer and wider than the frames, and hemmed upon the edges, and eyelet holes may be worked along the edges, two feet or less apart, in which cords may be fastened by which to stretch the cloth and tie it down closely over the frames to nails, hooks, or wooden pegs driven into the outer faces of the frame planks, three or four inches below the upper edges. Other devices will suggest themselves to the intelligent farmer, by which he can make the cloth covering effective, easily handled, and economical.

When the plants are nearly large enough to be set out this protecting cover should be taken off in the morning for two or three days and replaced in the afternoon, that the plants may be gradually hardened by exposure to the direct rays of the sun and better fitted for transplanting.

It often happens that a dry season occurs after the first drawing of plants, and those that remain on the bed cease to grow, turn yellow, and perhaps die. One or two planks and a few blocks of wood should be provided. A block on each side of the bed will support a plank, upon which the person drawing the plants should stand. Nothing injures a plant-bed so much as compacting it when wet, and as plants are almost always drawn when the soil is wet no pains should be spared to prevent treading upon or otherwise compressing the bed. If from any cause the plants begin to turn yellow and wither away shade must be provided by building over the bed a low arbor of green boughs and watering the surface copiously. This will almost always give new vitality to the enfeebled plants.

A practice of many good planters is to resow the beds with about half the quantity of seed originally used as soon as the first plants appear, so that if the first plants are destroyed in any manner the seed last sown will be undergoing the process of germination and a second crop of plants will be assured.

In Tennessee and in North Carolina plant-beds may be prepared and sown at any time from the 1st of November until the 1st of April. Prepared while wet or frozen, a plant-bed rarely does well. Beds are usually burned in February or March; but if the burning is done in the fall, when the soil is dry, less fuel is needed, and the prepared bed may be left to the meliorating influences of the winter freezing, to be sown in the early spring. Many good farmers sow the fall-burned beds as soon as prepared, but there is some risk in so doing. Heavy rains and melting snows are apt to wash or drift the seeds, and so disturb their uniform distribution. One of the best tobacco-growers in the South says that a rod of land well burned in the fall will furnish as many good plants as twice the area burned in February or March.

In some parts of Virginia and Maryland, and in districts where wood and brush are scarce, farmers have succeeded in growing good plants upon plats of clean soil without burning by the use of guano, raked into the surface, or as a top-dressing, applied at the time of sowing the seed, about 40 pounds per hundred square yards. Others select a standing bed, one that has produced plants well, in a warm location, neither too wet nor too dry; coulter over the bed after the planting season is past and before any grass or weeds have gone to seed upon the plat; cover with straw, leaves, or brush with the leaves on, or with all of them, so thick as to completely hide the surface and prevent vegetable growth. A bed is thus made ready for burning at some dry time from November to

January, or later, which is done by simply applying a torch. By this method a standing plant-bed can be annually prepared which, if heavily manured, will become better each succeeding year.

In Pennsylvania, New York, the New England states, and in Ohio, burning is rarely practiced, and then only so far as may be thought necessary to destroy weed and grass seeds in the upper surface soil. The same seed-bed is used for successive years, kept clear of grass and weeds throughout the year and heavily enriched by an addition of fresh loam from the woodlands, composts of stable manures thoroughly rotted, and so handled that no foreign seeds capable of germination are left therein, and frequently top-dressings of good commercial fertilizers are used. The most successful growers in Ohio and in New York use manures from the hog-pen, as not only the richest, but as most likely to be free from noxious seeds. In the New England states seed-beds are enriched with guano, castor pomace, well-rotted stable manure, the refuse of the fish-oil factories, or some one of the numerous manufactured fertilizers. In most of the northern states it is a very common practice to sprout the tobacco seed before sowing. The seeds are mixed with dark, rich loam, or, what is better, as in Wisconsin, with finely-pulverized rotten wood from the hollow of an old stump or log, and placed in a pan or dish in a warm place and kept moderately damp by frequent sprinkling with tepid water. The seeds germinate under such conditions in about two weeks, and are sown as soon as danger of frost is passed. Another plan is to spread the seeds very thinly upon a piece of dampened cotton cloth and cover them with another cloth, but of wool; the two are made into a loose roll, the woolen cloth outside. This roll is kept in a warm place, dipped in tepid water every day, and the white germs appear in from four to six days. In northern Illinois similar cloths are kept moist and warm in a pan of earth, of which there is a layer above as well as below the cloths. Great care is necessary in all these forcing processes. Sometimes the soil of the plant-bed is too wet, or otherwise not in proper condition when the seeds are ready, and when a delay of a day or two may render the sprouted seeds useless. The prudent man provides against such danger by preparing several lots of seed at intervals of several days.

The most common error in sowing tobacco seed, both north and south, is in using too much seed. Tobacco seeds are exceedingly small, an ounce containing about 340,000 seeds. One large, well-developed tobacco plant will produce seed enough to grow plants to set 10 acres certainly, and, should all of them germinate and grow, enough to set out 100 acres. Crowded plants must struggle for existence, are never strong and vigorous, and bear transplanting badly; those that have room enough to grow thriftily will have a thick tuft of roots, a low, stocky top, and a vigorous constitution, growing off quickly when transplanted. It is far better economy to increase the size of the bed than to attempt to produce a large number of plants by thick seeding.

A bed of 100 square yards will usually furnish plants enough to set 6 or 7 acres; sometimes a bed of this size will produce enough to set 10 acres. No tobacco-grower ever regrets having a surplus of plants, for in that case he can select the best and set out his whole crop early. On new land very small plants may be set, and at any time immediately after the late frosts without risk. For old lands plants should be a little more advanced than such as can be safely planted upon new lands, but as the season advances larger plants are required for both old and new lands.

INSECT ENEMIES OF THE TOBACCO PLANT.

From the first appearance of the minute seed-leaves in the plant-bed until the tobacco is cut and hung in the barn the patience and watchfulness of the farmer are taxed to guard against the depredations of insects.

Among the earliest to appear, often attacking the plants and destroying them so early as to make the planter doubt whether the seed had even germinated, are the "garden fleas", sometimes called "snow fleas" and "spring-tails" (*Smynthurus hortensis*). When viewed from the upper side (dorsal view), the most conspicuous divisions are a large head and an abdomen perfectly smooth and plump, without any segmental cross-lines. The thorax seems confluent with the abdomen. Beneath are some transverse wrinkles, indicating segmental divisions. The antennæ are three-fourths as long as the body, elbowed about the middle, and are composed of nine joints, six very short and three very long. Projecting from the posterior of the abdomen is a cone-shaped process, composed of three distinctly marked segmental lines, that appear to be a caudal termination of the body. On the lower side of the abdomen, and near its end, is a forked member (a spring-tail), which lies folded up against the under side and reaches as far forward as the head, in which lies its leaping power. Its feet, six in number, are united apparently to the front of the abdomen, which, from a ventral view, exhibits a rudimental sternum, compensating for the absence of the thorax usual in insects. This insect has neither wings nor wing covers, and from a top view might be mistaken for a small, black spider by a novice if he did not know that a spider has eight feet, and that the head and thorax are confluent, instead of the thorax and abdomen. These insects are capable of bearing a low temperature, and are frequently found upon the surface of the snow, from whence comes the name of "snow flea". Tobacco-growers complain of these pests under the name of "black fly", "black spider," etc. Their larval and pupal histories seem to be unknown. They are found in all the states of the Atlantic coast, but have not been observed in the interior. They appear as far north as Lancaster county, Pennsylvania, during the months of May and June, but by the first of July they have disappeared, and nothing more is seen of them until the following spring. As a remedy flour of sulphur has been highly recommended. These insects are very delicate in their structure, and cannot be taken between the fingers without crushing them. As it is evident that the first stages of their development must be passed underground and not far below the surface, it is suggested that where tobacco-beds are not burned the soil be prepared early, thoroughly pulverized, and copiously drenched with scalding water three or four times in as many days before the seed is sown.

From all parts of the United States come reports that the flea-beetle is the most persistent and most dreaded enemy of the young tobacco plants. Several species of these insects are well known to every farmer and gardener from the Gulf of Mexico to Canada. The cabbage flea (*Haltica striolata*) is found in North Carolina and Tennessee in the latter part of March or early in April, sometimes in immense numbers, in the newly-planted cotton-fields, feeding upon the seed-leaves of the young plants. Dr. Rathvon, of Pennsylvania, describes two species of the genus *Epitrix*, family *Halticidæ*, as follows: The *Epitrix cucumeris* is black all over, except the antennæ and the feet. The thorax is thickly punctured, and the wing covers conspicuously striated and punctured between the striæ. The *Epitrix pubescens* is slightly more oblong, and not quite so convexed as the former, but otherwise is about the same size. The whole of the body beneath is of a dull-black color, including also the posterior thighs. The feet, the antennæ (which are slightly serrated along the anterior margin), and the whole of the dorsal or upper part of the body, are of a honey-yellow color, except about a third of the middle portion of the wing covers, which is a dusky black. The thorax is of a much brighter color than the other upper portions of the body, and the eyes are very black, their composite character being more distinct than in the first-named species; and except the thorax, the upper and lower part of the whole body is pubescent. This pubescence is conspicuous in rows between the striæ of the wing covers and along the margins of the abdominal segments. This species is the most troublesome to the young cotton and cabbage plants of the middle southern states. They also attack the seed-leaves of beans and other leguminous plants, but appear to have an especial fondness for tobacco. These insects are about one-sixteenth to one-tenth of an inch in length.

The above-named and other species of the Halticans feed on a variety of plants. The sweet potato, cabbage, beet, turnip, radish, horseradish, common nettle, and the Jamestown weed are all infested by one or the other and often by the same species of this omnivorous family. When disturbed, the flea-beetles leap off the plants and hide themselves quickly in the dry soil or under small clods. Various solutions, poisonous or simply distasteful to these insects, have been used with successful results. Ashes, slaked lime, and soot, dusted upon melon, cucumber, potato, and turnip plants, and applied in the morning, when the dew is on the plants and while the beetles are sluggish, are effectual in most instances. Of various plans to keep them from tobacco-beds probably the only certain protection is to cover the seed-bed with cloth, as suggested heretofore.

Transplanted into the field, the tobacco plant is exposed to the attacks of other insects. The greasy cut-worm usually cuts off the plant just beneath the surface of the soil without cutting the top at all. When these worms are disturbed, they immediately coil themselves into a ring. They do not like the sunlight, and during the day bury themselves in the lower soil in the vicinity of the plant. When grown, they are from $1\frac{1}{4}$ to $1\frac{1}{2}$ inches long. They bury themselves beneath the soil to pupate. The pupa is three-fourths of an inch in length, of a shining or glossy light-brown color, and the anterior margin of the segments is dark brown. The anal segment is armed with two very small spines or points, by the assistance of which it pushes itself toward the surface about the time the moth is evolved. This moth is commonly called the Lance Rustic, from the dark-brown, lance-shaped spots on the anterior wings, which are a light brown in color. The hind wings are lustrous and whitish in color, with a grayish margin. The antennæ of the females are filamental or thread-like; but in the male, along the inner margin near the base, they are more or less pectinated. The body of the largest specimens is three-fourths of an inch in length, and the wings expand $1\frac{5}{8}$ inches from tip to tip. Cut-worms are largely preyed upon by hymenopterous and other parasites, and there is no better or safer remedy than hand-picking while they are yet in the larval state, discriminating in favor of the parasites when seen and known. Toads, lizards, snakes, and moles are all very useful in keeping these worms in check, and should be protected, excepting, of course, poisonous snakes. The cut-worms, in various stages of development, may be found in the earth during the entire winter, too torpid to feed until the return of warm weather. This accounts for their appearance and their advanced physical condition so early in the season. When cut-worms exist in large numbers, as in grass or clover sod or in fields not cleanly cultivated, fall or winter plowings, to expose as much as possible the upper soil to the severe freezings of midwinter, are absolutely necessary to secure a good stand of tobacco; but no matter how hard the frosts, nor how often the ground is plowed, some of the worms will survive, making daily inspection of the newly-planted field indispensable for an even stand of plants.

Wire-worms do not attack the leaf, but bore into the stems of the plants at the surface of the ground and work their way upward. After the tobacco gets a fair start in growth nothing is seen of these worms for the remainder of the season. They are the larvæ of "click-beetles", or "hammer-bugs" (*Elateridæ*). These worms are sometimes very numerous. In April and early in May, sometimes as late as the first of June, some of these species are very destructive in the corn-fields, especially upon lands which have been lying out for some years; but they are rarely troublesome in well-cultivated fields.

In Ohio, Pennsylvania, and perhaps farther northward, the *Heliothis armigera* (the southern boll-worm, or corn-worm) is sometimes found feeding upon the seed-leaves of young tobacco plants, but south of 35° these worms are rarely known to attack tobacco plants, since they find more appropriate food in abundance.

Some of the schedules returned state that in the earlier stages of growth in the field tobacco plants have been attacked by the *Epilachna borealis* (northern lady bird). This insect is shaped like the common "box turtle", is of a lemon-yellow color, spotted all over with black, and when caught in the hand emits a few drops of a clear yellow fluid of unpleasant odor. It is nearly as large as the Colorado potato beetle, but rather more hemispherical, and the larva, pupa, and *imago* are often found together on the same plant. They are usually found upon pumpkin, melon, and cucumber vines. The larva is a short, convexed slug, of a uniform bright yellow color, covered all over with short, bristly hairs, and has a pair of very black eyes. It undergoes all its transformations on the plants it infests, and the pupa is suspended by the adhesion of the caudal extremity. This species and several others of the same family hibernate beneath the rough outer bark of the wild cherry, and sometimes upon the apple trees in neglected orchards. These insects, as well as some others hereafter mentioned, are rarely found upon tobacco plants except near trees or shrubbery or close to fences.

Tree crickets (*Œcanthus niveus*) are often found upon tobacco plants in Tennessee, North Carolina, and other southern tobacco regions in July and August, and in Pennsylvania and farther north in August. Though usually found on trees, these crickets show a decided partiality for tobacco, perforating the tender top leaves about the time they are expanding. It does not kill the leaf nor arrest its growth, but the holes increase in size. Although these holes are circular when first made, they become oblong as the leaves lengthen, and always in the longitudinal direction of the leaf. These crickets, when young, either leap away or hide among the leaves when approached, but after their wings are fully developed they can both leap and fly to a considerable distance. The male tree cricket is nearly white, sometimes tinged with green; the wings lie flat on the back, one lapped over on the other; the legs are all long and slender, the posterior pair much the longest, and formed for leaping; the antennæ are very long and thread-like, and are generally thrown backward when the animal is at rest. The female is more robust and shorter in the body; the wings are short and deflexed, and her color is various shades of green and brown. Her legs and antennæ are also shorter than those of the male, and at the end of the abdomen she is provided with a sword-like ovipositor. She perforates the raspberry and blackberry canes, as well as the tender branches of other shrubbery, with this instrument, and deposits her eggs therein, where they remain all winter and hatch in the spring. Tobacco cultivators have noticed that these insects are most abundant on tobacco growing under or near trees. Clean culture, and the clearing up of fence corners and neglected spots about the tobacco fields, will do much to prevent injury by crickets.

Various species of grasshoppers, especially the meadow grasshopper (*Orchilemum vulgare*), sometimes feed upon the tobacco plant, eating the leaves of the newly-set plants while in a wilted condition, but the injury from this source is slight, and rarely occurs with any but late plantings.

Several species of hemipterous insects puncture tobacco plants. These insects are true bugs, and are not provided with mandibular organs. They do not eat the plant nor cut holes in it, but are provided with a sharp proboscis, with which they pierce the plant and suck out its juices. One of these, the *Phytocoris linearis*, is a small gray insect about a quarter of an inch long, having generally a conspicuous yellowish V-shaped mark on the back, occupying that part called the scutellum. This bug is found upon the potato, and has been observed in Tennessee upon parsnip, tomato, and late cabbage plants. The *Euschistus puncticeps* is a much larger insect than that last described, and is capable of greater injury. It belongs to the family *Scutellaridæ*, distinguished by a triangular lobe that extends from the base of the thorax downward on the wing covers. This insect is half an inch long and three-eighths of an inch across at the broadest part. Above, it is of a yellowish color, and closely punctured darkly, giving it a grayish hue; below, it is a light greenish yellow. It has a longer and more slender proboscis than the species that prey upon other insects; otherwise it might easily be confounded with them, and no doubt frequently is. It also lacks the thoracic spines; but these are very variable in their development, and not always a safe distinguishing characteristic. These bugs are found on mulleins, thistles, and other weeds, and have also been found upon tobacco plants in several localities, feeding upon the sap of the leaves, but it is doubtful whether any great injury can be charged to their account. The ordinary observer is apt to mistake the purpose for which many insects visit various plants. The spined tree-bug (*Podisus spinosus*), the large tree-bug (*Podisus cynicus*), the *Stiretrus diana* (a plant bug of a purple-black color, with red or orange marks on the thorax and scutellum), and the *Stiretrus fimbriatus*, the ground colors of which are orange or yellow, with black markings, are sometimes found upon or in the immediate neighborhood of tobacco plants. These bugs should not be destroyed, unless upon careful examination they are found actually feeding upon the juices of the leaves, as it is more than probable that their presence is beneficial, rather than injurious.

From the early part of June until the sharp frosts destroy their food in the fall the larvæ of the sphinx moths infest the tobacco. In Virginia, Maryland, Kentucky, Tennessee, and Missouri both the *Sphinx carolina* and the *Sphinx quinquemaculata* are found, and they are both reported as found in the tobacco-fields as far north as latitude 41° 30′. South of latitude 35° only the *S. carolina* has been observed. The larvæ of these two *Sphingidæ* are so well known to all tobacco-growers as to need no description here. They have always been regarded as the most inveterate enemies of the tobacco plant, and, despite plans adopted for their destruction, the horn-worms seem to be as numerous as ever. In some seasons there are comparatively few in certain localities, but it has been noticed that the fields of such districts are often visited late in July or August of the next year by a "heavy shower" of horn-worms

Comparative immunity for one season too often causes the farmer to neglect the destruction of the late brood of worms left upon the suckers which spring up after the crop is harvested, large numbers pupating and hibernating, protected by the forgotten and neglected trash of the tobacco-field. Catching the moths with ingeniously-contrived traps, poisoning them with sweetened cobalt dropped into the bloom of the Jamestown weed, or killing them with paddles as they hover about the tobacco plants after sunset, are all practiced. Recently, as in Tennessee, porcelain imitations of the blossom of the Jamestown weed have been introduced. These are fastened upon sticks, set up at short distances apart throughout the tobacco-field, and are supplied with a few drops of poisoned sirup. They are cheap, will last with ordinary care a lifetime, and are highly recommended by planters who have used them. A knowledge of the transformations of these insects will enable the observant farmer to do much to reduce their numbers, and if it were possible to secure prompt measures throughout a considerable section of country, or even by the growers of a large neighborhood, much disagreeable labor might be saved.

The moth deposits an egg of a sea-green color, not larger than a mustard-seed, upon the surface of the leaf. This egg gradually assumes a cream color, and from it, in due time, a tiny worm issues, not larger than a horse-hair, and about one-eighth of an inch in length. The process of hatching embraces from twenty-four to thirty-six hours, depending upon the condition of the weather. The worm begins to eat immediately, making first a small hole in the leaf, through which it passes in hot weather to the under side, and occasionally the eggs are there deposited by the moth. This worm, though voracious, does little damage for four or five days. Its power of destruction increases exceedingly with each day, and this makes it highly important to go over the field often in search of them.

When the horn-worm has attained full size it stops eating, comes down from the plant, and usually burrows into the ground close to its last feeding-place, but not unfrequently crawls away some distance to find soil sufficiently soft to enable it to get some inches below the surface. Here it becomes quiescent, casts off its larva skin, and assumes its pupal form. It is now oval in shape, four times as long as it is thick, about 1¾ inches in length, and the hard, glossy envelope is of a bright chestnut color. The forward end is prolonged into a long, tube-like appendage, bent backward and firmly attached to the chest, forming a loop like a pitcher-handle, this tube ensheathing the tongue, which is so remarkably developed in the perfect moth. Only under peculiar circumstances are these pupæ found at a greater depth than may be reached by deep plowing. A further means of reducing the number of these insects is therefore by fall or winter plowing the tobacco-fields. It must be said, however, that even if every egg, worm, moth, and chrysalid in a given neighborhood were destroyed, high winds, or even the lighter breezes of the summer evenings, bring other moths many miles. The tobacco-grower should instruct those in his employ not to destroy any horn-worm found with the cocoons of the parasite *Microgaster congregata* attached to its body. These cocoons are white, of a regular oval form, a little more than an eighth of an inch long and about one-sixteenth of an inch broad, and resemble small grains of rice. From ten to a hundred of these cocoons are found upon a single horn-worm. The worm so infested may be removed from the tobacco plant, but should be handled carefully and placed where the cocoons may not be injured, so that the parasites may hatch undisturbed. The flies which issue from the cocoons are black, with clear, transparent wings and legs of a bright tawny color, the hue of beeswax, with the hind feet and the tips of the hind shanks dusky.

The testimony of all tobacco-growers points to the one conclusion about insect enemies. No methods of prevention or destruction can justify a single day's neglect to search for and destroy cut-worms about newly-set plants and the eggs and larvæ of the sphinx moth upon the expanded leaves throughout the season.

DISEASES OF THE TOBACCO PLANT.

The tobacco plant is subject to certain diseases, few in number, however, and rarely resulting in very serious damage. Unfavorable seasons, too wet or too dry, often reduce the yield and impair the value of the product; but diseases, properly so called, seldom affect more than a few plants, or perhaps a small portion of a field. Schedules returned from widely-separated districts mention the same diseases, all of which result from deficiencies in the soil or its preparation, or from peculiarities of the seasons during growth.

A disease known in New England as "brown rust", and in the South as "firing" and "field-fire", prevails to some extent every year. It appears in very wet or very dry weather, and reports concur in the opinion that it is caused by violent changes from one extreme to the other. A plethoric plant with the supply of moisture suddenly cut off, and a lean plant forced by excessive moisture to rank growth—a leaf perishing in spots for lack of sustenance, and another from the opposite cause—present variable conditions, developing "rust" or "fire". This disease is not so prevalent in some districts as formerly, which is attributed by some planters to the substitution of new for old varieties; but it is more probably due to planting upon a different character of soil, or to more thorough drainage and improved culture. Sometimes, though rarely, the entire plant is involved, drooping and withering through excessive humidity. This is the "black fire", a strictly wet-weather disease. In dry weather the plant sometimes parches up, as if scorched. In uniform, ordinary seasons it does not appear. Injudicious use of heating manures is assigned as sometimes the cause of firing, and undoubtedly does occasionally produce "red" or dry-weather firing. Thorough drainage is regarded as the best preventive of this and its kindred diseases.

"Frenching", derived from the French *friser* (to curl), occurs almost exclusively upon cold, stiff uplands, having a close and stiff clay subsoil. During a wet season it is very prevalent upon clayey lands, and is sometimes found upon sandy soils in small basins during excessively rainy weather. This disease renders the plant worthless when it has progressed to any considerable extent. The effects are first seen in the buds of the plant, which become of a yellow color. The leaves afterward become thick and fleshy, have a semi-transparent or honey-colored appearance, and often curl around the edges downward, sometimes growing in long, narrow strips, with ragged outlines. When cured, the leaves are dull and lifeless in color, and very brittle. No remedy for the disease has been found. It is sometimes arrested by close plowing, or by giving the plant a vigorous pull, so as to break the tap root, but the only preventive measure is to avoid planting upon a soil not properly underdrained, either naturally or artificially.

"Walloon", or "water-loon", is of very common occurrence, and is closely akin to "frenching". The leaves, instead of curving over in graceful outlines, stick up like a fox's ears, whence the disease is known in some sections of the country as "fox-ears". When tobacco is thus attacked it becomes rough and thick, and is unfitted for any but the most inferior purposes. Excessive tenacity of the soil or defective drainage are causes of the disease.

"Hollow stalk" and "sore shin" rarely occur, except when the plants have been overflowed, and then mostly upon old lands. Some planters attribute "hollow stalk" to an insect feeding upon the pith of the lower stalk, or to the after effects of an attack by the wire-worm upon the young plant; others think it the effect of a bruise or a wound upon the stem of the young plant. The two names above given are descriptive of different appearances of the same disease. It is most probably produced by excessive absorption of water by the pith of the stalk while partially submerged and subsequent exposure to a high degree of temperature. It is not reported as occurring upon such lands as are never flooded by rain water, nor has it been observed upon soils well underdrained or overlying a porous subsoil. There is no remedy for it, and unless the plants are cut as soon as it appears they become worthless. The affected plant presents very much the same appearance as if nearly severed from the stalk, withering slowly without ripening.

"Frog-eye", or "white speck", sometimes occurs in tobacco thoroughly ripe. This disease, if it is such, is of rare occurrence, and is little understood. In Florida white specks are a sure indication of fine texture in the leaf, and this "frog-eye" appearance was at one time much esteemed. This particular marking seems to result from conditions of soil or climate, or from both, and some varieties are more frequently affected than others.

"White veins" occur in the cured product. By some they are believed to be caused by long-continued dry weather before and after cutting; by others they are ascribed to any check in the growth of the plant, whether for lack of manures, from deficient cultivation, drought, bad seed, or too much water. Some think they are caused by the absence of some soil constituent. All that can be said is that they do occur, very much to the injury of the leaf for wrapping purposes. As a general rule, the product from a field well prepared, well fertilized, and well cultivated, planted in good season, properly topped, and kept free of suckers, will show, when cured, very few white veins.

"Leprosy" is a name given to a fungoid mold which is occasionally found upon cured tobacco hanging in the barn during warm, moist winters. This mold affected a large portion of the crop of 1880 in the Ohio River valley, especially in southern Illinois, and in the lower Ohio River districts of Kentucky. This fungous plant increases with amazing rapidity wherever the spores find congenial lodgment, and even sound, dry tobacco is sometimes infected and seriously damaged. This disease, although not a new one, is imperfectly understood. Appearing to a serious extent only in weather congenial to its development, and propagated from spores which have escaped detection in badly-kept barns or tobacco-sheds, too many planters look upon it as of obscure or doubtful origin, or as an inevitable concomitant of unfavorable atmospheric conditions. The remedy is prevention. Thorough cleansing of the tobacco-barns, stripping, assorting, and packing rooms, and the careful destruction, by burning, of all the trash and dirt which accumulate about the premises, will secure well-handled tobacco against "leprosy", and perhaps other diseases of fungous origin.

TOBACCO STRIPS.

The making of strips, although a distinct branch of business, rarely, if ever, carried on by tobacco growers, is regarded as a part of the necessary preparation of the leaf when designed for shipment to English markets. This stemming process is employed almost altogether upon the heavier types of tobacco, so that the leaf, deprived of the midrib or stem, may be shipped in a dry condition. The tax in England on tobacco is 3*s*. 6*d*., about 84 cents, per pound. On a hogshead of tobacco weighing 1,000 pounds net a tax of $840 must be paid to the government. Assuming the tobacco to cost 15 cents per pound, the value of the hogshead, tax paid, would be $990, or 99 cents per pound. If it should have the capacity to absorb 15 per cent. of water, the profit from this would be $148 50. Tobacco selected for strips should therefore be porous and a "deep drinker". The greater its capacity for absorbing water, other things being equal, the larger the profit. Recently the government of Great Britain has taken cognizance of this source of profit, and now requires a duty of 3*s*. 10*d*., about 92 cents, to be paid on all tobacco containing less than 10 pounds of water to the 100 pounds.

Details of the manner of purchasing tobacco for stemming purposes, the types used, and the method of assorting, preparing, and putting up strips for export, will be found in the special reports upon the states of Indiana, Kentucky, and Virginia.

Of the crop of 1879 there were put up during the fall and spring of 1879-'80, as nearly as can be ascertained, 17,315 hogsheads of strips; or, assuming the average net weight at 1,200 pounds per hogshead, 20,778,000 pounds, requiring about 31,000,000 pounds of leaf.

The estimated make of strips from the crops of 1876 to 1879, inclusive, were as follows:

Year.	Section.	Hogsheads.
1876......	Virginia....................	3,500
	The West....................	26,000
1877......	Virginia....................	7,500
	The West....................	33,000
1878......	Virginia....................	6,000
	The West....................	10,000
1879......	Virginia....................	4,300
	The West....................	13,015

Of the strips made in 1879-'80 there were put up at—

	Hogsheads.	Pounds.
Richmond, Lynchburg, Petersburg, and Farmville, Virginia..	4,300	5,160,000
Henderson and Owensboro', Kentucky	5,575	} 12,240,000
Louisville, Russellville, and Paducah, Kentucky............	2,000	
Minor points..	2,625	
Evansville, Booneville, Corydon, Indiana, and other points	1,425	1,710,000
Clarksville, Paris, Springfield, and Nashville, Tennessee	1,290	1,548,000
Cairo, Illinois..	100	120,000

A small quantity of White Burley strips was put up on the Ohio river below Cincinnati as an experiment; also about 500 cases of seed-leaf at Miamisburg, Ohio.

The preparation of strips for export is a business of considerable importance in a few cities and towns, as in Henderson, Owensboro', and Louisville, Kentucky; Richmond and Lynchburg, Virginia; Clarksville and Paris, Tennessee, and Booneville, Indiana. In these places a large capital is invested in warehouses and the necessary appliances for handling large quantities of tobacco. This branch of industry can, however, be successfully and profitably managed on a small scale, and there seems to be an increasing disposition to carry it on in close proximity to the districts which produce the types best fitted for the purpose. The saving in cost of handling, transportation, etc., of over 30 per cent. of weight has assumed more importance since there is no longer a profitable market for the stems and other waste of the factories.

CONCLUSION.

The tobacco plant exhibits a facility for adapting itself to diverse conditions, rivaling that of Indian corn, and excelling that of the potato. All three are plants thriving best upon soils rich in the salts of potassium. In all sections of the Union any well-drained soil capable of producing Indian corn will produce tobacco, the latter exhibiting, however, much more strongly marked diversity of characteristic qualities, as affected by variations of soils and of climatic conditions.

The best types of fine tobacco in the southern states are grown upon soils poorly supplied with vegetable matter and are poor in albumen, although sufficiently rich in nicotine, while the best types of the northern tobacco districts are grown upon lands purposely enriched with nitrogenous manures, to promote rapid growth and early maturity, and are also poor in albumen, burning freely without disagreeable odor, and are at the same time fairly supplied with nicotine. That these similar results should follow unlike conditions of fertility of soil can be attributed alone to difference of climate.

The special reports herewith submitted present another apparent anomaly. In the southern tobacco-growing sections the use of commercial fertilizers, while generally increasing the yield of pounds, has not resulted in an improvement of quality; and, *per contra*, in the northern states these fertilizers have almost always bettered the quality of the product.

Both north and south, on the Atlantic border and in the far interior, the surest reliance for an increased yield is the free use of composted or well-rotted farm-yard and stable manures, and these are almost invariably accompanied by a parallel improvement in quality.

It is asserted, with some show of reason, that the color of the cured leaf is correlative to the color of the soil upon which the plant is grown; and it is certain that upon dark-colored soils, and especially upon those containing a large proportion of clay, the stronger, heavier, and darker types are produced. Although the seed-leaf varieties grow finer and make a really superior quality of tobacco upon sandy soils, fashion has dictated that darker colors are most desirable for cigar wrappers, and the colors most in demand are grown upon argillaceous and calcareous loams. The fine yellow types of North Carolina and Virginia are grown upon light-colored arenaceous soils.

Tobacco culture, perhaps more conspicuously than any other kind of farming, exhibits the condition of agricultural progress in the regions in which the staple is produced. The revenue tax has had the effect of discriminating in favor of good tobacco, has really been an incentive to the production of finer types and better grades, and has induced better cultivation and more careful management. Progressive enterprise in tobacco growing has had most beneficial effects upon other agricultural pursuits. The tobacco-field usually occupies but a few acres upon the farm, and in most cases gets a large share, if not all, of the manures saved at home. It is upon these limited areas, in all parts of the country, that the most carefully-conducted and best authenticated experiments have been made with commercial fertilizers. Wherever tobacco culture has been made profitable, there has been an increase of all farm products suited to the locality.

In the preparation of these reports the object has been to furnish abundant information as to the geological position, the lithological constitution, and the geographical location of all soils which have been found specially adapted to certain classes and types of tobacco.

Chapter XXI.

REPORT ON THE CHEMISTRY OF AMERICAN TOBACCOS, BY GIDEON E. MOORE, Ph. D.

Tobacco in commercial form represents the products of vegetable growth more or less changed by fermentative or putrefactive processes. The peculiarities of the different varieties are, therefore, of twofold origin, being due, first, to the diverse conditions of soil, climate, and mode of cultivation; and, second, to the effects of the processes of curing to which the harvested leaf has been subjected. While, therefore, it is permissible to trace out the relations between the nature and the relative amounts of the constituents of the finished commercial product and the properties upon which the technical application and commercial rank of the latter depend, the question of the influence of the diverse conditions, under which the cultivation of the different varieties has been effected, on the quality of the finished product, can only be decided from the results of the chemical examination when due regard is had to the modifying effects on the composition of the product, exerted by the processes of curing to which it has been subjected. These last consist either in simply drying the leaf by exposure either to the heat of the sun or to more or less carefully regulated artificial heat, in which case fermentative change is either avoided or reduced to a minimum; or they consist in a more or less perfect fermentation preliminary to, or simultaneous with, the operation of drying, and in this case result in essential modifications in the composition of the leaf and degree of adaptability to the different applications for which it is designed. The process of curing, however conducted, is only then regarded as complete and the tobacco fit for market after the leaf has undergone a supplemental process of fermentation, technically known as "sweating". This sweating occurs during the spring or summer following the curing proper. It is attended with elevation of temperature to 120° F., and results in essential modifications in the flavor and combustibility of the tobacco, and necessarily also in its chemical composition.

CONSTITUENTS OF THE TOBACCO LEAF.

The constituents hitherto detected in the leaf of the tobacco plant are as follows, viz:

NICOTINE ($C_{10}H_{14}N_2$).—A volatile oily substance, possessing a strong, acrid, tobacco odor. It is a powerful base, and forms well characterized compounds (salts), with the stronger acids. It is to this substance that the narcotic and toxical properties of tobacco are chiefly to be ascribed, especially when the leaf is chewed or the decoction is administered internally. When the tobacco is smoked, the nicotine is partly decomposed, and its decomposition products, together with those of the other constituents of the leaf, co-operate with the nicotine that sublimes unaltered to produce the physiological effects of the smoke.

Nicotine is present at a very early stage in the development of the tobacco plant. According to Nessler (*Der Tabak, seine Bestandtheile und seine Behandlung:* Mannheim, 1867, p. 12) it is present in the ribs and parenchyma of the leaves of the young plant when the leaves are only 1½ to 2 inches long. The following determinations by Nessler show the proportions present in leaves of different degrees of maturity:

	Percentage of nicotine in the *fresh substance.*	Percentage of nicotine in the *dry substance.*
1. Ribs of leaves 2 to 2¼ inches in length	0.164	1.636
2. Parenchyma of leaves 2 to 2¼ inches in length	0.379	2.840
3. Parenchyma of leaves 10¼ inches wide and 16 inches long	0.600	5.680
4. Parenchyma of leaves 3¼ inches wide and 8¼ inches long	0.225	1.496

The leaves marked No. 4 were the upper leaves from the same stalk that furnished the leaves marked No 3.

The foregoing results would show that the relative proportion of the nicotine increases with the age and development of the leaves. According to the same author, although the green leaves contain more nicotine than the fermented leaves, the nicotine odor is not perceptible in the former; it appears only after fermentation.

NICOTIANINE.—A volatile substance, of the consistence and appearance of camphor, possessing the odor of tobacco, and an acrid, aromatic, and bitter taste. According to the analysis of Barral (PELOUZE ET FRÉMY: *Traité de Chimie*, T. iv, p. 633), it possesses a composition in accordance with the formula $C_{23}H_{32}N_2O_3$. It is chemically an indifferent substance, forming no compounds with acids or alkalies, and is supposed to be the substance to which the characteristic odor and flavor of tobacco are chiefly due.

RESINOUS AND FATTY SUBSTANCES.—Tobacco contains a considerable proportion of resinous and fatty substances, concerning the nature of which as yet little is known. That the odor of the smoke is greatly influenced by these substances is more than probable, and this would appear to be especially true as regards the question of their resinous or fatty nature. The finely flavored tobaccos of Havana and Porto Rico are, according to Nessler (*op. cit.*, p. 29), richer in such substances than many European tobaccos, the smoke of which is strongly charged with the odor of burning fat, whence he infers that in the first named varieties the resinous substances are present in excess of the fats.

STARCH ($C_{36}H_{62}O_{31}$).—All tobaccos contain starch, usually in small proportions, although under certain conditions, as in the experiments of Schloesing (*Comptes-Rendus*, lxix, 253), the amount may rise to over 10 per cent. of the weight of the dry leaves.

SUGAR (glucose, $C_6H_{12}O_6$) is also present in the fresh (green) plant, usually in small proportions. When the tobacco is fermented in the operation of curing, the sugar usually disappears.

NITROGENOUS SUBSTANCES GENERALLY (ALBUMINOIDS).—Beside nicotine and nicotianine tobacco contains a large proportion of nitrogenous organic substances. Vauquelin (*Annales de Chimie*, lxxi, 139) found vegetable albumen in green tobacco, and his observations were confirmed by the investigations of Goupil (*Comptes-Rendus*, July, 1846, No. 1), made under the direction of Frémy, and by the analysis of Posselt and Reimann (*Pharm. Centralbl.*, 1847, 171). Tobacco that has become yellow or brown on drying, no longer contains the albuminous substance above noted. The nitrogenous substances extracted from harvested and dried tobacco are brown, and are to be regarded as the products of the more or less advanced alteration of the albuminous substances originally present in the green leaf. These brown nitrogenous substances approach closely in their properties to the (so-called) ulmic acid (PELOUZE ET FRÉMY, *op. cit.*, iv, 636).

PECTIC ACID ($C_{16}H_{22}O_{15}$, Frémy) occurs in varying proportions in tobacco, and gives strength and stiffness to the leaf. It has been generally assumed to exist in the tobacco in the state of calcium pectate.

CITRIC ACID ($C_6H_8O_7$), MALIC ACID ($C_4H_6O_5$) AND OXALIC ACID ($C_2H_2O_4$).—These acids are always present in tobacco, the first two in large, the last in small proportions. They exert a very important effect on the quality of the leaf.

ACETIC ACID ($C_2H_4O_2$) is present in varying, and usually small, proportions, and is either wholly or at least for the most part a product of fermentation.

NITRIC ACID (HNO_3) is present in certain cases in considerable quantity. According to Nessler (*op. cit.*, pp. 22 and 28) the presence of this substance in tobacco is to be ascribed, either wholly or in part, to the decomposition of other nitrogenous substances by fermentation with free access of air (nitrification). Reasons will be hereafter given which would appear to justify the opinion that this conclusion of Nessler's is erroneous, and that the nitric acid in tobacco has entered the plant through the processes of nutrition (absorption by the roots) during the period of its growth.

AMMONIA (H_3N) is present in all tobaccos, usually in small proportions. It is evidently a product of fermentative change. Nessler (*op. cit.*, p. 19) asserts that it does not occur in fresh (green) tobacco, and it is found to be evolved in large quantities during the fermentation of snuff. (PELOUZE ET FRÉMY, T. iv, pp. 654 *et seq.*)

CELLULOSE (CRUDE FIBER).—This material constitutes the frame-work or skeleton of the cellular tissue as distinct from the cell-contents. According to the proportion in which it is present, it bears a most important relation to the character of the leaf, as regards the texture, and, in the case of smoking tobaccos, the combustibility and general quality. According to Frémy (PELOUZE ET FRÉMY, T. iv, p. 647) the proportion is usually from 6 to 11 per cent. It is greatest in fine tobaccos of close texture and least in coarse tobaccos of thick tissue. According to Nessler (*op. cit.*, p. 29), the quality of tobacco (for smoking) improves to a certain extent as the proportion of woody fiber increases and that of the soluble organic (extractive) substances diminishes.

ORGANIC SUBSTANCES OF UNDETERMINED CHARACTER.—In addition to the substances previously enumerated, tobacco contains certain other substances, the nature of which has not been investigated. Among these are substances of a gummy consistence and indefinite chemical character, substances similar in properties to the humus substances, possibly also the decomposition products of tannin, which latter substance, while often present in the green leaf, is present only in faint traces in some of the less perfectly cured samples.

MINERAL INGREDIENTS (ASH).—The leaves of the tobacco plant are exceedingly rich in mineral ingredients, and the amount and nature of these is of essential influence on the quality of the material.

DISTRIBUTION OF THE DIFFERENT CONSTITUENTS IN THE PLANT.

From the investigations heretofore made concerning the distribution of the different constituents, it would appear that they are very unequally distributed throughout the different organs of the tobacco plant.

The results of Nessler have, as already stated, shown that nicotine is present in larger quantity in the substance of the leaves than in the ribs. Buchner (*Buchner's Repertorium*, xxxii, 38) found it in abundance in the seeds of the plant. In the leaves from plants grown under different conditions of soil, climate, and mode of cultivation, the percentage of nicotine varies greatly, as will be seen from the following analyses by Schloesing (*Ann. Chim. Phys.* [3] xix, 230):

PROPORTION OF NICOTINE IN LEAF TOBACCO, COMPUTED ON THE LEAF, DRIED AT 100° C.

Variety or source.	Percentage of nicotine.
Havana	2.00
Virginia	6.87
Kentucky	6.09
Maryland	2.29
Cigars (French, at 15 centimes)	2.00
Department Lot (French)	7.96
Department Lot-et-Garonne (French)	7.34
Department Nord (French)	6.58
Department Ille-et-Vilaine (French)	6.29
Department Pas-de-Calais (French)	4.94
Alsatia	3.21
Snuff	2.04

The amount of nicotine varies in different samples even among those from the same locality, and is influenced greatly by the character of the fermentation which the tobacco has undergone, as well as the length of time it has been kept, and the degree of exposure to which it has been subjected.

Nitric acid is very unequally distributed in the plant, being, as will be seen from the following table by Schloesing, (*Ann. Chim. Phys.* xl, 479), much more abundant in the midrib than in the substance of the leaf.

PROPORTION OF NITRIC ACID IN TOBACCO, COMPUTED ON THE LEAF, DRIED AT 100° C.

	Percentage of nitric acid in the leaf deprived of the midrib.	Percentage of nitric acid in the midrib.
FRANCE:		
Department Nord	1.49	5.00
Department Pas-de-Calais	1.74	5.99
Department Ille-et-Vilaine	0.48	2.10
Department Lot	0.60	2.08
Department Lot-et-Garonne	0.90	1.98
Alsatia	0.23	0.46
ALGIERS:		
Algérie des colons	0.74	6.10
Algérie des Arabes	0.14	1.04
EUROPE:		
Holland	2.00	5.12
Hungary (Szegedin)	0.39	3.11
Hungary (Debreczyn)	0.02	0.43
Macedonia	0.02	0.25
EXOTIC:		
Maryland	0.09	0.74
Kentucky	0.97	5.67
Havana	0.14	0.72
Brazil	0.08	1.80
Paraguay	1.80	4.70
Java	0.02	0.15

According to Schloesing, the percentage of nitric acid in the midrib diminishes as the latter contracts on approaching the apex of the leaf. The small lateral ribs contain nearly the same amount as the substance of the leaf. By the fermentation of tobacco, as in the manufacture of snuff, the percentage of nitric acid remains unchanged.

Pectic acid is contained in larger proportions in the ribs than in the substance of the leaves.

The mineral ingredients are distributed unequally in the different parts of the plant, as will be seen from the following table (PELOUZE ET FRÉMY, T. iv, p. 637):

PROPORTION OF ASH IN TOBACCO, DRIED AT 100° C.

	Per cent.
Leaves and ribs	17 to 24
Stalks	6 to 16
Roots	5 to 14

ANALYSES OF CERTAIN OF THE PRINCIPAL VARIETIES OF AMERICAN TOBACCO.

In Tables I, II, and III are given the results obtained in my analyses of samples of some of the principal varieties of American tobacco.

With the exception of No. 35, which was furnished by the producer, the samples were furnished by Colonel J. B. Killebrew, special agent for the investigation of the details of the cultivation and curing of tobacco. The samples were numbered and labeled as follows:

No. 3. Virginia tobacco. Sun-cured; for manufacturing plug tobacco.

No. 5. Virginia tobacco. Fire-cured; for the German and continental trade. Low grade.

No. 7. Tennessee tobacco. From Clarksville. Fire-cured; for the German and English markets. Gummy. Grown on rich, heavy loam, heavily manured.

No. 19. Kentucky tobacco (White Burley). From the Mason county district. Air-cured (in sheds, without artificial heat); for cutting or plug tobacco.

No. 10. North Carolina Yellow tobacco (Bright Wrapper). From Granville county. Grown on white or light gray sand.

No. 28. Louisiana tobacco. "Perique, cured in its juices." (Leaf deprived of midrib.)

No. 37. Louisiana tobacco. "Perique," air-cured. (Leaf deprived of midrib.)

No. 35. Connecticut Seed-Leaf. From New Milford. Grown on rich loamy soil, heavily manured. This sample was freshly cured, and had not undergone the "sweating" process.

No. 30. Connecticut Seed-Leaf. From Hartford, Connecticut. Grown on sandy soil.

No. 34. Pennsylvania Seed-Leaf. From Manor township, Lancaster county. Grown on a clearing, being the second crop after removing the timber. Eighty bushels of lime were used to the acre, but no manure.

No. 16. Ohio Seed-Leaf.

No. 22. New York State Seed-Leaf.

No. 25. Wisconsin and Illinois Seed-Leaf.

The details of the modes of curing and cultivation of these samples are fully set forth in the report of Colonel Killebrew. It is, however, desirable in this place to briefly recapitulate the leading features of the treatment to which the plants have been subjected, in so far as may be necessary for the correct interpretation of the results of the analyses.

Apart from the difference in character of the soil, the differences in the mode of cultivation between the different varieties relate chiefly to the length of time the plant is allowed to remain in the field after the "top" has been removed. As soon as the leaf ceases to expand, and the "granulation" due to the distension of the individual cells of the leaf through accumulation of intercellular substance begins, which, in good soil, and with favorable weather, will take place in from two to three weeks after "topping", the seed-leaf varieties are cut. The heavier tobaccos are, on the other hand, allowed to remain from four to six weeks before cutting, or, in the case of heavy shipping leaf (samples Nos. 5 and 7) until fully ripe and ready to decay.

Concerning the modes of curing: Sample No. 3 was cured by simple exposure to the sun on scaffolds. Samples Nos. 5 and 7 were cured by open wood fires in close barns, the heat being kept at or below 90° F. (32.2° C.) for two days, after which it was allowed to rise to 125° F. (51.6° C.) and then to 150° F. (65.5° C.), the last heat being continued for twenty-four hours, and the operation being complete in about four days and nights. No. 10 was cured by a very carefully regulated heat in close barns; the temperature being maintained for thirty-six hours at 90° F. (32.2° C.), and then carefully and systematically raised to 170° F. (76.6° C.), at which it remained for ten hours, the operation being complete in sixty to sixty-five hours, open coal fires or flues being used. Samples Nos. 19 and 37 and the seed-leaf samples (Nos. 35, 30, 34, 16, 22, and 25) were cured without artificial heat in sheds, ventilated by doors which are left open during the day, except in very damp weather, and closed at night.

From the foregoing it is evident that the samples Nos. 3, 5, 7, and 10 were cured with very little or no fermentation, whereas the other samples must have suffered considerable fermentative change. The process of curing, to which the sample No. 28 (Perique cured in its juices) was subjected, involves a very thorough and prolonged fermentation, with periodical applications of pressure, which last would tend to express the juices of the leaf from the cells and insure an exceedingly thorough and uniform fermentative process.

METHODS OF ANALYSIS EMPLOYED.

In preparing the samples for analysis, the leaves were exposed to the air at ordinary temperatures until thoroughly dry, the whole leaf, inclusive of the midrib, except Nos. 28 and 37, ground to fine powder and preserved in tightly stoppered glass bottles. The different determinations were then made on the air-dried leaf by the methods given below, and the results reduced to percentages in the substance, dry at 100° C.

1. MOISTURE.—Five grammes were dried for two hours in the air-bath at 100° C.

2. NICOTINE was determined in ten grammes by the method of Schloesing, as described by Grandeau (*Handbuch für Agricultur-chemische Analyse:* Berlin, 1879, p. 194), namely, by exhaustion with ether after making the sample strongly alkaline with ammonia, evaporation of the ether and titration of the residue with deci-normal sulphuric acid.

3. PECTIC ACID was also determined by the method of Schloesing, as described by Grandeau.

4. STARCH was determined in the residue from which the pectine substances had been removed by inversion to glucose by the method of Sachs (*Corr. Blatt d. Vereins analytischer Chemiker*, ii, 15, 21, and 25, and *Jour. Am. Chem. Soc.*, i, 546) and gravimetrical determination of the glucose with Fehling's solution, as described in the case of sugar.

5. SUGAR.—Ten grammes of tobacco were exhausted with 85 per cent. alcohol, the extract evaporated to remove the alcohol, the residue dissolved in water and made up to 500 cubic centimeters. One hundred cubic centimeters of the solution were then measured off, treated with excess of basic lead acetate, filtered, and the filtrate and washings of the precipitate brought to the volume of 200 cubic centimeters. The solution was then made alkaline with sodium carbonate, treated with a moderate excess of Fehling's solution and heated for twenty-five minutes to a temperature of 75° C. to 80° C. The cuprous oxide was then collected on a weighed filter and the equivalent of the precipitate in glucose calculated from the results of check determinations made under the same conditions with inverted cane sugar. A second portion of the original solution was then subjected to the process of inversion, after precipitation with lead acetate and treated as above with identical results—showing that no cane sugar was present.

6. NITRIC ACID was determined by exhausting the tobacco with 85 per cent. alcohol, evaporation of the extract, re-solution in water, and then proceeding by the method of Schultze (*Zeitschrift f. anal. Chemie*, 1870, 401); the error (a slight loss) incident to the method as originally described being compensated for by the addition to the solution under examination of a measured quantity of solution of sodium nitrate of known strength, the volume of gas yielded by the latter being deducted from the total volume obtained in the analysis. The graduated tube containing the soda solution was also caused to dip into mercury during the evolution of the gas, to prevent loss by the "churning up" of the gas with the liquid, and the attendant escape of small bubbles from the tube.

7. CITRIC, MALIC, OXALIC, AND ACETIC ACIDS were determined substantially by the methods of Schloesing, as described by Grandeau.

8. TOTAL NITROGEN was determined by the method of Dumas, and corrected by the results of "blank" combustions made under precisely similar conditions with pure sugar. In the case of the tobaccos which contained no nitric acid duplicate nitrogen determinations were made by the soda-lime method, with closely accordant results.

9. AMMONIA was separated from nicotine, and determined by the excellent method of Nessler (*op. cit.*, p. 144), namely, the ammonia was liberated with freshly ignited pure magnesia, distilled into dilute sulphuric acid, the solution carefully neutralized with sodium carbonate, and the nicotine precipitated with mercurio-potassic iodide. The liquid was then filtered, filtrate and washings treated with an excess of sodium mono-sulphide, the ammonia redistilled into deci-normal sulphuric acid, and the amount determined by titration.

10. RESINOUS AND FATTY SUBSTANCES.—The tobacco was exhausted, first with ether, then with absolute alcohol, the solutions evaporated to dryness, the residue digested with dilute sulphuric acid, thoroughly washed with water, dried at 100° C., and weighed.

11. CELLULOSE (CRUDE FIBER).—The determinations were made by the method described by Wolff. (*Chem. Untersuchung landwirthschaftl. Stoffe*, [3te *Aufl.*]: Berlin, 1875, p. 175.)

12. ALBUMINOIDS.—The figures under this heading were obtained by multiplying by 6.25 the residue left on deducting from the total nitrogen the nitrogen contained in the nicotine, ammonia, and nitric acid.

13. MINERAL INGREDIENTS.—The total percentage of mineral ingredients (ash) was determined by the method of Schloesing, as described by Grandeau (*op. cit.*, p. 6). The sample (10 grammes) was gently heated in a platinum boat in a porcelain tube, through which a slow current of carbonic acid was conveyed, until combustible gases ceased to be evolved. The combustion was then finished in a very slow current of oxygen, the tube being kept below a visible red heat during the whole experiment. The ash thus obtained was of about the same consistence as that of a cigar, no sign of fusion or "fritting" being observable, and was perfectly free from unburned carbon.

14. ASH ANALYSES.—The ash analyses, the results of which are given in Table II, were made substantially by the admirable method of Bunsen (*Annalen der Oenologie*, i, 3. See also Thorpe, *Ann. d. Chemie*, cxlix, 163). The phosphoric acid was separated from the insoluble ash by tin, as recommended by Bunsen, but the tin precipitate was not further treated for the determination of the phosphoric acid, as the latter was directly determined by the molybdate method of Finkener (*Berichte d. deutsch. Chem. Gesellsch.*, xi, 1638), in the second portion of the insoluble ash. The separations of potassium and sodium were made in duplicate, both by the platinic chloride and the indirect (chlorine) methods.

ANALYSES OF AMERICAN TOBACCOS.

TABLE I.—PERCENTAGE COMPOSITION OF TOBACCOS, DRIED AT 100° C.

Number of sample.	Variety.	Nicotine.	Resin and fatty substances.	Starch.	Glucose.	Albuminoids (N × 6.25).	Pectic acid (anhydride).	Citric acid (anhydride).	Malic acid (anhydride).	Oxalic acid (anhydride).	Acetic acid (anhydride).	Nitric acid (anhydride).	Ammonia.	Cellulose (crude fiber).	Sand.	Ash, exclusive of sand and carbonic acid.	Undetermined.	Total.
3	Virginia; sun-cured; for manufacturing plug tobacco.	3.26	4.15	5.80	6.80	16.00	6.10	2.12	5.02	0.84	0.42	0.00	0.30	9.58	0.55	12.41	26.26	100.00
5	Virginia; fired-cured; for the German and continental trade; low grade.	4.30	4.05	2.75	2.75	13.06	7.46	2.84	7.58	1.03	0.55	0.00	0.32	8.24	2.38	13.36	27.18	100.00
7	Tennessee, Clarksville; fire-cured; gummy; for the German and English markets; soil: heavy, rich loam.	5.20	4.90	3.54	0.00	16.54	6.01	2.09	5.51	1.30	0.30	1.55	0.98	9.68	2.25	14.37	24.61	100.00
10	Kentucky, Mason county; air-cured; for cutting or plug tobacco.	3.12	5.34	4.45	0.00	15.08	7.49	4.05	0.26	2.18	0.64	0.00	0.48	12.19	0.66	16.06	18.11	100.00
10	North Carolina, Granville county; bright wrapper; grown on white or light gray sand.	2.70	5.73	6.71	16.30	8.75	5.97	0.48	7.41	0.46	0.53	0.00	0.10	9.13	1.26	8.49	25.85	100.00
28	Louisiana "Perique" tobacco; "cured in its juices."	4.32	6.28	2.45	0.00	15.80	6.60	1.18	3.94	3.40	1.02	0.00	0.76	9.08	4.17	13.30	26.85	100.00
37	Louisiana "Perique" tobacco; air-cured.	4.25	7.26	2.70	0.00	16.50	7.43	4.31	7.00	2.06	0.28	1.65	1.65	8.80	0.76	15.54	10.32	100.00
35	Connecticut Seed-Leaf, New Milford; soil: rich loam.	4.06	4.29	3.22	0.00	18.09	8.26	5.80	10.09	0.02	0.31	3.23	0.65	10.61	1.34	15.10	16.00	100.00
30	Connecticut Seed-Leaf, Hartford; sandy soil	1.14	2.98	3.14	0.00	17.33	11.24	4.95	5.04	0.95	0.48	2.39	0.62	15.23	1.48	18.50	14.58	100.00
34	Pennsylvania Seed-Leaf; Lancaster county.	1.04	4.02	3.67	0.00	14.62	12.50	1.61	5.46	0.04	0.57	0.00	0.22	15.12	1.64	17.98	20.12	100.00
16	Ohio Seed-Leaf............................	1.92	3.67	3.19	0.00	15.80	7.46	3.46	6.58	1.42	0.42	3.41	0.92	12.67	1.85	14.22	23.11	100.00
22	New York State Seed-Leaf..................	2.35	3.02	2.63	0.00	10.20	9.88	4.42	8.27	1.11	0.41	2.29	1.20	12.15	1.94	15.50	18.56	100.00
25	Wisconsin and Illinois Seed-Leaf..........	0.86	3.28	4.15	0.09	20.34	11.61	2.00	9.99	1.07	0.68	1.22	0.63	12.97	1.53	15.43	16.36	100.00

TABLE II.—ASH ANALYSES.

Number of sample.	Variety.	Total ash.	Ash, exclusive of sand and carbonic anhydride.	Potash.	Soda.	Lime.	Magnesia.	Ferric oxide.	Alumina.	Manganous oxide.	Phosphoric anhydride.	Sulphuric anhydride.	Silicic anhydride.	Chlorine.
3	Virginia; sun-cured; for manufacturing plug tobacco.	14.29	12.41	34.16	0.26	31.76	7.91	0.58	1.22	0.00	3.61	4.98	1.39	13.92
5	Virginia; fire-cured; for the German and continental trade; low grade.	17.42	13.36	26.55	0.22	36.96	11.51	0.65	1.61	0.00	3.23	4.27	8.20	11.21
7	Tennessee, Clarksville; fire-cured; gummy; for the German and English markets; soil: heavy, rich loam.	19.28	14.37	33.15	0.15	36.48	11.65	0.51	0.05	0.25	4.42	6.16	3.43	2.66
19	Kentucky, Mason county; air-cured; for cutting or plug tobacco.	21.85	16.00	30.51	0.86	39.60	5.34	1.66	0.51	0.13	6.09	4.52	1.20	0.46
10	North Carolina, Granville county; bright wrapper; grown on white or light gray sand.	11.19	8.49	41.56	0.47	28.12	9.78	0.80	0.20	0.11	5.23	4.53	2.75	6.57
37	Louisiana "Perique" tobacco; air-cured (leaf deprived of midrib).	19.82	15.54	30.23	0.25	37.47	12.43	1.10	0.72	0.29	6.18	6.19	1.61	3.14
35	Connecticut Seed-Leaf, New Milford; soil: rich loam.	21.06	16.30	35.08	0.01	40.38	11.83	1.47	0.74	0.13	3.20	4.08	1.39	2.19
30	Connecticut Seed-Leaf, Hartford; sandy soil..	22.92	18.56	41.30	0.26	28.70	7.56	2.13	0.83	0.00	3.26	3.34	1.00	11.58
34	Pennsylvania Seed-Leaf; Lancaster county....	24.74	17.98	40.60	0.36	28.55	8.18	1.30	1.05	0.00	5.72	2.61	1.65	1.49
16	Ohio Seed-Leaf...............................	10.05	14.22	33.87	0.27	34.69	17.32	1.07	0.93	trace	4.20	3.48	3.07	1.51
22	New York State Seed-Leaf.....................	21.12	15.50	33.13	0.39	30.26	8.60	0.74	0.56	0.16	3.61	3.78	3.67	6.10
25	Wisconsin and Illinois Seed-Leaf.............	20.81	15.43	38.71	1.08	33.49	12.57	0.79	0.74	trace	3.09	3.89	4.65	0.09

TABLE III.—PROPORTION OF MINERAL INGREDIENTS, TOTAL NITROGEN, AND POTASSIUM CARBONATE, IN 100 PARTS OF THE LEAF, DRIED AT 100° C.

No. of sample.	Variety.	Potash.	Soda.	Lime.	Magnesia.	Ferric oxide.	Alumina.	Manganous oxide.	Phosphoric anhydride.	Sulphuric anhydride.	Silicic anhydride.	Chlorine.	Total mineral ingredients.	Nitrogen.	Potassium carbonate.
3	Virginia; sun-cured; for manufacturing plug tobacco.	4.24	0.04	3.94	0.98	0.07	0.15	0.00	0.47	0.82	0.17	1.73	12.41	3.41	1.87
5	Virginia; fire-cured; for the German and continental trade; low grade.	3.85	0.03	4.94	1.54	0.12	0 .24	0.00	0.43	0.57	0.44	1.60	13.36	3.21	1.41
7	Tennessee, Clarksville; fire-cured; gummy; for the German and English markets; soil: rich, heavy loam.	4.77	0.02	5.24	1.71	0.07	0.14	0.02	0.64	0.80	0.49	0.38	14.37	4.77	4.76
10	Kentucky, Mason county; air-cured; for cutting or plug tobacco.	6.34	0.14	6.38	0.86	0.25	0.08	0.02	0.96	0.73	0.19	0.08	16.06	3.49	8.25
10	North Carolina, Granville county; bright wrapper; grown on white or light gray sand.	3.53	0.04	2.39	0.83	0.05	0.03	0.01	0.44	0.38	0.23	0.56	8.49	2.03	4.21
37	Louisiana "Perique" tobacco; air-cured (leaf deprived of midrib).	4.71	0.04	5.82	1.93	0.18	0.11	0.04	0.96	0.96	0.30	0.49	15.54	5.10	4.39
35	Connecticut Seed-Leaf, New Milford; soil: rich loam.	5.30	trace	6.10	1.71	0.22	0.11	0.02	0.48	0.62	0.21	0.33	15.10	4.97	8.08
30	Connecticut Seed-Leaf, Hartford; sandy soil....	7.06	0.05	5.33	1.40	0.40	0.15	0.90	0.61	0.62	0.20	2.14	18.56	4.10	8.06
34	Pennsylvania Seed-Leaf; Lancaster county.....	8.02	0.06	6.13	1.47	0.25	0.19	0.00	1.08	0.47	0.19	0.27	17.98	2.70	11.91
16	Ohio Seed-Leaf..................................	4.75	0.04	4.93	2.46	0.15	0.13	trace	0.61	0.43	0.44	0.22	14.22	4.42	5.83
22	New York State Seed-Leaf.......................	5.13	0.06	6.96	1.33	0.11	0.08	0.02	0.56	0.39	0.57	0.95	15.50	4.59	4.86
25	Wisconsin and Illinois Seed-Leaf................	5.97	0.17	5.17	1.94	0.12	0.11	trace	0.48	0.60	0.72	0.15	15.42	4.23	7.83

PERCENTAGE OF NICOTINE IN THE PRINCIPAL VARIETIES OF AMERICAN TOBACCO.

In the following table are given the results of my determinations of nicotine on samples of the principal varieties of American tobaccos. In each case the air-dried leaves (including the midrib) were finely ground, and a careful average sample taken. The nicotine was determined on the air-dried sample by the method of Schloesing, and the percentage of moisture in a separate portion by drying at 100° C. The results are stated in percentages on the sample dried at 100° C.:

	Percentage of nicotine.
Virginia (heavily manured lots)........	5.81
Mexican Dalor (heavily manured lots)........	5.60
Clarksville, Tennessee (heavily manured lots)........	5.29
Virginia (French Régie)........	4.81
Virginia (heavy English shipping)........	4.72
North Carolina Yellow ($50)........	4.58
German Saucer (Kentucky)........	4.55
Perique, cured in its juices (stripped from midrib)........	4.32
German, low grade (Virginia)........	4.30
Perique, air-cured (stripped from midrib)........	4.25
West Tennessee Stemmer........	4.23
German (dark)........	4.14
New York (Wilson's hybrid)........	4.14
Connecticut Seed-Leaf (New Milford)........	4.06
French Régie, A........	3.90
Pennsylvania Seed-Leaf........	3.88
Wisconsin Havana Seed........	3.82
Connecticut Seed-Leaf (Hartford)........	3.49
Pennsylvania Seed-Leaf (Lancaster county)........	3.47
Virginia sun-cured, for plug........	3.27
Perique air-cured (whole leaf)........	3.25
North Carolina Yellow ($65)........	3.15
Mason county, cutting or plug........	3.12
Ballard county, Kentucky, bright wrapper........	2.92
Owen county, Kentucky, plug fillers........	2.80
North Carolina bright wrapper........	2.60
Hart county, Kentucky, bright wrapper........	2.54
New York domestic Havana........	2.53
Florida Seed-Leaf........	2.38
New York State Seed-Leaf........	2.35
Connecticut Havana Seed........	2.21
Owen county, Kentucky, cutting leaf........	2.19
Ohio Seed-Leaf........	1.93
Sweet-scented Wisconsin and Illinois........	1.33
Connecticut Seed-Leaf........	1.14
Pennsylvania Seed-Leaf........	1.02
Wisconsin and Illinois Seed-Leaf........	0.86
Little Dutch (Miami valley)........	0.63

ABSORPTIVE CAPACITIES OF CERTAIN VARIETIES OF AMERICAN TOBACCO.

The capacity of leaf tobacco to absorb and retain different flavoring substances added in the form of "sauces" is a matter of great importance to the manufacturer, and especially to the foreign importer of American tobaccos. In the following table I have given the coefficients of absorption of some of the principal varieties used for the manufacture of chewing tobacco. These coefficients give the amount of water which each type will absorb and retain without dripping, expressed in multiples of the weight of the air-dried leaf; they do not, of course, represent the actual amount of water that a given sample will absorb and retain when subjected to the usual operations of manufacture. It may be safely assumed, however, that the results obtained in practice will stand to each other in a relation that will not vary greatly from that indicated by the theoretical coefficients of absorption, and the latter may, therefore, serve as a sufficient basis for classification and comparison.

The coefficients of absorption were determined as follows: The air-dried leaf was carefully weighed, moistened with water until it had become pliable, then loosely coiled on the bottom of a beaker and water enough added to completely cover it. The whole was then left at rest for 48 hours. The leaf was then taken out, suspended over the beaker until it had ceased to drip, and weighed. The liquid in the beaker was then evaporated to dryness on the water-bath, the residual extract dried at 100 C°., and weighed. The coefficient of absorption was determined from these data by the equation

$$\frac{a+b-c}{c}=x$$

wherein a is the weight of the wet leaf, b the weight of the dry extract, c the weight of the dry leaf, and x the coefficient of absorption. The results were as follows, viz:

	Coefficient of absorption.
German, low grade (Virginia)	2.88
North Carolina bright wrapper	2.77
North Carolina Yellow ($65)	2.65
Owen county, Kentucky, cutting leaf	2.60
Owen county, Kentucky, plug fillers	2.55
Hart county, Kentucky, bright wrapper	2.54
North Carolina Yellow ($50)	2.39
Ballard county, Kentucky, bright wrapper	2.27
Mason county, Kentucky, cutting or plug	2.21
Régie Virginia Shipper	2.14
German Saucer	2.07
Mexican Baler	2.04
Virginia sun-cured for plug	2.02
English Shipper (Virginia)	1.95
West Tennessee Stemmer	1.92
Virginia (heavily manured)	1.92
Florida Seed-Leaf	1.79
Perique, air-cured	1.74
Ohio Seed-Leaf	1.73
Sweet-scented Wisconsin and Illinois	1.67
Clarksville, Tennessee, German	1.48
Virginia French Régie, A	1.41
Virginia German Shipper	1.12

VARIATIONS IN THE COMPOSITION OF TOBACCOS REFERABLE TO CAUSES ATTENDING THE GROWTH OF THE PLANT.

These are of twofold character, being due in the first place to peculiarities of climate and soil, and secondly to the special methods of cultivation employed.

Concerning the immediate effects of climate, but little is known. It would appear, from the observations of Nessler, already cited, that the tobaccos of the tropics are richer in resinous substances, while those of the north in some cases contain a larger proportion of fat. It would also appear, from the existing analyses, that the northern tobaccos are generally richer in nicotine than those of southern climates. Nevertheless, in default of analyses of the *fresh* tropical tobaccos, it is impossible to say that this difference may not be chiefly due to fermentative change, attended with loss of nicotine by volatilization.

The effects of the character of the soil on the quality of the product have been much better studied. Thus the seed-leaf tobaccos of New England, which are specially prized on account of their fine texture, combined with strength and elasticity, and the entire absence of distinctive flavor, which might interfere with that of the cigar filling with which they are used as wrappers, are stated by Professor S. W. Johnson, in his admirable report on tobacco (*Annual Report of the Secretary of the Connecticut State Board of Agriculture*, 1873, p. 384), to be produced only on light, sandy lands, and he adds that "if upon these very heavy crops are obtained by extra manuring, the gain in quantity is offset by loss in quality". The peculiarities in chemical composition which especially distinguish these varieties are chiefly, as will be seen from the analyses on Table I, the larger proportion of cellulose, pectic acid, and mineral ingredients, and the smaller proportion of fatty or resinous substances and nicotine. The difference between the two samples of Connecticut Seed-Leaf, Nos. 30 and 35, is very marked. Sample No. 30, which was grown upon sandy soil, agrees closely in composition with the other seed-leaf varieties; whereas sample No. 35, grown on rich and heavily manured loam (see soil analysis No. 1), approaches in its large percentage of nicotine, relatively smaller percentage of cellulose, ash, and pectic acid, more closely to the "plug" than to the seed-leaf class.

Of all the samples analyzed, however, the sample of North Carolina "Bright Wrapper", No. 10, shows to the most surprising extent the influence of the character of the soil on the composition of the plant.

The soil on which this sample was grown was a light gray sand (see analysis, in Tables V and VI), containing, as shown by the analysis, a surprisingly small proportion of the mineral constituents available for the nutrition of the plant. On reference to the analysis on Table I, it will be seen that this tobacco contains little more than one-half of the average amount of mineral ingredients contained in the other samples, the deficiency being, as will be seen from Table III, especially noteworthy in the case of the lime, ferric oxide, and sulphuric acid. In the matter of proximate organic constituents, the tobacco is especially rich in carbo-hydrates, notably in glucose, which reaches the unprecedented figure of 16.39 per cent. Equally remarkable is the deficiency in albuminoids, which latter substances are present in little more than half of the average amount present in the other tobaccos.

The views at present generally obtaining regarding the physiological processes attending the growth of the plant, teach that the first organic substances formed in the leaves under the influence of light are the carbo-hydrates, starch, and glucose, and that these primary products are under the influence of the mineral ingredients absorbed from the soil, then transformed through further metamorphosis into secondary products such as organic acids, and with the co-operation of nitrogenous compounds (nitric acid and ammonia), also absorbed by the roots from the soil into the albuminoids and other nitrogenous constituents of the plant. The amount of nicotine in this sample is greater than in any of the seed-leaf varieties, excepting only the sample No. 35, a fact that would indicate that the small proportion of albuminoids is not due exclusively to deficiency in total nitrogen, but to the lack of those mineral constituents which are essential for the transformation of the nitrogen into albuminoids. Noteworthy in this connection is the deficiency in sulphuric acid, shown in Table III, a substance usually deemed prominent in the formation of the albuminoids.

It is of special interest in this connection to recall the results obtained by Schloesing (*Comptes-Rendus*, xlix p. 253), in his ingenious and beautiful experiments for the purpose of ascertaining the effects on the composition of the plant of the reduction of the absorption of mineral ingredients by the roots, by retarding evaporation from the leaves. Two tobacco plants, each of a dry weight of 8 grammes, were placed in pots. One pot was covered with a glass bell jar through which air was drawn at the rate of 500 liters in twenty-four hours. The plant in the other pot was left freely exposed to the air. The plants developed into a healthy growth and each produced twelve leaves. Plant No. 1, grown under the bell jar, possessed a dry weight of 48 grammes; plant No. 2, grown in the open air, a dry weight of only 37.4 grammes. For every liter of water evaporated there was, in the case of No. 1, 5.1, and in the case of No. 2 only 1.3 grammes increase of dry substance, while the gain in mineral substances in No. 1 was 3.6, and 5.1 grammes in No. 2. The results of the analyses of the plants obtained in these experiments are given in the following table:

TABLE IV.—ANALYSES OF TOBACCOS GROWN IN SCHLOESING'S EXPERIMENTS.

Percentage composition of leaves, dried at 100° C.

	Nicotine.	Oxalic acid.	Citric acid.	Malic acid.	Pectic acid.	Resin.	Cellulose.	Starch.	Albuminoids.	Ash.
No. 1, grown under the glass bell.........	1.82	0.24	1.91	4.08	1.78	4.00	5.36	19.30	17.40	9.41
No. 2, grown in the open air..............	2.14	0.66	2.79	9.68	4.86	5.02	8.67	1.00	18.00	15.26

Analyses of the ash of the whole plant.

	Total ash.	Ash, less sand and carb. acid.	Potash.	Soda.	Lime.	Magnesia.	Ferric oxide.	Phosphoric acid.	Sulphuric acid.	Chlorine.
No. 1, grown under the glass bell.........	18.00	9.41	32.31	....	42.48	5.04	0.90	5.08	8.48	8.09
No. 2, grown in the open air..............	21.80	15.26	27.14	....	44.97	5.61	1.41	2.70	7.66	14.59

In the foregoing experiment the retardation of the evaporation of the water from the leaves of the plant under the bell jar was attended with a diminution in the absorption of mineral ingredients from the soil. The carbo-hydrates (in this instance starch), instead of undergoing transformation into other products, accumulated to an abnormal extent. The consequence was precisely similar in character to that resulting from the deficiency of mineral ingredients in the North Carolina tobacco (No. 10), only the accumulated carbo-hydrate in the last-named instance was sugar, whereas in the former instance it was starch, the difference in this respect being probably attributable to the difference in the other conditions of the experiment—among which perhaps the most noteworthy in this connection is the difference in the amount of albuminoids formed and in the percentage of sulphuric acid in the plant.

The differences in composition due to variations in the mode of cultivation are, apart from those arising from differences in manuring, chiefly to be referred to the greater or less length of time that the plant is allowed to remain in the field after it has been "topped". The operation of "topping", or removing the upper portion of the stalk, is designed to stop the further growth of the plant and to direct the whole vegetative energy to storing the cells already formed with the different organic substances, such as the organic acids, etc. The treatment of the seed-leaf and the smoking tobaccos in this respect is notably different from that to which the tobaccos destined for chewing are subjected. The former are allowed to remain on the stalk after "topping" until the expansion (*i. e.*, cessation of the growth of new cellular tissue, followed by "granulation", that is to say, distension of the individual cells from accumulation of cell-contents) commences, say two or three weeks, while the heavier shipping leaf is allowed to stand until fully ripe, *i. e.*, until the verge of decay is attained. During this period the increase in the cell-contents is very marked to the eye, by reason of the greater thickness of the leaf as well as in the granulation of the surface caused by the distension of the individual cells.

The leaf being in both cases allowed to remain on the stalk until the expansion of the leaf, *i. e.*, the formation of new cellular tissue ceases, it is evident that the larger proportional amount of cellulose in the seed-leaf varieties is due to a relatively more rapid production of ingredients other than cellulose in the other varieties during the period of growth subsequent to "topping" the plant. The smaller proportion of mineral ingredients, in spite of the fact that the chewing tobaccos are usually produced on soil rich in mineral plant-food, and the disappearance of the nitric acid, which is transformed into albuminoids and nicotine, would indicate that the removal of the "tops" has operated to diminish the absorption at the roots. That the nitric acid in the tobacco plant has entered through the process of absorption by the roots is clearly evident from the results obtained by Schloesing, and previously cited, which show that the nitric acid or nitrates are chiefly present in the midrib and in far smaller proportions in the substance of the leaf. This distribution is entirely inconsistent with the theory of Nessler (*op. cit.*, p. 28) that the nitric acid, as well as the ammonia, has resulted from the fermentative alteration of the albuminoids. In treating of the fermentation of tobacco it will be shown that while undoubtedly true of the ammonia, this theory is untenable in regard to the nitric acid. Meanwhile it may be mentioned that Nessler (*op. cit.*, p. 104) states that the total amount of nitrogen in the plant is greatest at the time of its strongest (most rapid) vegetation, *i. e.*, the middle of August, diminishes gradually from that time until the beginning of September, and then appears to remain constant until the point of absolute ripeness is attained or exceeded. The carbonate of potash in the ash increases until the middle of August, the period of strongest vegetation, and after that diminishes regularly until after the point of ripeness is attained.

CHANGES IN COMPOSITION OF TOBACCO INDUCED BY CURING.

According to the nature of the tobacco and the use to which it is to be applied, the operation of curing consists either simply in expeditious drying, with such precautions as may insure a regular progress of the operation and prevent the exudation of the juices which attends irregular and too rapid drying, or in drying preceded by or accompanied with fermentation.

As an instance of the first method may be mentioned the process of sun-curing, in which fermentation is probably reduced to a minimum. In the case of the methods of slower curing by carefully regulated artificial heat, a certain amount of fermentation probably takes place, although as shown by the large proportion of sugar retained by some tobaccos cured by this method, the fermentation must in these cases have been exceedingly slight, and probably restricted to those portions of the leaf that have been injured so as to expose the cell-contents to the air. The operation of slow curing by exposure to the air in barns or sheds is attended with a much greater fermentative change, accompanied by gradual oxidation, while the process of "curing in its juices"—to which Perique tobacco is subjected—represents a very thorough fermentation, with greatly reduced exposure to the air.

In order to understand the changes produced by fermentation, it is necessary to consider in detail the fermentative processes to which the different constituents of tobacco are liable.

1. SUGAR.—Of all the constituents of tobacco sugar is the most liable to change. As a rule the small quantities found in the green leaf disappear completely during the process of air-curing, so that it is generally stated that cured tobacco contains no sugar. While this is true of all of the air-cured samples analyzed, the sun-cured (No. 3) and fire-cured (No. 5) contain notable proportions, while in the case of the North Carolina yellow tobacco (No. 10), the carefully regulated drying by artificial heat has probably left almost the entire amount of sugar unchanged in the leaf.

2. CITRIC AND MALIC ACIDS.—These substances, especially in combination with bases are readily susceptible of fermentation. In the case of citric acid, Buchner (*Ann. Chem. Pharm.*, xxlviii, 208) found that under the action of ferments, alkaline citrates are gradually transformed, yielding first acetates, and subsequently carbonates of the alkaline base. Personne (*Comptes-Rendus*, xxxvi, 197) observed that crude calcium citrate (the juice of lemons neutralized with chalk) passes rapidly into fermentation, yielding acetic and butyric acids, and that the change is still more rapid when beer yeast is added.

Dessaignes (*Ann. Chem. Pharm.*, lxx, 102) observed the formation of succinic acid by the spontaneous fermentation of neutral calcium malate. Liebig (*ibid.*, lxx, 363) obtained the same results through fermentations produced by the addition of yeast or cheese in small proportions. If the temperature or the quantity of cheese exceed a certain degree or proportion, no succinic acid is formed, or that produced is immediately decomposed and there is produced butyric acid, some acetic acid and a colorless, volatile, oily substance possessing the odor of apples, the nature of which was not further determined, but which would seem to consist of the compound ethers of the acids formed in the fermentation.

3. ALBUMINOIDS.—These substances as a class, and in the moist state, are very susceptible to fermentative or putrefactive change. The only product of this decomposition that has been observed to form during the fermentation of tobacco is ammonia, which is evolved freely during the fermentation of tobacco for snuff. While undergoing such changes the albuminoids become active ferments. Pelouze (*Comptes-Rendus*, xliv, 118) has shown that in the absence of free mineral bases the decomposition of organic nitrogenous substances by fermentation or putrescence is unattended by the formation of nitric acid, but that, on the contrary, the nitrates, if already present, are decomposed with evolution of ammonia.

4. NITRIC ACID.—In spite of the fact just mentioned, and the additional fact communicated by Pelouze and Frémy (*op. cit.*, iv, 655) that the juice of tobacco, in a putrescent state, decomposes nitric acid, liberating nitrous oxide, it appears that nitric acid is not changed during the fermentation of tobacco. The following analyses made at the laboratory of the government tobacco manufactory at Paris show that even the prolonged fermentation to which snuff is subjected during the operations of manufacture does not cause any perceptible change in the proportion of nitric acid contained therein:

PROPORTION OF NITRIC ACID IN TOBACCO DURING THE DIFFERENT STAGES OF FERMENTATION FOR SNUFF.

Tobacco:	Per cent. of nitric acid.
Fermented in heaps	0.74
First fermentation in cases	0.73
Second fermentation in cases	0.70
Third fermentation in cases	0.72
Fourth fermentation in cases	0.72

5. OTHER CONSTITUENTS.—Concerning the other constituents of tobacco there is no evidence to show that they are liable to alteration during the processes of fermentation to which tobacco is subjected during the operation of curing.

Apart, therefore, from the destruction of sugar, it is manifest from the foregoing that the changes in composition attending the fermentation of tobacco must be restricted chiefly to the albuminoids and organic acids. The change in the albuminoids can only be observed in the general effect of fermentation on the quality of the tobacco, especially when used for smoking, and its extent is only measured to a certain degree by the evolution of ammonia and the attendant reduction in the percentage of total nitrogen. For the most part the albuminoids are transformed into substances of undetermined character, according to the statement of Pelouze and Frémy, already cited, substances similar to the humus bodies. That this change has an important effect on the quality is evident from the marked difference between the odor of the smoke of fermented and of unfermented tobaccos.

In the case of the organic acids (citric and malic acids) it will be seen from the foregoing that these acids are susceptible of several distinct species of fermentative change, of which the three following have been observed and studied:

1. Neutral calcium malate (Dessaignes and Liebig) is decomposed, with formation of succinic acid.

2. In presence of a large quantity of ferment, or in cases where the temperature is somewhat elevated, the fermentation yields only acetic and butyric acids, and a volatile substance of fruity odor (Liebig).

3. Alkaline citrates are transformed first into acetates, and finally into carbonates of the alkaline bases (Buchner), or they are transformed into acetates and butyrates (Personne).

In view of the fact that tobacco is very rich in albuminoids, which, when in a decomposing state form the most active ferments, the first species of fermentation of malic acid can hardly be supposed to occur. We have, therefore, to deal solely with the second and third cases.

The extent to which differences in composition may result from differences in kind and degree of fermentation in one and the same variety of tobacco is instructively shown by the two analyses of "Perique" tobacco; the one (28) "cured in its juices", the other (37) "air-cured". The sample "cured in its juices" contains but little over one-fourth of the citric acid, but one-half of the malic acid, and about six times the amount of acetic acid contained in the air-cured leaf. Details are not at hand concerning the length of time the plants were, in each of these cases, allowed to stand in the field after "topping", but the absence of nitric acid from the sample "cured in its juices" and its presence in the "air-cured" sample would lead to the inference either that the former had been allowed to remain longer in the field than the latter, or that the exceptionally prolonged and thorough fermentation had resulted in the destruction of the nitric acid originally present. The smaller proportion of ash would favor the first assumption.

In the case of the Perique tobacco "cured in its juices", therefore, we have manifestly an instance of the conversion of a large proportion of both the citric and the malic acids into acetic (and butyric) acid, and the agreeable fruity odor which this tobacco acquires during the fermentation, while partly due to these acids, would indicate the presence of substances similar to the volatile oil obtained by Liebig during the fermentation of malic acid. It is probable that this fermentation is similar in character to that which takes place whenever the drying of the leaf is retarded, and at the same time a moderate elevation of temperature is induced either spontaneously or through the cautious application of artificial heat. It will be observed that the increase in the acetic acid in the foregoing instance has not kept pace with the loss in citric and malic acids. This is no doubt partly due to the volatile character of the former and to the periodical exposure to the air to which the product is subjected during the curing.

In the case of tobaccos like the foregoing, intended chiefly for chewing purposes, the object of the fermentative part of the operation of curing is chiefly to produce or develop the flavor, and this is attained by the production of volatile acids, and probably of the ethers of these acids as above described. In the case of smoking tobaccos, the object to be attained is the improvement of the odor of the smoke and also the combustibility, on which moreover the former closely depends.

The fine aroma of good smoking tobacco is dependent on an exact regulation of the operation of combustion, so that a certain quantity of empyreumatic products may be formed and no more. It is hardly necessary to add that the nature of these products, as well as the quantity produced, depends upon the degree of completeness of the combustion. An absolutely complete combustion of tobacco produces only carbonic acid, water, and nitrogen, all absolutely inodorous substances. A simple destructive distillation of tobacco, without combustion, furnishes a mixture of liquid and gaseous products most offensive in odor even in the case of fine tobacco, and absolutely dissimilar from the perfume of the same tobacco when smoked. The operation of smoking tobacco, therefore, involves a nicely adjusted combination of destructive distillation and combustion. The more perfectly a tobacco burns the less odor it involves in burning; on the other hand, the slower and less perfectly it burns the stronger is the odor, until the point is reached when the odor becomes simply offensive and the tobacco becomes unfit for smoking.

The changes produced in the operation of curing smoking tobacco, must therefore be effected primarily with a view to modifying or, as uncured tobacco is always imperfectly combustible, to increasing the combustibility.

CAUSES UPON WHICH THE COMBUSTIBILITY OF TOBACCO DEPENDS.

Schloesing (*Comptes-Rendus*, l, 642 and 1027), to whom more than to any other investigator we are indebted for our present knowledge regarding the chemistry of tobacco, first pointed out in the year 1860 the existence of a connection between the "combustibility" of tobacco (*i. e.*, the property it possesses of remaining incandescent, glowing for some time after being ignited) and the percentage of potassium carbonate it yields on incineration. The conclusions attained by this author are as follows:

1. The soluble part of the ash of a combustible tobacco always contains potassium carbonate (tobacco contains, according to Schloesing, no sodium); or, in general, a tobacco is the more combustible the more alkaline the ash.

2. The soluble part of the ash of a difficultly combustible tobacco contains no potassium carbonate; it ordinarily contains lime, whence it follows that in combustible tobaccos the quantity of potash exceeds in equivalent proportion that of the sulphuric acid and chlorine, and that in difficultly combustible tobaccos the reverse is the case.

3. A difficultly combustible tobacco becomes combustible if the potassium salts of an organic acid (malic, citric, tartaric, oxalic, etc.) be added thereto in such quantity that the potash in the ash exceeds in equivalent porportions the sulphuric acid and chlorine.

4. A combustible tobacco becomes difficultly combustible if a mineral salt (sulphate or chloride of calcium, magnesium, ammonium, etc.) be added in such quantity that the sulphuric acid and chlorine exceed in equivalent proportions the potash in the ash.

Schloesing finds that while the presence of nitrates promotes the combustibility to a certain extent, their value is only secondary. Very combustible tobaccos have been found to be very poor in nitrates, while other, quite difficultly combustible tobaccos, were rich in nitrates.

Schloesing gives the following explanation of the results of his observations on the foregoing subject:

I have observed that the alkaline salts of malic, citric, oxalic, pectic, and tartaric acids, when heated in close vessels, swell up strongly, without doubt because they melt in decomposing, and leave a very voluminous coal that possesses little solidity and is very porous; while the lime salts under the same circumstances do not alter in volume, and leave a very compact and coherent coal. Now, every one knows that a porous coal remains longer incandescent than a compact one. On the other hand, if we examine the combustion of tobacco, *e. g.*, a cigar, we will observe that the action of heat produces two classes of effects. Volatile substances (smoke) and coal are formed, which latter chiefly sustains the combustion, as it burns out as it forms. If a cigar contains enough of those salts which, when ignited, swell up while decomposing, it will leave a porous coal, throughout which the other substances of the tobacco are finely distributed, and will consequently "hold fire" for a long time. If, on the other hand, the cigar contains little or no organic potash salt, but only sulphate or chloride, neither of which plays any rôle in the combustion, and if the malic, citric, etc., acids are combined with lime, the constituents of the tobacco do not swell up in burning, but leave a compact coal which does not long remain incandescent. In the latter case the cigar carbonizes, and the resulting coal still shows the structure of the leaf.

I will not say that in a difficultly combustible tobacco there are no organic potash salts, that all the potash is in the form of sulphate and chloride, but only that the combustibility of tobacco is independent of its thickness, porosity, ripeness, and composition. A tobacco, therefore, burns well if it contains enough organic potash salts; it burns badly or not at all if it contains too little, and the presence of carbonate of potash in the ash is a sign of the good combustibility of tobacco, as its absence is a sign of incombustibility.

The connection between the presence of carbonate of potassium in the ash and the combustibility of tobacco was also observed by Nessler (*op. cit.*, p. 32, *et seq.*) almost simultaneously with Schloesing. While the results obtained by him tend in general to show, in accordance with those of Schloesing, that the ash of "combustible" tobacco always contains a notable proportion of potassium carbonate, he has found, by quantitative determinations, that the combustibility is not so strictly proportional to the amount of potassium carbonate in the ash as Schloesing has assumed, at least not when comparison is instituted between tobaccos of different origin. Among the conditions that influence combustibility he mentions that tobacco containing larger quantities of albuminoids and fat may leave a difficultly combustible coal that will only then burn when much potash is present; and, on the other hand, that those tobaccos burn best that contain the most woody fiber.

Concerning the explanations of Schloesing in regard to the nature of the effect exerted by potassium carbonate in the ash, or rather by the substances that leave potassium carbonate on incineration, on the combustibility of the tobacco, Nessler mentions the following objections, based in part on his own observations and experiments:

First. In the case of slips of paper, as well as those of tobacco, the combustibility is essentially promoted by saturating them with carbonate or sulphate of potassium. A formation of organic potassium salts is in this case only possible when tobacco is impregnated with potassium carbonate, but not when the paper is so treated, and not when tobacco is treated with potassium sulphate.

Second. A swelling up of the coal behind the incandescent part, such as Schloesing assumes, is a sign of a bad and not of a good tobacco.

Third. Acetates of the alkalies do not swell up, or at least hardly do so, and nevertheless promote combustibility like the carbonates.

It will be observed that the authorities just cited admit two conditions as conducive to the perfect combustibility of tobacco, namely:

1. The presence of a notable proportion of potassium carbonate in the ash. (Schloesing–Nessler.)
2. The presence of a large proportion of woody fiber in the tobacco. (Nessler.)

Concerning these points it is to be observed that the presence of a larger proportion of woody fiber is equivalent to the presence of a smaller proportion of the other constituents of the leaf, and on reference to the analyses on Table I it will be seen that the seed-leaf varieties are especially rich in cellulose (crude fiber), while the chewing varieties, with the sole exception of the Kentucky tobacco, No. 19, are relatively poor therein.

Concerning the presence of potassium carbonate in the ash, it will be seen from Table III that great variations exist in the amounts yielded by the different samples, but that the seed-leaf varieties yield more potassium carbonate than the others, with the sole exception of No. 19. But among the seed-leaf varieties themselves the amount of carbonate of potash furnished on incineration does not stand in any simple relation to the combustibility, as will be seen from the following instances in which the combustibility was determined by the method of Nessler (*op. cit.*, p. 65): Pieces 1 to ½ inch wide were cut from the middle of each leaf, running from the edge to the midrib and avoiding the lateral ribs. These were pressed flat by gentle pressure after slight moistening, and exposed to the air for forty-eight hours. The strips were then ignited on the end, and the lapse of time noted between the first ignition and the extinction of the spark or glowing edge; the burnt edge was then removed with the scissors and the slip reignited, the operation being repeated until the whole slip had been burned from the edge to the midrib; the mean of the observations for the whole slip was then taken. When six slips had been burned, the maximum, minimum, and mean of the series were noted. The results of these tests, while showing great diversities in the combustibility of even different leaves from the same sample, were nevertheless in a measure characteristically distinct for the different brands.

Especially interesting were the results obtained with the samples of Connecticut Seed-Leaf, viz: No. 30 (Hartford), burned to end of strip 120–160 seconds; No. 35 (New Milford) maximum 16.0, minimum 2.7, mean 7.8 seconds. As will be seen from Table III, these samples yielded, on incineration, the same percentage of potassium carbonate. The percentage of cellulose is greater in No. 30; the percentage of citric and malic acids is greater in No. 35. This latter fact would suggest that a difference in the character of the organic salts, and especially a difference in the relative proportions of acids and bases therein, might have something to do with this marked difference in combustibility. As we are still ignorant of the modes of combination in which the mineral ingredients exist in the plant, and as we are still in uncertainty as to the chemical character (whether acid or indifferent) of the hitherto unstudied constituents of the leaf, it is not possible to say, with any certainty, from the results of the analysis, or even from the examination of the extracts or decoctions of the plant, precisely in what state of combination the constituents may have existed in the interior of the vegetable cell. Nevertheless, it is of some interest to compare the respective equivalence of the acids and bases found in the analysis with a view of ascertaining if this proportion bears any relation to the combustibility of the leaf. The equivalence is obtained by dividing the percentage of each ingredient by its molecular weight and multiplying the quotient by the atomicity. If we then deduct from the sum of the equivalents of the inorganic bases the sum of the equivalents of the inorganic acids of the ash, we have as the residue the equivalence of the inorganic bases (potash, soda, lime, etc.), that are to be compared with the organic acids and nitric acid of the plant. The equivalent ratio therefore expresses the relative equivalence of the organic acids and nitric acid (taken as unity) with that of the inorganic bases with which these acids may be supposed to be combined. Applying this process to samples Nos. 30 and 35, we have:

Nos. of samples.	Equivalent ratios.
30	Organic and nitric acids : Bases=1 : 1.345
35	Organic and nitric acids : Bases=1 : 0.970

From the foregoing it will be seen that the sample No. 30 contains a large excess of bases over the amount requisite to form neutral salts with the acids named above, or, in other words, the quantity of mineral bases in the sample No. 30, after deducting the amount required to form neutral salts with the inorganic acids of the ash, is about one-third greater than is required to form neutral salts with the organic acids and nitric acid of the leaf; whereas in the sample No. 35 the proportion of bases is less than is required to form neutral salts.

In this and the following calculations, both ammonia and nicotine are omitted, as on account of the volatility and readily decomposable character of the organic salts of these bases, and their relatively small amount, they cannot be supposed to materially affect the combustibility of the tobacco. Nitric acid has been included with the organic acids, for the reason that it is readily decomposed in contact with organic matter, and at a low heat, and, like the organic acids, leaves the base with which it was combined in the state of carbonate.

On the following table are given the equivalent ratios, proportions of potassium carbonate, and, for comparison, also the proportions of nitric acid, together with the results of the burning tests, for sample No. 37 and the different seed-leaf varieties:

RELATIONS BETWEEN EQUIVALENT RATIOS AND BURNING QUALITIES.

Number.	Nitric acid.	Potassium carbonate.	Equivalent ratios.	Burning tests.
			Acids. Bases.	*Max. Min. Mean.*
37	1.65	4.30	1 : 1.065	3.0 2.0 2.4 seconds.
35	3.23	0.08	1 : 0.970	10.0 2.7 7.8 seconds.
30	2.39	0.96	1 : 1.345	To end of strip, 120 to 160 seconds.
34	0.00	11.91	1 : 1.703	To end of strip, 110 to 120 seconds.
16	3.41	5.83	1 : 1.160	To end of strip, 80 to 230 seconds.
				Max. Min. Mean.
22	2.29	4.86	1 : 0.978	Dark .....15.6 8.4 12.2 seconds. Medium..60.8 34.7 46.0 seconds. Light..To en of strip, 140 seconds.
				Max. Min. Mean.
25	1.23	7.83	1 : 1.336	106.5 44.5 71.3 seconds.

The results communicated on the foregoing table show unmistakably the existence of a relation between the combustibility and the relative proportions of acids and bases present in the leaf. In general, those samples burn best wherein the excess of bases is most marked, and it will be seen that the relative combustibility is independent of the proportion of potassium carbonate the leaf yields on incineration, and, to a large extent, of the proportion of the nitric acid; nevertheless, the effects of the latter are quite apparent in the sample No. 16. In Nos. 25 and 30, while the equivalent ratios are nearly equal, the degree of combustibility—although both burn well—is quite different, possibly owing to the much larger percentage of albuminoids in No. 25. Sample No. 22 was composed of leaves of very diverse appearance, mostly dark in color, but sometimes light. One leaf, however, was very light and thin, and this specimen, as stated, burned to the end of the strip. The reactions of the aqueous extracts of these samples to test papers were as follows: No. 35, acid; Nos. 16, 22, and 37, neutral; Nos. 25, 30, and 34, alkaline. No. 34 was strongly alkaline.

The foregoing results would appear to indicate that the rational conduct of the operation of curing smoking tobaccos, and especially the seed-leaf varieties, would involve the destruction of a larger proportion of the organic acids (citric and malic acids) by fermentation, the operation being in some instances carried to the extent of transforming the salts of these acids, in part, into carbonates. It is hardly necessary to say that this operation would result in setting free a large proportion of the nicotine, which would volatilize during the process.

Nessler (*op. cit.*, p. 138), to improve the combustibility of tobacco, recommends that it should be moistened with a solution of acetate, or better, carbonate of potassium, adding "the best result was always obtained with an aqueous solution of potassium carbonate".

While it is quite conceivable that a marked improvement should be attained by adding potassium acetate to tobacco containing an excess of citric or malic acids, inasmuch as these acids would displace the acetic acid, it is improbable that any good result should accrue from the addition of alkaline citrates or malates on the general principle of increasing the percentage of organic salts in the tobacco, inasmuch as it is evident from the foregoing results that an increase in the absolute amount of citric and malic acids has a disadvantageous effect on the combustibility of the tobacco.

ANALYSES OF TOBACCO SOILS.

These analyses of soils were made on samples from: First, the Housatonic valley, at New Milford, Connecticut; second, the Clarksville district, Montgomery county, Tennessee, which produces the best variety of "shipping" or "export" tobacco; and third, Granville, North Carolina, where the best variety of the North Carolina Lemon Yellow tobacco is grown. The two samples last named were furnished by Colonel Killebrew, and, according to him, are fairly representative specimens of the best varieties of these respective soils. The first sample was taken by myself at New Milford, from a field which, according to my informant (Mr. Isaac B. Bristol), produces the best quality of Housatonic Valley Seed-Leaf tobacco.

The general character of the samples was as follows:

No. 1. *New Milford, Connecticut.*—Hill soil. Rich, dark loam, somewhat sandy in character. Average depth, about 12 inches, with loamy subsoil extending to the bed-rock (gneiss). Geological character of the surrounding rocks: Granite, gneiss, and mica, and hornblende slates. The rock fragments found in the sample were chiefly granite, quartzite, mica slate, and, more rarely, hornblende slate. The field had been under cultivation six years, exclusively on tobacco. Average yield, 1,500 to 1,800 pounds (dry weight) per acre of tobacco of fine quality. Manured in the spring with 20 cart-loads of barnyard and stable manure per acre. The sample was taken November 30, 1880. The last application of manure was in the spring of the same year.

No. 2. *Clarksville, Montgomery county, Tennessee.*—Virgin soil. Rich, dark, clayey loam. Average depth 5 to 6 inches. Incumbent upon a highly ferruginous clay, the latter being intercalated with beds of chert, varying from 1 to 3 feet in thickness. According to Colonel Killebrew this soil belongs, geologically, to the Lithostrotian bed of the Siliceous group of the Lower Carboniferous formation. The small quantity of rock fragments contained in the sample consisted chiefly of highly decomposed feldspar. The land adjoining the woods where this sample was taken, produced, when first opened, 1,500 pounds of most excellent tobacco per acre, and has continued to produce it, in rotation with wheat and clover, for twenty-two years, with but little diminution in fertility. The Clarksville tobacco, marked No. 7 on the schedules of tobacco analyses (Tables I to III), is, according to Colonel Killebrew, fairly illustrative of the character of that produced upon this soil.

No. 3. *Granville, North Carolina.*—Light, gray sand, with porous cream-colored subsoil. According to Colonel Killebrew this soil belongs to the Laurentine series of the Archæan age, and is derived from granitoid rocks and quartzites. Numerous trap or intrusive rocks are found in the vicinity, but the soil arising from the disintegration of these will not produce the yellow tobacco, nor does this tobacco attain a high degree of excellence on soils containing much ferric oxide. When the subsoil is red or clayey, heavy tobacco will grow, but not the yellow leaf. The rock fragments found in the sample consisted chiefly of quartz. The field from which the sample was taken had been used for tobacco for six years in succession, but was previously an "old field" that had been exhausted by long cultivation and allowed to lie untilled for some 14 years previous to being used for tobacco, and had become covered with "old-field pines" (*Pinus tæda*, Michaux), persimmon bushes, etc. Concerning the manuring to which this field was subjected, I quote the following from Colonel Killebrew: "The soil is simply a sponge, into which just enough fertilizing matter is put to bring the plants to the proper size, and no more."

METHODS OF ANALYSIS.

1. MECHANICAL ANALYSIS.—In the mechanical analysis of soils, which operation has for its object the separation of the particles of the soil according to their size and the determination of the proportional quantity of the particles of different sizes, the following method was adopted, viz:

The whole sample was first passed through a sieve of perforated metal having holes of 3 millimeters in diameter. The weight of the particles remaining on the sieve was then determined and also that of the portion passing through the sieve ("fine earth"). The last-named portion constituted the material for all of the subsequent operations of mechanical and chemical analysis.

Thirty grammes of the "fine earth" were boiled out repeatedly with water, as recommended by Wolff (*Chem. Untersuchung landwirthschaftlicher Stoffe*: Berlin, Wiegant & Hempel [3te Aufl.], 1875, p. 4), until the lumps were disintegrated and the clayey portions separated from the sand. The material was then successively washed through perforated metal sieves, the holes in which were respectively 1^{mm}, 0.5^{mm}, and 0.25^{mm} in diameter. The portions retained on the sieves were severally dried, ignited and weighed, and the finest portion, or that passing through the 0.25mm sieve was then submitted to the following process of separation, which is based upon the method of Knop, as described by Wolff (*op. cit.*, p. 10), but perfected by the employment of the principle of fractional separation.

The sediment and water passing through the 0.25mm sieve were placed in a glass cylinder 53 centimeters long and 37mm in internal diameter. The cylinder was closed at the bottom and was provided with a lateral tube inserted 6 centimeters above the bottom. Three other lateral tubes were inserted at intervals of 10 centimeters above the first tube, and a ring was etched into the cylinder 10 centimeters above the uppermost tube. The lateral tubes were closed with rubber tubes compressed by spring clips. The sediment being placed in the cylinder, water was added to the mark or ring, the cylinder closed with a rubber stopper, and vigorously shaken until the contents were thoroughly mixed. It was then placed upright, the stopper removed, and after standing undisturbed for five minutes the clip on the uppermost tube was opened and the water allowed to flow into a beaker. After five minutes further standing, the second clip was opened and the water drawn off into the same beaker; in the same manner the water was drawn off from the other tubes at intervals of five minutes until the level of the lowest tube was reached. The cylinder was then refilled with water to the mark, thoroughly shaken after inserting the stopper and the water again drawn off at intervals of five minutes, as before; the operation being repeated until the water drawn off was almost free from turbidity. The sediment remaining in the cylinder from this process of washing by subsidence is termed by Knop "fine sand", the material flowing off in suspension in the washing waters "dust", and the process of separation by Knop's original method ends here.

A little reflection will show that as far as a separation into particles of definite size is concerned, the foregoing method is very imperfect. While the repeated agitation of the sediment from each washing with fresh additions of water tends to remove the objection noted by E. W. Hilgard (*Silliman's Journal*, 1873, [3] vi, 288, 333) in his admirable paper on silt analysis, and to which all methods of continuous washing known previous to the invention of the method of Hilgard were subject, viz, the tendency of the particles of clay to ball together and sink with the coarser particles even in opposition to upward currents of water, it is nevertheless attended with the following defect to which Hilgard's method is also liable, and which, as far as the author is aware, has not hitherto received sufficient attention. In the case of a quiescent body of water containing suspended sediment, the particles of the latter sink to the bottom with varying degrees of rapidity, proportional to their size and specific gravity, or, as the mineral constituents of soils do not, for the most part, differ very greatly among themselves in specific gravity, chiefly proportional to their size. In course of their descent, however, the more swiftly descending particles collide with the more slowly descending, or, as we may say, "lighter" particles. The rate of descent is therefore influenced not only by the relative size of the particles of suspended matter, but also by the number and force of these collisions. These two last-named conditions vary according to the difference in size (and specific gravity) of the particles and also according to the relative number of the particles of each different size. It is evident, therefore, that the error arising from the cause just mentioned is not constant, but that it must vary in amount according to the specific character of each sediment, and that the results of separations by simple subsidence can never afford a basis for an exact comparison in the matter of the state of subdivision of sediments of diverse origin and differing in the relative proportions of the particles of the different sizes. The conditions above instanced as obtaining in the case of a subsidence from a liquid in a quiescent state, obtain with equal force in the case of subsidence from slowly moving upward currents, and undoubtedly constitute a source of material error in all methods of mechanical analysis by continuous subsidence.

In the method pursued by the author the defect above noted was obviated by the following means:

The "fine sand" from the first series of subsidences was placed in a separate vessel, the washings were allowed to remain undisturbed for twelve hours, the turbid liquid decanted off, and the sediment returned to the cylinder. Water was then added to the mark, the whole shaken up, and the liquid drawn off at intervals of five minutes, as in the first series. The sediment from this operation was placed in a separate beaker, the liquid "washings" returned to the cylinder, and again subsided as before; the sediment from this second subsidence was added to that from the preceding operation and the washings again returned to the cylinder, the operation being repeated as long as any sediment could be obtained from renewed treatment of the washings; the final washings were then placed in a separate vessel for subsequent microscopic measurements.

The collective sediments from the last series of operations were then returned to the cylinder and subsided with fresh additions of water, as in the case of the first series; the "fine sand" thus obtained being added to that from the first series, and the washings being collected in a large beaker. The latter were left at rest for twelve hours, and the sediment returned to the cylinder and treated as before until no further separation could be effected. The "fine sand" resulting from all of these operations was then dried, ignited, and weighed; the weight of the portion removed by the washing being determined by difference, as it was, owing to its excessively slow rate of subsidence, found impracticable to collect it for direct weighing. The size of the particles of "fine sand" was then determined by micrometric measurement, and was found to vary from 0.25mm to 0.009mm average diameter. Similar measurements were made on the material obtained by long subsidence from the washings from the foregoing operations, with the result of showing that the average diameter of the largest particles did not exceed 0.01mm.

The results of the foregoing processes of mechanical analysis were then computed in percentages on the ignited soil, and are given in the following table:

TABLE V.—MECHANICAL ANALYSES OF TOBACCO SOILS.

[Computed in percentages on the ignited soil.]

	New Milford, Connecticut.	Clarksville, Tennessee.	Granville, North Carolina.
Particles larger in diameter than 3.0mm	8.55	0.32	0.23
Particles of diameter from 3.0mm to 1.0mm	4.96	0.45	15.04
Particles of diameter from 1.0mm to 0.5mm	4.43	0.96	33.48
Particles of diameter from 0.5mm to 0.25mm	11.86	1.25	18.82
Particles of diameter from 0.25mm to 0.01mm	60.54	61.58	23.59
Particles smaller in diameter than 0.01mm	9.66	35.44	8.89
Total	100.00	100.00	100.00

2. CHEMICAL ANALYSES.—The chemical analyses of the "fine earth" embrace analyses of the extracts obtained by treating, first, the air-dried soil with cold hydrochloric acid; second, with hot hydrochloric acid; third, by treating the residue insoluble in hot hydrochloric acid with sulphuric acid, and analyses of the residues insoluble in sulphuric acid. The acid extracts were prepared according to the directions of Wolff (*op. cit.*, p. 12 *et. seq.*), and the analyses were made substantially according to the method of the author in question, with the exception of the analyses of the residues insoluble in sulphuric acid, which were made by the usual method of silicate analyses (fusion), the alkalies being determined by the method of Professor J. Lawrence Smith.

The results of the analyses are given in the following table, in which the method of Wolff has been in so far departed from that the horizontal columns of figures headed "soluble in hot hydrochloric acid", in lieu of representing the total substances extracted from the air-dried soil by hot hydrochloric acid, represent the constituents soluble in hot but insoluble in cold hydrochloric acid, while the horizontal columns headed "total" and printed in heavy type represent the percentage composition of the air-dried soils irrespective of the degree of solubility of the constituents.

TABLE VI.—CHEMICAL ANALYSES OF TOBACCO SOILS.

	Moisture (100° C.).	Organic and volatile substances.	Silicic anhydride in solution.	Silicic anhydride soluble in sodium carbonate.	Ferric oxide.	Alumina.	Manganous oxide.	Lime.	Magnesia.	Potash.	Soda.	Phosphoric anhydride.	Sulphuric anhydride.	Total.
NEW MILFORD, CONNECTICUT.														
Moisture at 100° C	1.8200													1.8200
Organic and volatile substances		6.8600												6.8600
Soluble in cold hydrochloric acid			0.0535	(?)	2.1433	3.4009	0.0173	0.2830	0.7047	0.1801	0.0074	0.1984	0.0378	8.1023
Soluble in hot hydrochloric acid			0.0724	4.2426	0.3833	1.2999	0.0000	0.0404	0.0205	0.0468	0.0072	0.0218	0.0378	6.1722
Soluble in sulphuric acid			0.0000	1.0188	0.0326	2.8121	0.0000	0.1080	0.0738	0.3767	0.0027	0.0000	0.0000	4.2797
Insoluble in acids			59.9632		0.8540	7.4694	0.0000	1.3658	0.4302	1.3155	1.5432	0.0749	0.0000	73.0162
Total	**1.8200**	**6.8600**	**65.3505**		**4.4132**	**14.8513**	**0.0173**	**1.5531**	**1.2592**	**1.9216**	**1.3605**	**0.2951**	**0.0756**	**100.3101**
CLARKSVILLE, TENNESSEE.														
Moisture at 100° C	1.3500													1.3500
Organic and volatile substances		4.3450												4.3450
Soluble in cold hydrochloric acid			0.0338	(?)	1.5800	1.4006	0.0873	0.2270	0.1218	0.0445	0.0018	0.0711	0.0105	3.5784
Soluble in hot hydrochloric acid			0.0808	3.2308	0.3167	1.8001	0.2104	0.0680	0.0714	0.0730	0.0013	0.0105	0.0009	5.8649
Soluble in sulphuric acid			0.0000	2.7230	0.1701	3.3385	0.0000	0.0547	0.0051	0.2561	0.0261	0.0000	0.0000	6.6065
Insoluble in acids			73.8330		0.3835	2.2123	0.0000	0.2772	0.1020	1.6484	0.2654	0.0507	0.0000	78.7586
Total	**1.3500**	**4.3450**	**79.8073**		**2.4303**	**8.7515**	**0.3037**	**0.0269**	**0.3903**	**2.0220**	**0.2866**	**0.1383**	**0.0114**	**100.5033**
GRANVILLE, NORTH CAROLINA.														
Moisture at 100° C	0.6050													0.6050
Organic and volatile substances		1.2050												1.2050
Soluble in cold hydrochloric acid			0.0060	(?)	0.1775	0.3523	0.0052	0.0533	0.0098	0.0115	0.0033	0.0203	0.0000	0.6488
Soluble in hot hydrochloric acid			0.1290	0.7021	0.2115	0.4737	0.0365	0.0174	0.0123	0.0046	0.0012	0.0000	0.0030	1.5841
Soluble in sulphuric acid			0.0000	0.3818	0.1542	0.8057	0.0000	0.0305	0.0044	0.0767	0.0016	0.0000	0.0000	1.5449
Insoluble in acids			92.1031		0.0843	0.7748	0.0000	0.1318	0.0577	0.4117	0.2831	0.0170	0.0000	93.9541
Total	**0.6050**	**1.2050**	**93.3035**		**0.6275**	**2.4065**	**0.0417**	**0.2330**	**0.0847**	**0.5045**	**0.2892**	**0.0379**	**0.0140**	**99.7025**

INDEX TO TOBACCO CULTURE.

O.

P.

www.ingramcontent.com/pod-product-compliance
Lightning Source LLC
Chambersburg PA
CBHW031407270326
41929CB00010BA/1358

* 9 7 8 3 3 3 7 1 8 7 2 1 7 *